Crime in Scotland 1660–1960: The Violent North?

CW01497157

Scotland has often been regarded throughout history as 'the violent North', but how true is this statement? Does Scotland deserve to be defined in this way, and upon what foundations is this definition based? This book examines the history of crime in Scotland, questioning the labelling of Scotland as home to a violent culture and examining changes in violent behaviour over time, it also considers how gender impacted on violence and how the level of Scottish violence fares when compared to incidents of violence throughout the rest of the UK.

This book offers a groundbreaking contribution to the historiography of Scottish crime. Not only does the piece illuminate the nature and incidence of Scottish criminality over the course of some three hundred years for the first time, but it also employs a more integrated analysis of gender than has hitherto been evident. This book sheds light on whether the stereotypical label given to Scotland as 'the violent North' is appropriate or in any way accurate, and it further contributes to our understanding of not only Scottish society, but of the history of crime and punishment in the British Isles and beyond.

Anne-Marie Kilday is Professor of Criminal History and Pro Vice-Chancellor (Student and Staff Experience) at Oxford Brookes University.

History of Crime in the UK and Ireland
Professor Barry Godfrey

Rarely do we get the opportunity to study criminal history across the British Isles, or across such a long time period. *History of Crime in the UK and Ireland* is a series which provides an opportunity to contrast experiences in various geographical regions and determine how these situations changed – with slow evolution or dramatic speed – and with what results. It brings together data, thought, opinion, and new theories from an established group of scholars that draw upon a wide range of existing and new research. Using case studies, examples from contemporary media, biographical life studies, thoughts and ideas on new historical methods, the authors construct lively debates on crime and the law, policing, prosecution, and punishment. Together, this series of books builds up a rich but accessible history of crime and its control in the British Isles.

Crime in England, 1688–1815
David J. Cox

Crime in England, 1880–1945
Barry Godfrey

Crime in England, 1815–1880
Helen Johnston

Land of White Gloves?
A history of crime and punishment in Wales
Richard Ireland

Crime in Scotland 1660–1960: The Violent North?
Anne-Marie Kilday

For more information about this series, please visit: www.routledge.com/ History-of-Crime-in-the-UK-and-Ireland/book-series/HCUKI

Crime in Scotland 1660–1960:
The Violent North?

Anne-Marie Kilday

Routledge
Taylor & Francis Group

LONDON AND NEW YORK

First published 2019 by Routledge

2 Park Square, Milton Park, Abingdon, Oxon OX14 4RN
605 Third Avenue, New York, NY 10017

Routledge is an imprint of the Taylor & Francis Group, an informa business

First issued in paperback 2021

Copyright © 2019 Anne-Marie Kilday

The right of Anne-Marie Kilday to be identified as author of
this work has been asserted by her in accordance with sections
77 and 78 of the Copyright, Designs and Patents Act 1988.

All rights reserved. No part of this book may be reprinted or reproduced or
utilised in any form or by any electronic, mechanical, or other means, now
known or hereafter invented, including photocopying and recording, or in
any information storage or retrieval system, without permission in writing
from the publishers.

Notice:
Product or corporate names may be trademarks or registered trademarks,
and are used only for identification and explanation without intent to
infringe.

Publisher's Note

The publisher has gone to great lengths to ensure the quality of this reprint
but points out that some imperfections in the original copies may be apparent.

British Library Cataloguing-in-Publication Data
A catalogue record for this book is available from the British
Library

Library of Congress Cataloguing-in-Publication Data
A catalogue record has been requested for this book

ISBN: 978-1-84392-945-1 (hbk)
ISBN: 978-0-367-48357-9 (pbk)

Typeset in Bembo
by codeMantra

For my beloved niece Grace Charlotte Kilday
and for her mum Laura, with much love.
Also for Rebecca Henderson, research assistant and bionic
woman, with thanks and awe.

Contents

List of figures   ix
Acknowledgements   xv

The Violent North – Fact or Fiction?
Introduction and Context   1

1   The Violent North? Fatal Violence, 1660–1960   27

2   The Violent North? Sexual Violence, 1660–1960   77

3   The Violent North? Violent Assault: Public and Private,
    1660–1960   113

4   The Violent North? Communal Violence, 1660–1960   153

5   The Violent North? Violence for Gain, 1660–1960   200

6   The Violent North or The Enterprising Scot, 1660–1960?   243

7   The Violent North – Fact or Fiction? Conclusion   289

Bibliography   295
Index   327

List of figures

1.1   Indictments for Homicide in Scotland, 1805–1899   36
1.2   Indictments for Homicide in Scotland by Gender, 1805–1899   36
1.3   The Gendered Nature of Homicide Indictments
      in Scotland, 1805–1899   36
1.4   Indictments for Homicide in Scotland, 1900–1960   37
1.5   Indictments for Homicide in Scotland by Gender, 1900–1960   37
1.6   The Gendered Nature of Homicide Indictments
      in Scotland, 1900–1960   38
1.7   Indictments and Convictions for Homicide
      in Scotland, 1805–1899   38
1.8   The Gendered Nature of Convictions for Homicide
      in Scotland, 1805–1899   39
1.9   Verdicts and Sentencing Related to Homicides in Scotland,
      1805–1899   39
1.10 Indictments and Convictions for Homicide in Scotland,
      1900–1960   40
1.11 The Gendered Nature of Convictions for Homicide
      in Scotland, 1900–1960   40
1.12 Verdicts and Sentencing Related to Homicides in Scotland,
      1900–1960   41
1.13 Indictments for Culpable Homicide in Scotland, 1805–1899   41
1.14 Indictments for Culpable Homicide in Scotland by Gender,
      1805–1899   41
1.15 The Gendered Nature of Culpable Homicide Indictments
      in Scotland, 1805–1899   42
1.16 Indictments for Culpable Homicide in Scotland, 1900–1960   42
1.17 Indictments for Culpable Homicide in Scotland by Gender,
      1900–1960   43
1.18 The Gendered Nature of Culpable Homicide Indictments
      in Scotland, 1900–1960   43
1.19 Indictments and Convictions for Culpable Homicide in
      Scotland, 1805–1899   44

1.20 The Gendered Nature of Convictions for Culpable
     Homicide in Scotland, 1805–1899   44
1.21 Verdicts and Sentencing Related to Culpable Homicides in
     Scotland, 1805–1899   45
1.22 Indictments and Convictions for Culpable Homicide in
     Scotland, 1900–1960   45
1.23 The Gendered Nature of Convictions for Culpable
     Homicide in Scotland, 1900–1960   45
1.24 Indictments for Infanticide in Scotland, 1805–1899   46
1.25 Indictments for Infanticide in Scotland, 1900–1960   46
1.26 Indictments and Convictions for Infanticide in Scotland,
     1805–1899   46
1.27 Indictments and Convictions for Infanticide in Scotland,
     1900–1960   47
2.1 Indictments for Rape in Scotland, 1805–1899   84
2.2 Indictments for Rape in Scotland, 1900–1960   84
2.3 Indictments and Convictions for Rape in Scotland, 1805–1899   85
2.4 Indictments and Convictions for Rape in Scotland, 1900–1960   85
2.5 Indictments for Attempted Rape in Scotland, 1830–1899   86
2.6 Indictments for Attempted Rape in Scotland, 1900–1960   86
2.7 Indictments and Convictions for Attempted Rape in
     Scotland, 1830–1899   87
2.8 Indictments and Convictions for Attempted Rape in
     Scotland, 1900–1960   87
3.1 Indictments for Attempted Murder in Scotland, 1830–1899   118
3.2 Indictments for Attempted Murder in Scotland by Gender,
     1830–1899   119
3.3 The Gendered Nature of Attempted Murder Indictments in
     Scotland, 1830–1899   119
3.4 Indictments for Attempted Murder in Scotland, 1900–1960   119
3.5 Indictments for Attempted Murder in Scotland by Gender
     1900–1960   120
3.6 The Gendered Nature of Attempted Murder Indictments in
     Scotland, 1900–1960   120
3.7 Indictments and Convictions for Attempted Murder in
     Scotland, 1830–1899   121
3.8 The Gendered Nature of Convictions for Attempted Murder
     in Scotland, 1830–1899   121
3.9 Indictments and Convictions for Attempted Murder in
     Scotland, 1900–1960   122
3.10 The Gendered Nature of Convictions for Attempted Murder
     in Scotland, 1900–1960   122
3.11 Indictments for Assault of Authority in Scotland, 1805–1914   123
3.12 Indictments for Assault of Authority in Scotland by Gender,
     1805–1914   123

3.13 The Gendered Nature of Assault of Authority Indictments
      in Scotland, 1805–1914   124
3.14 Indictments and Convictions for Assault of Authority in
      Scotland, 1830–1914   124
3.15 The Gendered Nature of Convictions for Assault of
      Authority in Scotland, 1830–1914   125
3.16 Indictments for Assault in Scotland, 1805–1899   125
3.17 Indictments for Assault in Scotland by Gender, 1805–1899   125
3.18 The Gendered Nature of Assault Indictments in Scotland,
      1805–1899   126
3.19 Indictments for Assault in Scotland, 1900–1960   126
3.20 Indictments for Assault in Scotland by Gender, 1900–1960   126
3.21 The Gendered Nature of Assault Indictments in Scotland,
      1900–1960   127
3.22 Indictments and Convictions for Assault in Scotland,
      1805–1899   127
3.23 The Gendered Nature of Convictions for Assault in
      Scotland, 1805–1899   127
3.24 Indictments and Convictions for Assault in Scotland,
      1900–1960   128
3.25 The Gendered Nature of Convictions for Assault in
      Scotland, 1900–1960   128
3.26 The Proportion of Recidivism amongst Indictments for
      Assault in Scotland, 1836–1896   128
3.27 The Proportion of Recidivism amongst Indictments for
      Assault in Scotland, 1897–1960   129
3.28 Plan of Crime Scene – Case Against Henry Watson, 1914   141
4.1   Indictments for Mobbing and Rioting in Scotland,
      1805–1913   160
4.2   Indictments for Mobbing and Rioting in Scotland by
      Gender, 1805–1913   160
4.3   The Gendered Nature of Mobbing and Rioting Indictments
      in Scotland, 1805–1913   161
4.4   Indictments for Offences Against Public Order
      in Scotland, 1925–1960   161
4.5   Indictments for Offences Against Public Order in Scotland
      by Gender, 1925–1960   162
4.6   The Gendered Nature of Indictments for Offences Against
      Public Order in Scotland, 1925–1960   162
4.7   Indictments and Convictions for Mobbing and Rioting in
      Scotland, 1830–1913   163
4.8   The Gendered Nature of Convictions for Mobbing and
      Rioting in Scotland, 1830–1913   163
4.9   Indictments and Convictions for Offences Against Public
      Order in Scotland, 1925–1960   163

4.10 The Gendered Nature of Convictions for Offences Against
      Public Order in Scotland, 1925–1960   164
5.1   Indictments for Attempted Robbery
      in Scotland, 1830–1882   203
5.2   Indictments for Attempted Robbery in Scotland
      by Gender, 1830–1882   203
5.3   The Gendered Nature of Attempted Robbery Indictments
      in Scotland, 1830–1882   204
5.4   Indictments and Convictions for Attempted Robbery
      in Scotland, 1830–1882   204
5.5   The Gendered Nature of Convictions for Attempted
      Robbery in Scotland, 1830–1882   205
5.6   Indictments for Robbery in Scotland, 1805–1899   205
5.7   Indictments for Robbery in Scotland by Gender, 1805–1899   206
5.8   The Gendered Nature of Robbery Indictments
      in Scotland, 1805–1899   206
5.9   Indictments for Robbery and Attempted Robbery
      in Scotland, 1900–1960   206
5.10 Indictments for Robbery and Attempted Robbery in
      Scotland by Gender, 1900–1960   207
5.11 The Gendered Nature of Robbery and Attempted Robbery
      Indictments in Scotland, 1900–1960   207
5.12 Indictments and Convictions for Robbery in Scotland,
      1805–1899   207
5.13 The Gendered Nature of Convictions for Robbery
      in Scotland, 1830–1899   208
5.14 Indictments and Convictions for Robbery and Attempted
      Robbery in Scotland, 1900–1960   208
5.15 The Gendered Nature of Convictions for Robbery and
      Attempted Robbery in Scotland, 1900–1960   208
5.16 Colour Portrait of Gilder Roy   216
6.1   Indictments for Non-Violent Property Crime in Scotland,
      1836–1899   249
6.2   Types of Non-Violent Property Crime Indicted in Scotland,
      1836–1899   249
6.3   Indictments for Non-Violent Property Crime in Scotland by
      Gender, 1836–1899   250
6.4   The Gendered Nature of Non-Violent Property Crime
      Indictments in Scotland, 1836–1899   250
6.5   Indictments for Non-Violent Property Crime
      in Scotland, 1900–1960   251
6.6   Types of Non-Violent Property Crime Indicted
      in Scotland, 1900–1960   251

6.7   Indictments for Non-Violent Property Crime
      in Scotland by Gender, 1900–1960   252
6.8   The Gendered Nature of Non-Violent Property Crime
      Indictments in Scotland, 1900–1960   252
6.9   Indictments and Convictions for Non-Violent Property
      Crime in Scotland, 1836–1899   253
6.10 The Gendered Nature of Convictions for Non-Violent
      Property Crime in Scotland, 1836–1899   253
6.11 Indictments and Convictions for Non-Violent Property
      Crime in Scotland, 1900–1960   253
6.12 The Gendered Nature of Convictions for Non-Violent
      Property Crime in Scotland, 1900–1960   254
6.13 Indictments for Resett in Scotland, 1836–1899   254
6.14 Indictments for Resett in Scotland by Gender, 1836–1899   254
6.15 The Gendered Nature of Resett Indictments in Scotland,
      1836–1899   255
6.16 Indictments for Resett in Scotland, 1900–1960   255
6.17 Indictments for Resett in Scotland by Gender, 1900–1960   255
6.18 The Gendered Nature of Resett Indictments in Scotland,
      1900–1960   256
6.19 The Proportion of Recidivism amongst Indictments for
      Non-Violent Property Crime in Scotland, 1836–1896   256
6.20 The Proportion of Recidivism amongst Indictments for
      Non-Violent Property Crime in Scotland, 1897–1960   256
7.1   Criminal Indictments in Scotland 1832–1896.   291
7.2   Criminal Indictments in Scotland 1897–1960.   291

Acknowledgements

This book was a significant undertaking and simply would not have been possible without a Research Excellence Award from Oxford Brookes University. This enabled me to hire two research assistants: Daniel Vicars who worked with me in various Scottish archives collecting data and original source material and Rebecca Henderson who undertook the collation of judicial statistics for Scotland between 1805 and 1960. Both Daniel and Rebecca were highly industrious and hugely supportive, and their ongoing fascination for the project was a relentless motivator for me. Rebecca became seriously ill not long after the completion of this work. Her ongoing bravery and determination of will is humbling. I am proud to know her and to call her my friend. Significant thanks also goes to Pamela Fortescue who helped immeasurably in the production of this work, not least in her dedication to detail when it comes to graphs and charts of all shapes and sizes!

To my other colleagues at Oxford Brookes University, I owe a great debt. They have kept me sane and cheerful through some difficult times of late and I know this work is richer for their input, suggestions and unstinting encouragement. Particular thanks go to David Nash and Cassie Watson, my partners in crime. In addition, I would like to thank Adrian Ager, Joanne Begiato, Gary Browning, Dan Croft, Alistair Fitt, Beth Hill, Linda King, Simon Kövesi, Mike Henderson, Michelle Montgomery and Melanie Reynolds. Thanks too, go to Bill Knox and Billy Kay for our various discussions on the history of Scottish criminality which were enlightening, fruitful and fun!

My editor at Routledge, Hannah Catterall deserves a special mention in these acknowledgements for her perpetual patience with me and for all her support and guidance. In a similar vein, I would like to thank the staff at the Central Library (Edinburgh), the Mitchell Library (Glasgow), the National Records of Scotland (Edinburgh), the National Library of Scotland (Edinburgh), and the University of Glasgow Archives for all their help and for answering my innumerable questions. I would also like to express my gratitude to Roddy Flinn, Legal Secretary to the Lord President at Parliament House and to James Hamilton, Research Principal at the Signet Library in

Edinburgh, for allowing me special access to papers I would not otherwise have been able to consult.

Finally, as ever, I would like to thanks my family for their love and support and to Daniel for making everything better, always. The Kilday clan got a little bit larger recently, with the arrival of my gorgeous niece Grace and it is to her smile, her laughter and her enormous sense of fun, that this work is dedicated. Final thanks then must go to my brother John-Paul, and especially to his wife Laura, for the gift of Grace...

The Violent North – Fact or Fiction? Introduction and Context

The Violent North Thesis – Fact or Fiction?

In his topographical survey of Great Britain and Ireland produced in 1586, historian and antiquarian, William Camden promulgated an image of the Scots as a wild and barbarous people saying '…they drink the blood out of the wounds of the slain, they ratifie [ratify] their leagues with mutual draughts of blood,…and true Scots think their honour greater or less, in proportion to the numbers they have slain.'[1] Commentaries such as this heavily influenced opinion at home and abroad in the Middle Ages and beyond, with the French author Claude Jordan de Colombier, writing in 1697, describing the Scots as barbarian savages from the North.[2] When Daniel Defoe visited Scotland at the dawn of the eighteenth century, he too complained that the natives he encountered were quick-tempered and brutish: '…the steadyest Unsettled people Ever I met with. They are a hardened, refractory and Terrible people.'[3] A further depiction of the Scottish nation and its people was offered by Robert Chambers in the first volume of his *Domestic Annals of Scotland* written in 1858. He noted that:

> …every picture of noble humanity has its reverse – it is forced upon us that the Scots were, a fearfully rude and ignorant people…ruder than the England of that day, ruder than many other European states. Men carried weapons and were apt to use them on light occasion. Men were accustomed to violence in all forms, as to their daily bread.[4]

Even in the modern era, surveys and reports have apparently supported the proposition that Scotland is a violent nation and the Scots, a violent people. Indeed, one account produced by the United Nations in 2005, offered data which indicated that Scotland, at that time, was the most violent country in the developed world.[5]

Clearly this notion of Scotland as a lawless, uncivilised and savage nation contrasts sharply with the inoffensive tartanry and romanticised shortbread-tin history propounded by elements of the Scottish tourist industry. Nevertheless, and as is evident from these examples, the notion of 'the violent North' is clearly a historic trope or motif, often repeated and unquestionably enduring. But where did this idea originate and why has it seemingly persisted? Has this portrayal been a form of propaganda in perpetuity, utilised at different junctures in history by powerful internal or external neighbours, competitors and enemies in order to score political points, to suggest an innate primitiveness, or to offer an excuse for the failure of others to assimilate, suppress, or wholly colonise this northern nation? To what extent have the Scots themselves been complicit or active participants in the derivation and persistence of the notion of Scotland being a violent nation? Was this suggestion a form of audacious bravado, a self-defence tactic, or merely erroneous jest? Most importantly, to what extent does the actual reality of Scottish criminality bear out this supposition and justify the nation's label as a lawless, barbarous place? This monograph examines the accuracy of this ancient and long-held assumption and establishes the extent to which it is a truth or a fallacy. In so doing, it will be the first ever historical research to chart the long-term history of Scottish crime and in particular, Scottish violence.

The Violent North – Early Perceptions and Scholarship

As is evident from the quotes at the start of this chapter, the notion of Scotland as a violent nation has long endured and has been caught up, to some extent, in anti-Scottish sentiment (Scotophobia[6]) from various quarters and for a range of reasons at different historical moments. Fiona Watson has argued that Scotland is a country with '...a long and supposedly tormented past.'[7] The nation, she argues, '...is, and always has been, a complex melting pot of disparate groups, many of which have sat uneasily alongside the mainstream, but were equally often at odds with it.'[8] From the earliest times through to the Roman and Viking invasions and beyond, the cosmopolitan early peoples of Scotland were labelled as 'savages' in order to set them apart, as a distinctive threat, rival or enemy to other 'native' tribes and social groups.[9] The notion of Scotland as a violent nation then, at least in its earliest conception, was not a label early Scottish peoples gave to themselves, it was a constructed characterisation given to them by others, to establish them as different, or 'the other'.[10]

Whilst there is evidence to suggest that the early Scots could be fatally fractious on occasion and they undoubtedly did engage in bloodshed and brutality from time to time (such as during border raids or intra-tribal battles for supremacy), such behaviour was not as endemic or as serious as early commentators suggested. Violence in early Scotland was seemingly sporadic and deliberate, rather than common and gratuitous.[11] Nevertheless, irregular instances of violence and bloodshed were reported by early writers and their comments undoubtedly served to fuel and shape the initial conception of

Scotland as a violent nation. Indeed, over time, and through continual reiteration using prevailing localised examples, it became an accepted negative stereotype utilised as political propaganda during periods of internal and external conflict in an attempt to paint the entire northern nation and its people as primitive, uncivilised and easily subjugated.[12]

Yet, in actual fact, it was the Highland region, more than any other part of Scotland, that seemed to cause the most concern and which made the most significant contribution to this national trope of belligerence.[13] During the Wars of Independence in the thirteenth and fourteenth centuries and for several centuries afterwards, the far North was pretty much left to its own devices in terms of formal governance, resulting in violent clan conflicts between families. Chroniclers such as John of Fordun castigated the Highlanders for their lawlessness and their unruly, savage behaviour, and even Lowland Scots saw themselves as being distinct from their uncivilised more northern compatriots.[14] Over time, the Highland reputation for bad behaviour and indifference to authority intensified to such a degree that King James VI was forced to deploy various initiatives to bring the area to heel in the early years of the seventeenth century. However, the ill-thought-through experiments he introduced and the policy decisions he made only served to raise antagonisms and fuel unwillingness to conform.[15] Despite this, it could be argued, once again, that the true nature and extent of violent criminality in the Highland region seems to have been overblown and exaggerated as recent scholarship has indicated.[16]

In any event, it is evident that specific instances of violent atrocities coming to light from the Highland context served to re-energise the negative stereotypes tied to Scottish identity. Similarly, the concept of the blood feud also did much to bolster outsiders' notions of Scotland as a violent nation and the Highlands in particular, as an area beyond control.[17] The blood feud, a customary form of justice practiced across Europe during the Middle Ages, was typically applied after an episode of deliberate murder. In this era there was no state-sanctioned redress relating to criminal matters and so by this custom, the murder victim's nearest kin had an obligation to retaliate against the killer. This premodern form of vendetta, was subject to certain rules concerning the type of vengeance permissible, and these shaped the amount of compensation that could be exacted (known in Scotland as assythment), the location at which the reparation was to be made, and the circumstances in which such compensation was *not* required (such as in the defence of nobility or a female family member or if a known thief had been killed).[18]

The blood feud seems to have lasted longer in Scotland compared to elsewhere and specifically in the Highland region. This suggests that it was *needed* in Scotland for longer than in other European nations as a consequence of the nation's primitive and uncivilised governance and the inadequate provision and acceptance of a more centralised system of justice. The continuation of the blood feud in Scotland provided onlookers and commentators with a further unfortunate example suggesting not only that the country's inhabitants were violently anarchic and lawless but also that the prevailing governance structures could not secure order, control criminality or foster disciplined behaviour.[19] However, closer analysis of the Scottish experience of the blood feud suggests that this form of customary justice lasted longer because it was tremendously effective and typically did an excellent job of preventing existing antagonisms from escalating to a point where further bloodletting became inevitable. The detailed negotiations that transpired and the weight placed upon the 'bonds of manrent' or compensation agreements that were drawn up, worked well to shut down and thereafter control waywardly violent tendencies, not just in the Highland region, but across the country more widely.[20]

Regardless of how the blood feud worked in reality, it was still used, alongside various other infamous violent episodes in wider Scottish history, to suggest that the violent character of the Scottish people was utterly entrenched and irreversible. Commentators greedily fed on news of violent intrigue at the royal court, violent politicking between noble families, violent feuding and skirmishes in the Borders region, violent clan rivalries in the far North and violent religious-based rebellions and popular revolts everywhere else. Their reportage of these events (individually and collectively) undoubtedly augmented the trope of Scottish truculence and fuelled its persistence.[21] The Unions of 1603 and 1707 did nothing to quell the notion of Scotland as an untamed and ruthless nation either, and problems with the seemingly 'savage' and 'rebellious' Highlands continued, with the Jacobite campaigns providing further fuel to negative connotations associated with the Scottish character.[22] It is clear, once again, that this was not a self-derived or self-perpetuated viewpoint. Rather it was one that was applied from without, rather than from within. Indeed, into the more modern era too, the highlighting of isolated and localised examples of popular disturbance and radicalism in order to sustain political pressure, ensured that Scotland's reputation for unrest and aggression, alluded to by Daniel Defoe at the start of this chapter in relation to the eighteenth century, was set to endure.[23] But what have historians said about the accuracy of this?

Whilst the history of Scottish crime is relatively under-researched in comparison with many of its European counterparts, and there has, until now, been no national or historical survey of its nature and incidence, the issue of Scotland's seemingly violent nature has nonetheless sparked something of a historiographical debate.[24] According to Christopher Whatley, the '...uninflammability of the Scottish people and the relative quiescence of Scottish society' is something that has long been accepted by Scottish historians, especially in relation to the eighteenth and early nineteenth centuries.[25] What he has deemed an '...orthodoxy of passivity'[26] has seemingly stemmed from the work of renowned scholars such as Thomas Devine, T.C. Smout and Hamish

Fraser who have argued that, contrary to the image portrayed in the negative stereotype, the Scots were largely a 'tame' people, not a violent one.[27]

As this acquiescent characteristic of national identity has been so widely accepted for so long, much of the prevailing historiography has concentrated on providing explanations as to why this was the case. Devine, Smout and others have insisted that the existence of flexible multi-layered systems of support and 'social control' functioned to minimise unrest and disquiet. Even in more rural areas during the premodern period, where many other European countries experienced unrelenting waves of violent, popular protest, the Scottish experience was seemingly distinct in its relative tranquillity.[28] This quiescence arguably continued into the more modern era, where economic growth meant that more of the population were able to enjoy a higher standard of living and were thus not so commonly disposed to disorder. Moreover, those that were not exposed to these advances always had the safety valve of social and geographical mobility to deploy when times became tough.[29] On those rare occasions when hostility did break out, government interventions, by the twentieth century at least, were largely effective in curbing disquiet quickly so that it did not spread.[30]

Whilst far from accepting the blanket stereotypical notion of Scotland as a violent nation, Christopher Whatley sees this historiographical 'orthodoxy of passivity' as too simplistic and in need of reassessment. He argues that the nature of the Scots has been '...underestimated and imperfectly understood' for too long.[31] Moreover, he has found evidence of numerous forms of resistance and examples of persistent tensions in existence across Scottish society (particularly in urban areas) during the eighteenth and nineteenth centuries. Whilst he acknowledges that these instances may not be as significant as those experienced in other countries at the same time, nor was the evident defiance necessarily uniform or endemic, he insists, nonetheless, that the examples are worthy of note as they link to a broad range of complaints regarding diverse issues such as taxation and the collection of duties, food shortages and the formulation of the military, to name but a few.[32] Callum Brown also adds his weight to this revisionist approach by arguing that the premodern religious context in Scotland was one that experienced regular episodes of angst-based disorder which could result in physical manifestations of grievance.[33] For the nineteenth century too, William Knox and Alan McKinlay further develop this historiographical riposte by providing more modern examples of sectarian conflict, political radicalism, strike activity, gang-based criminality and episodes of juvenile delinquency, all of which challenge the suggestion that the Scots were a tamed and peaceable people.[34] The conclusions of these historians suggest that the Scottish character is much more nuanced and complex than previous scholars have acknowledged and long-held negative stereotypes have allowed.

The historiography of Scottish violence clearly has its disagreements and limitations as the analysis thus far has concentrated on specific time periods and thus the nature and incidence of Scottish violence has not been considered over a long chronology. This makes it difficult to make any unambiguous conclusions regarding lasting historical character traits. In addition, the perspectives presented have focused on forms of disorder or protest very specifically, and not upon violent criminality more broadly. Moreover, disorder is perhaps not the best index to use when determining whether violent behaviour or aggression was an intrinsic part of Scottish national identity. For one thing, as we will see in Chapter 5 of this volume, protest is spontaneous and collective by nature and is typically based on identifiable causes or grievances. More importantly perhaps, and as we will see, Scottish riots were not habitually bloodthirsty affairs.

The portrayal of the Highlands as a particularly wild and lawless place has similarly been the subject of unresolved historiographical debate. Scholars such as David Stephenson, Michael Fry and Bruce Lenman have all testified to the violence and lawlessness of the region, especially in the seventeenth and eighteenth centuries.[35] However, their work has been criticised by revisionist historians such as Allan Macinnes and especially Allan Kennedy, who insist that the '...blanket characterisations' that had been presented hitherto by these individuals, have been insufficient, and inaccurate. Crucially, they have not taken into account the fact that contemporaries may have exaggerated reports of Highland criminality or brutality for political effect.[36] Macinnes and Kennedy argue that Highland lawlessness was localised and infrequent, but when it *did* emerge, it was for economic or opportunistic reasons, rather than being instances of unfocussed callousness or viciousness.[37] In many respects therefore, they contend that the Highland experience of crime and criminality – violent or otherwise – was not particularly unusual or substantially different from anywhere else.[38]

Further factors which argue against the notion of Scotland as a violent nation emerge when the broader social history of the country is considered. It is soon evident, for instance, that various mechanisms for social control existed within and across Scottish society which should have acted to curb illegality and any inherent tendencies towards aggression and excessive use of force.[39] The first of these pertains more to the premodern period and relates to the combined influences of Kirk and community which utilised the power of entrenched religious influence and shame-based punishments as a means to foster moral adherence.[40] In addition to the influential governance structures already in existence and the prevailing bonds of kinship (attested to above in the discussion of the blood feud), the Church commanded considerable respect and wielded significant authority in premodern Scotland. The effectiveness of this apparent hegemony was undoubtedly strengthened by the fact that church discipline was explicitly interlinked – in both a theoretical and a practical sense – with other jurisdictions and alternative methods of social control, such as the judicial system.[41]

As I have discussed elsewhere, the system of justice that prevailed in Scotland before 1700 was innately complex.[42] Numerous jurisdictions based on legal entitlements and geographical boundaries existed and were underpinned by kinship agreements, territorial rights and other arrangements.[43] In general, the application of justice tended to be local and unprofessional in nature, and related to the maintenance of good order and daily adherence to regulations.[44] The absence of centralised control of judicial matters in pre-Enlightenment Scotland (largely due to the weakness of the Privy Council and the hereditary nature of many of the judicial offices) certainly influenced the prevailing perception of Scotland as a backward and lawless nation. It also meant that in addition to a lack of consistency in judicial decisions, there was also minimal regulation of the legislative process and those who controlled it. Likewise it was evident in discrepancies in the range of punishments meted out for similar offences across different jurisdictions.[45]

Although historians have testified to the gradual introduction of centralised justice in Scotland, such as the adoption of Justices of the Peace from the early seventeenth century onwards, significant change was nonetheless slow in coming.[46] Indeed, the real watershed for Scottish judicial practice did not occur until 1747 with the passing of the Heritable Jurisdictions Act.[47] This Act, which was part of a more general legislative programme concerned with pacifying the Highlands in the wake of the Jacobite Rebellions, abolished hereditary offices and effectively made some jurisdictions, like the barony and regality courts, obsolete. The Act also diminished the power of other local jurisdictions such as the burgh courts, whilst at the same time strengthened the judicial reach of the more 'superior' courts. As Stephen Davies describes, the Act '...brought about the final demise of a complex and distinctive legal system in favour of a formally structured order which has continued, by and large, to our own day.'[48]

Law, rationality and discipline were seen as crucial elements of Scotland's Enlightenment culture, as at least in theory, they enabled and encouraged the formation of a more civilised and sophisticated society.[49] In light of this, and in consequence of the changes in judicial provision described above, the business of the courts started to increase after 1750. As a result of this, criminal matters came increasingly to be heard in Scotland's central judiciaries and the Sheriff Court, Justiciary Court and, to a lesser extent, the Justice of the Peace Court. Although the Sheriff Court and the Justice of the Peace Court could in theory deal with a wide variety of offences by 1750, most of the *serious* criminal cases were brought before the Court of Justiciary.

The High Court of Justiciary was formally established in 1672 and was presided over by the Lord Justice General, the Lord Justice Clerk and five Lords of Session. The High Court was to sit in Edinburgh every Monday during the session, and for the first time, additional circuit courts were organised, with the country divided into three associated jurisdictions. The North Circuit related to courts held in Perth, Aberdeen and Inverness. The West

Circuit managed the courts held in Glasgow, Stirling and Inverary, and the South Circuit dealt with the courts held in Ayr, Dumfries and Jedburgh. Initially at least, these circuit courts met once a year, presided over by two Lords. After 1747, however, the increased volume of business caused by the absorption of work from the aforementioned dissolved jurisdictions, meant that the court had to go on circuit twice a year.[50]

The Justiciary Court had a wide remit when dealing with criminal offences. In the early modern period it dealt with petty crimes and moral offences, but these were increasingly assigned to the 'inferior' jurisdictions over the course of the eighteenth century. In the main, therefore, the Justiciary Court dealt with 'serious' offences such as political and treasonous crimes, the four pleas of the Crown (murder, rape, robbery and arson) and other felonious activities. These latter included counterfeiting and fraud, assault, infanticide, riot, sodomy and bestiality, theft, and the sale of stolen goods (known in Scotland as resett), as well as a variety of other misdemeanours.

It has been argued that in addition to developments related to the judicial system and its processes, there was also a growing awareness of the need for public displays of authority emanating from this more centralised form of justice. According to Jenny Wormald, for instance, by the late seventeenth and early eighteenth centuries, the Scottish state had moved away from conciliatory forms of atonement to more explicitly violent forms of penality to demonstrate power and authority to the wider populace, not simply to control criminality but also with respect to governance more generally.[51] Yet, the chronology of Professor Wormald's observation is misplaced and inaccurate. Whilst it is true to say that the nation had something of a notorious reputation for enacting tough justice, and the Scots were not unfamiliar with particularly gruesome displays of judicial violence such as the pre- and post-mortem amputation of convict limbs,[52] prolonged and painful death by drowning or burning at the stake[53] or the drawing, quartering and beheading of treasonable felons,[54] such instances had become very unusual by the eighteenth century.[55] Indeed, Scotland rarely deployed the ultimate sanction at all by this time and came to be described as a nation which had an 'innocence of the noose'.[56] However, we should not take from this that the Scottish Justiciary court was lenient or unduly sympathetic to the plight of the criminal, compared to that of the victim: far from it. Evidence from this volume and elsewhere suggests that the Scottish acquittal rate was low and convictions were commonplace.[57] Thus we can see that it was the gravity and opprobrium associated with the indictment and trial process, along with the unpredictable use of a myriad of penal sanctions, which historically combined to function as a tool of social control, and not (as has often been assumed), the spectacle of judicial violence. Capital punishment was never commonly or extensively utilised North of the Tweed and by the middle of the eighteenth century it had effectively become obsolete to be replaced firstly by transportation and latterly by imprisonment.[58]

The final mechanism for social control which prevailed in the Scottish context was policing. To some extent, the notion of policing was in existence in Scotland before it prevailed elsewhere, with the very word 'police' first being used in relation to the Scottish context in official documentation sanctioned by Queen Anne in 1714.[59] Before that time, and indeed throughout the eighteenth century, 'policing' in Scotland was done in part by the militia (especially in relation to instances of popular disturbance) and in the main by elders and members of the Kirk, who regularly 'detected' crimes and misdemeanours amongst their parishioners and then either reported these to the judicial authorities or dealt with them 'in-house' as described above.[60] However, the authority of the Kirk and the ability of its ministers to function in this way had deteriorated by the end of the eighteenth century in response to changes brought about by urbanisation and industrialisation, and so the idea of developing an alternative agency was cultivated.[61]

Rather than being concerned with the prevention of crime or the maintenance of order, which we now commonly associate with the activities of 'law enforcement', the main purpose of early Scottish policing was to promote the public good through the development of a rudimentary system of welfare provision. This did involve some basic surveillance of the populace, but only in terms of overseeing their health, safety and prosperity.[62] To this end, private police acts proliferated towards the end of the eighteenth and start of the nineteenth centuries in large urban centres across Scotland, but in actuality, it was the more rural areas that would eventually take the lead in establishing the kind of police 'force' that we are more familiar with today.[63]

Over the course of the early nineteenth century, the prevention and combatting of crime came to be blended with the original welfare objectives of policing and in 1833, the first public statute relating to Scottish policing – 'An Act to Enable the Burghs in Scotland to Establish a General System of Police' – was passed.[64] The impact of this act was not as revolutionary as might have been expected, however, because its plan for a centralised system of control was neither swiftly nor uniformly accepted.[65] However, increasing concerns about rising criminality and a particular anxiety regarding the perceived link between vagrancy and criminal activity did expedite matters, so that by 1857, new legislation compelled all Scottish counties to set up a force of their own.[66] Even then, however, development was not entirely uniform or consistent, as some burghs rejected attempts to assimilate them into a broader county-based provision. Nonetheless, by mid-century, policing throughout Scotland was on a firmer footing and it was regarded as being an effective mechanism for social control, with its role now firmly entrenched in the prevention of crime and the detection and capture of lawbreakers.[67]

The history of policing alongside the preceding commentary suggest that the very existence of these collective and collaborative mechanisms would make it unlikely that Scotland should necessarily be a *more* violent nation than anywhere else at any given time. If anything, and if these mechanisms operated fully effectively as is commonly suggested, then Scotland should have been a more *peaceable* nation than its neighbours and contemporaries.

The Persistence of the Violent Scot?

One of the factors which has undoubtedly contributed to the notion of Scotland as a violent nation, alluded to above, has been the attention focussed on a number of especially violent or brutal episodes which occurred throughout the country's past. The Jacobite rebellions of 1715 and 1745 for instance, undoubtedly demonised the Scottish nation for some audiences and aided the construction of narratives which associated the Scots with wanton bloodshed and violence. Yet, the importance of such episodes in perpetuating the notion of Scotland as a violent nation further intensified with the introduction of forms of mass media in the nineteenth century. Indeed, arguably, these sensational events (both individually and collectively) have served to create something akin to a historic moral panic which, at its simplest level, unremittingly equates the Scottish nation with violence, and its people with especially truculent tendencies. Indeed, as one early Victorian publication put it, these cases (referring to examples such as the grave robbers Burke and Hare, the robber-poisoners John Stewart and his wife Catherine Wright, and the brutal double-murderer Robert Edmond), Scotland had been '…disgraced by the commission of a series of crimes so novel in their character, and arguing such a degree of hardened depravity or calculating villainy upon the part of the perpetrators, as to astonish the whole world.'[68] One such example, also referred to in the same broadside, comes in the very middle of the three-hundred-year period scrutinised in this present work. Described as '…foul and unnatural',[69] this episode occurred at a transformative time in the history of Scotland. As we have seen, urbanisation and industrialisation were gathering pace, the power of the Kirk was waning, the policing initiative was being expanded because of concerns about the prevalence of criminality and violent criminality in particular, and the powers of centralised justice had firmly taken hold as the old feudal forms of social control withered on the vine.[70]

On the 12th of July 1830, two men – John Thomson and David Dobie were indicted at the High Court of Justiciary in Edinburgh for the rape, robbery and murder of a woman called Margaret Paterson.[71] The court heard how Thomson and Dobie had met Margaret Paterson in a pub at Liberton (near Edinburgh) on the 17th of April 1830, and after they had drunk there together for some time, the men agreed to give their new friend a cart-ride to the village of Gilmerton, some one-and-a-half miles away, as her feet were sore and it was on their journey home.[72] Near to their destination, one or both of the accused 'wickedly and feloniously' attacked Margaret Paterson, and after throwing her onto her back and holding her down by force and against her will, they '…did pull up her petticoats…did use indecent liberties with her and did attempt to have carnal knowledge of her person.' Witness evidence presented in court suggested that the men were likely too inebriated to complete their assault on Paterson to their satisfaction.[73] So, and perhaps on account of their apparent frustration, their attack on their victim escalated further at this point and they:

> ...did strike her several severe blows with their fists, and did kick her on the head and sides, and other parts of her body, whereby she was rendered quite insensible, and did thrust an angular piece of stone, a quantity of hay, and a number of small piece of coal and coal dust into the private parts of the said Margaret Paterson...They then also did thrust the stick of the corsets then worn by the said Margaret Paterson, or some other instrument to the Prosecutor unknown, up her fundament, and did thrust two angular pieces of stone up her fundament, whereby the said Margaret Paterson was grievously cut and torn in the inward parts of her body to the severe injury of her person, and great effusion of her blood.[74]

Thomson and Dobie (or 'The Gilmerton Monsters' as they were dubbed in contemporary publications[75]) then 'cruelly and inhumanely' abandoned Margaret Paterson at the roadside, but not before stealing various items from her person. The indictment lists the stolen effects as being: one gold earring, one small tin box, two pawn tickets for gowns (one worth 3s. 6d. and the other 4s.), one key, one checked cotton or muslin handkerchief, one green shawl, one coarse towel, three shillings and sixpence in silver money and a random selection of bread, meat and cardboard pieces.[76]

Margaret Paterson lay insensible in a ditch for some time before she attempted to get some assistance by crawling along the road in the direction of some nearby houses. Local woman Violet Armour found Margaret Paterson lying cold and trembling on the ground at the entrance to her property and called upon her sister-in-law, Mrs Gillon, for help.[77] Gillon helped Margaret to the house of her estranged father (who lived in nearby Dalkeith) and offered to tend to her there. She noted that upon arrival, Margaret seemed very frightened. Her clothes were filthy and her petticoats in particular were '...a sight in blood'.[78] Gillon then testified that although Paterson did not complain to her that she had '...been hurt about the private parts', she observed '...drops of blood falling from the woman's clothes on to the floor.'[79] She reported that whilst in her care, the victim '...constantly complained of a pain in the lower part of her belly' and that when Paterson '...made water' she '...seemed to feel great pain' and that the urine she produced was bright red.[80] After a few days, Mrs Gillon 'perceived a very disagreeable smell, like what she supposed to be the smell of mortification' coming from Margaret Paterson. Upon examination, Gillon discovered the victim's clothes to be 'drenched with a stuff which was bloody.'[81]

Five days after the attack, Margaret Paterson died after succumbing to her injuries. According to her parents, her final days were ones where she suffered terrible agonies. According to her father, for instance, Margaret's arms and sides were covered in so many bruises that she could not lie down comfortably. One broadside suggested that these marks had been made by '…the infliction of blows from some heavy or blunt weapon, such as a carter's rack pin or wrench.'[82] Mr Paterson further described how he witnessed '…a great deal of blood come from her' and saw his daughter '…suffer excruciating pain.'[83] Margaret's mother, for her part, was hugely distressed when she testified in court. She became particularly upset when she described how she witnessed a Dr Morrison trying to remove various items which had been forcibly stuffed into her daughter's body. She explained that some material was able to be recovered premortem, but other items (stones and knots of hay) were only removable postmortem. Mrs Paterson went on to explain that although her daughter had disclosed *some* of the details of the assault she had endured, her shame at what had happened to her, had '…prevented her from telling all that she could.'[84] Nevertheless, Mrs Paterson was categorical in the testimony she offered based on her discussions with her daughter on her deathbed. Margaret Paterson, unequivocally described to her mother how *both* of the men had '…used every kind of freedom with her', that '…*they* abused her…*they* forced her…and *they* then rendered her insensible by ramming her own wooden corset sticks up her private parts.' When Mrs Paterson sought clarification '…on which of the men had used her worst…her daughter had answered that they were *both* alike.'[85]

The report from the postmortem carried out on the body of Margaret Paterson at Dalkeith on the 23rd of April 1830, revealed the extent of the victim's injuries and the savagery of the abuse she had endured. Firstly, the medical men observed that:

> The external surface of the abdomen was of a bluish yellow colour, particularly the lower and lateral parts, the upper part of the thighs were livid [bruised] and emphysematous [swollen]. The anus was much contused and lacerated, the lower portion of the rectum gangrenous and detached from its natural connections, the external parts of generation also much contused with abrasion of the external surface of the vagina from which a quantity of hay was extracted. On examining the external part of the abdomen, we found the peritoneum very much inflamed [common in instances of assault where abdominal injuries have been inflicted] and there was a considerable effusion of seropurulent [pus] matter into the general cavity of the abdomen.[86]

It was their learned conclusion that '…death was in this instance, occasioned by external violence.'[87]

Although the evidence against the two men may at first glance seem circumstantial, as the crime was not witnessed and there was no obvious or direct evidence which linked Thomson and/or Dobie to the crime as described, further evidence which effectively sealed the men's fate came to light during the trial. For one thing, a man called Walter Dingwall, testified to having found several items in a cart belonging to his neighbour, David Dobie. Alongside a green shawl, Dingwall discovered a bundle of pieces of bread and boiled meat which had been parcelled up in a coarse towel. Walter Dingwall was sure these articles did not belong to either David Dobie or John Thomson, and the prosecution noted that they matched some of the items alleged to have been taken from Margaret Paterson.[88] In addition, the declarations and statements emitted to the court on the part of the accused also aided the prosecution's cause and testified to the contumeliousness and fundamental lack of remorse of the accused.

John Thomson, for his part, submitted two declarations to sheriff officers on the 22nd and 29th of April. In these statements he admitted having met the victim in a pub just as the prosecution had asserted, but he claimed that Margaret Paterson had come in to the premises already intoxicated and that she '...seemed to be entirely "done" with the drink' by the end of their drinking session and '...was unable to walk'. Thomson claimed he tried to help Paterson along the road but he could not support her weight and so he left her in a ditch to recover and went home to bed.[89] David Dobie, also tried to use the fact that Paterson was inebriated whilst in the two men's company to insinuate that she was a woman of bad character. However, he went a stage further in his two declarations made on the 29th of April and the 13th of May 1830.

Dobie claimed that after the left the pub with his two companions, he fell asleep in his cart due to his inebriation. He awoke due to noises that were caused by Thomson who '...was having to do with the woman in the cart and that he did so, two or three times again, to the point at which she was not able to walk.' He noted that '...the woman was not calling or resisting in any way... that she was heartily drunk...that her petticoats were apart and her legs bare...and he thought she could not be a very decent woman.' Moreover, Dobie was at pains to suggest that as '...the woman was drunk, she might be as willing as Thomson.'[90] Consequently, not only did Dobie incriminate his co-accused in the alleged assault, robbery and murder in his statement before the sheriff, but he also insinuated that Margaret Paterson was an enthusiastic participant in what had transpired. Dobie then said he had subsequently witnessed Thomson interfering with Margaret Paterson whilst she was 'insensible' and specifically saw that '...he had cut the woman with her corset sticks or thrust stones or hay into her person.' Dobie latterly saw Margaret Paterson '...yowling like a cat in the ditch' and described his witnessing of this entire episode as '...a sair [sore] sight to see.'[91]

David Dobie's account of what transpired on the 17th of April 1830 between himself, John Thomson and Margaret Paterson, which was intended to exonerate him from any wrongdoing, was undermined, to a large extent, by three factors which were brought to the court's attention. The first was

Dobie's admission before the sheriff at his final interview that he had not told the entire truth of what had happened. Dobie then announced that he was willing to do this, but only if the authorities agreed to revoke all of the charges against him, and instead, allow him to become a witness for the prosecution.[92] The sheriff refused Dobie's request. Next came witness testimony presented at the trial which declared that David Dobie had made crude, incriminatory and boastful jests to friends, colleagues and neighbours about the attack made on Margaret Paterson. Individuals recounted hearing Dobie say, on more than one occasion, that he *and* Thomson '…had made a woman, that she will neither hold in wind nor water.'[93] Finally, it was revealed during the trial that a significant sum of money had been found in a tin box on David Dobie's person upon his arrest. The value of the coinage discovered, as well as the description of the box it was in, exactly matched the prosecution's description of possessions stolen from Margaret Paterson.[94] This evidence, when considered collectively, may have made Dobie's declaration in court that he was '…as innocent as the child that's unborn' seem rather unlikely to the attentive assize.[95]

Indeed, once all the testimony had been heard, the jurors enclosed, but they deliberated upon their verdict for only a few minutes before declaring both prisoners guilty of murder, robbery and assault with intent to ravish. The rape charge against them was found not proven.[96] The three judges who heard the case at the High Court were so affected by the testimony they heard, that they each made a speech to the court before the inevitable sentence was delivered. Lord Meadowbank (Alexander Maconochie, 1777–1861) began by saying:

> It is hardly possible to imagine that persons living in this Christian land could have brought their minds to the commission of such atrocious crimes…I have not words to express the feelings which the details of this day have excited in my bosom.[97]

Lord Moncrieff (Sir James Wellwood Moncrieff, 1776–1851) then took his turn saying that the case:

> '…beggared all his powers of language to describe, and all his terms of condemnation to characterise. It was not to be wondered that it should sicken the heart of any honest man, much less a Christian man, to hear the details of it. This was a case, in which were exemplified the workings of the great enemy of the human race, and the dreadful lengths in wickedness to which the human heart will go, when left to itself. To think of the poor creature against whom these detestable things were done, it was impossible not to shudder.' He continued to say that the two convicts '…had degraded themselves into little better than beasts of prey, making this helpless woman their victim; they then left her, without

one particle of feeling, lying on the road in a state of insensibility…such atrocious criminals.'[98]

Finally, the Lord Justice Clerk (David, Lord Boyle, 1772–1853) addressed John Thomson and David Dobie directly. He said:

> I feel that no words that I can use are capable of describing the unparalleled brutality, cruelty, and wickedness of the foul transaction disclosed this day. The exhibition which you have made is calculated to make every man blush. Such wickedness and brutal abomination could not have been believed had it not been sworn into evidence…Rest assured that if ever there was a case in which the law will take its full course, it is yours.[99]

He then proceeded to sentence both men to execution at Edinburgh on the 18th of August and further ordained that their bodies be given over to Dr Alexander Munro (1773–1859), Professor of Anatomy, for public dissection.[100] Contemporary broadside material reports that the sentence was carried out to its full effect before a large crowd of onlookers.[101] Subsequent evidence came to light from intercepted correspondence between David Dobie and his wife whilst he languished in jail prior to his execution, that he at least, had seemingly become penitent by the time of his death. In his letters he acknowledged '…the enormity of our crimes…which were of the rudest and deepest dye' and admitted that both he and Thomson had

> …recall to mind many idle-spent Sabbaths and the Church we often neglected and passed by as if it were a ruinous heap…making scoff of such that attended it while we went to the public house and wallowed in all the abominations the human mind can picture.[102]

Clearly the assault perpetrated upon Margaret Paterson was a brutal, abhorrent and senseless crime. Crucially for our purposes, though, it occurred at a time when, as we have established, there was an evident moral panic regarding the nature and incidence of violent crime in Scotland. Due to the needless extreme violence involved and the lurid details which were made available in largely uncensored form to the Scottish populace, media coverage of the trial of Thomson and Dobie was intense, ubiquitous and persistent. Whether this case *triggered* the moral panic or was merely one of several sensational cases which acted as catalysts at specific points in the nation's history to prolong the moral panic is difficult to determine. Certainly, one evident legacy of the Thomson and Dobie case is that it was regularly used by social and moral commentators to defend the notion that Scotland was indeed a violent nation.[103] Indeed, just a little over a decade later, Archibald Alison bemoaned '…the astonishing increase in human depravity…and the rapid progress of wickedness' in Scotland, where crime rates were significantly outstripping the contemporary demographic upsurge.[104]

Yet, can a media storm and the public scrutiny of just a few select cases necessitate labelling an entire nation as violent in perpetuity? How valid is this portrayal and how typical were cases like that of Thomson and Dobie in Scottish criminal history? This book will answer these questions in detail and will determine the extent to which the notion of Scotland as a violent nation is hyperbolic, inaccurate and overblown. Was Scottish crime predominantly violent in nature and were Scottish criminals excessively aggressive when they offended? When Jenny Wormald reminded her fellow Scottish historians some thirty-five years ago, that '...we need to set the level of Scottish violence in its proper context'[105], her call went unanswered. This volume, now many years later rectifies that silence. Chapter 2 analyses the history of fatal violence in Scotland between 1660 and 1960 and Chapter 3 does the same with sexual violence. Chapters 4 and 5 examine forms of interpersonal violence over the same period, encompassing both individual and collective forms of direct action nationwide. Chapter 6 investigates violent activity where the motive was personal or economic gain and offers a counterpoint to Chapter 7 which looks at forms of Scottish criminality where the actions of the participants could more accurately be labelled as 'enterprising' rather than 'enraged'. The volume then offers a brief conclusion which summarises its key findings and directions for future work. Each chapter begins with an investigation into the legal context of the crimes considered. This is followed by an incidence analysis based on reported crime rates for the nineteenth and twentieth century periods and a broader chronological discussion of typical offenders, victims, methodologies and motives. A series of case studies is then presented to illuminate these aspects in more detail and to present a more qualitative picture of the history of crime in Scotland between 1660 and 1960.

Sources and Methodology

Although this monograph utilises an eclectic range of primary source evidence including songs, poems, broadside confessions, newspapers and interviews, the bulk of the material consulted (and upon which the statistical analysis presented is based) relates to a forensic examination of the rich records of the Scottish Justiciary Court over the 1660–1960 period.[106] It is worth reiterating that this work is the first to consider Scottish crime, and Scottish violence more especially, over a long chronology. Yet, it must be acknowledged that, the picture offered here may not be wholly complete. This is for several reasons. The first relates to a problem most historians of crime face, and that is the so-called 'dark figure' of unreported and thus unknown crime. As official crime statistics can only relate to crime that has been reported to the authorities, we may never know the full extent of its true nature and incidence. Although this problem is likely mitigated by the fact that this work is dealing with serious offences which were more likely to be reported, it is nonetheless a consideration that needs to be borne in mind about the accuracy of the data presented.[107] To that end, this work will use a mix of quantitative and qualitative case-study evidence to provide the fullest and most accurate possible picture.

The second issue which may impact upon the data presented in this volume is that the evidence provided largely relates to indictments at the Justiciary Court. As the supreme jurisdiction in Scotland, this court was far more likely than any other to indict serious or violent offenders. Of course, this makes a study of the provenance and business of this court absolutely essential for any investigation of violent criminality North of the Tweed in the 1660–1960 period. However, it also means that certain forms of criminality are not part of the picture painted by this work. Petty offences, even if violent, but dealt with in the minor courts of Scotland are not addressed in any depth, save for in the fourth chapter on violent assault and the seventh chapter on non-violent property crimes. Juvenile offences and offenders which were dealt with by specific and alternative jurisdictions from the second half of the nineteenth century do not form a detailed part of this analysis, nor will the violent criminality of gangs through extortion and blackmail as so much of this behaviour tended to operate within in a separate criminal underworld with its own retributive system of 'justice' which negated the use of the courtroom.[108] Although the data utilised in this monograph does have the potential to skew or exaggerate the picture of criminality in the Scottish context, as the Justiciary Court dealt with the most serious crimes and was thus more likely to deal with crimes of violence, it nonetheless remains the obvious and most appropriate jurisdiction within which to prove or disprove the notion of Scotland as a violent nation.

Notes

1 W. Camden (1722 edition) [Translated by Edmund Gibson] *Britannia: Or a Chorographical Description of Great Britain and Ireland, Together with the Adjacent Islands* (London: M. Matthew) [Found at https://archive.org/details.gri_331250111 16247 and accessed 14/03/2018].
2 C. Jordan de Colombier (1709 edition) *Historiques de Toutes Les Cours de L'Europe avec L'Espion des Cours – Tome* IV (Brussels: Francois Foppens), p. 140.
3 P.N. Furbank and W.R. Owens (2016 edition) *A Political Biography of Daniel Defoe* (London: Routledge), p. 69.
4 R. Chambers (1858) Domestic Annals of Scotland: From the Reformation to the Revolution – Volume I (Edinburgh: Chambers), p. 5.
5 See *The Guardian*, 19th September 2005. For criticisms of the report and its contents see *The Scotsman*, 19th September 2005.
6 Historian William Ferguson uses this phrase to reflect what he calls a long-held form of '…racial prejudice' against the Scots by the English. In my view, it could be argued that this racism has broader origins. The phrase can be defined as an

intense hostility or aversion towards Scotland, its people and its culture. For further discussion see W. Ferguson (1998) *The Identity of the Scottish Nation: A Historic Quest* (Edinburgh: Edinburgh University Press), p. 227.

7 F. Watson (2002 edition) *Scotland: A History, 8000 B.C. – A.D. 2000* (Stroud: Tempus), p. 13.

8 *Ibid*, p. 14. See also R. Mitchison (2002 edition) *A History of Scotland* (London: Routledge), p. ix and M. Lynch (2000) *Scotland: A New History* (London: Pimlico), p. 53.

9 *Ibid*, p. 26, p. 39, p. 46 and pp. 77–79. See also T.O. Clancy and B.E. Crawford (2001) 'The Formation of the Scottish Kingdom' and D. Ditchburn and A.J. MacDonald (2001) 'Medieval Scotland, 1100–1560' both in R.A. Houston and W.W.J. Knox (eds.) *The New Penguin History of Scotland: From the Earliest Times to the Present Day* (London: Allen Lane), pp. 28–95 at p. 33 and pp. 96–181 at p. 150 respectively and K. Forsyth (2005) 'Origins: Scotland to 1100' in J. Wormald (ed) *Scotland: A History* (Oxford: Oxford University Press), pp. 1–38 at p. 28.

10 The notion of the contribution made by other cultures in the shaping of Scottish national identity is a point acknowledged by Scottish historians, see for instance R.A. Houston and W.W.J. Knox (2001) 'Introduction: Scots and their Histories' in Houston and Knox (eds.) *The New Penguin History of Scotland*, pp. xiii–lviii at p. xvii.

11 See for instance Watson (2002 edition) *Scotland*, pp. 34–35, p. 39, p. 47, p. 49 and p. 117 and Houston and Knox (2001) 'Introduction', p. xlix and p. liv.

12 For examples see Ferguson (1998) *The Identity of the Scottish Nation*, pp. 25–26 and Watson (2002 edition) *Scotland*, p. 121 and p. 125.

13 See Houston and Knox (2001) 'Introduction', p. xviii.

14 See M. MacGregor (2009) 'Gaelic Barbarity and Scottish Identity in the Later Middle Ages' and D. Broun (2009) 'Attitudes of *Gall* to *Gaedhel* in Scotland before John of Fordun' both in D. Broun and M. MacGregor (eds.) *Mìorun Mòr Nan Gall, 'The Great Ill-will of the Lowlander?' Lowland Perceptions of the Highlands, Medieval and Modern* (Glasgow: University of Glasgow Press), pp. 7–48 and pp. 49–82 respectively. See also Lynch (2000) *Scotland*, pp. 67–68.

15 See M. Brown and S. Boardman (2005) 'Survival and Revival: Late Medieval Scotland' in Wormald (ed) *Scotland*, pp. 77–106 at p. 84; K.M. Brown (2001) 'Reformation to Union, 1560–1707' in Houston and Knox (eds.) *The New Penguin History of Scotland*, pp. 182–275 at pp. 223–224 and p. 237 and Watson (2002 edition) *Scotland*, p. 175.

16 See for instance A. Kennedy (2016) 'Crime and Punishment in Early-Modern Scotland: The Secular Courts of Restoration Argyllshire, 1660–1688', *International Review of Scottish Studies*, 41, pp. 1–36 at pp. 11–28; C.A. Whatley (2010) 'Order and Disorder' in E. Foyster and C.A. Whatley (eds.) *A History of Everyday Life in Scotland, 1600–1800* (Edinburgh: Edinburgh University Press), pp. 191–216 at p. 191 and D. McCormack (2014) 'Highland Lawlessness and the Cromwellian Regime' in S. Adams and J. Goodare (eds.) *Scotland in the Age of Two Revolutions* (Woodbridge: Boydell Press), pp. 115–133.

17 See Lynch (2000) *Scotland*, p. 69.

18 For a broader European perspective of blood feud see R. Fletcher (2004 edition) *Bloodfeud: Murder and Revenge in Anglo-Saxon England* (Oxford: Oxford University Press) and I. Wood (2006) '"The Bloodfeud of the Franks": A Historiographical Legend', *Early Medieval Europe*, 14, 4, pp. 489–504. For the Scottish perspective see K.M. Brown (1986) *Bloodfeud in Scotland 1573–1625* (Edinburgh: John Donald).

19 For evidence of this see Brown (1986) *Bloodfeud*, p. 13.

20 *Ibid*, p. 4, p. 14, p. 22 and p. 43. For further evidence of this see also J. Wormald (1980) 'Bloodfeud, Kindred and Government in Early Modern Scotland', *Past and Present*, 87, pp. 54–97 at p. 73 and J. Wormald (1985) *Lords and Men in Scotland: Bonds of Manrent, 1442–1603* (Edinburgh: John Donald), p. 116 and pp. 127–128.

21 See Brown (2001) 'Reformation to Union', p. 234; Watson (2002 edition), *Scotland*, pp. 131–139, p. 141, p. 167, pp. 181–182 and p. 196 and E.J. Cowan and R. Finlay (2000) *Scotland Since 1688: Struggle for a Nation* (London: Cima Books), p. 62.

22 Watson (2002 edition), *Scotland*, pp. 203–212.

23 *Ibid*, p. 220.

24 Some significant works on Scottish history and Scottish national identity have completely omitted consideration of crime and violence such as W.C. Dickinson and A.A.M. Duncan (1977 edition) *Scotland from the Earliest Times to 1603* (Oxford: Clarendon); J.D. Mackie (1991 edition) *A History of Scotland* (London: Penguin); T.M. Devine and P. Logue (2002) *Being Scottish: Personal Reflections on Scottish Identity Today* (Edinburgh: Polygon); R. Mitchison (2002 edition) *A History of Scotland* (London: Routledge) and E.J. Cowan and L. Henderson (eds.) *A History of Everyday Life in Medieval Scotland, 1000 to 1600* (Edinburgh: Edinburgh University Press). I have written elsewhere about the lacunae of research into the history of Scottish crime, see A-M. Kilday (2007) *Women and Violent Crime in Enlightenment Scotland* (Woodbridge: Boydell), Chapter 1 and (2014) 'The Barbarous North? Criminality in Early Modern Scotland' in T.M. Devine and J. Wormald (eds.) *The Oxford Handbook of Modern Scottish History* (Oxford: Oxford University Press), pp. 386–404. However, as well as my own work (which will be utilised throughout this volume and thus not replicated here) and the scholarship cited in this introduction, thankfully there are now many more academic contributions which contribute greatly to our burgeoning understanding of criminal history in the 1660–1960 Scottish context. These include (in chronological order): K.J. Logue (1979) *Popular Disturbances in Scotland 1780–1815* (Edinburgh: John Donald); M.A. Crowther (1992) 'Scotland: A Country with No Criminal Record', *Scottish Economic and Social History*, 12, pp. 82–86; M.M. Stewart (1995) 'In Durance Vile: Crime and Punishment in the Seventeenth and Eighteenth Century Records of Dumfries' and M.A. Crowther (1995) 'Criminal Precognitions and their Value for the Historian' both in *Scottish Archives: The Journal of the Scottish Records Association*, I, pp. 63–74 and pp. 75–84 respectively; I. Donnachie (1995) '"The Darker Side": A Speculative Survey of Scottish Crime during the First Half of the Nineteenth Century', *Scottish Economic and Social History*, XV, pp. 5–24; D.A. Symonds (1997) *Weep Not for Me: Women, Ballads and Infanticide in Early Modern Scotland* (University Park: Pennsylvania State University Press); R.A. Houston (2006) 'Poor Relief and the Dangerous and Criminal Insane in Scotland, c.1740–1840', *Journal of Social History*, 40, 2, pp. 453–476; P.T. Riggs (2010) 'Prosecutors, Juries, Judges and Punishment in Early Nineteenth-Century Scotland', *Journal of Scottish Historical Studies*, 32, 2, pp. 166–189; L.A. Jackson and A. Bartie (2011) '"Children of the City": Juvenile Justice, Property and Place in England and Scotland, 1945–60', *The Economic History Review*, 64, 1, pp. 88–113; P. King (2011) 'Urbanization, Rising Homicide Rates and the Geography of Lethal Violence in Scotland, 1800–1860', *History*, 96, 3, pp. 231–259; L. Abrams (2013) 'The Taming of Highland Masculinity: Inter-Personal Violence and Shifting Codes of Manhood, c. 1760–1840', *Scottish Historical Review*, 92, 1, pp. 100–122 and W.W.J. Knox (2015) 'Homicide in Eighteenth Century Scotland: Numbers and Theories', *Scottish Historical Review*, 95, 1, pp. 48–73.

25 C.A. Whatley (1990) 'How Tame were the Scottish Lowlanders during the Eighteenth Century' in T.M. Devine (ed) *Conflict and Stability in Scottish Society 1700–1850* (Edinburgh: John Donald), pp. 1–30 at p. 1.

26 *Ibid*, p. 3. For further discussion see also C.A. Whatley (2000) *Scottish Society 1707–1830: Beyond Jacobitism, Towards Industrialisation* (Manchester: Manchester University Press), p. 143.

27 See for instance Devine (1999) *The Scottish Nation 1700–2000* (London: Penguin), p. 102; T.C. Smout (1969) *A History of the Scottish People 1560–1830* (London: Fontana), p. 417 and W.H. Fraser (1988) 'Patterns of Protest' in T.M. Devine and R. Mitchison (eds.) *People and Society in Scotland– Volume I: 1760– 1830* (Edinburgh: John Donald), pp. 268–291. See also R.A. Houston and I.D. Whyte (1989) 'Introduction: Scottish Society in Perspective' in R.A. Houston and I.D. Whyte (eds.) *Scottish Society 1500–1800* (Cambridge: Cambridge University Press), pp. 1–36 at p. 25 especially; K.J. Logue (1980) 'Eighteenth Century Popular Protest: Aspects of the People's Past' in E.J. Cowan (ed) *The People's Past* (Edinburgh: Polygon), pp. 108–130 at p. 109; Houston and Knox (2001) 'Introduction' and Brown (2001) 'Reformation to Union' both in Houston and Knox (eds.) *The New Penguin History of Scotland* (London: Allen lane), pp. xiii–lviii at p. xlix and pp. 182–275 at p. 224 respectively.

28 For further discussion see for instance B. Lenman and G. Parker (1980) 'Crime and Control in Scotland, 1500–1800', *History Today*, XXX, pp. 13–17; B. Lenman (1981) *Integration, Enlightenment and Industrialisation: Scotland 1746–1832* (London: Edward Arnold), *passim*; T.M. Devine (1978) 'Social Stability and Agrarian Change in the Eastern Lowlands of Scotland, 1810–1840', *Social History*, 3, pp. 331–346 and T.M. Devine (1988) 'Unrest and Stability in Rural Ireland and Scotland, 1760–1840' in R. Mitchison and P. Roebuck (eds.) *Economy and Society in Scotland and Ireland 1500–1939* (Edinburgh: John Donald), pp. 126–139.

29 For further discussion see for instance Devine (1999) *The Scottish Nation*, p. 217.

30 For further discussion see J. Foster (2001) 'The Twentieth Century, 1914–1979' in Houston and Knox (eds.) *The New Penguin History of Scotland*, pp. 417–493 at p. 437.

31 Whatley (2000) *Scottish Society*, p. 144.

32 See for instance Whatley (1990) 'How Tame?', pp. 3–24; Whatley (2000) *Scottish Society*, p. 151, pp. 163–175 and pp. 187–189 and C.A. Whatley (2010) 'Order and Disorder', pp. 202–211.

33 C.G. Brown (1990) 'Protest in the Pews: Interpreting Presbyterianism and Society in Fracture during the Scottish Economic Revolution' in Devine (ed) *Conflict and Stability*, pp. 83–105.

34 For further discussion see W.W.J. Knox and A. McKinlay (2010) 'Crime, Protest and Policing in Nineteenth-Century Scotland' in T. Griffiths and G. Morton (eds.) *A History of Everyday Life in Scotland, 1800 to 1900* (Edinburgh: Edinburgh University Press), pp. 196–224 at pp. 206–212.

35 See D. Stevenson (1980) *Highland Warrior: Alisdair MacColla and the Civil Wars* (Edinburgh: Birlinn); M. Fry (2005) *Wild Scots: Four Hundred Years of Highland History* (London: John Murray) and B.P. Lenman (1995) *The Jacobite Clans of the Great Glen 1650–1784* (Dalkeith: Scottish Cultural Press).

36 See A. Macinnes (1996) *Clanship, Commerce and the House of Stuart, 1603–1788* (East Linton: Tuckwell Press), *passim* and especially A. Kennedy (2014) *Governing Gaeldom: The Scottish Highlands and the Restoration State, 1660–1688* (Leiden: Brill), p. 66 and p. 70. The suggestion that Highland attitudes to violence might be more nuanced than first thought had also been made by an earlier scholar, see E. Richards (1973) 'How Tame were the Highlanders during the Clearances?', *Scottish Studies*, 17, pp. 35–50.

37 For further discussion see Macinnes (1996) *Clanship, passim* and especially Kennedy (2014) *Governing Gaeldom*, p. 72, p. 81 and pp. 107–108.
38 See, in particular, Kennedy (2014) *Governing Gaeldom*, p. 106 and p. 111.
39 See for instance Whatley (2010) 'Order and Disorder', pp. 193–202; Whatley (2000) *Scottish Society*, pp. 145–149 and Houston and Knox (2001) 'Introduction', p. xlix.
40 For further discussion see M. Todd (2002) *The Culture of Protestantism in Early Modern Scotland* (London: Yale University Press), pp. 10–11, pp. 135–149; M.F. Graham (1996) *The Uses of Reform: 'Godly Discipline' and Popular Behaviour in Scotland and Beyond, 1560–1610* (Leiden: Brill), *passim* and G. Parker (1988) 'The "Kirk By Law Established" and the Origins of "The Taming of Scotland": St Andrews 1559–1600' in L. Leneman (ed) *Perspectives in Scottish Social History – Essays in Honour of Rosalind Mitchison* (Aberdeen: Aberdeen University Press), pp. 1–32 at pp. 12–14.
41 For further discussion of this point see B. Lenman (1984) 'The Limits of Godly Discipline in the Early Modern Period with Particular Reference to England and Scotland' in K. Von Greyerz (ed) *Religion and Society in Early Modern Europe 1500–1800* (London: George Allen and Unwin), pp. 124–145 at p. 137 and p. 139; Parker (1988) 'The "Kirk"', pp. 4–6 and p. 10; Brown (2001) 'Reformation to Union', p. 187 and p. 224 and also Lenman and Parker (1980) 'Crime and Control', p. 13 and p. 16.
42 Kilday (2007) *Women and Violent Crime*, pp. 26–38. See also M.B. Vasser (1995) 'Violence and the Central Criminal Courts in Scotland, 1603–1638' (Unpublished PhD thesis, Columbia University).
43 For further discussion see S.J. Davies (1980) 'The Courts and the Scottish Legal System, 1600–1747: The Case of Stirlingshire' in V.A.C. Gatrell, B. Lenman and G. Parker (eds.) *Crime and the Law: The Social History of Crime in Western Europe since 1500* (London: Europa), pp. 120–154; I.D. Whyte (1995) *Scotland Before the Industrial Revolution: An Economic and Social History: c. 1050–1750* (Harlow: Longman), pp. 210–218; J.W. Cairns (2000) 'Historical Introduction' in K. Reid and R. Zimmermann (eds.) *A History of Private Law in Scotland, II: Obligations* (Oxford: Oxford University Press), pp. 14–184 and A.E. Whetstone (1981) *Scottish County Government in the Eighteenth and Nineteenth Centuries* (Edinburgh: John Donald), Chapter 1.
44 Houston and Whyte (1989) 'Introduction', p. 26.
45 Davies (1980) 'The Courts', pp. 151–154.
46 See for instance Wormald (1985) *Lords and Men*, p. 164; Brown (1986) *Bloodfeud*, pp. 242–43, pp. 247–249 and p. 258 and especially J. Findlay (2000) *All Manner of People: The History of the Justices of the Peace in Scotland* (Edinburgh: Saltire Society).
47 20 Geo II, c. 43 (1747).
48 Davies (1980) 'The Courts', pp. 120. See also L. Farmer (1997) *Criminal Law, Tradition and Legal Order: Crime and the Genius of Scots Law, 1747 to the Present* (Cambridge: Cambridge University Press), Chapter 3.
49 See for instance N.T. Phillipson (1976) 'Lawyers, Landowners, and the Civic Leadership of Post-Union Scotland: An Essay on the Social Role of the Faculty of Advocates, 1661–1830, in Eighteenth-century Scottish Society', *Juridical Review* (New Series), XXI, pp. 97–120 at p. 107 and Farmer (1997) *Criminal Law*, Chapter 4. For further discussion of the concept of the 'civilising process' see N. Elias [translated by E. Jephcott] (1994) *The Civilising Process: The History of Manners and State Formation and Civilization* (Oxford: Wiley-Blackwell) and for more on its potential application in a Scottish context see Kilday (2007) *Women and Violent Crime*, concluding chapter.

50 For further discussion of the jurisdiction of the Justiciary Court in Scotland see Baron D. Hume (1797) *Commentaries on the Laws of Scotland Respecting Trial for Crimes – Volume I* (Edinburgh: Bell and Bradfute), Chapter 1; W. Croft Dickinson (1958) 'The High Court of Justiciary' in *An Introduction to Scottish Legal History* (Edinburgh: Stair Society, Series XX), pp. 408–412; Cairns (2000) 'Historical Introduction', pp. 122–123 and P. Raynor, B. Lenman and G. Parker (1982) *Handlist of Records for the Study of Crime in Early Modern Scotland (to 1747)* (London: Swift), p. 30 and p. 32.

51 Wormald (1985) *Lords and Men*, pp. 165–166.

52 See for instance the fate of Jannet Shanks indicted for infanticide at the South Circuit on the 18th of December 1710. She was convicted and sentenced to be hanged with her hand amputated postmortem and to be set up in Dumfries (the town nearest to where the crime was committed) for all to see: National Records of Scotland (NRS), Justiciary Court, Books of Adjournal, JC3/3 and NRS, Justiciary Court, South Circuit Minute Books, JC12/1 and JC12/2. See also National Library of Scotland (NLS), (1711) *The Last Words and Declaration of Jannet Shank* (Edinburgh: John Reid), Special Collections (SpC), 6.314 (28) 104.

53 See for instance the fate of John Muir who was convicted of multiple acts of bestiality at Lanark on the 17th of July 1654 on account of his own confession and was ordered to be burnt at the stake: NRS, Justiciary Court, Process Papers, JC26/16/1 and JC26/16/2/1. See also the fate of the so-called Wigtown Martyrs, Margaret MacLauchlan and Margaret Wilson, on the 11th of May 1685 after their refusal to swear the Oath of Abjuration (declaring James VII as head of the Church). At hastily arranged local court proceedings, government commissioners ordered that they to be tied to palisades fixed in the sand at Wigtown, but within the tidemark of the sea, and were to stand there until '...the flood o'erflowed them' see NRS, Records of Church of Scotland Synods, Presbyteries and Kirk Sessions, Records of Penninghame Kirk Session, CH2/1387/1 and Records of Kirkinner Kirk Session, CH2/228/1 as well as G. Fraser (1885) *The Story of the Wigtown Martyrs* (G. Ferguson: Wigtown) [NLS, Ref. APS.1.78.188] and H. Macpherson (1947) 'The Wigtown Martyrs', *Records of the Scottish Church History Society*, IX, pp. 166–184.

54 See for instance the fate of John Baird and Andrew Hardie, the so-called 'Bonnymuir Prisoners' after their conviction for high treason amidst a radical uprising in the West of Scotland. After state trials were heard against eighteen individuals at Stirling on the 13th of July 1820, six men were convicted. At execution, Baird and Hardie, after being hanged and their bodies left on the gallows for thirty minutes, were both beheaded before a crowd of onlookers. It took several blows to remove each man's head with the axe selected for this purpose. Both men were also ordered to be quartered as part of their sentence, but there is no evidence of that specific punishment having taken place. See NLS (1820) *The Following is a Particular Account of the Trial and Sentence: The Bonnymuir Prisoners For High Treason* (Edinburgh: W. Carse), SpC, L.C. Fol. 73 (009); NLS (1820) *Trials: A Particular Account of the Proceedings on the State Trials Which Commenced at Stirling on the 13th July, 1820* (Glasgow: John Muir), SpC, L.C. Fol. 73 (008); NLS (1820) *A Full, True and Particular Account of the Execution of Andrew Hardie and John Baird* (Edinburgh: William Cameron), SpC, Ry III a. 2 (12) and NLS (1820) *Execution: A Particular Account of the Execution of John Baird and Andrew Hardie who were Hanged and Beheaded at Stirling, on Friday the 8th day of September, 1820, convicted of High Treason* (Glasgow: John Muir), SpC, L.C. Fol. 73 (014).

55 For further discussion of the use of judicial violence in Scotland see C. Jackson (2005) 'Judicial Torture, the Liberties of the Subject, and Anglo-Scottish

Relations, 1660–1960' in T.C. Smout (ed) *Anglo-Scottish Relations from 1603 to 1900* (Oxford: Oxford University Press), pp. 75–101; C.N. Johnston (1907) 'The Punishment of Crime', *Juridical Review*, XX, pp. 316–340; J. Cameron (1983) *Prisons and Punishment in Scotland: From the Middle Ages to the Present* (Edinburgh: Canongate), p. 11 and R.E. Bennett (2018) *Capital Punishment and the Criminal Corpse in Scotland, 1740–1834* (Basingstoke: Palgrave), pp. 7–8, p. 138, p. 140 and p. 187.

56 V.A.C. Gatrell (1994) *The Hanging Tree: Execution and the English People 1770–1868* (Oxford: Oxford University Press), p. 8. See also S.J. Connolly (1999) 'Unnatural Deaths in Four Nations: Contrasts and Comparisons' in S.J. Connolly (ed) *Kingdoms United? Great Britain and Ireland Since 1500* (Dublin: Four Courts Press), pp. 200–214 at pp. 210–213; Cameron (1983) *Prisons*, p. 52 and Bennett (2018) *Capital Punishment*, p. 2

57 See for instance Kennedy (2016) 'Crime and Punishment', pp. 21–28 and A-M Kilday (1998) 'Women and Crime in South-west Scotland: A Study of the Justiciary Court Records, 1750–1815, (Unpublished PhD thesis, University of Strathclyde), Chapter 6.

58 For further discussion see Bennett (2018) *Capital Punishment*, pp. 32–33. For further discussion of the variety and flexibility of sanctions deployed by the Scottish judiciary see also Kilday (1998) 'Women and Crime', Chapter 6; Cameron (1983) *Prisons*, *passim* as well as A. Bartie and L.A. Jackson (2011) 'Youth Crime and Preventive Policing in Post-War Scotland (c.1945–71)', *Twentieth Century British History*, 22, 1, pp. 79–102 for the more modern era.

59 K. Carson and H. Idzikowska (1989) 'The Social Production of Scottish Policing 1795–1900' in D. Hay and F. Snyder (eds.) *Policing and Prosecution in Britain 1750–1850* (Oxford: Oxford University Press), pp. 266–297 at p. 270.

60 Kilday (2007) *Women and Violent Crime*, p. 28.

61 D.G. Barrie (2011 edition) *Police in the Age of Improvement: The Origins and Development of Policing in Scotland, 1775–1865* (Abingdon: Taylor and Francis), p. 48.

62 See Carson and Idzikowska (1989) 'The Social Production', pp. 270–272 and Barrie (2008) *Policing*, p. 7 and p. 13.

63 *Ibid*, pp. 271–272.

64 3 & 4 Wm. IV, c. 46 (1833).

65 For further discussion see Barrie (2008) *Policing*, pp. 3–5 and Carson and Idzikowska (1989) 'The Social Production', pp. 273–274.

66 20 & 21 Vict., c. 72 (1857). For more on the perceived link between increasing vagrancy and rising crime see Carson and Idzikowska (1989) 'The Social Production', pp. 288–293 and for further discussion on the impact that the panic about crime rates more generally had on the development of Scottish policing see D.G. Barrie (2008) *Policing*, p. 82.

67 See Knox and McKinlay (2010) 'Crime', pp. 214–227; Barrie (2008) *Policing*, p. 48 and p. 214 and for the more modern era R. Sparks, L. Jackson, N. Davidson, L. Fleming and D. Smale (2017) 'Police and Community in Twentieth-Century Scotland: The Uses of Social History', *British Journal of Criminology*, 51, 1, pp. 18–30.

68 NLS, (1830) *Melancholy Accident, with Further Particulars Relative to the Gilmerton Murder* (Edinburgh: F. O'Neill), SpC, F.3.a.13(7). For a similar use of case studies to emphasise a crime problem in early Victorian Scotland see also NLS (1830) *Lines on the Gilmerton Murder* (Edinburgh: Robert Hodge), SpC, F.3.a.14(56).

69 *Ibid*.

70 For further discussion of the contemporary view of Scotland with respect to the nature and incidence of crime in the 1830s, 1840s and 1850s see A. Alison

(1844) 'Imprisonment and Transportation – The Increase in Crime', *Blackwood's Edinburgh Magazine*, LV, CCCXLIII, pp. 533–545 and A. Alison (1850) 'Crime and Transportation', *Essays Political, Historical and Miscellaneous – Volume I* (Edinburgh: William Blackwood and Sons), pp. 543–617. See also Devine (1999) *The Scottish Nation* who describes this era as 'the dangerous times' at p. 224.

71 NRS, Justiciary Court, Indictment, AD14/30/334/2.

72 NRS, Justiciary Court, Indictment, AD14/30/334/2.

73 See for instance the testimony of David Dobie's own wife to this effect at NRS, Justiciary Court, Precognition, Testimony of Mrs Dobie, AD14/30/334/1.

74 NRS, Justiciary Court, Indictment, AD14/30/334/2. See also NLS (1830) *Trial and Sentence: A Full and Particular Account of the Trial and Sentence of John Thomson and David Dobie, Carters, Gilmerton, Who Are to be Executed at Edinburgh, on Wednesday the 18th of August 1830, for the Assault, Rape, Murder and Robbery of Margaret Paterson, and Their Bodies to be Given for Dissection!* (Edinburgh: W. Robertson), SpC, F.3.a.14(57).

75 See for instance NLS (1830) *Murder – Fourth Edition – Authentic Particulars* (Forbes and Owen: Edinburgh), SpC, F.3.a.14(53); NLS (1830) *Trial and Sentence of the Gilmerton Monsters* (Edinburgh: Forbes and Owen), SpC, F.3.a.14(58); NLS (1830) *Third Edition of the Gilmerton Murders* (Edinburgh: n.p.), SpC, F.3.a.14(59); NLS (1830) *Trials for Rape, &c. of D. Dobie, J. Thomson and D. Bertie before the High Court of Justiciary – July 12 and 14* (Edinburgh: n.p.), SpC, F.3.a.14(60) and NLS (1830) *Thomson and Dobie's Lamentation* (Edinburgh: n.p.), SpC, F.3.a.14(62).

76 *Ibid.*

77 NRS, Justiciary Court, Precognition, Testimony of Violet Armour, AD14/30/334/1.

78 NRS, Justiciary Court, Precognition, Testimony of Mrs Gillon, AD14/30/334/1.

79 *Ibid.*

80 *Ibid.*

81 *Ibid.*

82 NLS (1830) *Murder – Fourth Edition.*

83 NRS, Justiciary Court, Precognition, Testimony of William Paterson, AD14/30/334/1.

84 NRS, Justiciary Court, Precognition, Testimony of Mrs Paterson, AD14/30/334/1.

85 *Ibid.* [Author's emphasis in italics.]

86 NRS, Justiciary Court, Precognition, Medical Report, AD14/30/334/1. [Author's additions in parenthesis.]

87 *Ibid.* See also NLS (1830) *Murder – Fourth Edition.*

88 NRS, Justiciary Court, Precognition, Testimony of Walter Dingwall, AD14/30/334/1.

89 NRS, Justiciary Court, Process Papers, Declarations of John Thomson, JC26/1830/346/4 and JC26/1830/346/5.

90 NRS, Justiciary Court, Process Papers, Declarations of David Dobie, JC26/1830/346/2 and JC26/1830/346/3. For further insinuation by David Dobie that the assault upon Margaret Paterson was nothing more than a '...drunken frolic', see NLS (1830) *The Recent Gilmerton Murder! The Latest Account of Interesting Particulars Relevant to These Most Iniquitous and Horrid Transactions, Which Lately Took Place Near Gilmerton, in the County of Edinburgh* (Edinburgh: John Craig), SpC, F.3.a.14(54).

91 *Ibid.* [Author's additions in parenthesis.]

92 *Ibid.*

93 NLS (1830) *The Trial, Sentence and Behaviour of John Thomson and David Dobie, Who Are to be Executed at Edinburgh, on Wednesday the 18th of August Next, and*

Their Bodies Given for Dissection, for the Assault, Murder and Robbery of Margaret Paterson; Together with the Speeches of The Lords Justice Clerk, Meadowbank, and Moncrieff before Passing Sentence (Edinburgh: R. Menzies), SpC, F.3.a.14.f61, p. 7. See also NLS (1830) *Melancholy Accident.*

94 A handkerchief belonging to Margaret Paterson was also found in the pocket of John Thomson upon his arrest. See NRS, Justiciary Court, Process Papers, Declarations of David Dobie, JC26/1830/346/2 and NLS (1830) *The Trial, Sentence and Behaviour,* p. 7.

95 NLS (1830) *The Trial, Sentence and Behaviour,* p. 6.

96 *Ibid,* pp. 7–8.

97 *Ibid,* p. 8.

98 *Ibid,* pp. 8–9. For additional contemporary commentary which refers to Thomson and Dobie as '...dogs or beasts of prey' see also NLS (1830) *Lamentations as of John Thomson and David Dobie* (Edinburgh: n.p.), SpC, F.3.a.14(63).

99 *Ibid,* p. 9.

100 *Ibid,* pp. 9–10.

101 NLS (1830) *An Account of the Execution of John Thomson and David Dobie for the Assault, Murder and Robbery of Margaret Paterson,* SpC, F.3.a.13(11). See also NLS (1830) *Execution and Confession: An Account of the Execution of David Dobie and John Thomson, at Edinburgh, on Wednesday the 18th August 1830, with an Account of Their Behaviour in Jail and on the Scaffold* (Edinburgh: n.p.), SpC, F.3.a.14(65); NLS (1830) *Execution of the Gilmerton Murderers, Dobie and Thomson* (Edinburgh: Forbes and Owen), F.3.a.14(66); NLS (1830), *Lives and Transactions of the Gilmerton Murderers, Dobie and Thomson* (Edinburgh: n.p.), SpC, F.3.a.14(68) and NLS (1830) *The Gilmerton Murderers, &c. A Sketch of the Conduct, Transactions and Behaviour of David Dobie and John Thomson Who Were Executed on Wednesday the 18th of August for Assault, Murder and Robbery, with Their Last Dying Confession and Behaviour on the Scaffold* (Edinburgh: R. Menzies), SpC, F.3.a.14(69).

102 NLS (1830) *The Gilmerton Murders: Melancholy Address of Dobie and Thomson, with Dobie's Letter to His Wife* (Edinburgh: Forbes and Owen), SpC, RB1. 238 (62). For similar broadsides that point to irreverence and drunkenness as causal factors in this case, see NLS (1830) *Execution and Confession.*

103 See for instance NLS (1830) *Lines on the Gilmerton Murder.*

104 A. Alison (1844) 'Causes of the Increase of Crime', *Blackwood's Edinburgh Magazine,* LVI, CCCXLV, pp. 1–14.

105 Wormald (1985) *Lords and Men,* p. 136.

106 The statistical evidence presented from Chapter 2 onwards relates to an exhaustive analysis of judicial statistics from their first inception in 1805 until the end of period of study for this project in 1960. Although extensive data was also collected for the late seventeenth and eighteenth centuries, the production of national statistical evidence from this material was wholly impossible as the data was incomplete due to unsystematic record keeping in some regions of the country. Consequently, the analysis had to be restricted to commentary on the regional experiences of crime and criminality up to the beginning of the nineteenth century. The vast datasets created from the research of judicial statistics published in Parliamentary Papers and available at https: //parlipapers-proquest. com (which records every single reported crime nationwide for one hundred and fifty-five years between 1805 and 1960) are available on open access from the research data repository of Oxford Brookes University at https://radar. brookes.ac.uk/radar/home.do. In the main, the statistical data relates to indictments from the Justiciary Court, but material from other jurisdictions (such as the Sheriff and Burgh courts) have been included when provided. Typically

this relates to 'lesser' offences including assault, public order offences and non-violent theft.

107 For further discussion of these problems see Kilday (2007) *Women and Violent Crime*, pp. 2–3.

108 In any case, this topic has already been dealt with eloquently by Andy Davies in relation to twentieth century Glasgow see – A. Davies (2013) *City of Gangs: Glasgow and the Rise of the British Gangster* (London: Hodder and Stoughton). Moreover, another monograph project on the history of criminality and power relations in modern Britain which will include offences such as these is already contracted to the author.

Chapter 1

The Violent North? Fatal Violence, 1660–1960

Introduction

As we saw in the introductory chapter, contemporaries perceived sixteenth-century Scotland to be a violent place. In 1582, for instance, the Privy Council announced that:

> ...his Majesties peciable gude subectis ower all his realme hes bene troublit havelie with bludescheid, stowth, reiff, masterfull oppressionis, convocationis and utheris enormiteis, to thair great hurt and skaith, without redres or puneisment of the offendouris...[1]

Effectively, this tract confessed that violence in Scotland, and fatal violence in particular, was widespread and out of control. By the seventeenth century, however, and internally at least, greater peace and stability had come to the Scottish nation through the actions of the new King, James VI. Externally, however, the Scots retained their reputation for violence and bloodshed at this time in a comparative European context. Episodes of casual violence were widely reported upon and contemporary commentators referred to daily slaughter, much blood being shed and what was in effect, an epidemic of murder in Scotland.[2]

Much of what was written at this time about Scotland as a violent nation was hyperbole which had largely derived from perceptions of the Scottish blood feud. Certainly feuds could be very brutal and sometimes could last for years or even decades, and as a result, other nations perceived the Scottish blood feud as something that was identifiably uncivilised, which promoted bloodshed and acts of random barbarity.[3] However, and as we have already observed, in practice, the blood feud was not as savage as it seemed, '...it was neither anarchic nor without restraints'[4] and it did not encourage fatal violence to occur. Rather, the Scots recognised the value of peace and used the blood feud to defuse tensions and to maintain order, rather than to detract from it.[5] Despite its apparent merits, and as we saw in the preceding chapter, the blood feud was nonetheless gradually displaced over the course of the seventeenth century, when the Crown introduced a judicial system with a more centralised version of social control.[6] Many saw this as a key turning point in Scotland's transformation to being more civilised.[7] Moreover, it also expedited a greater concentration or focus (at least in a practical sense) on individual criminals and their offences, in contrast to the vague, generalised perceptions of collective regional or national behaviour that had long held sway.

Fatal Violence and the Law

Although a full and detailed history of the criminal law is lacking for Scotland for the 1660–1960 period, we can still piece together some of the key elements of the judicial context for fatal violence over that time span through the work of various legal scholars and commentators. Indeed, it is evident that an understanding of the judicial context in Scotland is absolutely essential when formulating a view of how this category of crime and its perpetrators were regarded by the Scottish authorities and the extent to which their opinions changed over time. This better facilitates our analysis of Scotland as a violent nation.

(a) Homicide

Fiona Brookman argues in relation to the present day that 'Homicide is the most serious form of violent crime. It is uniquely harmful and strikes at the very heart of what most of us hold most precious – our life.'[8] Judicial attitudes towards homicide in Scotland have altered very little over the three centuries dealt with in this volume and largely agree with the gravity of this statement. One of the earliest and most influential commentators on Scots Law, Baron David Hume (1757–1838), for instance, defines homicide as a crime which is '…the highest of any, and of which nature has most abhorrence…by which life is taken away, and the person of a human creature is destroyed.'[9] By and large, Hume's two volume *Commentaries on the Law of Scotland Respecting the Description and Punishment of Crimes*, written in 1797, has stood the test of time and has only been slightly edited, rather than fundamentally altered, by his successors. This magisterial work remains integral to legal discussions of homicide (and indeed other offences) in Scotland today.[10] Hume argues that in relation to homicide, there are four conditions that have to be fulfilled for an offence of that nature to be indicted under Scots law. First, and somewhat obviously '… it is necessary to all conviction of homicide, that a person have been actually killed.'[11] Second, '…it must be shown that the person died of the harm or mischief libelled; if that whereof the pannel was actor or art and part.'[12] Third, '…the slaughter must be of a person, or existing human creature.'[13] Finally, '…the manner of death [must] be such, wherein the act of the pannel plainly and palpably, and not by suspicion and conjecture only, appears.'[14]

According to Hume, there are four categories of homicide in Scots Law. The first is murder 'free from all blame' where, in effect, the killer concerned is not liable to be subjected to any pain for the events that have transpired. This is because the act of fatal violence has either been 'casual' (occasioned by 'pure misadventure') or it has been 'justifiable' (perhaps committed intentionally, but 'may be vindicated on the principles of duty').[15] The second category of homicide is probably the most complicated in terms of legal argument, but nevertheless, it is the one most often applied to instances of fatal violence in the Scottish courtroom during the 1660–1960 period as we will see in the section below on trends in fatal violence, and that is 'culpable homicide'. One of the main reasons for the wider use of this category of homicide is because it can result in a more measured or flexible judicial approach. As Hume explains, culpable homicide '…implies blame in the killer, and is followed with punishment, more or less considerable, according to the quality of the fault.'[16] In other words, in instances of culpable homicide, the punishment befits the nature and extent of the crime. Typically, culpable homicide occurs when an individual acts (either legally or illegally) without '…due caution and circumspection for preventing injury to others.' More seriously, however, it can occur when an individual behaves in a manner that is purposefully harmful, but crucially, there can be no deliberate intention to kill unless the 'mortal purpose' in question has been suddenly encouraged through significant provocation or threat. In other words an indictment for murder may be mitigated to a charge of culpable homicide if there is irrefutable evidence that the incident was either an act of self-defence or a killing in hot blood.[17]

The third category of homicide is that of 'wilful murder' which is a homicide '…done wilfully and out of malice aforethought.'[18] The use of a 'lethal weapon' is required in instances of wilful murder, but the actual nature of the weapon deployed is often less important than how it is used (i.e. the force, repetition and context involved).[19] The severity of the crime and the explicit intent involved renders atonement impossible for the offence amongst civilised nations, according to Hume, and thus, the only possible sentence for wilful murder is death.[20] The author references various measures used by the Scottish courts in particularly 'atrocious cases' to introduce further suffering or indignity to the convicted in wilful murders in the premodern period. These included striking off the hand prior to execution (see the case study of Robert Irving below), hanging the body in chains postmortem, quartering the executed corpse, and fixing the head and/or limbs of the perpetrator to '…conspicuous places, to keep up the memory and terror of the example' (again, see the Irving case study below).[21] In addition, the Murder Act of 1751 included a provision '…for better preventing the horrid crime of murder', Scottish individuals convicted of particularly heinous crimes were publicly dissected prior to burial. In the 1830s this practice had largely fallen out of favour and the law was repealed.[22]

The fourth and final category of homicide recognised in Scots law was 'aggravated murder'. In these instances, as Hume explains, '…either on account of some peculiar baseness or cruelty in the mode of the deed, or on account of the relative situation of the parties, our custom proceeds against the murderer with more than usual severity.'[23] Essentially what this meant in practice is that cases of this type were dealt with swiftly as pleas in mitigation were rarely allowed. Furthermore, the offender, if convicted, would be executed (with no chance of remission) and with aggravations to their punishment as described above.[24] Examples of homicides where an indictment of aggravated murder might result include assassination, 'murder under trust', parricide (the act of killing one's parents or another close relative in a position of authority) and poisonings where malice and intent were entirely obvious.[25]

In the more modern era, these categories of homicide were largely retained (if not regularly applied) and the absolute seriousness of this kind of fatal violence remained intact. The standard modern definition of murder is that which was set out by the advocate J.H.A. Macdonald in his *Practical Treatise on the Criminal Law of Scotland* in 1867 where he said:

> Murder is constituted by any wilful act causing the destruction of human life, whether plainly intended to kill, or displaying such utter and wicked recklessness, as to imply a disposition depraved enough to be wholly regardless of the consequences.[26]

We can clearly see echoes of Baron Hume in this and in subsequent commentaries on the subject, but the key characteristic of this particular definition of murder is its emphasis on the fact that '…unlike any other crime, the degree of seriousness is not based on the act committed, but on the intention of the actor.'[27] With the gradual rise of humanitarian feeling and the consequent restrictions on the scope of capital punishment, the notion of intent came to be increasingly debated in the Scottish courts and, as Lindsay Farmer explains, there was an evident '…narrowing of the factual circumstances in which the death penalty could apply' even in instances of fatal violence. Moreover, juries became inclined to acquit individuals charged with murder rather than send them to the gallows.[28] We can see this trend in the data below.

Consequently, and over the course of the first half of the nineteenth century, the use of culpable homicide as a charge in its own right, and as an alternative to murder, grew in favour amongst the Scottish judiciary owing to its considerable malleability.[29] This evolution had various ramifications. For instance, it meant that individuals could be prosecuted for both 'act' and 'omission': they could be charged for failing to act to prevent danger from happening, as well as being the instigator of danger.[30] In addition, and perhaps more significantly, it meant that the culpability of offenders came to be chiefly articulated according to their state of mind at the time of transgression. As we can see from the data in the subsequent section of this chapter, this paved the way for mitigation via 'diminished responsibility' or mental incapacity and thus psychiatric testimony regarding the accused was increasingly heard in Scottish courtrooms alongside medical evidence pertaining to the injuries sustained by the victim (evident from Peter Manuel's appeal in the case study below).[31]

The only other key legislative change to the legal context of murder in Scotland between 1660 and 1960 was the Homicide Act of 1957.[32] Although various sections of this legislation did not apply in the Scottish context, Part II of the Act did and it restricted liability for the death penalty to so-called 'capital murders' alone. The introduction of this legislation was an evident continuation of the 'civilising' desire to abolish capital punishment which was effectively achieved in 1965.[33] It could be argued that in essence, this category of murder was simply a more detailed, nuanced and modernised version of the category of 'aggravated murder' that Hume had determined some one hundred and sixty years earlier. Five types of capital murder were defined by the Act[34]:

a   any murder done in the furtherance of theft;
b   any murder by shooting or by causing an explosion;
c   any murder done in the course of or for the purpose of resisting or avoiding or preventing a lawful arrest, or effecting or assisting an escape or rescue from legal custody;
d   any murder of a police officer acting in the execution of his duty or of a person assisting a police officer so acting;
e   in the case of a person who was a prisoner at the time when he did or was a party to the murder, any murder of a prison officer acting in the execution of his duty or of a person assisting a prison officer so acting.

Between 1957 and 1965 then, a capital conviction and sentence for murder in Scotland (and indeed elsewhere in Great Britain) could only result from one of these five circumstances, as the case study of Peter Manuel below perfectly illustrates.

(b) Infanticide

Explanations for the introduction of explicit legislation regarding newborn child murder in England and Wales during the seventeenth century have hinged on contemporary concerns about protecting infant life, curbing maternal malpractices and, in particular, controlling the rates of illegitimacy which had significant financial implications for parishes and communities. In Scotland, however, according to Baron Hume at least, 'The Act Anent Murdering of Children', passed in 1690 in Scotland was created in direct response to an unprecedented surge in infanticidal behaviour in the early 1680s.[35] It read:

> Our Soveraigne Lord and Lady the King and Queens Majesties Consider-
> ing the frequent Murthers that have or may be committed upon innocent
> infants, whose mothers doe conceale their being with childe and doe not
> call for necessary assistance in the birth whereby the new borne childe
> may be easily stifled or being left exposed in the condition it comes to the
> world it must quicklie perish, For preventing whereof Their Majesties
> with advice and consent of the Estates of Parliament, doe statute enact
> and declare that if any woman shall conceale her being with child during
> the whole space and shall not call for and make use of help and assistance
> in the birth, the child being found dead or amissing the mother shall
> be holden and repute the murderer of her own childe, And ordaines all
> criminall Judges to sustaine such processes, and the lybell being remitted
> to the knowledge of ane inqueist, it shall be sufficient ground for them
> to returne their verdict finding the Lybell proven and the mother guiltie
> of murder tho there be no appearance of wound or bruise upon the body
> of the Childe, And ordaines this act to be printed and published at the
> mercat Cross of the head burghs of the severall shyres and to be read in
> all the paroch Churches be the Reader of the parish.[36]

As we can see, the Scottish tract makes a direct link between concealment of pregnancy and intending to commit murder. This is largely absent from the equivalent legislation south of the Tweed which was passed sixty-six years earlier in 1624.[37] Moreover, and as Hume points out, the Scottish statute had a far wider range of circumstances which were grounds for an indictment for this offence. In addition to concealing the death of the infant concerned, if a woman had concealed her condition throughout the entirety of her preg-nancy; if she had not called for assistance at the time of parturition; and, if the infant in question was now either dead or was missing, a charge of newborn child murder could result.[38]

For the purposes of this volume, an act of infanticide is considered to mean the killing of a newborn infant under the age of one. Although the Scottish infanticide legislation, for reasons that remain unclear, had a wider remit than its English and Welsh equivalent, indictments for this type of offence could be difficult to achieve especially in the absence of a cadaver. First, it had to be proven that the accused individual had recently been pregnant. In the premodern period, this necessitated some rather crude tests to be done by midwives to establish whether parturition had occurred and lactation had begun. Often these proved inconclusive, at least to the satisfaction of the Scottish judiciary. Second, it had to be proven that the suspect had not re-vealed her pregnancy to another and that she had not called for assistance in the birth. Suspects regularly brought relatives and acquaintances to court who were willing to testify that the woman's condition had been revealed to them. Alternatively, suspects brought baby clothes and child-rearing artefacts to the courtroom as rather flimsy evidence to suggest that they had prepared for their child's imminent arrival and intended to do it no harm. Third, some women were able to suggest that the child they had borne had been still-born or had been miscarried. Once again, the unsophisticated autopsy tests adopted to prove or disprove such claims were, unsatisfactory in removing all doubt from the minds of impressionable jurors. Finally, it was difficult to convict a married woman or indeed any accomplice of the crime of newborn child murder due to the wording of the 1690 statute which had essentially been constructed to police the activities of unmarried mothers alone.[39]

There was a further offence related to infant killing that was indictable under Scots law and that related to the murder of an infant through desertion and exposure. Cases of this type were relatively rare in Scotland, certainly in comparison with indictments for newborn child murder, and the offence was not considered capital in nature. Hume suggests that this is because in instances of murder via desertion or exposure, the crime was considered a variant of culpable homicide by the Scottish courts. This was because the key issue for consideration seems to relate to wilfulness in what happened to the child. As the child had been abandoned and exposed to risk, such practice *was* deemed a criminal offence. However, as the child was not directly or wilfully killed by the suspect in question, the offence could not be deemed a 'murder'.[40] Although there was no victim age specification associated with this offence and the characteristics of the accused were not elaborated on in any legal treatise (for instance in relation to gender or marital status), in theory anyone could be indicted for this 'species' of child murder. However, in practice, and as was the case with infanticide 'proper', those accused tended to be young, desperate, unmarried women.

In England and Wales, a lot of dissatisfaction was voiced by political and legal commentators over the initial legislative provision for child murder as it was thought to be too harsh and therefore increasingly unenforceable as the number of successful prosecutions had dwindled.[41] In Scotland, criticism of the legislation was arguably more humanitarian in nature. Despite Hume's concerns regarding the obstacles to conviction in Scottish infanticide cases, guilty verdicts for the offence were significant in number at the start of the eighteenth century in particular.[42] However, this judicial standpoint diminished fairly rapidly from 1750 onwards, but not on account of difficulties in proving liability as one might assume from Hume's comments. Rather, the Scottish courts introduced an unofficial get-out clause for women indicted for newborn child murder. Suspects were able to petition the court for life banishment from Scotland, without admitting culpability to any crime, so as to avoid the risk of a capital trial. Scottish legal professionals considered the 1690 legislation to be too tough and sought to mitigate it where possible. They preferred to avoid the use of the ultimate sanction of execution in these cases, reserving that punishment for those women who had behaved in an overtly aggressive manner and had thus blatantly transgressed accepted gender and maternal norms of behaviour.[43]

Eventually, in 1809, the Scots decided to revise the statute of 1690 and introduced a new law which enacted that:

> if, from and after the passing of this Act, any Woman in that Part of Great Britain called Scotland, shall conceal her being with Child during the whole Period of her pregnancy, and shall not call for and make use of Help and Assistance in the Birth, and if the Child be found dead or be amissing, the Mother being lawfully convicted thereof, shall be imprisoned for a Period not exceeding Two years, in such Common Gaol or Prison as the Court before which she is tried shall direct and appoint.[44]

Once again, the Scottish version of the legislation was quite different from the approach adopted by her southern neighbours in their equivalent law of 1803.[45] First of all, the Scots denoted concealment to be an entirely distinct offence. This enabled them to legislate against those women who had acted criminally, but had not intentionally killed their child. Consequently, and as a result of this new legislation, trials for infanticide 'proper' were not considered separately in Scotland, and instead, they were assimilated into homicide indictments. Scots law now felt that it had the various aspects of this offence covered and as it had created the opportunity for a more flexible and nuanced approach to instances of newborn child murder, the need for complex judicial debate regarding mitigation, which became so prevalent in indictments for this offence south of the border, was wholly unnecessary in the Scottish context. This was certainly true in relation to indictments for concealment after 1809, but in instances of infanticide as homicide, mental health testimony related to the accused became more prevalent in attempts to qualify intent and thereby mitigate the offence and avoid a capital conviction.

We can also see from the wording of the 1809 statute that although the maximum penalty for concealment was the same north and south of the border, the Scottish definition of what constituted concealment was much broader than that found in the 1803 Act. More significantly, whilst the new legislation was gendered, it did not restrict liability to unmarried mothers alone and thus it could be applied to any woman suspected of concealment. If we consider the potential flexibility of this legislation in terms of its application, it would appear that the Scottish version of the legislation was arguably more modern and progressive than its southern equivalent.[46]

The merits of the Scottish legislative system in relation to newborn child murder must go some way to explain why the Scots did not adopt a separate legislative provision for infanticide as was the case elsewhere across Europe and beyond at the start of the twentieth century.[47] England, for instance, did so in 1922.[48] The Scots likely considered this step unnecessary, due to the various indictment options in existence for the offence north of the border, which increasingly included the adoption of the lesser charge of culpable homicide in instances of 'proper' newborn child murder or as we have come to term it, infanticide as homicide.[49] The Scottish judiciary also continued to develop their use of diminished responsibility in serious criminal trials during the more modern era; something they had initiated in the mid-nineteenth century, far in advance of their English neighbours.[50] The Scots had long recognised that this concept was more appropriate to their needs when prosecuting instances of newborn child murder and they were more accustomed to deploying that provision.[51] Consequently, they did not need to enter the complicated legislative territory of trying to establish causal links between parturition, lactation, mental illness and infanticide in the legal provision they chose to adopt.[52] The more simplified judicial approach in Scotland was arguably more effective in delivering swifter, proportionate, and compassionate justice in relation to the traumatic and tragic instances of newborn child murder brought to the courts' attention.

Trends in Fatal Violence and its Punishment

As explained in the introduction, the trends in criminality presented in this work are based on the judicial statistics published since 1805. In the main, these refer to the work of the Justiciary Court, but cases heard at the Sheriff Court have also been analysed. Accurate longitudinal data before this time is not available for all the offences covered by this work, but in any event, and in relation to fatal violence more particularly, scholarship has already indicated the existence of a low homicide rate but a far higher infanticide rate in Scotland before the nineteenth century.[53] As we might expect, various factors affect the completeness of crime data. The so-called 'dark figure' of unknown or unreported crime is probably not as significant in data on homicide as it might be for other offences such as infanticide since the latter was predicated on an act of concealment. Nonetheless, we should remember that the entirety of activities which resulted in fatal violence may not be wholly represented in the data below. In addition, the impact of differing legal definitions and alterations in how crimes were categorised from the nineteenth century onwards means that there is some fluidity of the data across the boundaries of homicide, culpable homicide and infanticide. Furthermore, the opaque classification carried out in relation to *locus operandi* (where the crime took place) in the published judicial statistics, means that it is almost impossible to precisely determine the proportion of offences in urban as opposed to rural areas, but suffice to say that the bulk of criminality was committed where the majority of people resided. In other words, as urbanisation and social migration to towns occurred as part of Scotland's process of industrialisation, established patterns of criminality followed.[54]

Figures 1.1 and 1.4 below show the indictment pattern for homicide in Scotland between 1805 and 1960. Whilst the number of indictments for

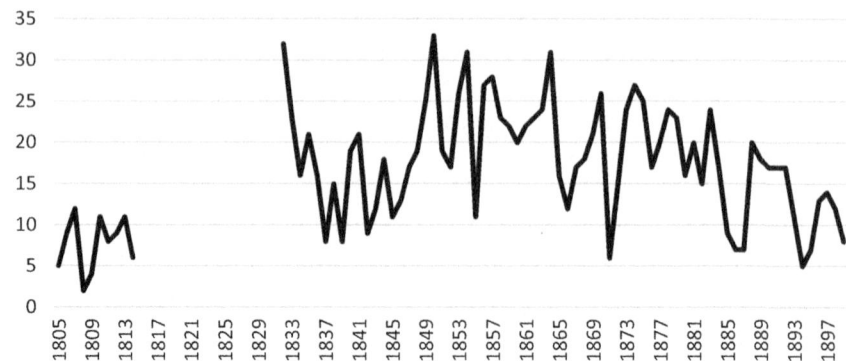

Figure 1.1 Indictments for Homicide in Scotland, 1805–1899.

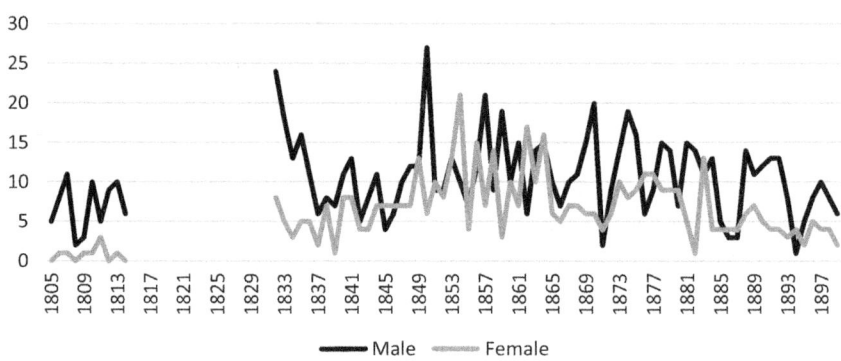

Figure 1.2 Indictments for Homicide in Scotland by Gender, 1805–1899.

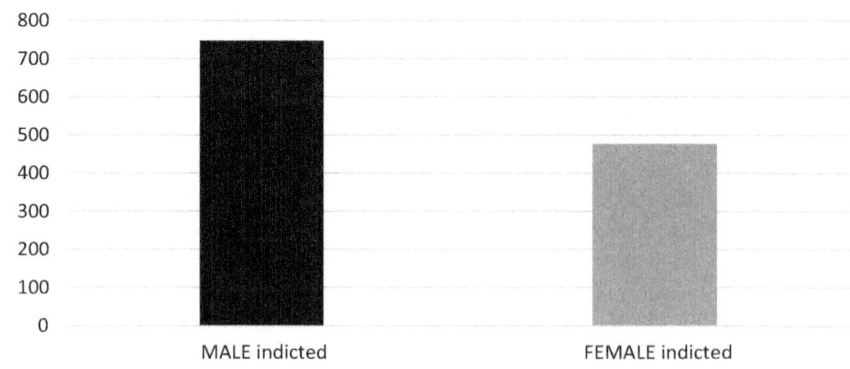

Figure 1.3 The Gendered Nature of Homicide Indictments in Scotland, 1805–1899.

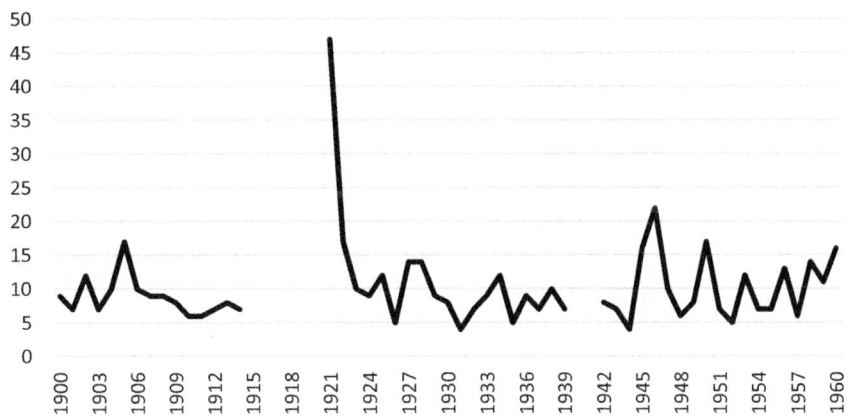

Figure 1.4 Indictments for Homicide in Scotland, 1900–1960.

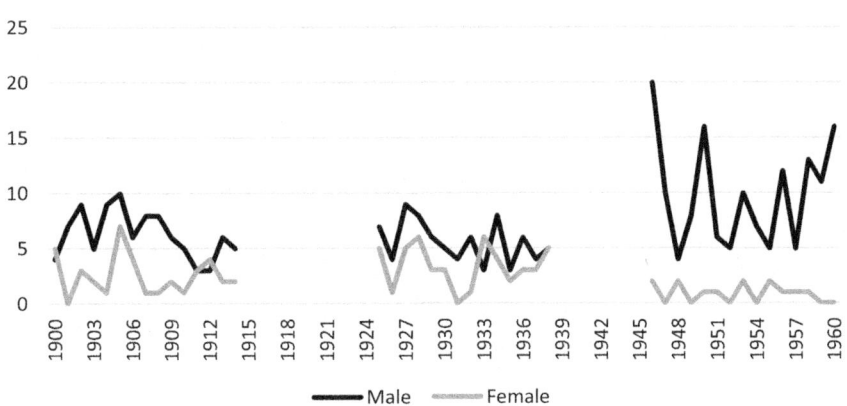

Figure 1.5 Indictments for Homicide in Scotland by Gender, 1900–1960.

homicide in the nineteenth century is far higher than that of the twentieth century, there is, nonetheless, a gradual decline in this kind of fatal violence over time. In general over the century and half, the incidence of indictments was never very great, save for a few post-war spikes in activity, caused by cumulative data being published to account for the years when statistics were not produced. Certainly, this data does not provide evidence for a particularly violent nation where homicide was commonplace. Rather, it is more in line with scholars who have argued that the incidence of fatal violence contracted over time, although it should be noted that to date, no other national comparative dataset has been completed.[55]

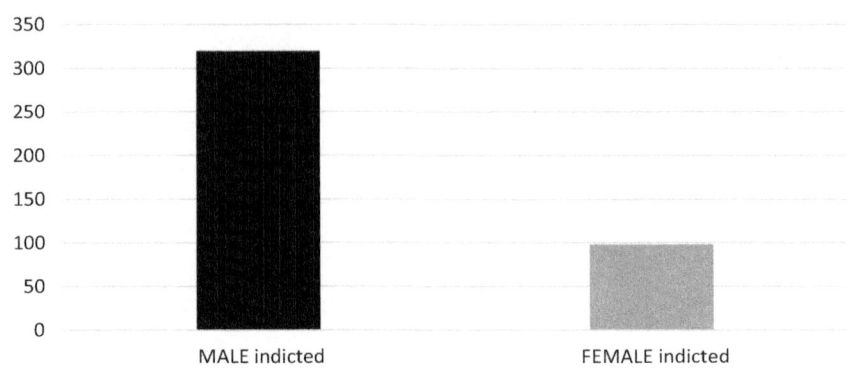

Figure 1.6 The Gendered Nature of Homicide Indictments in Scotland, 1900–1960.

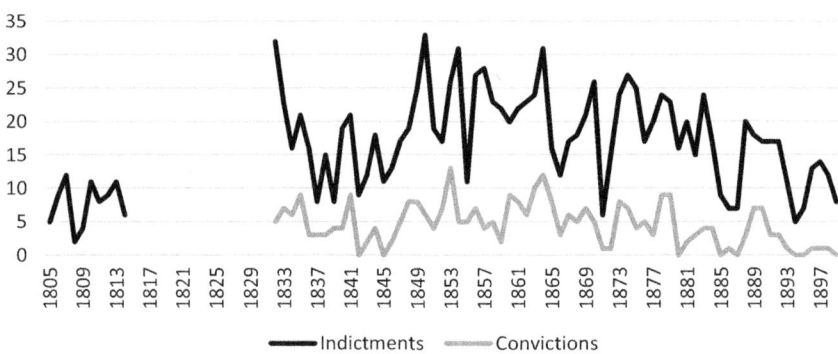

Figure 1.7 Indictments and Convictions for Homicide in Scotland, 1805–1899.

Figures 1.7 and 1.10 above demonstrate the low conviction rate for homicide in Scotland in the 1805–1960 period and Figures 1.8 and 1.11 show that it was the women accused of this offence who particularly benefitted in this respect. Figures 1.9 and 1.12 illustrate that execution was still used ahead of the abolition of capital punishment for convicted homicidal offenders as the law dictated, but aligned with the low conviction rate, there was an evident tendency amongst the higher Scottish courts to mitigate the full extent of the law, and its associated penality, through the use of insanity verdicts. As aforementioned, these became more commonplace over time.

Figure 1.13 above shows the increasing dominance of charges of culpable homicide in the nineteenth century Scottish courts when instances of fatal violence were brought to the judiciary's attention. The drift in this direction

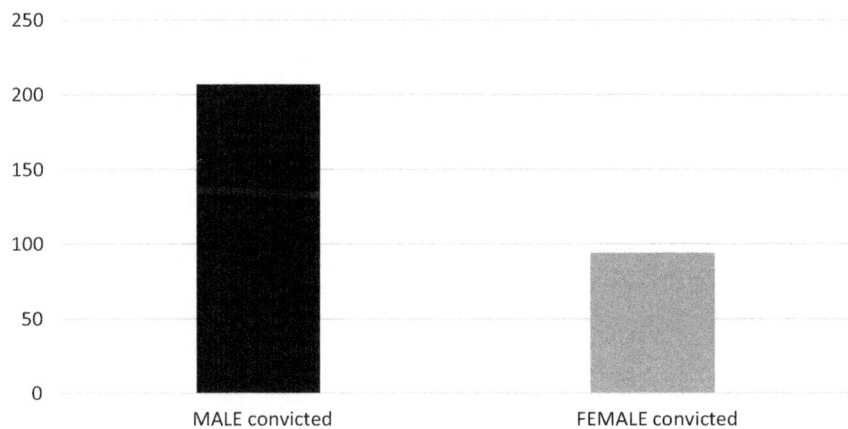

Figure 1.8 The Gendered Nature of Convictions for Homicide in Scotland, 1805–1899.

Figure 1.9 Verdicts and Sentencing Related to Homicides in Scotland, 1805–1899.

was discussed earlier in this chapter. Although a downward trend in indict-ments for culpable homicide is evidenced for the more modern period in Figure 1.16, this mirrors the decline in fatal violence more generally by that time, and which we have already seen evidenced above. The relatively high numbers of this kind of fatal violence could be indicative of more violent ten-dencies being prevalent in a Scottish context. However, we have no compar-ative data with which to test the accuracy of this suggestion and in any case, we should remember that we are dealing with what the authorities deemed to be less serious episodes of fatal violence here, those lacking in wilful intent or

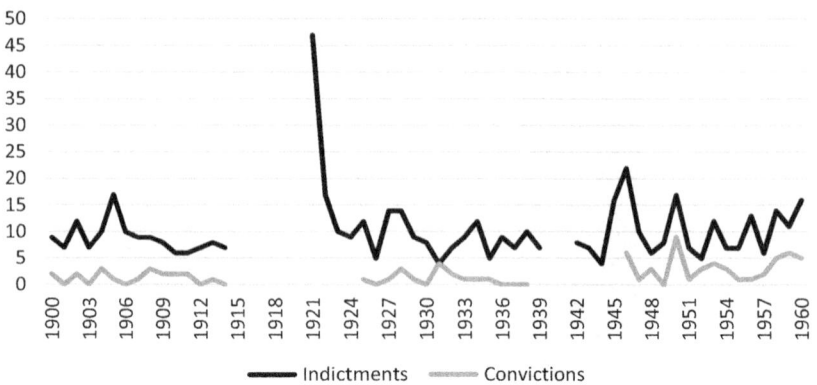

Figure 1.10 Indictments and Convictions for Homicide in Scotland, 1900–1960.

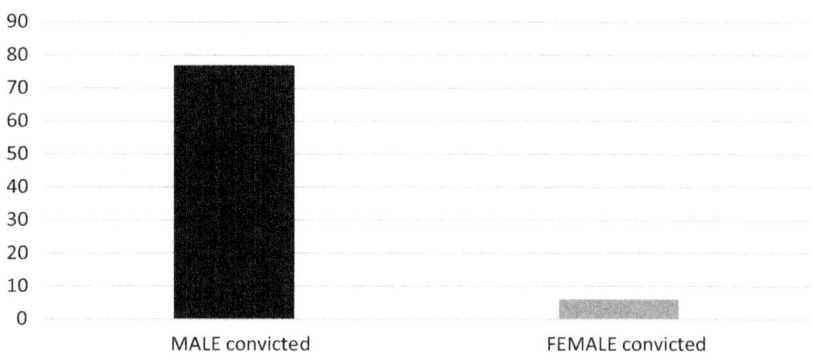

Figure 1.11 The Gendered Nature of Convictions for Homicide in Scotland, 1900–1960.

premeditation. Figures 1.14, 1.15, 1.17 and 1.18 all demonstrate that women were never significantly involved in indictments for culpable homicide and indeed, this kind of fatal violence could be deemed a gender-specific crime which was almost entirely dominated by male perpetrators based on the evidence presented here.

The trend towards a low conviction rate evidenced in relation to homicidal activity in Scotland between 1805 and 1960 is mirrored in the data for culpable homicide too as Figures 1.19 and 1.22 above demonstrate. However, it is worth noting that, after the Second World War, the gap between indictments and convictions narrowed substantially, probably on account of improved detection techniques or a greater determination to only prosecute

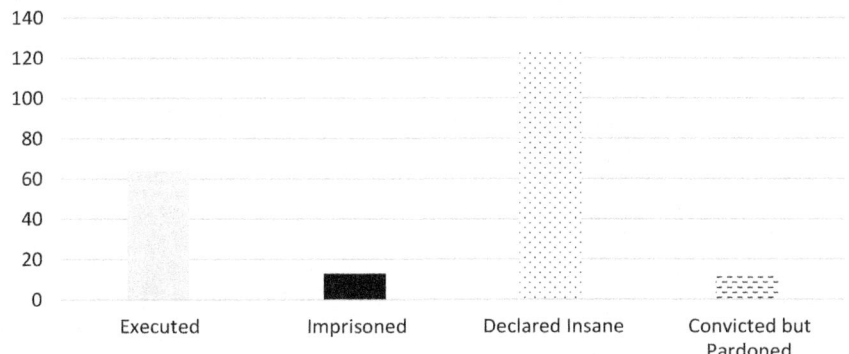

Figure 1.12 Verdicts and Sentencing Related to Homicides in Scotland, 1900–1960.

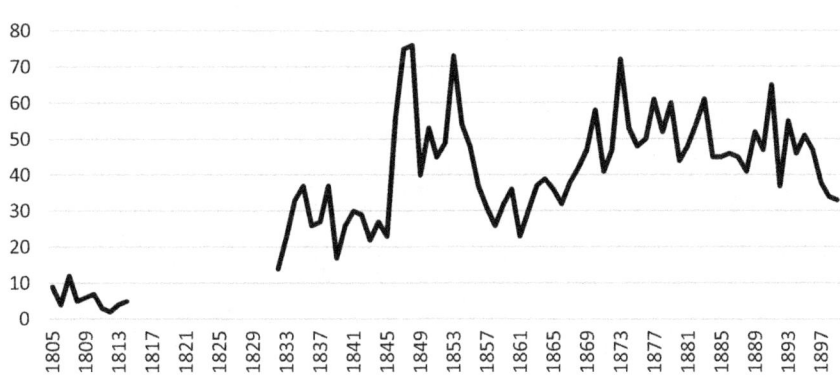

Figure 1.13 Indictments for Culpable Homicide in Scotland, 1805–1899.

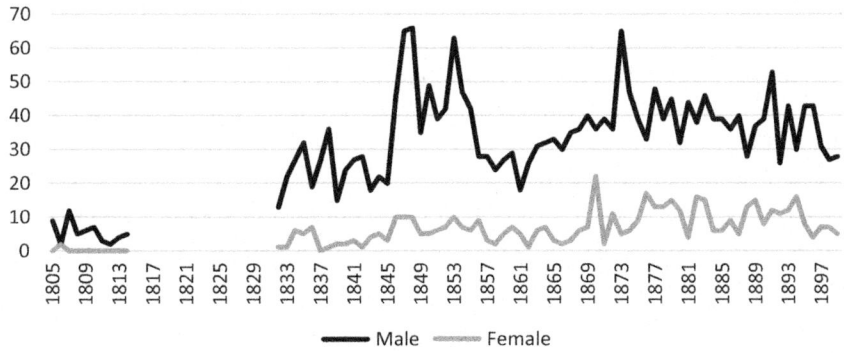

Figure 1.14 Indictments for Culpable Homicide in Scotland by Gender, 1805–1899.

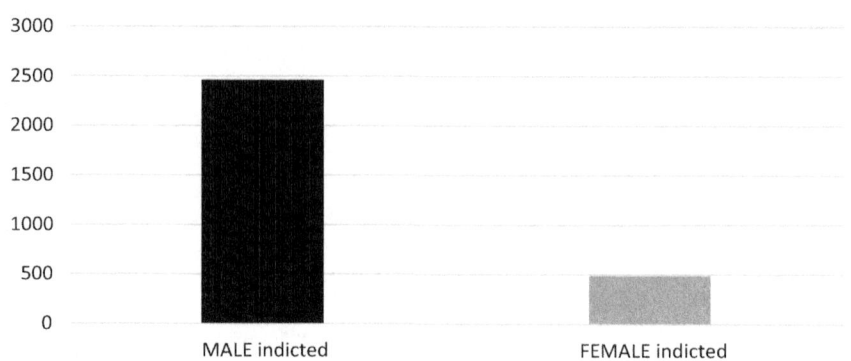

Figure 1.15 The Gendered Nature of Culpable Homicide Indictments in Scotland, 1805–1899.

Figure 1.16 Indictments for Culpable Homicide in Scotland, 1900–1960.

cases where the evidence was strong enough to warrant a conviction. Once again (as shown in Figures 1.20 and 1.23) the female conviction rate lagged significantly behind the male, but in any event, and as the law provided, it was sentences of imprisonment (typically penal servitude) that dominated the penal policy for this type of offence during the nineteenth century as Figure 1.21 shows. Indeed, *all* convictions for culpable homicide after 1900 similarly resulted in imprisonment. There were, unlike homicides proper, only a handful of insanity defences accepted in relation to culpable homicide over the century and a half in question, undoubtedly because there was no need to seek mitigation of the ultimate sanction at law for this offence.

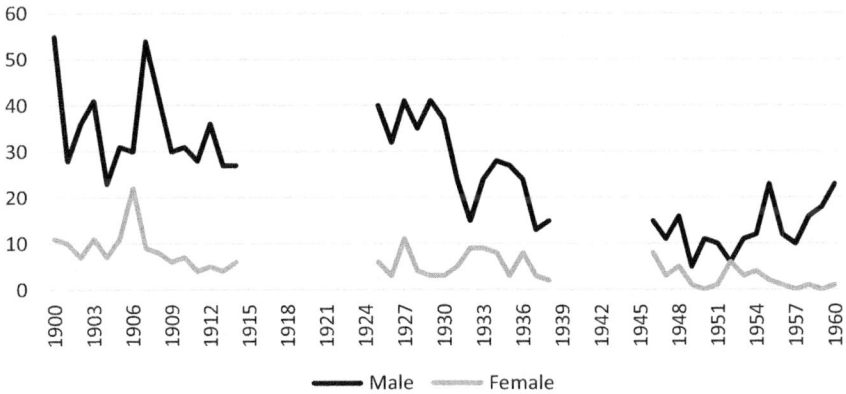

Figure 1.17 Indictments for Culpable Homicide in Scotland by Gender, 1900–1960.

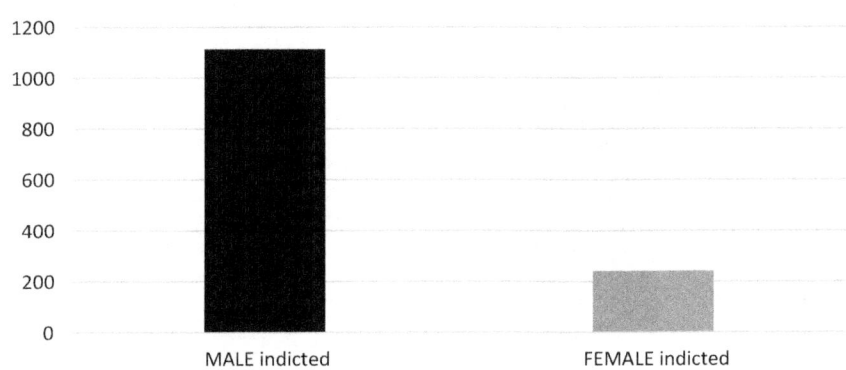

Figure 1.18 The Gendered Nature of Culpable Homicide Indictments in Scotland, 1900–1960.

Figures 1.24 and 1.25 show the trend in indictments for the kind of fatal violence which was dominated by female assailants: infanticide. In the nineteenth century the indictment numbers, whilst erratic from year to year, show no discernible trend upwards or downwards until the latter decades of the century. Although the numbers *per annum* may seem relatively high, given that we are analysing a crime which resulted in a fatality, we should remember that they are roughly on par with female involvement in culpable homicide seen above. In the more modern era, there is a more evident reduction in infanticide charges being brought before the Scottish courts over time probably on account of a more relaxed attitude to illegitimacy and

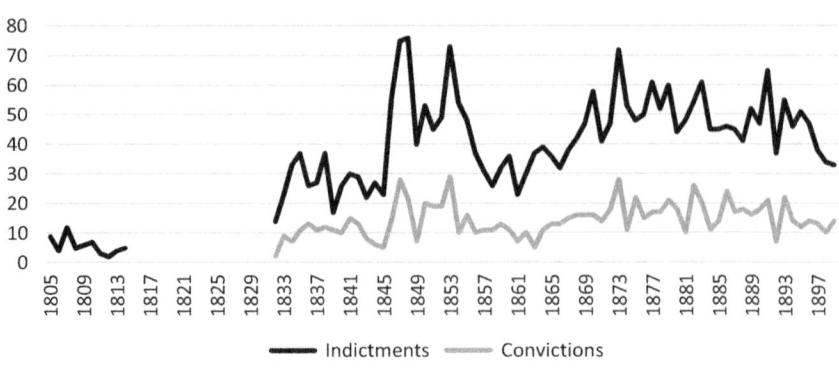

Figure 1.19 Indictments and Convictions for Culpable Homicide in Scotland, 1805–1899.

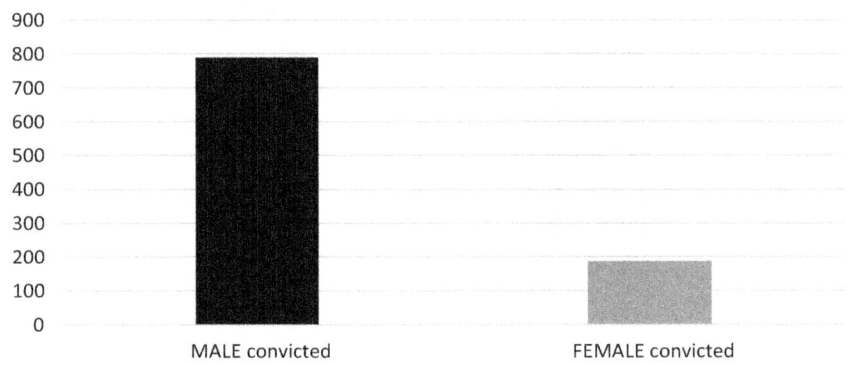

Figure 1.20 The Gendered Nature of Convictions for Culpable Homicide in Scotland, 1805–1899.

the increased availability of methods of birth-control (including abortion). Figure 1.26 below shows the gap in indictments and convictions for infanticide between 1830 and 1899 and Figure 1.27 shows the narrowing of this over the twentieth-century period, when evidence in mitigation was easier to deploy and when imprisonment came to dominate penal provision. It was undoubtedly easier to convict individuals when the punishment meted out could more readily fit the crime committed and the context in which it occurred.

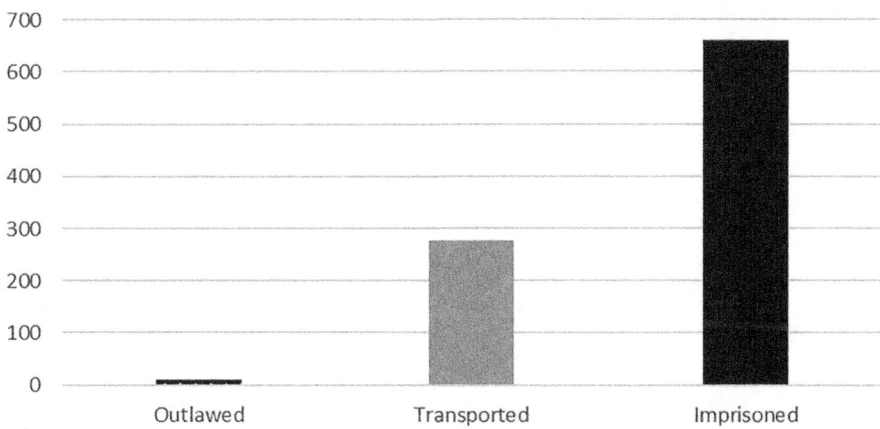

Figure 1.21 Verdicts and Sentencing Related to Culpable Homicides in Scotland, 1805–1899.

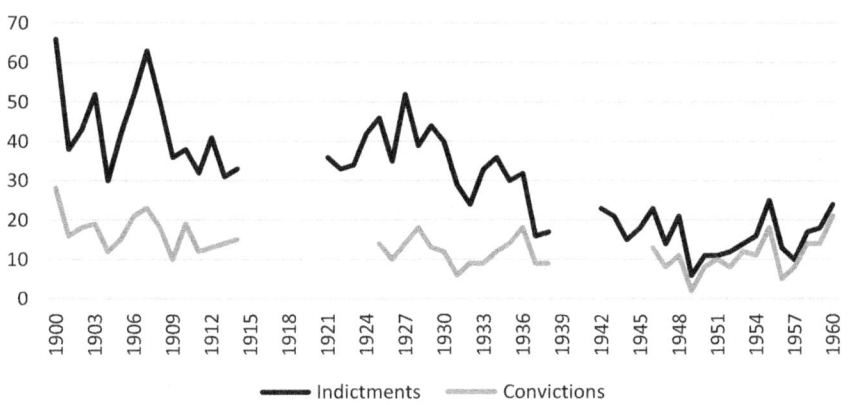

Figure 1.22 Indictments and Convictions for Culpable Homicide in Scotland, 1900–1960.

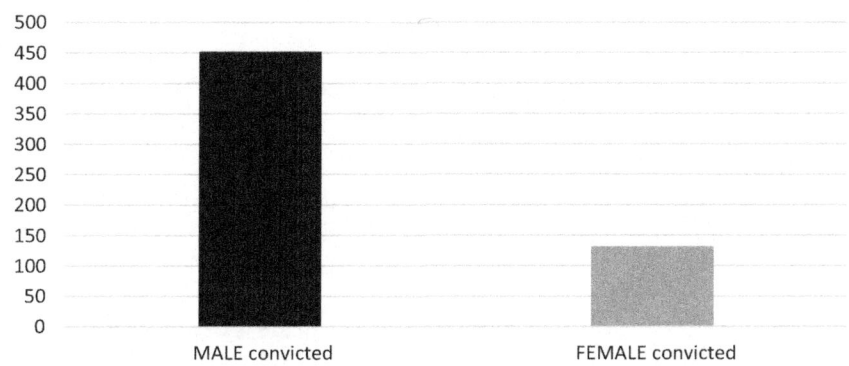

Figure 1.23 The Gendered Nature of Convictions for Culpable Homicide in Scotland, 1900–1960.

Figure 1.24 Indictments for Infanticide in Scotland, 1805–1899.

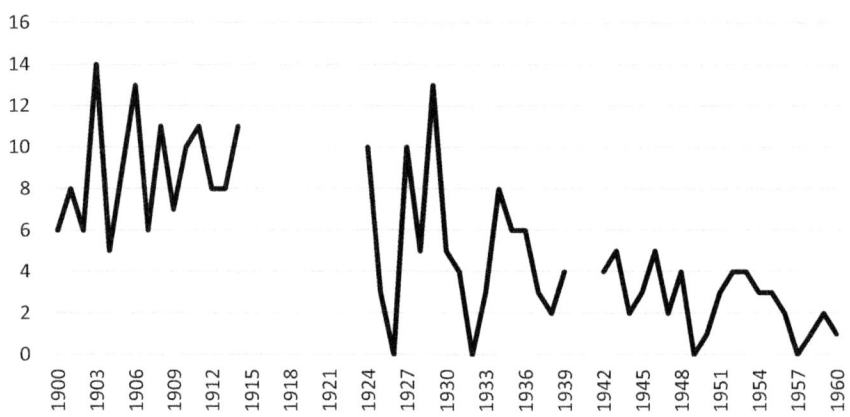

Figure 1.25 Indictments for Infanticide in Scotland, 1900–1960.

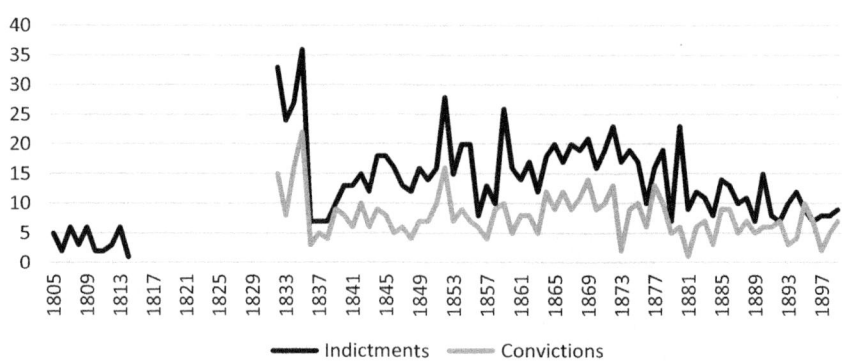

Figure 1.26 Indictments and Convictions for Infanticide in Scotland, 1805–1899.

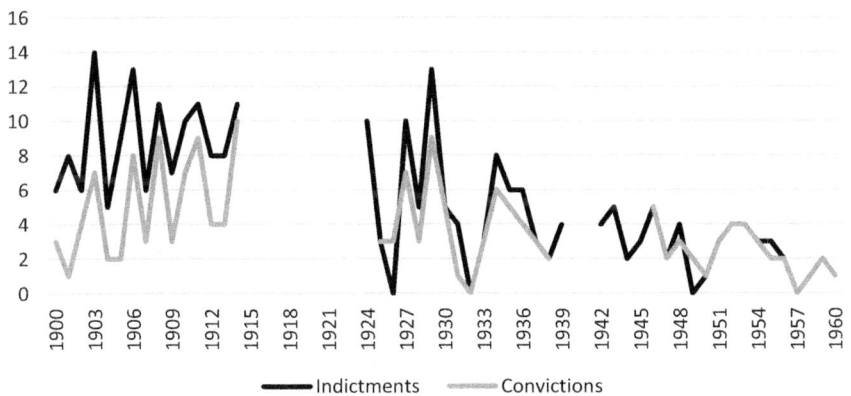

Figure 1.27 Indictments and Convictions for Infanticide in Scotland, 1900–1960.

Offenders, Victims, Methods and Motive

As evidence from this chapter and elsewhere has already shown, Scottish homicide in the premodern period was a gendered crime where males predominated. Men were more likely to perpetrate murder and culpable homicide in Scotland and they were also more likely to be the victims of such offences. Women, on the other hand, were far less likely to commit fatal violence during this era and if they did get involved in episodes which resulted in killing, it was usually in the role of victim and in the context of domestic unrest of one kind or another.[56] The limited involvement of women in episodes of fatal violence has led some historians to suggest that women could not participate in serious crime as independent actors in their own right as they lacked the necessary physical strength and the single-minded aggression required. Instead, it has been argued that women experienced violence only when it was at the instigation of men or when they had no choice in the matter, as they were the unfortunate victim of the violence that had transpired.[57] Yet, detailed analysis of Justiciary Court indictment material has shown that whilst Scottish women did not participate in murder and culpable homicide to the same extent and frequency as their male counterparts prior to the nineteenth century, they could be just as assertive, uncompromising and ferocious in their murderous instincts when the situation demanded it.

The gender disparity evident in Scottish homicide continued during the nineteenth century and into the more modern era. Although women were indicted for murder and culpable homicide more often during this period than ever before, as the above data shows, they were still significantly outnumbered by their male counterparts.[58] One explanation given for this was the more restricted social role afforded women until their comparative liberation from the domestic sphere in the second half of the twentieth century. Although there is plenty of evidence to suggest that Scottish women did venture out of the home to engage in work, philanthropy and duties of citizenship even in the seventeenth and eighteenth centuries,[59] the fact that the vast majority of the fatal violence they perpetrated was committed in the domestic sphere throughout the 1660–1960 period shows that there may be some merit to what we might call the 'domestic proximity thesis'. As men operated in a much wider sphere of influence in comparison to their female counterparts in relation to work and leisure – especially in Scotland's rapidly expanding urban areas – they were more likely to encounter and engage in random drink-fuelled brawls and episodes of often casual violence with relative strangers. These instances could, on occasion (and in the absence of swift medical provision until the more modern era), result in fatality and in subsequent charges of murder or culpable homicide.[60]

Another species of homicide linked to 'domestic proximity' and indeed to gender was infanticide or newborn child murder. Unlike murder or culpable homicide however, Scottish women were almost exclusively the protagonists of this kind of fatal violence throughout the entire 1660–1960 period.[61] As we have seen, by the very nature of the statutory provision for this offence, it was the mothers of illegitimate infant victims found dead or thought to be missing who were prosecuted. Accomplices were indicted on occasion, but were rarely convicted.[62] In the early modern period, it is possible to determine a specific offender profile in instances of infanticide. Suspects were typically young, unmarried domestic servants reliant on remaining childless if they were to stay in paid employment.[63] This profile becomes blurred over the course of the nineteenth century and irrelevant by 1900, as newborn child murder by that time was committed by a wide range of individuals in a variety of circumstances.[64]

Perceptible traits and characteristics amongst those men and women indicted for other forms of fatal violence in Scotland between 1660 and 1960 are far more difficult to discern, and reflect the largely spontaneous and unpredictable nature of the offence as we will see below. Very obviously in episodes of infanticide, and as was the case with fatal violence more generally, the victim and the offender were typically 'known' to one another to a lesser or greater extent. Although, as we have seen, men were more likely to engage in fatal 'casual violence' than women, even in such instances, the individuals involved tended to be acquaintances, even if the extent of their relationship was simply hours-old rather than established. Fatal violence against complete strangers, such as that evident in the Peter Manuel case study below, and the type of event which might well be associated with a particularly violent nation, were actually a rare phenomenon in Scotland.[65]

Premeditated violence (such as that described in the Robert Irving case study below) also seems to have been relatively rare amongst indictments for fatal violence in Scotland in the three hundred years after 1660.[66] However, there were two exceptions to this general observation. First were homicides committed in the furtherance of another offence and considered particularly heinous by the Scottish courts. These types of offences were thought to be increasing in significant numbers over the nineteenth century (particularly in Scotland), although there is little evidence to substantiate this perception.[67] Second, it could be argued that the crime of newborn child murder might involve malice aforethought to some degree. It might be supposed, for example, that in instances of deliberate infanticide, the killing of the infant may have been planned or at least contemplated at some point during the gestational period. Again however, this is hard to substantiate and was rarely, if ever, admitted to by the Scottish women indicted for the offence. In the main, then, fatal violence in Scotland typically related to episodes of spontaneous or hot-blooded violence, rather than cold, calculated criminality.[68] The weapons used to facilitate fatal violence in Scotland between 1660 and 1960 largely bear out this contention.

Up until the middle of the nineteenth century at least, the weapons of male and female killers in Scotland tended to be implements that were close to hand when tempers frayed: irons, tongs, knives of varying descriptions, axes, scissors, cutlery, crockery, sticks, stones and even garden tools were used.[69] Women tried for infanticide 'proper' in premodern Scotland overwhelmingly favoured using razors to dispatch their innocent victims after parturition, but this is probably because it was an implement they were used to using as part of their domestic chores such as food preparation. Increasingly, after 1850, we see more victims suffering fatal beatings with fists and more individuals kicked to death. Poison was used more frequently to murder over the course of the nineteenth century too, but aside from a few sensationalised cases, this *modus operandi* was never adopted with the same extent or frequency as was seemingly the case elsewhere in Britain at this time.[70] Drownings and the use of fire were rarely employed. However, one significant change that *did* emerge in relation to weapon use in Scotland after 1850 was the increasing prevalence of firearms in episodes of fatal violence involving adults. Guns were most commonly deployed when murder or culpable homicide was committed in the furtherance of another crime such as theft (as we can see in the Peter Manuel case below), but they also appeared with some frequency in episodes of hot-blooded murder too, particularly in the first half of the twentieth century when their availability became more widespread as a consequence of munitions production for the two world wars.[71]

In the same way that the weaponry for fatal violence varied from case to case in Scotland between 1660 and 1960, so did the motives behind this kind of criminal activity, and neither set Scotland apart as being an unusually violent nation. Explanations for fatal violence often tend to be very personal to an individual offender and the circumstances he or she finds herself in at the point at which killing occurs. Nevertheless, it is interesting to note that the factors that often lay behind homicidal activity remained relatively consistent in Scotland in the three hundred years in question. Some motives were easy to establish from the circumstances of a case or from the explanations given by a suspect, such as jealousy, greed, insult and acting in self-defence after prolonged and extreme provocation.[72] In infanticide cases, the shame of rearing an illegitimate child alongside the prospect of enduring solitude and poverty were regularly given as explanations for newborn child killing as were psychological imbalances in the context of conception or parturition and its aftermath.[73] There were also instances where homicides were obviously committed to facilitate another crime or to cover up evidence of other wrongdoing (as was the case in the Mary Braid trial outlined below).[74] Finally, there were episodes of fatal violence that were difficult to explain, such as murders committed during a drunken rage but for no obvious reason, killings committed by insane individuals in a moment of mania and various other episodes when the issues involved were obscure or less than clear-cut.[75] Motives for murder in Scotland were seemingly as varied as the individuals who perpetrated the offence.

Case Studies and Attitudes to Fatal Violence

(a) Mr Robert Irving (Eighteenth Century)

On the 28th of April 1717, John and Alexander Gordon (sons of the wealthy burgess and merchant James Gordon) had concluded their lessons with their chaplain, Mr Robert Irving, and were encouraged to go out for a walk in the fields near Multrees Hill in Edinburgh. Irving went with his charges and after reaching a picturesque spot where they stopped to play and pick some flowers, Irving first attacked John Gordon, grabbing him and cutting his throat with a pen knife. He died instantly. Seeing what had happened to his brother, a terrified Alexander Gordon ran off, but Irving soon caught up with him and pinning him to the ground, he dispatched the boy with the same vicious treatment. Robert Irving then tried to commit suicide. First he cut his own throat with the pen knife and then when that did not prove fatal, he threw himself in a water-filled quarry hole.[76] Unfortunately for Irving, neither of these attempts at self-slaughter were successful.

To make matters worse (for Irving at least), the entire episode was witnessed by a gentleman taking an evening constitution on Castle Hill who subsequently raised the alarm.[77] When he was being apprehended, Irving first tried to throw himself into the Waters of Leith and then tried to tear at the wound in his throat with his own fingers to facilitate his demise, but his captors bound his hands together during his arrest.[78] Irving was brought in a cart to prison '…and there chained down to the floor, as if he had been a wild beast.'[79] Matters grew graver still for Irving during his subsequent interrogation. Although he could give no explanation for his 'horrid wickedness' save for '...a temptation of the Devil', he did admit however, that '...he designed to prosecute the said Barbarous Murder Three of Four Days before the same was Committed.'[80] As Irving was caught '...with the red hand' (red-handed) and owing to his open admission of 'forethought felony', he was tried before Charles Hope and George Haliburton, two honourable Baillies of the Barony of Broughton the very next day after his arrest. He was promptly convicted and sentenced to death.[81]

Irving was visited in jail, prior to his execution by three fellow religious ministers, who all tried to ascertain more of the motives that lay behind Robert Irving's horrendous acts on two 'innocent', 'tender-aged' boys. At first, Irving refused to co-operate, simply saying that he had '...been a great Sinner, and had never spent so much as one Day as he ought to have done.'[82] All Irving seemed to be concerned about was how he would fair in the afterlife. He feared that his sins were too heinous to merit God's mercy and instead, 'That Snares, Fire and Brimston would be his Portion, and that the Tribulation and Anguish threatened against the Wicked would fall upon him.'[83] Eventually however, and after the bloody clothes of his victims were brought before him in prison, Irving became '...much affected, and broke out into Groans and Tears'.[84] He confessed that he had regularly attempted to debauch the servant girl of his employer James Gordon, but '...had never Committed any Uncleaness with her.' On one of these occasions, however, the two young Gordon boys had witnessed Irving's forceful attempts at seduction and had told their father what they had seen. James Gordon upbraided Irving for his behaviour but ultimately decided to retain his services on condition that such immorality would cease.[85] Irving claims to have been utterly ashamed by the entire episode. This opprobrium was then apparently channelled into murderous intent when Irving became heavily influenced by the writing of Presbyterian clergyman John Flavel (1627–1691). Flavel was an outspoken critic of the dangers of antinomianism and its link to the principles of predestination and had been ejected from the pulpit in 1662 for his nonconformist views.[86] It was in consequence of reading this material (and in the context of his embarrassing detection and shameful rebuke), that Robert Irving became determined to kill his two young charges.

Regardless of his explanation or his apparent remorse, on the 30th of April, just two days after the murderous incident, Irving was taken to the area called the Greenside in Edinburgh. He had both of his hands hacked off by the hangman and was then hung on a gibbet until he was dead. The execution of Robert Irving turned out to be something of a grisly spectacle for those who witnessed it as they not only saw a double premortem amputation, but the act of hanging aggravated the self-inflicted wound in Irving's throat to such an extent that '...blood gushed out in great Abundance.'[87] Unusually, the Baillies ordered that Irving's hands be fixed to stakes on the top of the Tolbooth of

Broughton for everyone to see and that Irving's body be interred near the scene of his crimes.[88] In the immediate aftermath of these events, the grieving father James Gordon erected a sundial in the garden of Ellon Castle in Aberdeenshire (a property he purchased in 1706) in fond memory of his two beloved sons. The memorial remains standing to this day, not only as a reminder of the tragic events that transpired and the young innocent victims who lost their lives, but also of the 'monstrous sinner' – Mr Robert Irving – and his ultimate fate.[89]

This case highlights some specific aspects of murder in early modern Scotland which have been illuminated in this chapter. First, and as was typical for this period at least, the offender was a male, a lone offender and his victims were individuals who were known to him. Although methods and motives vary from case to case as we have seen, the Irving example shows that murder could be brutal and extreme on occasion, but was regularly based on emotions and/or circumstances that were very specific and personal to the offender concerned. The fact that the murders of James and Alexander Gordon had been witnessed first-hand meant that justice was swift and the punishment inevitable in this instance. Yet, this was not necessarily the case with all the Scottish judiciary in the premodern period as centralised judicial processes became more important and complex and the role of professional lawyers and the nature of evidence grew in importance alongside these developments. The Irving case also generated publicity and popular reaction in its time with the publication and circulation of various broadsides and pamphlet material detailing the events that transpired. The intensified interest in the killings and in Robert Irving himself is likely explained by the age and class of the victims, the fact that they were killed by someone in a position of trust and especially by the various religious connotations of the case. The Irving case presented a fascinating and strange mix of debauchery, opprobrium, revenge and premeditated barbarity which stood in stark contrast to the piety and flawless morality which was unerringly expected of religious individuals in Calvinist Scotland during the early modern era. It must have worried and repelled some, but fascinated others, just as numerous murder cases have done since.

(b) Mary Braid (Nineteenth Century)

A sensational trial began at the High Court of Justiciary in Edinburgh on the 27th of January 1884.[90] Thomas Braid and his sister Mary were charged with two crimes: incest (which was still considered a capital crime) and child murder (which was not deemed to be a capital offence in Scotland after 1809, as we have seen). The court heard how over an eighteen-month period in their mother's house at Liberton near Edinburgh, Thomas and Mary '...did cohabit together as husband and wife and on various occasions...were there in naked bed together and did abuse your bodies with each other.'[91] Moreover, it was claimed that after repeatedly having 'wicked' and unlawfully carnal incestuous intercourse with one another, Mary found herself to be pregnant with her brother's child and she subsequently gave birth to a daughter on the 10th of April of 1833.[92] It was alleged that four months after this, on the 16th of August 1833, Thomas and Mary Braid killed their newborn baby by throwing her into the Glasgow Union Canal at Port-Hopeton near Edinburgh.[93] The couple had allegedly fastened a rope around the baby's neck with '…a stone, or some other heavy substance, likewise attached to the said rope, for the purpose of sinking its body into the water.' However, the weight they had allegedly attached was insufficient, and the child's corpse was found floating in the canal by a passer-by.[94]

The case was described by one of the judiciary at the time as '…most foul, abominable and unnatural…one of the most miserable and lamentable that ever was presented in this Court.'[95] What is interesting about this quote is that the judicial authorities were at pains to emphasise that the nature of this case was particularly unusual and that the behaviours exhibited by the suspects involved could never be countenanced in a 'civilised' society. In effect, the authorities were offering a counter-argument to the prevailing suggestions that Scotland was a nation where violence was endemic.

Thirty-six witnesses were adduced for the prosecution in this case and the trial lasted over eighteen hours, which was substantially longer than any other contemporary proceedings.[96] However, because of the nature of the evidence, the trial progressed behind closed doors and thus the details of what transpired were not open to the public's purview. Nevertheless, and probably because of the court's attempts at public censorship, interest in the case remained unabated and was indeed further heightened, by a series of broadsides and newspaper reports produced during and after the trial outlined the grisly details that the public evidently craved.[97] A case which combined sexual deviancy with child murder was tantalising to a nineteenth-century audience already fascinated by the aberrant and the macabre. Moreover, the trial occurred at a time when there was a groundswell of popular and authoritative interest in infant care; when debates over the causes of maternal malpractice proliferated and calls for infant protection burgeoned.

The child murder charge against Thomas Braid was found not proven by the assize, largely because it was very difficult to bring a man to account for infanticide under the terms of the prevailing legislation. However, he was convicted (by a majority verdict) of incest which, according to the judges in this case Lord Mackenzie and Lord Meadowbank, made him '…hardly a human being'.[98] Once again, the authorities took the time to challenge the notion of Scotland as a violent nation by emphasising that criminals like Braid should be considered anomalous social outcasts, rather than conventional members of a 'civilised' Scottish society. Thomas Braid was sentenced to be banished from Scotland for the rest of his natural life. Thomas responded to his sentence by exclaiming:

> My innocence will protect me, I hope;
> in this bloody country I have got no justice.[99]

Mary Braid, described at this point in the proceedings as being '…in a state of dejection and debility'[100] was found guilty of both charges libelled. Mary's blatant lies to various individuals and her ever-changing testimony and declarations had evidently not aided her cause.[101] The judges in the case blatantly criticised the couple's behaviour as '…shocking and disgusting' and Mary's offences in particular as '…abhorrent to the better feelings of our nature [and] which if not checked by severe punishment, would be most fatal to the purity of females and to the happiness of society.'[102] In consequence of this, Mary was sentenced to death and the judges ordered that her body be buried in the precincts of the gaol.[103] A broadside produced ahead of Mary's execution described the parting of the siblings, their evident atonement (standard fare for this type of state sanctioned publication) and Mary's preparedness to meet her fate saying:

As thus she sat in deep sorrow drowned,
Her frail body with many a chain being bound,
Beside her stood, in anxious thought,
Her brother, partner of her guilt.
Their looks betrayed their inward pain,
As they struggled a self-command to gain
To take a last and solemn farewell
Of each other they loved so fatally well.

At length spake the brother, while his tears ran down,
Farewell, dearest Mary, our time now is flown;
Though death is your doom, how freely could I
With you exchange places, and in your stead die.
But, alas! I'll be hurried to a foreign land,
Where hard-hearted tyrants shall o'er me command,
Without the least prospect of comfort or peace,
Till death's welcome message shall give me release.

Scarce able to speak, in his arms then she fell,
As she faulter'd these words, dear Thomas, farewell!
Repent of your sins, be Religion your guide,
And Heaven will bless you whatever betide.
For me do not grieve – I go hence in full hope
Of receiving free pardon through Jesus my God;
In which blessed hope I trust I shall die,
And wake in the blessed assembly on high.[104]

The case did not conclude with Mary's execution as had been expected, however. This is because a petition for clemency was lodged at the Home Office in London on her behalf. One hundred and fifty-two individuals had countersigned the document. The petition claimed that although Mary was guilty of incest with her brother, it was *he* who had 'betrayed' *her* and had killed the child '...without her knowledge'. Moreover, and as part of the clemency submission, Thomas Braid had offered a signed confession to the same.[105] Interestingly, a close reading of the original judicial sentencing speeches in this case suggests that Lord Mackenzie and Lord Meadowbank had been much more convinced of Thomas Baird's culpability in the episode of child murder than the jury had been.[106] In any event, Mary Braid craved that she be banished overseas and that her elder daughter, presumably from a previous relationship, be allowed to accompany her.[107]

Much debate ensued between legal authorities north and south of the border in the aftermath of this appeal because in Scotland, incest was a capital crime, but in England it was not.[108] Furthermore, Mary had not only acknowledged her guilt of that offence but a jury had convicted her of it also and by a unanimous verdict. The Home Office was also presented with evidence that Mary Braid had become unwell whilst languishing in gaol awaiting her fate. She had contracted 'a severe fever' and was said by surgeons to be gravely ill.[109] Weighing all of this evidence together, alongside the fact that the case against Thomas Braid could not be opened after the fact despite his confession, the Right Honourable Lord Viscount Melbourne decided that '... both prisoners should receive equal sentences' and ordered Mary Braid's sentence to be commuted to life banishment.[110] It is unknown whether she and Thomas met up again after the resolution to the case, but both individuals can be traced to the Van Dieman's Land penal colony (now Tasmania) on convict ships. Thomas went in 1834 on the *William Metcalfe* where he appears to have made a living as a barber to other transportees.[111] Mary sailed on the *Hector* in 1835 and by 1841 she had found work in the service of a local magistrate Samuel R. Dawson as a cook, housemaid and needlewoman.[112]

The case of Thomas and Mary Braid was scarcely a typical episode of Scottish infanticide for various reasons. First, the child victim was not newborn and second, if we are to believe Thomas's later confession, the perpetrator of the infanticide was male rather than female. Furthermore, by the nineteenth century and certainly by the 1830s, it was relatively rare for a sentence of execution to result from an indictment for child murder, due to the flexible judicial approach to the crime as we have already seen. This makes the Braid case significant however, as it is likely that it was one of the very last infanticide trials where this type of sentence was meted out by the Scottish courts. However, it is evident that the events had been deemed aggravated by the accompanying incest charge which seemed to have overshadowed much of the trial proceedings given that as the case occurred after the new child murder legislation of 1809, it was the only capital offence indicted. Moreover, we have to remember that ultimately, and despite the evidence put to the court, it was clemency and subsequent transportation, rather than any sort of physical punishment that marked the judicial outcome in this case. In this respect, the Braid case highlights one of the key changes in trials for newborn child murder in the 1660–1960 period.

From the early nineteenth century onwards, as we have seen, the Scots introduced a more flexible and nuanced approach to cases of newborn murder. Either indictments accused the suspect of homicide (by infanticide) or they charged the individual with the lesser offence of concealment. Although in theory, this negated the need to introduce prolonged legal debate regarding the psychological status of the accused at the time of the infanticidal act, in cases of infanticide as homicide, such evidence increasingly encroached upon the Scottish courtroom. Psychological status was used to determine culpability in the precise moment and far less attention was given to considerations of intent or premeditation as would be the case in 'regular' homicide trials. The courts scarcely relished trying infanticidal women as too obviously these women had transgressed accepted gender and maternal norms. Consequently, if their actions could be explained away through mental aberration of one kind or another, then the judicial authorities in Scotland (and indeed elsewhere) were more than happy to accept such an explanation.[113] Scottish women accused of infanticide were still prosecuted and convicted in the nineteenth century and beyond, but their actions were far more likely to be mitigated by psychological pressures associated with parturition and lactation. As such, and indeed as we have seen from the analysis of judicial punishments given above, they were more inclined to be given what might be considered relatively lenient sentences, considering that an infant's life had been deliberately or even negligently extinguished. Although the Braid case did not discuss the mental health of either of the accused, the clemency shown to Mary Braid in particular,[114] was symptomatic of an ongoing sympathy amongst the Scottish judiciary for women who found themselves accused of this tragic and emotive crime.

(c) Peter Manuel (Twentieth Century)

Peter Thomas Anthony Manuel was born in Manhattan, New York on the 15th of March 1927, the son of Scottish emigrants. The Manuel family returned to their homeland in 1932 and proceeded to be energetically peripatetic, moving around various towns and cities primarily in England, before settling in the Motherwell area in 1946. Even by this time, and whilst still a teenager, Peter Manuel had an extensive criminal record and had made regular appearances in juvenile courts across Britain. Most of Manuel's criminal exploits, up to this point at least, related to theft and housebreaking and he was typically sent to approved schools upon conviction but then escaped and went on to reoffend. There were also instances of violence in Manuel's early criminal history too, however. For instance, he once attacked an individual with a hammer in their own home and in December of 1942 (aged just fifteen) he robbed and indecently assaulted the wife of someone who worked at the school he was attending. After this latter incident, he was sent to borstal but was released two years later, just as his family returned to Scotland.[115]

Another change of scene did nothing to quell Manuel's criminal tendencies, and in March of 1946, he was indicted on fifteen separate charges of housebreaking and was sentenced to one year in an adult prison. He was just nineteen years old. Whilst serving this particular sentence, Manuel was concurrently convicted of rape and sentenced to a further eight years imprisonment.[116] The nature of his offence meant that he had to serve his time alongside many other sexual predators at Aberdeen's Peterhead Prison, and it was acknowledged at the time that he was one of their youngest-ever inmates. Eventually, and although the authorities acknowledged that it was unlikely that Manuel could reform, he earned some remission from his sentence on account of good behaviour and was released from prison to live with his parents in Birkenshaw, Lanarkshire.[117] Initially at least, things seemed to improve for Manuel, as he became engaged to a local girl and managed to hold down some steady employment. However, this welcomed prosperity and conventional happiness did not last long. Manuel was regularly cruel and malicious to his fiancé, and so she ended their engagement citing religious differences for their break-up. Soon after this, Manuel found himself in trouble with the law time and again. In the mid-1950s, he was prosecuted and convicted mostly for relatively petty offences.[118] However, closer analysis of his criminal history reveals several instances of sexual violence at this time for which Manuel was charged but not convicted. These included one instance where Manuel successfully acted in his own defence in court against an allegation of aggravated sexual assault.[119]

On the 14th of January 1958, Manuel was arrested by police at his parent's house on suspicion of his involvement in a multi-victim fatal robbery in Uddingston. They had a warrant to search the premises and to remove Manuel's clothing for forensic examination.[120] Samuel Manuel, Peter's father was also arrested at the time on charges of theft and reset (or receiving stolen goods) and in order to clear his father from any wrongdoing, Peter Manuel confessed to his own, sole culpability in a series of vicious and seemingly senseless crimes in the local area.[121] Although Manuel later tried to claim that the said confession had been elicited through emotional blackmail and was part of a significant police conspiracy against him, as we will see, when he appeared before Lord Cameron at Glasgow's Justiciary Court on the 11th of May 1958, he was accused of eight separate offences relating to what was latterly described as '…one of the darkest series of events in British criminal history.'[122] The indictment[123] accused him of:

1   *The capital murder of Anne Kneilands on the 2nd of January 1956 by striking her repeatedly on the head with a piece of iron or similar instrument and robbing her of a watch, a pair of earrings, a French coin, a belt and a handbag.*

Anne Kneiland's body was found on a golf course in East Kilbride. She had planned to meet her boyfriend Andrew Murnin on the evening she was attacked, but he failed to show up at their agreed rendezvous point.

Her clothing had been rearranged and some items (a stocking and her knickers) were missing from the crime scene. Medical reports delivered in court did not indicate that sexual intercourse had taken place, despite the evidence suggesting that this was a sexually motivated attack.[124] It has been suggested by criminologists with the benefit of hindsight that in this instance (as in other sexual offences alleged to have been committed by Manuel) that he had ejaculated on his own clothing before penetration could occur.[125] Despite seven Glaswegian businessmen offering a £900 reward for information about the case, and local newspapers printing a picture of Peter Manuel as someone interviewed and suspected by the police at the time of the murder, no public response was forthcoming and no arrest was made at the time.[126]

2   *Breaking into the Platts' house at Bothwell sometime between the 12th and the 15th of September 1956 and (a) stealing an electric razor, some tools and certain other articles and (b) maliciously damaging a mattress by firing a loaded firearm into it.'*

3   *Breaking into the Martins' house at High Burnside between the 15th and 17th of September 1956 and stealing two rings, four pairs of nylon stockings and six shillings.*

These two break-ins in the Lanarkshire area (along with another for which Manuel was suspected but not indicted) all occurred when the victims were away on holiday. It is interesting for us to consider whether Manuel knew this detail ahead of committing these offences, or whether, given his later *modus operandi* that this fact was merely incidental and wholly fortuitous for the individuals involved. Although the items stolen in these break-ins were not valuable, these crimes are significant for three key reasons. Firstly, some of the items stolen were recovered by the police from amongst Peter Manuel's possessions (most notably the relatively unusual electric razor). Secondly, the calibre of bullet fired into the mattress at the Platt family home matched the bullet used in the Watt family murders (see indictment charge (4) immediately below).[127] And thirdly, when conducting these break-ins the culprit made a fair amount of mess (for instance food was scattered around the properties or left uneaten and muddy footprints were found on carpets and bed linen).[128] This vandalistic 'signature' was something that was repeated in the later robbery homicides[129] and along with the chain of evidence described, was thus an aspect which not only linked these various crimes together, but also linked Peter Manuel to their perpetration.

4   *Breaking into the Watts' house at High Burnside on the 17th of September 1956 and the capital murder by shooting of Mrs Watt, Mrs Brown and Vivienne Watt.*

The bodies of the invalided Mrs William Watt, her sister Mrs Margaret Brown and her daughter Vivienne were found by the family's home help the morning after they were killed in their beds. All three of the victims had been shot in the head at close range. Evidence from the crime scene showed little signs of a struggle in relation to the two older women, although Mrs Watt's pyjama bottoms had been ripped from the waist down her right leg. The time of death for their killings was estimated at 6am. Vivienne on the other hand was thought to have been killed some three and a half hours later and had been found wearing just an unbuttoned pyjama top and cardigan. Her bra and pyjama bottoms had seemingly been ripped from her by force and extensive bruising was evident on her thighs and other parts of her body, including her genitals. Despite appearances, none of the victims had been sexually assaulted.[130] Initially, and understandably given some witness testimony which questioned his whereabouts at the time of the murders, Mr William Watt, respectively husband, brother-in-law and father to the victims was arrested for the Burnside killings. He was eventually released from Barlinnie Prison some sixty-seven days later.[131]

5   *Breaking into the Reverend Alexander Houston's house at Mount Vernon on 25th of December 1957 and stealing a camera, a pair of gloves, a sock and £2.*

The lull in criminal activity between the time of the Watt murders to this instance of housebreaking, can be explained by the fact that Manuel was in Barlinnie Prison from the 2nd of October 1956 until the 30th of November 1957 serving consecutive and concurrent sentences for petty acts of criminality.[132] During this time inside, and in a somewhat bizarre twist of fate, Peter Manuel met William Watt and discussed the Burnside murders at length with him to pass the time. The Houston house break-in occurred less than a month after Manuel's release. Moreover, nearly every aspect of this offence mirrors that of the break-ins indicted in charges (2) and (3) of the indictment.[133]

6   *The capital murder of Isabelle Cooke on the 28th December 1957, tearing off her clothing and tying a brassiere round her neck and a headscarf round her face and mouth, and robbing her of a pair of shoes, a brush, a fan, a stole, a pouchette of cosmetics and a handbag.*

Three days after Christmas in 1957, seventeen-year-old Isabelle Cooke left her parents' house to go to a dance in Uddingston with a classmate. Isabelle did not meet up with her friend as planned and simply vanished instead. As part of his initial confession to police, Peter Manuel took officers on a macabre cross-country clue hunt where they picked up some of Isabelle's possessions which had been scattered around the immediate locale, mirroring Manuel's aforementioned disarray 'signature' found at other crime scenes.[134] Eventually, Manuel led police to the spot where her body was buried. Isabelle was found wearing just a cardigan, a suspender belt, a pair of nylon stockings and some jewellery. Bruises were found about her face and as the indictment details suggests, the cause of her death had been asphyxiation via a double ligature. Once again, there was no evidence of any penetrative sexual assault on the victim.[135]

7   *Breaking into the Smarts' house at Uddingston on the 1st of January 1958 and the capital murder by shooting of Mr and Mrs Smart and their son Michael; also*

robbing Mr Smart of £30 and a number of keys and Mrs Smart of a pair of gloves, a purse and eighteen shillings.

Peter Smart was a civil engineer and successful entrepreneur who lived with his wife and eleven year old son Michael in Uddingston. The Smart family were likely killed at some point during the New Year celebrations of 1958, although their bodies were not discovered until a week later. As with the Watt family murders, the Smart family had all been shot in the head at close range whilst in their beds. In this instance, however, there was no evident disarray at the scene (although food had been consumed by the assailant) and the victims had not been touched or moved pre- or postmortem. Evidence recovered from the scene and gleaned from witness testimony regarding the curtains in the Smarts' front room which changed from open to closed on an *ad hoc* but regular basis, suggests that the culprit stayed in the *locus operandi* for some time after the killings had been perpetrated. It was in the aftermath of this particular crime that the net closed in on Peter Manuel as the lead suspect in the eight crimes indicted. The police were tipped off in very early January that a young man who had been bemoaning his poverty to friends prior to Hogmanay was now spending freely and there seemed to be no explanation for his newfound wealth. Moreover, this same man (who had scratches on his face and was known to the police) was using blue bank notes which matched the type that Peter Smart had withdrawn from his savings account immediately before his untimely death. On the basis of the information received, the police arrested Peter Manuel.[136]

8   *The theft on the 1st of January 1958 of Mr Smart's motor-car.*

Various individuals came forward to testify that Peter Manuel had given them a lift in Mr Smart's car – which was later found abandoned. In another bizarre aspect of the case, one of the passengers that Manuel aided was a Constable Robert Smith who needed a lift to continue searching the River Calder for the remains of the missing schoolgirl Isabelle Cooke.[137]

As is evident from the indictment above, Peter Manuel was accused on four counts of 'capital murder'. As is evident from discussion elsewhere in this chapter, prior to the Homicide Act of 1957, all acts of murder (but crucially not all killings) were considered to be capital and, upon conviction, death was the only punishment that could be meted out. After the 1957 Act was passed however, distinctions were drawn between *types* of murder, with only so-called 'capital murders' warranting a death sentence upon conviction. Two types of 'capital murder' are evident in the eight-count indictment against Peter Manuel: murder committed via shooting and murder committed in the furtherance of another crime – theft.[138]

Although something of a moot point given the outcome of the trial, it is worth noting that Scottish indictments, as is evident in the Manuel case, can contain multiple accusations, whereas their English counterparts would indict only one offence at a time. Individuals accused of multiple offences in Scotland were permitted to ask for the charges against them to be separated out, but this was rarely done. The Scots judiciary practiced this system so that no other accusations could be brought against an accused at the point of trial. Under the new legislation of 1957, a murder case became capital if the offender had a previous conviction for murder (regardless of intent or methodology). Consequently, this could have applied to some of the charges in the Manuel case if the indictments had been separated out and conviction achieved in relation to an initial murder charge. In other words, more 'capital murder' convictions could have resulted from the Manuel indictment if he had committed his offences south of the border and been tried in an English court.[139]

Prior to Manuel's arrest, the seemingly indiscriminate nature of the attacks caused fear and terror to spread around the West of Scotland.[140] Women and children did not go out at night and hardware shops in the area sold out of home security provisions. Consequently, once a suspect was unmasked and subsequently charged with the offences, the curiosity of the public was well and truly piqued. According to J.G. Wilson, the trial of Peter Manuel '…aroused more public interest than any other in living memory in Scotland and special arrangements were made to regulate admission to the court.'[141] But it was Peter Manuel the individual who attracted much of the attention at the time of his trial, rather than the crimes which he was alleged to have committed, brutal and sensational though they undoubtedly were. The press reported that members of the public queued through the night outside the court in order to get a seat at the proceedings,[142] and it is evident that Manuel attained something of a celebrity status in the summer of 1958, with women in particular seemingly transfixed by the defendant.[143] Rival newspapers battled it out to seek exclusive interviews with the Manuel family and acquaintances of Peter, and Manuel himself was offered £3,000 for an exclusive interview in the course of his trial which the courts disallowed.[144]

The strength of the prosecution's evidence at the trial was initially rather flimsy as it concentrated on testimony from known members of the Glasgow Underworld and other convicted felons with regard to how Peter Manuel came to be in possession of two hand guns – a Webley revolver and a Beretta automatic – which were both recovered by police divers from the River Clyde in the wake of Manuel's arrest.[145] Unusually for a murder case, there was little in the way of indicative medical or forensic evidence pointing to a specific suspect. Yet eventually the trial did turn more in the prosecution's favour, after it won an extensive legal debate over the admissibility of the evidence from Manuel's detailed confessions to police.[146] Said evidence was communicated in great depth by the prosecution[147] and in one of the most sensational moments of the trial, Inspector McNeill recalled how Manuel concluded his confession by saying to him (in the presence of his parents): 'There is no future for me. I have done some terrible things.'[148] Manuel was infuriated by this turn of events. He promptly sacked his legal team and, just as he had done on previous occasions, he decided to mount his own legal defence against the charges before him. This brought him some latitude from the judge who allowed him some time to regroup, but confronted with his own repeated admissions of culpability, he faced an uphill battle to persuade the jury of nine men and six women of his innocence.[149]

There are a variety of 'special defences' that an accused individual can put forward to the Scottish judiciary. These are self-defence, alibi, insanity and impeachment or blaming another individual for the crime or crimes charged. Peter Manuel put forward *both* impeachment and alibi in his defence. He claimed via impeachment that one Charles Tallis and his partner Mary Bowes had committed the Martin housebreaking and that William Watt had killed his wife, daughter and sister-in-law in the Burnside killings. He also claimed *via* alibi, that at the time of the Smart family killings, he was at home in the company of his parents, siblings and another family friend and that his presence there could be proven irrefutably.[150] Using evidence from Manuel's confessions however, the prosecution was able to undermine most of his defence *via* alibi.[151] They were also able to dismantle his arguments of impeachment too, through Manuel's own words and the testimony of various witnesses who were able to forcefully contradict his claims regarding the whereabouts of William Watt at the time of the Burnside murders.[152]

Peter Manuel insisted nonetheless that the confession evidence submitted in court by the prosecution was a fabrication and that he had been bullied and intimidated into making false statements by the police as part of a significant conspiracy against him. He argued that this plot had been borne out of police frustration when they had failed to convict him on a previous occasion when he had successfully acted as his own defence in court. In summing up his own defence, Peter Manuel said: 'I can assure you I have never been the confessing type and have never been considered by the police to be the confessing type.'[153]

In his summing up, the trial judge, Lord Cameron noted that Manuel had made no defence of insanity and that there was no evidence to support a mitigation of any of the homicide charges down to culpable homicide. However, he did give the jury the specific direction that as there was insufficient evidence linking the defendant to the murder of Anne Kneilands, a conviction could not and should not be merited against that charge. All the remaining elements of the indictment were left for the jury to determine.[154] They took a little more than two hours to reach their verdict on the seven charges before them. The jury found Peter Manuel guilty of all charges, except the Kneilands murder of which he was found 'not guilty' as directed by the judge and the Houston housebreaking which was found to be 'not proven'. The prosecution moved that sentencing be restricted to the murder convictions alone and to that end, the judge pronounced that Peter Manuel was to be imprisoned in Barlinnie jail until the 19th of June, when he was to be hanged in the prison grounds between 8 and 10 that morning.[155]

Peter Manuel employed legal counsel to launch an appeal against his conviction and won a temporary stay of execution. There were six grounds for his appeal: that his confessions were inadmissible as evidence; that the jury had been misdirected in relation to the burden of proof required in special defences; that the verdict in the Martin case was contrary to the evidence presented; that the jury was misdirected in relation to the motive for the Watt murders which had relied on the uncorroborated testimony of William Watt (suspect in the eyes of the defence at least); that the evidence of defence witnesses (Taylor and Morrison) was unfairly reviewed before the jury; and, that there was misdirection to the jury in relation to evidence in the Cooke murder thought to corroborate the accused's alleged confession.[156] Obviously the first point of appeal was the most important, as much of the prosecution's case hinged on whether the confessions entered by Manuel had been obtained voluntarily and without coercion. It is interesting to note that Manuel did not contest his conviction relating to the Smart family murders in his appeal. This meant that even if all of his other claims were substantiated, he would still be convicted of 'capital murder' three times over.[157] In any event, the Appeal Court Judge, Lord Clyde, dismissed all six of Manuel's claims in short shrift and the 11th of July was fixed as the date of execution.[158] Peter Manuel was hanged at one minute past eight on the morning decreed. He was thirty-one years old.[159]

In the wake of Manuel's execution order, a lot of effort was expended to try to understand why he had committed the offences for which he came to be indicted and to determine whether there were any mitigating factors (such as mental health problems) that ought to be taken into consideration should any petitions for reprieve be received by the Home Office. Much of the information on which these deliberations were based was taken from psychological evaluations and reports made about Manuel's behaviour dating from his time at approved school, borstal and during the various spells of imprisonment that he had served over the course of his relatively short life. Comments from authority figures who encountered Manuel as an adolescent and young adult for instance, describe him variously as '…a slippery customer', '…a great nuisance locally', '…an unruly character' and '…an absolute pest'.[160] He was regarded as a fantasist and someone who could be unbearably cocky, often to his own detriment. More menacingly, and as time went on, Manuel is referred to in more threatening terms such as '…a danger to the neighbourhood' and even '…an aggressive psychopath.'[161] His sexual promiscuousness, heavy drinking and routine temper tantrums are referred to at regular intervals in his case files and even his sister was at pains to point out that she thought he was 'a psychopath' with a 'split mind'.[162] Nevertheless, and according to the psychiatrists that interviewed Peter Manuel ahead of his Appeal in 1958:

> They found no evidence that he was insane or suffering from an aberration of mind…they believed him to be an abnormal man, showing many of the traits usually acknowledged to be characteristic of psychopathic personality, but…they did not believe that these constituted in his case a psychopathic state of such degree to diminish responsibility for his actions.[163]

One further thing that was clear from the psychiatric and psychological evidence lodged in Peter Manuel's case files, and indeed from how he conducted himself during his trial, was that he thrived upon being the centre of attention and had '…a morbidly inflated ego'.[164] This narcissism did not dissipate even when he was facing the hangman's noose. For instance, whilst preparations were being made to hear his appeal in Edinburgh, Peter Manuel appeared to develop a sudden, curious illness whilst in his cell in Barlinnie gaol.[165] He was found in his cell by a warder '…lying on his back, twitching his limbs, contorting his face and frothing at the mouth'.[166] Seemingly, the effects of this condition had rendered him '…haggard and withdrawn' to the extent that he developed '…a shuffling gait and his muscular movements became clumsy and abnormal' and eventually he refused all sustenance and blanked all attempts to communicate with him.[167] The press picked up on what was happening and provided daily updates on Manuel's mystery condition. Newspapers initially questioned whether he had been poisoned, but soon headlines asked: 'IS HE INSANE?' and pondered whether doctors would be able to earn Manuel a reprieve on the grounds of insanity or diminished responsibility.[168]

A petition for a reprieve (signed by a paltry fifty-nine individuals) was forthcoming for Peter Manuel, but it was not submitted by physicians as, after much deliberation and completing a barrage of tests on Manuel, they could find nothing (either mentally or physical) wrong with him. They concluded instead, that his recent ill-behaviour was '…assumed and consciously motivated.'[169] It seemed merely a ruse to prolong his life and garner popular and media attention. The plea for clemency that *was* eventually submitted to the Home Secretary was written by playwright Edward Bond, a staunch figure in the movement to abolish capital punishment.[170] Bond was far more interested in making a point about the cruelty of state executions than he was about saving the life of Peter Manuel *per se* and this plea unsurprisingly fell on deaf ears as we know.

Peter Manuel was suspected of other contemporaneous killings and, shortly before his death, the *Sunday Pictorial* newspaper (which became the *Sunday Mirror* in 1963) reported that Manuel had confessed to the murder of Helen Carlin, a prostitute found strangled in Pimlico, London, in September 1954; the murder of Anne Steele, a spinster found battered to death in Glasgow in January 1956; and, the murder of Ellen Petrie found stabbed to death also in Glasgow in June of the same year. These apparent confessions have never been substantiated, and moreover, the *modus operandi* employed in each of these cases is sufficiently different from Manuel's approach to cast doubt on his involvement. However, on the 28th of July 1958 Peter Manuel was convicted by Newcastle Crown Court of the murder of a taxi driver Sydney Dunn in County Durham in December of 1957. Dunn had been shot through the head at close range in his taxi which had been parked on moorland. His throat had also been cut and his taxi vandalised. The victim's possessions had been scattered around the *locus operandi* as per the Manuel 'signature'. Some forensic evidence was recovered from the crime scene which linked Manuel to the murder and it was evident from witness testimony that Peter Manuel had been in the area at the time.[171] The Dunn killing had not been added to the eight-count 1958 indictment against Peter Manuel as the killing had occurred outside Scottish jurisdiction. In addition, as Manuel had already been executed by the time of this further conviction, sentencing in this case could not be expedited.[172]

The Peter Manuel case is important in this chapter and indeed the wider scope of this work as it highlights many aspects of continuity and change in relation to fatal violence in Scottish history. As has been shown elsewhere in this chapter, murder has and largely remains a gendered crime predominated by lone, male offenders. Weapons are still overtly used in instance of Scottish homicide as they were in the past, but as can be seen in the Manuel case, we see the increasing use of firearms in criminal trials involving fatal violence over the course of the twentieth century. One aspect of modern murder in particular that the Manuel case especially illuminates is the fact that individuals can, and indeed do, kill multiple victims. Some individuals have argued that Peter Manuel was not a true example of a 'serial killer' (defined as someone who murders two or more victims over a relatively short time period on account of an abnormal need for psychological gratification[173]) as he had no fixed victim type. Yet, it is undeniable that he exemplified other traits or characteristics associated with this type of modern offender such as a methodological 'signature', a fixed geographical zone of operation, 'trophy' collection, tangential involvement in the related police enquires and a lack of obvious or explicit motive (save for the apparent pleasure he gained from terrorising his victims).[174]

Another key issue associated with modern homicide that is highlighted by the Manuel case relates to aspects of offender profiling. It is evident that more concerted and deliberate efforts were made to better understand killers in the twentieth century and the triggers that made them commit their crimes. Consequentially, psychiatric reports became part and parcel of homicide case files in the modern era and could often dominate trial or appeal proceedings as we saw in the Manuel case in particular. Occurring in tandem with the rise in prominence of the psychiatric profession from the late nineteenth century onwards, in some ways the provision of this kind of 'medical' information was done in order to try to prevent future crimes from being perpetrated and thereby minimise the risk to the public. However, it was also done in order to ostracise violent individuals from the rest of society and explain their violent tendencies as the actions of individuals who were mentally 'diminished' or who knew no better. Finally, and perhaps more typically, evidence regarding mental capacity was increasingly provided in mitigation, especially at a time when capital punishment was still part of Britain's penal policy.

The final aspect of homicide illuminated by the Peter Manuel case is the historic and ongoing public fascination with murderers and their crimes in the Scottish context. This interest was evident to some extent in the case of Robert Irving way back in 1717 and had been heightened further by the time of the Mary Braid case in 1834. Since then, and through the evolving mechanisms of the modern media, our preoccupation with murderous offenders has intensified to an unprecedented and arguably an unhealthy degree. Certainly, press and public interest encouraged the spotlight to fall on Peter Manuel in the late 1950s. As we have seen, throngs of individuals hung out near the court to get a place in the gallery or to catch a glimpse of the accused. Manuel thrived on the attention he received during and after his trial. He played to this as it fuelled both his ego and his fantasist tendencies.[175] Unquestionably, Peter Manuel became global front-page news during the entirety of his trial[176] and the Scottish populace seemed especially fascinated by the monster in their midst who famously described himself as 'The foulest beast on earth... ...a reptile in disguise...Scotland's Frankenstein.'[177] Our obsession with individuals who commit fatal violence and especially those who kill multiple victims, shows little sign of diminishing and Peter Manuel was arguably first in a burgeoning line of Scottish offenders who have attained a degree of infamy in the annals of Scottish crime.[178] Scotland's fascination with these types of individuals throughout history must contribute, at least in part, to perceptions which relate to the nature of a given place and the behaviour of its people.

Conclusion – The Violent North?

We would expect, that in a nation deemed to be persistently lawless and rebellious throughout its history, fatal violence would be ubiquitous and extreme. However, despite a legal context which clearly provided for the prosecution of murder, culpable homicide and infanticide, such episodes were not commonly brought to the Scottish courts' attention during the 1660–1960 period. Although there is a lack of judicial statistics for the period before 1805, it is nonetheless evident, that if we take into account contextual factors such as the development of centralised justice, the establishment of an effective system of policing and the inexorable increase in population across Scotland since the dawn of the nineteenth century, the relatively minimalistic nature of Scottish fatal violence over that time is significant. Although the Scottish judiciary had harsh sanctions to utilise upon murderous individuals, they rarely deployed these as the bulk of offenders were either deemed insane or were convicted of the lesser charge of culpable homicide. In terms of court business then, fatal violence was more the exception rather than the rule in the Scottish context.

Most episodes of fatal violence in Scotland between 1660 and 1960 were committed by men (with the exception of newborn child murder) and most were committed in hot blood, between individuals who knew one another. Motives for killing were diverse and typically related to the specific circumstances of each episode. Weapons were quite often utilised, but on the whole, there was nothing particularly extraordinary about fatal violence in Scotland. The perpetration of homicide in Scotland was not that dissimilar from elsewhere in terms of who committed it, how it was done and why. So why then, has there been a long-held belief in the violent nature of Scottish society and in what ways has fatal violence contributed to this?

Ironically, it may be the very uncommon nature of fatal violence in Scotland that is to blame for the ongoing and false proposition regarding the nation's character. By having fewer cases to focus on, more attention has been afforded to those episodes of fatal violence that *have* occurred and attention has been magnified still further, when the context of those cases have the potential to be especially melodramatic or sensational. Just as the case studies in this chapter perfectly illustrate – a trusted schoolmaster who kills his pupils, an incest case which results in a clandestine murder, and a home-grown serial killer who shows no remorse – all three episodes offer significant fascination for audiences at home and afar, not only at the time of their perpetration but in the years beyond too. The public zealously pour over cases like these in order to extract every single piece of salacious information and in the process, the criminals concerned are effectively turned into cult-based celebrities. In the Scottish context it would seem that the publicity generated by cases such as these has fuelled the historic, but unsubstantiated notion that fatal violence, as with violence more generally, was endemic, entrenched and out of control between 1660 and 1960. The extent to which a more realistic portrayal of Scottish criminality can be achieved will be explored in the rest of the volume, beginning with an investigation and analysis of sexual violence, a subject which hitherto, has been completely ignored by Scottish historians.

Notes

1 D. Masson (2004) (ed) *The Register of the Privy Council of Scotland – Volume III: 1578–1585* (Burlington: Tanner Ritchie Publishing), p. 500.

2 See K.M. Brown (1986) Bloodfeud in Scotland 1573–1625: Violence, Justice and Politics in an Early Modern Society (Edinburgh: John Donald), p. 13 and J. Wormald (1985) Lords and Men in Scotland: Bonds of Manrent, 1442–1603 (Edinburgh: John Donald), p. 115.

3 For further discussion and examples see *ibid, passim* and A. Grant (2013) 'Murder Will Out: Kingship, Kinship and Killing in Medieval Scotland', a working

paper, published by the University of Lancaster, p. 2 and found at http://eprints. lancs.ac.uk/67711/1/GRANT_03_MURDER_WILL_OUT_REF_3_ FINAL_CORRECTION_25.11.2013.pdf.

4 Brown (1986) *Bloodfeud*, p. 22.

5 For further discussion see *ibid*, p. 22 and p. 43; Grant (2013) 'Murder', p. 27; Wormald (1985) *Lords and Men*, pp. 127–128 and J. Wormald (1980) 'Bloodfeud, Kindred and Government in Early Modern Scotland', *Past and Present*, 87, pp. 54–97 at pp. 72–74.

6 For further discussion see Brown (1986) *Bloodfeud*, pp. 242–243 and pp. 258–259 as well as Wormald (1985) *Lords and Men*, pp. 164–166.

7 See Wormald (1980) 'Bloodfeud', pp. 96–97.

8 F. Brookman (2005) *Understanding Homicide* (London: Sage), p. 1.

9 Baron D. Hume (1797) Commentaries on the Laws of Scotland Respecting the Description and Punishment of Crimes – Volume I (Edinburgh: Bell and Bradfute), p. 260.

10 See for instance G. Maher (2010) '"The Most Heinous of all Crimes": Reflections of the Structure of Homicide in Scots Law' in J. Chalmers and F. Leverick (eds.) *Essays in Criminal Law in Honour of Sir Gerald Gordon* (Edinburgh: Edinburgh University Press), chapter thirteen; C.H.W. Gane, C.N. Stoddart and J. Chalmers (2009 edition) *A Casebook on Scottish Criminal Law* (Edinburgh: W. Green), *passim* and C. McDiarmid (2010 edition) *Criminal Law Essentials (Scots Law Essentials)* (Edinburgh: Edinburgh University Press), *passim*.

11 Hume (1797) *Commentaries – Volume I*, p. 260.

12 *Ibid*, p. 263.

13 *Ibid*, p. 274.

14 *Ibid*, pp. 278–279. Author's addition in parenthesis.

15 For further discussion see *ibid*, pp. 283–352.

16 *Ibid*, p. 352.

17 For further discussion see *ibid,* pp. 352–390.

18 Ibid, p. 390.

19 *Ibid*, p. 400.

20 For further discussion see *ibid*, pp. 390–452.

21 *Ibid*, p. 447.

22 25 Geo 2 c. 37 (1751). For further discussion see *ibid*.

23 *Ibid*, p. 452.

24 For further discussion see *ibid*, pp. 452–462.

25 *Ibid*, p. 452.

26 J.H.A. Macdonald (1867) *A Practical Treatise on the Criminal Law of Scotland* (Edinburgh: W. Paterson), p. 140.

27 L. Farmer (1997) Criminal Law, Tradition and Legal Order: Crime and the Genius of Scots Law, 1747 to the Present (Cambridge: Cambridge University Press), p. 146.

28 *Ibid*, p. 147 and p. 149.

29 For further discussion see *ibid*, pp. 151–160.

30 *Ibid*, p. 155.

31 See *ibid*, p. 154 and p. 158.

32 5 & 6 Eliz 2 c. 11 (1957).

33 The Murder (Abolition of Death Penalty) Act (1965), pp. 1–11. The last execution in Scotland actually took place in 1963 at Craiginches Prison, Aberdeen after John Henry Burnett was found guilty of the 'capital murder' of seaman Thomas Guyan.

34 The Murder (Abolition of Death Penalty) Act (1965), p. 3.

35 Hume (1797) *Commentaries – Volume I*, p. 463.
36 The Acts of the Parliaments of Scotland – Volume IX: A.D. M.DC.LXXXIX – A.D. M.DC.XCV (1822) (London: HMSO), p. 195 [Bodleian Library K5.354/9].
37 21 Jac. 1 c. 27 (1624). For further discussion of the differences between the two pieces of legislation see A-M. Kilday (2013) *A History of Infanticide in Britain c. 1600 to the Present* (Basingstoke: Palgrave), pp. 15–21.
38 For further discussion see Hume (1797) *Commentaries – Volume I*, p. 463.
39 For further discussion of these problems see *ibid*, pp. 466–485.
40 For further description of this variant of child murder see *ibid*, pp. 487–488.
41 See Kilday (2013) *A History of Infanticide*, p. 113.
42 *Ibid*, pp. 45–49.
43 *Ibid*, pp. 113–118.
44 49 Geo. 3 c. 14 (1809).
45 43 Geo. 3 c. 58 (1803).
46 Kilday (2013) *A History of Infanticide*, p. 117.
47 *Ibid*, p. 193, especially note 69.
48 12 and 13 Geo. 5 c. 18 (1922).
49 Kilday (2013) *A History of Infanticide*, p. 193.
50 For further discussion see N. Walker (1968) *Crime and Insanity in England – Volume One: The Historical Perspective* (Edinburgh: Edinburgh University Press), pp. 142–144.
51 For further discussion see M.N. Marks and R. Kumar (1996) 'Infanticide in Scotland', *Medicine, Science and the Law*, 36, pp. 299–305 at pp. 299–300.
52 Kilday (2013) *A History of Infanticide*, p. 193.
53 For the earlier homicide rate see W.W.J. Knox (2015) 'Homicide in Eighteenth-Century Scotland: Numbers and Theories', *The Scottish Historical Review*, XCIV, 238, pp. 48–73 at pp. 61–62 and A-M. Kilday (2007) *Women and Violent Crime in Enlightenment Scotland* (Woodbridge: Boydell), pp. 43–44. For the earlier infanticide rate see Kilday (2013) *A History of Infanticide*, p. 30 and p. 46.
54 See P. King (2011) 'Urbanization, Rising Homicide Rates and the Geography of Lethal Violence in Scotland, 1800–1860', *History*, 96, 323, pp. 231–259.
55 See T.R. Gurr (1981) 'Historical Trends in Violent Crime: A Critical Review of the Evidence', *Crime and Justice*, 3, pp. 295–353; M. Eisner (2003) 'Long-Term Historical Trends in Violent Crime', *Crime and Justice*, 30, pp. 83–142 and J.S. Cockburn (1991) 'Patterns of Violence in English Society: Homicide in Kent 1560–1985', *Past and Present*, 130, pp. 70–106.
56 For further discussion see Kilday (2007) *Women and Violent Crime*, Chapter three. For further evidence of the lack of female involvement in fatal violence see Knox (2015) 'Homicide', p. 65; A. Brown (2013) 'Social History of Scottish Homicide, 1836–1869' (Unpublished PhD Thesis, University of Leicester), p. 82 and P.E.H. Hair (1971) 'Deaths from Violence in Britain: A Tentative Secular Survey', *Population Studies*, XXV, pp. 5–24 at p. 18.
57 See for instance F. McLynn (1991 edition) *Crime and Punishment in Eighteenth-Century England* (Oxford: Oxford University Press), chapters six and seven; J.M. Beattie (1975) 'The Criminality of Women in Eighteenth-Century England', *Journal of Social History*, 8, pp. 80–116 at p. 90 and C. Emsley (1996) *Crime and Society in England, 1750–1900* (London: Longman), pp. 158–162.
58 See for instance D.A. Symonds (2006) Notorious Murders, Black Lanterns and Moveable Goods: The Transformation of Edinburgh's Underworld in the Early Nineteenth Century (Akron, OH: University of Akron Press); A. McGregor (2005) The Law Killers: True Crime from Dundee (Edinburgh: Black and White Publishing); J. McLennan (2009) Blood in the Glens: True Crime from the

Scottish Highlands (Edinburgh: Black and White Publishing) and M. Archibald (2014 edition) Glasgow: The Real Mean City – True Crime and Punishment in the Second City of the Empire (Edinburgh: Black and White Publishing).

59 See for instance E.C. Sanderson (1996) *Women and Work in Eighteenth-Century Edinburgh* (Basingstoke: Palgrave); R.A. Houston (1989) 'Women in the Economy and Society of Scotland, 1500–1800' in R.A. Houston and I.D. Whyte (eds.) *Scottish Society, 1500–1800* (Cambridge: Cambridge University Press), pp. 118–147; C.A. Whatley (1994) 'Women and the Economic Transformation of Scotland', *Scotland Economic and Social History*, XIV, pp. 19–40 and various essays in E. Ewan and M.M. Meikle (1999) (eds.) *Women in Scotland, c. 1100–c. 1750* (East Linton: Tuckwell Press).

60 See for instance Brown (2013) 'Social History', p. 82.

61 See Kilday (2007) Women and Violent Crime, p. 59 and also Kilday (2013) A History of Infanticide, passim.

62 See I. Donnachie (1995) '"The Darker Side": A Speculative Survey of Scottish Crime During the First Half of the Nineteenth Century', *Scottish Economic and Social History*, 15, pp. 5–24 at p. 14.

63 See Kilday (2007) *Women and Violent Crime*, pp. 70–73 and Kilday (2013) *A History of Infanticide*, chapter two.

64 For further discussion see Kilday (2013) *A History of Infanticide, passim*.

65 See Kilday (2007) *Women and Violent Crime*, p. 51. For a similar conclusion in relation to the late nineteenth century see C.A. Conley (2008) 'Atonement and Domestic Homicide in Late Victorian Scotland' in R. McMahon (ed) *Crime, Law and Popular Culture in Europe, 1500–1900* (Cullompton: Willan Publishing), pp. 219–238 at p. 220 and pp. 223–235; M. Archibald (2014) *Bloody Scotland: Crime in Nineteenth Century Scotland* (Edinburgh: Black and White Publishing), p. 146; C.A. Conley (2007) *Certain Other Countries: Homicide, Gender and National Identity in Late-Nineteenth Century England, Ireland, Scotland and Wales* (Columbus: Ohio State University Press), p. 36 and C.A. Conley (2001) 'Homicide in Late-Victorian Ireland and Scotland', *New Hibernia Review*, 5, 3, pp. 66–86 at p. 84. The lack of fatal violence against strangers has also been identified in other historical studies of this type of offending see for instance Gurr (1981) 'Historical Trends', p. 299.

66 See Kilday (2007) *Women and Violent Crime*, p. 53. The lack of premeditated fatal violence has also been identified in other historical studies of this type of offending see for instance Eisner (2003) 'Long-Term Historical Trends', p. 84 and Hair (1971) 'Deaths from Violence', p. 19.

67 For studies that make mention of this see Archibald (2014) Bloody Scotland; A. Adamson (2011) Murder, Poaching and Lemonade: Crimes and Court Cases from Nineteenth Century West Lothian (London: CreateSpace); M. Archibald (2012) A Sink of Atrocity: Crime in Nineteenth Century Dundee (Edinburgh: Black and White Publishing); J. House (2002 edition) Square Mile of Murder: Horrific Glasgow Killings (Edinburgh: Black and White Publishing); D. Brandon and A. Brooke (2010) Edinburgh Murders and Misdemeanours (Stroud: Amberley Publishing) and L. Wilson (2012) Murder and Crime: Stirling (Stroud: The History Press).

68 Other studies have also identified that fatal violence was typically hot-blooded in nature – see Knox (2015) 'Homicide', pp. 70–71; Brown (2013) 'Social History', p. 82 and p. 211; Gurr (1981) 'Historical Trends', p. 300 and Hair (1971) 'Deaths from Violence', p. 19.

69 For a similar conclusion see Knox (2015) 'Homicide', p. 59 and Gurr (1981) 'Historical Trends', pp. 306–308.

70 For further discussion see Archibald (2014) *Bloody Scotland*, chapter sixteen; K.J. Merry (2010) 'Murder by Poison in Scotland During the Nineteenth and Early Twentieth Centuries' (Unpublished PhD Thesis, University of Glasgow) and K.D. Watson (2007 edition) *Poisoned Lives: English Poisoners and Their Victims* (London and New York: Hambledon and London).

71 For evidence that firearms were rarely used in Victorian Scotland see Conley (2007) *Certain Other Countries*, p. 63 and p. 65 and Conley (2001) 'Homicide', pp. 71–72. For more on the growth of firearms in modern Scotland see D.M. Fraser (2010) *The Book of Glasgow Murders* (Glasgow: Neil Wilson).

72 For similar conclusions but in relation to the nineteenth century see Brown (2013) 'Social History', p. 6 and p. 219 and Conley (2007) *Certain Other Countries*, p. 154.

73 For further discussion see Kilday (2007) *Women and Violent Crime*, pp. 73–78 and Kilday (2013) *A History of Infanticide*, chapter six.

74 For the mid-nineteenth century see Brown (2013) 'Social History', pp. 236–245.

75 Several scholars have noted that drink is more commonly linked to episodes of fatal violence in Scotland in comparison with other countries, particularly in the nineteenth century – see for instance King (2011) 'Urbanization', p. 252; Brown (2013) 'Social History', p. 212 and p. 248; Conley (2007) *Certain Other Countries*, p. 23, p. 25 and p. 141; Archibald (2014) *Bloody Scotland*, p. 171; Conley (2001) 'Homicide', pp. 73–75 and Conley (2008) 'Atonement', p. 220, p. 227 and pp. 233–234.

76 National Library of Scotland (hereafter NLS) (1717) *A Declaration of Mr Robert Irving Who Murdered John and Alexander Gordon's* (Edinburgh, n.p.), Special Collections (SpC), Ry. III. c.36 (034f).

77 R. Chambers (1861 edition) Domestic Annals of Scotland: From the Revolution to the Rebellion of 1745 – Volume III (Edinburgh and London: W. & R. Chambers), p. 423.

78 NLS, (1717) The Whole Trial, Confession and Sentence of Mr Robert Irving: Chaplain to Baillie Gordon, Who Was This Day Execute at the Green-side Betwixt Leith and Edinburgh, for Murdering of John and Alexander Gordons (Edinburgh, n.p.), SpC, Ry. III. c.36 (034g).

79 Chambers (1861 edition) *Domestic Annals*, p. 423.

80 Ibid.

81 J. Grant (1880) *Old and New Edinburgh – Volume III* (London: Cassell, Petter, Galpin and Co.), chapter twenty-five, p. 183.

82 NLS (1717) The Last Confession of Mr Robert Irvine Who was Execute May 1st 1717. near Brughton between Leith and Edinburgh, for Murdering John and Alexander Gordons, Sons to James Gordon of Allan on Sunday the 28th of April 1717 (Edinburgh, n.p.), SpC, Ry. III c.36 (034h).

83 Ibid.

84 Ibid.

85 Chambers (1861 edition) *Domestic Annals*, pp. 422–423.

86 See for instance J. Flavel (1840 edition) *A Blow at the Root of Antinomianism* (Philadelphia: Presbyterian Board of Publication). An on-line version of this tractate can be found at www.monergism.com/thethreshold/articles/onsite/blowatroot. html. I am grateful to Professor David Nash (Oxford Brookes University) for sharing his expertise on this subject with me.

87 Ibid.

88 NLS (1717) 'The Whole Trial.'

89 For a drawing of the sundial see E.V.G. Boyle (1900) *Seven Gardens and a Palace (with illustrations by F.L.B. Griggs and Arthur Gordon)* (London and New York:

John Lane – The Bodley Head), frontispiece. See also I.A.G. Shepherd (2006) *Aberdeenshire, Donside and Strathbogie: An Illustrated Architectural Guide* (Newcastle: Rutland Press).

90 National Records of Scotland (hereafter NRS), Justiciary Court, Precognition Papers, AD14/34/361/1.

91 Ibid. See also NLS (1834) Trial and Sentence: A Full Account of the Trial and Sentence of Thomas and Mary Braid Who Were Tried for Incest and Murder (Edinburgh, n.p.), SpC, F.3.a 13 (116).

92 See the testimony of numerous witnesses who had observed Mary Baird being with child and who each reported to the local minister that they believed Thomas Baird to be the father. See NRS, Justiciary Court, Precognition Papers, AD14/34/361/30 and AD14/34/361/32. From evidence presented as part of the trial proceedings it is clear that the victim in this case was in fact Mary's second child. She had another daughter with her husband Robert Morrison not long before his death. This daughter was aged eleven at the time of the 1834 trial – see NRS, Justiciary Court, Precognition Papers, AD14/34/261/32 and NRS, High Court of Justiciary, Process Papers, JC26/1834/354.

93 Friends and neighbours of Mary Baird testified in court that although they did not hear or see Mary Baird giving birth, Mary eventually told them that she had been delivered of a child and had placed the infant with a wet nurse in the city. See the testimony of various witnesses at NRS, Justiciary Court, Precognition Papers, AD14/34/361/30 and AD14/34/361/32. Mary, in her own declaration to the court, altered her story once more, claiming that she had given the infant over to its father, but she would not name him – see NRS, Justiciary Court, Precognition Papers, AD14/34/261/32.

94 NRS, Justiciary Court, Precognition Papers, AD14/34/361/1 and AD14/34/361/2. For evidence relating to the medical examination carried out on the body of the infant where the cause of death was deemed '...the united effects of strangulation and drowning' see – NRS, Justiciary Court, Precognition Papers, AD14/34/361/32.

95 *Caledonian Mercury*, 30th January 1834, Issue 17560, p. 4.

96 NRS, High Court of Justiciary, Process Papers, JC26/1834/354.

97 See for instance ibid which reports that the trial '...created a great deal of interest' as well as NLS (1834) Lamentation of Mary Braid, Who is to Be Executed at Edinburgh on the 17th day of February for Incest with Her Brother and the Murder of Her Own Child, Etc. (Edinburgh, n.p.), SpC, F.3.a 13 (117) and The Morning Chronicle, 31st January 1834, Issue 20104, p. 3; The Lancaster Gazette and General Advertiser, 8th February 1834, Issue 1704, p. 1 and The Bury and Norwich Post, 12th February 1834, Issue 2694, p. 1. For further discussion of murder broadsides during this period see K. Bates (2014) 'Empathy or Entertainment? The Form and Function of Violent Crime Narratives in Early-Nineteenth Century Broadsides', Law, Crime and History, 4, 2, pp. 1–27.

98 *Caledonian Mercury*, 30th January 1834, Issue 17560, p. 4.

99 *The Belfast News-Letter*, 4th of February 1834, Issue 10084, p. 1.

100 Ibid.

101 See NRS, Justiciary Court, Precognition Papers, AD14/34/361/30 and AD14/34/361/32.

102 *Caledonian Mercury*, 30th January 1834, Issue 17560, p. 4. Author's addition in parenthesis.

103 NLS (1834) 'Lamentation.'

104 Ibid.

105 Thomas Braid's confession was reported in the press – see *Caledonian Mercury*, 13th of February 1834, Issue 17566, p. 3.

106 See for instance *Caledonian Mercury*, 30th January 1834, Issue 17560, p. 4.

107 National Archives (hereafter NA), Home Office Criminal Petitions (Scotland), HO 17/21/67, petition dated 1st of February 1834 and letters dated the 3rd and 9th of February and the 10th of April 1834.

108 See for instance *ibid*, letters dated the 3rd and 5th of February and the 4th of July 1834.

109 See *ibid*, letters dated the 8th and 9th of February 1834.

110 Reported in *The Morning Post*, 18th February 1834, Issue 19720, p. 2.

111 www.founders-storylines.com/mugsheets/convicts/profile/6712/thomasbraid [accessed 24/10/2016].

112 www.founders-storylines.com/mugsheets/convicts/profile/6027/marybraid [accessed 24/10/2016].

113 For further discussion see Kilday (2013) *A History of Infanticide*, pp. 166–179.

114 The judge in the case said that '...it was with a degree of pain and distress which I cannot express...' that he found himself having to inflict a capital sentence on Mary Baird – see the *Caledonian Mercury*, 30th January 1834, Issue 17560, p. 4.

115 For more on Peter Manuel's early history see the *Evening Times*, 25th June 1958, p. 5; J.G. Wilson (1959) *The Trial of Peter Manuel: The Man Who Talked Too Much* (London: Secker & Warburg), pp. 229–230; J. Carron (2012) *Ghosts of Barlinnie: Ten Men, Ten Murder Trials, Ten Executions* (Edinburgh: Amenta Publishing), pp. 88–91; H. MacLeod and M. McLeod (2010 edition) *Peter Manuel: Serial Killer* (Edinburgh: Mainstream Publishing), pp. 28–53 and A.M. Nicol (2008) *Manuel: Scotland's First Serial Killer* (Edinburgh: Black and White Publishing), pp. 1–3. For a list of his prior convictions see NRS, Crown Office Criminal Appeals, AD24/62/7/1/91-92.

116 For further discussion of this particular part of Manuel's criminal career see J. Bingham (1973) The Hunting Down of Peter Manuel: Glasgow Multiple Murderer (Written in Association with Detective Chief Superintendent William Muncie, Lanarkshire County Police) (London: Macmillan), pp. 20–29.

117 On the authorities opinion of Manuel up to the point of his release from Peterhead Prison see MacLeod and McLeod (2010 edition) *Peter Manuel*, pp. 55–57.

118 See for instance the indictment regarding theft by housebreaking from 1956 found in NRS, Justiciary Court, Trial Reports, AD21/24/1.

119 For further discussion see the references at note 15 above especially Nicol (2008) *Manuel* at pp. 23–25 and also Bingham (1973) *The Hunting Down*, pp. 36–48.

120 See Wilson (1959) *The Trial*, pp. 29–31.

121 See *ibid*, pp. 134–137 and also Nicol (2008) *Manuel*, chapters twenty-seven to twenty-eight.

122 Bingham (1973) *The Hunting Down*, p. 6.

123 For the full indictment served see NRS, Justiciary Court, Trial Reports, AD21/22/1 and also *The Glasgow Herald*, 12th May 1958, p. 8.

124 For further details regarding this crime see *The Scotsman*, 13th May 1958; Wilson (1959) *The Trial*, pp. 14–15 and pp. 106–107; Nicol (2008) *Manuel*, chapters thirteen through to fifteen and Bingham (1973) *The Hunting Down*, pp. 46–62.

125 For further discussion of the likelihood that Manuel suffered from sexual dysfunction such as premature ejaculation or paraphilia (the need for abnormal stimulus to achieve orgasm) see Carron (2012) *Ghosts*, p. 92; Nicol (2008)

Manuel, p. 359; MacLeod and McLeod (2010 edition) *Peter Manuel,* p. 67 and Bingham (1973) *The Hunting Down,* p. 219.

126 See Wilson (1959) *The Trial,* pp. 15–16.

127 See *ibid,* p. 21.

128 For further details of these crimes see Bingham (1973) *The Hunting Down,* pp. 74–75 and pp. 79–80 and Nicol (2008) *Manuel,* pp. 89–90 and pp. 101–103.

129 See Wilson (1959) *The Trial,* p. 20 and Carron (2012) *Ghosts,* p. 90.

130 For further details regarding this crime see *The Scotsman,* 13th–15th May 1958; *The Glasgow Herald,* 14th–15th May 1958; Wilson (1959) *The Trial,* pp. 18–20 and pp. 107–109; Nicol (2008) *Manuel,* chapters seventeen through to nineteen and Bingham (1973) *The Hunting Down,* pp. 66–74.

131 Bingham (1973) *The Hunting Down,* pp. 85–109.

132 Wilson (1959) *The Trial,* p. 23.

133 For further details of this crime see Bingham (1973) *The Hunting Down,* pp. 117–118 and Nicol (2008) *Manuel,* chapter twenty-three.

134 See Bingham (1973) *The Hunting Down,* p. 118.

135 For further details regarding this crime see Wilson (1959) *The Trial,* pp. 23–25 and p. 109. See also Bingham (1973) *The Hunting Down,* pp. 119–126.

136 For further details of this crime see Wilson (1959) *The Trial,* pp. 25–28 and pp. 109–110. See also Bingham (1973) *The Hunting Down,* pp. 128–138 and pp. 144–155 and Nicol (2008) *Manuel,* chapters twenty-four and twenty-five and pp. 133–137.

137 See Wilson (1959) *The Trial,* pp. 91–92.

138 *Ibid,* p. 35.

139 *Ibid,* pp. 36–38.

140 See D. Wilson (2009) *A History of British Serial Killing* (London: Sphere), p. 133 and Carron (2012) *Ghosts,* p. 88. For drawings of the *locus operandi* in these crimes see NRS, Justiciary Court, Trial Reports, AD21/23/3.

141 Wilson (1959) The Trial of Peter Manuel, p. 45.

142 See for instance *The Scotsman,* 15th May 1958, p. 1.

143 For further discussion see Carron (2012) *Ghosts,* p. 88 and p. 94 and Nicol (2008) *Manuel,* p. 156.

144 MacLeod and McLeod (2010 edition) *Peter Manuel,* pp. 159–160.

145 See for instance *The Glasgow Herald,* 14th May 1958. See also Bingham (1973) *The Hunting Down,* pp. 213–216 and Wilson (1959) *The Trial,* pp. 57–68, pp. 98–102 and pp. 122–123.

146 See *The Times,* 20th May 1958, p. 6.

147 For more detail of the trial testimony see the coverage in *The Times,* 14th–30th May 1958 and in *The Manchester Guardian,* 14th–24th May 1958. See also Bingham (1973) *The Hunting Down,* pp. 176–197 and Nicol (2008) *Manuel,* chapters thirty through to fifty.

148 The *Evening Times,* 21st May 1958, p. 9.

149 See *The Times,* 23rd May 1958, p. 6.

150 For more detail on the special defences adopted by Peter Manuel see *The Glasgow Herald,* 12th May 1958, p. 1 and *The Manchester Guardian,* 13th May 1958, p. 3. See also Wilson (1959) *The Trial,* pp. 39–40.

151 See for instance the details provided in the *Evening Times,* 21st May 1958, p. 1.

152 See The Scotsman, The Glasgow Herald, The Times and The Manchester Guardian, 15th May 1958. See also Wilson (1959) The Trial, pp. 69–72.

153 See The *Evening Times,* 26th and 27th May 1958, p. 1; the *Daily Record,* 27th May 1958, p. 1 and *The Times,* 26th May 1958, p. 10. For the police perspective on

these crimes and on the hunt for Peter Manuel see W. Muncie (1979) *The Crime Pond: Memoirs of William Muncie formerly Assistant Chief Constable, Strathclyde Police* (Edinburgh: Chambers), chapter six.

154 For further detail of the summation see *The Times*, 29th May 1958, p. 6 and Wilson (1959) *The Trial*, pp. 202–213.

155 For full details of the verdict and sentence see the *Evening Times*, 29th May 1958, p. 1; *The Times*, 30th May 1958, p. 6 and Bingham (1973) *The Hunting Down*, p. 199.

156 For full details of Manuel's appeal see the *Evening Times*, 6th June 1958, p. 1.

157 A point made in Wilson (1959) *The Trial of Peter Manuel*, p. 216.

158 See the *Evening Times*, 25th June 1958, p. 1 and the *Scottish Daily Express*, 26th June 1958, p. 1.

159 For details of the death certificate see NRS, Crown Office Criminal Appeals, AD24/62/7/1/11. For reports of Manuel's death see for instance The *Evening Times*, 11th July 1958, p. 1. See also Nicol (2008) *Manuel*, chapter fifty-four.

160 See NRS, Crown Office Criminal Appeals, AD24/62/7/1/40-41.

161 See *ibid*, AD24/62/7/1/41.

162 See *ibid*, AD24/62/7/1/38 and AD24/62/7/1/44.

163 See *ibid*, AD24/62/7/1/21.

164 See *ibid*, AD24/62/7/1/42.

165 See also the *Evening Times*, 21st June 1958, p. 1.

166 See NRS, Crown Office Criminal Appeals, AD24/62/7/1/43.

167 See *ibid* as well as *The Manchester Guardian*, 21st June 1958, p. 2 and the *Evening Times*, 24th June 1958, p. 1. See also MacLeod and McLeod (2010 edition) *Peter Manuel*, pp. 333–345.

168 See the *Scottish Daily Express*, 26th June 1958, p. 1 and MacLeod and McLeod (2010 edition) *Peter Manuel*, pp. 257–260.

169 See the commentary found in NRS, Crown Office Criminal Appeals, AD24/62/7/1/21-44 and AD24/62/7/1/76-85. See also NRS, Justiciary Court, Murder Cases, HH60/703/1/108-117, HH60/703/1/184-195, HH60/703/1/217-220 and HH60/703/1/269-284.

170 See correspondence sent by Edward Bond to the press on this issue –*The Manchester Guardian*, 6th July 1958, p. 4 as well as NRS, Crown Office Criminal Appeals, AD24/62/7/1/103-106. See also Nicol (2008) *Manuel*, p. 341.

171 See Bingham (1973) *The Hunting Down*, pp. 110–116 and Nicol (2008) *Manuel*, chapter twenty-two.

172 *The Manchester Guardian*, 29th July 1958, p. 4. For more details of this case see the *Scottish Daily Express*, 26th June 1958, p. 1.

173 For a further explication of this definition see R.M. Holmes and S.T. Holmes (eds.) (2010 edition) *Serial Murder* (Thousand Oaks, CA: Sage), *passim*.

174 For further discussion of serial offender characteristics see P. Vronsky (2004) *Serial Killers: The Method and Madness of Monsters* (New York: Penguin). For more on this in relation to the Manuel case specifically see Nicol (2008) *Manuel*, pp. 360–367.

175 For further detail on Manuel's fantasist nature see *ibid*, p. 27–28.

176 See MacLeod and McLeod (2010 edition) *Peter Manuel*, p. 257.

177 This quote is taken from a poem purportedly written by Manuel in prison during his 1958 trial. It was found in the private papers of Duncan Mackenzie, Governor of Barlinnie gaol at the time – see the *Daily Record*, 11th April 2009.

178 Arguably, others Scots who are in this list include Archibald Hall, Ian Brady, Dennis Nilsen, Angus Sinclair, Robert Black and Peter Tobin. For further

discussion of what I have termed 'the cult of the criminal' and our enduring fascination with homicide see A-M. Kilday (2016) 'Britain's Most Wanted: Homicide and Serial Murder Since 1900' in D.S. Nash and A-M. Kilday (eds.) *Murder and Mayhem: Crime in Twentieth Century Britain* (Basingstoke: Palgrave), chapter one and A-M. Kilday (2016) 'Constructing the Cult of the Criminal: Kate Webster – Victorian Murderess and Media Sensation' in A-M. Kilday and D.S. Nash (eds.) *True Crime Histories: Micro-Histories in Law, Crime and Deviance since 1700* (London: Bloomsbury), chapter six.

Chapter 2

The Violent North? Sexual Violence, 1660–1960

Introduction

This chapter analyses the nature and incidence of sexual violence in Scotland between 1660 and 1960. In comparison with the other chapters of this volume, the multifarious complexities of the offences concerned and associated categorisation issues rendered the content of this chapter particularly challenging. For instance, indictments for rape, and especially for sodomy and bestiality were often reported to the Scottish courts in summary form due to the perceived need to shield the public from the abhorrent details, so it is incredibly difficult for the scholar to make determinations about these offences.[1] Should bestiality be considered a violent offence when it is committed against an animal rather than a person? How can we determine whether an act of sodomy was consensual or not, or indeed violent or otherwise, when both individuals were indicted for the offence, the details of what transpired are largely obscured, and the line between perpetrator and victim is wholly blurred? How can we accurately determine what is meant when offences are defined by the court as an instance of 'sexual assault' or 'indecent assault' when the details of instances of sexual violence have been substantially censored, and how can we know whether such categorisations were applied consistently across the Scottish judiciary over time?

The research conducted for this chapter raised a significant number of questions which cannot be answered in a broad study such as this and which will necessitate a more focussed and significant analysis by the author in a subsequent research project. For the purposes of this chapter then, although a range of so-called 'sex crimes' will be referred to in the content which follows, the piece will largely concentrate on the crimes of rape and attempted rape. As the various case studies at the end of the chapter clearly show, rape in itself was one of the most persistent but also one of the most nuanced and complex crimes of violence brought before the Scottish courts. However, the details of these offences were *less* obscured by court officials when compared to other crimes of a sexual nature and this enables scholars to track instances of this kind of offence and reactions to its perpetration more easily over time in order to assess its contribution to notions of Scotland as an inherently violent nation.

Sexual Violence and the Law

(a) Bestiality and Sodomy

Although, and as has already been articulated above, it is often difficult for the scholar to come to understand the specific details associated with the 'crimes' of bestiality and sodomy, until the modern era at least, these offences were nevertheless regarded with horror and loathing by the Scottish authorities.[2] In Scots Law, bestiality and sodomy were deemed to be capital offences, despite the fact that this ruling was not based on any statutory provision. This makes these offences highly unusual in a Scottish context and the northern approach towards these offences is also somewhat incompatible with that of England where statutes passed against 'buggery' in 1533 and 1548 established a clear prosecutory pathway for these types of offences. As Peter Maxwell-Stuart has explained, the law north of the Tweed appears to have made illicit carnal intercourse a capital crime on the basis of chapter eighteen of Leviticus,[3] where it is written:

> You shall not lie with a male as with a woman; it is an abomination. And you shall not lie with any beast and defile yourself with it, neither shall any woman give herself to a beast to lie with it: it is perversion…If a man lies with a male as with a woman, both of them have committed an abomination; they shall be put to death, their blood is upon them…If a man lies with a beast, he shall be put to death; and you shall kill the beast…If a woman approaches any beast and lies with it, you shall kill the woman and the beast; they shall be put to death, their blood is upon them.[4]

In other words, bestiality and sodomy were considered more *sinful* than criminal and furthermore, they were regarded as sins that were both against God *and* against nature.[5] This probably goes a long way to explain why so many of these cases were brought to the courts' attention by the Church authorities in Scotland, rather than by sheriff officers or other judicial officials. In addition and perhaps more interestingly, as there was no statute upon which to base these offences, the judges in proven cases of sodomy or bestiality were permitted, or at least they permitted themselves, to mete out explicitly *exemplary* sentences of capital punishment to those convicted of these crimes. As we saw in Chapter 1, sodomy and bestiality felons in Scotland after 1600 could be strangled, burnt at the stake or more commonly drowned prior to being hung on a gibbet by the common hangman, as according to Baron David Hume, the offender's '…very presence is a pollution to the society of his fellow creatures.'[6]

In addition to the staunch legal provision of sorts that existed in the pre-modern for bestiality and sodomy, we can see from the gravity of the language used in indictments and in the courtroom itself that these offences were taken very seriously by the judicial authorities and by the public more generally. In the early modern period, Scottish trial advocates used phrases like '...these shameful and unnatural lusts', '...a maist detestable, odious and abominable crime', '...a vile and filthy crime' and '...a fearful and unnatural acte of evil' in their opening arguments. In witness testimonies too, although the mechanics of the actual act of sodomy or bestiality were often shrouded in vague and complicated language such as 'unnatural connection', 'sowing the dirty seed', 'carnal capture' and 'obscene assembly', by and large, the language used evidently illustrates that these offences were regarded as sinful and aberrant in nature. As we saw in the previous chapter, such commentary and language indicate efforts at labelling this kind of behaviour as aberrant, in order to re-emphasise the conventionally 'civilised' state of Scottish society. Although attitudes to consensual acts of sodomy have slowly changed over the course of the twentieth century, culminating in the legalisation of homosexuality in Scotland in 1980,[7] bestiality cases brought before Scottish courts in the more modern era still seem to adopt this historic rhetoric of bewilderment, censorship and condemnation. However, neither bestiality nor sodomy has received any scholarly attention in the post-1750 Scottish context as yet and what is provided in this chapter serves merely as a clarion call for further research in these areas.[8]

(b) Incest and Child Sexual Abuse

I have chosen to separate out forms of child abuse from rape and sexual assault in this chapter, as in my view, these offences were treated very differently by the Scottish courts when compared to instances when the victim was considered to have reached maturity, although a separate legal provision was not clarified until 2009.[9] Although as we will see in the section below, a charge of rape or sexual assault could be applied to episodes of sexual violence involving pre-pubescent Scottish victims, arguably such indictments were dealt with in a swifter and more routine fashion by the Scottish courts for three reasons.

First, this was because less emphasis was placed on the interrogation of victims in cases of child sexual abuse. Second, the courts went to great lengths to censor the material contained in these court cases and as a result trials were often heard summarily and behind closed doors. And thirdly, owing to the uniformly condemnatory attitude of judicial officials and the populace at large towards individuals suspected of child sexual abuse, convictions were clearly craved from the prosecutions that did come before the court. However, as the standards of proof required for conviction in instances of serious sexual offences were complicated by various contextual elements and evidentiary problems that were specific to cases involving young victims, prosecutions were commonly laid for *lesser* offences – such as attempted ravishment, indecent assault or even lewd behaviour – in order to secure a guilty verdict and punishment.[10] Consequently, the evidence required was less onerous for all concerned and hearings were more concise and successful as a result.

One type of sexual offence, which often involved children, which was considered heinous and which was punishable by death in premodern Scotland on the basis of it being '...a very gross and shameful immorality', was incest.[11] We have already encountered a case study involving this offence (amongst others) in the previous chapter, and it was evident how the Scottish authorities regarded relations deemed to be '...violations of the duty of a decent and well-disposed citizen.'[12] Defined by Baron Hume as '...carnal knowledge between persons who are of near kin,'[13] the advocate went to some lengths to try to determine which kinds of relationships would qualify as incestuous and which would not. In the end, he seemed to include the entirety of the family circle (including relations by marriage rather than just by blood) and so incest, in Scots Law at least, seems to have a particularly wide catchment.[14]

The exemplary punishments that came to be associated with this particular offence once again stemmed from incest being regarded as more *sinful* than criminal.[15] As was the case with bestiality and sodomy, chapters eighteen and twenty of Leviticus once again seems to have provided direction to the Scottish legal context on how to approach and regard this type of felonious activity.[16] In addition, and according to Baron Hume, indictments for incestuous connections can only be laid if the parties involved knew they were related to one another and continue to have relations with one another in that knowledge.[17] He also acknowledged, that unless the accused confessed to their 'crimes', as occurred in our case study from chapter two, incest was a very difficult offence to prove beyond reasonable doubt, as corroborating evidence was typically lacking and this was especially problematic in instances where one of the participants was a minor.[18]

Similar problems of proof were evident in relation to other forms of child sexual abuse brought before the Scottish courts between 1660 and 1960.[19] Although the Scottish authorities and the Scottish populace were united in their distaste and outright abhorrence of this type of offending, cases of this type were problematic to prosecute nonetheless, particularly if the charge was more serious in nature. For instance, sometimes the victim was simply too young and too innocent to understand or describe what had happened to them in sufficient depth, or with sufficient confidence. Sometimes they were incapable of offering a verbal or written declaration detailing the events because of the trauma and/ or injury they had endured, or owing to the terror they felt at having to relive their experiences at a young age in the public sphere of the courtroom.

Sometimes child victims were scarcely supported by their immediate family and their testimony was doubted by those nearest and dearest to them, especially when alleged assailants were friends or family members who could produce convincing explanations for what had transpired. Sometimes medical testimony and forensic evidence was inadequate or inaccurate and unable to substantiate claims of abuse, particularly in the era before the use of this kind of professional evidence became a matter of routine. Consequently, and as is evident from the Edward Hand case study from 1822 analysed below, it was common for Scottish individuals to be indicted for less serious sex crimes against children, which were easier to prove.

Tragically too, and as we have only recently come to recognise today, some child victims simply remained wholly silent about their abuse as they had normalised their experiences over time and their suffering went unnoticed. Although, the majority of sexual assault prosecutions in premodern Europe related to instances of child abuse rather than adult rape, the numbers were still remarkably low and the statistics unlikely to reflect anything like real levels of offending.[20] As many scholars have convincingly argued, unreported cases of child abuse (and incest) must have made (and continue to make) a significant impact upon the 'dark figure' of unknown sexual offences perpetrated in Scotland and beyond.[21] When this suggestion is set alongside the persistent prosecutorial problems referred to above, and the historic lack of convictions for sexual offences against children explored in the section on trends in offending below, it would seem that our approach towards child sexual abuse in Scotland and indeed elsewhere, has remained archaic and wholly unsatisfactory for too long.[22]

(c) Rape

Throughout history, rape has always been considered a very serious offence by the Scottish judiciary. Formerly, for instance, it was one of the Four Pleas of the Crown alongside murder, robbery and wilful fire-raising where the monarch held exclusive jurisdictional rights to try defendants accused of these offences.[23] As Baron David Hume has explained, the 'filthy crime' of rape (as he terms it) is held to be a grave offence in Scots Law as it is:

> …one of the most grievous injuries than an individual can sustain being a robbery of that wherein a woman's honour, her place in society, and her estimation in her own eyes depend, and being also, in the perpetuation of it, necessarily accompanied with great alarm and terror, and with actual violence to the person.[24]

Although Hume's description is gendered and excludes the possibility of male victims of this offence,[25] it does at least capture some of the nuances of experience related to rape. Moreover, and unlike his exceedingly limited discussion of the legal context for sodomy and bestiality, Hume does provide a detailed definition of rape and explains the conditions necessary for such a charge to apply to an individual (or individuals) accused of this offence.

According to Hume, in Scots Law rape is defined as '…the unlawful carnal knowledge of the woman's person, forcibly, and against her will.'[26] Proof of the use of force against the victim's will (her non-consent) as well as evidence of an unstinting resistance to the assault were thus both necessary for a conviction to be achieved in these cases, unless the victim was a minor and therefore likely to be physically incapable of resisting.[27] More specifically, and although the abduction of the victim was not required for a rape charge to result (as it was in Roman Law) '…there must be carnal knowledge of the woman's person, by penetration of her privy parts, or entry of her body.'[28] Hume points out however, that no emission was necessary for a rape charge to be laid, that it was not necessary for disclosure of the assault to be immediate, nor was there an issue regarding the age of the victim either, as in Scots Law, it made no difference to the charge whether the victim concerned had reached puberty or not.[29] Thus, the problems which beset English courts when dealing with child rape in relation to confusion over the relevance of the age of consent did not occur north of the Tweed.[30]

From the research conducted for this project, and as is evident from the case studies below, some aspects of Hume's commentaries were accurate and valid in relation to prosecutions for rape and others were not. Emission, for instance, was not a focus for court proceedings in premodern Scotland as Hume points out. However, as we can see from the 1948 case study below, the increased use of forensic and medical evidence in sexual assault cases meant that proof of emission did grow in importance over time. Hume was also accurate in saying that child victims were largely treated the same as adult victims, although as testimony always had to be corroborated in the Scottish courtroom, rape cases were notoriously difficult to prove. For instance, and as the case studies in this chapter illustrate once again, proving *both* the use of force and non-consent in these situations was extremely difficult as it was highly unusual for a third party to witness what had transpired.[31] Indeed, this fact may go some way to explain why Hume's dismissal of the importance of the quick disclosure of sexual assault is one aspect of his commentary that is not supported by evidence from indictments for this kind of offence. Arguably, the evident difficulties with proving these cases necessitated other tangential aspects of the alleged events – such as whether disclosure had been prompt – to take on more significance than might otherwise have been the case.[32]

In addition to these prosecutorial parameters for rape indictments, Hume was also at pains to point out that both the motive for rape and the moral character of the victim were wholly irrelevant to the proving of a given case.[33] As he explained:

> As the crime of rape is independent of the age of the female, so it is also independent of her situation, be she maid, wife or widow, and even of her character and way of life, though it were that of a strumpet…For the person of this woman, as much as that of any other of the King's subjects is under the safeguard of the law…in fixing the character of any crime, and deciding whether it has been committed, the constant course is to attend to the act itself, and never to the person, to consider the immediate and fundamental thing that has been done – the violation of order, peace, or

security – and to pay no regard to the merits of the sufferer, nor attempt to trace the precise degree of evil which follows it in the particular case.[34]

Once again, there are accuracies and inaccuracies about Hume's commentary here. For instance, the determination of motive on the part of the alleged protagonist did not seem to play an important part in rape trials in Scotland between 1660 and 1960. On this matter, the evidence concurs with Hume. In relation to his suggestion that the character of the victim should have no bearing on the case, however, Hume's comments seems somewhat naïve and erroneous. As *all* of the case studies below show and as various scholars have clearly demonstrated in relation to a variety of different judicial contexts, one of the central and persistent strategies of defence teams in rape cases has been to manipulate the past sexual history, background, opinion, character and even the dress-sense or style of alleged rape victims in order to discredit them in the eyes of jurors.[35] Arguably, the interrogation of the victim in this fashion has happened more explicitly in rape prosecutions than for trials relating to any other type of offence, violent or otherwise. Defence lawyers garner any 'ammunition' they can to undermine the victim's testimony in order to call into question the degree of resistance offered to an assailant and to add uncertainty to considerations regarding whether sex had been consensual or otherwise. Indeed, the scale and extent of how rape victims were treated in the courtroom, particularly in our period of study 1660–1960, has led some to acknowledge that such practices rendered them feeling victimised a further time.[36] Certainly, these experiences must explain why, as we will see in the next section of this chapter, so many rape victims in Scotland and elsewhere throughout history have been reluctant to report the crimes committed against them and to accuse their attackers.[37]

In the final sections of his commentary on the legal context of rape, Baron Hume noted that in Scotland if the violation of a person was attempted but penetration was not accomplished, an individual could still be indicted, but for 'assault with intent to ravish.'[38] He also made it plain that 'The punishment of rape is death, by immemorial custom.'[39] This sentence was the case until 1841 when the Substitution of Punishments of Death Act abolished capital punishment for this offence.[40] He further notes that in Scots Law, a husband cannot rape his wife, as technically upon marriage she becomes his property. However, as with other individuals who assist in the perpetration of rape, a husband can be charged art and part.[41] Surprisingly, the exemption for marital rape was not abolished until as late as 1989 in Scotland and 1992 elsewhere in the United Kingdom.[42] Finally, Hume emphasises the importance of the victim's testimony in rape prosecutions (or their declaration if underage) and its centrality to achieving a successful conviction. In order to avoid false accusations made against innocent individuals '…the credit to be given to her testimony must depend on the probity of her story (all circumstances considered) and the concurrent evidence which supports it.'[43] This final point is an important one as it relates to a premodern preoccupation and a prolonged 'moral panic' which associated rape prosecutions with attempts to blackmail wealthy individuals.[44]

Trends in Sexual Violence and its Punishment

As the number of indictments for bestiality and sodomy was insubstantial over the 1660–1960 period and tended to be assimilated into the judicial statistics of relatively minor so-called 'unnatural offences' including exposing the person and other 'lewd and libidinous practices', a chronological incidence analysis of these offences was not possible.

Figures 2.1 and 2.2 above show trends in indictments for rape in Scotland between 1805 and 1960. Although the data for the nineteenth century shows an encouraging upward rate of indictments for this offence, this trend is not

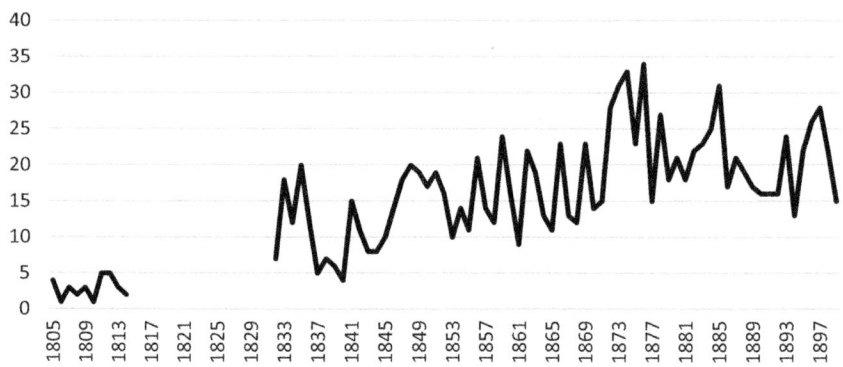

Figure 2.1 Indictments for Rape in Scotland, 1805–1899.

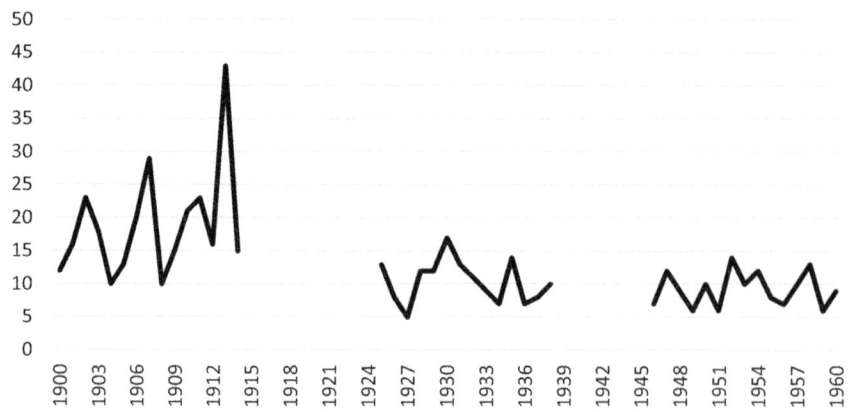

Figure 2.2 Indictments for Rape in Scotland, 1900–1960.

continued into the twentieth century. Moreover, and as Figures 2.3 and 2.4 clearly illustrate, the conviction rate in Scottish rape trials has been woeful, especially in the more modern era, when at times there is an evident inverse relationship between indictments and convictions (see between 1912 and 1915 and again between 1935 and 1938). Clearly, successful rape prosecutions were hard to achieve and knowledge of this must have impacted upon the readiness of victims to report assaults to the authorities over time. The full force of the law was only very rarely used upon individuals convicted of rape in the Scottish context between 1805 and 1960. Instead, sentences of transportation, or penal servitude of typically five to seven years in duration, were more commonly deployed.

The trends in incidence for attempted rape in Scotland 1805–1899 and 1900–1960, shown in Figures 2.5 and 2.6 above are not too dissimilar from that of rape proper, although the numbers of actual indictments are higher

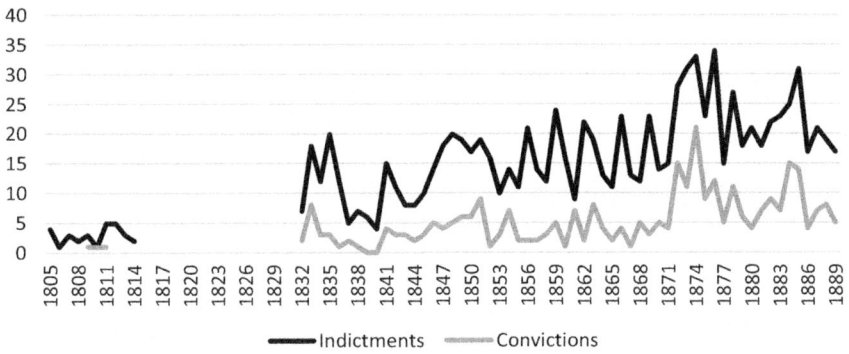

Figure 2.3 Indictments and Convictions for Rape in Scotland, 1805–1899.

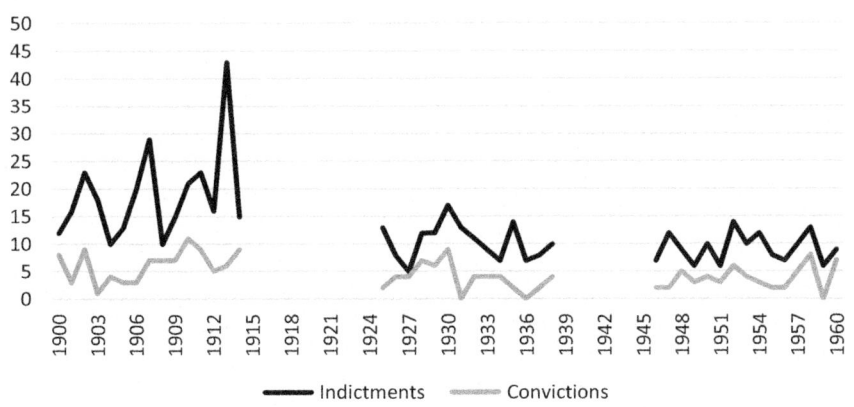

Figure 2.4 Indictments and Convictions for Rape in Scotland, 1900–1960.

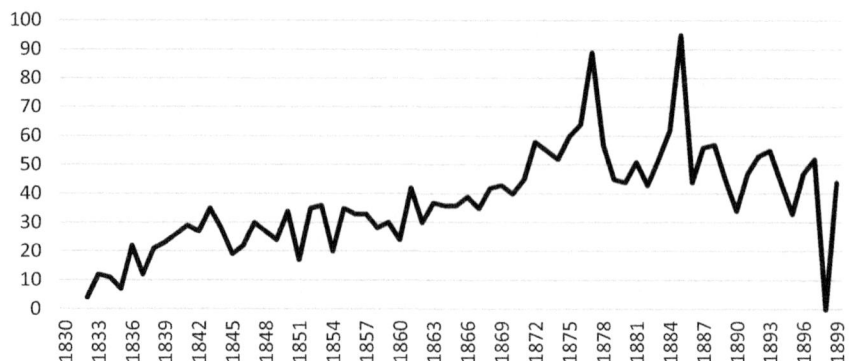

Figure 2.5 Indictments for Attempted Rape in Scotland, 1830–1899.

Figure 2.6 Indictments for Attempted Rape in Scotland, 1900–1960.

as attempted rape was deemed easier to prosecute than its more serious counterpart. Perhaps for this reason, the relationship between indictments and convictions is closer for attempted rape as shown in Figures 2.7 and 2.8. However, once again, we see a significant downward trend in both indictments and convictions from the mid-1920s, probably due to the under-reporting of the offence coupled with a reluctance to prosecute unless unequivocal evidence was available, which as we know was not common to episodes of sexual assault. Punishments for Scottish individuals convicted of attempted rape between 1805 and 1960 were relatively insignificant in nature, with fines and short stays of imprisonment being typical. Moreover the lenient outcome of these cases may well have further contributed to the evident under-reporting and unwillingness to prosecute.

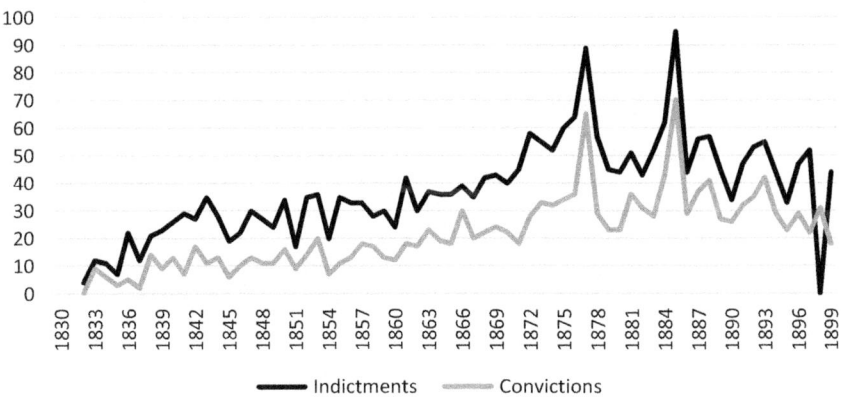

Figure 2.7 Indictments and Convictions for Attempted Rape in Scotland, 1830–1899.

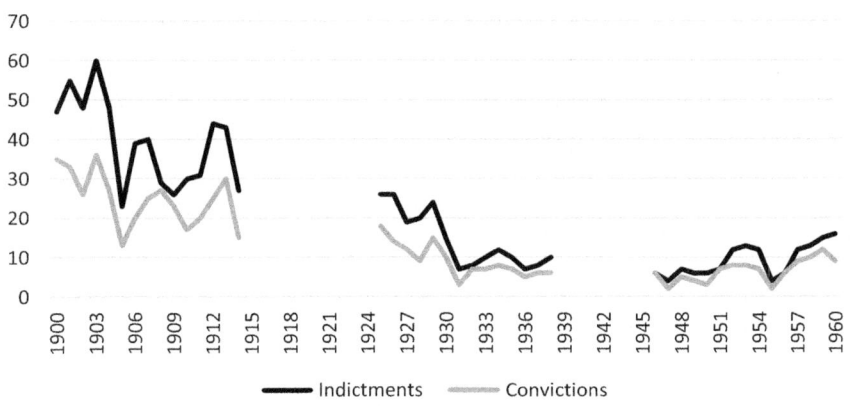

Figure 2.8 Indictments and Convictions for Attempted Rape in Scotland, 1900–1960.

Offenders, Victims, Methods and Motive

Until very recently, crimes involving sexual violence were considered explicitly gendered. Normally offenders have been male and victims female.[45] We have already seen in this chapter how, in the premodern period at least, many of the victims in prosecuted cases were children. However, the significant number of unreported sex crimes during this era and in the more modern period makes it difficult for scholars to accurately establish a typical offender or a typical victim profile in relation to this type of offending. Certainly, the majority of reported cases brought before the Scottish courts between 1660 and 1960 related to lone assailants, although on occasion, and as is exemplified by the Glasgow Green case study below from 1948, gangs of sex attackers were not unheard of and likely became more common in the post-1970s period when we came to realise the existence of sex trafficking industries and child abuse 'rings' where multiple offenders used new technologies to further despicable criminal exploits.

Victims of sexual violence had many barriers to overcome if they were to see their assailants prosecuted and convicted. First, they had to disclose what had happened to them. Second, they had to be believed, so they had to have appropriate and persuasive evidence to substantiate their claims. Third, they had to have the courage to face their attacker and to relive their experiences in court. And fourth, they had to ensure that they revealed the details of their experiences to maximise the credibility of their testimony and to limit any criticism regarding their behaviour. Thus victims had to describe what had occurred without sounding particularly experienced in sexual matters, as this would potentially jeopardise portrayals of their 'innocent' character.[46] The fact that so many of the victims of sexual violence were assaulted by someone from their immediate family, or someone well known to them, also undoubtedly made their task harder and more traumatic. Typically in these cases, the outcome often came down to the jury favouring one person's word against another, even in the face of overwhelming forensic, medical or circumstantial evidence as can be seen in both of the case studies from 1822 below.[47]

Evidence of premeditation in these cases was rare within our period of study as, more often than not, sex crimes committed by lone assailants were opportunistic in nature rather than planned. Weapons were often employed in order to threaten victims or to get them to comply with their protagonist's wishes, but were rarely used.[48] However, this is not to suggest that sexual assaults were non-violent. Brute force was regularly involved in the instances of rape, sexual assault and non-consensual sodomy (male rape) brought before the Scottish courts between 1660 and 1960. Victims were often bruised and bloodied after the fact, either from the aggressive sex act itself or from being battered and abused before or afterwards.[49] In addition, many victims suffered intense emotional and mental trauma which persisted long after the attack had ceased. It is arguably only in the more modern period that we have better come to realise the full extent of the psychological impact that sexual offences have upon victims both young and old.

As with so many violent crimes against the person, the motives in sexual assaults are difficult to discern and typically vary from one offence and offender to another. We have already seen in this chapter that establishing motive in these offences was far less important to the court authorities than establishing proof that an assault had occurred, that resistance had been offered and that the event was non-consensual. Nevertheless, some analysis has been conducted into the rationale behind these kinds of crimes and certainly, the conventional view that sexual offences were caused by uncontrollable or unnatural lusts is now regarded as a significant oversimplification and inaccurate. As court cases of non-consensual sodomy are so difficult to distinguish from consensual ones across our period, and indeed as we have seen prosecutions are so few, it is impossible to work out how many of these episodes were not offences at all, but were instances of normal homosexual relationships and encounters and therefore the motives involved were sexual or joyful rather than deviant or criminal. In instances of bestiality, several motives can be discerned from the evidence at hand and particularly from the confessions that some offenders gave before the courtroom. Some individuals said they had sex with animals because of a lack of opportunity for sex with females in the area where they lived. Some had done so to avoid getting their usual sexual partners pregnant. Some confessed to experimentation and an imitation of animals in the field. Some had engaged in bestiality in a deliberate manner within the confines of a perceived 'relationship' of sorts.[50]

In instances of the sexual assault or abuse of children one common motive that can be discerned from the evidence is that a significant number of attacks in the premodern period were caused by the myth that having sex with a virgin cured adult men of venereal disease. Scholarship has shown that this apologue and associated practice was certainly perpetuated in Scotland well into the twentieth century, and it was probably one of the key reasons more of these cases came to light in comparison with adult sexual assaults where victims often chose to remain silent about their experiences. As we can see from the Edward Hand case study from 1822 below, mothers occasionally discovered their children's underclothes to be soiled with discharges associated with sexually transmitted diseases and promptly took their suspicions about the cause to the authorities.[51]

Aside from this despicable practice, the other motives for the sexual assault and abuse of children were seemingly not substantially different from those involving adult victims. Although drink was often present in these abusive situations, it was not regarded by the courts as either an explanation or a mitigation.[52] Some individuals had been romantically rebuffed by their victims and had latterly taken out their frustrations over their failed courtship on their erstwhile partners.[53] Power, control, the need to assert or reassert authority, the enjoyment of gratuitous violence and mental health problems have also been suggested by scholars to explain the motives behind the perpetration of sexual violence and the reasons why men have dominated the perpetration of this type of offending over time and across all cultures. However it is evident that in the Scottish context at least, insanity verdicts or declarations were exceedingly rare in trials for sexual violence.[54]

Case studies and Attitudes to Sexual Violence

(a) John and James Sword (Eighteenth Century)

An interesting case was brought before the West Circuit Court in Glasgow on the 25th of May 1769. Two merchants from the city, John and James Sword were charged with raping (or 'ravishing') a woman called Janet Orr who was married to a local bookseller named John Brown. The very first thing that the men's defence team did was to make a statement to the court which said that:

> ...the Crime of Rape is of very difficult investigation, it requires the utmost degree of Attention, not only to the Import of the Evidence, but to the Credibility of the Witnesses who emitt it.[55]

The lawyers then went on to claim that rather than this indictment be one against the defendants for sexual assault, it should have been an indictment against the alleged victim and her husband for extortion. This may go some way to explain why, when the victim came to testify in court, she seemed to be more preoccupied with defending her right to bring a prosecution in the first place, rather than presenting the details of the assault that had been seemingly perpetrated against her.

Eventually, nonetheless, the court heard that Janet Orr and her husband John Brown had been walking back to Glasgow from Paisley on the 9th of July 1768 when they were joined by the two defendants (both of whom she described as 'being in Liquor') and a third man called James Boyd, who had originally been part of the indictment but had been subsequently admonished in order to give evidence at the trial.[56] The victim alleged that John Sword laid hold of her by the arm and insisted that she walk with him separately. Janet's husband was displeased by this suggestion and explained that the couple were married, but John Sword was undeterred and said '...she is not your wife she is some Whore whom you have pick't up upon the Road.' After parting company for some short time, the defendants caught up with the couple once more, and again John Sword grabbed Janet by the arm and said rather crudely he would '...have the Girl...and that a standing prick and a Sallow Cunt were good for such a cold night as this.' He then proceeded to thrust his hand inside her petticoats and with the help of James Sword, the co-accused, they pulled her into a field whilst James Boyd restrained her husband from coming to her rescue.[57]

The men threw her down to the ground upon her back and whilst holding her down with force they took it in turns to have 'carnal knowledge' of her body. Janet Orr claimed that although she fainted during the course of the attack, she managed to recover her senses enough to observe the assault upon her and indeed, she was able to recollect it in fairly vivid detail. The victim was very clear that she had endeavoured to resist her attackers, that she cried out 'Murder!' and for her husband to come to her aid several times but he did not. Some fifteen minutes after the alleged incident had occurred, Janet Orr's husband John Brown returned to the scene, bringing several men with him to help escort his wife to a nearby house. However, a scuffle broke out between the parties concerned and John Brown proceeded to hit one of the accused with a stone hammer, whereupon the three men set upon him and beat him quite badly whereby he sustained a head injury. Eventually the fighting died down and the individuals went their separate ways.[58]

There were several issues that came to light during the trial proceedings which served, rightly or wrongly, to cast serious doubt on both the prosecution's case and the validity of Janet Orr's testimony. In the first instance, and in the aftermath of the alleged attack against her, the victim recalled that she was '…weeping but unable to speak' at that time, so she did not immediately inform her husband (or anyone else) of the violence she had been subjected to. Instead, she went to the authorities to complain about the beating *her husband* had received by the assailants. The defence lawyers thought that Janet Orr's initial non-disclosure was rather odd, given the fervency of her subsequent accusations, so they pushed her to explain her silence on the supposed rape. Janet Orr explained that as her husband was already suspicious of her infidelity and had threatened her that '…if ever she had dealings with any other Man he would Stick her through the Body', she had 'concealed' the details of the assault upon her from her husband for some thirty-six hours after it had occurred. Moreover, she testified that even when she had admitted to her husband that two men had thrown her to the ground, she had wholly and repeatedly denied that she had been in any way ravished. Similarly, she admitted that when she was rescued, her husband inquired whether the alleged assailants '…had got her wronged' and she had replied '…that she thanked God they had not.' Then, when asked the same question by a female witness who lived in the house she was taken to after the skirmish, she acknowledged that she had replied '…they had done her no wrong and had only tussled about her knees.'[59]

The second factor which served to undermine Janet Orr's testimony and the strength of the prosecution's case was the provision of defence testimony from men like Thomas King and Robert Tannahill which portrayed her as a woman of historically loose morals. Indeed, various witnesses separately testified to her being '…habite and repute to be free of her person with men', that they never saw her refuse the advances of men, that she was often drunk or very merry through drink and that '…men handled her very freely, putting their hands up her coatts and that she did not pretend to make any resistance.'[60]

The third and perhaps most significant problem with the testimony provided by Janet Orr and indeed the prosecution's case as a whole, was that the individuals she had initially named as her assailants were not the two men who were now being prosecuted for her rape. Originally, Janet Orr had named James Boyd and a man called John Haldon as her abusers. However, the court heard that after a visit from James Boyd's wife a few days after she had made her initial accusation, Janet Orr switched her story to implicate James and John Sword instead. Further inconsistencies, which served to undermine the prosecution case, continued to emerge when it was John Brown's turn to testify. Although at first glance, he appeared to entirely corroborate his wife's story in terms of the precise and intimate details of the assault perpetrated upon her, and in his description of her bruises and ripped clothing in the wake of the attack, his testimony was in fact exceedingly problematic as his wife had already testified that he was unaware of what had actually transpired as he had been absent at the time of the alleged assault.[61]

Then came the evidence of James Boyd. His testimony implied that the events that transpired had all been an elaborate and well-planned ruse by Janet Orr and her husband to extort money from innocent men. He told the court that Janet Orr behaved very strangely when the three men met her and her husband on the road from Paisley. He recalled that whilst she stopped to rest at the side of the road, her husband continued on walking to the tollbar. Then, whilst chatting with James Boyd and the two accused, Janet Orr suddenly loudly cried out 'Murder!' for no reason. At no point, he argued, did anyone lay a hand on the victim nor impose any violence or force upon her of any kind. Yet, when her husband returned along with individuals he had roused in the town, he started to attack the group with a stone hammer and engaged in a random and unprovoked fist fight with them.[62] David Cross and James Osburn who both came to help escort Janet Orr to a house of safety in the wake of the alleged assault further testified that they '...observed no Marks of Violence about her' and '...observed nothing wrong about her Cloaths, but that she was as genteel as ever she was.' Their evidence was entirely contrary to that given by John Brown, the victim's husband.[63]

Finally, came the damning testimony of Isobell McIntyre (the woman who tended to Janet Orr in the safe house after the alleged affray), James George, a tobacconist in Glasgow, and Robert Auchincloss, a cooper in the same city. Isobell McIntyre told the court that in the wake of the alleged incident, Janet Orr had asked her to broker payment to the value of five pounds sterling from John Sword with his wife acting as intermediary. As part of this deal, John Brown had said that he would absent himself from court as a witness, but that he would require one hundred pounds sterling to cover the fine he would incur, in addition to the five pounds currently being offered. John Sword's wife then offered ten pounds sterling to the couple, but negotiations broke down after this when she refused to increase her offer further and instead craved that the trial commence.[64]

Attempts at brokering a settlement did not end there however. The court then heard from James George that he had been asked by John Brown to broker a deal between John Sword, James Sword and James Boyd where John Brown would offer to absent himself from court as a witness. More specifically, James George was told that if he could persuade the three men to pay John Brown forty pounds sterling a piece, then '...he would make them as free as he was.' Ultimately, however, it was the testimony of Robert Auchincloss that was crucial in determining the outcome of this case. He testified that in discussions he had with John Brown, Brown admitted to wanting money from the accused men to recompense him for the assault *against him* and for the loss of business accrued as he had taken time off work to recover from his injuries. Brown also said that he believed James Boyd when he had told him that '...no attempt had been made upon his wife' and claimed instead that '...his wife behooved to be a base Jade.'[65]

Whilst the testimony of these three individuals did little to categorically prove or disprove the allegation that a rape or ravishment had occurred, it did a lot to undermine Janet Orr's testimony, who had previously categorically stated before the court that '...there never was any offers made to her or to her husband so far as she knows of money or any other Consideration to persuade them to compromise this prosecution.'[66] It also cast doubt on the character and motivation of her husband John Brown as it now seemed that the charge of extortion implied by the defence lawyers at the start of the trial had more weight to it than may have been first thought. This was especially so, if we consider that every attempt to achieve some sort of financial settlement had been initiated and instigated by either Janet Orr or her husband and not by the accused men John and James Sword. Perhaps unsurprisingly, the jury unanimously found the two accused not guilty of the crime charged against them. They were exonerated and set at liberty.[67]

This case is interesting for many reasons, not least because even though a conclusion is reached in relation to the prosecution, there remains no certainty over what did or did not happen to Janet Orr on the 9th of July 1768. Was she indeed raped, but her assailants escaped justice due the naïve and arguably ill-judged attempts of her and her husband to either attain some compensation through an out-of-court settlement or to avoid the ignominy of a court case played out in public? Or was this an instance of the kind of barefaced blackmail and extortion efforts that authorities believed were very common in relation to sexual violence during the eighteenth and nineteenth centuries?

Clearly, it is impossible to come to a firm conclusion, but the testimony of so many separate and independent witnesses would seem to support the suggestion that Janet Orr and John Brown were confidence tricksters of sorts whose actions evidently lent weight to the general and prevailing assumption that victims of rape and sexual assault typically fabricated accusations against other individuals either for their own benefit, or on account of their own fantasist tendencies. We have also seen here, as elsewhere in this chapter, that defence lawyers did their best to undermine the character and credibility of victims in these cases. Indeed, this was done with more rigour and with greater frequency in relation to prosecutions for sexual violence than in any other type of criminal trial. Indeed, and as was evident in this case, the defence team's strategy could on occasion invert the roles of victim and alleged perpetrator in the courtroom. This not only had a devastating impact on 'real' victims of sexual violence, but it also dissuaded other victims from coming forward to prosecute their assailants. Thus it can be argued, as indeed this chapter has done, that rape has probably made the most significant contribution to the so-called 'dark figure' of unknown or unrecorded crime throughout history. This makes it exceedingly difficult for us to determine the extent to which crimes of this nature contributed to the prevailing assumption regarding the violent character of the Scottish nation and its people.

(b) Edward Hand and James Burtney (Nineteenth Century)

In 1822, in closed sessions of the Justiciary court, two men were separately indicted for acts of sexual violence against a minor in the western lowlands of Scotland and their cases reflect the historic nature of the complications and difficulties associated with prosecuting child sexual abuse. More than this too, when compared with one another, both prosecutions reflect the centrality of the initial charge laid in prosecutions for sexual violence in terms of the proof required and the punishment resulting upon conviction. It also highlights the challenges brought about by the testimony of victims who were not considered to be 'of age.'

Edward Hand (a thirty-four-year-old glass blower from Renfrewshire) was indicted at the West Circuit Court in Glasgow on the 17th of September 1822.[68] Married with one child, he was accused of 'attempting to ravish' twelve-year-old Mary Ann Smart, the young daughter of his employer, on the 20th of July 1822 within her own house at Finnieston, Renfrewshire.[69] It was alleged in the indictment that Edward Hand had laid hold of Mary Ann Smart, threw her down on the bed and attempted to have '…carnal knowledge of her person forcibly and against her will.'[70]

Interestingly, the court heard from the victim herself and her account of events was clearly crucial in determining both the nature of the charge levied against Edward Hand and indeed the outcome of the prosecution. Mary Ann explained that Hand had come to her father's house whilst her parents were absent. She recalled that he had been drinking but was not insensible from it. Hand gave Mary Ann's four-year-old sister a half-penny and sent her off to buy sweets and then asked Mary Ann to go and cut him some parsley. She duly did this and was going to go and fetch a tub for him to take it away in, when he called to her and gave her some money: a silver sixpence. When she asked Hand what the money was for, he told her it was a present for herself and that she should keep it, so she thanked him and put the money in her pocket. Mary Ann's testimony explained that at this moment, Hand

> …caught hold of her by her two sides and threw her down upon her own bed and turned up her petticoats and got upon the top of her, and opened

his breeches. That she cried out for help, but nobody came, and Hand laughed at her and said "Hold your bother you old slut." That her person was fully exposed and so was Hand's. That Hand was upon her top for about five minutes and he would not let her up though she repeatedly asked him but always told her to hold her bother...[71]

Mary Ann told the court that she was very much frightened and '...did not know what Hand was doing but she did not think that he got into her body.' She testified that '...although he tried all he could to have connection with her, he did not hurt her much...nor was she sensible of anything being left on her person.' Edward Hand charged her not to tell her mother and father what had transpired. Mary Ann did what Edward Hand asked, but seemingly this was less on account of her fear of him and more on account of her fear of what her mother, in particular, would say or do. As Mary Ann explained in court '...she was afraid her mother would thrash her' if she recounted what had happened. Despite Mary Ann's claim that Edward Hand had not injured her in any way, she did testify that in the aftermath of the assault, she '...felt sore.' When questioned by the prosecution lawyer with regard to where that pain had emanated from, she explained that about three days after Hand's assault upon her, she '...felt a pain in her belly...' but once again, she maintained her silence on its cause.[72]

The circumstances of what had happened to Mary Ann were eventually revealed when some time afterwards her mother (Elizabeth Savage) was about to do the washing and noticed '...an unusual stain' on her daughter's shift. When she asked Mary Ann about the cause of the mark, her daughter simply said that '...something had been coming from her that she did not understand.' Elizabeth Savage was not satisfied that this reply was any sort of explanation and pushed Mary Ann to explain what had happened and eventually, she made her daughter '...tell all' in relation to the abuse she had suffered. In her opinion, her daughter's naivety and innocence made it impossible to tell from the details she recounted what exactly had transpired. Mary Ann admitted to her mother that since she had been assaulted she had felt unwell and so her mother took her to see a doctor.[73]

Dr Alexander Gibson observed Mary Ann Smart on the 2nd of August 1822, nearly two full weeks after the alleged incident had occurred. From his examination of Mary Ann, the doctor was able to ascertain that she had become infected with a sexually transmitted disease as '...she had a discharge of purulent matter from the vagina.' He also noted however that '...there were no symptoms of violence having been done to the parts and the inflammation of the parts was very slight.' He added that in his view '...from the age of the patient and the size of her person it was physically impossible she could have complete carnal connection with a man.' Latterly, the doctor inspected Edward Hand and found him to be suffering from a receding case of gonorrhoea. Doctor Gibson concluded that '...he had little doubt that the disease affecting Mary Ann Smart had been communicated by Edward Hand.'[74]

The accused pled not guilty to the charges against him. He told the court that although he remembered going to visit the house of Benjamin Smart and his wife Elizabeth Savage, he had no recollection of what transpired when he was there as he was slightly the worse for drink. Despite his protestations, the jury convicted him nonetheless. There were three elements to his punishment which, when combined, made for a pretty severe penalty for what was prosecuted as an 'attempted' rape case. First, Hand was imprisoned in the Tolbooth of Glasgow for eight days. After this, he was ordered to be whipped through the streets of Glasgow by the hands of the common hangman. Finally, he was sentenced to be transported for life from Scotland and if he ever returned to his native land, it was ordained that he would 'suffer death.'[75]

Contemporary newspaper accounts focussed on the public flogging inflicted on Hand in particular. They reported that 'Although the day was very wet, an immense crowd attended; and all the windows of the shops in the streets through which the cavalcade passed were shut up.' Hand received eighty lashes in total and afterwards '…his back was much lacerated and bleeding profusely.' Press coverage was also at pains to point out that the specific crime for which Hand was convicted had '…become very frequent in this country…bringing to light a depravity of morals, and an indulgence of passions of such a black and brutal nature, that we thought existed not in any class of the community.'[76] Once again, and as with the preceding two chapters, we see the influence that a particular case could have on general perceptions regarding the nature and incidence of Scottish criminality.

Evidence that this commentary was perhaps not mere hyperbole on the part of the press came when another well-publicised prosecution for child sexual assault was brought within a few months of the Edward Hand case. On the 18th of November 1822, James Burtney was indicted at the High Court of Justiciary in Edinburgh charged with '…the rape of child under the age of puberty.' Burtney was also accused of the sexual assault and *attempted* rape of the victim in the same indictment.[77] Dual-charge indictments of this sort were quite a common ploy by the Scottish courts at this time and reflected the difficulties inherent in securing convictions for this kind of offence. Prosecution lawyers had to be perspicacious and lay as many charges as possible if they were to achieve any measure of success.

James Burtney was said to have assaulted eight-year-old Janet Anderson at Prestwick on the 14th of September 1821. The court heard that:

> …having forcibly seized hold of her, and having thrown her down on the ground, you did then and there, wickedly and feloniously ravish her, and had carnal knowledge of her person, forcibly and against her will, notwithstanding every resistance in her power…[78]

The details of this case and how the assault came to be discovered were articulated to the assize when the judge permitted testimony from the young victim about the events that had occurred, despite protracted protestations from the defendant's legal team. They tried to claim, for instance, that Janet Anderson was '...originally of weak intellect' and that since the time of the alleged assault she had entered '...a state of total derangement of mind, and is, even now, weak in her mind, and subject to fits of nervousness and partial incapacity of understanding.'[79] However, the judge in the case rejected their claims, and allowed the victim's testimony to be heard *via* a declaration she had previously given to court authorities. This enabled her to avoid the trauma of a court appearance where she would have had to face her would-be attacker once more. The only meaningful effect of the defence team's legal wrangling in this instance then, was to emphasise the grave impact that the assault had clearly had upon the unfortunate and innocent victim.

Piecing together evidence from both the victim and from other witnesses testifying for the prosecution in this case, it is evident that James Burtney and the family of the victim were neighbours who shared access to a plot of land where they had planted potatoes. Janet Anderson and her older brother Thomas had gone to the potato field on the morning of the alleged assault to dig up some produce. They met James Burtney there and after they had assisted him in digging up some of his potatoes, they bagged up their vegetables and started off for home together. Some way along the journey, James Burtney sat down for a rest. He encouraged Thomas to go on his way and said that he would bring Janet with him once he got his breath back.[80]

Burtney returned to the homestead around fifteen minutes after Thomas Anderson. At roughly the same time, Janet Anderson entered her house and her mother (Agnes Shields) immediately 'challenged' her after noticing that the back of Janet's clothes seemed wet. When Janet's mother investigated her daughter's garments more closely, '...she saw a good deal of blood on the backside of her petticoats' and assumed that Janet must have got herself torn when walking through the bushes or clambering over a dyke. However, Agnes realised that all was not well with her daughter who appeared somewhat traumatised and out-of-sorts. After pressing Janet to explain what had transpired, she simply explained that James Burtney '...had hurt her.' Agnes lifted her daughter's petticoats to discover '...that her private parts were bleeding and [there was] a good deal of blood on her thighs.'[81] Janet explained to her mother, more specifically, that Burtney had:

> ...gripped her when she was following her brother and had carried her in to the side of a dyke and laid her down and took up her petticoats and shift and took down his breeches and got on the top of her and had bruised her with his knee and his kneeve [fist] and hurt all her belly... That he had put two large potatoes in her mouth and after she got the potatoes out he put in his hand and prevented her crying and lay upon her sometime and during all the time she was much affrighted and felt

great pain from the place where she makes her water and she felt him pressing something into that place.[82]

After hearing what had transpired, Agnes Shields instantly went out to challenge James Burtney over what he had done to her daughter. Burtney denied having done anything to Janet saying that she was already in that state before they had left the potato field and he promptly walked off. Agnes returned to nurse her daughter who collapsed in a faint. She gently washed Janet's legs and private parts with warm water and milk but noticed that she was still bleeding profusely. After the attack Janet Anderson was confined to bed and according to her mother at least, '...she was feverish and in a state of stupor and complains much of pains in her loins and belly.'[83] Agnes Shields then called for some medical assistance. Doctor William Whiteside examined Janet Anderson in the immediate aftermath of the assault against her and found her to be 'much bruised and wounded' in her private parts as '...the hymen was swollen, ruptured and inflamed and lacerated wounds of about half an inch in length appeared at the lower and back parts of the vagina.' He noted that he found the girl in '...a state of nervous excitement and irritability' and that she had been suffering from related 'convulsions' brought about by the trauma of her experience. He also testified that upon the arrest of James Burtney, he went to examine the defendant and found him to be wearing a shirt which had splatters of blood at its 'front tail' and the said shirt was collected as evidence for the prosecution.[84]

James Burtney offered no evidence in defence. The assize enclosed and after '...only a few minutes' they unanimously found the defendant guilty of rape. In delivering sentence, the judge addressed the prisoner saying:

> In this case a rape had been committed under the most atrocious circumstances and of the most abominable nature – one more abhorrent to human nature had never, he believed, been before a Court of Justice. He cautioned the prisoner against entertaining any idle hopes of any mitigation of punishment, as there was no circumstances in his case that court warrant such an idea.[85]

He then ordered that Burtney be taken back to the Tolbooth of Edinburgh and imprisoned there for seven days before being transported on to the Tolbooth of Ayr. He was to remain a prisoner there for three weeks before being executed on a gibbet.[86] There was to be no reprieve for him and, unlike in the Edward Hand case, the evidence presented in court was conclusive and damning.

It would seem from the testimony heard in the Edward Hand case that something more than *attempted* ravishment had taken place between him and his victim. Her fairly detailed description of the assault itself, the pain she felt afterwards and the incontrovertible evidence of her contracting a sexually transmitted disease all pointed to *actual* rape, rather than anything less than this. However, the testimony presented in court also revealed why an indictment for rape in this instance would have been difficult to prove. It was evident, for instance, that few of the witnesses in this case believed that it was even possible for a girl of such tender years to be abused in a physical sense by a male adult. Then, of course, we heard from the victim herself who seemed convinced that penetration had not occurred despite clear circumstantial evidence to the contrary. Crucial too, was the fact that the victim did not reveal the circumstances of the crime committed against her immediately. Rather, it was nearly a fortnight later that disclosure was given. As we have seen elsewhere in this chapter, revelations of sexual violence had to occur promptly as otherwise the veracity of victims and their claims was likely to be challenged.

In the case against James Burtney, on the other hand, the evidence presented to court was more immediate, precise and corroborated which meant that conviction was effectively the only possible outcome for the accused. Perhaps this was particularly inevitable given contemporary concerns that this type of crime had become rife and that the verdict and sentence given to other individuals tried earlier in 1822 (such as Edward Hand) was now held to be insufficient to curb the slide of the nation into further depravity. The concerns voiced by the press in relation to the Hand case were indeed echoed once more in relation to the trial of James Burtney. However, this time, it was a local sheriff officer, rather than a journalist, who voiced his fear about the state of criminality in early nineteenth century Scotland,. Upon the arrest of Burtney, Ayshire Sheriff William Eaton argued:

> This is a most cruel and aggravated case, and one that is turning too common in this country and therefore I would suggest that the culprit be tried and meet with that punishment which the enormity of the crime deserves.[87]

Further evidence of a clear determination to bring James Burtney to justice amongst both the authorities and the Scottish populace more broadly comes in the precognition material relating to his trial. Papers recount the extensive manhunt launched for Burtney after his altercation with Agnes Shields, the mother of his young victim. After a reward of five guineas was posted for his apprehension for instance, it was recounted that '...the muirs [moors] were covered with people in quest of him.'[88] Moreover, and according to Sheriff Eaton, who saw Burtney being apprehended: 'If I had not been present...I really believe the inhabitants would have murdered him.'[89] Although it was clearly evident that both of these assaults were brutal and horrific experiences for the young girls concerned and that there was a formidable strength of feeling against individuals suspected of such heinous offences, the outcome of trials such as these was generally difficult to predict. They were often determined by a myriad of factors which were only indirectly or tangentially related to the sexual offence alleged. Once again we can see that the weight given to the multifarious *contextual* elements related to instances of sexual assault made the content, tone and reaction to these prosecutions very different to judicial trials relating to other types of interpersonal violence in the premodern era.

(c) The Glasgow Green Gang Rapes of the 1940s (Twentieth Century)

One of the first crimes to grip public attention in Scotland in the aftermath of the Second World War was the infamous 'Glasgow Green Case.' As it involved a gang of protagonists and multiple victims, it was a highly complicated legal affair with various indictments laid and different individuals on trial at different times but for the same suite of violent sexual offences. This case study investigation concentrates on the last and arguably most significant of the indictments related to this case which was brought before the High Court in Glasgow on the 14th of February 1948 and was laid against John McKenzie McPike (17), John Anderson (20), Hugh Dearie Docherty (20) and John Docherty Calikes (19).[90] Each man was accused of rape and assault. By this point, two other individuals had already been convicted in this case: James Bell Martin (then prisoner in the Criminal Lunatic Department of Perth Prison) and Alexander Bannan (then prisoner in Barlinnie Prison).[91]

The court heard that on the 1st of August 1947, a couple (who we will refer to as Female A and Male A) were sitting on Glasgow Green near the King's Bridge. While they were chatting, two individuals came up to them wanting a cigarette and they asked Male A what gang he belonged to. Male A replied that he didn't belong to any gang as he had just been demobbed out of the army. The individuals initially went away but returned a short time later with two other men, just as the couple were leaving to go home. They shouted after Male A and asked to speak to him once more. Whilst Male A went to speak to the men, one of the four came towards Female A and as she explained in court:

> …he tried to kiss me, and I objected. He had hold of my arm and I objected. I was frightened when I saw him at first. Then there was another man came over and I started to cry and he asked me what I was crying for, and I just told him that I wanted to go home. A chap then came over and took a razor out of his pocket and he put it back again. They pulled me over to the embankment. The chap who had the razor knocked me down on the embankment. I tried to struggle but it was no use. I was screaming and two of the chaps caught me by the throat. The chap that knocked me down the embankment took off my underwear. I was struggling. One of the fellows started interfering with me. He got on top of me. There were two chaps holding me down.[92]

Female A then described to the court how this process was then repeated again and again by all of the men present at the scene, excepting her helpless boyfriend. When asked by the prosecution how many men in all abused her, the victim answered: 'Eight.'[93] Medical evidence provided in court by W.D. Richardson (Acting Casualty Surgeon, Glasgow Royal Infirmary), J.A. Imrie (Lecturer in Forensic Medicine at the University of Glasgow) and John Glaister (Professor of Medical Jurisprudence at the University of Glasgow) revealed the presence of some bruising on the legs of Female A and her 'private parts' showed signs of swelling, tenderness, tearing and bleeding '...consistent with recent defloration and forced penetration.' No other marks of violence were found on the victim's body but trace evidence of blood and semen were found on her under-slip and it was noted that the victim was '...somewhat agitated and shaky.'[94]

At this point in the proceedings the victim was asked some pretty testing, inappropriate and arguably irrelevant questions. Crucially, however, these were not posed by lawyers acting to defend the accused, but instead, the questions came from the legal team acting on behalf of the victims in this case. They asked:

'Were you wearing knickers at the time?'
'Did you allow them to do this?'
'Was anything done to frighten you?'
'Did you see any weapons?'
'What did you think was taking place?'
'Did you stop struggling or did you go on struggling all this time?'
'Did you yield yourself willingly to any of these men?'
'Did you consent to what they did?'[95]

Managing to keep her composure, Female A emphasised that although she became exhausted during the course of the attack against her, she continued to struggle throughout her ordeal and at no point did she consent to what was done to her. In court, the victim managed to positively identify Hugh Dearie Docherty as one of the rapists and it was noted that she had picked out formerly indicted Alexander Bannan in an earlier identification parade too.[96] Male A identified both Hugh Dearie Docherty and John McKenzie McPike as two of the assailants and, in his testimony he explained his frustration and shame at not being better able to defend his girlfriend but that being threatened with a revolver, a bayonet, a bread-knife and a razor, he had been rendered powerless.[97] For their part, the counsel for the defence, tried to make Female A contradict her testimony by using the fact that she had been attacked by eight different men to confuse her identification of Docherty and her recounting of events. They claimed that Female A had misunderstood Docherty's actions: he was actually trying to defend her and persuade the other men present to leave her alone. Female A refuted such arguments and steadfastly stuck to her testimony, emphasising once again the persistent nature of the struggle she offered her assailants and her absolute noncompliance with what had transpired.[98]

Another couple (who we will refer to as Female B and Male B) testified to having suffered a similar fate at the hands of the Glasgow Green rapists in the exact same location and on the very same day as the assault previously described. Indeed, Female B actually testified to having witnessed the assault conducted on Female A and corroborated her story entirely.[99] In an attempt to divert an attack upon them, Female B and Male B pretended to be married, thinking that this would put off their assailants. It did not. Female B's testimony of the assault carried out upon her was very similar to that of Female A, although arguably, Female B's experience was even more horrendous as she testified that in addition to being raped and terrorised, she had been viciously punched and kicked by her attackers throughout her ordeal. One of the group had also plainly threatened her saying: 'If you squeal I will stick a razor in you.'[100] Female B was able to positively identify both McPike and Docherty in court as two of the individuals who had attacked her.[101]

Male B similarly seemed to have suffered a worse fate than Male A during the second attack as he claimed to have been repeatedly punched about the head and body and assaulted with a bayonet. The three men called to provide professional medical evidence in this case substantiated Male B's claims, testifying to the presence of long incised wounds on the victim's head which had effectively scalped him in two places. In their opinion the wounds '…were consistent with injury due to a sharp instrument such as a bayonet.'[102] The medical evidence presented in court in relation to Female B's injuries seems to have been wholly inconclusive and aside from some abrasions noted on the victim's knees and trace evidence of semen on her clothing, little evidence was offered by the three medical professionals to support her claims of rape, indecent assault or aggravated assault.[103]

Despite Male B corroborating his girlfriend's story and his identification in court of McPike, John Anderson and John Docherty Calikes as assailants in this case, his testimony was undermined somewhat by the defence counsel who were able to show that in the immediate aftermath of the alleged assault, Male B had picked out a completely innocent individual as one of the attackers in an identification parade. Male B thus came to be portrayed as an unreliable and confused witness.[104] The defence team then set about trying to dismantle the testimony of Female B by meticulously cross-examining her about the statements she had made in court. When this strategy failed to have the desired effect, the defence lawyers then asked Female B to provide the court with the details of her sexual history. Female B explained that she had lost her virginity at the age of fifteen. Despite this being a clear attempt to suggest that the victim was sexually promiscuous and had likely consented to the sexual activity described, it was evident from a close reading of Female B's testimony at this juncture of the proceedings that her loss of virginity at a fairly young age, was on account of sexual abuse that had been conducted against her will.[105]

The defence counsel proceeded with no exculpatory evidence for John McKenzie McPike, John Anderson or John Docherty Calikes. A few character witnesses were submitted in defence of Hugh Dearie Docherty but their testimonies were somewhat superficial and lacked detail and after the judge summed up the 'ghastly' and 'disgusting' details of the case, the verdict was deliberated on by the assize. Unanimously, the jury found John McKenzie McPike and Hugh Dearie Docherty guilty of one charge of rape and indecent assault and guilty of two further charges of aggravated assault. They found John Anderson guilty of two charges of indecent assault and two charges of aggravated assault and they also found John Docherty Calikes guilty of one charge of indecent assault and one charge of aggravated assault.[106]

In the wake of the jury's decision, the court then sentenced Docherty to fifteen years penal servitude, McPike twelve years penal servitude, Anderson five years penal servitude and Calikes three years penal servitude.[107] The contemporary press thought that the punishment inflicted on the four young men convicted in this case was 'heavy', despite the 'reign of terror' the gang inflicted over Glasgow's courting couples.[108] Perhaps in the wake of such commentary and immediately after their trial had concluded, McPike and Docherty launched appeals against both their convictions and the sentences received which they too argued were excessive. Anderson and Calikes (both of whom had no known previous convictions) also launched appeals at this time, but against their convictions alone.[109] All four men argued that the verdicts against them had been 'unreasonable' and not supported by the evidence presented in court. They argued that 'insufficient evidence of their direct involvement in the crimes charged' had been provided in the trial proceedings, that the judge had misdirected the jury and that their case was thus 'a miscarriage of justice.'[110]

Anderson and Calikes were successful with their appeals and their convictions and sentences were subsequently quashed. On the other hand, McPike and Docherty's appeals were unsuccessful and the verdict and sentence against both young men stood.[111] This decision sparked repeated appeals for the early release of both John McKenzie McPike and Hugh Dearie Docherty which originated from various quarters of Scottish society and which persisted over the duration of their respective confinements.[112] Clemency was craved on the grounds of their youth, their belief that the jury had been prejudiced by newspaper publicity at the time of the offences, their good behaviour whilst incarcerated and on account of the fact that they had received harsher sentences than most reprieved murderers of the same era.[113] However, '...the dastardly and appalling nature of the crimes for which they were convicted' negated any pleas in mitigation and they both served the entirety of their sentences '...to act as a strong deterrent to similar criminals of an abhorrent character.'[114]

The gang rapes committed on Glasgow Green in the late 1940s and the subsequent trial proceedings, contained certain key aspects which appear to have been common amongst indictments for sexual violence in modern Scotland and indeed earlier in the history of the prosecution of this type of criminality. Although it was evident that such offences were roundly condemned by the general populace and were taken extremely seriously by the Scottish authorities as was evident from the sentencing in this case study, it is also plain that trials for rape and violent sexual assault unequivocally added further trauma to the experiences of the victims in these cases. First, and as happened to Females A and B in this case study, a victim had to undergo a humiliating, often painful, degrading and harrowing medical examination where they were digitally penetrated by medical professionals trying to ascertain whether sexual activity had occurred and whether penetration had required force. Their trauma did not end there, however. Indeed it has become clear from the findings of this chapter and from other scholarship that historically, the victims of sexual offences have been wholly disadvantaged in comparison to the victims of other types of crimes, violent or otherwise. Not only did victims have to report sex crimes committed against them immediately despite the shock, terror, injury and potential shame they felt, they also had to prove in court that they had resisted their attacker at every stage of the crime committed against them and they had to demonstrate that they had clearly and repeatedly articulated their non-consent to sexual activity. The onus was on the victim to provide this evidence and often corroboration was impossible as sexual offences were rarely witnessed and medical testimony was regularly imprecise or inaccurate. Accused individuals on the other hand were not expected to prove that they had consent or that force was unnecessary in the events that had transpired.

The whole emphasis of court trials where sexual violence was alleged was to undermine the victim's evidence and to test their resolve. To do this, lawyers from both the prosecution and the defence routinely went to great lengths to question and re-question the victim and her version of events. Then, as we saw in the case study, the sexual history and moral character of victims became exposed to public scrutiny and past behaviours were debated at length to determine their impact upon the causality of events. Yet typically, the moral fibre of the accused was not dismantled in sexual violence prosecutions to anything like the same extent and indeed, if we compare these kinds of cases to other forms of criminality, there were few instances where the victim of an offence appeared to be more on trial than his or her alleged assailant. As academic and campaigner for women's rights Sue Lees has pointed out, if a female victim reports a burglary at her house, she is automatically assumed to be telling the truth and her credibility and integrity are not questioned. This does not occur when a woman reports that she has been raped or sexually assaulted.[115]

When we take the experiences together, it is evident why incidents of sexual violence are so under-reported even in the present day, as well as why convictions in these cases remain a rarity, rather than the norm. Although improvements to the victim experience have definitely been made as we have seen, there are still undoubted problems with prosecutions for sexual violence in present-day Scotland where archaic practices and demeaning attitudes still persist. What is also unequivocal is that those victims who have managed to come forward to disclose their traumatic experiences of sexual violence over the centuries should be considered brave and heroic for doing so. Clearly, they were, and indeed still deserve our empathy, our attention and our appropriate conduct.

Conclusion – The Violent North?

Sexual violence is a very difficult subject to study with any definitive precision due to under-reporting, the routine censorship of trial details and an ongoing uncertainty regarding the best course of action in dealing with crimes of this nature. It is also a relatively diverse category of 'crime' potentially involving consensual and non-consensual acts of a sexual nature, given former attitudes to homosexuality. Prosecutions for bestiality and sodomy were relatively rare (unless witnessed first-hand) over the 1660–1960 period, although the punishments for these offences upon conviction were serious and exemplary. The same could not be said of indictments for rape and attempted rape. Although these offences were more commonly brought before the Scottish courts between 1805 and 1960, they were rarely proven and, when convictions did result, culprits were given remedial sentences of little consequence. For rape and attempted rape, the staunch set of legal provisions available were evidently more ineffective in practice and this likely contributed to the under-reporting of sexual violence and an unwillingness to try crimes of this nature when the odds were so heavily and routinely stacked in favour of the defence rather than the prosecution.

As several of the case studies in this chapter illustrate, rape (or sexual assault) was a considerably violent and invasive crime, typically perpetrated by men against women or children, and in many instances, the victim and the assailant were related or at least known to one another. Motives for this type of criminality were hard to glean or indeed to fathom, especially in relation to episodes involving child victims, but a desire to dominate and appropriate control in sexual matters seems to have been one explanation commonly offered by assailants in the more modern era at least. The historic and ongoing uncertainty regarding the true nature and incidence of sexual violence in Scotland between 1660 and 1960 means that it is impossible to assess the contribution that crimes of this nature made to perceptions of the violent character of the Scottish nation. However, in this chapter, as earlier in this volume, there is some evidence to suggest that specific well-publicised cases had a significant part to play in the persistent notion that Scotland had an entrenched and inherent crime problem that it could not resolve.

Notes

1 For further discussion of the difficulties associated with researching these crimes see, for instance, R. Trumbach (1989) 'Sodomitical Assaults, Gender Role, and Sexual Development in Eighteenth-Century London' in K. Gerard and G. Hekma (eds.) *The Pursuit of Sodomy: Male Homosexuality in Renaissance and Enlightenment Europe* (New York and London: Harrington Park Press), pp. 407–429 at p. 420; A.N. Gilbert (1978) 'Sodomy and the Law in Eighteenth- and Early Nineteenth-Century Britain', *Societas – A Review of Social History*, VIII, 3, pp. 225–241 at pp. 226–227 and H. Cocks (2003) *Nameless Offences: Homosexual Desire in the Nineteenth Century* (London: I.B. Taurus), p. 17, 20, 25 and 28.

2 See B.P. Levack (2010) 'The Prosecution of Sexual Crimes in Early Eighteenth-Century Scotland', *The Scottish Historical Review*, LXXXIX, 228, pp. 172–193 at p. 177.

3 P.G. Maxwell-Stuart (2002) '"Wild, Filthie, Execrabill, Detestabill, and Unnatural Sin": Bestiality in Early Modern Scotland' in T. Betteridge (ed) *Sodomy in Early Modern Europe* (Manchester: Manchester University Press), pp. 82–93 at p. 83.

4 (1952) *The Holy Bible– The Old Testament: Revised Standard Version* (New York and Glasgow: Collins), Leviticus chapter eighteen, verses 22–23 and chapter twenty, verses 13, 15 and 16.

5 For further discussion of this notion of bestiality and sodomy as sinful rather than criminal, see K. Crawford (2007) *European Sexualities, 1400–1800* (Cambridge: Cambridge University Press), p. 156; C. Bingham (1971) 'Seventeenth-Century Attitudes Towards Deviant Sex', *The Journal of Interdisciplinary History*, 1, 3, pp. 447–468 at p. 447; E. Fudge (2000) 'Monstrous Acts: Bestiality in Early Modern England', *History Today*, 50, 8, pp. 20–25 at p. 21; J. Liliequist (1992 edition) 'Peasants against Nature: Crossing the Boundaries between Man and Animal in Seventeenth- and Eighteenth-Century Sweden' in J.C. Fout (ed) *Forbidden History: The States, Society and the Regulation of Sexuality in Modern Europe* (Chicago and London: University of Chicago Press), pp. 57–87 at p. 57; C.A. Conley (1991) *The Unwritten Law: Criminal Justice in Victorian Kent* (New York and Oxford: Oxford University Press), p. 187 and J. Grosclaude (2014) 'From Bugger to Homosexual: The English Sodomite as Criminally Deviant', *Revue Française de Civilisation Britannique*, 19, 1, pp. 33–48 at pp. 35–38.

6 For further discussion see Baron D. Hume (1797) *Commentaries on the Laws of Scotland Respecting the Description and Punishment of Crimes – Volume II* (Edinburgh: Bell and Bradfute), pp. 335–336. For examples of exemplary punishments given in other jurisdictions outside of Scotland for these types of offences see J. Peakman (2004) *Lascivious Bodies: A Sexual History of the Eighteenth Century* (London: Atlantic Books), chapter five and pp. 256–259.

7 The Criminal Justice [Scotland] Act (1980) decriminalised homosexual acts between men over the age of twenty-one and in private. The age of consent was then reduced to eighteen in 1994 and then again to sixteen in 2001. See R. Davidson and G. Davis (2014 edition) *The Sexual State: Sexuality and Scottish Governance, 1950–1980* (Edinburgh: Edinburgh University Press), chapters three and four; Grosclaude (2014) 'From Bugger', p. 46 and www.stonewallscotland. org.uk.

8 The exception to this is in relation to sodomy at least is Jeffrey Meek's magisterial work on the post-war period which contains a chapter on the subject see

J. Meek (2015) *Queer Voices in Post-War Scotland: Male Homosexuality, Religion and Society* (Basingstoke: Palgrave Macmillan), chapter two.

 9 See the Sexual Offences [Scotland] Act (2009). For further discussion see C.H.W. Gane, C.N. Stoddart and J. Chalmers (2009 edition) *A Casebook on Scottish Criminal Law* (Edinburgh: W. Green), chapter nine.

10 For evidence of this approach elsewhere in the premodern period see J.R. Ruff (2001) *Violence in Early Modern Europe* (Cambridge: Cambridge University Press), p. 145 and L. Jackson (2000) *Child Abuse in Victorian England* (London: Routledge), pp. 22–23.

11 Hume (1797) Commentaries – Volume II, p. 299.

12 *Ibid*, p. 288.

13 Ibid.

14 *Ibid*, pp. 292–298.

15 See *ibid*, p. 298.

16 (1952) *The Holy Bible*, Leviticus chapter eighteen, verses 6–18 and chapter twenty, verses 11–14, 17 and 19–21.

17 Hume (1797) Commentaries – Volume II, p. 301.

18 *Ibid*. For further discussion on the development of the law of incest in a Scottish context albeit later than the scope of this present volume see W. Leeming (1996) 'New Taboo? Some Observations on the Late Arrival of Changes to the Law of Incest in Scotland', *Journal of the Sociology of Law*, 24, pp. 313–336.

19 For further discussion of the difficulties associated with evidence relating to alleged child abuse cases across history and within different jurisdictions see E. Snell (2012) 'Trials in Print: Narratives of Rape Trials in the Proceedings of the Old Bailey' in D. Lemmings (ed) *Crime, Courtrooms and the Public Sphere in Britain, 1700–1850* (Farnham: Ashgate), pp. 23–41 at p. 34; J. Gammon (1995) '"A Denial of Innocence": Female Juvenile Victims of Rape and the English Legal System in the Eighteenth Century', in A. Fletcher and S. Hussey (eds) *Childhood in Question: Children, Parents and the State* (Manchester: Manchester University Press), pp. 74–95 at p. 86; C. Emsley (2005 edition) *Crime and Society in England, 1750–1900* (Harlow: Longman), p. 28; L.A. Jackson (1999) 'The Child's Word in Court: Cases of Sexual Abuse in London 1870–1914' in M. Arnot and C. Usborne (eds) *Gender and Crime in Modern Europe* (London: UCL Press), pp. 222–237; Jackson (2000) *Child Abuse*, p. 71 and p. 80; C. Smart (2000) 'Reconsidering the Recent History of Child Sexual Abuse, 1910–1960', *Journal of Social Politics*, 29, 1, pp. 55–71 at pp. 63–66 and K. Stevenson (2016) 'Offences Against Children: Incest and Child Sexual Abuse' in D.S. Nash and A-M. Kilday (eds.) *Murder and Mayhem: Crime in Twentieth Century Britain* (Basingstoke: Palgrave), pp. 125–47 at pp. 128–129 and p. 134.

20 For further discussion of the significant numbers of child victims in prosecutions for sexual assault in Britain through history see G. Walker (2013) 'Everyman or Monster? The Rapist in Early Modern England, c.1600–1750', *History Workshop Journal*, 76, pp. 5–31 at p. 18; J. Gammon (2013) 'Researching Sexual Violence, 1660–1800: A Critical Analysis' and K. Barclay (2013) 'From Rape to Marriage: Questions of Consent in Eighteenth-Century Britain' both in A. Greenfield (ed) *Interpreting Sexual Violence, 1660–1800* (London: Pickering and Chatto), pp. 13–22 at p. 20 and pp. 35–44 at p. 42 respectively; L. Jackson (1999) 'Family, Community and the Regulation of Child Sexual Abuse: London, 1870–1914' in A. Fletcher and S. Hussey (eds) *Childhood in Question: Children, Parents and the State* (Manchester: Manchester University Press), pp. 133–151 at p. 135 and Jackson (2000) *Child Abuse*, p. 18 and p. 20.

21 For evidence of the likely contribution of child abuse to the so-called 'dark fig-ure' of unreported sexual violence see M. Ingram (2001) 'Child Sexual Abuse in Early Modern England' in M.J. Braddick and J. Walter (eds) *Negotiating Power in Early Modern Society* (Cambridge: Cambridge University Press), pp. 63–84 at p. 64 especially; A.S. Wohl (1978) 'Sex and the Single Room: Incest Among the Victorian Working Classes' in A.S. Wohl (ed) *The Victorian Family: Structure and Stresses* (London: Croom Helm), pp. 197–216 at p. 200; Jackson (1999) 'Family, Community', p. 135 and Jackson (2000) *Child Abuse*, p. 25 and p. 46.

22 For further evidence of a lack of convictions relating to trials for child sexual abuse across time and in relation to different jurisdictions see J. Hurl-Eamon (2005) *Gender and Petty Violence in London, 1680–1720* (Columbus, OH: Ohio State University Press), p. 39; Ingram (2001) 'Child Sexual Abuse', p. 65 and Stevenson (2016) 'Offences Against Children', pp. 132–134.

23 Levack (2010) 'The Prosecution of Sexual Crimes', p. 179.

24 Hume (1797) Commentaries – Volume II, p. 1.

25 Within our period of study male rape not recognised officially as a crime by the Scottish law courts. Indeed, this did not change fully until the Sexual Offences [Scotland] Act of 2009. As there were no prosecutions for this offence between 1660 and 1960, male rape cannot be included in this work, but for scholarship on this topic in the modern English context see R.J. McMullen (1990) *Male Rape: Breaking the Silence on the Last Taboo* (London: GMP Publishers); G.C. Merely and M.B. King (2000 edition) *Male Victims of Sexual Assault* (Oxford: Oxford University Press) and S. Lees (1997) *Ruling Passions: Sexual Violence, Reputation and the Law* (Buckingham: Open University), chapter five.

26 Hume (1797) Commentaries – Volume II, p. 2.

27 *Ibid*, p. 9. For evidence of the need to prove resistance and use of force in other judicial contexts and across time see Crawford (2007) *European Sexualities*, p. 154; G. Walker (2013) 'Rape, Acquittal and Culpability in Popular Crime Reports in England, c. 1670-c.1750', *Past and Present*, 220, pp. 115–142 at p. 135; K. Stevenson (2010) '"Most Intimate Violations": Contextualising the Crime of Rape' in A.-M. Kilday and D.S. Nash (eds) *Histories of Crime: Britain 1600–2000* (Basingstoke: Palgrave Macmillan), pp. 80–99 at p. 84 and S. Lees (1997 edition) *Carnal Knowledge: Rape on Trial* (London: Penguin), p. 112.

28 Hume (1797) Commentaries – Volume II, p. 2.

29 *Ibid*, pp. 2–3 and p. 14. Evidence that emission was considered an important proof in England from the early modern period until 1828 can be seen in Walker (2013) 'Rape', p. 129 and in M.R. Block (2013) '"For the Repressing of the Most Wicked and Felonious Rapes and Ravishments of Women": Rape Law in England, 1660–1800' in A. Greenfield (ed) *Interpreting Sexual Violence, 1660–1800* (London: Pickering and Chatto), pp. 23–33 at p. 32.

30 For further discussion see Walker (2013) 'Rape', p. 128; Jackson (2000) *Child Abuse*, p. 13 and S. D'Cruze (1998) *Crimes of Outrage: Sex, Violence and Victorian Working Women* (London: UCL Press), p. 168.

31 For more on the difficulties with successfully prosecuting individuals for rape due to the standards of proof required throughout history see Levack (2010) 'The Prosecution of Sexual Crimes', p. 179; Walker (2013) 'Rape', p. 125 and p. 128; J. Kelly (1995) '"A Most inhuman and Barbarous Piece of Villainy": An Exploration of the Crime of Rape in Eighteenth-Century Ireland', *Eighteenth-Century Ireland*, 10, pp. 78–107 at p. 83; C.A. Conley (1986) 'Rape and Justice in Victorian England', *Victorian Studies*, 29, 4, pp. 519–536 at p. 520; J. Bourke (2013 edition) *Rape: A History from 1860 to the Present* (London: Virago Press), p. 23; Stevenson (2010) 'Most Intimate Violations', p. 80 and Lees (1997 edition) *Carnal Knowledge*, p. xiii and p. xvi.

32 There is some evidence that prosecutions for sexual violence held before the Scottish ecclesiastical courts *did* require immediate disclosure in the seventeenth and eighteenth centuries – see R. Mitchison and L. Leneman (1989) *Sexuality and Social Control: Scotland 1660–1780* (Oxford: Basil Blackwell), p. 194.

33 Hume (1797) Commentaries – Volume II, p. 9.

34 *Ibid*, pp. 7–9.

35 See for instance S. D'Cruze (1993) 'Approaching the History of Rape and Sexual Violence: Notes Towards Research', *Women's History Review*, 1, 3, pp. 377–397 at p. 389; Walker (2013) 'Rape', p. 140; Conley (1986) 'Rape', pp. 530–532; Lees (1997) *Ruling Passions*, p. 66, p. 81 and p. 88 and Lees (1997 edition) *Carnal Knowledge*, pp. 129–158.

36 See for example Hurl-Eamon (2005) *Gender and Petty Violence*, p. 37; A. Clark (1987) *Women's Silence: Men's Violence – Sexual Assault in England 1770–1845* (London and New York: Pandora), p. 50; Bourke (2013 edition) *Rape*, p. 5; D'Cruze (1998) *Crimes of Outrage*, pp. 160–161 and Lees (1997) *Ruling Passions*, p. 54.

37 See for instance M. Chaytor (1995) 'Husband(ry): Narratives of Rape in the Seventeenth Century', *Gender and History*, 7, 3, pp. 378–407 at p. 378; G. Walker (1998) 'Rereading Rape and Sexual Violence in Early Modern England', *Gender and History*, 10, 1, pp. 1–25 at p. 1; Bourke (2013 edition) *Rape*, p. 16 and p. 394; D'Cruze (1998) *Crimes of Outrage*, p. 2 and pp. 19–20 and Lees (1997 edition) *Carnal Knowledge*, p. 24.

38 Hume (1797) Commentaries – Volume II, p. 15.

39 *Ibid*, p. 10.

40 4 and 5 Vict. c. 56 (1841).

41 Hume (1797) Commentaries – Volume II, p. 10.

42 For further discussion of marital rape see Bourke (2013 edition) *Rape*, p. 327 and especially Lees (1997) *Ruling Passions*, chapter six.

43 Hume (1797) Commentaries – Volume II, p. 15.

44 For further discussion see A.E. Simpson (1986) 'The "Blackmail Myth" and the Prosecution of Rape and its Attempt in Eighteenth Century London: The Creation of a Legal Tradition', *The Journal of Criminal Law and Criminology*, 77, 1, pp. 101–150; L. Edelstein (1998) 'An Accusation Easily to be Made? Rape and Malicious Prosecution in Eighteenth-Century England', *The American Journal of Legal History*, 42, 4, pp. 351–390 and Bourke (2013 edition) *Rape*, pp. 28–41.

45 For further discussion of the historic gendered nature of sexual violence see H.V. McLachlan and J.K. Swales (1994) 'Sexual Bias and the Law: The Case of Pre-Industrial Scotland', *International Journal of Sociology and Social Policy*, 14, 9, pp. 20–43 at p. 40; Hurl-Eamon (2005) *Gender and Petty Violence*, p. 32; Emsley (2005 edition) *Crime and Society*, p. 107; Jackson (2000) *Child Abuse*, p. 108; Conley (1986) 'Rape', p. 532; Clark (1987) *Women's Silence*, p. 1 and Stevenson (2016) 'Offences Against Children', pp. 133–134.

46 For further discussion of the need to give evidence of sexual violence in a certain way in court see Gammon (1995) 'A Denial', p. 75; Hurl-Eamon (2005) *Gender and Petty Violence*, pp. 33–34; K. Stevenson (2000) '"Ingenuities of the Female Mind": Legal and Public Perceptions of Sexual Violence in Victorian England, 1850–1890' and J. Jones (2000) '"She Resisted With All Her Might": Sexual Violence against Women in Late Nineteenth Century Manchester and the Local Press' both found in S. D'Cruze (ed) *Everyday Violence in Britain, 1850–1950: Gender and Class* (London: Pearson), pp. 89–103 at p. 93 and pp. 104–118 at p. 108, p. 113 and p. 116 respectively.

47 For further evidence that reported instances of sexual violence were typically committed by individuals known to their victims see Ingram (2001) 'Child

Sexual Abuse', pp. 74–76; Ruff (2001) *Violence*, p. 142; T. Dunning (2007) 'Narrow Nowhere Universes, Child Rape and Convict Transportation in Scotland and Van Diemen's Land, 1839–1853', *Scottish Historical Review*, 86, 1, pp. 113–125 at p. 117; Jackson (2000) *Child Abuse*, p. 31 and Lees (1997) *Ruling Passions*, p. 61.

48 For further evidence of threats used in relation to instances of sexual violence see Ingram (2001) 'Child Sexual Abuse', p. 71.

49 For further evidence of the physical violence often involved in sex crimes see Ingram (2001) 'Child Sexual Abuse', p. 70; Conley (1986) 'Rape', p. 525 and Clark (1987) *Women's Silence*, p. 39.

50 For further discussion of the confessed testimony of Scottish individuals indicted for this offences see A-M. Kilday (2007) 'A Strange Kind of Loving? Bestiality in Early Modern Scotland' paper given to the European Social Science History Conference (Dublin). For similar material from other jurisdictions in the premodern period see Liliequist (1992 edition) 'Peasants', pp. 76–77 and G. Parker (1986) 'Is a Duck an Animal? An Exploration of Bestiality as a Crime', *Criminal Justice History – An International Annual*, VII, pp. 95–109 at pp. 104–105.

51 See for instance A. Gollapudi (2013) 'The Disordered Fundament: Sexual Violence on Boys and Sodomy Trial Narratives in the Old Bailey Proceedings' in A. Greenfield (ed) *Interpreting Sexual Violence, 1660–1800* (London: Pickering and Chatto), pp. 45–56 at p. 45 and p. 49; Ingram (2001) 'Child Sexual Abuse', p. 70; Gammon (1995) 'A Denial', pp. 78–79; Dunning (2007) 'Narrow Nowhere Universes', p. 120 and p. 123; Jackson (1999) 'Family, Community', pp. 136–137; Jackson (2000) *Child Abuse*, p. 33; Smart (2000) 'Reconsidering', pp. 59–60 and especially R. Davidson (2000) *Dangerous Liaisons: A Social History of Venereal Disease in Twentieth Century Scotland* (Amsterdam: Rodopi), pp. 86–87 and pp. 170–171 and R. Davidson (2001) '"This Pernicious Delusion": Law, Medicine, and Child Sexual Abuse in Early-Twentieth-Century Scotland', *Journal of the History of Sexuality*, 10, 1, pp. 62–77.

52 See for instance the case study of Edward Hand from 1822 in this chapter as well as J. Mills (2009) 'Rape in Early Eighteenth-Century London: A Perversion "So Very Perplex'd"' in J. Peakman (ed) *Sexual Perversions, 1670–1890* (Basingstoke: Palgrave Macmillan), pp. 140–166 at p. 158 and Dunning (2007) 'Narrow Nowhere Universes', p. 123.

53 For further discussion see for instance D'Cruze (1998) *Crimes of Outrage*, p. 134.

54 For further discussion of the motives behind rape and other forms of sexual violence see Simpson (1986) 'The 'Blackmail Myth', p. 107; Jackson (1999) 'Family, Community', p. 147; Jackson (2000) *Child Abuse*, p. 117; Clark (1987) *Women's Silence*, p. 6 and Lees (1997) *Ruling Passions*, p. 53.

55 National Records of Scotland (NRS), Justiciary Court, West Circuit Minute Books, JC13/16.

56 Ibid.

57 Ibid.

58 Ibid.

59 Ibid.

60 Ibid.

61 Ibid.

62 NRS, Justiciary Court, Process Papers, JC26/189.

63 NRS, Justiciary Court, West Circuit Minute Books, JC13/16.

64 Ibid.

65 Ibid.

66 Ibid.

67 NRS, Justiciary Court, Process Papers, JC26/189.

68 NRS, Justiciary Court, West Circuit Minute Books, JC13/53.
69 NRS, Justiciary Court, Precognition Papers, AD14/22/149.
70 *Ibid*.
71 Ibid.
72 Ibid.
73 Ibid.
74 Ibid.
75 NRS, Justiciary Court, West Circuit Minute Books, JC13/53. For a contemporary newspaper account of this case see National Library of Scotland (NLS) (1822), *Trials and Sentences of All the Different Prisoners who have Stood their Trials at the Circuit Court of Justiciary, which Opened at Glasgow on Monday the 16th of September 1822* (Glasgow: John Muir), Special Collections (SpC), L.C. Fol. 73 (038).
76 See NLS (1822) An Account of the Public Flogging of Edward Hand through the Streets of Glasgow, on Wednesday the 25th of September 1822, for Committing a Violent Assault on the Person of a Young Girl under 12 Years of Age at Greenock (Glasgow: John Muir), SpC, L.C. Fol. 73 (039).
77 NRS, Justiciary Court, High Court of Justiciary, Minute Books, JC4/13.
78 Ibid.
79 *Ibid*. The case was originally held at the West Circuit of the Justiciary Court in Ayr but due to the legal debate over the permissibility of the victim's testimony, the prosecution was deferred twice before being transferred to the High Court in Edinburgh – see *The Scots Magazine*, XI, June-December 1822, p. 621.
80 NRS Justiciary Court, Precognition Papers, AD14/22/227.
81 *Ibid*. My addition in parenthesis.
82 *Ibid*. My addition I parenthesis: I am grateful to Mr Daniel Vicars for advising me with regard to the definition of 'kneeve.'
83 Ibid.
84 Ibid.
85 For the judge's summation see NLS (1822) Trial and Sentence of James Burtney before the High Court of Justiciary at Edinburgh, on Monday the 18th of November 1822 for Violating the Person of a Girl under Nine Years of Age at Prestwick, near Ayr (Glasgow: John Muir), SpC, L.C. Fol. 73 (041).
86 NRS, High Court of Justiciary, Minute Books, JC4/13.
87 NRS, Justiciary Court, Process Papers, JC26/1822/180.
88 NRS, Justiciary Court, Precognition Papers, AD14/22/227.
89 NRS, Justiciary Court, Process Papers, JC26/1822/180. The contemporary press also praised the activity displayed by the public and the authorities in the apprehension of the culprit see NLS (1822) *Trial and Sentence of James Burtney*.
90 See *The Glasgow Herald*, 27th February 1948 and NRS, Justiciary Court, Books of Adjournal, JC13/145 and JC15/59. I am very grateful to the Lord Advocate for granting me access to the papers in this case and for our lengthy discussions regarding the legal complexities associated with this trial. It should be noted that as the names of the accused are a matter of public record, they have been included in this work. The names of the victims on the other hand have been anonymised due to the sensitive nature of the material and in order to protect their identity.
91 NRS, Justiciary Court, Appeal Process Papers, JC34/2/240.
92 NRS, Justiciary Court, Process Papers, JC26/1948/34.
93 Ibid.
94 NRS, Justiciary Court, Appeal Process Papers, JC34/2/240.
95 NRS, Justiciary Court, Process Papers, JC26/1948/34.

 96 Ibid.
 97 NRS, Justiciary Court, Appeal Process Papers, JC34/2/240.
 98 NRS, Justiciary Court, Process Papers, JC26/1948/34.
 99 Ibid.
100 Ibid.
101 Ibid.
102 NRS, Justiciary Court, Appeal Process Papers, JC34/2/240.
103 Ibid.
104 NRS, Justiciary Court, Process Papers, JC26/1948/34.
105 Ibid.
106 NRS, Justiciary Court, Books of Adjournal, JC13/145 and JC15/59 and *The Glasgow Herald*, 27th May 1948.
107 NRS, Justiciary Court, Books of Adjournal, JC13/145 and JC15/59. It is worth noting the court's recommendation that John McKenzie McPike (who had been indicted for theft when he was just nine-years-old on the 14th of November 1940 but had been admonished from the charge) serve his sentence in a borstal due to his 'criminal tendencies' – see NRS, Justiciary Court, Appeal Process Papers, JC34/2/240.
108 For commentary on this case which not only reflects the divergent views of public opinion as well as the global reach of this case see for instance *The Times*, 27th February 1948, Issue 51006 and *The Mirror* (Perth, Western Australia), 13th March 1948.
109 *Ibid* and NRS, Justiciary Court, Appeal Process Papers, JC34/2/240.
110 NRS, Justiciary Court, Process Papers, JC26/1948/34.
111 See *The Glasgow Herald*, 28th May 1948.
112 See for instance NRS, Justiciary Court, Criminal Case File, HH16/269/2.
113 For further detail on these attempts see for instance the material on Hugh Dearie Docherty available at NRS, Justiciary Court, Criminal Case File, HH16/269/1.
114 Ibid.
115 Lees (1997 edition) *Carnal Knowledge*, p. 116.

Chapter 3

The Violent North?
Violent Assault: Public and
Private, 1660–1960

Introduction

Fatal violence and sexual violence, whilst significant in terms of the serious nature of the offences involved, were two categories of crime that were committed relatively rarely in Scotland between 1660 and 1960, as previous chapters have shown. Consequently, when analysing the extent to which Scotland could be deemed 'a violent nation' over the three centuries in question, it is important to investigate the nature and incidence of the more 'mainstream' or 'everyday' acts of pugnacity. Thus, this chapter looks at offences which come under the broad category of interpersonal assault and examines them in relation to both public and private contexts. Although often less sensational than homicides or infanticides, instances of interpersonal assault tell us much about the ways in which men and women reacted to the situations they faced in their everyday lives, and are thus a useful mechanism for investigating the forms and causes of more 'usual' violence. Moreover, as assault (considered in its broadest definition) was the most commonly indicted crime of violence perpetrated in Scotland throughout our period of study, a closer scrutiny of this type of offence is vital for any consideration of the violent nature of the nation as a whole.

Violent Assault and the Law

In Scotland, the definition of interpersonal assault had been clearly defined since the early modern period as '…an intentional physical attack upon the person, either seriously threatened or actually accomplished.'[1] Yet, when a given case came before the Scottish courts, the categories of the offence were described in much more specific terms. Attempted murder, common aggravated assault, aggravated assault of authority, deforcement, some forms of sexual assault, hamesucken and a serious of minor offences such as gross insult and abuse, violent threatenings and writing incendiary letters, were all possible charges and could be regularly combined with one another.[2] This was the case from the late seventeenth century to the mid-Victorian era. However, after that time, there was greater consolidation of the charges laid and the categories of accusations diminished accordingly. Consequently, after 1850, a much closer reading of indictment material is required in order to determine the precise nature of the offence or offences being prosecuted. In any event, this chapter of the volume concentrates on hamesucken, the assault of authority and common and/or aggravated assault (including attempted murder).

(a) Hamesucken

Hamesucken is defined as '…the felonious seeking and invasion of a person in his dwelling-place or house.'[3] We might have assumed that hamesucken would have been one of the offences subsumed into the general category of assault in the move to summary justice described above, but prosecutions for hamesucken are still evident in Scottish court records today, albeit rarely.[4] Historically, in Scotland, hamesucken had been considered a capital offence, akin to rape and robbery as '…in its own nature, it far exceeds the guilt of an ordinary assault, and is a crime of that bold and heinous character, which makes it a fit companion of those high transgressions.'[5] Baron David Hume explained in more detail why hamesucken was considered such a serious offence in his writings of the late eighteenth century saying:

> For nothing can well be attended with greater terror and alarm, or more break in upon a person's peace, and opinion of security for the future, than the sudden uruption and attack of a ruffian in that place which is most peculiarly a man's own and which the law has carefully fenced for him, as his sanctuary and surest refuge, from all manner of harm.[6]

In addition to this, the fact that instances of hamesucken were considered premeditated or conducted with malice aforethought, rendered them particularly serious and distinctively aggravated in the Scottish legal context. Yet, despite the 'highest pains' being available to prosecutions for this offence, it is evident that capital punishment was rarely resorted to by the Scottish courts when convictions for hamesucken actually occurred.[7] However, as is evidenced by the Campbell and MacKinnon case study below, in the early modern period at least, a non-capital outcome was not necessarily guaranteed.

There was one essential condition that had to be fulfilled in order for a hamesucken charge to result: the victim had to be 'assaulted' within the place where they resided. In the Scottish legal provision for hamesucken, the protection afforded to the chief resident extended to all of his household – wife, children, servants, in-laws – and the household ought to consider itself secure from harm whether the 'master' was present or not. In other words, a hamesucken could still occur and be prosecuted against even if the master of the household was not present at the time. The chief resident need not be a home owner either, he could simply be a tenant at a given property, but if he resided there and the private space of his household was invaded, then a hamesucken charge would likely result. Physical injury need not have occurred for a charge of hamesucken to be laid. Nor did the invasion of the household have to have been carried out with force. If an individual was forcibly removed from his or her property and assaulted elsewhere, it was still regarded as a hamesucken, as personal security had been breached.[8] It is worth noting that the degree of violence perpetrated as part of the assault conducted did have a bearing on the severity of the sentence delivered upon conviction. The more violent the hamesucken, the more severe the punishment. The case against Sir William Bruce presented below demonstrates nearly all of the different legal facets of hamesucken in action.

(b) Assault of Authority

The legal context for the offence of assault of authority was quite compli-cated in Scotland, at least in comparison with attempted murder or common aggravated assault. Although the assault of authority was only an offence at common law, the Scottish courts typically dealt with those convicted of this type of crime far more harshly than those found guilty of other variants of interpersonal violence. Essentially, this was because, to legal minds at least, the assault of authority was closely associated with treason and seditious prac-tices. Therefore, this type of crime was not only seen as a threat to the social order in the place it was committed, but also to the wider authority of the state throughout the nation as a whole. As Baron Hume describes:

> The reprehension due to it, is not only on account of the high damage which may attend the hindrance in the particular instance, but also, and more especially, because it is a contempt of the authority of the King, as represented by his courts of justice, and in the course of legal process, and is thereby a matter of evil and most dangerous example, which tends to the unhinging of government, and to intercept the benefits of the state of civil union. The servants and executors of the law, how low soever their rank, are part of the great plan of judicial establishment, and are the necessary instruments of the courts of justice, without whose assistance the orders of those tribunals would be fruitless. And having, for this important purpose been regularly installed by public authority, and under surety for their proper deportment, they have a just claim to the obedience of all the lieges in their office, and to the same inviolability of person as the Magistrates in whose service they minister…' Thus, he explained '…it is necessary that all hindrance and molestation of them in their office be set down as a high crime, and strictly forbidden under pain of severe correction.[9]

Those convicted of the assault of authority, regardless of gender or class, had to be made examples of in order to deter others from behaving in a similar manner. As a result, the courts applied the most severe punishments available to them within the boundaries of non-capital discipline. The weighty con-sideration given to this type of offence by the legal authorities in Scotland is probably the main reason why indictments for the assault of authority were historically more prevalent at the higher courts than in lesser jurisdictions, until Burgh Police Courts were introduced to Scotland in the first third of the nineteenth century. Indeed, from the meticulous work conducted by David Barrie and Susan Broomhall relating to that judicial context, it is evident that the assault of authority was still branded a distinct and aggravated version of common assault in the more modern era and still regarded as a serious offence by the authorities by the start of the twentieth century.[10]

A charge of the assault of authority (sometimes referred to as 'oppression' or 'deforcement') was said to apply in Scotland '...wherever, either by any sort of actual violence, or by plain shew and preparation of mischief, or by the wilful opposing of real impediments in his way, the officer has been hindered, or disabled, from proceeding with the execution of his duty.'[11] There were several conditions in Scots Law which had to be met in order for a charge of this nature to result. First, the person assaulted or 'deforced' must be a lawful officer; someone employed to act diligently on behalf of the crown or state. Second, he must have notified individuals of his official capacity and intention. Third, he must have proceeded to do his duty in a lawful manner. Finally, the degree of violence offered in the assault was unimportant; an offence was committed as long as the officer was hindered from doing his duty. As can be seen, nearly all the conditions which have to be met in order to validate a charge of the assault of authority are concerned with the behaviour of the victim rather than the assailant. This makes this sort of offence rather unusual in Scots law but it demonstrates a determination on the part of the legal authorities that indictments for the assault of authority should be obvious and transparent in order to maximise convictions, and to enable the courts to use whatever punishments they deemed appropriate. The effectiveness of this approach is indeed borne out by the data below (see Figure 3.14).

(c) Common and/or Aggravated Assault

In general terms in Scotland, other instances of interpersonal assault brought to the authorities' attention were considered non-capital, common law crimes, and were punished according to the discretion of the court and the circumstances of a given case.[12] In the same way that the nature of assault could be broad and wide ranging, the nature of punishments that went with a conviction for common assault were also multifarious in design and degree. Moreover, and as will be clear from the subsequent sections of this chapter, instances of aggression and interpersonal violence could be settled out of court, or alternatively, and particularly from the late eighteenth century onwards, sections of the judiciary could be used more as a tool for mediation and reconciliation than as source of prohibition, sanction and punishment.[13]

In cases of attempted murder or 'common' or 'aggravated' assault (typically an assault committed in combination with other offences) there was only one central condition to be met for a charge to result. This was that regardless

of the instrument used to facilitate the assault, the attack itself had to be '...
attended with *immediate* pain and distress, as by bringing the person to the
ground, effusion of blood, or contusion of body.'[14] Apart from this, the legal
context related to interpersonal assault was concerned with the degree of violence involved and whether the attack had been provoked, committed with
'mortal purpose', or had occurred in self-defence. Clearly the Scottish courts
were interested in hearing explanations for outbursts of aggression, as well as
determining the degree of culpability of those involved.

Unlike many of the other serious violent offences examined in this book,
prosecutions for assault were not the sole provenance of the Justiciary Court.
The Justiciary Court, the supreme criminal court in Scotland, would deal
only with the most series assault cases – typically attempted murder or aggravated assault – instances where the violence offered was brutal and difficult to
excuse and was typically perpetrated with a weapon of one sort or another.
Other Scottish courts heard indictments for lesser forms of assault – 'common'
assault or 'simple' assault – or could, especially from the 1820s, register warrants of arrest for those individuals suspected of these versions of the offence.
Consequently, and in order to get a good sense of the extent to which assault
contributed to notions of Scotland as a 'violent nation', the material analysed
in this chapter pertains to a much broader volume of source material than that
utilised in other sections of the volume. Judicial statistics have been gathered
for this purpose from the Sheriff Courts and the Burgh Courts in addition to
the Justiciary Court between 1805 and 1960.[15]

The Scottish legal context for 'common' or 'aggravated' assault and for
the other offences in this particular category of interpersonal violence has
not changed substantially since 1660 in terms of the definitions, necessary
preconditions and judicial attitudes related to this type of offence. However,
there are two notable exceptions to this. In 1937, the Children and Young
Persons (Scotland) Act was passed alongside a raft of measures designed to
better protect the lives and livelihoods of Scottish children. This piece of
legislation explicitly criminalised cruelty to persons under the age of sixteen for the first time. If an individual was convicted of wilfully assaulting,
ill-treating, neglecting or abandoning a child or exposing a child to suffering or injury, then they would be liable to a fine not exceeding £100 and/
or imprisonment of two years or less.[16] However, the Act did not result in a
plethora of prosecutions for child assault for historic reasons that will be explained in due course and owing to the fact that the concept of 'child abuse'
was yet to be recognised as a real social problem until the late 1960s. Indeed,
substantial and specific legislation was not passed again on this issue in Scotland until 1995.[17]

The second exception to the Scotland's legal stasis regarding interpersonal
assault since 1660 relates to domestic violence. However, judicial recognition
of this issue north of the Tweed occurred even later than was the case for
child assault. In England, domestic violence, especially amongst the working

classes, was taken relatively seriously from the 1860s period onwards and specifically outlawed by legislation in 1853, 1868, 1882 and 1891. However, it is
fair to say that many of the measures introduced were subsequently repealed or
modified and the issue was left dormant under the surface of English society
during the first half of the twentieth century, largely on account of the disruption caused by the two World Wars.[18] Nevertheless, in Scotland by contrast,
legislative recognition of domestic abuse as a serious social problem was far
slower in coming. It was not until the Protection from Abuse (Scotland) Act
of 2001 and then the Domestic Abuse (Scotland) Act 2011 that the issue was
properly considered by the Scottish judiciary.[19] Shockingly, this means that
during the entire three centuries covered by this work, no legislation was
passed to specifically protect the victims of domestic abuse in Scotland, despite
the fact that assaults of this nature were some of the most commonly indicted
offences brought before Scottish courts particularly from the 1830s. Indeed,
even today, Scots Law does not recognise domestic abuse as a specific crime.[20]

Trends in Violent Assault and its Punishment

Figures 3.1 and 3.4 above show the erratic incidence of indictments for attempted murder in Scotland between 1830 and 1960 with no real discernible
trend in evidence, although the numbers concerned were not significant in any
given year.[21] As Figures 3.2, 3.3, 3.5 and 3.6 demonstrate, women were only
occasionally prosecuted for this offence in the Scottish context and this trend
explains the lack of convictions against female offenders seen in Figures 3.8 and
3.10. Figures 3.7 and 3.9 show that conviction rates for attempted murder in
Scotland persistently fell behind indictment rates and despite the introduction
of better detection techniques and evidence-gathering methods over the course
of the twentieth century, the gap widened. The vast majority of individuals
convicted of this offence were imprisoned, but typically for less than a year.

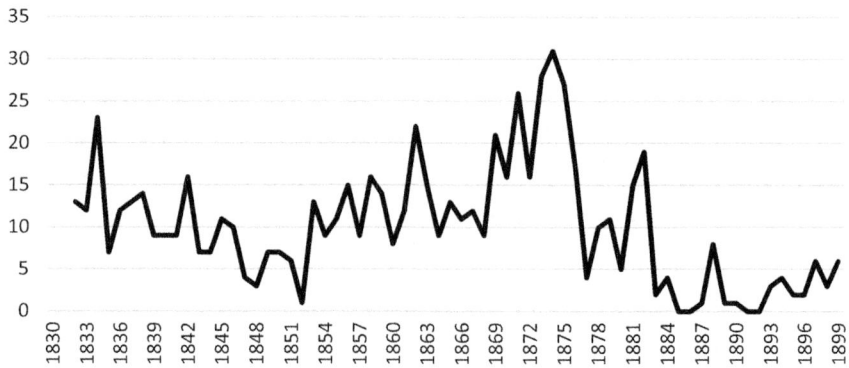

Figure 3.1 Indictments for Attempted Murder in Scotland, 1830–1899.

Figure 3.2 Indictments for Attempted Murder in Scotland by Gender, 1830–1899.

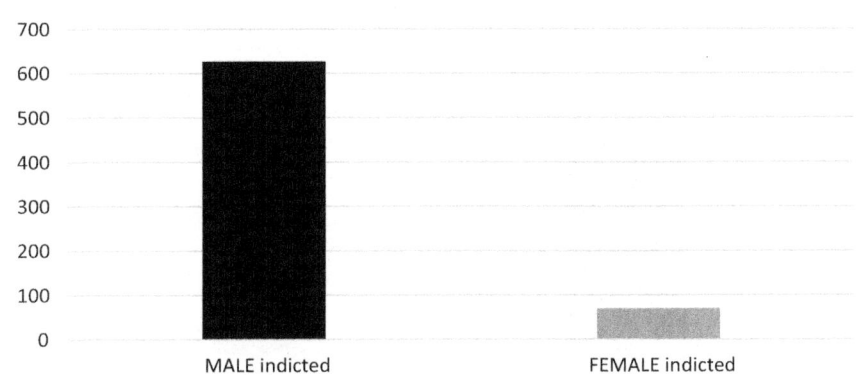

Figure 3.3 The Gendered Nature of Attempted Murder Indictments in Scotland, 1830–1899.

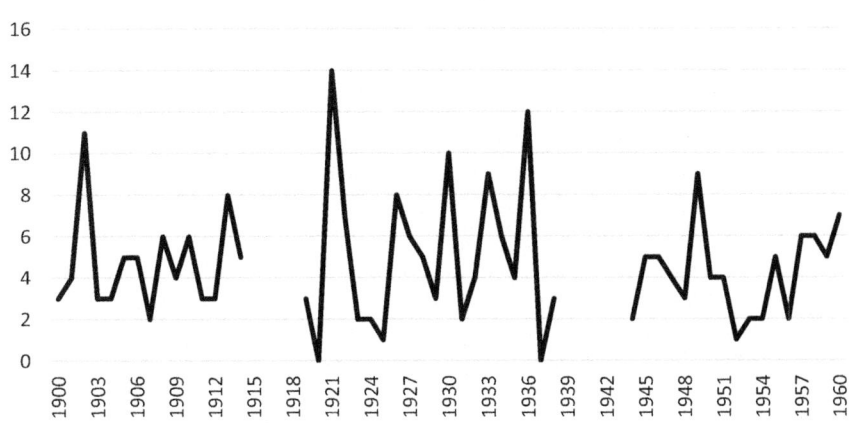

Figure 3.4 Indictments for Attempted Murder in Scotland, 1900–1960.

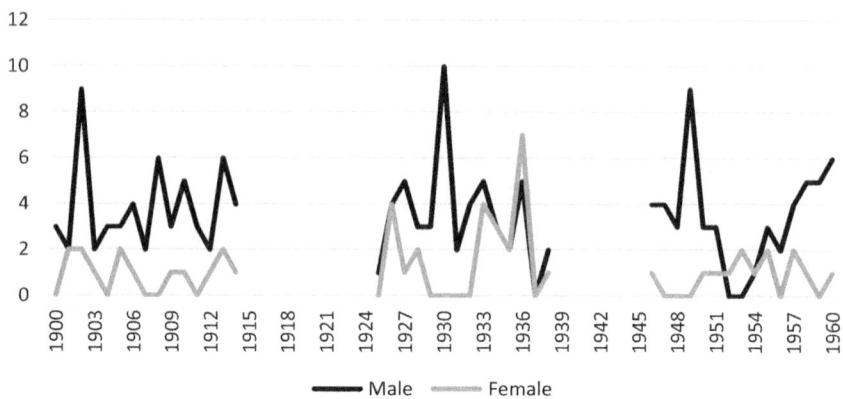

Figure 3.5 Indictments for Attempted Murder in Scotland by Gender, 1900–1960.

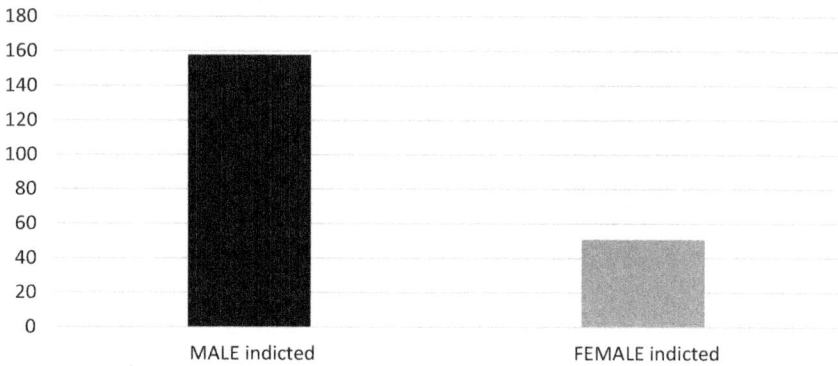

Figure 3.6 The Gendered Nature of Attempted Murder Indictments in Scotland, 1900–1960.

The statistical evidence related to the assault of authority in Scotland shows that this offence was far more regularly prosecuted than attempted murder, although discreet data on this specific form of assault exists only until 1914, as after that time, all assault indictments became assimilated into one single category.[22]

Figure 3.11 above shows the trend in indictments from 1805 to 1914 which is generally downward until the start of the twentieth century. This latter up-turn is probably caused by the amalgamation of court records in the judicial statistics, rather than an increased incidence of offending. As Figures 3.12, 3.13 and 3.15 demonstrate, women did not have a significant part to play in indictments (and thus convictions) for the assault of authority and this is interesting, given their particularly notable participation in this type of offence

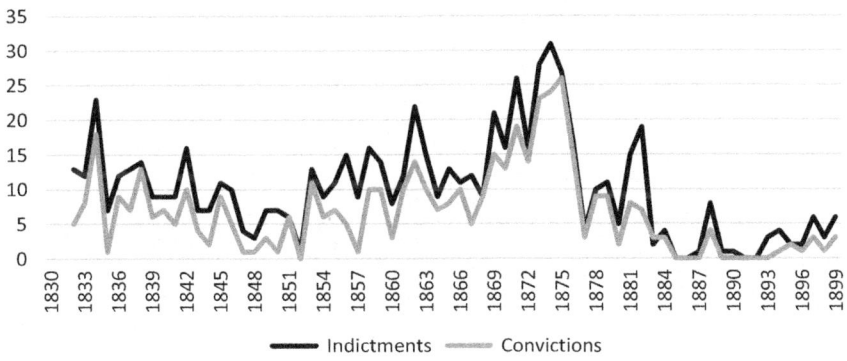

Figure 3.7 Indictments and Convictions for Attempted Murder in Scotland, 1830–1899.

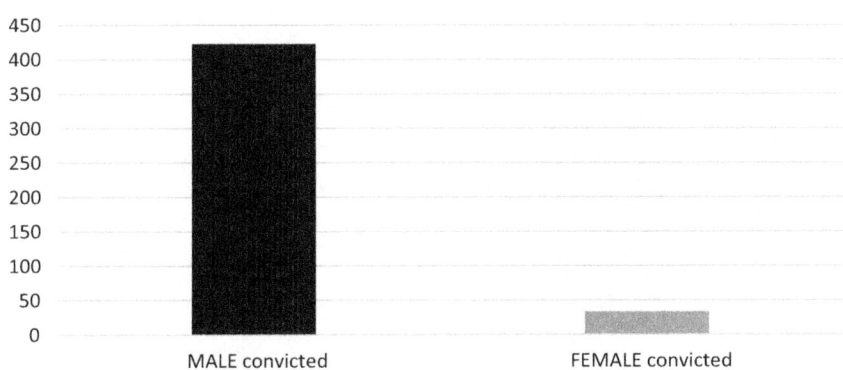

Figure 3.8 The Gendered Nature of Convictions for Attempted Murder in Scotland, 1830–1899.

in the preceding century.[23] As we have observed earlier in this chapter, the precise legal provision for this offence meant that the relationship between indictments and convictions would likely be closer in relation to the assault of authority than in many other offences brought to the judiciary's attention, and this is indeed what we see in Figure 3.14. Punishment for those convicted of the assault of authority in the Scottish context typically involved short spells of imprisonment.

Indictment rates in the judicial statistics for the broader category of assault (see Figures 3.16 and 3.19 below) show recorded incidences of this offence to be at a higher level than any other form of interpersonal violence investigated in this study. A largely downward trend is evident, which does not continue into the more modern era, probably due to differing data categories being assimilated after 1914. Although more women were indicted for assault in

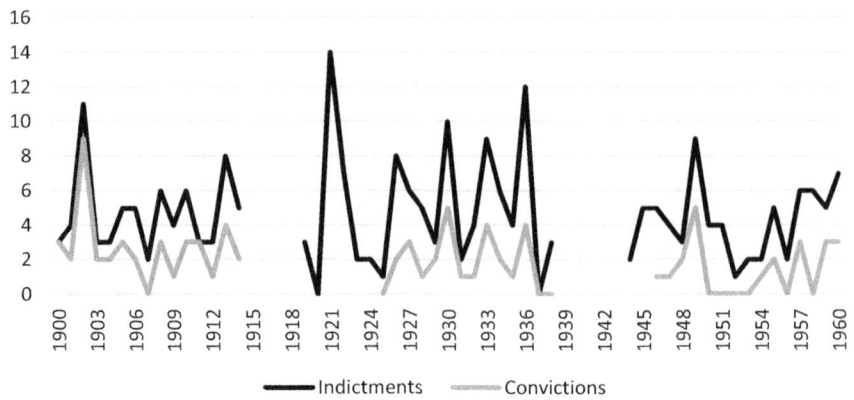

Figure 3.9 Indictments and Convictions for Attempted Murder in Scotland, 1900–1960.

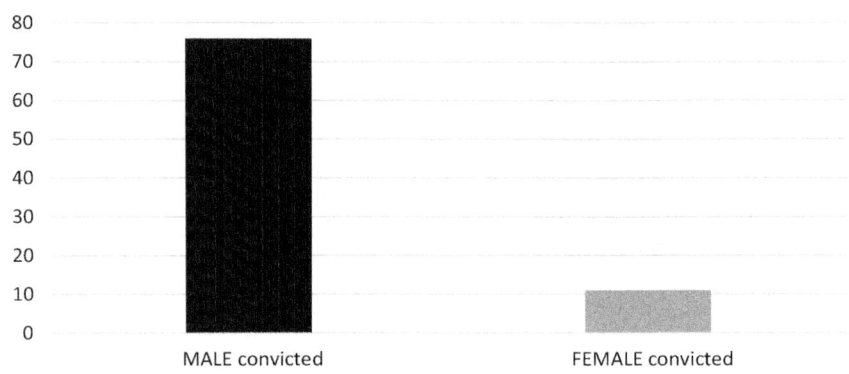

Figure 3.10 The Gendered Nature of Convictions for Attempted Murder in Scotland, 1900–1960.

Scotland than for any other form of violent crime between 1805 and 1960, their proportionate contribution to indictment numbers was insignificant to that of their male counterparts as Figures 3.17, 3.18, 3.20 and 3.21 illustrate. They are thus under-represented in conviction statistics for this offence too (see Figures 3.23 and 3.25).

It is interesting to note two further distinctive characteristics of the judicial statistics for assault in Scotland between 1805 and 1960. Firstly, juvenile offenders were indicted fairly regularly for this offence, albeit not in high numbers and secondly, there was a relatively serious issue with recidivism related to assault across the entirety of the period as shown in Figures 3.26

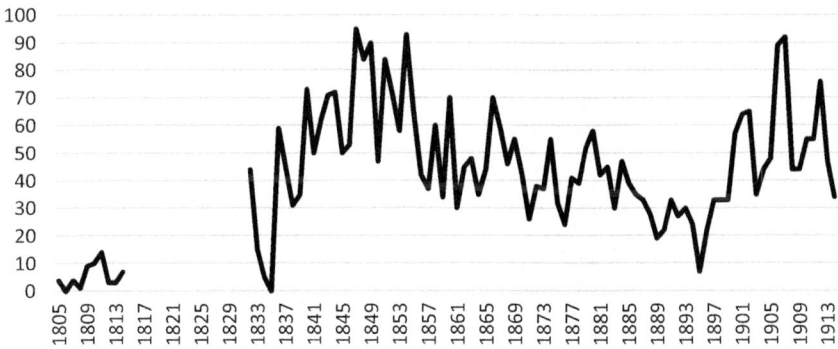

Figure 3.11 Indictments for Assault of Authority in Scotland, 1805–1914.

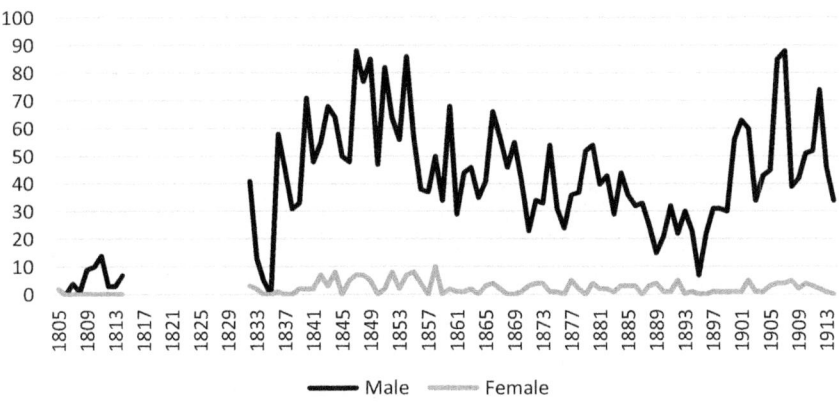

Figure 3.12 Indictments for Assault of Authority in Scotland by Gender, 1805–1914.

and 3.27. To date, scholarship on recidivism has largely been restricted to property offences and wholly in relation to the English context as we will see in Chapter 6, but the evidence from this study suggests that a broader investigation of repeat offending is warranted. Not only would an analysis of this sort have much to say about the effectiveness of contemporary judicial and policing measures, but it would also enable us to determine whether the actions of persistently violent individuals had an impact upon notions of Scotland as a violent nation.

Interestingly, and as Figures 3.22 and 3.24 show, there was a distinct and persistent gap between the indictment rate and the conviction rate for assault in Scotland over the 1830–1960 period. When compared to the trends in the assault of authority above, this is notable, and suggests that until the aftermath

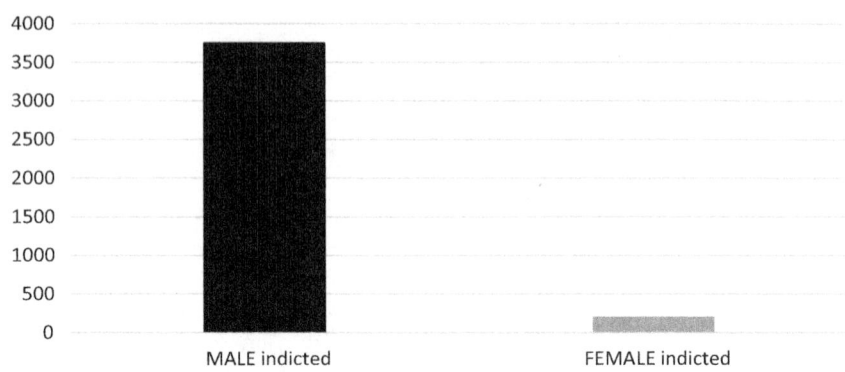

Figure 3.13 The Gendered Nature of Assault of Authority Indictments in Scotland, 1805–1914.

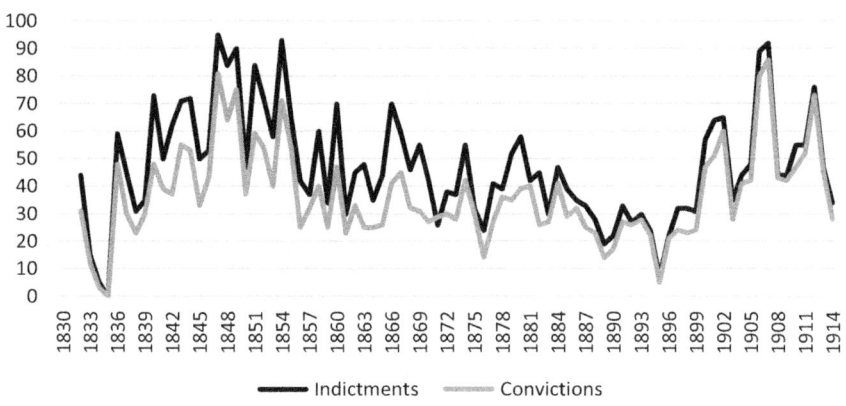

Figure 3.14 Indictments and Convictions for Assault of Authority in Scotland, 1830–1914.

of the Second World War, guilty verdicts in trials for this offence were not common and standards of evidence for less serious offences may have been problematic. There was a far greater variety of punishments deployed by the Scottish courts for those convicted of assault between 1830 and 1960 in comparison with those for other forms of interpersonal violence over that period. In the nineteenth century, for instance, imprisonment was often used, but sentences of transportation and fines were also common. By the more modern era, a mix of imprisonment, probation and sureties for good behaviour were more typically dispensed.

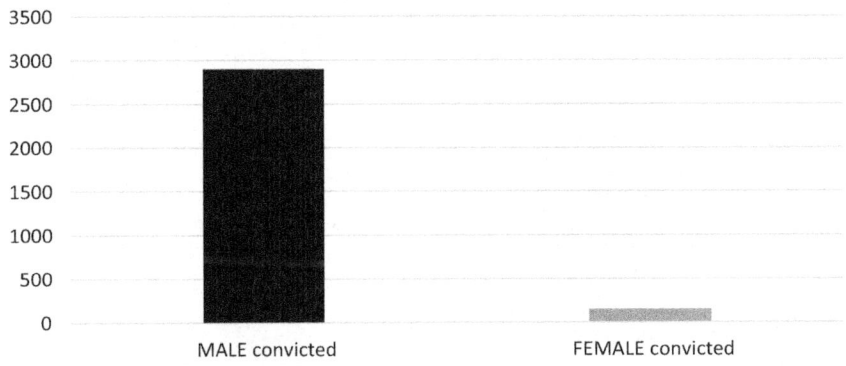

Figure 3.15 The Gendered Nature of Convictions for Assault of Authority in Scotland, 1830–1914.

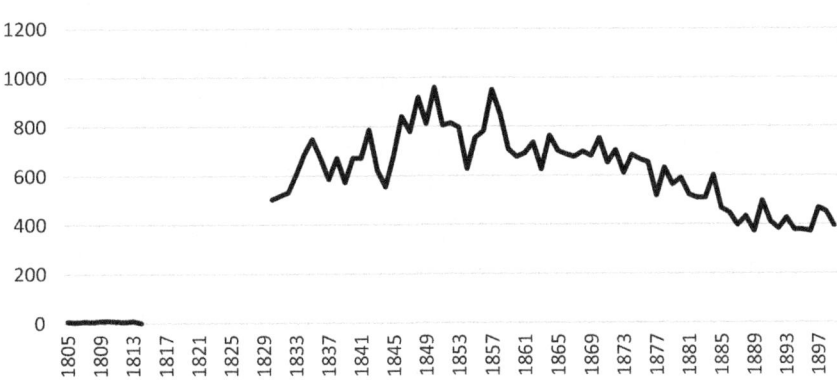

Figure 3.16 Indictments for Assault in Scotland, 1805–1899.

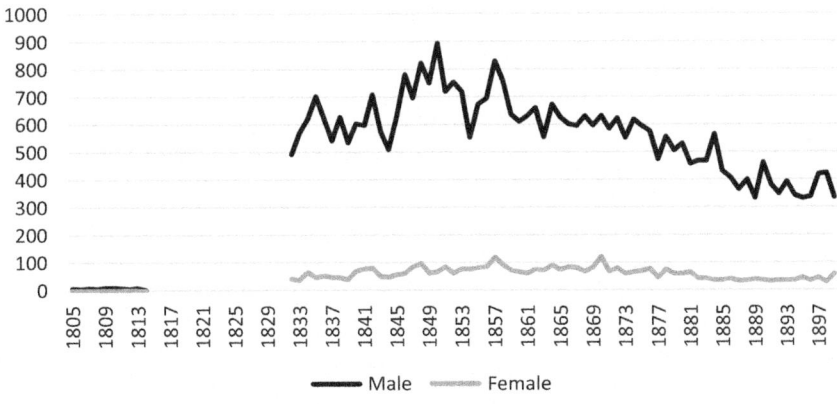

Figure 3.17 Indictments for Assault in Scotland by Gender, 1805–1899.

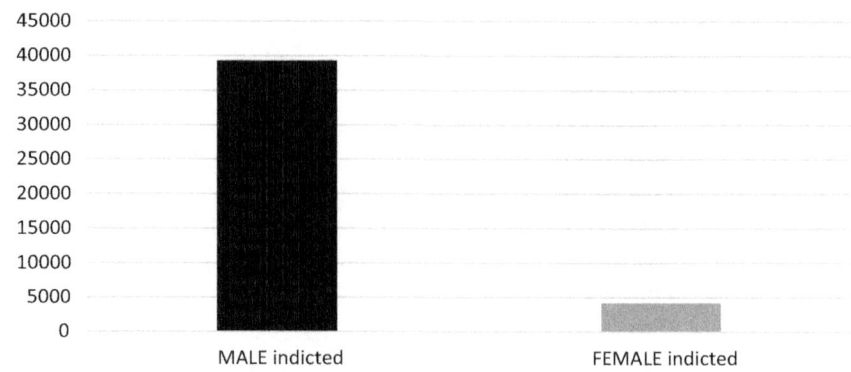

Figure 3.18 The Gendered Nature of Assault Indictments in Scotland, 1805–1899.

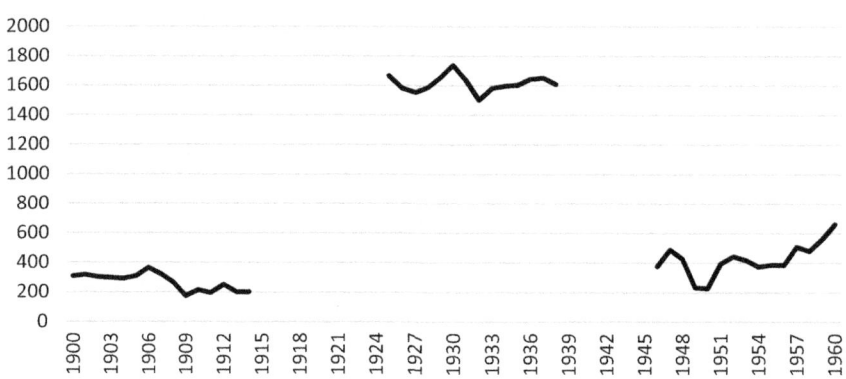

Figure 3.19 Indictments for Assault in Scotland, 1900–1960.

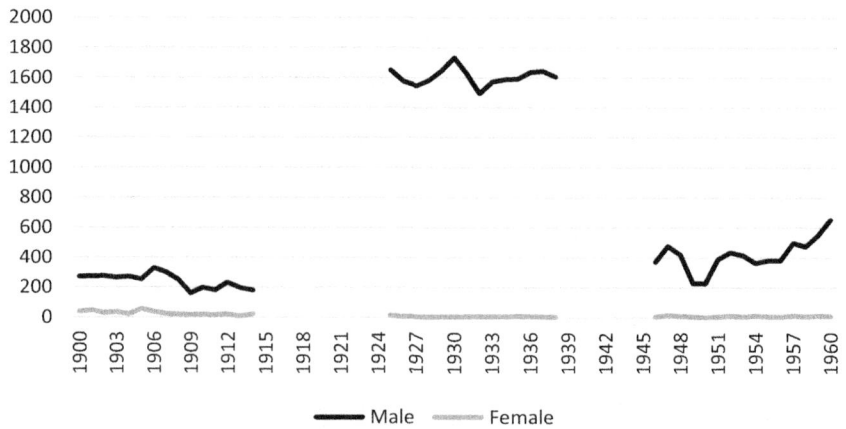

Figure 3.20 Indictments for Assault in Scotland by Gender, 1900–1960.

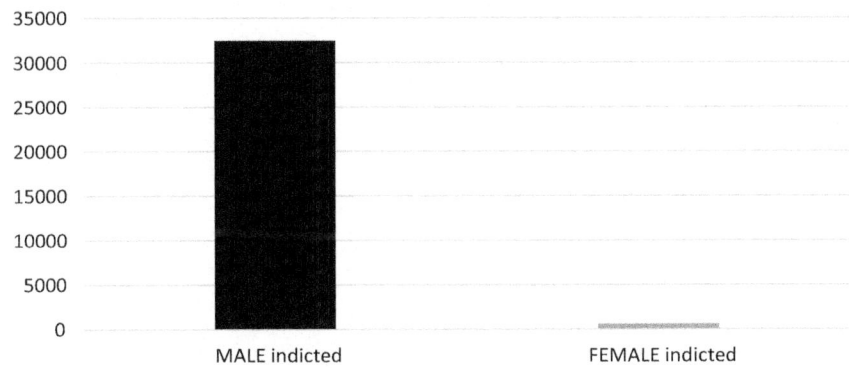

Figure 3.21 The Gendered Nature of Assault Indictments in Scotland, 1900–1960.

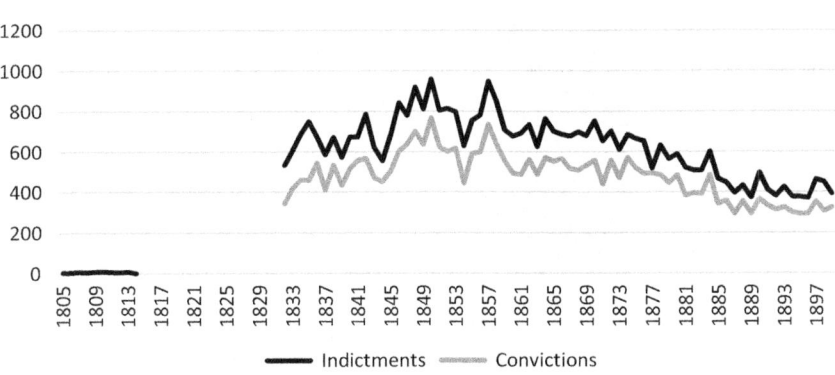

Figure 3.22 Indictments and Convictions for Assault in Scotland, 1805–1899.

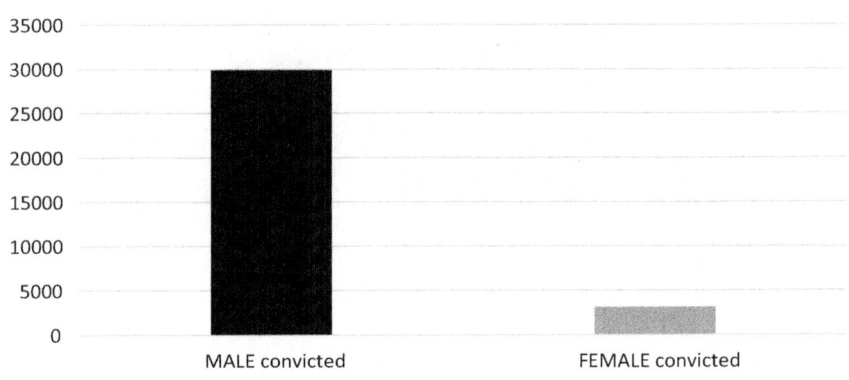

Figure 3.23 The Gendered Nature of Convictions for Assault in Scotland, 1805–1899.

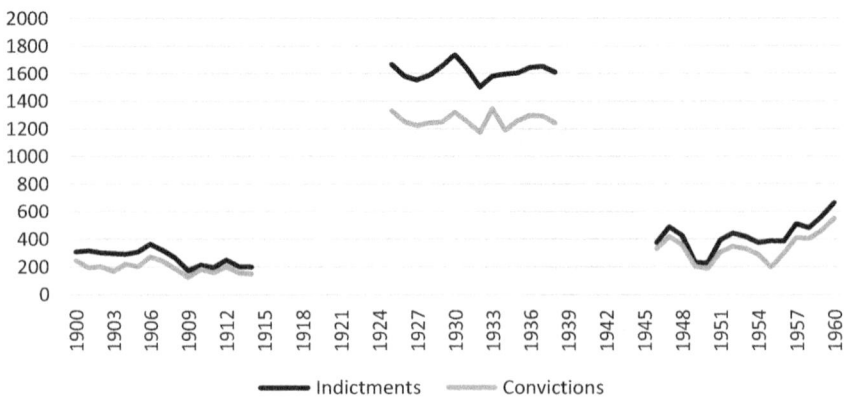

Figure 3.24 Indictments and Convictions for Assault in Scotland, 1900–1960.

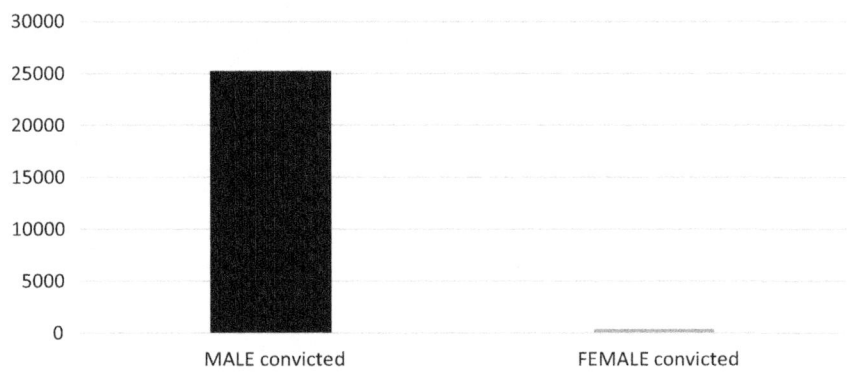

Figure 3.25 The Gendered Nature of Convictions for Assault in Scotland, 1900–1960.

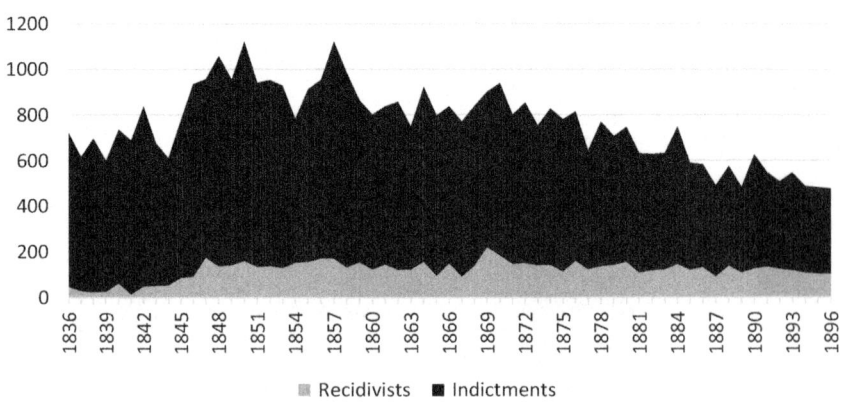

Figure 3.26 The Proportion of Recidivism amongst Indictments for Assault in Scotland, 1836–1896.

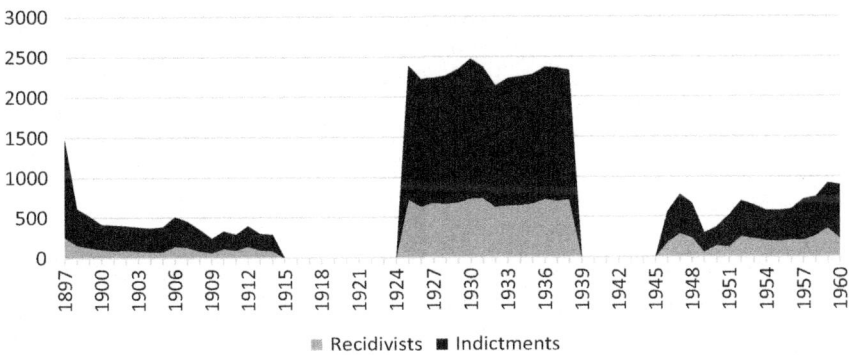

Figure 3.27 The Proportion of Recidivism amongst Indictments for Assault in Scotland, 1897–1960.

Offenders, Victims, Methods and Motive

For the most part, interpersonal violence in Scotland between 1660 and 1960 was dominated by male assailants and women victims. This is not to say that Scottish women could not be violent. Far from it. There are numerous examples throughout Scottish history of vicious instances of husband-beating, brutal assaults committed by Scottish women typically against other women and, in the period before 1820, evidence shows us that aggravated assaults of authority were more often committed by females rather than males north of the Tweed.[24] Clearly, Scottish women did not lack aggression. Nonetheless, in quantitative terms, they were still outnumbered by their male counterparts.[25] We have already seen that to some extent the gender disparity in interpersonal assault may have been affected by the 'dark figure' of unreported crime, especially in relation to male victims who may have been reluctant to admit being emasculated and abused by a female. However, the dominance of male offenders in the interpersonal assault statistics in Scotland would suggest that such under-reporting would only have a minimal impact on the broader offender profile.

The victims of interpersonal assault in Scotland between 1660 and 1960 usually knew or were acquainted with their attacker. This was most obviously evident in cases of domestic violence against children, servants and spouses, but was also apparent in episodes of hamesucken and common or aggravated assault perpetrated within a given community. Even in instances of male on male brawling, which could be instigated quite quickly given the right circumstances, the individuals involved had usually met on a prior occasion or had conversed with one another prior to an attack.[26] The exception to this was in aggravated assaults of authority figures where often the assailants did not know the individual officer concerned. However, as they felt legitimised in carrying out their assault, the rather random nature of their violence was to some extent mitigated, in their own minds at least.[27] The other thing that was unusual about the assault of authority in comparison to other acts of interpersonal assault was that it was typically conducted by groups of offenders rather than lone assailants.[28] Certainly there was safety in numbers, as the authorities found it difficult to round up and arrest all of the individuals involved as evidenced by the McGaa and Alexander case study below. In addition however, assailants tended to band together in these instances as there was a common grievance or purpose in mind. As we will see in the next chapter, if community members felt disempowered, subjugated or disadvantaged, they could, on occasion, come together to challenge authority and its representatives.

Access to power, control and dominance seems to have been the predominant and over-arching motive for instances of interpersonal assault in Scotland between 1660 and 1960.[29] Although historians have cited challenges to honour and to masculinity as key factors which have played a part in triggering and/or escalating violent behaviour, these issues are usually wrapped up within more substantial physical and mental conflicts over an individual or group's right to superiority over another.[30] The triggers for the initiation of such conflict could be relatively minor or ambiguous: refusal to do a prescribed task, criticism over the performance of domestic duties, accusations of impropriety in relationship, etc.[31] However, the ramifications of assaults could be significant in terms of the physical injuries suffered and the emotional scars received. Moreover, if these attacks are carried out against wives, servants and children under the sanction of patriarchal correction, they could be prolonged and inescapable.[32] Such victims would be incapable of removing themselves from any cycle of abuse, or indeed of even revealing its occurrence, because of their financial dependency on the head of the household and due to fear of the escalation of said violence in the longer term.[33]

Many historians have considered drink to be an important trigger to instances of interpersonal assault in the past, largely because so many violent skirmishes occurred in pubs and spaces of sociability where alcohol was served.[34] Certainly, whether drink was evident in an assault episode was something of a preoccupation amongst the Scottish judiciary where, as we saw in Chapter 1, its presence in a given case was seen as an aggravating factor, rather than an excuse in mitigation.[35] As can be seen from the evidence presented in the Henry Watson case study below, whether or not the accused had been drinking at the time of the incident and whether he had a habitual 'relationship' with alcohol consumption were questions asked of all the witnesses in the case. However, a closer analysis of instances of interpersonal violence more generally reveals that alcohol tended to inflame an

argument, rather than be something which provoked a disagreement to occur in the first place. Tangentially, drink could be a factor in some instances
of intimate violence where the husband had spent too much of his weekly
wages on drink and a fight had ensued between husband and wife over who
had ultimate control over domestic resources and how they were spent.[36]

With the exception of hamesucken, some instances of assaults against authority and some cases of domestic abuse, most interpersonal assault was
'hot-blooded' in nature rather than premeditated and planned.[37] As we
saw in the chapter on fatal violence, the spontaneous nature of physical
assault was reflected in the weapons chosen to perpetrate that kind of criminality. Items were grabbed which were close at hand when fighting broke
out: crockery, pokers, tongs, irons, etc. Interestingly, the evidence of interpersonal assault in Scotland suggests that fists were the most common
weapon deployed in the variants of interpersonal assault, and as the Henry
Watson case study demonstrates, they could do as much damage to a victim
as any other weapon utilised for that purpose.[38] Moreover, it is important
to remember that the ritualised or symbolic methodology of physical assault
tended to target certain parts of the body (head and upper torso) and to
tear hair and clothing which, when combined by verbal abuse and threats,
maximised the domination and humiliation of the victim.[39] Again, this emphasises that the primary objective in interpersonal assault was supremacy
and control.

One feature that was common to many instances of interpersonal assault
in Scotland between 1660 and 1960 was the unwillingness of bystanders to
intervene when violence was taking place, even if one of the parties was
evidently suffering and being brutalised in front of witnesses. The Campbell and MacKinnon hamesucken case study below is thus fairly unusual
in this respect. In assaults against authority for instance, it was very rare
that a member of the public would step forward to protect the officer under attack. This seems evident from the McGaa and Alexander case study
outlined below and was probably because onlookers either fully supported
the assailants in the action they had chosen to take, or because to intervene
would be to challenge the popular view within a given community and
such a treacherous move would not easily be forgotten by neighbours or
kinfolk. In instances of common or aggravated assault, individuals were
typically just left to get on with fighting things out between themselves.[40]
Conflict resolution was essentially completed through violent combat of
one sort or another.

In domestic violence cases, interventions were similarly uncommon, although family members did what they could from time to time.[41] Yet, even
by the modern era, the notion of patriarchal legitimacy in the control of
wifely behaviour still largely prevailed and predominated.[42] A husband had
the right to discipline his wife as long as his methods of correction were

relatively restrained, although the definition of what this constituted remained unclear and uncertain over time. Even by the twentieth century, as we can see clearly from the example of the Henry Watson case below, marital disputes were seen as private affairs, even though local communities were fully aware of what was going on through their comparatively close surveillance of each other's lives.[43] Intervention in these instances was rare unless an individual was in evident mortal danger.[44] Sadly, it seems that the authorities tended to take a similar reticent view until more recent times, although on the odd occasion (as the Henry Watson case shows) things could turn out more favourably for the victim through the determined efforts of professional agencies.[45]

Case Studies and Attitudes to Violent Assault

(a) Sir William Bruce [1718] (Hamesucken)

On the 14th of June 1718, Sir William Bruce of Stenhouse (fourth baronet of Stenhouse and Airth in Stirlingshire[46]), his wife Margaret Boyd, their son William and two of their servants (Hellen Lawson and Jannet Russell) were all prosecuted at the High Court of Justiciary in Edinburgh. All five were charged with the hamesucken, spulzie (plunder), invasion, threat and assault of Thomas Spence, his wife Margaret Rockhead and their children and servants on the 8th and the 10th of November 1715. The offences were said to have occurred at Stenhouse Chapel where Spence and his family resided and it was noted in the court proceedings that they had rented the property from Sir William Bruce on a lengthy lease which still had seventeen years to run.[47]

The court heard that Sir William Bruce and his wife first ransacked the complainant's barn and trampled over all the corn he kept there. A few days after this incident, Sir William, along with the four other accused individuals were said to have come to the complainant's house, whilst Thomas Spence was away in Ayr on business. At this juncture, Hellen Lawson (in the presence of Lady Margaret Boyd) apparently called the complainant's wife, Margaret Rockhead, a 'whore's burd', threw dirt and stones at her and threatened to 'burn down the house upon her.'[48] Jannet Russell also verbally abused Margaret Rockhead on this occasion, '…threatening to tread her under foot.' Lady Margaret Boyd also became directly involved in the incident when she extinguished the fire burning in the house and then

> …in a violent and outrageous manner turned the said Margaret Rockhead, her children, nurse and Sucking Child and Servants out of doors, locking the door and carrying away the key, and afterwards riffling and away taking the whole household furniture, beds, bed cloathes and Every thing Else valuable therein without either Inventar [inventory]

or Appretiation, Leaving the said Margaret Rockhead her Children and Servants to Shift for accommodation in the midst of a Rigorous Season destitute of all accommodation of Bedding or Bed Cloathes, and at a tyme when the Country was in the Confusion of a Rebellion and in a place thereof where accommodation was not Easy to be had...[49]

The court further heard that Lady Margaret Boyd and her accomplices also proceeded to seize and carry off all of the grain stored in the complainer's barn and a dairy cow belonging to him too.

Thomas Spence claimed that as a result of the hamesucken and confiscation inflicted, he and his family, '...were robbed of all necessaries of Life and exposed to hardships; destitute both of food, cloathing and habitation.'[50] In order to make ends meet, he explained that he had been forced to sell his remaining cow and two horses, and thus he no longer had any possessions whatsoever to call his own. He reiterated that he had entered into a lawful leasehold agreement with Sir William Bruce which was still legally binding at the time of the alleged incident, and that it was only on the 10th of February 1716, some three months after this violent intrusion had occurred, that he received a retrospective eviction notice from his landlord. Thomas Spence thus craved that the court find the defendants guilty as charged, punish them to the full letter of the law and order them to make a reparation payment of four thousand merks Scots. The prosecution summed up his position saying:

> This crime was '...a violent oppression...an unheard of barbaritie...A man's own house has, in all civiled [civilised] nations, been Looked upon as the most inviolable Sanctuary, where men even find protection in some Cases against the very Law itself, as well as the unjust Resentments of our fellow subjects...[51]

The defence counsel in this case made strenuous efforts to refute the charges laid. First, they pointed out that the retrospective eviction notice, which according to Thomas Spence at least contained an acknowledgement of guilt on the part of the defendants, had been mislaid by the complainant and had thus not been admitted as evidence to court. As a result, they argued, the document should not have been referred to in the judicial proceedings. Second, the defence stated that as neither Sir William Bruce nor his son had been mentioned in the details of the indictment as having had any part to play in the crimes as alleged, or even said to have been present when the incident occurred, they should not be listed as accused and the libel against them should be dismissed. Moreover, and in any event the defence claimed, Sir William Bruce's son was too young to be prosecuted in this matter. Third, and perhaps more problematically, the defence pointed out that if the servants indicted in this case were acting on the orders of their master/mistress, they ought not to be prosecuted for fulfilling their duties and behaving as compelled by their betters. With this particular argument, the defence lawyers were clearly treading a fine line between the point they were trying to make and admitting the culpability of either Sir William Bruce or Lady Margaret Boyd or indeed both parties![52]

The fourth and final argument offered by the defence team was the most telling and arguably the most cunning. The lawyers challenged the validity of the entire indictment by pointing out that although the indictment had been brought to court in June of 1718, the alleged crime had occurred in November of 1715. As such, the Act of Indemnity (also known as the Act of Grace and Free Pardon) which was passed in July of 1717 applied to these proceedings.[53] This particular piece of legislation was ratified in the wake of the 1715 Jacobite Rebellion in an attempt to curb further unrest. In the Act, King George I gave an amnesty and free pardon to all his subjects charged or convicted of any crimes alleged or proven to have been committed before the 6th of May 1717.[54] Sir William Bruce's defence lawyers therefore submitted that no criminal prosecution could be brought for an offence committed between the rebellion and that date. The High Court of Justiciary agreed with this contention and dismissed the *criminal* charges against the five defendants, but made a specific order which reserved the right of Thomas Spence to bring the matter to a *civil* court if he desired to do so. Sadly, no evidence exists of the complainant's decision in the aftermath of this Justiciary court ruling.

(b) Mr Archibald Campbell and Mr Donald MacKinnon [1725] (Hamesucken)

On the 11th of March 1725 another case of hamesucken was brought to the Sheriff Court of Inverness and charged against Archibald Campbell and Donald MacKinnon. Exactly one month before these proceedings began, Campbell and MacKinnon arrived armed with weapons '…under silence and cloud of night', at the house of Alexander Fraser at Popachy in Invernesshire.[55] With other unknown accomplices, Campbell and MacKinnon proceeded to force open an outer door of the dwelling place, and '…with swords drawn in their hand' they rushed into the room that Alexander Fraser usually resided in swearing and shouting 'That they would have his head and Intraills.' Alexander Fraser was not in the room, however, and so the invaders went from room to room in the house trying to find him '…with the design of Murdering him'. Eventually, they made their way into a room where some of the children slept and

> …they seized one of them…and holding their naked swords to her neck, Swore and threatn'd they would take away her life if she did not reveal where her father was…which they no doubt would have perpetuated,

if the servants of the family and others of the neighbourhood…had not interposed.[56]

A fight then broke out between the invaders and the neighbours who came to help the household. As well as threatening one local man (Thomas Bayn) with a 'cock'd pistol', they fired a gun at James Lobban which fortunately misfired, so they proceeded to assault him and others nearby '…with their said swords wounding severalls of them to the great effusion of their blood, and by which means, the accomplices made their escape.'[57]

The court heard in defence that Campbell and MacKinnon were employed as watchmen by local landowners and it was their job to patrol the area and prevent cattle theft from occurring. On the night in question, however, the two men had got drunk – apparently for the first ever time in their lives – and proceeded upon an inebriated foot patrol of the district. The accused claimed that after some time they heard a lot of noise and commotion coming from the Popachy area and, when they went to investigate, they saw some men that they had met earlier that evening involved in a skirmish '…with some local country people.' Campbell and MacKinnon were then attacked themselves by the said 'country people' outside a house they were unfamiliar with and thereafter they were apprehended for wrong-doing that they were unaware of committing and claimed to be entirely innocent of.

Campbell and MacKinnon's defence team offered four arguments which challenged the capital indictment against their clients. First, they pointed out that as Alexander Fraser was not home at the time of the alleged incident, a charge of hamesucken was redundant. Yet, as we have already seen from the legal context to this offence, this argument was not likely to be sustained by the judiciary. The home owner did not need to be present and any attack on his dwelling house (and any of his 'property' within it – including children and servants) or indeed any threat made to his person within that dwelling house, was still pertinent under law. The second argument lodged by the defence was that the complainant had not named the accomplices referred to in the indictment. Once more, the defence team's attempt at curbing the full strength of the indictment was refuted and the naming of other assailants deemed unnecessary.

Next, Campbell and MacKinnon's lawyers tried to use the fact that they were drunk as a mitigation, arguing that what had transpired was spontaneous and not premeditated. They also suggested that their clients' occupation legitimised their actions and gave them the right to stop and search properties or people if they suspected foul play to have occurred or to be in progress. With hindsight, these defence tactics seem rather desperate, as they seem to acknowledge partial culpability at the very least. Moreover, and as we have already seen in this chapter, alcohol consumption was regarded by some judges as an aggravating factor in instances of interpersonal violence and by others as something that assuaged bad behaviour to a greater or lesser degree, so adding in this argument to the defence proceedings seems to have been something of a gamble.

Indeed, the gamble did not pay off in this instance and the court chose to reject all of the defence team's arguments. After a wealth of prosecution testimony was heard, the assize enclosed to reach a decision on the indictment. The jury were unanimous in returning a verdict of guilty against both men and Campbell and MacKinnon were duly sentenced to death by hanging scheduled for the 24th of March 1725 at the Gallows Hill of Inverness.[58] As indicated earlier in this chapter, it was exceedingly rare for a capital sentence to result from a charge of hamesucken upon conviction, even though the law allowed for this. In reality, hamesucken was treated by the Scottish judiciary as a species of assault and typically punished with the same arbitrary 'pains' as other instances of interpersonal assault. The severity of the verdict in the Campbell and MacKinnon case did not go unnoticed and the executions were postponed by the Lords of Justiciary who discussed the matter at a meeting in Edinburgh on the 1st of June 1725. In essence, the Lords believed that the sentence meted out by the Sheriff Court was disproportionate to the crimes proven to have been committed. Consequently, they formally decreed that if an application was made to them to suspend Campbell and MacKinnon's sentence before the 16th of June, they would intervene to that effect. However, no application was forthcoming, and so the original verdict and sentence stood and the executions effected. The reasons why Campbell and MacKinnon's once very vocal defence team had latterly become silent are unknown, but according to some commentators, the ultimate fate of the two men rested in 'legal neglect' rather than criminal wrong-doing.[59]

Both of these case studies of hamesucken in eighteenth century Scotland highlight the complexities associated with prosecutions of this type of interpersonal assault at that time. The severity of the legal context for the crime meant that accusations of the offence were taken very seriously and were hotly debated in the courtroom. Indeed hamesucken indictments generated more intense legal debate than any other type of violent offence prosecuted in the Scottish criminal courts. Descriptions of the actual nature of the offence could vary widely from case to case given the broad parameters of the crime. As we can see from the first example, sometimes threatening behaviour within someone else's household was sufficient for an accusation of hamesucken to be relevant. On other occasions, verbal abuse, violence with weapons and significant bloodshed occurred and had to be remedied as the Campbell and MacKinnon case exemplified. And sometimes, what transpired was something in between.

Evidently hamesucken confused the Scottish authorities. On the one hand they wanted to ensure that the Scottish populace felt protected within their own homes for the maintenance of the common peace and facilitation of social stability, during an era where Scotland had experienced a great deal of disruption and unrest in a range of different contexts. However, and at the same time, the authorities did not necessarily want to get involved in local or personal disagreements and long-standing tit-for-tat retaliations which often came to light in prosecutions for hamesucken and other forms of interpersonal assault at this time. In an enlightened Scotland, such everyday rebellions ought be mediated and mitigated by religious and community-based authorities rather than judicial ones. Consequently, attitudes to hamesucken in the eighteenth century are hard to pin down and verdicts and sentences could be unpredictable, eccentric and surprising as we have seen.

(c) Mrs Janet McGaa and Mrs Helen Alexander [1781] (Assault of Authority)

An indictment brought at the South Circuit Court held at Ayr on the 18th of May 1781 charged a gang of individuals with violent deforcement as well as the forcible carrying off of goods which had been confiscated by a revenue officer.[60] More specifically, revenue officers in Port William (Wigtownshire) had seized a box of tea which they believed had been smuggled without proper payment of duty. Robert Lindsay, Thomas Maxwell, Susan Agnew, Janet McGaa and Helen Alexander, on the other hand, claimed that the tea belonged to them. According to the prosecution, these five individuals became determined to rescue the tea, and at the instigation of Helen Alexander, Robert Lindsay and Thomas Maxwell, Officer Hugh Hannah was violently assaulted by Susan Agnew and Janet McGaa. The women forcibly held Hannah down on the ground and battered him '...most cruelly with stones about the face and otherways upon his body to the great effusion of his blood and danger of his life.'[61] The pair then stripped Hannah naked and then resumed their vicious treatment of him, brutally stoning him once more at close quarters. During the ongoing melee, the other members of the gang calmly carried off the tea and secured it in a safe location. The court heard that as a result of the savage assault he had received, Hugh Hannah lost an eye in the incident and was critically disfigured, '...being left in a most miserable condition.'[62]

In the court case that ensued, only Janet McGaa and Helen Alexander were tried under the indictment. The other three defendants failed to appear in court to face the charges against them and they were consequently declared fugitate (officially named outlaws from justice) and all their goods and gear were ordered to be forfeited to the rights of the Crown.[63] In court, Janet McGaa pleaded guilty to holding the revenue officer down whilst the tea was carried off. Helen Alexander, for her part, acknowledged that she had encouraged others to assist in the tea being carried off. As both defendants had pleaded guilty to an aspect of the indictment, the prosecution declared that they were happy to restrict the libel to 'an arbitrary punishment'.[64] The case was heard quickly, summarily and without recourse to witness testimony, as this was now deemed unnecessary. The assize accordingly found the accused guilty in line with the content of the confessions they had each submitted. The judge in the case, Lord Kennet, sentenced both Janet McGaa and Helen

Alexander to eight days imprisonment in the Tolbooth of Ayr and thereafter, ordained that they should be set at liberty.[65]

Although this example does not contain the same level of detail as is evident in the other case studies in this chapter, it nevertheless illuminates various aspects of the assault of authority and how it came to be regarded by the Scottish authorities. In the first instance, the example clearly shows that deforcement was not a solitary form of criminal activity. Groups tended to be formed largely on an *ad hoc* basis, rather than being scrupulously planned in advance of the assault taking place. They also often involved both male and female protagonists working together, and the members involved (as was the case in this current example) were not necessarily related to one another. One thing that such groups did have in common however, was that they believed they had some legitimising notion or right to assault authority figures if they felt they were being treated unjustly or unfairly. As in many other instances of deforcement, the Port William gang believed that the tea had been unlawfully confiscated from them and they felt assured that by assaulting Hugh Hannah, they were simply pointing out this fact and reminding him who was in the right and who had ultimate authority in a given community.

The case against Janet McGaa and Helen Alexander also exemplifies the fact that women were prepared to be aggressive and independent actors in violent criminality outside the home as well as within the domestic sphere. The actions of Janet McGaa and Susan Agnew could not be described as timid and were not conducted at the behest of men or with male support. The assault was initiated and indeed carried out by the women of the group. The men were seemingly bystanders who were reluctant to get directly involved. McGaa and Agnew's assault on Hugh Hannah also illuminate some of the more symbolic aspects of this kind of interpersonal violence discussed earlier in the chapter. Their use of stones, the fact that their attack focused on the face of their victim, as well as their decision to strip Hugh Hannah of all his garments and possessions, all point to efforts in ritualised humiliation where the protagonists were making a very explicit point about power and control and who owned the right to implement it. This behaviour was very common in instances of deforcement and the assault of authority in Scotland during the seventeenth and eighteenth centuries.

Finally, we know from the legal context associated with this kind of interpersonal violence that the assault of authority was taken very seriously by the Scottish judiciary at least. Such instances were regularly treated as 'aggravated assault' and, as this chapter has already identified, the penalties upon conviction could be quite severe – typically imprisonment for a lengthy period of time or even banishment abroad. However, enforcing absolute justice within this context in practice proved tricky for the Scottish authorities on the ground. For instance, it was very rare that *all* of the individuals involved in an assault on authority would face trial. Either, they fled the scene and were not arrested, or as was the case here, the defendants absconded from justice in the run up to their trial. Moreover, and on some occasions, it was clear that the victim was not willing to prosecute all of the individuals responsible for a particular attack, no matter how bloody or barbarous the assault had been. If local officials wanted to retain any authority within a given community, and if they wanted to maintain decent relations with individuals from the locality, it was sometimes more prudent to select just a few of their known assailants for prosecution. By this action officers demonstrated that they could be discretionary, merciful and sympathetic to the plight of their charges, but they still had to remind the populace that the deforcement of state-sanctioned authority was intolerable in a civilised society.

Successful convictions of *all* the individuals involved in assaults against authority were hard to come by in seventeenth and eighteenth century Scotland and beyond. The absence of key defendants from the courtroom made prosecutions difficult as gaps in evidence became the norm rather than the exception and as a result, lawyers often resorted to negotiating the outcome of the cases between themselves. Prosecution teams were acutely aware of the serious regard with which the judiciary held the assault of authority and deforcement, and so they were under a lot of pressure to secure convictions in instances where the weight of evidence was insufficient to merit conviction. As a result, they often encouraged defence counsels to plead guilty to a lesser charge, so that a conviction *was* delivered but at a reduced or limited cost to the defendant. This was exactly what transpired in the McGaa and Alexander case. The defendants pleaded guilty to misdemeanour offences rather than aggravated assault, the indictment was restricted accordingly, and convictions resulted, showing that violence against authority was unacceptable. Nonetheless, the defendants were given very lenient punishments and the end result was thus likely considered acceptable to all concerned, except perhaps for the victim Hugh Hannah who had to live the rest of his life disfigured.

(d) Mr Henry Watson [1914] (Domestic Violence)

Labourer Henry Watson was a man already known to the Glaswegian police. In April 1912 he had been convicted of the assault of Agnes Watson (36) after they had been married for around a year and he was sentenced to twenty-one days in prison.[66] On the 20th of August 1914 he was in trouble again. He was brought before the Sheriff Court in Glasgow charged with another assault. The indictment explained that within their dwelling place at 53 Green Street in Bridgeton, Henry Watson abused his wife once more and '…did beat her with your fists and with three chairs or parts thereof, a stool, a kerb, and a metal winter, to her serious injury and the danger of her life.' At this time, due to the extent of her injuries, Agnes Watson was a patient in the Royal Infirmary.[67]

The precognition papers in this case reveal a wealth of detail about what transpired before, during and after the assault described above. The testimony of Martha McWilliams, Agnes Watson's sister was probably the most revealing.

Martha explained that her sister married widower Henry Watson in 1911. He already had four children from his first marriage, when Agnes gave him a fifth, a son called Sidney who was born the same year that the couple were wed. Martha pointed out several times in her testimony that Henry Watson was '…a sober man' who was not given over to drink and that he was '…a regular worker.' She explained that despite these good habits, the relationship between Henry Watson and her sister had been a turbulent one. After just five weeks of marriage, Agnes left her husband telling her sister '…it was because he was in use to assault her.' She stayed away from him for five months before returning. A few months after this Agnes was violently assaulted once again by Watson and this episode resulted in the 1912 conviction referred to earlier.[68] In addition, Martha testified that her sister had complained to her on multiple and separate occasions that the accused had assaulted her.

After the 1912 incident, Agnes Watson left her husband and since that time she had not resided with him. This separation greatly displeased Henry Watson and he repeatedly tried to persuade Agnes to come back home. She declined, but in turn asked Henry for aliment (alimony), which he refused.[69] Agnes told her sister that she '…would have to go with her every place she went because she was afraid of him assaulting her.' By June of 1914 however, it seems that relations between the couple had thawed to some extent as they went on a shopping trip together and bought some clothes for their son. In the following month, Agnes agreed to go on three separate holiday trips with Henry and the five children to Millport, West Kilbride and Helensburgh. It is likely that Henry believed a reconciliation would be imminent, especially as he had gone to so much trouble and considerable expense to convince his wife that they would be happier together than apart. After further time spent together, a few more excursions and various presents being given to Agnes by her husband, Henry came to visit his wife (who was staying at Martha's house in Bridgeton) on the 26th of July 1914 and asked her to come back and stay with him once more. She refused. Henry threatened Agnes that if she did not come with him, he would '…take the boy'. Agnes swore she would not let that happen and Henry Watson left the premises.[70]

Watson returned later that evening to his sister-in-law's house and asked Agnes to go with him to the Olympia Theatre. She refused. He then asked her why she would not return to the family home and Agnes replied saying '…she would not go back as it would just be the same over again, as he never gave her place in the home.' Henry called her a liar and asked Martha what she thought. Martha said that '…when they couldn't agree they would be better separated…that she had given him a chance before but that he was far worse when she went back.' Henry asked Agnes if she '…had another man' and she replied 'No' adding '…that if he wanted to marry another woman he could divorce her.' Henry said 'I'm not going to have another woman' and their conversation began to escalate into a heated argument. Henry demanded that Agnes give him back the presents he had recently bought for her – a brooch and a pair of gloves. Both were on shelf above where Agnes was sitting. As she reached up to retrieve them, Martha recalled how '...he struck her with both fists on the face and head as hard as he could. He continued to strike her standing right in front of her. I tried to pull him away from her but could not. I then ran out calling "MURDER" and "Police".'[71] Once Martha had run off to get help, Henry Watson closed and locked the door behind her, leaving him alone with his wife. Eventually, and around thirty minutes later, Martha returned to her house with the police constable George Paul in tow. She was able to open the door with her spare key and she describes the carnage they discovered:

> I found my sister alone in the house. She was lying on her right side in front of the fire-place, her head being in a pool of blood. My sister made no answer when I spoke to her. I saw that three chairs, a wooden footstool, a kerb, a grate winter or slider and a kettle were all broken and lying on the floor. All of them seemed to be more or less bespattered with blood. There were three china or delf jugs broken also. There were spots of blood in front of the grate. The constable lifted my sister to another part of the floor. Her head was bleeding. Her hands and arms were also bleeding. An ambulance was brought and my sister was removed to the Royal Infirmary.[72]

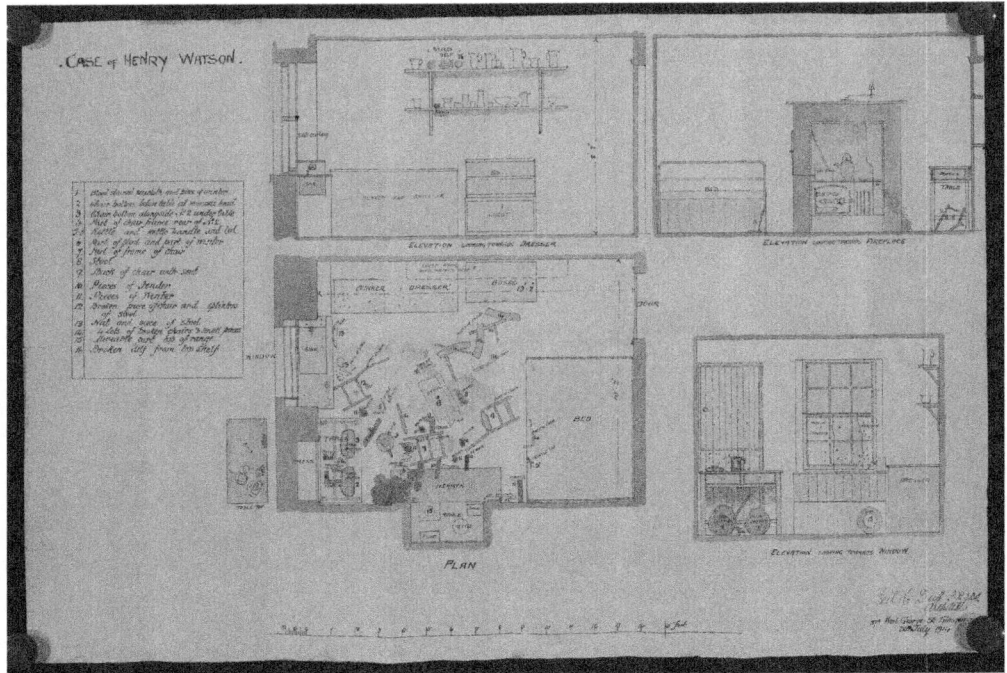

Figure 3.28 Plan of Crime Scene - Case Against Henry Watson, 1914.

The extent of the violence perpetrated against Agnes Watson was skilfully depicted in a detailed drawing of the crime scene requested by the police officer who headed up the investigation into the assault, Chief Detective Inspector John Dempster. Figure 3.28 clearly shows the damage done to the room the couple were in and the volume and scope of the bloodshed carefully recorded indicates the severity of the assault carried out upon the victim.[79]

Testimony regarding the assault was also provided from a range of other individuals including two of Henry Watson's children, who seemed to get on well with their step-mother but were not willing to suggest that their father was in any way directly implicated in what happened to her. However, it was alleged that when his sixteen-year-old daughter, also called Agnes, had heard about the incident she exclaimed 'Oh, what has my father done now', which suggests that she may well have been aware of previous altercations and abuse.[74] Another of Agnes's sisters, Isabella McWilliams testified to the history of the abuse between the couple reporting that, from what she had witnessed, her sister Agnes lived '...in a state of great terror' whilst she was with Henry Watson. Agnes had told her that her husband had repeatedly been '...locking her up in the house, striking her and pulling her by the hair' and that this kind of abuse had occurred when she was pregnant with their child. Yet, despite knowing this, when the couple stayed with her one time and an argument broke out between them, Isabella did not intervene in the quarrel going on, and Agnes was assaulted once more.[75]

In a similar vein, although various neighbours came forward to offer testimony to the couples 'frequent quarrels', to the repeated 'screaming' of Agnes Watson and to the assault which occurred in July of 1914, few of them could give specific details of what actually transpired within 58 Green Street, Bridgeton, that evening as they too had refused to interpose in the episode. One woman said she was 'too afraid' to do so and a man said he '...did not want to get into any trouble myself.'[76] What this testimony does reveal however, is further clues to the factors which made this marriage so unhappy and so turbulent. One neighbour, Jeannie Campbell, who lived next door to the couple when she lived in Rutherglen after Henry and Agnes were first married noted that Watson '...thrashed her when something was done in the house that he did not approve of.' For instance, when their son Sidney was newly-born, Agnes had bought a feeding bottle for the child, but Henry objected and wanted her to feed the child by spoon. This particular disagreement, resulted in the brutal assault in 1912 for which Henry was imprisoned.[77]

On the 5th of August 1914 Dr James Maxtone Thom, Superintendent at Glasgow's Royal Infirmary provided a written report to the police on the condition of his patient Agnes Watson when she first arrived at the hospital in the immediate aftermath of the assault on the 27th of July 1914. He noted:

> On admission she was unconscious and suffering from considerable shock. Her pulse was 120, respiration 30, and temperature sub-normal...On

examination it was found that she had eight different scalp wounds which extended down to the cranial bones. These wounds were distributed mostly over the front part of the scalp area and two extended about an inch down to the forehead. The right ear was completely severed in two parts – the soft tissues for about half an inch in front and behind the ear were also out in line with the ear wounds. No fracture of the skull could be found. Her right arm and right and left hands showed cuts and bruises. Her eyes were both ecchymosed (blackened). She was apparently suffering from concussion. She remained unconscious for three days when she gradually regained consciousness…When spoken to she replies very slowly…I believe her mental condition is not absolutely normal at present… [and] She is slightly deaf. Her life was endangered at the time of injury, but at present I think her out of danger. I cannot at present state that her present mental condition will be permanent, but it is possible it may be.[78]

The police arrested Henry Watson soon after the incident. They testified that his clothes and personal effects '…bore stains of blood' and that one of his hands showed signs of recent injury with his thumb, knuckle and finger wounded. They also reported that when the accused was in custody and was being charged with the assault he said in reply to the officers present: 'I did not strike her with my fists. I lost my temper.' The officers described Watson as being '…quite sober but a little excited.' [79]

When preparing the case for trial, Dr Maxtone Thom was contacted once more by the police and the Procurator Fiscal to determine whether they would be able to call Agnes Watson as a witness for the prosecution in the trial against her husband. Maxtone Thom wrote a letter in reply to this request for information on the 19th of August 1914 saying that although Mrs Watson had recovered from many of the physical injuries she had received '…I do not consider she is able to make an intelligent statement at present. It is beyond any power to say whether she will be fundamentally defective mentally. There is a possibility that she may be.'[80] In the wake of the receipt of this commentary, the prosecution pressed ahead with the trial without hearing testimony from the victim, being determined nonetheless to get a conviction in this case. Indeed, in his letter outlining his decision not to call Agnes Watson as a witness, the Procurator Fiscal, James N. Hart states: 'The assault was undoubtedly a brutal one and [the] accused is well deserving of penal servitude.'[81]

Although it is often highly unusual to glean any evidence of the state of mind of either a defendant or a victim in interpersonal assault cases of this type, we do see a glimpse of the kind of man Henry Watson was, from a letter he wrote to his children whilst in Duke Street Prison on the 1st of August 1914.[82] In this note it is evident that Watson was a man who cared deeply for his children and who looked after them to the very best of his ability. He reminds the older children of a medical appointment that one of their younger siblings need to keep at the Eye Infirmary and advises them on how to make ends meet whilst he is incarcerated, giving them his permission to sell any of his belongings if it ensures they '...be as happy as comfortable' as possible. He describes himself as being 'sad' as it was soon to be his birthday and he was spending it alone, but encouraged the children to visit and to write long letters to him which he would be 'anxious' to receive.

Any sympathy the neutral observer might feel towards the accused when reading this correspondence dissipates somewhat when Henry Watson discusses the incident for which he was imprisoned. He states:

> This is a terrible example for a father to show his children, but mother altogether refused to return home and bring back your little brother Sidney and I felt so disappointed and miserable with her refusal to return and complete the family circle that I assaulted her I doubt seriously.

As well as an admission of guilt, this comment seems to apportion some of the blame for the assault on the victim and her decision not to return to an abusive relationship with her young child. It also indicates that Henry Watson did not fully appreciate the seriousness of the assault he had conducted; that the injuries he had inflicted on his wife may have done long-term damage to both her hearing and her mental capacity.

In any event, no trial in this case actually took place. This is because on the 25th of August 1914, the Procurator Fiscal received a letter from the lawyers acting on behalf of Henry Watson saying that the accused would plead guilty to the charges against him on condition that reference to a kerb being used in the assault was dropped from the indictment.[83] Did Henry Watson learn the extent of the damage he had done to his wife rendering him more remorseful for what he had done? Did he simply tire of waiting for the case to be resolved? Or was this decision one which his lawyers had encouraged, based on the weight of evidence against him? We cannot know the answer to these questions. What we do know is that this request was accepted by the prosecution. Henry Watson consequently entered a guilty plea to the revised indictment and was remitted to the High Court of Justiciary in Edinburgh to learn his punishment.[84] On the 16th of September 1914, Lord Guthrie sentenced Henry Watson to nine months imprisonment.[85] From what we have seen with regard to sentencing in cases like these, this particular punishment was unusually severe, and was undoubtedly due to the involvement of the High Court in the decision-making process and the accused's violent recidivism.

The case against Henry Watson highlights and indeed illuminates much of what has been considered in this chapter in relation to domestic interpersonal violence in the Scottish context since 1600. In the first instance, the case shows that informal separations could occur without recourse to the law courts, depending on the specific preferences or needs of the individuals involved.[86] Although it was easier to obtain a divorce in Scotland compared to

England until 1923 as most wives were largely financially dependent on their husbands, recourse to a formal separation was limited to wealthier individuals who could afford the court fees and the alimony arrangements after the fact.[87] In any case, divorce on the grounds of cruelty was not permitted in Scotland until the Divorce (Scotland) Act of 1938, so Agnes Watson could not have brought a petition on those grounds in 1914.[88] She could have applied to the Court of Session for a formal separation instead, but again, the expense of this process, the highly unpredictable nature of the outcome, and the social stigma associated with any sort of legal proceedings regarding marital relationships may have deterred her.[89]

The Watson case also highlights that within a context of violence (perhaps especially when a young child was involved) women would tolerate abuse only to a certain extent and were quite prepared to lean upon local and kinship networks to support them when things became too difficult. However, and as we have seen, those networks were only able, or prepared, to offer a limited degree of assistance. The private sphere of the home, or rather, the private sphere of the marital relationship was still bounded, and to some extent impenetrable, even by the early twentieth century. Change, if it was to occur in the context of a violent relationship, had to be enacted by the husband or the wife concerned. Intervention by others, was limited and its consequences unpredictable.

The Henry Watson case also indicates that, as with many instances of domestic violence, the abuse had occurred over a long history and often the aggressor in the relationship had previous convictions for interpersonal assault. In terms of prevailing motives for this ongoing abuse, it is of note that drink was evidently *not* a catalytic factor in this case study, but may well have been in numerous other like instances. Instead, it seems that power and control were the key factors which triggered violence between Henry and Agnes Watson. Agnes thought that domestic duties were her domain in the household. However, Henry had other ideas and his constant intervention and reprimanding of Agnes in these matters inevitably caused tensions. When Agnes then tried to defend her practices or behaviour to her husband, he took this to be a challenge to his patriarchal authority and sought to control his wife and restore her diligence and subservience through violent means. The fact that Henry often carried out his assaults in the full view of witnesses, including two of his sisters-in-law, suggests that he believed he had more than a degree of legitimacy in deploying aggressive forms of correction. Alternatively, and as the letter he wrote to his children arguably suggests, perhaps Henry Watson naively assumed that his aggression was not particularly serious and would not have a significant impact or legacy. As we have seen elsewhere in this chapter, the kind of situation depicted in this case study was not new: the battle for domestic supremacy in Scottish households was long and bloody and indeed, seems to be far from over.[90]

Finally, and on a more positive note, we can see something of a deter-mined attitude amongst and between the police, medical professionals and the judicial authorities in this case. All of the agencies involved were dogged in their resolve to get a conviction against Henry Watson in order to protect Agnes from further abuse. Whilst it is evident from content elsewhere in this chapter that such determined efforts were more the exception than the norm, and that the courts were often used as a tool for mediation rather than sanc-tion, it is clear that by the more modern era, the Scottish authorities, slowly but surely came to realise that domestic violence was a significant problem that needed to be addressed and ought to no longer be hidden behind closed doors and closed relationships. Although the degree of success they have had to date is certainly debatable, in this particular instance in 1914, the detailed investigations and collaborative working of the professional services involved (including pushing the sentencing to the High Court to guarantee that a stiff penalty ensued) ensured that the right result was delivered in the end. Whether Henry Watson continued to be a violent man after his release from prison is not known.

Conclusion – The Violent North?

Non-fatal interpersonal violence in Scotland between 1660 and 1960 was overwhelmingly dominated by male assailants. They tended to attack indi-viduals they knew and did so in order to dominate or control their victims or because they felt they had a legitimate grievance which could only be resolved by conflict. Often, and as is ably demonstrated by the domestic violence case study above, the abuse and aggression involved in such attacks could be pro-longed and excessive, but it was typically unplanned. Forms of assault, in both the public and the private context, were by far the most commonly indicted forms of interpersonal violence in Scotland between 1660 and 1960. However, the data presented above does not necessarily point to endemic violence in the Scottish context. Rather the levels of this form of criminality are largely inconsistent over time and, if anything, a general downward trend in incidence is apparent from the post 1805 period onwards. Indeed, even in relation to the highest data points in evidence, the number of cases concerned are proportionately small in comparison to assault prosecutions brought be-fore English magistrates' courts alone over the same period.[91] Once again then, the supposedly pervasive nature of violence in Scotland is not borne out by the statistical evidence regarding recorded instances of assault. However, interesting evidence which suggests the existence of a persistent problem with violent recidivism in the Scottish context along with evident examples of extreme but occasional violence throughout the nation's history, indicate that some nuances may yet be required regarding this conclusion should further research allow.

Notes

1 A.M. Anderson (1904 edition) *The Criminal Law of Scotland* (Edinburgh: Bell and Bradfute), Part II, p. 158.

2 As sexual assault has already been investigated in the previous chapter it will not be re-examined here. In addition, due to the limits of space, this section will not consider indirect forms of interpersonal assault such as insult, slander, defamation and threatening in either verbal and/or written form. For more on these offences in early Scottish history see E. Ewan (2002) '"Many Injurious Words": Defamation and Gender in Late Medieval Scotland' in R.A. McDonald (ed) *History, Literature, and Music in Scotland, 700–1560* (London and Toronto: University of Toronto Press), pp. 162–186; J.R.D. Falconer (2013) *Crime and Community in Reformation Scotland: Negotiating Power in a Burgh Society* (London: Pickering & Chatto), chapter four and G. Parker (1988) 'The "Kirk By Law Established" and the Origins of "The Taming of Scotland": St Andrews 1559–1600' in L. Leneman (ed) *Perspectives in Scottish Social History – Essays in Honour of Rosalind Mitchison* (Aberdeen: Aberdeen University Press), pp. 1–32.

3 Baron D. Hume (1797) Commentaries on the Laws of Scotland Respecting the Description and Punishment of Crimes – Volume II (Edinburgh: Bell and Bradfute), p. 20.

4 See for instance a recent case at Kilmarnock Sheriff Court in 2015 –*Daily Mail*, 9th July 2015, p. 6.

5 Hume (1797) Commentaries – Volume II, p. 20.

6 *Ibid*, pp. 20–21.

7 *Ibid*, p. 21.

8 For further discussion of the different legal conditions relating to this offence see *ibid*, pp. 24–36

9 *Ibid*, pp. 165–166.

10 See D.G. Barrie and S. Broomhall (2014) Police Courts in Nineteenth-Century Scotland: Volume 2 - Boundaries, Behaviours and Bodies (Farnham: Ashgate), pp. 36–40.

11 Hume (1797) Commentaries – Volume II, p. 184.

12 For an exception to this see A.-M. Kilday (2016) '"Sugar and Spice and All Things Nice"? Violence against Parents in Scotland, 1700–1850', *Journal of Family History*, 41, 3, pp. 318–335.

13 For further discussion see A.-M. Kilday (2007) *Women and Violent Crime in Enlightenment* Scotland (Woodbridge: Boydell Press), chapter five. See also Hume (1797) *Commentaries – Volume II*, p. 55–56. For more on the courts as mediator especially in instances of domestic violence see J. Carter Wood (2004) *Violence and Crime in Nineteenth-Century England: The Shadow of Our Refinement* (London: Routledge), pp. 60–61 and especially A. Hughes (2010) 'The "Non-Criminal" Class: Wife-Beating in Scotland (c. 1800–1949)', *Crime, History and Societies*, 14, 2, pp. 31–54 at p. 32 and pp. 48–52.

14 Hume (1797) *Commentaries – Volume II*, p. 47. My addition in parenthesis.

15 It should be noted that indictments for hamesucken were too insignificant in number to warrant a trend analysis over the 1805–1960 period.

16 *Parliamentary Papers*, 1 Edw. 8 and 1 Geo. 6 c. 12 (1937).

17 Although legislation relating to the appropriate parties to investigate child abuse was passed in Scotland in 1968, it was not until the Children (Scotland) Act of 1995 that the issue was seriously considered within the Scottish legal context – see *The Guardian*, 18th May 2005, p. 17. For further discussion of the late recognition of child abuse as a problem see M. May (1978) 'Violence in the Family: An

Historical Perspective' in J.P. Martin (ed) *Violence and The Family* (Chichester: John Wiley and Sons), pp. 135–167 at pp. 150–162; M.D.A. Freeman (1979) *Violence in the Home: A Socio-Legal Study* (Farnborough: Gower), pp. 13–107 and especially M. Flegel (2009) *Conceptualizing Cruelty to Children in Nineteenth-Century England: Literature, Representation, and the NSPCC* (Farnham: Ashgate).

18   For further discussion see R. Phillips (1988) *Putting Asunder: A History of Divorce in Western Society* (Cambridge: Cambridge University Press), pp. 330–331; M.J. Wiener (2001) 'Alice Arden to Bill Sikes: Changing Nightmares of Intimate Violence in England, 1558–1869', *Journal of British Studies*, 40, 2, pp. 184–212 at pp. 211–212; A. Clark (2000) 'Domesticity and the Problem of Wifebeating in Nineteenth-Century Britain: Working-class Culture, Law and Politics' in S. D'Cruze (ed) *Everyday Violence in Britain, 1850–1950* (Harlow: Pearson), pp. 27–40; Freeman (1979) *Violence*, pp. 127–239 and especially M.E. Doggett (1993) *Marriage, Wife-Beating and the Law in Victorian England* (Columbia, SC: University of South Carolina Press).

19   See C. Connelly (2015) 'Effecting Change in the Legal Response to Domestic Abuse', *A History of Working-Class Marriage – Learning from the Past, Looking to the Future: Session 1 – Domestic Abuse and the Law* (University of Glasgow) available at   http://workingclassmarriage.gla.ac.uk/wp-content/uploads/2013/11/clare_connelly.mp3, accessed 24th October 2016.

20   For further discussion see *ibid*.

21   It should be noted that no indictment data was available for this offence in the judicial statistics prior to 1830. In addition, there was no conviction data available for any of the offences investigated in this chapter prior to 1830, so the analysis of the indictment to conviction rate was carried out from that date onwards.

22   It should be noted that in relation to the judicial statistics of the assault of authority and the general category of assault, the years 1897–1899 were problematic as this was when data from the Burgh and Police Courts was introduced to the published material. For these years, the judicial statistics were recorded as sums of cumulative data from all the preceding years of the nineteenth century when the material from these courts had been recorded but not published. The significant numbers thus recorded for 1897–1899 falsely skew the time series data to an overwhelming degree. Thus, to rectify this problem, the published data was removed and linear extrapolation calculations were used instead.

23   See Kilday (2007) *Women and Violent Crime*, pp. 97–102.

24   See for instance E. Ewan (2011) 'Impatient Griseldas: Women and the Perpetration of Violence in Sixteenth-Century Glasgow', *Florilegium*, 28, pp. 149–168; E. Ewan (2010) 'Disorderly Damsels? Women and Interpersonal Violence in Pre-Reformation Scotland', *The Scottish Historical Review*, 84, 2, pp. 153–171; Kilday (2007) *Women and Violent Crime*, chapter five; A.-M. Kilday (2013) '"Outrageous Acts and Everyday Rebellions": Criminal Women in Eighteenth-Century Scotland' in K. Barclay and D. Simonton (eds) *Women in Eighteenth-Century Scotland: Intimate, Intellectual and Public Loves* (Farnham: Ashgate), pp. 253–270; K. Barclay (2011) *Love, Intimacy and Power: Marriage and Patriarchy in Scotland, 1650–1850* (Manchester: Manchester University Press), pp. 193–914 and Barrie and Broomhall (2014) *Police Courts*, pp. 60–75.

25   For similar evidence of a gender disparity in interpersonal assault see Falconer (2013) *Crime and Community*, pp. 124–125; J. Warner and A. Lunny (2003) 'Marital Violence in a Martial Town: Husbands and Wives in Early Modern Portsmouth, 1653–1781', *Journal of Family History*, 28, 2, pp. 258–276 at p. 261; M. Hunt (1992) 'Wife Beating, Domesticity and Women's Independence in Eighteenth-Century London', *Gender and History*, 4, 1, pp. 10–33 at pp. 18–19; D.D. Gray (2009) *Crime,*

Prosecution and Social Relations: The Summary Courts of the City of London in the late Eighteenth Century (Basingstoke: Palgrave), p. 96; J. Bailey (2003) *Unquiet Lives: Marriage and Marriage Breakdown in England, 1660–1800* (Cambridge: Cambridge University Press), p. 110 and N. Tomes (1978) 'A "Torrent of Abuse": Crimes of Violence Between Working-Class Men and Women in London 1840–1875', *Journal of Social History*, 11, 3, pp. 328–345 at p. 330.

26 For further evidence of this see Kilday (2013) 'Outrageous Acts', pp. 246–265 and J. Ruff (2001) *Violence in Early Modern Europe, 1500–1800* (Cambridge: Cambridge University Press), p. 117.

27 See for instance Kilday (2007) *Women and Violent Crime*, p. 99.

28 See for instance *ibid*.

29 The same also appears to have been the case in earlier Scottish history see J.R.D. Falconer (2010) "Mony Utheris Divars Odious Crymes": Women, Petty Crime and Power in Later Sixteenth Century Aberdeen', *Crimes and Misdemeanours*, 4, 1, pp. 7–36 at p. 18, 20 and 33. For evidence of supremacy as a key factor in instances of intimate assault in Scotland within the 1660–1960 period see Barclay (2011) *Love*, p. 183 and pp. 186–192 and A. Hughes (2002) 'Working Class Culture, Family Life and Domestic Violence on Clydeside, c. 1918–1939 – A View from Below', *Scottish Tradition*, 27, pp. 60–94. For evidence of this elsewhere see E. Foyster (2005) *Marital Violence: An English Family History, 1660–1857* (Cambridge: Cambridge University Press), pp. 8–9 and p. 39; E. Ross (1982) '"Fierce Questions and Taunts": Married Life in Working-Class London, 1870–1914', *Feminist Studies*, 8, 3, pp. 575–602; S. D'Cruze (1998) *Crimes of Outrage: Sex, Violence and Victorian Working* Women (London: Routledge), p. 68 and Freeman (1979) *Violence*, p. 142 and 146.

30 See for instance J.R.D. Falconer (2008) 'A Family Affair: Households, Misbehaving and the Community in Sixteenth-Century Aberdeen' in E. Ewan and J. Nugent (eds) *Finding the Family in Medieval and Early Modern Scotland* (Farnham: Ashgate), pp. 139–150 at p. 139; Ruff (2001) *Violence*, p. 117 and 124 and J. Archer (2000) '"Men Behaving Badly"?; Masculinity and the Uses of Violence, 1850–1900' in D'Cruze (ed) *Everyday Violence*, pp. 41–54 at p. 43 and 47.

31 For further discussion see Kilday (2007) *Women and Violent Crime*, chapter five; Gray (2009) *Crime*, p. 96; Bailey (2003) *Unquiet Lives*, pp. 117–121; Tomes (1978) 'A "Torrent of Abuse"', p. 331 and A.J. Hammerton (1992) *Cruelty and Companionship: Conflict in Nineteenth-Century Married Life* (London: Routledge), pp. 45–46.

32 For more on the abuse of children and servants in the domestic arena see P. Rushton (1991) 'The Matter in Variance: Adolescents and Domestic Conflict in the Pre-Industrial Economy of Northeast England, 1600–1800', *Journal of Social History*, 25, 1, pp. 89–107; Bailey (2003) *Unquiet Lives*, p. 117; R.B. Shoemaker (1991 edition) *Prosecution and Punishment: Petty Crime and Law in London and Rural Middlesex, c. 1660–1725* (Cambridge: Cambridge University Press), pp. 174–175; E.A. Foyster (1999) 'Silent Witnesses? Children and the Breakdown of Domestic and Social Order in Early Modern England' in A. Fletcher and S. Hussey (eds) *Childhood in Question: Children, Parents and the State* (Manchester: Manchester University Press), pp. 57–73; Foyster (2005) *Marital Violence*, pp. 128–161 and D. Hay (2000) 'Master and Servant in England: Using the Law in the Eighteenth and Nineteenth Centuries' in W. Steinmetz (ed) *Private Law and Social Inequality in the Industrial Age: Comparing Legal Cultures in Britain, France, Germany and the United States* (Oxford: Oxford University Press), pp. 226–264.

33 For further discussion see Gray (2009) *Crime*, pp. 100–101; Foyster (2005) *Marital Violence*, p. 16 and 24; Hammerton (1992) *Cruelty*, p. 40; A. Hughes (2004)

'Representations and Counter-Representations of Domestic Violence on Clyde-side Between the Two World Wars', *Labour History Review*, 69, 2, pp. 169–184 at p. 178 and E.A. Stanko (1985) *Intimate Intrusions: Women's Experience of Male Violence* (London: Routledge), p. 57.

34 The importance of alcohol and interpersonal violence has been debated by historians see Ruff (2001) *Violence*, pp. 126–128; Gray (2009) *Crime*, p. 97; Hammerton (1992) *Cruelty*, pp. 46–47; Carter Wood (2004) *Violence*, p. 62, 76 and 103; D'Cruze (1998) *Crimes of Outrage*, p. 66; J. Rowbotham (2000) '"Only When Drunk": The Stereotyping of Violence in England, c. 1850–1900' in D'Cruze (ed) *Everyday Violence*, pp. 155–169; Archer (2000) '"Men Behaving Badly"?', p. 49; Foyster (2005) *Marital Violence*, p. x; Freeman (1979) *Violence in the Home*, p. 138; Hughes (2004) 'Representations', pp. 169–184 and L. Stone (1990) *Road to Divorce: England 1530–1987* (Oxford: Oxford University Press), p. 198.

35 See L. Leneman (1997) '"A Tyrant and Tormentor": Violence against Wives in Eighteenth- and Early Nineteenth-Century Scotland', *Continuity and Change*, 12, 1, pp. 31–54 at p. 42; S. Broomhall and D.G. Barrie (2012) 'Making Men: Media, Magistrates and the Representation of Masculinity in Scottish Police Courts, 1800–35' in D.G. Barrie and S. Broomhall (eds) *A History of Police and Masculinities, 1700–2010* (London: Routledge), pp. 72–101 at p. 80; C.A. Conley (2007) *Certain Other Countries: Homicide, Gender and National Identity in Late Nineteenth Century England, Ireland, Scotland and Wales* (Columbus: Ohio State University Press), p. 25 and Hughes (2010) 'The "Non-Criminal" Class', p. 39–41 and 51.

36 For further discussion in a modern Scottish context see A. Hughes (2010) *Gender and Political Identities in Scotland, 1919–1939* (Edinburgh: Edinburgh University Press), pp. 130–131. See also Foyster (2005) *Marital Violence*, p. 52; Ross (1982) 'Fierce Questions', pp. 576–584 and D'Cruze (1998) *Crimes of Outrage*, pp. 66–67.

37 For further discussion see Kilday (2007) *Women and Violent Crime*, chapter five; D.D. Gray (2007) 'The Regulation of Violence in the Metropolis: The Prosecution of Assault in the Summary Courts, c.1780–1820', *The London Journal*, 32, 1, pp. 75–87; Gray (2009) *Crime*, p. 104 and Archer (2000) '"Men Behaving Badly"?', p. 45.

38 For similar evidence regarding the nature of weapons used in intimate violence elsewhere see Bailey (2003) *Unquiet Lives*, p. 124 and D'Cruze (1998) *Crimes of Outrage*, p. 67.

39 See for instance Kilday (2013) 'Outrageous Acts', p. 268 and D'Cruze (1998) *Crimes of Outrage*, p. 67.

40 For similar evidence of this elsewhere see Ruff (2001) *Violence*, p. 129 and p. 137 and Archer (2000) '"Men Behaving Badly"?', p. 46.

41 See for instance Barclay (2011) *Love*, p. 181; Bailey (2003) *Unquiet Lives*, p. 123; Tomes (1978) 'A "Torrent of Abuse"', p. 329 and Ross (1982) 'Fierce Questions', p. 592.

42 See Tomes (1978) 'A "Torrent of Abuse"', pp. 336–338; Hammerton (1992) *Cruelty*, pp. 53–54, p. 164 and p. 169; Carter Wood (2004) *Violence*, p. 61, 53 and 125 and especially Hughes (2010) 'The "Non-Criminal" Class', p. 52; Stanko (1985) *Intimate Intrusions*, p. 50 and R.E. Dobash and R.P. Dobash (1992) *Women, Violence and Social Change* (London: Routledge), *passim*.

43 Such surveillance was evident early on in Scottish history and persisted through the centuries under consideration in this volume see for instance J. Nugent (2010) '"None Must Meddle Between Man and Wife": Assessing Family and the Fluidity of Public and Private in Early Modern Scotland', *Journal of Family History*, 35, 3, pp. 219–321 at pp. 222–227.

44 For further discussion in the Scottish context see *ibid*, pp. 219–231. For elsewhere see Tomes (1978) 'A "Torrent of Abuse"', p. 335; Hammerton (1992) *Cruelty*, p. 43 and D'Cruze (1998) *Crimes of Outrage*, p. 69 and 76.

45 For further discussion see Hughes (2010) 'The "Non-Criminal" Class', p. 32.

46 See www.thepeerage.com for further details.

47 National Records of Scotland (NRS), High Court of Justiciary, Books of Adjournal, JC3/8.

48 *Ibid*. The phrase "whore's burd" which was underlined in the indictment, effectively means 'bastard' or child of a prostitute – see G. Williams (1994 edition) *A Dictionary of Sexual Language and Imagery in Shakespearean and Stuart Literature* (London: Athlone Press), Volume III, p. 1527.

49 *Ibid* – my addition in parenthesis.

50 Ibid.

51 NRS, High Court of Justiciary, Books of Adjournal, JC3/8 – my addition in parenthesis.

52 For the legal debate that ensued in this case see *ibid*.

53 *Parliamentary Papers*, 4 Geo. I (1717).

54 Although there were some notable amnesty exemptions stated in this Act (largely Jacobite supporters directly involved in the 1715 Rising), in the main, the legislation did seem to suggest that its application ought to be very broad – see A. Boyer (1717) *The Political State of Great Britain – Volume XIV* (London: T. Warner), pp. 59–72.

55 For the details of this case see NRS, Miscellaneous Small Collections of Family, Business and Other Papers, GD1/616/67.

56 Ibid.

57 *Ibid* – my addition in parenthesis.

58 Ibid.

59 For further discussion see M. Maclaurin (1774) Arguments and Decisions In Remarkable Cases, Before the High Court of Justiciary, and other Supreme Courts in Scotland (Edinburgh and London: Bell and Dilly), pp. 142–143.

60 NRS, High Court of Justiciary, South Circuit Minute Books, JC12/17.

61 NRS, High Court of Justiciary, Process Papers, JC26/161.

62 Ibid.

63 NRS, High Court of Justiciary, South Circuit Minute Books, JC12/17.

64 Ibid.

65 Ibid.

66 NRS, Justiciary Court, Precognition Papers, AD15/14/35 – Note to this effect found on 'List of Productions' printed on the back of the 1914 indictment. See also the commentary of James N. Hart, Procurator Fiscal dated 29th July 1914 in the same file and NRS, Justiciary Court, Process Papers, Extract from the Police Court of Rutherglen, JC26/1914/105.

67 NRS, Justiciary Court, Precognition Papers, Indictment, AD15/14/35.

68 NRS, Justiciary Court, Precognition Papers, Testimony of Martha McWilliams, AD15/14/35/1.

69 Aliment is the sum paid or allowance given in Scots Law in respect of the reciprocal obligation of parents and children, husband and wife, grandparents and grandchildren, etc. to contribute to each other's maintenance.

70 NRS, Justiciary Court, Precognition Papers, Testimony of Martha McWilliams, AD15/14/35/1.

71 Ibid.

72 *Ibid*. A kerb was used to keep coal from falling out of the fire-place. A winter was a grate taken from the oven to keep plates of food warm on a table. 'Delf' was

Delft china purchased for everyday use. Police Constable George Paul corroborated the description of the scene provided by Martha McWilliams – see *ibid*, Testimony of George Paul, Constable, Eastern District Glasgow Police.

73 NRS, Plan of Crime Scene in the Case Against Henry Watson by Neil Duff Architect, RHP 140365, reproduced with the kind permission of The National Records of Scotland. Although precognition papers could include drawings of wounds received to bodies and maps of crime locations, to date I have never come across another detailed drawing of a crime scene like this, so I am unsure how common the production of such illustrations were in court. See also NRS, Justiciary Court, Precognition Papers, Testimony of John Dempster, Chief Detective Inspector, Eastern District Glasgow Police, AD15/14/35/1.

74 NRS, Justiciary Court, Precognition Papers, Testimony of Agnes Hay Duncan Watson, AD15/14/35/1.

75 *Ibid*, testimony of Isabella McWilliams.

76 See for instance *ibid*, testimonies of Margaret McInnes, Janet Purves, Hannah Logan Kerr, Jane Logan McAlpine and Joseph Kerr.

77 *Ibid*, testimony of Jeannie Campbell.

78 *Ibid*, medical notes of J. Maxtone Thom dated 5th April 1914. My addition in parenthesis.

79 *Ibid*, testimony of John Dempster, Chief Detective Inspector, Eastern District Glasgow Police and NRS, Justiciary Court, Precognition Papers, Testimonies of William Rae, Lieutenant and Andrew Cooke, Detective Constable, both Eastern District Glasgow Police, AD15/14/35/2.

80 *Ibid*, letter from J. Maxtone Thom dated 19th April 1914.

81 *Ibid*, letter from James N. Hart, Procurator Fiscal dated 20th August 1914. My addition in parenthesis.

82 NRS, Justiciary Court, Process Papers, Transcript of Letter from Henry Watson to his Children dated 1st August 1914, JC26/1914/105.

83 NRS, Justiciary Court, Precognition Papers, Letter to James N. Hart, Procurator Fiscal dated 25th August 1914, AD15/14/35.

84 *Ibid*, see telegram reporting the same dated 31st August 1914 as well as a letter from James N. Hart, Procurator Fiscal of the same date.

85 *Ibid*, notes on sentence dated 16th September 1914.

86 L. Leneman (1996) '"Disregarding the Matrimonial Vows": Divorce in Eighteenth and Early Nineteenth Century Scotland', *Journal of Social History*, 30, 2, pp. 465–482.

87 For further discussion see C.J. Guthrie (1910) 'The History of Divorce in Scotland', *Scottish Historical Review*, 8, 29, pp. 39–52 and L. Leneman (2000) '"A Natural Foundation in Equity": Marriage and Divorce in Eighteenth and Nineteenth-Century Scotland', *Scottish Economic and Social History*, 20, 2, pp. 199–215. For more on the English experience of divorce by comparison, see Stone (1990) *Road to Divorce, passim*.

88 *Parliamentary Papers*, 1 and 2 Geo. 6 (1938).

89 For further discussion see L. Leneman (1998) *Alienated Affections: The Scottish Experience of Divorce and Separation, 1684–1830* (Edinburgh: Edinburgh University Press).

90 See for instance www.gov.scot/Topics/People/Equality/violence-women/Key-Facts as well as www.scottishwomensaid.org.uk/ and www.abusedmeninscotland.org/.

91 See for instance C. Emsley (2005) *Hard Men and Violence in England Since 1750* (London: Hambledon and London), p. 23.

Chapter 4

The Violent North? Communal Violence, 1660–1960

Introduction

A study of popular disturbances is important to any work undertaking an analysis of criminal activity in a given place over a long chronology as, according to historian John Stevenson, it can provide '…historians with a "window" on the attitudes and assumptions of otherwise inaccessible sections of the population.'[1] In Scotland, particularly before the franchise was fully extended and provided an alternative outlet for local and national grievances, there appeared to be something of a tradition of resistance.[2] The nation's history shows that fleeting but intense episodes of communal violence occurred throughout the country at different intervals across time, and for a multifarious range of reasons. Although Scotland did not experience popular disturbances on a dramatically collective scale, as was arguably the case elsewhere in Europe during the premodern period,[3] resistance at a more local level was nonetheless an endemic feature of Scottish social life and something akin to what historian Bill Knox has termed a 'riotous culture' evidently prevailed, as this chapter will demonstrate.[4]

Unlike the other categories of interpersonal violence investigated thus far, communal violence and violence for gain (or robbery which we will address in the next chapter), are offences which have undergone significant transformation over time with regard to the nature, function and format of the criminal enterprises involved in their perpetration. Although there have been some changes in the perpetration of homicide and types of assault in Scottish history, these changes have been principally to do with nuances in methodology and enhanced visibility through the more dedicated detection and reporting of offences, rather than any shifts in perpetration that could be considered transformative. In this chapter and the next, therefore, an extra section of analysis will be added to scrutinise the changing chronology of some types of offending in Scotland from 1660 to 1960.

A Chronology of Scottish Communal Violence

As has already been alluded to in the introductory chapter, one of the most in-teresting and intense debates to occupy Scottish scholarship in recent decades is the extent to which communal violence prevailed in Scotland during the seventeenth and eighteenth centuries. As we have seen, some historians, such as T.C. Smout and T.M. Devine, have put forward the so-called 'orthodoxy of passivity' thesis, where they argue that aside from a few sporadic riotous episodes, Scotland was largely exempt from the kind of popular disturbances evident elsewhere in the early modern period. Social calm prevailed, not social revolt.[5] Although this historiography has been nuanced over time to suggest that there was perhaps a regional dimension to this 'orthodoxy of passivity', with the lowland area of the country seen as effectively stable and parts of the highlands seen as more rebellious, by and large this thesis empha-sises the general acquiescence of the Scots to changes affecting their everyday lives.[6] It has been explained that a range of factors mitigated against resistance and ensured compliance in the Scottish context.[7]

Contemporaries, however, thought the Scots to be somewhat different in character from their portrayal in this thesis of passivity. On the 19th of July 1784, the Lord Justice Clerk Thomas Miller wrote to his peers in London of his fears regarding Scottish rioters saying:

> For some time past, a spirit of disorder, a contempt of the laws, and a *proneness* to resist the execution of them has infected the minds of the lower class of people very generally. So that in every part of the country, and more every part of the country, and more particularly in populous towns and citys, we have a lawless force of Mob, ready, upon any emer-gency to execute what their own imagination or a hint from a secrete enemy to the public peace may suggest.[8]

Moreover, recent academic research has shown that these opinions do not appear to be sensationalised hyperbole. Scholarship based on exhaustively detailed analysis of archival records has rejected the 'orthodoxy of passivity' or at least suggested that it needs to be substantially redrawn. Whilst, it is true to say that Scotland did not experience riots on the scale of those elsewhere, as has already been established above, there is evidence to support the no-tion that the Scots were frequently involved in more local, community-based skirmishes and rebellions of one sort or another which have hitherto been ignored by historians or dismissed as isolated incidents.[9] Anti-Union and anti-taxation rebellions, routs concerning forced conscription into the mi-litia, patronage protests and other religious disputes, food riots, political tu-mults, disturbances related to industrial grievances, the writing and sending of incendiary letters, episodes of arson and wilful property damage, minor lawbreaking as protest (such as illegal trespass and ritualised vandalism) and countless assaults on authority figures are routinely documented in the indictment records of the seventeenth and eighteenth century Scottish courts.[10] Considered collectively, these episodes of resistance arguably point to a prevailing orthodoxy of 'participation' rather than 'passivity' when it came to airing grievances, maintaining traditional practices or craving change in Scottish society. In addition, far from being subtle or 'low level' examples of Scottish resistance as some historians have suggested,[11] the evidence relating to the tactics and methodologies deployed by Scottish rioters in the premodern period indicates an explicit determination by some to participate in violent and forceful collective action to ensure the success of the popular will in the face of outside threats.

Whilst participation in popular disturbances of the type clearly continued into the nineteenth century in Scotland,[12] change was nonetheless beginning to occur in relation to the purpose and practice of riotous activity, as well as in attitudes towards its perpetration. The American historian, sociologist and political scientist, Charles Tilly has attempted to chart the nature and evolution of collective violence in Western Europe from the seventeenth century to the present day. He categorised three main forms of this kind of activity. The initial stage involved 'primitive' collective violence which was communal in nature and usually localised and small scale (for example the family feud). This form of disturbance had almost completely died out by the modern period. The second stage, of what he termed 'reactionary' collective violence, was also communally based, but, in contrast, grew out of opposition to national socio-economic and political change (for example the food riot). This phase covers the early modern period which has been addressed in the preceding section of this chapter and extends to the 1830s when it is superseded by the final category, that of 'modern' collective violence, which is based not on communal association but on specific interest groups which promote change rather than resist it (for example the political demonstration).[13] Although Tilly's approach can be criticised for its rigidity, it does suggest nonetheless that there was a transformative nature to European popular disturbances over time.[14]

Scholars of Scottish history have agreed with Charles Tilly and have evidenced gradual changes to the nature and causes of popular disturbances after 1830. For instance, Stana Nenadic has shown that the extension of the franchise across Scotland from this point onwards did dissipate the need for individuals to unite for riotous purposes as often as they had done previously.[15] Violence gave way to voice. In addition, when collective action did occur, it was increasingly in relation to issues of national concern, rather than matters which were localised or of personal interest to the participants.[16] In large part this was because protest (and indeed the populace more widely) became more politicised in Scotland during the nineteenth century.[17] The data below show that riots still occurred during and after this period, and when they did occur, they were less explicitly about socio-economic grievances and more about defending territory, promoting fairness and transparency, and, most importantly, championing the rights of the people.[18] Groups got together to campaign for a cause rather than to resist change, as per Tilly's typology.

As Scotland became more urbanised, the industrial arena became the focal point for much of the collective action which occurred in Scotland after 1830,[19] but in addition to a change in the principle context for protest, the methodology of this kind of disturbance was in the process of changing too. The threat of collective violence, which was so eloquently articulated by certain eighteenth century social and political commentators, was arguably one of the key factors which encouraged the establishment of a police force in Scotland.[20] One of the key duties to be performed by this force was to suppress tumultuous activity and to maintain order. By and large, the police became reasonably effective at this, although on occasion (as shown in two of the three case studies below) they needed reinforcements to quash certain rebellions and reinstate calm. In the face of this state-sanctioned suppressive force, collective *violence* became problematic and protestors had to seek other mechanisms by which to legitimately voice their grievances.[21] Consequently, printed forms of protest, peaceful public demonstrations or strikes came to replace riots, tumults and other acts of communal violence.[22] This was certainly the chronology of collective action in the Scottish Lowlands, but in the Highlands there is an entirely different picture. There, the clearance of impoverished tenants or crofters from their land to make way for sheep, then deer and then fanciful sporting estates, meant that bitter, violent resistance to change via popular protest endured well into the twentieth century.[23] Collective violence in the very North of Scotland did not evolve into peaceful protest akin to the lowland experience till much later on.

By the twentieth century, strikes (and to a lesser extent public demonstrations) had largely replaced riots as the chief mechanism by which collective grievances were voiced in Scotland and indeed elsewhere in Britain.[24] Essentially, and as historian James Cronin has argued, protest was relocated from the marketplace to the workplace.[25] These episodes of collective action varied in size, scale, duration and impact and were both inconsistent and unpredictable in relation to the levels of success they enjoyed.[26] Certainly, the policy of legitimising collective action continued as protest of this sort became even more aligned to politics by the more modern era.[27] Consequently, violence tended to be curbed (typically through the intervention of official or unofficial trade unions and shop stewards) unless antagonism and conflict broke out between the police and the protestors as evidenced by the third case study in this chapter.[28] The causes of strikes and demonstrations were not too dissimilar from the issues that triggered popular protest in earlier periods. The three most divisive features of Scottish society at this time were skill, trade and religion and participants in collective action tended to convene and congregate along these lines.[29] Solidarity was to be found amongst those living a shared experience. Twentieth century protestors, just like their forbears from the early modern period, persisted in their demands for equity and fairness and for greater control over the matters that impacted upon their everyday lives. Evidently, some aspects of collective action and collective violence had been transformed over the course of Scottish history, and some had not.

Communal Violence and the Law

In the same way that the methodology and causes of communal violence and popular protest have changed over time, so too has the legal response to this type of activity. Prior to the centralisation of justice in Scotland from around the middle of the eighteenth century, there seemed to be a fair degree of self-policing by communities when it came to episodes of popular disturbance, and burghs could be served heavy corporate fines by the government if they failed to keep their citizens in order.[30] Later on in the eighteenth century, and within the newly developed legislative context, attitudes to popular disturbances changed and the authorities became more intent on bringing riotous participants to justice. According to the contemporary legal commentator Baron David Hume, this resulted in riot becoming the crime which occupied the largest portion of the Justiciary Court's time.[31]

The specific criminal act involved in popular disturbances, which separated this kind of activity from assault, was that of mobbing, (sometimes referred to as tumult). As Hume explains, in Scots Law, 'Under this general appellation "of mobbing"...our practice seems to reduce the several degrees and stages of disorder, which are known in the law of England, by the names of riot, rout and unlawful assembly.'[32] He goes on:

> For whether the convocation proceed to execute their violent purpose, which the law of England calls a *riot*; or only take some step toward the execution, which is a *rout*; or have simply met with the intention of doing some mischief, which is an *unlawful assembly*; this is a consideration which, in our practice, serves to affect only the measure of the punishment, and in no-wise the proper style to be applied to the offence, in drawing the indictment: Provided always the meeting be attended with those circumstances of disorder and alarm, which makes it a punishable meeting.[33]

It is clear from Hume's comments that any description of what constitutes an act of mobbing was relatively complex in the Scottish legal context and clearly distinct from English understanding of the same offence. Indeed, Hume provides no statutory definition of the crime of mobbing. Instead, he suggests four 'particulars' which must be apparent, in order for an indictment to be laid. The first is that a crowd of people must be assembled: '...it is, in the appearance of power, as well as disposition to execute their unlawful purposes, of their own will and authority, that the alarm and danger of such assemblies lie.'[34] In English common law, the lowest number necessary to constitute a mob was three people. However, in Scots Law this determination appears to have been left to the discretion of individual prosecutors considering specific cases. The second 'particular' explored by Hume was that in order for a charge of mobbing to apply, the crowd had to disturb the public peace and behave in a violent or threatening manner so as to cause fear amongst the populace.[35]

Thirdly, the assembly must not only tend towards violence and disorder, but it must also consist of individuals who have combined together for that purpose. As Hume explains:

> It is the *union* and resolution of a multitude, who are in league to defy authority, and execute their pleasure by means of force, by these means which it belongs to the supreme power alone to employ, that is the aggravated quality of the crime of mobbing.[36]

In this description, mobbing was distinguished in Scots Law from its English equivalent, which included participants in 'casual affrays' and even mere spectators of popular disturbances in charges of this nature. Essentially then, in premodern Scotland, if a crowd gathered together with a uniform intention, then that was sufficient to warrant a charge of mobbing, whether they went on to behave riotously or not, as it was the threat of what they *could* do and the disturbance to the public peace of their assembly, that was deemed problematic.[37] The final 'particular' which must have been apparent for a charge of mobbing to be levelled was that the disorder had to arise from a matter of 'private' concern. The word 'private' in this context referred to matters of specific or local interest, such as an attempt to reduce the price of grain in a certain market rather than a more national concern or interest of the State, such as an attempt to challenge or depose the government, which would be considered sedition or treason.[38]

Although open to ambiguous interpretation and the manipulation of prosecutors depending on the circumstances of a given case, these four 'particulars' were the basis for an indictment of mobbing to be held valid by the Justiciary Court. However, the court could also indict participants of popular disturbances *via* an entirely separate legal provision too. The Riot Act of 1715 had evolved from older Scots and English laws relating to collective protest.[39] Once a magistrate had read the Riot Act, it was a capital offence if more than twelve individuals remained in 'assembly' and did not disperse.[40] The Act also made it a non-clergyable felony if the crowd attempted to prevent the magistrate's proclamation, or if any property damage was committed during the reading of the Act.[41]

Despite various peculiarities linked to the 1715 Riot Act, such as the fact that it did not apply if the rioters dispersed after fifty-nine minutes or if there were only eleven individuals assembled, it was frequently referred to in indictments at the Scottish courts. It appears to have been particularly common for the prosecutor to apply this charge if he had serious misgivings about his ability to achieve a conviction for mobbing, in the face of an assize that might sympathise with those accused. The last reading of the Riot Act in Scotland occurred in 1919 at George Square in Glasgow during a tumultuous melee linked to the Forty Hours' Strike.[42] An analysis of the events associated with this disturbance, makes up the third case study below.

The wide-ranging legal provision for popular disturbances suggests that the authorities were determined to control the incidence of this type of crime in premodern Scotland. Yet when cases actually came to trial, the attitudes of the courts did not necessarily reflect this resolve in terms of the punishments meted out to those convicted. It was extremely rare, for instance, for a convicted rioter to receive the ultimate sanction from Scottish judges. Executions for this offence were rare between 1660 and 1960. It was far more common in the initial decades of the eighteenth century at least, for riotous individuals to be imprisoned (sometimes at hard labour) or fined. From the 1760s, banishment or transportation became the favoured sanction for these convicts, although this could be coupled with flogging in episodes where the authorities thought a show of judicial force was necessary.

The increased use of transportation at this time was more a reflection of changing punishment preferences for crime in general, than a shift in judicial attitudes towards rioting *per se*. The authorities considered the punishment of a few unruly offenders, through imprisonment or banishment, to be enough of an exemplary deterrent to other would-be rioters, and as a result the execution of rioters could be avoided. This was especially important if the rioters' cause was one that elicited widespread sympathy. Fierce disturbances could ensue from an unpopular hanging, as was exemplified by the Porteous riots in Edinburgh in 1736 and such instances had to be avoided in an age when there was a basic lack of resources for 'formal' social control.[43]

The final reason that the authorities shrank from executing rioters in the premodern period was that it was frequently very difficult to arrest *all* of the individuals involved. This, coupled to the fact that measuring the precise degree of culpability in an episode of collective action was particularly difficult to achieve,[44] meant that only petty sanctions could be deployed. Moreover, once the Combination Acts of 1799 and 1800 (which outlawed anti-government amalgamations) were repealed in 1824,[45] it became almost impossible to convict individuals for assembly with riotous intent alone, as this legislative turn wholly undermined the very principle upon which Scots law was able to sanction indictments for mobbing and riot as we have seen. Consequently, and after this time, it was only really when explicit violence was witnessed against authority figures during an episode of poplar protest that prosecutions followed in the Scottish context. Indeed, the difficulties associated with bringing rebellious individuals to justice did not dissipate over time and explain why throughout the nineteenth century and into the more modern era, Scottish individuals convicted of being involved in forms of protest or disturbance were effectively given sentences appropriate to breach of the peace or public order offences, as in effect, that was all that the law could allow.[46] Moreover, and as we can see from the data below, the changing nature of Scottish protest meant that there was a diminishing need for authoritative intervention over time in any case.

Trends in Communal Violence and its Punishment

Figures 4.1 and 4.4 demonstrate the evident decline in indictments for mobbing and rioting in Scotland in the 1805–1960 period.[47] Although there were peaks of activity at certain times, on the whole, the data shows a sharp decline in Scottish collective violence after 1870, which mirrors the transformation to more modern forms of protest described above. The high indictment levels

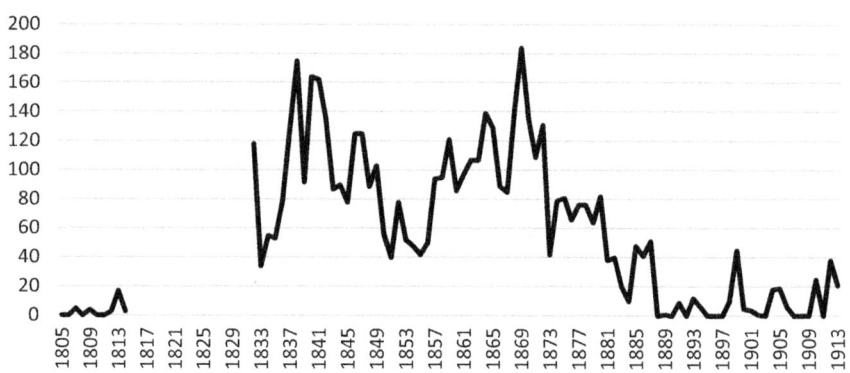

Figure 4.1 Indictments for Mobbing and Rioting in Scotland, 1805–1913.

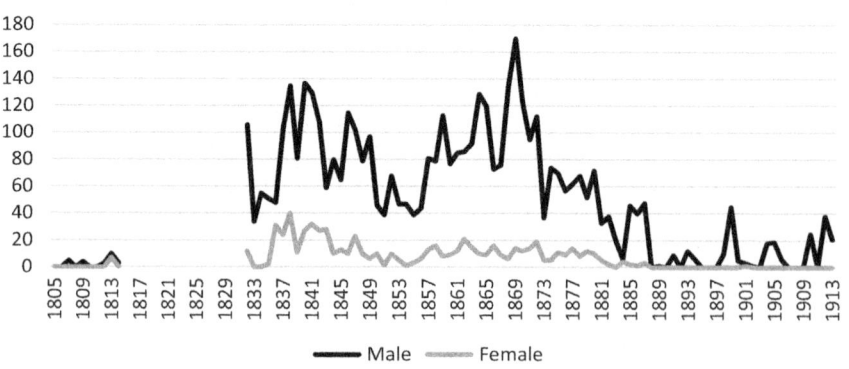

Figure 4.2 Indictments for Mobbing and Rioting in Scotland by Gender, 1805–1913.

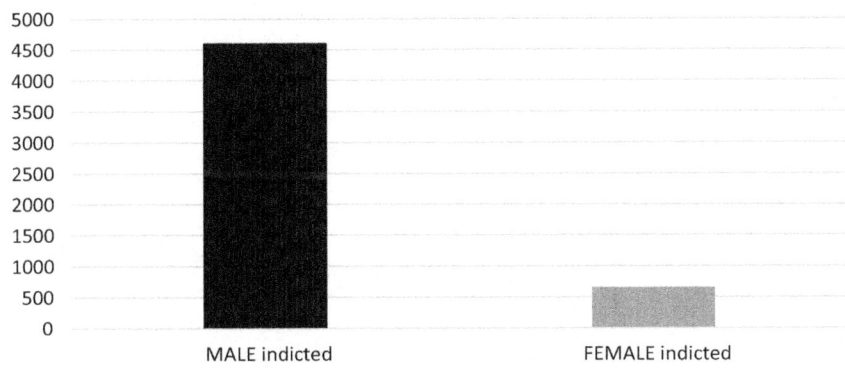

Figure 4.3 The Gendered Nature of Mobbing and Rioting Indictments in Scotland, 1805–1913.

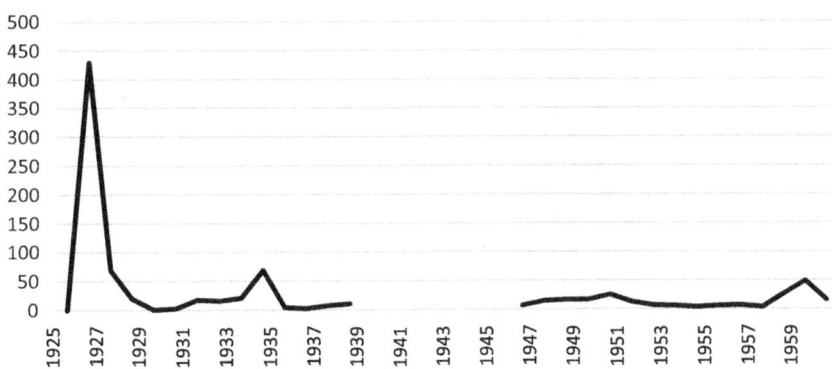

Figure 4.4 Indictments for Offences Against Public Order in Scotland, 1925–1960.

seen in 1925 are indicative of cumulative data reporting for previously un-published years across multiple jurisdictions, and not a sudden surge in crim-inality. Figures 4.2, 4.3, 4.5 and 4.6 illustrate the atypical involvement of women in Scottish collective action after the mid-nineteenth century. This contrasts with their involvement in earlier periods but compares well with historic gender patterns in the assault of authority shown in the previous chapter. Evidently, Scottish women's involvement in collective violence sig-nificantly diminished over time.

Figures 4.7 and 4.9 show a close correlation between indictments and con-victions in Scotland over time. Although prosecutions were tricky to initiate and difficult to conclude successfully for the reasons alluded to above, when trials did come before the various sections of the Scottish judiciary, they were

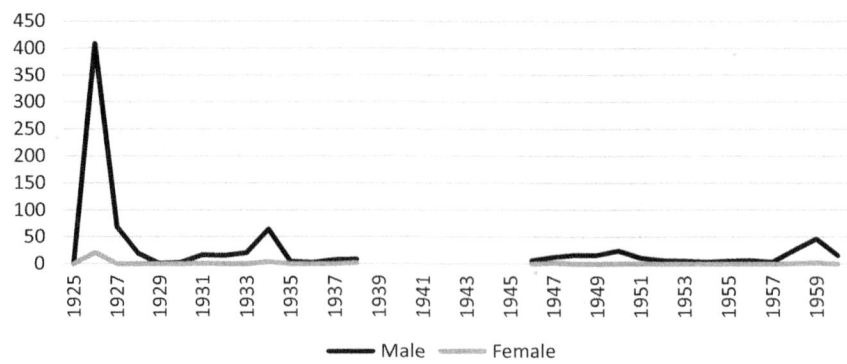

Figure 4.5 Indictments for Offences Against Public Order in Scotland by Gender, 1925–1960.

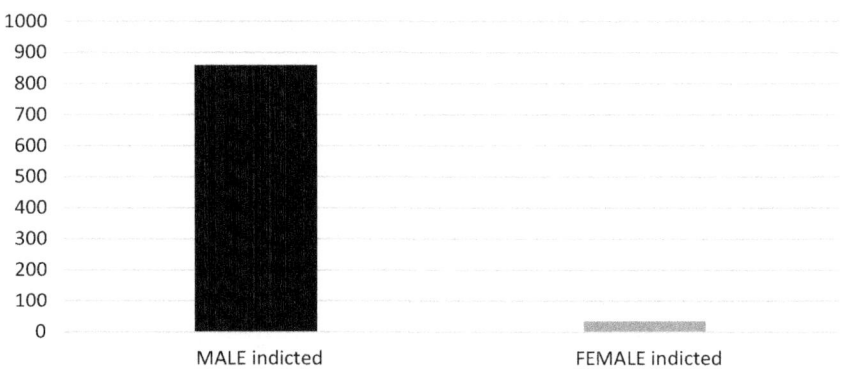

Figure 4.6 The Gendered Nature of Indictments for Offences Against Public Order in Scotland, 1925–1960.

regularly sound and based on unequivocal evidence which tended to include eyewitness testimony provided by notable figures from the community in which the riot took place. This, coupled with the seriousness with which collective violence was viewed by the Scottish authorities, meant that convictions were far from uncommon. However, not all participants in episodes of Scottish collective violence were brought to justice between 1805 and 1960, and as we have seen, the frequency of convictions may have had a lot to do with the flexibility afforded to the courts in their use of sanctions. Certainly, and as Figures 4.8 and 4.10 illustrate, women were rare recipients of guilty verdicts related to collective violence, in large part because of their infrequent involvement in this type of criminal activity once protest had become politicised and had less to do with matters that directly impacted upon their domestic arrangements or the familial experience.

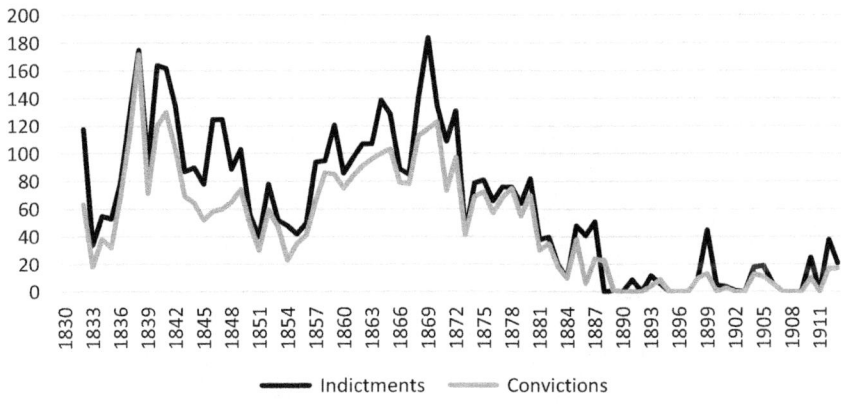

Figure 4.7 Indictments and Convictions for Mobbing and Rioting in Scotland, 1830–1913.

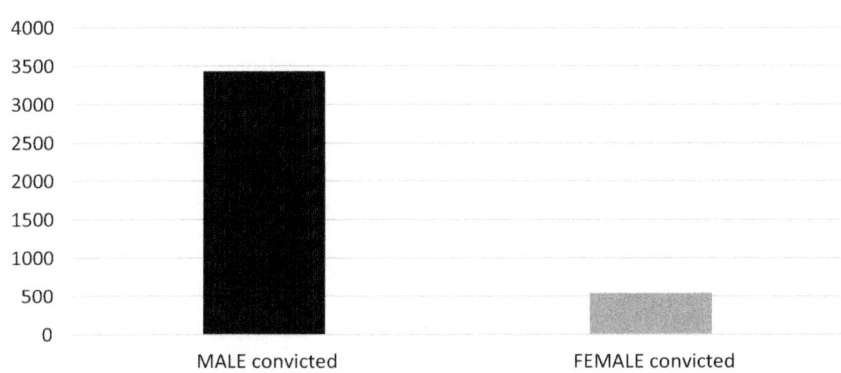

Figure 4.8 The Gendered Nature of Convictions for Mobbing and Rioting in Scotland, 1830–1913.

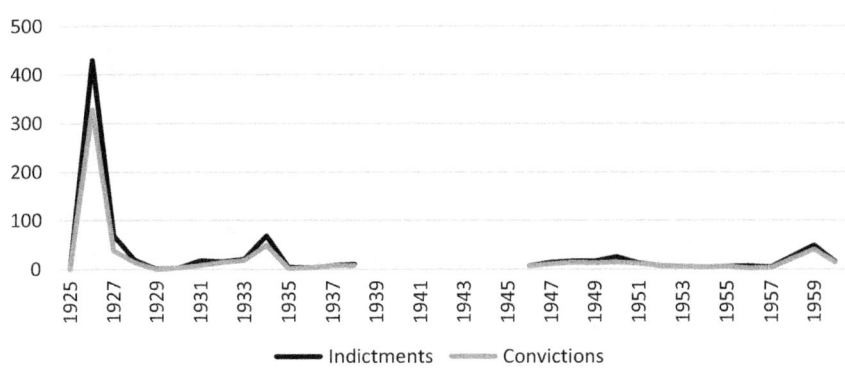

Figure 4.9 Indictments and Convictions for Offences Against Public Order in Scotland, 1925–1960.

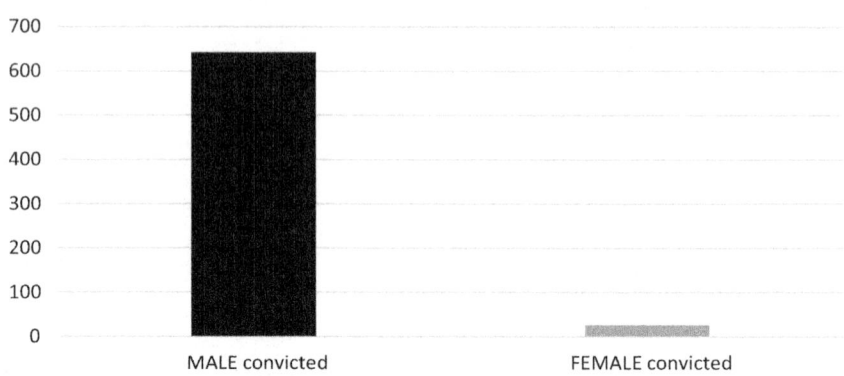

Figure 4.10 The Gendered Nature of Convictions for Offences Against Public Order in Scotland, 1925–1960.

Offenders, Victims, Methods and Motive

If we consider the range of types of popular protest that prevailed in Scotland between 1660 and 1960 and the varied grievances that underpinned this behaviour, then it is perhaps not that surprising to learn that the individuals involved in these episodes were heterogeneous in their characteristics and backgrounds. Both men and women participated in riotous activity, although it was regularly females that made up the vanguard in the more explicitly violent examples of disturbance in the early modern era. Perhaps this was determined by the particular issue or cause being promoted by the rioters, or perhaps this was because of a prevailing belief that they would be treated more leniently by the authorities than would their menfolk.[48] Youths were often involved in recorded episodes of communal violence in Scotland (as exemplified by the second case study below) but this does not mean that mobs were solely made up of known criminal elements from a particular community.[49] Rather than socially marginal people, rioters in Scotland and indeed elsewhere, were individuals who hailed from varied backgrounds and were not confined to any particular social class, although they did often have a shared trade or occupational experience and, more often than not, they knew each other but were not related.[50]

Recorded evidence suggests that Scottish mobs were sizeable in terms of the number of constituent individuals, but this may be more to do with the kinds of tumult reported upon, rather than a normative characteristic of this particular type of offending.[51] Scottish riots, at least in their early phase, tended to be local in terms of how they were initiated, but depending on the issues involved, they could intensify, spread and escalate to form protest which took on a cross-county or even a national significance. Collective violence in Scotland was typically spontaneous in origin and although planning may have gone into organising individuals to assemble together in the first place, any violence perpetrated thereafter tended to be hot-blooded and reactionary on the whole, rather than premeditated.[52]

One characteristic which has been long accepted by historians as common in popular disturbances throughout history, is the evident *lack* of violence committed during riotous episodes.[53] Typically described as 'fleeting but intense',[54] forms of collective protest across European history were considered remarkable due to the evident restraint shown by the rioters involved. For many, riot was considered a last resort to resolve a dispute or conclude a grievance.[55] Although intimidation was commonplace, and methodologies could be varied,[56] riotous mobs were said to have deployed a ritualised code of behaviour which only permitted certain types of behaviour to be instigated in the pursuit of common goals. For instance, violence against people was *not* acceptable and violence against property was tolerated only on certain occasions.[57]

In Scotland, evidence from court records paints a slightly different picture of the nature and experience of popular protest compared to that elsewhere. Whilst Scottish mobs did engage in ritualised forms of protest in terms of their selection of particular targets or in relation to how they committed certain types of riotous activity,[58] they were more violent than we might expect from depictions of disorder elsewhere. North of the Tweed, violence – and typically violence against the person – was the norm, not the exception amongst the offences reported to the Scottish courts.[59] For instance, weapons (such as sticks, cudgels and stones) were typically deployed by Scottish protestors determined to get their message across to the authorities and the wider public.[60] Moreover, and as we will see in the case studies below, Scottish rioters could be brutal and vicious in their treatment of individuals who got in their way. These situations were sometimes exacerbated by excessive alcohol consumption and often innocent bystanders as well as authority figures could get caught up in the melee that ensued.[61] As Scottish mobs often escalated in size and intensity as the protest persisted, and as such episodes were typically peripatetic, the damage done by a Scottish riot could be substantial, and its impact both far-reaching and long-lasting with extended paths of destruction and injury regularly traceable.

We should not conclude from this, however, that Scottish mobs engaged in collective violence just for the sake of it. As with their peers in popular protest elsewhere, Scottish rioters had clear objectives in mind when they participated in popular protest. Although disturbances were clearly motivated by a wide variety of grievances, some of which were very personal to the individuals involved, scholars have tried to categorise the common factors which resulted in episodes of communal violence.[62] Historians such as Robert Shoemaker and Adrian Randall have convincingly argued that economic issues were the dominant causal factor in early modern European riots.[63] Others have suggested that resistance to change was of more significance and some, such as John Stevenson have pointed to disorder being caused by an unwillingness to accept interference of any kind in the machinations of everyday life.[64] In all likelihood, riots were caused by all of these issues and more, and sometimes multiple causal factors could be at play.

All popular protest, however, seems to have one thing in common that scholars more or less agree upon which was that rioters believed their actions to be entirely legitimate. In the early modern period, the general populace had no formal or indeed informal mechanism by which to facilitate change or raise a grievance with their superiors. Even by the more modern era, when enfranchised, they could still feel that their views were regularly subjugated or ignored. Consequently, sections of the populace felt that collective action in the form of popular protest was the only way to establish or reaffirm what the late historian E.P. Thompson has described as a 'moral economy' within their particular neighbourhood and indeed within wider society.[65] By protesting, rioters reminded their betters that new commercially-oriented malpractices ought to be shunned, that forms of paternalism should be encouraged and in particular, that the many traditional rights and customs which were once afforded to the people but had been subsequently disregarded or abolished must be reinstated, preserved or even enriched. This 'moral economy' would ensure that communities were fair and just and places where the rich and the poor, the weak and the powerful, could live together in an atmosphere of mutual respect. The need to defend the 'moral economy' or aspects of this concept, was what gave rioters in Scotland and elsewhere a 'legitimising notion' for their participation in communal violence across the 1660–1960 period, regardless of what particular grievance acted as the initial trigger for protest.[66]

In the next section, three case studies demonstrate the kinds of passions that could be enflamed when the Scots became determined to defend rights which they considered were now being abused or were under serious threat. The loss of the right to influence decisions at a parochial level, the encroachment of perceived external threats, the loss of protectionism and the abuses associated with authoritative suppression were all rallied against by Scottish rioters across the 1660–1960 period. For many then, collective violence was considered a justified means to an end in the ongoing battle for power and supremacy amongst the different layers of Scottish society.[67] Within this enduring conflict, riot often functioned as a safety valve when frustrations boiled over or when change was slow in coming.[68]

Popular protest articulated these vexations in an explicit physical sense, but often, the ideological battle continued once the damage had been cleared and order restored.

Case Studies and Attitudes to Communal Violence

Understanding the underlying context to episodes of communal violence is absolutely essential to appreciating why they occurred.[69] Although, as we have seen, the notion of a 'moral economy' explains the ideological background to many popular disturbances in a generic sense, each riotous episode is different and so prior to the discussion of each particular case study below, a specific contextual section for each example is also provided.

(a) Patronage Riot (Eighteenth Century)

According to Callum Brown, religious protests were an endemic feature of Scottish life in the period between 1730 and 1870.[70] Although other scholars, such as R.H. Campbell, dispute the significance of these events,[71] the evidence provided by Brown is compelling and points to the significant reach and impact of religious disturbances upon the very fabric of Scottish society during the eighteenth and nineteenth centuries. Brown points to four causes of religious-based protest during that era: pewing, reform of worship, inadequate church accommodation and patronage.[72] It is the last of these issues which relates to the case study immediately below and Brown insists that in relation to the premodern Scottish context, 'By far the most important spark to religious disputes was patronage.'[73]

In an attempt to enhance its role in the political control of Scotland's affairs at a local level, the Crown restored patronage in 1712, just a little over two decades since it had been abolished for being too incompatible with the tenets of Presbyterianism.[74] Patronage was the system whereby a hereditary patron (typically an individual under the direct influence of a wealthy local landowner) had the right to select and present a minister for a Church of Scotland parish.[75] In effect, this practice sidelined the views of both parishioners and church elders regarding who should minister to them; a right of selection which they had hitherto enjoyed and routinely exercised.[76] This ostracisation resulted in intense wrangling at a local and national level between church authorities, and, as we will see below, it could, on occasion, result in instances of communal violence. Indeed, historians Richard Sher and Alexander Murdoch have gone as far as to describe such instances collectively, as 'the Scottish patronage <u>wars</u>'.[77] Such episodes typically occurred when attempts were made to prevent the presentation of the hereditary patron's choice of minister. Human barricades were set up to scupper access to the parish church and rioters threw missiles at either the church itself or the assembled parties ready to induct their selected charge.[78]

Brown argues that 'During the whole period of patronage, from 1712 until 1874, a conservative estimate would be that between a third and a half of Scotland's parishes suffered a disputed settlement, with a significant minority experiencing more than one dispute.'[79] Not only were the participants in these disputes motivated by their inability to influence the selection of their own minister at a local level, they were also evidently perturbed by the more general encroachment of the views and influence of unfamiliar grandees upon their daily lives. As Brown explains 'The overall complaint of Presbyterian protesters was that the elites were usurping the people's place in the Kirk, eroding a whole catalogue of traditional popular rights, privileges and symbols.'[80] The resulting power struggle between what we might call privilege and principle ravaged Scottish society for some time and evidently involved a wider range of social issues than simply religion.[81]

On the 8th of October 1764, ten individuals were arrested and charged with 'convocating or assembling together numbers of persons in a tumultuous, riotous and invasive manner and assaulting our lieges' after a violent incident in Ayrshire.[82] Some fifteen days later, on the 23rd of October 1764, Alexander Thomson, William Wylie, James Crawfurd, John Hill, Adam White, David Dunlop, William Nimmo, William Davies, Hugh Thomson and Robert Creelam were brought to the South Circuit of the Justiciary Court for trial. These men were all from Kilmarnock and all had respectable jobs as shoemakers, glovers, bonnet-makers and carriers. They certainly could not be described as economically or socially marginal, nor could they be regarded as 'criminals' or 'troublemakers', as none of them had previously been in trouble with the law.

Yet, by the time of the court case, the indictment against them had become more specifically violence-laden, accusing them of being '...armed with stones or other offensive weapons, and without just cause or provocation, invading and assaulting the lieges, and bruising and wounding them to the hurt of their persons.'[83] Moreover, the case was said to have been 'aggravated' by the fact that the victims of the disorder had been attacked when 'assembled at the publick [public] Worship of God.'[84] This meant that the accused individuals were not only indicted under the laws against riotous behaviour discussed earlier, but they were also accused of contravening legislation passed during the reign of King James VI in 1587, which made the disturbance of a religious service a criminal offence.[85]

The court heard that on the 12th of July 1764, certain Church of Scotland Ministers from the Presbytery of Irvine had travelled to the Parish Church of Kilmarnock in Ayrshire to preside over the admission of a new minister there: the Reverend Mr Lindsay. It is clear from other sources that the presentation of the new minister had been the subject of considerable debate. The Presbytery of Irvine, for instance, had vehemently opposed Mr Lindsay's appointment when it was first mooted in 1762, chiefly because he had been selected not by them or by church officials, but by the principle landowner of the area, the Earl of Glencairn (William Cunningham). In his work on the history of Kilmarnock produced in 1858, Archibald McKay explains the reasons for this dissention and the context in which it occurred in more depth. First, he pointed out that 'The people of Kilmarnock have long been noted as a religious and church-going people...and the Sabbath... was kept so strictly sacred, that the town on that day had all the appearance of a place deserted by its inhabitants.'[86] However, he then explains that '... though thus respecting the clergy, and the religious usages of the land, there were times when acrimonious feelings would arise in the community on subjects connected with the church.' One such issue was patronage, which '...was then looked upon as an evil of no small magnitude' and which caused '...the peace of the town to be disturbed by the bitter animosity and opposition of its enemies.'[87]

McKay also provides us with specific detail on why the opposition to Mr Lindsay was so fervent and he uses extracts from the minute books of the Kirk Session of Kilmarnock to substantiate his contentions. First, and as has been stated above, the Presbytery of Irvine were aggrieved that the Earl of Glencairn's selection of a replacement minister had been accepted without consultation. Indeed, it was alleged that the appointment was an example of insidious favouritism as Mr Lindsay's wife, Margaret Lauder, had once been housekeeper or governess to the Glencairn family, and that this friendship had influenced the Earl's decision.[88] Moreover, the Presbytery had it on good authority that Mr Lindsay '...held not a very elevated place as a preacher' and that his religious opinions were overly liberal in nature.[89] Consequently, the Presbytery (strongly supported by the Town Council) informed the General Assembly that they '...unanimously declared their disapprobation both of the manner of the Presentation and acceptance' stating that they could not concur with the decision '...as this congregation are strangers to him and he to them and never got a hearing of him' and because he is '...commonly reported to be a man unfit (and in their opinion unqualified) for such as a charge as that of minister in Kilmarnock.'[90] Opinions were so entrenched on this matter that eventually, the General Assembly of the Church of Scotland had to step in to settle the issue, ordering the Presbytery to accept the decision and to ensure Mr Lindsay was admitted to his new parish.[91]

Heretors of the parish, heads of families and other parishioners consequently convened at the Parish Church in Kilmarnock in July of 1764, alongside the aforementioned Church of Scotland officials to welcome Mr Lindsay and 'divine service' began with the singing of psalms. Then, whilst prayers to 'Almighty God' were being offered up from the pulpit by one of the ministers in attendance,

...a great number of riotous and disorderly persons...having convo-
cated and assembled themselves in a lawless manner, did, in defiance of
the laws and in contempt of all decency and of the solemn worship of
God, forcibly attack and brake [break] open the doors of the said Church
and did assault the Ministers and Congregation assembled as said is, by
throwing many and large stones at them, whereby certain of the persons
there assembled for the publick [public] Worship of God were Bruised
and Wounded...The Minister officiating was put on fear of his life and
obliged to leave the Pulpit, a tumult or fray was raised, and the Congregation was disordered, troubled and dispersed.[92]

As the testimony from the twenty-four prosecution witnesses was not recorded in the minute books for this trial, it is unclear whether the Riot Act
was read during the disturbance. In addition, and as was typically the case
with prosecutions for communal violence in the early modern period as we
have seen, the court papers did not single out particular actions by specific
individuals, nor identify any named victims of the events that transpired.
However, they do indicate that not all of the individuals directly involved in
the riot had been properly brought to justice: a number had seemingly fled
the scene and evaded capture.

The vague and imprecise nature of the indictment was used by the defence
team in this case. They argued, for instance, that they should not be asked
to derive a defence for a case which had no named victims and where the
charge was so general in content. They also argued that the 1587 legislation
had gone into desuetude and could not be sustained. Finally, they pointed to
two other issues of relevance in the defence of this case: first, that the riot had
been caused by overzealous baron officers who had actively prevented parishioners from entering the Church to participate in 'divine worship' rather than
by individuals attempting to disrupt the service. Secondly, that some of the
accused rioters had already been inside the church at the time of the tumult
and were themselves victims of the disturbance rather than its instigators.[93]
The defence team made a series of strong arguments in this case and were
able to play on the confusion which often surrounded the details of riotous
assemblies, given the numbers typically involved. After legal debate between
the two sides, the defence managed to get the judge to concede that if the ten
men accused were found guilty, the libel would be restricted to an arbitrary
punishment.

More detail on the precise circumstances of the evident tensions and violent opposition relating to the settlement of Mr Lindsay is available from contemporary sources other than court records, such as the *Caledonian Mercury*
newspaper which recounts:

As soon as it was generally known that Mr Lindsay was to be admitted
their pastor, a portentous murmur of discontent was heard among the

inhabitants in every street and nook of the town; and, as the time of the settlement drew near, their dissatisfaction waxed louder and louder. Every sort of missile they secreted as ammunition with which to assail their opponents. At length the much-talked-of day arrived; and, according to all accounts, a scene of disorder and tumult ensued such as never before was witnessed in Kilmarnock. Labour seemed altogether suspended; numerous parties assembled on the streets, and, ere the hour of induction had come, surrounded the church, determined to oppose the proceedings. A mere outline of the affray is all we are enabled to give. The mob, who had placed themselves in a convenient position for attack, no sooner observed the patron and the clergyman approaching than they assailed them with a storm of execrations, and pelted them to such a degree with mud, dead cats, and other filthy substances, that it was with the greatest difficulty they gained the interior of the church. Here a scene of confusion and uproar took place, which even Hogarth, so noted for his faithful delineations of the ludicrous, would, we believe, have failed to depict. Several volleys of the missiles we have spoken of were discharged at the devoted heads of those friendly to Mr Lindsay's appointment. All indeed, was riot, noise, and disorder. The precentor, William Steven, had his wig torn from his head. The wig of one of the magistrates, too, was tossed into the air, amid the cheers of the mob; the Earl of Glencairn was struck on the cheek with a dead cat; and one of the clergymen belonging to the neighbouring village of Fenwick, convinced of the truth of the old saying that *"ae pair o'heels is worth two pair o'hands"*, mounted his horse and fled from the scene in the utmost consternation.[94]

This report is fascinating, as not only does it successfully bring the story of this particular popular disturbance to life with dramatic detail, but it is also, crucially, somewhat at odds with the evidence presented in court. For instance, the newspaper report suggested that the riot did not begin *during* the church service as the court had been told, but rather it began *outside* the church, when the key participants were en route there. If this were true, it would negate the prosecutions attempts to apply the Act of 1587 to this case. In addition, the press account suggests that the aggravated assault of key notables should also have been added to the list of indicted charges due to the evident abuse that they suffered. In any event, after deliberation, the jury announced its verdict, finding (by a majority) just three of the ten men guilty. The other seven were released from prison and set at liberty. The three convicts – Alexander Thomson, William Wylie and James Crawfurd – were sentenced to twenty days imprisonment in the Tolbooth of Ayr, ordered to be whipped through the Streets of Ayr by the common hangman '…receiving the ordinary number of stripes upon their naked backs at the usual places and at the accustomed time of day', and thereafter were to be reincarcerated until they could pay a £10 bail bond promising good behaviour and to keep the peace for the next twelve months.[95]

This case displays several of the key characteristics of popular disturbances from the early modern period in a Scottish context. First, there was an evident lack of specific detail in the written record of court cases accusing individuals of involvement in episodes of communal violence and also a lack of clarity with regard to who did what to whom and why. This imprecision, as well as the number of assailants typically involved, rendered the successful indictment and subsequent prosecution of *all* the individuals involved incredibly difficult to achieve. Indeed, in this particular episode, it was only after local magistrates offered a reward of ten pounds for help with arresting the guilty parties, and an individual called 'Lang Tam' took them up on their offer and gave the authorities the names of the ringleaders, that a prosecution was possible.[96]

As well as illuminating the difficulties the authorities faced, the case also highlights the fact that rioting was not an activity which typically involved criminal delinquents or the poorest members of society as some commentators have suggested. Rather, the background of protagonists tended to be more respectable or more socially diverse than that. Participants typically coalesced with riotous intentions when they perceived that certain rights and expectations, which had been traditionally afforded to them, had now been abandoned, displaced or lost. As was evident in this case, the issue of patronage was a particularly inflammatory and shared grievance across Scotland during the early modern period. The imposition of ministers chosen by wealthy landowners, rather than by parishioners or local church authorities caused upset, consternation and violence too on occasion. The centralisation of authority in this matter and others, resulted in numerous ideological and physical battles regarding the control of power and rights, in which rioters often believed they had a 'legitimising notion' for their tumultuous actions.

(b) Anti-Irish Riot (Nineteenth Century)

As historian Tom Gallagher has explained, although emigration from Ireland to Scotland had occurred on an *ad hoc* basis for a long period of time, it was only in the early nineteenth century that this in-migration equated to a considerable influx of people.[97] Prior to the 1840s, it was pull factors such as the demand for low-cost labour in certain parts of Scotland that encouraged this kind of social mobility. After that time, however, push factors such as the Irish famine and technological advances in transportation also contributed to the unprecedented Irish diaspora that unfolded.[98]

Hostility to Irish immigrants became more evident in Scottish society when seasonal migration increasingly became permanent from the end of the eighteenth century onwards and when the numbers of non-natives in Scottish cities became increasingly obvious.[99] Alongside cultural and religious differences, which often made the Irish seem a people set apart in the Scottish context, it was the perceived threat that they posed to the livelihood of native Scottish workers that caused entrenched resentment.[100] As one commentator noted in 1829 (the year the Catholic Emancipation Act was passed which allowed Catholics to be elected to Parliament):

> ...the lower orders in the west of Scotland were very naturally ever ready to do anything which, in their opinion, would press and keep back the Irish Catholics who pour in upon them almost with every tide, coming to compete with them successfully in all their occupations, and thereby materially lowering the rate of wages.[101]

Assimilation of the Irish was seemingly always going to be difficult to achieve, especially when they gained a reputation for striking, insubordination and rebellion in the workplace.[102] This, coupled to fact that so many aspects of their character and way of life distinguished them from their Scottish hosts, resulted in what historian Bill Murray has described as '...a virtual state of apartheid' prevailing in parts of nineteenth century Scotland.[103] Indeed, and as Tom Gallagher has noted, 'In order to make themselves acceptable in Victorian Scotland, the Irish would have needed to make themselves invisible.'[104] However, this was something they would find almost impossible to achieve, due to the conspicuous nature of their religious beliefs and because they tended to congregate together in distinctive enclaves for their own protection.[105]

Although anti-Irish prejudices were evident and did endure in some areas of Scottish society,[106] violent incidents related to this underlying sentiment were relatively rare, making the following case study of a riot in Dundee in 1830 something of an anomaly.[107] Indeed, Dundee, in particular, was thought by scholars to be a place that was notable because '...such divisiveness was surprisingly absent', despite it being a key place of Irish settlement.[108] This lack of 'intercommunal strife' in Dundee was arguably due to its prevailing multi-culturalism and diversity, alongside its evident prosperity.[109] However, and as we have seen elsewhere in this chapter, underlying tensions could easily erupt in Scottish society given the right conditions and regardless of past tranquillity. In addition, some historians have noted an evident bravado amongst the Irish in the city, rather than a sense of acquiescence, where they '...would not countenance criticisms from outside and neither, for that matter, would their priests...' suggesting that although the Irish were prepared to be assimilated in Dundee, it had to be on their own terms.[110] The potential for conflict in the city was perhaps stronger than some scholars have assumed.[111] Indeed, and as we will now establish, riots could be triggered easily and for insignificant reasons if the mood and context allowed. Popular disturbances could quickly escalate into episodes of communal violence if broader social tensions (which had hitherto been hidden) suddenly come to the surface of society and erupt.

On the 2nd of June 1830, near the village of Hanslope on the Northamptonshire border, an illegal prize-fight was arranged between the champion of Ireland, Simon Byrne and his Scottish equivalent, the reputed 'Highland Hercules', Alexander (Sandy) McKay. The winner would take home the princely sum of two hundred pounds. Both boxers had fought each other once before, and it was Byrne that had been the clear victor on that occasion. This fight was the long-anticipated rematch between the two and it was clear from newspaper reports leading up to the fight, that both men had trained long and hard for the bout.[112] However, when trying to determine a favourite for the match, the press reported that not only had Simon Byrne sprained his ankle in the weeks prior to the fight, he was also suffering from a bad cold and chest infection. Indeed, according to one report, he was '...forced to admit that he was anything up to the mark, whilst Sandy McKay was pronounced as fine as a star.'[113] Moreover, the physical descriptions provided of both men, clearly indicated who the press believed would prevail.

> McKay, although not above five feet ten in height, exhibited a frame of most gigantic dimensions. His weight was allowed to be fourteen stone ten pounds, while his bone and muscle seemed, like those of Atlas, suffi- cient to near the globe itself. His legs and arms were of prestigious bulk, and his hands looked like a pair of sledge hammers. His chest was expan- sive, while his shoulders bore a hump like that of a dromedary, although not quite so protrusive...he had a fierceness of aspect... and from his demeanour, victory was already in his grasp.[114]

According to reports, little betting took place at the bout itself, owing to the:

> ...unpromising features of Byrne, whose countenance was pale and somewhat agitated, whose weight was scarcely thirteen stone, and the colour of whose flesh wanted that clearness and freshness which are the true indications of good training.[115]

The fight itself was typical of bare-knuckle boxing matches in the early nine- teenth century: it was protracted, bloody and brutal.[116] Things were pretty even between the two men and knock-out punches were scored by both until round thirty-one, where – to the amazement of spectators – Simon Byrne gradually gained the upper hand and was eventually proclaimed the winner. His victory was not roundly celebrated by the crowd of spectators however, as throughout the fight he had repeatedly 'gone down' to evade the punches of his opponent and to tire him out over the duration of the fight. Whilst a per- fectly legitimate tactic, these actions had swayed the crowd to champion the 'courageous' McKay who had stayed on his feet throughout until knocked out, and whom they roundly referred to as 'the brave Caledonian'.[117]

A few days after the bout, newspapers reported that the conclusion to the fight had taken a tragic turn. Sandy McKay, who had been '...most cruelly beaten...[had] received many heavy blows about his left temple and his face

was so frightfully cut and disfigured that his features were lost in a confused mass of gore and bruises' had remained insensible since the conclusion
of the fight and, despite valiant efforts to 'restore animation' had died the
next day.[118] A subsequent inquest by the coroner, '...described death to have
been occasioned by an effusion of blood upon the brain, which might have
been produced by blows or falls.'[119] The inquest jury subsequently returned
a verdict of manslaughter against Simon Byrne. Byrne was duly arrested and
arraigned to stand trial.[120]

The press described the subsequent trial of Simon Byrne, which began at
Buckingham Assizes on the 22nd of July 1830, as one where 'The court was
crowded throughout the day almost to suffocation, and the galleries were
filled with men of the highest respectability in the county.'[121] Evidently,
wealthy individuals had come to court to lend their support to the pugi-
list movement, as the death of McKay had initiated a rather half-hearted
campaign, limited to just some sections of the press, to outlaw bare-knuckle
boxing matches of this sort.[122] It was not surprising to learn, therefore, that
Simon Byrne himself was to be dutifully defended by an impressive five-man
legal team, all paid for by keen patrons and boxing promoters alike who
principally argued that McKay's death may have resulted from the impact of
a recent fall he had suffered.[123] The jury deliberated on their verdict for just
ten minutes. They all agreed that Simon Byrne was not guilty of the 'killing
and slaying' of his erstwhile opponent.[124] According to press reports, the
decision of the assize '...was received with the loudest and most boisterous
acclamations, which it required some exertions on the part of the officers in
court to suppress, and which were warmly animadverted upon by the learned
judge, as most indecorous.'[125]

Prior to the commencement of Byrne's trial and long in advance of the
announcement of this verdict, when news of the fight and the tragic events
that had transpired eventually reached Sandy McKay's homeland, anti-Irish
riots broke out in some Scottish cities.[126] It would seem that Scottish attitudes to Simon Byrne were such that they considered the Irishman to be
a cheat, a brute and a killer. The most notable of these riots occurred in
Dundee. On the 5th of July 1830, an altercation began in a pub in the city
centre between a local man named Heron, and an Irishman and his two
sons by the name of Thurrel. A heated argument erupted between the men
after they disagreed over why McKay had lost the fight against Byrne, with
Heron arguing that the Irish contender had not fought fairly.[127] Others
also voiced their suspicions (repeated in the press) that McKay had been
poisoned in the midst of the bout via a sleeping draught added to his water
bottle.[128] The Thurrel family and other Irishmen present took great offence
at these allegations and the developing dispute quickly divided along national lines. When Heron and Thurrel decided to resolve their disagreement
through a fight on Dundee Law, crowds of supporters followed the men
to witness the ruckus. When the fight began, Heron was knocked down

pretty quickly and Thurrel proceeded to viciously and repeatedly kick his opponent whilst he was down on the ground.[129] This infuriated the native contingent in the crowd and a melee ensued between the Scottish and Irish factions, which rapidly escalated in both size and intensity across the city, as a host of underlying racial tensions rapidly came to the surface with violent repercussions.[130]

Although one contemporary press report suggested that the number of individuals involved in the riot could have been as many as eighteen thousand, this was probably hyperbole.[131] Nevertheless, it is likely that the prevailing mob was of a substantial size, given that three hundred special constables were drafted in to restore order to the city, substantial amounts of property was damaged or destroyed in the wake of the tumult, and significant casualty figures were reported in the immediate aftermath.[132] By piecing together contemporary accounts and the testimony provided in court, it can be estimated that at the height of the troubles, some fifteen hundred rioters marauded the streets of Dundee in July 1830. Yet, the eventual court case that resulted indicted just three individuals: John Adamson, a weaver from Dundee, William Robertson, a baker there, and a thirteen-year-old boy also from the city, named Nathan Croll.[133] Clearly, many more individuals were involved in the disturbance than the indictment papers suggest. However, as we have seen above, it was routinely difficult to round up all the participants in popular disturbances even by the nineteenth century when the police rather than the army were more likely to be involved in maintaining order and exacting justice. This was seemingly especially true when the participants were particularly numerous and when the riot concerned was peripatetic, occurred at night and/or lasted for a lengthy period of time. In this specific episode, all four of these criteria were met. Indeed, whilst the original arrest warrant in the case clearly testifies to the fact that attempts were made to indict additional individuals and multiple arrest warrants were served, they proved unsuccessful. As one constable commented: 'From the density of the crowd and the dusk of the light, I had much difficulty in getting any of the rioters identified.'[134]

The three indicted individuals, Adamson, Robertson and Croll, were charged with two offences: mobbing and rioting. More specifically, they were accused of coming together with others '...with the wicked and felonious intent of attacking the persons and destroying the houses and property of all Irishmen, and driving them out of Dundee.'[135] The court heard how the mob surrounded the house of Irish labourer Andrew Savage in Blinshall Street, and proceeded to

> ...throw showers of stones into the windows of the said house until they were broken and destroyed; and the said Andrew Savage having come to the door to defend his property, a stone struck his head, by which he was severely cut, to the effusion of his blood.[136]

Notwithstanding this, the mob rushed into the property, '...rummaged the same and did violently seize and carry off two pairs of blankets, a pair of sheets and a chaff mattress.'[137] The indictment did not accuse Robertson, Adamson or Croll with the theft or confiscation of these items, or with aggravated assault, but with being 'actively engaged' in the mob.

The accusations against the three men extended to the second day of the riot, the 6th of July 1830, when they were indicted for assembling '...in a riotous, menacing, and tumultuous manner' with the same hibernophobic intention, but this time the focus was the house of a different Irishman, a weaver called William Coyle who lived in the Hilltown area of the city. As well as inflicting significant damage by repeatedly stoning the property, it was also alleged that the mob entered his house, '...and did rummage the same, and destroy and carry off a pair of blankets, and a sheet therein, and did smash to pieces and destroy a quantity of plates and cups.'[138] Once again, Adamson, Robertson and Croll were *only* indicted for mobbing and riot in relation to what transpired on the second day of the disturbance and not for theft or wilful property damage.

Although the indictment brought in this case was restricted to two very specific events which occurred in the midst of this popular disturbance, the court heard additional evidence which testified to the scale and significance of this riot, the extent of the violence perpetrated against both property and person, as well as the evident strength of anti-Irish sentiment which clearly prevailed in Dundee at the time. Officer David Jack, for instance, Sergeant in the Dundee Constabulary, testified to multiple mobs running through the city on the 5th of July 1830 which eventually converged at a junction and

> ...continued to cheer and huzza for about ten minutes and the declarant saw it was hopeless for him to attempt to take any of them. There was a dense mass which extended for a long way and the declarant was crushed up against a wall without the ability to move.[139]

As well as attacking the person and property of Andrew Savage and William Coyle as described in the indictment, the rioters then proceeded to go from door-to-door

> ...and began searching out the houses of all those whom they knew to be natives of our sister kingdom, dragging them out of their beds, and beating them most unmercifully, breaking all their windows, and even tearing away and burning the very wooden stairs that led to their habitations.[140]

If any Irishman was recognised, '...he was instantly knocked down and mistreated.'[141] As one local man Alexander Farquharson recounted '...the declarant heard part of the mob exclaiming against "the Irish buggers" and to "bring them out"; and it was evident to him that the fury of the mob was di-rected against the Irishmen.'[142] Irish women received similar treatment if they failed what was known as 'the Irish test'. Dundonian resident Janet Lawson explained in court that rioters 'furiously' approached random individuals in the city, herself included, and asked them to say the word "guinea".[143] How their reply was judged to be enunciated dictated whether they had passed or failed 'the Irish test' and determined what treatment would then befall them.

The court also heard that by day two of the riot, the 6th of July 1830, the mob had swelled still further and became vehemently determined ('...with the police not daring to interfere with so numerous a mob'[144]) to rid the city of its Irish contingent once and for all. To that end,

> ...they paraded the streets in every direction, in a riotous and unruly manner, and swearing aloud they would not leave a single Irishman in Dundee...searching out the poor Irish and chasing them out of the town, which they were glad to leave with their lives.[145]

Soon, the Roman Catholic Chapel became the focus of the rioters' attention. The mob attacked the building rendering it '...partially destroyed, breaking all the windows, and other articles in the interior.'[146] The house of the Irish-born priest, Constantine Lee, was also badly damaged.[147] The desecration of the chapel in particular, that seems to have roused the authorities into action as the riot had seemingly morphed from being a private dispute over a boxing match, to an aggressive hibernophobic disturbance, to a large-scale anti-Catholic rout in a matter of days. The military were sent for, and eventually, with the help of the aforementioned extra constables who were drafted in to the city, order was eventually restored, but nonetheless, Dundee was left in disarray and hundreds of its citizens were left bruised, battered and frightened for their lives.

Contemporary newspapers and commentators debated the true cause of the riot in Dundee in the summer of 1830. Some were in no doubt that the root cause of the disturbance was hardened anti-Catholicism.[148] Some tried to downplay this or the anti-Irish element evident in the disturbance, prefer-ring instead to argue that a recent influx of unemployed Irish labourers from Aberdeen, who offered to work in the city for lower wages than its natives, had chiefly irritated the people of Dundee. This disgruntlement, when placed alongside the dispute over the pugilistic contest between Byrne and Mackay, was said to have triggered 'open hostilities' where racist tendencies had sur-faced but largely on account of socio-economic concerns.[149] In terms of the motives of the indicted individuals more specifically, this is pretty hard to glean from the testimony presented in court which was dedicated to proving the three men's involvement in the mob, rather than their rationale for doing so. One eye-witnesses, Thomas Forbes, did testify that he had seen William Robertson commit random acts of violence against property and persons during the riot.[150] Another local woman, Ann Wilson recounted that she witnessed John Adamson, '...seize a large square stone and dash it through the window of a house, shouting with great vehemence, "Damn you, I'll knock you all to hell!"'[151] She was convinced that Adamson, like so many of the rioters, was the worse for drink on the evenings in question. Interestingly, no evidence was brought to court which implicated Nathan Croll in the riot (either directly or indirectly), although a note in the marginalia of the precognition papers may explain why his involvement had been assumed by the authorities. It read: 'Croll is only thirteen or fourteen years of age – is of very bad character and has been nine times convicted of theft in the Dundee Police Court.'[152] In any event, and largely based on flimsy evidence which lacked detail and specificity with regard to their involvement, all three men were found guilty of mobbing and riot and were each sentenced to six months imprisonment.[153]

This case study, not unlike the one which preceded it, demonstrates the difficulties local and judicial authorities faced when attempting to arrest and successfully prosecute individuals involved in riotous behaviour. In this particular episode, the sheer numbers involved hindered the police in controlling the populace and bringing them to order. The episode also highlights the kind of issues and sentiment that bubbled under the surface of Scottish society in the premodern period and which, on occasion, could trigger tumultuous behaviour amongst the populace. Although there may have been more of a boisterous or drunken element to this riot in comparison with the patronage dispute from 1764, once again, we can see that the rioters felt legitimated in their actions and behaviour as they believed they were protecting their livelihoods and interests from a perceived encroachment of one sort or another. Perhaps the rioters would have been better off if they had heeded the epitaph written on the tombstone of their apparent hero whose death had at least in part instigated the tumult that occurred. The grave of Sandy McKay, the erstwhile 'Highland Hercules' is inscribed:

> Strong and athletic was my frame
> Far from my native home I came
> And bravely fought with Simon Byrne
> Alas, but never to return.
> Stranger take warning from my fate
> Lest you should rue your case too late
> If you have ever fought before
> Determine now to fight no more.[154]

(c) Riot on Red Clydeside (Twentieth Century)

At the High Court in Edinburgh, on the 7th of April 1919, twelve men were indicted for their part in a riot that occurred in and around George Square in Glasgow on the 31st of January.[155] More specifically, Emmanuel Shinwell,

William Gallagher, David Kirkwood, Joseph Brennan, George Ebury and Harry Hopkins were charged with inciting individuals to riot and all six, plus David McKenzie, Robert Loudon, Neil Alexander, James Murray, Daniel Stewart Oliver and William McCartney were further accused of being part of the actual mob itself. The indictment related to this case may have seemed pretty peculiar and opaque to contemporary audiences, in that it then went on to detail the riotous events that transpired in January 1919 without directly accusing any of the twelve prisoners of their involvement in the specific episodes mentioned. However, as we have seen, this was not untypical of indictments for communal violence where due to the sheer numbers involved, it was often difficult to pinpoint culpability. Indeed, this may have been especially true of this case as the indictment estimates the number of rioters to be somewhere in the region of '…20,000 evil-disposed persons'[156] and eye-witnesses described the streets of Glasgow to be '…black with bodies.'[157]

The context for this particular protest was a strike and demonstration related to the duration of the working week. Although national negotiations had established a forty-seven hour week for men employed in the shipbuilding and engineering industries, this was deemed insufficient by some militant groups and by the Clyde Workers' Committee in particular. They insisted that a forty-hour working week was more appropriate to protect jobs and wages on Clydeside in the aftermath of the First World War and the socio-economic problems its secession had brought.[158] Moreover, the national negotiations had resulted in the workers forfeiting their morning tea break and this was widely resented by many. Consequently, a so-called 'Joint Committee' of members of the Scottish Trades Union Council, the Allied Trades Council and various shop stewards was created to organise a strike. Despite the fact that such a move was not supported by the majority of the Trade Union organisations that prevailed in Scotland at the time, some 40,000 Glasgow workers came out in support of the strike on Monday 27th of January 1919, and by the next day, a further 30,000 workers had joined the cause.[159]

The strike continued throughout the rest of that week and was to culminate in a mass meeting at George Square on the Friday. A deputation of the strike leaders visited the Lord Provost in the City Chambers that day (31st of January 1919), to see if he had government support to accede to the strikers' wishes. They articulated their unease '…that the men's blood was on the boil';[160] a seemingly accurate prediction of what was to follow given that in the midst of their deliberations, a full-scale riot broke out in the square which bordered the very building they were in.

In the trial that ensued in the aftermath of the disturbance, the court heard how the assembled mob:

> …acting of common purpose did conduct itself in a violent, riotous and tumultuous manner to the great terror and alarm of the lieges, and in breach of the public peace, and did forcibly stop various tramway cars,

the property of the Corporation of Glasgow, and smash windows of said tramway cars and of shops and other premises situated in George Square and in North Frederick Street and in Cathedral Street, all in Glasgow.[161]

Prosecution witnesses testified to the fact that the tramway cars were evidently the initial focus for the rioters. The mob 'wilfully' and 'deliberately' encroached on the rails, blocking the passage of the cars and '...attempts were also made to pull the trolley off the live wire', trapping one female tramway driver in her car.[162] The police pushed forward upon seeing this, and 'attempted to push the crowd aside'. However, as one eyewitness recounted, the crowd

> ...had become very dense and many deep, and after giving way slightly to the Police, they began to push them back, and it became fairly clear... that the Police were in danger of being swept clear of the rails and overwhelmed by the weight of the crowd.[163]

Consequently, the Chief Inspector, who was standing at the front of one of the tramway cars, drew his baton and led a charge of his men. Whilst witnesses thought this action 'well merited' and 'unavoidable',[164] it proved futile not only in a practical sense as there were only one hundred and twenty-nine officers available to face down a crowd which was one hundred and fifty times larger, but perhaps more significantly, it also served to ignite the fury of the mob.[165]

Indeed, it was evident from the testimony presented to court by the one hundred and nine witnesses called for the prosecution, that after this point in the proceedings, the tumult intensified and the mob began to attack people as well as property. The court heard how their '...noise became very great and quite a number of the more active members of the crowd were gesticulating, shouting and roaring'[166] and that the rioters then proceeded to:

> ...assault Owen McQuade...who was then in charge of a licensed shop at 46 North Frederick Street...and strike him bottles and threaten to shoot him with a revolver, and attempt to rob him of the bottles of stout then under his charge in said shop and did rob George Binnie...who was then in charge of a vehicle in North Frederick Street...of the bottles and boxes then under his charge on said vehicle, and did throw bottles and missiles and perform other acts of violence to the danger of the lieges.[167]

Similar tumultuous practices and aggravated assaults of innocent bystanders were replicated in Argyle Street, Trongate, Saltmarket Street, Jail Square, East Clyde Street, Great Clyde Street and Paisley Road West as the tentacles of disorder extended their reach across the city.

Arguably, even more serious allegations were to come, with the evidence that related to the mob's involvement in the assault of authority. The court heard that immediately after the baton charge in George Square, '…the demeanour of the crowd became more menacing'[168] and the mob 'flew' at the police and:

> …did assault Alastair Oswald Morison Mackenzie, K.C., Sheriff of Lanarkshire, and strike him with a bottle or other missile, and snatch from his hand a copy of the Proclamation from the Riot Act from which he was then making proclamation to the lieges.[169]

Additionally, the rioters proceeded to variously assault twenty-four officers who were then on duty at various locations in the city. In the main, the police officers affected had been hit by stones, glass, bottles and other projectiles in the so-called '…dangerous swirl of humanity'[170] that occurred and they sustained scalp and head contusions as a result.[171] However, some officers fared worse and were attacked, badly beaten and kicked whilst on the ground by multiple but unspecified assailants.[172] As Constable Campbell Smart recalled:

> We were quite unable to cope with crowd. I was struck on the head with a large bottle and on the hands and legs with stones and bottles. I was completely stunned by the blow on the head. I had to be assisted. I came through some bad times in France and I think whilst it lasted, this was as bad as anything.[173]

Others received life-threatening injuries, such as Alexander Ferguson Mennie, the Assistant Chief Constable who was brutally stabbed and Constable Charles Cochran who had been beaten senseless with an iron bar.[174] Whilst there were no fatalities recorded, it is clear nonetheless, that what had transpired had been a bloody example of the excesses of communal violence[175] which had '…upset every business and every industry and had meant complete paralysis of the whole city's interests.'[176]

The government considered this riot to be a very serious incident indeed, especially in the wake of what had happened in Russia in 1905 and on account of press reports and other localised publications which introduced their descriptions of the tumult with sensational and provocative headlines such as 'Glasgow's Bloody Friday', 'Bolshevist Uprising', 'Terrorism on the Clyde', 'Revolution!' and 'The George Square Massacre.'[177] The cabinet threatened to invoke articles of the Defence of the Realm Act (1914) in order to arrest and deport the strike leaders if caught.[178] They then sent an estimated 10,000 English troops to Glasgow in order to ensure the riot quelled and to maintain order.[179] Scottish troops stationed at the nearby Maryhill barracks were available for this purpose, but it was thought they might be too sympathetic to the rioters given the burgeoning strength of anti-government feeling being voiced by recently demobilised military men regarding the nature of the socio-economic conditions they had returned home to. Finally, tanks and troops were ordered to be stationed in the Saltmarket area of the city as a symbolic gesture of force to locals, rather than a declaration of intent should further disturbances occur.[180] In any event, and by the 10th of February 1919, the forty-hours strike was over and whilst the striking workers had not achieved their stated aim, those in the engineering and shipbuilding industries did return to a forty-seven hour week, which was some ten hours less than they had been working prior to the strike.[181] However, and as has been noted above, agreement over reducing the working week to this extent had already been negotiated and agreed before the riot began, repudiating any positive impact of the popular disturbance that had occurred and which the press described as '…a debauchery…a disgrace to Scotland…and a spectacle unparalleled in modern times.'[182] Once again, and as with previous chapters in this volume, we see commentary which attempts to decry violence in the Scottish context and define such behaviour as atypical rather than commonplace.

The prosecution's case against the strike leaders Emmanuel Shinwell, William Gallagher, Harry Hopkins and David Kirkwood for inciting the riot was complex and rather ironically, this aspect of the indictment was repeatedly undermined during the course of the trial, by evidence provided by Crown witnesses. Although individuals like Duncan Weir, Chief Detective Inspector of the Central Division of Glasgow Police reported that he heard crowds being enthused and encouraged to maintain the strike after attending rallies and public speeches made by the three men, these orations had occurred days *before* the riot began and, he admitted, had stopped short of promoting violent collective action.[183] Other testimony, recounted hearing the strike leaders say to their supporters that they would take possession of certain buildings in the city on an unspecified occasion in order to showcase the strength of the strike and pointed to the fact that the accused William Gallagher had exclaimed 'We have kindled a fire which the authorities of Glasgow will never put out.' However, under cross-examination, although these witnesses believed the accused had been 'hostile to the police', they had to admit that no direct instructions to riot or rebellion had been given by the men standing in the dock.[184] Then, the Sheriff of Lanarkshire, himself assaulted and injured in the midst of the melee in George Square, testified to both men's attempts at quelling, rather than stoking, the mob's intensions.[185]

Only, one witness, John Steele, a sergeant in the Glasgow city force, gave specific and damning testimony regarding the strike leaders. He testified that he saw David Kirkwood:

> …in a wild state, running towards the crowd with both arms above his head waving to the crowd and at the same time shouting "Come on men, come on men, rally round men, rush the buildings, rush them!"…I was

standing quite near to him at the time. I ordered him to go away. He was very excited and angry. He said "To hell with you." I had my baton in my hand and I struck him with it on the back and shoulders and he fell. I apprehended him and conveyed him into the City Chambers where he was detained in custody.[186]

Steele was alone in his description of what transpired as no other testimony was provided which could corroborate his version of events. Moreover, both sides of the courtroom deemed Steele's use of force against Kirkwood to be inappropriate and overzealous, and it was clear that his conduct and behaviour was not roundly condoned.

Evidence to support the direct involvement of the indicted men in the actual riot itself, was similarly piecemeal, unsubstantiated and largely problematic. Constable Thomas Turner from the Central District of Glasgow's Police Force for instance testified to seeing the accused William Gallagher run after the Chief Constable and catching up to him he '...seized him by the sleeve, turned him round and hit him a severe blow on the face.'[187] Turner continued his evidence saying 'I think Gallagher had a stick in his hand at the time but of that I could not be certain. I saw that the Chief Constable's face was bleeding.'[188] He then recounted how when trying to arrest Gallagher for his actions, another of the accused – Neil Alexander – '...rushed forward and...in a very infuriated state like a madman...he seized hold of Gallagher with both arms round his waist, and tried to drag him from our custody.'[189] However, Turner's seemingly damning testimony was not corroborated by any other witness. Likewise, although Sergeant William Ferguson from the Southern Division of the Glasgow force apprehended the accused William McCartney in the aftermath of the riot and found two unopened bottles of 'invigorating' stout and a butcher's knife in his possession, no evidence could be found which unequivocally linked him with the violent events that transpired.[190] Similarly, Frederick Cameron, temporary constable with the St Rollox District of the Glasgow Police and his colleague Constable James Smillie came across the accused James Murray in Charles Street, the day before the riot. Cameron testified that Murray addressed him saying 'There will be a brick for your heads tomorrow and especially for those buggers in the Central District!'[191] Cameron subsequently recounted spotting Murray the next day in the midst of the mob that were running away from the police, and saw that he was carrying an iron bar.[192] Once again, however, there was no further evidence presented to the court which directly linked Murray with any of the subsequent assaults on the police or public, even though, as we have already noted, medical evidence insisted that iron bars were indeed used in the violence that ensued.

The lack of detail supporting the charges as laid, was a point made by the accused men's defence team in their objection to the libel and in the special defences entered into court. In addition, they pointed out that although several of the men were principally indicted for incitement to riot, the bulk of the evidence heard in court related to the events of the riot itself, rather than the factors which encouraged tumult to occur in the first place, and so the defence craved that the incitement part of the charges be dropped. Moving on to the accusations of riotous activity, six of the accused men (Shinwell, Kirkwood, Brennan, Ebury, Hopkins and Oliver) entered special defences which proved that they were not present at any of the locations across the city where communal violence was alleged to have occurred. They asked that these parts of the indictment against them be dismissed.[193]

These earnest pleas fell on deaf ears. Nevertheless, in his lengthy summation to the jury, the judge did point out the evidential problems related to proving this case. He questioned, for instance, whether the jury could convict an individual of a serious crime on the basis of a single witness whose testimony was uncorroborated by others or on the basis of disputed evidence. He pondered the issue of interpretation and the extent to which behaviours and gesticulations can appear menacing to one individual and yet harmless or indeed inspirational to another, depending on a person's outlook and views at any given time. He wondered whether, it was possible to positively identify an assailant in a melee which involved thousands and thousands of people and which occurred in a relatively confined space and he considered the extent to which being deemed present at a crime scene was tantamount to being involved in criminal activity, if there was no evidence to support direct involvement. All in all, the judge seemed to be at pains to emphasise the weaknesses of the case placed before the jury, rather than its merits and strengths.[194]

Curiously, in this case, the court records include two separate and very different accounts of the jury's verdict. One typed version, clearly states that the assize found all twelve men guilty as charged. The problem with this document is that it does not match the judge's sentencing in this case and therefore its purpose, accuracy or validity is questionable and unclear.[195] The second, hand-written version of the jury's verdict seems more plausible as it *does* match with the subsequent sentencing of those individuals convicted. It notes that by a majority decision of fourteen to one, the jury deemed Emmanuel Shinwell and William Gallagher guilty of incitement to riot and deemed James Murray and William McCartney guilty of rioting. The jury then declared that the eight other individuals Harry Hopkins, Daniel Stewart Oliver, Neil Alexander, Joseph Brennan, George Ebury, David McKenzie, Robert Loudon and perhaps most surprisingly of all, David Kirkwood, were not guilty as charged. Kirkwood had likely escaped a guilty verdict, due to his very public 'assault' at the hands of a senior police officer.[196] Finally, the jury in this case very specifically craved leniency for William Gallagher '...in consideration of the efforts he made to induce the crowd to disperse peacefully' when he realised the extent of what was likely to transpire.[197] The judge took this and the time already served in prison into account when sentencing the four convicts. Shinwell was sentenced to five months imprisonment, whereas Gallagher, Murray and McCartney received sentences of three months' imprisonment each.[198]

Once again, this case highlights the difficulties associated with prosecuting and convicting all of the individuals involved in riotous assembly. By the more modern era, popular protest tended to be conducted on a mass scale and revolved around issues that were typically of national concern, rather than being related to more localised grievances. The articulation of popular opinion in this way, through public demonstrations or strikes was considered wholly legitimate, but only if conducted decorously. Communal violence, of any kind, was deemed wholly unacceptable and had to be quickly suppressed by the authorities. This often involved the use of force on the part of the police as we have seen in various instances across the more modern era, but on occasion, and arguably as we have seen in this case, shows of strength and potency could easily backfire and accusations of unnecessary and excessive brutality could follow.

Indeed, the judge in the Glasgow Square riot felt compelled to address this very issue in his summation of the case. He addressed the defence team's insinuation that the police, rather than the strike leaders should have been on trial, due to their overzealous use of force in quelling the riot where innocent individuals had been rendered victims. The judge said:

> …I confess I think it would be very unfortunate if the idea got abroad that police have to be regarded as men who just wantonly, for no purpose except the purpose of hitting a man's head, hit him. That is not a view I hold of the police…when a baton charge takes place I am afraid it often happens that many innocent people are hit and suffer, but that is just one of the evils that arise from mobbing and rioting, that even some of the guilty escape and some of the innocent suffer, and that is one of the reasons why mobbing and rioting is such a serious offence.[199]

In this commentary, the judge squarely laid the blame for any potentially intemperate reaction of the part of the authorities on the individuals who instigated and/or engaged in riotous behaviour. In effect, he argued that innocent victims were an unfortunate by-product of the evils of mob rule.

Conclusion – The Violent North?

Episodes of communal violence seem to have had a significant part to play in the historic belief that Scotland was a violent nation over the 1660–1960 period, and undoubtedly, there is a wealth of examples of popular disturbances (both large and small scale) that testify to the persistent recalcitrance of the Scottish people. Evidently, and as the case studies in this chapter testify, instances of rioting and mobbing in the Scottish context could turn violent with weapons regularly being deployed against anyone who tried to curb popular protest or prevent its articulation. Yet, what this chapter has also shown is that riotous episodes were not instances of violence for its own sake where individuals happily came together to engage in random acts of bloody boisterousness or to rebel because they could. Rather the violence perpetrated was resorted to when no other appropriate or effective outlet for grievance was available or likely to be effective. Writing in *The Guardian* newspaper on the 2nd of April 1990 in the wake of the Strangeways Prison riot, journalist Martin Kettle noted:

> People riot when they have a sense of grievance and when they feel em-boldened by circumstances to commit acts of defiance or destruction which require a certain bravery and example. Riots normally start when people witness specific acts of injustice which no longer seem tolerable in the circumstances. Riots then frequently develop indiscriminately, according to the rioters' shared assumptions of what is, in their eyes, legitimate. This should not mean that rioting is justifiable, only that it is explicable.[200]

This statement was just as true in the seventeenth century as it is in the twentieth century and as we have seen, individuals involved in public protest in Scotland throughout the period 1660–1960, felt legitimated in their actions and ideologically united in their efforts to be heard.

The varied nature of the causes of popular protest across Scottish history has meant that all sorts of individuals have been involved in the perpetration of this crime. It is very evident, however, that whilst Scottish women were at the forefront of riotous action in the first half of our period, they had all but disappeared from this type of criminality by its end. Moreover, we have also seen that over the course of our period, the very nature of Scottish collective violence changed, moving away from campaigns which resisted change to ones which promoted it. To repeat a phrase used earlier in the chapter: violence gave way to voice in the modern era and instances of Scottish collective violence became infrequent. In sum then, this chapter suggests that if collective action did have a part to play in notions of Scotland as a violent nation, then its contribution was largely confined to the period before 1850 when men *and* women were prepared to come together and were determined to do whatever it took to protect interests that they held dear.

Notes

1 J. Stevenson (1992 edition) *Popular Disturbances in England 1700–1832* (London and New York: Longman), p. 4.
2 See A-M. Kilday (2007) *Women and Violent Crime in Enlightenment Scotland* (Woodbridge: Boydell Press), p. 105 and T.C. Smout (1998 edition) *A History of the Scottish People 1560–1830* (London: Fontana Press), p. 205. For further discussion on the impact that the lack of a vote had on the proliferation of

riots in Scotland see K.J. Logue (1979) *Popular Disturbances in Scotland 1780–1815* (Edinburgh: John Donald), p. 1; C.A. Whatley (2000) *Scottish Society 1707–1830: Beyond Jacobitism, Towards Industrialisation* (Manchester: Manchester University Press), p. 161.

3 For further discussion see for instance the essays in A. Charlesworth (1983) (ed) *An Atlas of Rural Protest in Britain 1548–1900* (London: Croom Helm) and A. Charlesworth, D. Gilbert, A. Randall, H. Southall and C. Wrigley (1996) (eds) *An Atlas of Industrial Protest in Britain 1750–1990* (London: Macmillan Press) as well as A. Wood (2002) *Riot, Rebellion and Popular Politics in Early Modern England* (Basingstoke: Palgrave); J.E. Archer (2000) *Social Unrest and Popular Protest in England 1780–1840* (Cambridge: Cambridge University Press); I. Gilmour (1992) *Riot, Risings and Revolution: Governance and Violence in Eighteenth-Century England* (London: Hutchinson); E. Hobsbawm and G. Rudé (2001 edition) *Captain Swing* (London: Phoenix Press); G. Rudé (1964) *The Crowd in History: A Study of Popular Disturbance in France and England 1730–1848* (London and New York: John Wiley and Sons); C. Bloom (2010 edition) *Violent London: 2000 Years of Riots, Rebels and Revolts* (Basingstoke: Palgrave Macmillan); D.J.V. Jones (1973) *Before Rebecca: Popular Protest in Wales 1793–1835* (London: Allen Lane); D. Williams (2011 edition) *The Rebecca Riots: A Study in Agrarian Discontent* (Cardiff: University of Wales Press) and W. Sheehan and M. Cronin (2011) (eds) *Riotous Assemblies: Rebels, Riots and Revolts in Ireland* (Cork: Mercier Press).

4 W.W. Knox (2012) 'The Attack of the "Half-Formed Persons": The 1811–12 Tron Riot in Edinburgh Revisited', *Scottish Historical Review*, 91, 232, pp. 287–310 at p. 295. See also K. Logue (1980) 'Eighteenth-Century Popular Protest: Aspects of the People's Past' in E.J. Cowan (ed) *The People's Past* (Edinburgh: Polygon), pp. 102–123 at p. 122.

5 See for instance Smout (1998 edition) *A History of the Scottish People*, p. 206 and 211. The thesis is outlined in detail in C.A. Whatley (1992) 'An Uninflammable People?' in I. Donnachie and C. Whatley (eds) *The Manufacture of Scottish History* (Edinburgh: Polygon), pp. 51–71 at p. 52 and in Whatley (2000) *Scottish Society*, pp. 142–145.

6 For further discussion of regional differences relating to the 'orthodoxy of passivity' thesis see especially T.M. Devine (1989) 'Social Responses to Agrarian "Improvement": The Highland and Lowland Clearances in Scotland' in R.A. Houston and I.D. Whyte (eds) *Scottish Society 1500–1800* (Cambridge: Cambridge University Press), pp. 148–168 and to some extent I.A. Whyte (1995) *Scotland Before the Industrial Revolution: An Economic and Social History c1050-c1750* (London and New York: Longman), p. 221.

7 For further discussion see Whatley (2000) *Scottish Society*, p. 142 and p. 145; C.A. Whatley (1990) 'How Tame were the Scottish Lowlanders during the Eighteenth Century?' in T.M. Devine (ed) *Conflict and Stability in Scottish Society 1700–1850* (Edinburgh: John Donald), pp. 1–30 at p. 1 and pp. 15–16; C.A. Whatley (2012) 'Custom, Commerce and Lord Meadowbank: The Management of the Meal Market in Urban Scotland, c.1740-c.1820', *Journal of Scottish Historical Studies*, 32, 1, pp. 1–27 at pp. 2–4; T.M. Devine (1995) *Exploring the Scottish Past: Themes in the History of Scottish* Society (East Linton: Tuckwell Press), chapter thirteen; W.H. Fraser (1988) 'Patterns of Protest' in T.M. Devine and R. Mitchison (eds) *People and Society in Scotland – Volume I: 1760–1830* (Edinburgh: John Donald), pp. 268–291 at p. 269 and pp. 273–275.

8 Unreferenced quotation cited in H.W. Meikle (1909) 'The King's Birthday Riot in Edinburgh, June, 1792', *Scottish Historical Review*, 7, 25, pp. 21–28 at pp. 24–25.

9 See for instance Whyte (ed) *Scottish Society*, p. 219.

10 For further discussion of these examples in a premodern Scottish context see Kilday (2007) *Women and Violent Crime*, chapter six; Whatley (2000) *Scottish Society*, p. 157, pp. 168–172 and chapter five; Whatley (1992) 'An Uninflammable People?', p. 61 and p. 63; Whatley (1990) 'How Tame?', pp. 5–6, p. 8, p. 14 and p. 22; C.A. Whatley (2010) 'Order and Disorder' in E. Foyster and C.A. Whatley (eds) *A History of Everyday Life in Scotland, 1600 to 1800* (Edinburgh: Edinburgh University Press), pp. 191–216 at pp. 192–193 and p. 203; C.G. Brown (1990) 'Protest in the Pews: Interpreting Presbyterianism and Society in Fracture During the Scottish Economic Revolution' in T.M. Devine (ed) *Conflict and Stability in Scottish Society 1700–1850* (Edinburgh: John Donald), pp. 83–105 and V. Wallace (2010) 'Presbyterian Moral Economy: The Covenanting Tradition and Popular Protest in Lowland Scotland, 1707-c.1746', *Scottish Historical Review*, 84, 227, pp. 54–72. For older historiography which also challenges the 'passivity thesis' see Logue (1979) *Popular Disturbances*, chapters one through to eight; Fraser (1988) 'Patterns of Protest', pp. 268–291 and Logue (1980) 'Eighteenth-Century', *passim*.

11 Whatley (2010) 'Order and Disorder', p. 206.

12 See for instance W.W.J. Knox and A. McKinlay (2010) 'Crime, Protest and Policing in Nineteenth-Century Scotland' in T. Griffiths and G. Morton (eds) *A History of Everyday Life in Scotland, 1800 to 1900* (Edinburgh: Edinburgh University Press), pp. 196–224.

13 C. Tilly (1969) 'Collective Violence in European Perspective' in H.D. Graham and T.D. Gurr (eds) *Violence in America: Historical and Comparative Perspectives* (New York: Praeger), pp. 83–118 at pp. 89–97.

14 For an exploration of Tilly's argument see S.J. Connolly (1987) 'Violence and Order in the Eighteenth Century' in P. O'Flanagan, P. Ferguson and K. Whelan (eds) *Rural Ireland, 1600–1900: Modernisation and Change* (Cork: Cork University Press), pp. 42–61 at pp. 57–58.

15 S. Nenadic (1990) 'Political Reform and the "Ordering" of Middle-Class Protest' in T.M. Devine (ed) *Conflict and Stability in Scottish Society 1700–1850* (Edinburgh: John Donald), pp. 65–82 at p. 66. See also Knox and McKinlay (2010) 'Crime', pp. 196–197.

16 Nenadic (1990) 'Political Reform', p. 68.

17 For further discussion see V. Honeyman (2008) '"A Very Dangerous Place"?: Radicalism in Perth', *Scottish Historical Review*, 87, 224, pp. 278–305 at pp. 285–292; Fraser (1988) 'Patterns of Protest', pp. 272–277 and pp. 283–287; W.H. Fraser (2010) *Chartism in Scotland* (Pontypool: Merlin Press) and for the origins of this see W.H. Fraser (1988) *Conflict and Class: Scottish Workers 1700–1838* (Edinburgh: John Donald).

18 For further discussion see W.W. Knox (1992) 'Whatever Happened to Radical Scotland? The Economic and Social Origins of the Mid-Victorian Political Consensus in Scotland' in R. Mason and N. Macdougall (eds) *People and Power in Scotland: Essays in Honour of T.C. Smout* (Edinburgh: John Donald), pp. 218–239 at pp. 221–230 and pp. 233–234 as well as Knox and McKinlay (2010) 'Crime', p. 218.

19 See for instance Fraser (1988) 'Patterns of Protest', pp. 277–282. This transformation was also evident in north-east England too see G. Morgan and P. Rushton (1998) *Rogues, Thieves and the Rule of Law: The Problem of Law Enforcement in North-east England, 1718–1800* (London: Routledge).

20 Rioting and tumultuous activity was increasingly associated with the so-called 'criminal classes' see Knox (2012) 'The Attack', p. 291 and Knox and McKinlay (2010) 'Crime', p. 201. For a detailed analysis of the introduction of policing

in Scotland see D.M. Barrie (2011 edition) *Police in the Age of Improvement: The Origins and Development of Policing in Scotland, 1775–1865* (Abingdon: Taylor and Francis).

21 For further discussion of this in a Scottish context see Nenadic (1990) 'Political Reform', pp. 65–82; Knox and McKinlay (2010) 'Crime', p. 196, pp. 200–201 and p. 213 and C.A. Whatley (1992) 'Royal Day, People's Day: The Monarch's Birthday in Scotland, c. 1660–1860' in R. Mason and N. Macdougall (eds) *People and Power in Scotland: Essays in Honour of T.C. Smout* (Edinburgh: John Donald), pp. 170–188 at p. 179. For discussion of the suppression of popular disturbances over time elsewhere see A. Gray (2006) *Crime and Criminals of Victorian London* (Chichester: Phillimore and Co), p. 91 and D. Waddington (1992) *Contemporary Issues in Public Disorder: A Comparative and Historical Approach* (London and New York: Routledge), p. 96.

22 For evidence of this change in Scotland and elsewhere see Nenadic (1990) 'Political Reform', pp. 68–69; Morgan and Rushton (1998) *Rogues*, p. 199 and S. Tarrow (1998 edition) *Power in Movement: Social Movements and Contentious Politics* (Cambridge: Cambridge University Press), pp. 52–53.

23 For further discussion see for instance Logue (1979) *Popular Disturbances,* chapter two; Devine (1995) *Exploring the Scottish Past,* chapter nine; Devine (1989) 'Social Responses', pp. 148–168; and especially E. Richards (2008 edition) *The Highland Clearances: People, Landlords and Rural Turmoil* (Edinburgh: Birlinn); E. Richards (1974) 'Patterns of Highland Discontent, 1790–1860' in R. Quinault and J. Stevenson (1974) *Popular Protest and Public Order: Six Studies in British History 1790–1920* (London: George Allen and Unwin Ltd), pp. 75–114; M. MacLean and C. Carrell (1986) *As an Fhearann (From the Land): Clearance, Conflict and Crofting* (Edinburgh: Mainstream Publishing) and I.J.M. Robertson (2013) *Landscapes of Protest in the Scottish Highlands after 1914: The Later Highland Land Wars* (Farnham: Ashgate).

24 For further discussion see J.E. Cronin (1989) 'Strikes and Power in Britain, 1870–1920' in L.H. Haimson and C. Tilly (eds) *Strikes, Wars, and Revolutions in an International Perspective* (Cambridge: Cambridge University Press), pp. 79–100 at pp. 83–84 and p. 87; J. Cronin (1979) *Industrial Conflict in Modern Britain* (London: Croom Helm), p. 5, p. 9 and pp. 45–46 as well as Tarrow (1998 edition) *Power*, pp. 31–32 and pp. 99–100.

25 Cronin (1989) 'Strikes', p. 87.

26 For further discussion see Cronin (1979) *Industrial Conflict*, pp. 13–14, p. 17 and pp. 47–48; Cronin (1989) 'Strikes', p. 99 and Hain (1986) *Political Strikes*, pp. 14–15 and chapters four to eleven.

27 For further discussion of the burgeoning alignment between protest and politics in the modern era see Charlesworth *et al* (1996) (eds) *An Atlas of Industrial Protest*, p. 154; Cronin (1989) 'Strikes', p. 81 and pp. 99–100 and Waddington (1992) *Contemporary Issues*, p. 92.

28 For further discussion see J. Foster (1992) 'A Proletarian Nation? Occupation and Class Since 1914' in T. Dickinson and J.H. Treble (eds) *People and Society in Scotland – Volume III: 1914–1990* (Edinburgh: John Donald) pp. 201–240 at p. 218; Charlesworth *et al* (1996) (eds) *An Atlas of Industrial Protest*, p. 151; Cronin (1979) *Industrial Conflict*, p. 13 and Hain (1986) *Political Strikes*, p. 13, pp. 68–69 and chapters four to eleven.

29 See for instance Foster (1992) 'A Proletarian Nation?', p. 217; P. Hain (1986) *Political Strikes: The State and Trade Unionism in Britain* (London: Penguin), pp. 49–50; A. Davies (2006) 'Football and Sectarianism in Glasgow during the 1920s and 1930s', *Irish Historical Studies*, 35, 138, pp. 200–219 and Knox and

McKinlay (2010) 'Crime', p. 199 and pp. 206–209 as well as the references that relate to the second and third case studies below.

30 See Smout (1998 edition) *A History of the Scottish People*, p. 210.

31 Baron D. Hume (1797) Commentaries on the Laws of Scotland Respecting the Description and Punishment of Crimes – Volume II (Edinburgh: Bell and Bradfute), p. 226.

32 Ibid.

33 Ibid.

34 *Ibid*, p. 227.

35 *Ibid*, pp. 227–228.

36 *Ibid*, p. 230.

37 For more detailed discussion see *ibid*, pp. 232–234.

38 *Ibid*, pp. 231–232.

39 *Parliamentary Papers*, 1. Geo. I. c. 5 (1715).

40 *Ibid*, Section I.

41 *Ibid*, Section V.

42 See   http://news.bbc.co.uk/1/hi/scotland/glasgow_and_west/7859192.stm [accessed 29/10/2016].

43 For further discussion of the Porteous Riots see H.T. Dickinson and K. Logue (1976) 'The Porteous Riot: A Study of the Breakdown of Law and Order in Edinburgh, 1736–1737', *Journal of the Scottish Labour History Society*, 10, pp. 21–40.

44 For further discussion of these problems in relation to the Scottish context see Kilday (2007) *Women and Violent Crime*, chapter six; Whatley (2000) *Scottish Society*, p. 199; Whatley (2010) 'Order and Disorder', p. 204 and Logue (1979) *Popular Disturbances*, p. 211. For further discussion of these problems also existing elsewhere see J.R. Ruff (2001) *Violence in Early Modern Europe* (Cambridge: Cambridge University Press), p. 191; Jones (1973) *Before Rebecca*, pp. 225–226; R.B. Shoemaker (1987) 'The London "Mob" in the Early Eighteenth Century', *Journal of British Studies*, 26, 3, pp. 273–304 at p. 277 and p. 296; Stevenson (1992 edition) *Popular Disturbances*, p. 309 and Gray (2006) *Crime*, p. 94.

45 *Parliamentary Papers*, 39. Geo. III. c. 81 (1799), 39 & 40 Geo III c. 106 (1800) and 5 Geo. 4 c. 95 (1824).

46 For further discussion of this in the wider British context see Hain (1986) *Political Strikes*, *passim*.

47 It should be noted that the data from this section relates to judicial statistics gleaned from the Burgh and Police Courts, the Sheriff Courts and the Justiciary Courts over the 1805–1960 period. It should also be noted that in 1925 mobbing and rioting were no longer recorded as separate categories in the judicial statistics but became assimilated into a broader, more amorphous category: 'Public Order Offences'. The graphs presented have been constructed accordingly and in relation to available data (i.e. there are no statistics on convictions prior to 1830).

48 For further discussion of this characteristic in a Scottish context see Kilday (2007) *Women and Violent Crime*, chapter six; Whatley (2010) 'Order and Disorder', p. 203; Whatley (2000) *Scottish Society*, pp. 197–198; Whatley (1990) 'How Tame?', p. 13; Logue (1979) *Popular Disturbances*, p. 199 and p. 203. For evidence of this characteristic in other contexts see Ruff (2001) *Violence*, p. 187 and p. 206; A. Randall (2006) *Riotous Assemblies: Popular Protest in Hanoverian England* (Oxford: Oxford University Press), pp. 312–313; Shoemaker (1987) 'The London "Mob"', p. 285 and R.B. Shoemaker (2004) *The London Mob: Violence and Disorder in Eighteenth-Century England* (London and New York: Hambledon and London), p. 112 and p. 138.

49 For examples see Whatley (1990) 'How Tame?', pp. 9–10; S.G.E. Lythe (1967) 'The Tayside Meal Mobs 1772–3', *Scottish Historical Review*, 46, 141, pp. 26–36 at p. 35 and Knox (2012) 'The Attack', p. 299.

50 For further discussion of the social class of rioters involved in popular protest in Scotland see V. Honeyman (2012) '"That Ye May Judge For Yourselves": The Contribution of Scottish Presbyterianism Towards the Emergence of Political Awareness Amongst Ordinary People in Scotland between 1746 and 1792', Unpublished PhD Thesis, University of Stirling, p. 285; Kilday (2007) *Women and Violent Crime*, p. 112; Logue (1979) *Popular Disturbances*, p. 191; Lythe (1967) 'The Tayside Meal Mobs', p. 35 and Knox (2012) 'The Attack', p. 292. For similar conclusions that relate to disturbances elsewhere see Ruff (2001) *Violence*, p. 187 and p. 205; Stevenson (1992 edition) *Popular Disturbances*, p. 3; Shoemaker (2004) *The London Mob*, p. 137 and p. 139; Shoemaker (1987) 'The London "Mob"', p. 281 and p. 284 and Waddington (1992) *Contemporary Issues*, p. 9 and p. 74.

51 See for instance Whatley (1990) 'How Tame?', p. 7.

52 For evidence of the spontaneity of popular protest in a Scottish context see Logue (1979) *Popular Disturbances*, p. 210 and p. 214; Whatley (2010) 'Order and Disorder', p. 204 and Knox (2012) 'The Attack', p. 298. For evidence of this in other contexts see Shoemaker (2004) *The London Mob*, p. 113; Shoemaker (1987) 'The London "Mob"', p. 281; Morgan and Rushton (1998) *Rogues*, p. 195 and Waddington (1992) *Contemporary Issues*, p. 10.

53 See for example Stevenson (1992 edition) *Popular Disturbances*, p. 105; J.M. Beattie (1986) *Crime and the Courts in England 1660–1800* (Oxford: Oxford University Press), p. 133; Shoemaker (2004) *The London Mob*, p. 130 and Shoemaker (1987) 'The London "Mob"', pp. 297–298.

54 Jones (1973) *Before Rebecca*, p. 203.

55 See Randall (2006) *Riotous Assemblies*, p. 18.

56 See for example *ibid*, p. 208; Ruff (2001) *Violence*, p. 186; Stevenson (1992 edition) *Popular Disturbances*, p. 12 and Logue (1979) *Popular Disturbances*, p. 210.

57 For further discussion see Ruff (2001) *Violence*, p. 191 and p. 201; Jones (1973) *Before Rebecca*, p. 206; Shoemaker (2004) *The London Mob*, pp. 115–120 and p. 131; Shoemaker (1987) 'The London "Mob"', p. 273; Morgan and Rushton (1998) *Rogues*, p. 192 and Randall (2006) *Riotous Assemblies*, p. 11 and pp. 308–309.

58 See for example Whatley (2000) *Scottish Society*, p. 161 and p. 173; Whatley (1992) 'Royal Day', p. 177 and p. 182 and Fraser (1988) 'Patterns of Protest', p. 281.

59 Scottish protestors also deployed violence against property as well against person in their tumultuous activities see for instance Whatley (1990) 'How Tame?', p. 5 and p. 16; Whatley (1992) 'Royal Day', p. 178 and p. 182 and Knox (2012) 'The Attack', p. 307.

60 See for example Kilday (2007) *Women and Violent Crime*, p. 113, p. 117 and p. 121 and Whatley (2012) 'Custom', pp. 12–13.

61 See for instance and for further discussion Honeyman (2012) 'That Ye May Judge', pp. 280–284; Logue (1980) 'Eighteenth-Century', pp. 113–114; Whatley (1992) 'An Uninflammable People?', p. 65; Kilday (2007) *Women and Violent Crime*, pp. 114–115 and Whatley (1992) 'Royal Day', p. 176. In the more modern era see the references related to case studies below and M. Rosie (2004) *The Sectarian Myth in Scotland: Of Bitter Memory and Bigotry* (Basingstoke: Palgrave Macmillan); Davies (2006) 'Football and Sectarianism', pp. 200–219; J. Phillips (2012) *Collieries, Communities and the Miners' Strike in Scotland, 1984–85* (Manchester: Manchester University Press) and found at http://news.bbc.co.uk/onthisday/hi/dates/stories/march/12/newsid_2540000/2540175.stm [accessed 30/10/2016].

62 For further discussion of the variety of grievances which have triggered episodes of collective violence in European history see Ruff (2001) *Violence*, p. 185; Logue (1979) *Popular Disturbances, passim*, Whatley (2010) 'Order and Disorder', p. 204; Shoemaker (1987) 'The London "Mob"', p. 275 and p. 277; Shoemaker (2004) *The London Mob*, p. 111 and Knox and McKinlay (2010) 'Crime', pp. 196–224.

63 See Shoemaker (2004) *The London Mob*, p. 113 and Randall (2006) *Riotous Assemblies*, p. 18 as well as Lythe (1967) 'The Tayside Meal Mobs', pp. 27–28 and p. 31 and Whatley (1990) 'How Tame?', p. 12.

64 For further discussion see Stevenson (1992 edition) *Popular Disturbances*, p. 308 and p. 318; Ruff (2001) *Violence*, pp. 184–186; Kilday (2007) *Women and Violent Crime*, p. 123; Logue (1980) 'Eighteenth-Century', p. 114 and p. 121; Whatley (2000) *Scottish Society*, p. 151; Whatley (2012) 'Custom', p. 6 and p. 11 and Whatley (2010) 'Order and Disorder', p. 207.

65 E.P. Thompson (1971) 'The Moral Economy of the English Crowd in the Eighteenth Century', *Past and Present*, 50, pp. 76–136.

66 For further discussion see especially the collection of essays in A. Randall and A. Charlesworth (2000) (eds) *Moral Economy and Popular Protest: Crowds, Conflict and Authority* (Basingstoke: Macmillan Press) and Randall (2006) *Riotous Assemblies*, p. 17, pp. 69–121, pp. 304–306 and p. 312 as well as Ruff (2001) *Violence*, p. 188 and p. 193; Logue (1979) *Popular Disturbances*, pp. 211–212; Honeyman (2008) '"A Very Dangerous Place"?', p. 286; Whatley (2000) *Scottish Society*, p. 196; Whatley (1990) 'How Tame?', p. 14; Kilday (2007) *Women and Violent Crime*, pp. 117–119; Shoemaker (2004) *The London Mob*, p. 130; Whatley (1992) 'An Uninflammable People?', p. 65; Shoemaker (1987) 'The London "Mob"', p. 279 and p. 286 and Fraser (1988) 'Patterns of Protest', p. 271 and p. 293.

67 See for example Honeyman (2012) 'That Ye May Judge', p. 280 and p. 285; Honeyman (2008) '"A Very Dangerous Place"?', p. 295; Whatley (2010) 'Order and Disorder', p. 204; Whatley (1992) 'Royal Day', p. 181; Knox (2012) 'The Attack', p. 288 and Waddington (1992) *Contemporary Issues*, p. 94 and p. 205.

68 For further discussion see Whatley (2000) *Scottish Society 1707–1830*, p. 203; Whatley (1992) 'An Uninflammable People?', p. 67; Whatley (1992) 'Royal Day', pp. 182–184 and Fraser (1988) 'Patterns of Protest', p. 281.

69 See Whatley (2010) 'Order and Disorder', p. 204.

70 Brown (1990) 'Protest', p. 83.

71 See for instance R.H. Campbell (1983) 'The Influence of Religion on Economic Growth in Scotland in the Eighteenth Century' in T.M. Devine and D. Dickson (eds) *Ireland and Scotland 1600–1850: Parallels and Contrasts in Economic and Social Development* (Edinburgh: John Donald), pp. 220–234 at p. 230 and p. 232.

72 Brown (1990) 'Protest', p. 91.

73 *Ibid*, p. 97.

74 See A.L. Drummond and J. Bulloch (1981) *The Scottish Church 1688–1843 – The Age of the Moderates* (Edinburgh: The Saint Andrew Press), p. 124 and also Logue (1979) *Popular Disturbances*, p. 168. For further discussion of the history of patronage in Scotland see R. Sher and A. Murdoch (1983) 'Patronage and Party in the Church of Scotland, 1750–1800' in N. Macdougall (ed) *Church, Politics and Society: Scotland 1408–1929* (Edinburgh: John Donald), pp. 197–220 and Honeyman (2012) 'That Ye May Judge', pp. 57–62.

75 See R.B. Sher (2015 edition) *Church and University in the Scottish Enlightenment* (Edinburgh: Edinburgh University Press), pp. 47–48.

76 Brown (1990) 'Protest', p. 97. For further discussion of the reasons patronage was so strongly objected to see Logue (1979) *Popular Disturbances*, p. 168, p. 172 and p. 176 as well as Honeyman (2012) 'That Ye May Judge', pp. 55–57.

77 Sher and Murdoch (1983) 'Patronage', p. 198 with my emphasis added. See also Honeyman (2012) 'That Ye May Judge', pp. 280–285.

78 See Brown (1990) 'Protest', p. 97, Logue (1979) *Popular Disturbances*, pp. 169–171 and Sher and Murdoch (1983) 'Patronage', p. 199.

79 Brown (1990) 'Protest', p. 98.

80 *Ibid*, p. 99. See also Honeyman (2012) 'That Ye May Judge', p. 260 and N.C. Landsman (1995) 'Liberty, Piety and Patronage: The Social Context of Contested Clerical Calls in Eighteenth-Century Glasgow' in A. Hook and R.B. Sher (eds) *The Glasgow Enlightenment* (East Linton: Tuckwell Press), pp. 214–226 at p. 221.

81 For further discussion of the patronage issue as a stimulus to the politicisation of the Scottish people see Honeyman (2012) 'That Ye May Judge', chapter six.

82 National Records of Scotland (hereafter NRS), High Court of Justiciary, Process Papers, JC26/171/1/6. The phrase 'lieges' refers to the ordinary peaceable citizens residing in the specific location referred to.

83 NRS, Justiciary Court, South Circuit Minute Books, JC12/11.

84 NRS, High Court of Justiciary, Process Papers, JC26/171/1/2. My addition in parenthesis.

85 NRS, Acts of the Parliaments of Scotland, PA2/13, ff.81r–v (16th July 1587).

86 A. McKay (1858 edition) *The History of Kilmarnock* (Kilmarnock: Archibald McKay), p. 114.

87 *Ibid*.

88 *Ibid*, p. 115. This aspect of the case is also referred to, in condemnatory terms, in the poem 'The Ordination' by Robert Burns, written in 1787. This is perhaps somewhat ironic, given that the Earl of Glencairn eventually becomes a key patron for the poet. See J. Kinsley (1968) (ed) *The Poems and Songs of Robert Burns – Volume I Text* (Oxford: Clarendon Press), pp. 213–217.

89 McKay (1858 edition) *The History of Kilmarnock*, p. 115.

90 *Ibid*, p. 116.

91 *The Scots Magazine*, XXVI, May 1764, p. 287. See also (1840 edition) *Annals of the General Assembly of the Church of Scotland from the Origin of the Relief in 1752, to the Rejection of the Overture on Schism in 1766, Volume II* (Edinburgh: John Johnstone), pp. 289–290.

92 NRS, High Court of Justiciary, Process Papers, JC26/171/1/2. My addition in parenthesis.

93 *Ibid* and JC26/171/1/5.

94 *Caledonian Mercury*, 21st July 1764. See also J. Paterson (1866) *History of the Counties of Ayr and Wigtown – Volume III: Cunninghame – Part Two* (Edinburgh: James Stillie), pp. 400–401. The riotous scenes played out inside the church are also detailed in an anonymous poem entitled 'Verses Written in 1764, On the Violent Induction of the Rev. Mr. Lindsay' and found in a pamphlet of clerical satires said to have been collected by Robert Burns and published in 1852. The pamphlet is entitled: *The Kirk's Alarm: Or, A Present for the Priest Ridden* (Edinburgh: H. Robinson) – see www.ayrshirecollections.co.uk/the-kirks-alarm/ [accessed 15/10/2016].

95 NRS, Justiciary Court, South Circuit Minute Books, JC12/11 and see also sealed verdict found in High Court of Justiciary, Process Papers, JC26/171.

96 McKay (1858 edition) *The History of Kilmarnock*, p. 122.

97 T. Gallagher (1987) *Glasgow: The Uneasy Peace – Religious Tension in Modern Scotland* (Manchester: Manchester University Press), p. 7 and J.E. Handley (1945 edition) *The Irish in Scotland 1798–1845* (Cork: Cork University Press), p. 3.

 98 Gallagher (1987) *Glasgow*, p. 7 and Handley (1945 edition) *The Irish*, p. 34, p. 37, p. 57 and p. 80. See also B. Collins (1991) 'The Origins of Irish Immigration to Scotland in the Nineteenth and Twentieth Centuries' in T.M. Devine (ed) *Irish Immigrants and Scottish Society in the Nineteenth and Twentieth Centuries* (Edinburgh: John Donald), pp. 1–18.

 99 See S. Bruce, T. Glendinning, I. Patterson and M. Rosie (2004) *Sectarianism in Scotland* (Edinburgh: Edinburgh University Press), p. 10 and R.B. McReady (1998) 'Irish Catholicism and Nationalism in Scotland: The Dundee Experience, 1850–1922', *Irish Studies Review*, 6, 3, pp. 245–252 at p. 245.

100 For further discussion see for instance Gallagher (1987) *Glasgow*, pp. 13–14; Handley (1945 edition) *The Irish*, p. 82, p. 142 and p. 171; Bruce *et al* (2004) *Sectarianism*, pp. 12–13 and B. Murray (2000 edition) *The Old Firm: Sectarianism, Sport and Society in Scotland* (Edinburgh: John Donald), p. 76.

101 Sir M.S. Stewart quoted in I.A. Muirhead (1973) 'Catholic Emancipation: Scottish Reactions in 1829', *Innes Review*, 24, 1, pp. 26–42 at p. 41 cited in Gallagher (1987) *Glasgow*, p. 10.

102 For further discussion see Gallagher (1987) *Glasgow*, p. 15 and Murray (2000 edition) *The Old Firm*, p. 80.

103 Murray (2000 edition) *The Old Firm*, p. 78.

104 Gallagher (1987) *Glasgow*, p. 16.

105 For further discussion see *ibid*, pp. 17–18; T. Gallagher (1991) 'The Catholic Irish in Scotland: In Search of Identity' in T.M. Devine (ed) *Irish Immigrants and Scottish Society in the Nineteenth and Twentieth Centuries* (Edinburgh: John Donald), pp. 19–43; B. Aspinwall (1996) 'Scots and Irish Clergy Ministering to Immigrants, 1830–1878', *Innes Review*, 47, 1, pp. 45–68 and W.M. Walker (1972) 'Irish Immigrants in Scotland: Their Priests, Politics and Parochial Life', *The Historical Journal*, 15, 4, pp. 649–667 at p. 651.

106 See for instance R.K. Donovan (1979) 'Voices of Distrust: The Expression of Anti-Catholic Feeling in Scotland, 1778–1781', *Innes Review*, 30, 1, pp. 32–76; S.K. Kehoe (2010) *Creating a Scottish Church: Catholicism, Gender and Ethnicity in Nineteenth-Century Scotland* (Manchester: Manchester University Press), chapter one; Muirhead (1973) 'Catholic Emancipation', pp. 26–42 and E.W. McFarland (1990) *Protestants First: Orangeism in Nineteenth Century Scotland* (Edinburgh: Edinburgh University Press), chapter four.

107 For further discussion of the potential reasons why violence of this kind was rare within the Scottish context see Gallagher (1987) *Glasgow*, pp. 33–37.

108 *Ibid*, p. 32. See also Gallagher (1991) 'The Catholic Irish', p. 27. For further discussion of the settlement of the Irish in Dundee in the nineteenth century see also M. Anderson and D.J. Morse (1990) 'The People' in W.H. Fraser and R.J. Morris (eds) *People and Society in Scotland – Volume II: 1830–1914* (Edinburgh: John Donald), pp. 8–45 at p. 18; McReady (1998) 'Irish Catholicism', pp. 245–247 and Rev. A.S. Canon MacWilliam (1967) 'Catholic Dundee: 1787 to 1836', *Innes Review*, 18, 2, pp. 75–87 at p. 75, p. 83 and p. 86.

109 See Gallagher (1987) *Glasgow*, p. 32 and Gallagher (1991) 'The Catholic Irish', p. 27.

110 Walker (1972) 'Irish Immigrants', p. 660.

111 For further discussion see Bruce *et al* (2004) *Sectarianism*, p. 21.

112 *The Morning Chronicle*, 3rd June 1830, Issue 18962.

113 *Ibid*.

114 *Ibid*.

115 *Ibid*.

116 For further discussion see J. Anderson (2001) 'Pugilistic Prosecutions: Prize Fighting and the Courts in Nineteenth Century Britain', *The Sports Historian*, 21, 2, pp. 37–57; D. Brailsford (1988) *Bareknuckles: A Social History of Prizefighting* (Cambridge: Lutterworths Press); J.G. Bohun Lynch (2008 edition) *Knuckles and Gloves* (London: Collins) and 'The Fight at Salcey Green' found at http://mkheritage.co.uk/hdhs/fight.html [accessed 16/10/2016].

117 *The Bury Norwich Post*, 9th June 1830, Issue 2502.

118 *The Examiner*, 6th June 1830, Issue 1166. See also *The York Herald*, 12th June 1830, Issue 3009.

119 *The Morning Chronicle*, 7th June 1830, Issue 18964.

120 *The Morning Chronicle*, 8th June 1830, Issue 18965 and *The Leicester Chronicle*, 12th June 1830, Issue 1013.

121 *The Standard*, 23rd July 1830, Issue 996 and *The Caledonian Mercury*, 26th July 1830, Issue 17011.

122 See for instance a commentary in *The Times* published on the 5th June 1830.

123 *The Standard*, 23rd July 1830, Issue 996.

124 *The Caledonian Mercury*, 26th July 1830, Issue 17011.

125 *The Standard*, 23rd July 1830, Issue 996.

126 See for instance reports of riots in Glasgow in the aftermath of the fight in *The Hull Packet*, 15th June 1830, Issue 2378.

127 For further elaboration of the issues that sparked the commencement of the riot see a broadside found in the National Library of Scotland (hereafter NLS) (1830) 'Rioting!! A Full and Particular Account of the Great Riots and Mobs that took Place at Dundee, on Tuesday, Wednesday and Thursday last, the 6th, 7th and 8th July, 1830', Special Collections (SpC), L.C. Fol. 74 (189).

128 For more on this particular rumour of corruption regarding the bout see 'The Fight at Salcey Green' found at http://mkheritage.co.uk/hdhs/fight.html [accessed 16/10/2016].

129 B. King (2011) *Undiscovered Dundee* (Edinburgh: Black and White Publishing), p. 63.

130 NLS, 'Rioting'.

131 See *ibid*.

132 See *ibid* and also King (2011) *Undiscovered Dundee*, pp. 65–66. Whilst the broadside referenced here reports three fatalities afforded to the riot, this detail is not repeated in any other account of the incident, including the associated court material and once again, it is likely that the report was exaggerated for sensational effect.

133 NRS, Justiciary Court, Precognition Papers – Indictment AD14/30/51.

134 See details of the arrest warrant dated 25th July 1830 and found in *ibid*.

135 *Ibid.*

136 *Ibid.*

137 *Ibid.*

138 *Ibid.*

139 *Ibid*, testimony of David Jack.

140 NLS, 'Rioting'.

141 *Ibid.*

142 NRS, Justiciary Court, Precognition Papers – Testimony of Alexander Farquharson, AD14/30/51.

143 *Ibid*, testimony of Janet Lawson.

144 NLS, 'Rioting'.

145 *Ibid.*

146 *Ibid.*

147 King (2011) *Undiscovered Dundee*, p. 65.
148 See for instance the commentary provided in *ibid*.
149 See for instance, *The Caledonian Mercury*, 15th July 1830, Issue 17006.
150 NRS, Justiciary Court, Precognition Papers – Testimony of Thomas Forbes, AD14/30/51.
151 *Ibid*, testimony of Ann Wilson, AD14/30/51.
152 NRS, Justiciary Court, Precognition Papers – Indictment, AD14/30/51.
153 King (2011) *Undiscovered Dundee*, p. 66.
154 *Ibid*, p. 62.
155 NRS, Justiciary Court, Process Papers – Indictment, JC26/1919/85. The case had originally been indicted in Glasgow on the 28th of March 1919, but latterly transferred to the High Court in the nation's capital.
156 *Ibid*.
157 NRS, Justiciary Court, Precognition Papers – Testimony of Constable William McClennan, Partick District, Glasgow Police, AD15/19/11.
158 Clydeside had something of a historic reputation for industrial agitation and the evident socio-economic tensions after the war exacerbated these tensions. See for further discussion W. Kenefick (2007) *Red Scotland! The Rise and Fall of the Radical Left, c. 1872 to 1932* (Edinburgh: Edinburgh University Press), chapter four; J. Jenkinson (2008) 'Black Sailors on Red Clydeside: Rioting, Reactionary Trade Unionism and Conflicting Notions of "Britishness" Following the First World War', *Twentieth Century British History*, 19, 1, pp. 29–60; A. Charlesworth, D. Gilbert, A. Randall, H. Southall and C. Wrigley (1996) *An Atlas of Industrial Protest in Britain* (Basingstoke: McMillan Press), chapter nineteen; I. McLean (1983) *The Legend of Red Clydeside* (Edinburgh: John Donald), chapter ten; T.C. Smout (1997 edition) *A Century of the Scottish People 1830–1950* (London: Fontana Press), pp. 259–270; T.M. Devine (2000 edition) *The Scottish Nation 1700–2000* (London: Penguin), pp. 309–315 and M. Craig (2011) *When the Clyde Ran Red* (Edinburgh and London: Mainstream Publishing), p. 160.
159 See H. McShane (1919) *Glasgow 1919: The Story of the 40 Hours Strike* (Glasgow: The Molendinar Press) [Bodleian Library Ref. 23215 d.42]; I. McLean (1974) 'Popular Protest and Public Order: Red Clydeside, 1915–1919' in Quinault and Stevenson (1974) *Popular Protest*, pp. 215–242 at p. 228 and 'Bloody Friday: Glasgow's General Strike of 1919' found at http://urbanglasgow.co.uk/archive-bloody-friday-glasgow-s-general-strike-of-1919._o_t_t_792.html [accessed 23/10/2016].
160 NRS, Justiciary Court, Precognition Papers – Testimony of Sir John Lindsay, Town Clerk, City of Glasgow, AD15/19/11.
161 *Ibid*.
162 *Ibid*, testimony of Alastair Mackenzie, K.C. Sheriff of Lanarkshire.
163 *Ibid*.
164 *Ibid*, testimony of Charles Robertson (local resident), AD15/19/11.
165 *Ibid*. For details of the roll call of officers on duty at the time of the riot see *ibid*, testimony of James Verdier Stevenson, Chief Constable, City of Glasgow Police.
166 *Ibid*, testimony of Sir John Lindsay, Town Clerk, City of Glasgow.
167 NRS, Justiciary Court, Process Papers – Indictment, JC26/1919/85. For further details see the *Dundee Courier*, 1st February 1919, Issue 20489 and *Yorkshire Evening Post*, 1st February 1919, Issue 8856.
168 NRS, Justiciary Court, Precognition Papers – Testimony of James Verdier Stevenson, Chief Constable, City of Glasgow Police, AD15/19/11.
169 NRS, Justiciary Court, Process Papers – Indictment, JC26/1919/85. See also NRS, Justiciary Court, Precognition Papers – Testimony of Alastair Mackenzie, K.C. Sheriff of Lanarkshire, AD15/19/11.

170 *Yorkshire Evening Post*, 31st January 1919, Issue 8855.
171 See for instance NRS, Justiciary Court, Precognition Papers – Testimonies of Constable William McClennan, Patrick District, Glasgow Police and Sergeant William Ferguson, Southern Division, Glasgow Police, both AD15/19/11.
172 *Ibid*, testimonies of Constables Thomas Burke and Charles Smith, both Glasgow Police.
173 *Ibid*, testimony of Constable Campbell Smart, St Rollox Division, Glasgow Police.
174 *Ibid*, testimonies of Alexander Ferguson Mennie, Assistant Chief Constable and Constable Charles Cochrane, both City of Glasgow Police.
175 For a full list of the police victims and the injuries they sustained see ibid, testimony of Dr R.T. Halliday, Physician to the Glasgow Police Force. See also the details provided in the *Aberdeen Journal*, 1st February 1919, Issue 19996.
176 See NRS, Justiciary Court, Precognition Papers – Testimony of Sir John Lindsay, Town Clerk, City of Glasgow, AD15/19/11. For further detailed descriptions of the riot see *Western Daily Press*, 1st February 1919, Issue 18892; *Aberdeen Journal*, 1st February 1919, Issue 19996 and *Western Times*, 1st February 1919, Issue 21708.
177 See respectively *The Strike Bulletin*, 1st February 1919, *The Scotsman*, 30th January 1919, the *Evening Times*, 31st January 1919; *The Glasgow Herald*, 31st January 1919 and *The Strike Bulletin*, 2nd February 1919.
178 *Parliamentary Papers*, 4 & 5 Geo. 5 c. 29 (1914).
179 *Derby Daily Telegraph*, 3rd February 1919, Issue 12287.
180 For further discussion see McLean (1974) 'Popular Protest', pp. 229–31'; Glasgow Digital Library, *Red Clydeside: A History of the Labour Movement in Glasgow 1910–1932*, 'Photograph of Tanks and Soldiers in Saltmarket Area of Glasgow, Feb 1919', found at http://sites.scran.ac.uk/redclyde/redclyde/rc025.htm [accessed 23/10/2016]. For further discussion see also McShane (1919) *Glasgow 1919*, *passim*.
181 See McLean (1983) *The Legend of Red Clydeside*, pp. 126–127 and McShane (1919) *Glasgow 1919*, *passim*.
182 *Aberdeen Journal*, 1st February 1919, Issue 19996.
183 NRS, Justiciary Court, Precognition Papers – Testimony of Chief Detective Inspector Duncan Weir, Glasgow Police, AD15/19/11.
184 See for instance *ibid*, testimonies of Inspector Neil Gillies, Eastern District, Glasgow Police Superintendent Matthew McCulloch, Lanarkshire Constabulary.
185 *Ibid*, testimony of Alastair Mackenzie, K.C. Sheriff of Lanarkshire.
186 *Ibid*, testimony of Sergeant John Steele, City of Glasgow Police.
187 *Ibid*, testimony of Constable Thomas Turner, Central District, Glasgow Police.
188 *Ibid*.
189 *Ibid*.
190 *Ibid*, testimony of Sergeant William Ferguson, Southern District, Glasgow Police.
191 *Ibid*, testimony of Temporary Constable Frederick Cameron, St Rollox District, Glasgow Police.
192 *Ibid*.
193 See NRS, Justiciary Court, Process Papers – Note of Objection to the Relevancy of the Indictment, JC26/1919/85/41 and NRS, Justiciary Court, Process Papers – Special Defences for Emmanuel Shinwell and Others, JC26/1919/85/40.
194 See NRS, Justiciary Court, Trial Transcript – Charge to the Jury, JC36/31/10.
195 See NRS, Justiciary Court, Process Papers – Paper E: Shinwell and Others, JC26/1919/85.

196 For instance, a photograph was taken of David Kirkwood being tended to whilst lying on the ground unconscious after having been struck by a police baton, see Glasgow Digital Library, *Red Clydeside,* 'Photograph of David Kirkwood, 31 Jan 1919', found at http://sites.scran.ac.uk/redclyde/redclyde/rc052.htm [accessed 23/10/2016].
197 See NRS, Justiciary Court, Process Papers – Verdict, JC26/1919/85.
198 See NRS, Justiciary Court, Trial Transcript – Sentence, JC36/31/10. Numerous appeals for the men's release were subsequently made by a range of individuals from various political parties and trade unions to the Secretary for Scotland see NRS, Justiciary Court, Criminal Case File: Glasgow Strike Riots, HH16/152, HH16/153, HH16/154 and HH16/155.
199 NRS, Justiciary Court, Trial Transcript - Charge to the Jury, JC36/31/10.
200 *The Guardian,* 2nd April 1990.

Chapter 5

The Violent North? Violence for Gain, 1660–1960

Introduction

An understanding of robbery offending is central to any history of violent crime. This is for several reasons, but especially because the nature of robbery offending, arguably more than any other type of interpersonal crime, regularly manifests key aspects of technological and social change over time. Although traditional rudimentary 'smash-and-grab' robberies still pervade the records of criminal statistics today just as they did in the early modern period, the methodology of robbery has nonetheless been transformed if we consider (albeit rather crudely) the change from the highwayman or pirate preying upon wealthy travellers in the seventeenth century, the footpad and garrotter attacking victims on the street in the eighteenth and nineteenth centuries, and then the more elaborate, pre-planned technologically advanced heists of the more modern era. It can be argued that the study of robbery offers an insight into the evolution of criminality over time and in a given context. Moreover, in our analysis we are more cognisant of the various factors which influence fluctuations in patterns of offending and alterations in approach, because these are wholly explicit in the changing nature of robbery offending itself. Few other offences map on to societal change and development as effectively as robbery.[1]

Another reason why robbery is pivotal to any work that investigates the history of crime is that the nature and incidence of robbery was (and still is) commonly regarded as a touchstone for how violent a place is, or is at least *perceived* to be.[2] The reason robbery holds this prominence over other offences is partly to do with the fact that it is both a crime against the person and a crime against property, and because it is one that involves violence of a direct and confrontational nature.[3] Furthermore, it has long been regarded as an indicator of national stability. It was widely recognised that the security of streets, homes and premises is essential to personal well-being, the facilitation of good communications and the continued commercial resilience of a given location. Consequently, if people were unable to travel along public roads, sleep in their homes at night or leave their businesses unattended without fear of being robbed, then this would have serious implications for the authorities and the general populace alike.[4]

It is clear that throughout history, there has been a popular sensitivity regarding rates of robbery offending that were not articulated as explicitly with respect to other types of interpersonal crime. Consequently, and as we will see in a subsequent section of this chapter, when reports from individuals indicated that robbery was rife or when crime statistics appeared to show a surge in this kind of offending, moral panics tended to quickly ensue, causing widespread anxiety and angst which in turn forced authoritative reaction of one kind or another.[5] Typically, however, these instances were rarely rooted in the reality of robbery's prevalence and were instead based on sensational media-based exaggeration.[6] Indeed, the widespread recognition of this pre-disposed sensitivity regarding robbery was such that it could be argued that on some occasions in Scotland and elsewhere between 1660 and 1960, moral panics were deliberately ignited by those in power to expedite a particular judicial change or facilitate the introduction of what might normally have been thought of as a controversial form of social control.[7]

Although the content of this particular section of the volume will be concerned with the crime of robbery, the concept of 'violence for gain' has been used in the title of this chapter and also occasionally in the body of the text to delineate the precise nature of the offending being discussed. It is evident that the term 'robbery' has been used erroneously throughout history and even in the present day to describe *both* violent and non-violent acts of theft, but it is solely the history of the former activity that concerns us here.[8] It should also be recognised (as was alluded to in the introductory chapter) that the analysis in this work will not extend to violence amongst street gangs in the Scottish historical context. This is for two reasons. First, the *raison d'être* for violence within Scottish gang culture was not normally *material* gain as such. Rather, violence was deployed to intimidate, retaliate or attain supremacy, to win revenge over a rival, or to gain some sort of territorial advantage.[9] Second, the kind of gang violence which we *could* associate with material gain (such as extortion or demanding money with menace) did not really come to the attention of the authorities, the populace or indeed the media in Scotland or elsewhere in Britain, until *after* the 1960s which is the endpoint of this study.[10] Thus, although we do have evidence in both this chapter and the next, of enterprising individuals who came together for the purposes of felonious activity, they were not street gang members as such. The nature of the relationships within these groupings tended to be tenuous, temporary, non-hierarchical and wholly unrelated to spatial supremacy, making them wholly unlike the ties that bound gang members together.[11]

Violence for Gain and the Law

Robbery can be defined as 'the taking and carrying away of [the] personal property of another, from the person and against his will, by force or violence or by assault and putting in fear with intent to steal.'[12] In Scotland, this variant of violence for gain was sometimes referred to as *stouthrief* in early court records, but as that particular term came to be associated with all sorts of elaborate theft, whether violent or otherwise, robbery was the preferred lexis in instances where aggression was evident and a capital charge deemed appropriate. In England, the 1691 Robbery Act was the statutory provision established for the prosecution of this kind of offence, as well as the necessary qualification of violence or fear being evident in an episode of theft to make it a robbery, this legislation also determined the monetary value of the plunder and the location from which the goods were stolen to be important too.[13] The situation in *ancien régime* France was even more complicated in this respect. There, an offence was deemed a robbery or an aggravated theft depending on a variety of circumstances. These included the nature of the object stolen, the way in which the crime was committed, the place and time the robbery occurred and even the rank and status of the individuals involved.[14]

In Scotland, robbery was a capital crime at common law and there were two simple and logical qualifications that had to be met for an indictment of this nature to arise. First, something had to be stolen and second, the thief must have used violence. An indictment for robbery did not require that the violence be applied to the victim. If the victim had surrendered his or her possessions merely because of the threat of being assaulted, this was enough to constitute a robbery according to Scots law.[15] The simplicity and clarity of the legislative approach to robbery north of the Tweed may go some way to explain why the Scottish authorities did not feel compelled to sanction amendments, introduce additional statutes or modify penal policy to broaden the definition and scope of the offence, as was evidently the case elsewhere between 1660 and 1960.[16]

As robbery regularly involved direct physical confrontation between victim and offender, it was regarded by the Scots as '...the prime instance of forcible theft' and one of the most serious crimes brought to trial.[17] Moreover, and as we have already identified, robbery was also deemed a particularly serious felony due to the recognition that the extent of its prevalence in any particular era was an indicator of regional or national stability and on account of the threat that it posed to personal and wider economic security too.[18] The gravity of regard for the offence was reflected in the punishment meted out to those convicted of its perpetration in Scotland and elsewhere. This was especially evident during the premodern period where a death sentence was the typical outcome, with few remissions and additional, particularly macabre pre- and postmortem aggravated punishments being regularly deployed at the judges' discretion. It was only by the second half of the nineteenth century, that penal servitude and imprisonment were eventually deemed appropriate alternative sanctions for individuals convicted of this type of violent theft.[19]

Trends in Violence for Gain and its Punishment

Figures 5.1, 5.6 and 5.9 below show trends in indictments for robbery and attempted robbery in Scotland between 1660 and 1960.[20] Although recorded rates of *attempted* robbery were never very significant in any given year, the number of successfully perpetrated robberies recorded was more substantial and offending rates for this offence were far higher in the nineteenth century in comparison with all forms of fatal violence, all types of sexual violence and recorded instances of both attempted murder and the assault of authority. This is striking when we consider the seriousness of the offence and is hugely significant for our analysis given the historic extrapolation of robbery rates in perceptions regarding generic trends in violent behaviour. Might this evidence go some way to explain why Scotland has been regarded as a violent nation for so long? In addition, the data also shows an upward trend in recorded instances

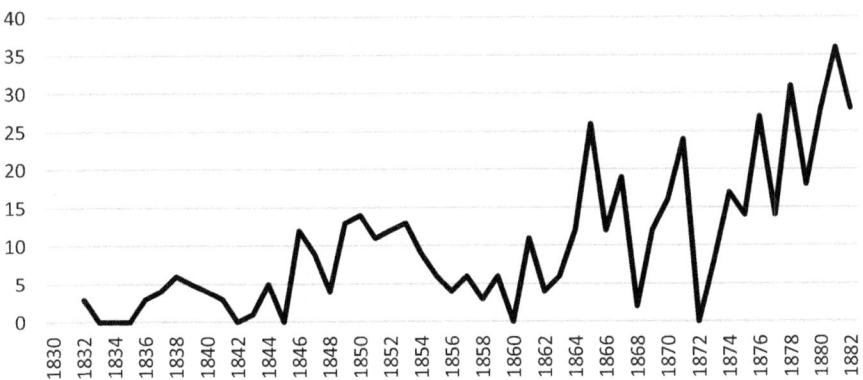

Figure 5.1 Indictments for Attempted Robbery in Scotland, 1830–1882.

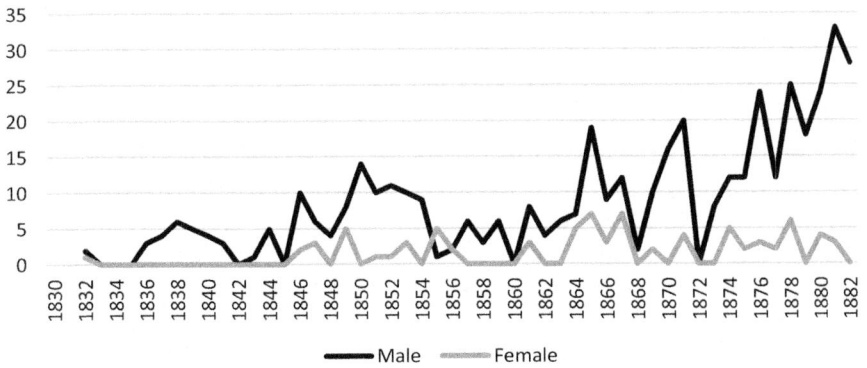

Figure 5.2 Indictments for Attempted Robbery in Scotland by Gender, 1830–1882.

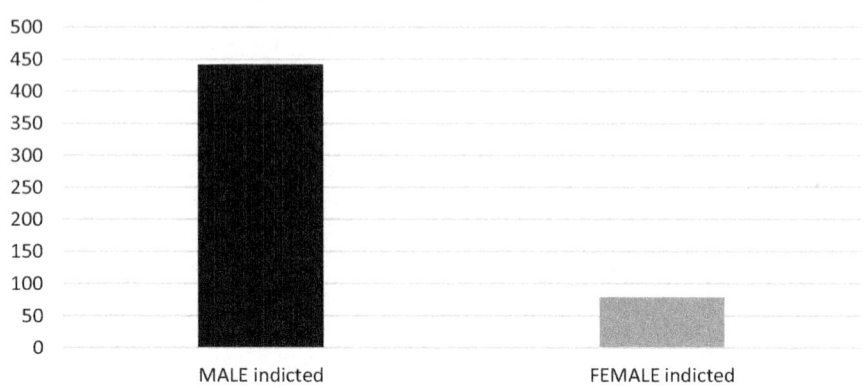

Figure 5.3 The Gendered Nature of Attempted Robbery Indictments in Scotland, 1830–1882.

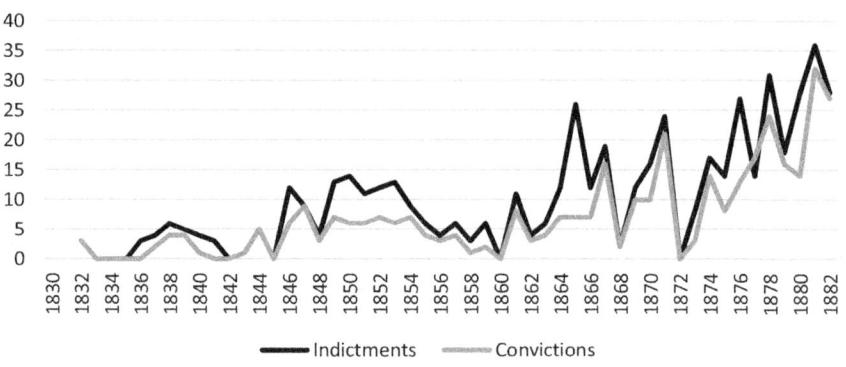

Figure 5.4 Indictments and Convictions for Attempted Robbery in Scotland, 1830–1882.

of both robbery and attempted robbery in the second half of the nineteenth century, in contrast to all of the other types of violent crime analysed in this volume. Although this pattern is not maintained in the twentieth century, there is evidence of a post-war rise in offending nonetheless. It is interesting to consider whether the atypical pattern of indictments for violence has also influenced perceptions of violent offending in Scotland more broadly and furthered a wholly false impression of the historic criminality of the nation.

Figures 5.2, 5.3, 5.7, 5.8, 5.10 and 5.11 above indicate that the perpetration of robbery in Scotland was largely a male enterprise in the 1805–1960 period. Women's involvement in robbery proper, whilst persistent and more significant than their involvement in other crimes of interpersonal violence (furthering trends observed in the eighteenth century) was still dwarfed by

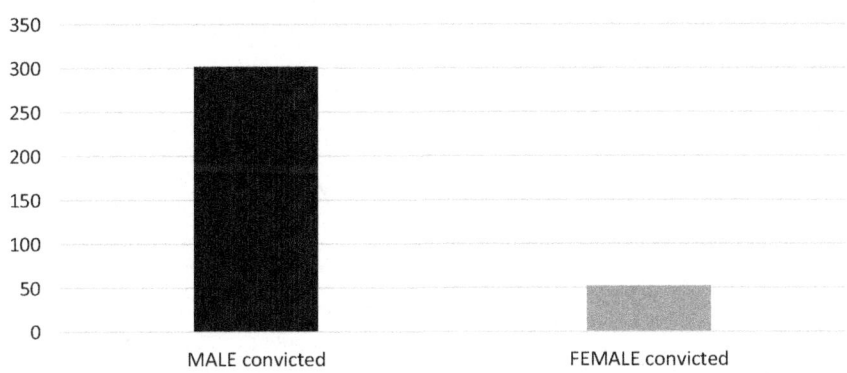

Figure 5.5 The Gendered Nature of Convictions for Attempted Robbery in Scotland, 1830–1882.

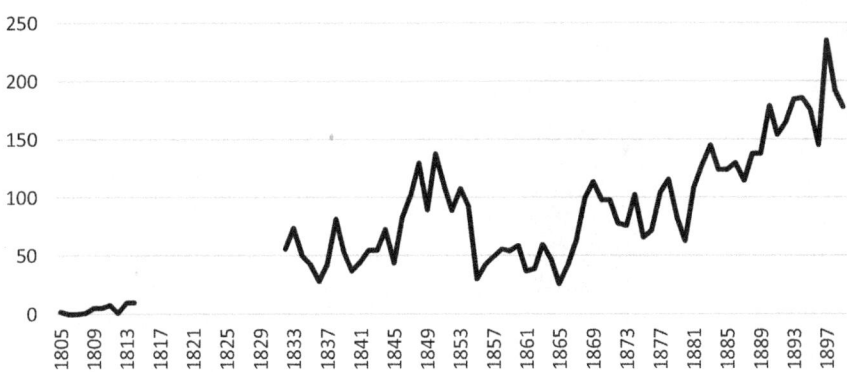

Figure 5.6 Indictments for Robbery in Scotland, 1805–1899.

that of their male counterparts.[21] This trend continues in the gendered nature of convictions rates (seen in Figures 5.5, 5.13 and 5.15) although it is evident from the data presented in Figures 5.4, 5.12 and 5.14, that convictions for robbery and attempted robbery were more likely in the twentieth century, in comparison to the previous era where the historic reluctance to capitally convict Scottish criminals is evident once again in the gap between indictments and convictions. This conclusion may seem strange to us, given the prevailing staunch legal opinion regarding these particular offences and the sensitive attitudes of contemporaries to their perpetration. Arguably, however, these trends may have more to do with prevailing standards of evidence, prosecutorial capabilities or the stance taken regarding the deployment of the ultimate state sanction, rather than attitudes towards those individuals convicted of committing crimes of violence for gain *per se*.

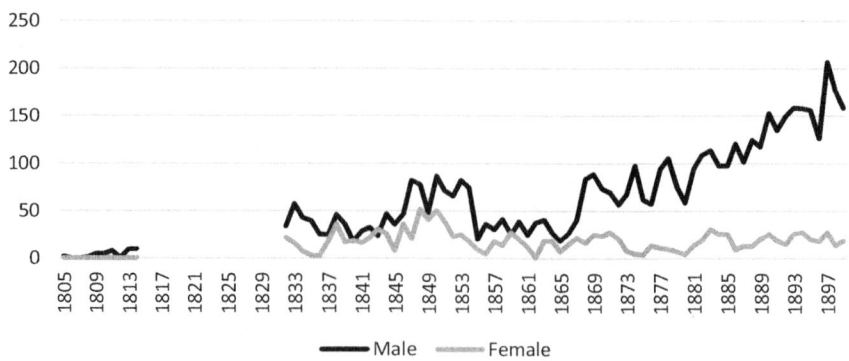

Figure 5.7 Indictments for Robbery in Scotland by Gender, 1805–1899.

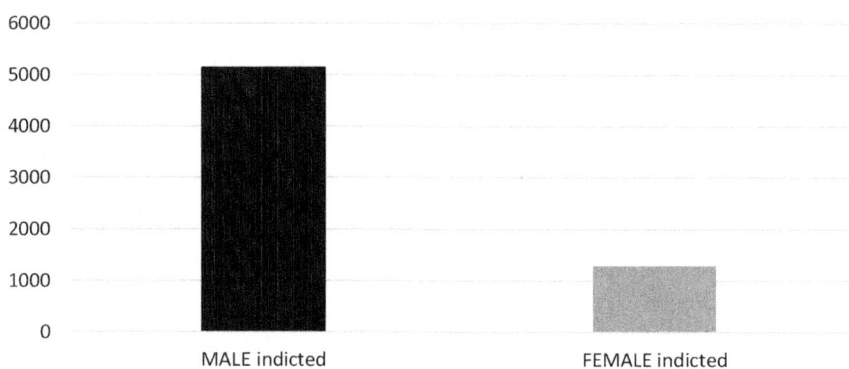

Figure 5.8 The Gendered Nature of Robbery Indictments in Scotland, 1805–1899.

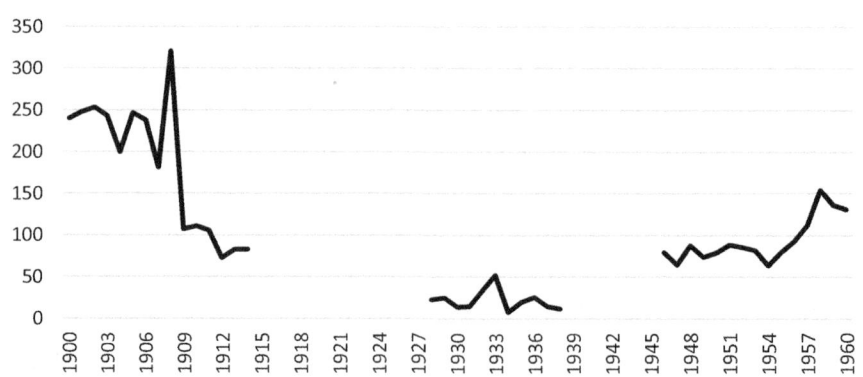

Figure 5.9 Indictments for Robbery and Attempted Robbery in Scotland, 1900–1960.

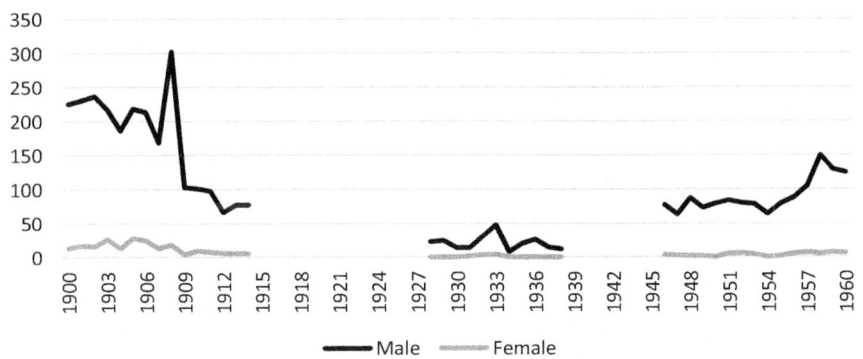

Figure 5.10 Indictments for Robbery and Attempted Robbery in Scotland by Gender, 1900–1960.

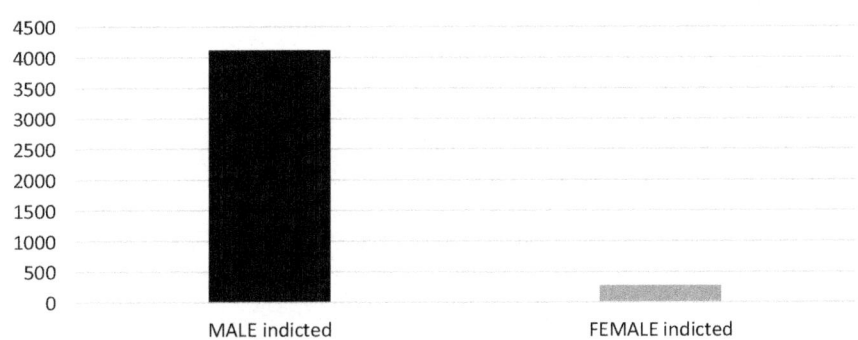

Figure 5.11 The Gendered Nature of Robbery and Attempted Robbery Indictments in Scotland, 1900–1960.

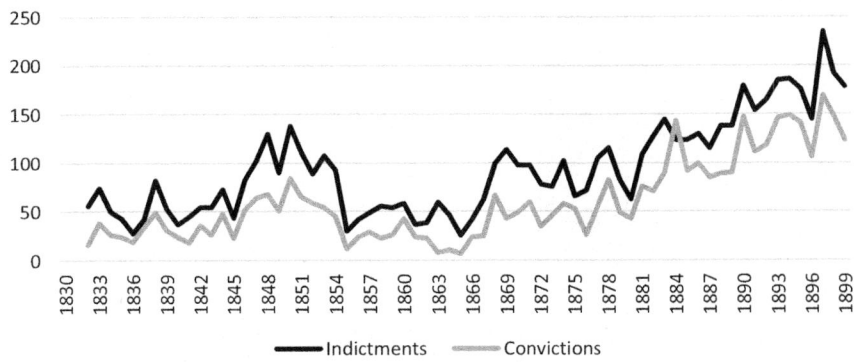

Figure 5.12 Indictments and Convictions for Robbery in Scotland, 1830–1899.

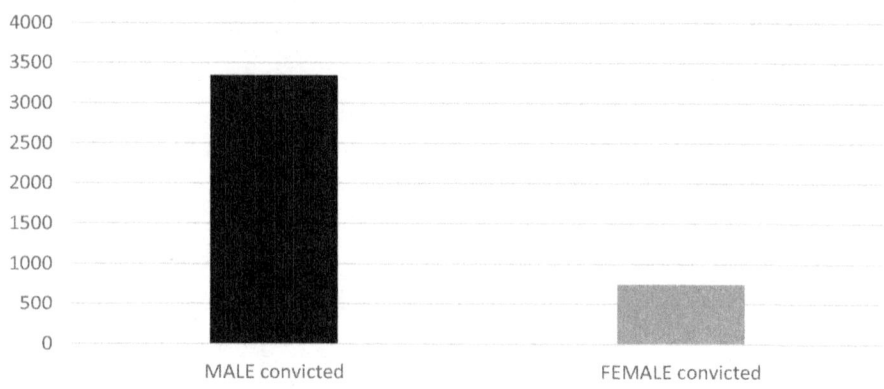

Figure 5.13 The Gendered Nature of Convictions for Robbery in Scotland, 1830–1899.

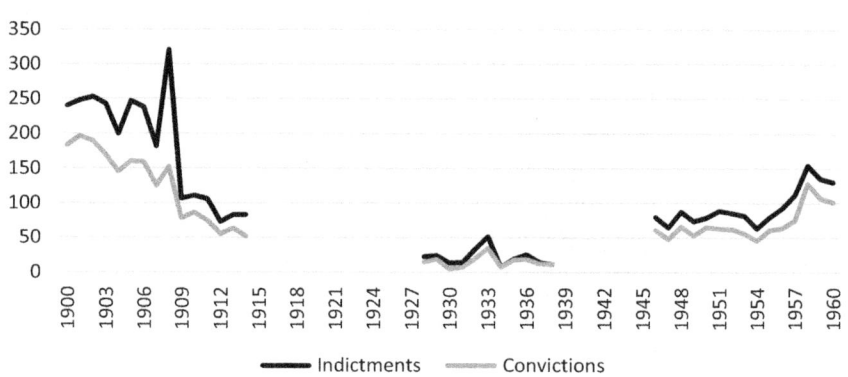

Figure 5.14 Indictments and Convictions for Robbery and Attempted Robbery in Scotland, 1900–1960.

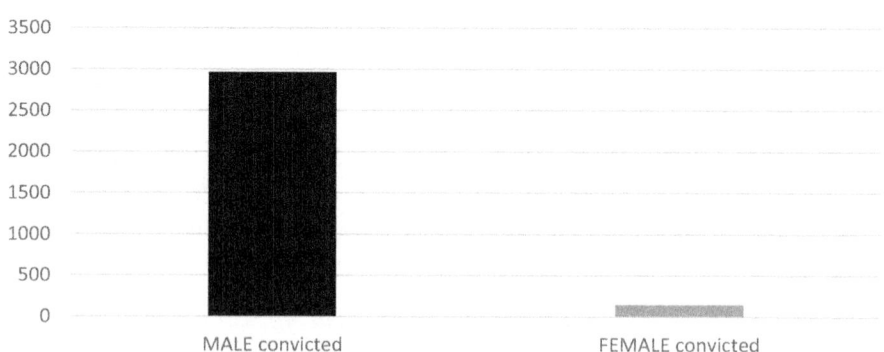

Figure 5.15 The Gendered Nature of Convictions for Robbery and Attempted Robbery in Scotland, 1900–1960.

Methods, Offenders, Victims and Motive

The case studies in the subsequent section of this chapter illustrate just some of the numerous and diverse methodologies utilised by Scottish robbers between 1660 and 1960. No robbery was typical and the ways in which the offence was carried out varied significantly across time in accordance with factors such as the skills and customary practice of the perpetrator, the perceived likely level of resistance offered by the victim, the technology available at the time, and the specific context in which the crime took place. The earliest example analysed – the case of Gilder Roy – relates to highway robbery. From the early seventeenth century onwards, the desire to improve commercial activity, coupled with advancements in technology, resulted in an increase in the number of travellers using horse-drawn carriages on the roadways that were emerging between the main population centres across Scotland. The intensification of road use improved social mobility as individuals (and produce) could travel greater distances more rapidly than before. However, this development also provided opportunities and would-be victims for highway robbers, especially as improvements in the reliability of firearms during the early modern period meant that individuals could perpetrate hold-ups or robberies of that sort, a feat which would have required a gang of outlaws to accomplish in earlier times.[22]

However, highway robbery was never very prevalent in Scotland and it seems to have been concentrated in and around the most densely populated urban areas of the Lowlands. This is probably because there were few rich pickings in rural areas and because the geography and geology of the country made travel to more northern destinations fairly difficult given that the provision of roads and highways was not uniform across the country until much later in the nineteenth century. Moreover, by that time of course, highway robbery had all but died out. The construction of tolls which made travelling unnoticed more difficult to achieve; the advent of the railway which offered a more convenient and secure mode of transport to the Scottish populace; the arming of coach operators to mitigate against attacks; the creation of an established police force; and, the introduction of more sophisticated methods of banking and commerce which largely eliminated the need to transport untraceable capital, coinage and valuables along insecure thoroughfares, were all factors which contributed to the demise of robbery on the highway.[23]

The methodology of the highway robber could be contrasted with that of the urban street robber, who, from formal indictment evidence at least, was far more common in the Scottish context. These robbers were said to be more threatening than those who operated on horseback as they could not make a getaway as easily and therefore they had to deploy more violence and brutality towards their victims in order to achieve subjugation and subsequent escape.[24] In England, social commentators were quick to categorise and label these sorts of offenders according to the precise methodology they employed. So, in the eighteenth century, we hear of 'footpads' robbing on foot and 'cut-throats' brutalising victims and in the nineteenth century, we learn of 'garotters' who choked their marks.[25] The Scots on the other hand did not compartmentalise or qualify their descriptions of robbers in this way, largely because the broad judicial definition of the offence rendered this unnecessary. Men like Hugh Bisland, who we meet in the second case study below, were simply regarded as violent thugs who robbed innocent individuals.

Street robbery, or mugging as it is commonly referred to now, persisted across Scotland during the 1660–1960 period and beyond, as it was essentially unsophisticated and opportunistic in nature. Robbers saw a potential victim, attacked them, took what they could and ran off. The longevity of this basic interpersonal version of the smash–and–grab approach is evidenced by the case study relating to Anthony Miller and James Denovan from 1960. Often criminals employed a practiced methodology that they were comfortable with. Simplicity was not to be baulked at if it proved effective. Yet, alongside these rudimentary robberies were more elaborate, pre-planned ones targeted at attaining more valuable rewards and more often aimed at institutions or businesses, rather than specific individuals. The nineteenth century episode of violence for gain presented in this chapter is a case in point. Individuals were threatened, intimidated and indeed assaulted in these more complex instances, but this was largely because they got in the way of what was planned, rather than because they themselves were the target of the intended robbery.[26]

In the more modern era, the methodology of robbery became much more diverse and fluid with offenders adopting a range of tactics and technologies to facilitate their criminal actions and avoid capture.[27] For instance, the motor car was initially used as a tool to enhance the chances of escape in heist-type situations, but its use subsequently evolved and it came to be utilised to facilitate direct entry into premises via ram-raids.[28] Evidently, robbers in Scotland, as elsewhere, had to constantly change their approach in order to keep up with the challenges offered by more advanced security, and in order to best utilise the available technology to maximise their chances of success.[29]

One implication of the changing nature of robbery offending over time, is that the characteristics of both the perpetrators and the victims of the offence have varied hugely. Robbers themselves came from all walks of life, and although there is some suggestion that early highway robbers were impoverished members of the nobility who were unwilling to beg and too lazy to work to pay their dues and fund their extravagant lifestyles,[30] this characterisation does not seem to apply to the Scottish experience, where, in any event, highwaymen and highwaywomen were not prevalent. The majority of robbers over the 1660–1960 period were men,[31] but there is evidence to suggest that in Scotland, more women participated in this type of offence, particularly in the premodern period, than seemed to be the case elsewhere.[32] Certainly, indicted Scottish female robbers did not engage in the offence by taking timorous, minor or subsidiary roles such as acting as a decoy or a look-out as some historians have suggested.[33] Rather, these women were direct, independent and autonomous criminal actors who regularly perpetrated violence with relish and with enthusiasm.[34]

Robbery victims too were wildly diverse. For instance, they could be individuals or institutions and sometimes multiple individuals were attacked in a single criminal episode.[35] Throughout history, robbers have essentially acted as opportunists. They have not tended to discriminate by gender, class, race or by age; but rather they have preyed on targets that they believed would generate the most reward.[36] Yet, on other occasions (as we see in several of the case studies below) the selection of targets was even more random than this. One thing that *is* common amongst the victims of robbery offending in Scotland and elsewhere between 1660 and 1960, is that they rarely knew their assailants. Robbery was a violent, interpersonal crime committed against strangers and that typology does set this offence apart from many other kinds of violent crime where there was often a relationship of some sort between victim and assailant.[37] Moreover, it was the public's evident vulnerability to these unpredictable, intimidating and violent marauders, which created the persistent fear and recurring panic about robbery offending acknowledged above.

The direct and deliberate violence commonly offered in episodes of robbery from the early period to the modern era certainly sets this offence apart from many of the others examined in this volume. Scottish robbers, alongside their counterparts elsewhere in Britain, were typically relentless and unforgiving in their use of violence and aggression whilst perpetrating their crimes, as it was through these means that the offence was effected.[38] The more violence that could be offered during a robbery, the greater the guarantee of success for the perpetrators involved and thus all sorts of weapons were deployed in the furtherance of the offence, although firearms tended to be threatened rather than used.[39]

In any event, indictment evidence suggests that the Scots were particularly fearsome with respect to crimes of violence for gain in the premodern period in particular. Scottish robbers, at that time, did not tend to just threaten violence, they actuated and perpetrated it, with the majority of Scottish individuals indicted for robbery also being indicted for serious aggravated assault.[40] Certainly, this behaviour seems far removed from the opinion of Sir John Fortescue, once a Chief Justice of the King's Bench who noted in the latter part of the fifteenth century that the Scots were rarely ever indicted for robbery because they did not have the stomach to commit it![41] However, we must take some care with the overall depiction of the Scottish robber as 'ultra-violent'. As there were so few highwaymen north of the Tweed in the premodern period, more street robberies were recorded and prosecuted by the courts. Consequently, our perspective of the nature of Scottish robbery has arguably become distorted to emphasise the more violent and more feared type of offender who was very far removed from the romantic folk-hero character typically portrayed in the contemporary English context.[42]

In any case, a further common characteristic of robbery which undoubtedly intensified the fear associated with its perpetration relates to the fact that it was typically perpetrated by multiple assailants. Bands of robbers were common in Scotland between 1660 and 1960 as many of the case studies below illustrate.[43] However, unlike in episodes of non–violent property crime, where accomplices were often used to facilitate the planning, getaway or aftermath of a theft via the criminal networks they belonged to, robbers were more likely to work in partnerships or groups to perpetrate the actual act of violence for gain itself. Usually this was because the practical requirements of robbery necessitated several participants. In interpersonal 'smash-and-grab' attacks for instance, at least one individual was needed to subdue the victim and one to purloin his or her property or possessions. Working in a group also offered extra pairs of hands in those situations where the victim offered more resistance than had been predicted and to expedite a clean escape.

The common use of accomplices in instances of robbery suggests that some preparation was necessary in order to best effect the perpetration of the offence and to maximise the benefit of engaging multiple individuals in the crime, although victim selection was still random. This seems to have been especially true in the more modern and relatively more complex episodes of this type of violence for gain where security systems had to be bypassed and getaway routes carefully plotted.[44] Yet, as we will see in the case studies below, planning of some sort was an endemic feature of robbery offending, even in the more opportunistic and precipitous instances, and as a result, robbery has long been considered a premeditated crime.[45] Certainly, Scottish robberies seems to have involved a degree of forethought relating to knowledge of targets, techniques of appropriation, methods of flight and means of disposal.[46]

Scottish robbers could be described as 'professional' in their criminal exploits in terms of the planning and organisation involved, their willingness to carry weapons, and evidence from the judicial statistics which suggests that recidivism was common especially after 1870.[47] However, this label of professionalism only applies in part. Robbery never really became a full-time occupation for those who perpetrated the offence. For instance, repeat offending was caused by the paltry levels of reward typically gleaned from this type of activity (especially in the period before more modern and large-scale heists were perpetrated) rather than because robbery had become a career or a way of life for the individuals involved.[48] Moreover, and as stated above, the membership of robber gangs was essentially too fluid and impermanent to be considered truly professional. Robbers tended to band together momentarily for a distinct or specific criminal purpose and once that was achieved, they then drifted apart and went their separate ways; it was safer for them to operate in this way as it increased their chances of remaining undetected.[49]

Historians contend that offenders chose to commit robbery rather than other types of property crime because the plunder involved was usually money. According to J.E. Conklin, this meant that robbers avoided the time-consuming, inconvenient and risky process of converting property into cash.[50] Whilst this may have been true to some extent, as can be seen from the case studies below, Scottish robbers also often stole light and readily portable items such as watches, keys, hats, gloves, pocket books and jewellery as well as lucre. Historian Brian Henry's comment about robbery in late eighteenth-century Dublin has a broader chronological and geographical reach and can certainly be applied to Scottish robbers across the 1660–1960 period. Henry said:

> Robbers stole a dizzying array of saleable items. They were motivated by greed as well as need, wanting things just to keep up with the changing fashions. A flourishing black market followed in the footsteps of a rapidly expanding consumer society…reflecting the materialism of the age.[51]

Therefore, although some offenders participated in robberies in order to be provided quickly and directly with cash, it appears that other individuals particularly favoured this type of property theft to supply them with immediate and fashionable additions to their wardrobes, or, more commonly, to provide them with the alternative opportunity of the sale of stolen goods at a later stage.

The specific motivations of the individuals indicted for robbery at the Scottish Justiciary Court are difficult to discern from the evidence. This is largely because throughout our period of study, understanding the rationale behind a property crime, even if violent, was not deemed relevant to the case of either the prosecution or the defence. Most historians and criminologists contend that the motivations for robbery are linked to economic conditions. Some assert that offenders committed robbery as a form of supplementary employment which could add to their meagre wages and others suggest that robbery was perpetrated to mitigate against the high price of staple goods and the relative opportunity of employment at any given time.[52] In his essay on the causes of robbery in eighteenth-century London, the contemporary commentator Henry Fielding offered various other suggestions why men and women committed this type of criminal activity during that period.[53] But to what extent can any of his arguments be applied to latter periods and to the Scottish experience of this offence more specifically?

Firstly, Fielding argued that the flaunting of luxuries by the upper classes encouraged the lower orders to crave possession of items which they simply could not afford. Secondly, he suggested that the widespread drunkenness of society caused people to be more violent and thus more willing to carry out robberies. Next, he pointed to the great increase of gambling houses that occurred during the eighteenth century as a cause of robbery, in that debtors often turned to this type of crime in their desperate attempts to recoup their losses. Fielding also claimed that inadequate Poor Law provision, reflected in the vast number of wandering vagabonds, motivated destitute individuals to commit this type of violent property theft. Finally, the inability of the authorities to break down criminal networks effectively or to apprehend, prosecute or convict individuals was also said to encourage robbery. These inefficiencies, along with the frequent pardoning of the few culprits who were found guilty, motivated robbers to re-offend as they perceived they could readily get away with their crimes. In addition, according to Fielding, the weakness of the judicial system also encouraged previously innocent individuals to engage in violent property crime as it seemed unlikely that they would ever be caught.[54]

Whether any of these stimuli affected Scottish robbers between 1660 and 1960 is difficult to ascertain. Certainly, very few of the indicted individuals were described as being drunk at the time of their offence or as owing substantial amounts of money, and none were referred to as vagabonds or vagrants. Nevertheless, as has been shown above, in terms of the types of goods stolen, perhaps Scottish robbers did crave frivolous 'luxury' items of to some extent. Also, given the evidence which suggests that a proportion of the indicted individuals were recidivists and the data presented above which points to the gap between indictment and conviction rates, Fielding was perhaps right to suggest that authoritative weakness encouraged some robbers to re-offend. However, it could also be said that they did this out of an entrepreneurial spirit and in order to make their criminal activities financially worthwhile. It is more probably the case that it was economic factors (whether stemming from hardship, greed or to a lesser extent criminal dependency) which encouraged men, and to a lesser extent women, to rob their contemporaries. However, there is one further motive that we might want to add to Fielding's list, which seems to be more pertinent to the twentieth century experience of robbery. This relates to the real relish some offenders have for the power and excitement that interpersonal violence brings. We see this to some extent in the last of our four case studies and it is an offered rationale which has only recently been acknowledged by criminologists and psychologists in their analysis of the mind-sets and behaviours of seriously violent offenders.[55]

Case Studies and Attitudes to Violence for Gain

Violent robbers have long held a fascination amongst the Scottish populace but as we have seen, unlike the case with the English history of this crime, Scottish perpetrators of violence for gain were not celebrated. They did not tend to become cult figures or attain what we might call folk-hero status following their attacks on wealth and their evasion of authority, but rather they were vilified and condemned, probably on account of their explicitly aggressive tendencies and determined criminal nature.[56] As we have seen in previous chapters, the resolute condemnation of illegality and violence by the Scottish authorities in particular, served as a reminder that such behaviour was unusual rather than endemic. The persistently negative popular attitude to robbery and the perpetrators of this offence in Scotland can arguably be traced back to the early seventeenth century and the randomly brutal exploits of the highland highwayman Gilder Roy (depicted in Figure 5.16 below).[57]

Gilder Roy suddenly became a rich young man when in 1623, at the age of just twenty-one, he inherited a large estate in Perthshire upon his father's death. The estate brought him an annual income of eighty merks a year, but Gilder Roy squandered all of his new-found wealth in less than eighteenth months and the estate had to be sold to pay off his debts. Initially, Gilder Roy's mother supported him financially as he declared himself to be '...reduced to the most extreme necessity', but she soon saw that this was pointless, as her son frittered away what income she had on luxuries neither could afford.[58] She withdrew her aid and advised her boy to make his own future path. Gilder Roy was incensed at this decision and decided to take his mother's advice, or at least his interpretation of it. In what was latterly described as an '...unparalleled piece of barbarity which filled the whole country round with horror', Gilder Roy entered his mother's bedroom whilst she slept and cut her throat from ear to ear. He then raped his sister and a maidservant, and after tying them up, he removed everything of value from the house and set the property on fire, killing everyone inside.[59]

Gilder Roy then fled from the authorities and went abroad for three years to France and then Spain where he made a living through fraud, petty theft and highway robbery. He always managed to evade capture by the authorities, despite their best efforts. Upon his return to Scotland, he became the leader of a notorious band of robbers who inflicted extreme violence on random targets across the Highland counties in order to extort items of value and large sums of money from their victims. Gilder Roy's reputation became such, that he was said to be '...dreaded as much as a common enemy in time of war.'[61] His violence was unpredictable, status-blind in terms of target

Figure 5.16 Colour Portrait of Gilder Roy.[60]

selection and savage. For instance, after some time, three of Gilder Roy's men were captured and imprisoned in the Tolbooth of Edinburgh. Although they tried to escape, they were soon recaptured and then promptly convicted, executed and gibbeted. Gilder Roy vowed revenge on the authorities who did this to his partners in crime, and more specifically, he set out to capture the judge who had passed sentence upon his friends.[62] One evening, to fulfil this ambition, a rampaging Gilder Roy and his gang viciously attacked a coach transporting the said judge. The gang stripped, bound and then drowned the coachman and two footmen. They needlessly killed the four coach horses, smashed the vehicle to pieces and robbed the judge of all his valuables, before taking him to where the executed gang members were gibbeted and hanged him alongside them.[63]

By this point in his criminal history, Gilder Roy was evidently fearless and insolent and was said to '…spread an inexpressible fear in every part where he haunted.' His behaviour was tempered to some extent by a well-publicised proclamation and offer of a reward of one thousand merks to anyone able to bring him to the Scottish authorities dead or alive, but Gilder Roy was used to living beyond his means and he had to continue to rob in order to fund the extravagant and opulent lifestyle to which he had become accustomed.[64] Unbeknownst to him, however, his mistress, Elizabeth (Peg) Cunningham had heard the proclamation and had decided to betray her lover in return for the handsome reward. One night, she invited a body of men to surround the house where she and Gilder Roy resided. Gilder Roy heard a noise however, and was quick to realise what was afoot. He savagely killed Peg by ripping open her belly. He then proceeded to attack and kill several of his adversaries, before he was eventually brought down by the sheer number involved.[65] Gilder Roy was arrested and imprisoned with irons loaded on to his hands, feet and waist to prevent his escape. Just three days after his capture, he was executed in 1636 at the age of thirty-four and his body, like those of his erstwhile comrades, was hung in chains on a specially erected gibbet between Edinburgh and Leith.[66] His end was not mourned, but celebrated by the relieved Scottish populace.

(a) Hugh Bisland (Eighteenth Century)

On the 24th of May 1765, Hugh Bisland, a carter from Glasgow, was prosecuted at the Justiciary court on a charge of robbery.[67] Unusually, when the indictment was read to the assize, they learnt that Bisland was actually accused of carrying out *two* acts of robbery in the one night, but in his defence, he claimed to have a cast-iron alibi. Clearly, this was going to be an interesting and highly contested prosecution as was often the case in robbery trials, where as we have already seen, convictions were notoriously difficult to achieve. Prosecutorial problems occurred for a whole host of reasons. Victims had often been brutalised and threatened during the assault upon them and were therefore reluctant witnesses for the Crown. Robbery was typically perpetrated in darkness making accurate identification of any assailant problematic. Moreover, as robbers were often very adept at fleeing the scene of their crime and had a myriad of underground criminal networks at their disposal, a detailed investigation after the fact often proved difficult and rarely yielded compelling prosecution evidence, especially in the premodern period when policing was in its infancy. We will see some of these issues at play in the trial brought against Hugh Bisland.

In the very early hours of the morning of the 28th of December 1764, shoe-maker Alexander Brown heard a cry of 'Murder!' in the street below his bed-room window in Glasgow's city centre. When he looked out, he saw a man lying on the street who was later identified as one Mr Colhoun of Kenmuir. The victim seemed to be surrounded by four men, and so Alexander Brown '...gave the alarm to the neighbourhood' and rushed downstairs to investi-gate. He found a dazed but relatively uninjured Mr Colhoun sitting on the street recounting that some men had come up behind him and given him two violent blows on the neck and shoulders which had knocked him to the ground. Whilst incapacitated and fearing for his life, the men then robbed him of a gold watch. Mr Colhoun was quick to point out that he did not know, nor did he see any of his assailants and indeed, he offered no testimony in the trial to supposedly redress the crime perpetrated against him.[68]

The witness Alexander Brown was also at a loss to describe any of the four robbers he had seen standing above the victim and the subsequent Crown witness, William Shearer (another Glaswegian shoemaker), was also unable to identify, describe or distinguish the individuals he saw running away from the victim '...due to the prevailing darkness of the hour' when the crime took place.[69] Next came John Thomson (an iron smith) who lived near the crime scene and had rushed to the area after hearing a great deal of commotion whilst making his way home. Upon nearing Blackfriars Steps, he suddenly ran into a man who inexplicably '...gave him a severe stroke upon the face with a thick stick which beat him down to the ground.' John Thomson was unable to identify or describe his attacker in any detail, except to say '...he was above the common size and had dark cloaths [clothes] on.' When pressed by the prosecution to determine whether he recognised the accused, Hugh Bisland as his attacker, the witness said '...he could not.'[70] This was a rather curious response as surely the stock answer in these circumstances would have been to say '...he *did* not.' Did this reply suggest that Thomson could have identified the defendant, but was not prepared to do so? At any rate, thus far in this capital criminal trial, the defence must have been quietly confident of a favourable verdict for their client. The evidence against him was scant at best. However, the fortunes of the defence team were about to change.

The next witness to testify before the court was the second victim of a street robbery in the early morning of the 28th of December 1764, John Shaw. He was a merchant who had lived in Glasgow all of his life. John Shaw was walking home on the night in question when a man stopped him to ask the time. This same individual then began to walk with John Shaw along the road whilst he got out his watch. They were then soon joined by another individual who proceeded to 'lay hold' of the victim's watch and whilst they struggled together, John Shaw asked the first man for assistance. Instead, the first man went to the aid of the second man in facilitating the robbery and the men started battering and abusing their victim to make him relinquish his property. During the ongoing melee, a third assailant became involved and he brutally felled John Shaw with one violent blow, which swiftly knocked him to the ground. The robbers then made off with the seal from his gold watch and a pocket book containing important papers.[71]

Although John Shaw was unable to identify the first two assailants that attacked him, he was able to identify the third man for three reasons. Firstly, because that individual attacked him from the front rather than from behind. Secondly, because there was a lamp lit at the very spot at which this particular part of the robbery took place which illuminated the right side of the attacker's face. Thirdly, and most unluckily for Hugh Bisland, John Shaw unmistakably recognised this third robber as someone he knew. John Shaw testified that he had known Bisland for two years and he was able to impart a detailed description of what his assailant had been wearing on the night of the robbery, which matched Bisland's appearance in the courtroom. John Shaw had certainly been brave in positively identifying one of the men who assaulted him in an open and public forum. However, his trepidation and reluctance to do this, which so typically pervaded robbery prosecutions as we have seen, prevailed once again in this case. Shaw insisted, in closing his testimony, that '...as he had received several blows before he saw the person he took to be Bisland and that the light was imperfect, it was possible he might be mistaken' with regard to his identification.[72]

The prosecution then presented some evidence to support their belief that Hugh Bisland was part of a violent band of street robbers who attacked innocent individuals going about their business on the streets of Glasgow. They described how the robbers (or 'Black Guards' as they were deemed by the Lord Advocate) would knock their victims to the ground and then take hats, cloaks and any other valuables or possessions they could seize quickly before making off unseen into the night almost in the fashion of an interpersonal 'smash-and-grab raid'.[73] Although, some evidence was beginning to stack up against Hugh Bisland, it was largely circumstantial and based on gossip or hearsay and at this point in the trial proceedings a conviction was still far from certain. However, the prosecution then played their trump card and they effectively signed Hugh Bisland's death warrant with the testimony from their last two witnesses.

Robert Reid and James Jack appeared in court to testify for the prosecution. Both were Glaswegian teenagers and both were sometime members of the robber gang referred to above. Reid and Jack had been advised by the authorities that if they testified against Hugh Bisland, they would not be prosecuted for their part in any of the robberies alleged to have occurred. They decided to take up this offer, although both were quick to state that they held no ill will or malice against the accused. The evidence of both young men corroborated and strengthened the somewhat tentative and imprecise evidence of previous witnesses in describing their involvement in a series of violent criminal exploits. They admitted to the robberies of Mr Colhoun and Mr Shaw, but took great care to directly implicate Hugh Bisland in these violent endeavours, essentially testifying that it was he who carried out the violence, whilst they carried out the less aggressive thievery.[74]

By the time it was the defence's turn to offer evidence to provide Hugh Bisland with an alibi, the trial was effectively over. The testimonies of Reid and Jack were damning in the extreme and thus, no one really listened to Margaret Black who lodged Hugh Bisland in her home and said he never went out on the night of the alleged robberies. Moreover, when she testified that she went to bed at ten o'clock, it soon became evident that Bisland's alibi was somewhat less than cast iron. He could have easily slipped out of the house when his landlady was fast asleep and perpetrated all manner of offences on the streets of Glasgow without her knowing.[75] Unsurprisingly, given the strength of evidence available, the jury reached a unanimous verdict in the case against Hugh Bisland. They found him guilty of two counts of robbery and the judge ordered the convicted felon to be taken back to the Tolbooth of Glasgow to be imprisoned for forty-four days before being hanged upon a gibbet at the common place of execution in the burgh.[76] No remission or reprieve was forthcoming and so Bisland met his end on the 10th of July 1765.[77]

(b) George Gilchrist, James Brown and William Gilchrist (Nineteenth Century)

The case against George Gilchrist, James Brown and William Gilchrist brought before Edinburgh's High Court of Justiciary in July 1831 was a highly complex but hugely interesting episode which is arguably pivotal to our understanding of the history of violent property crime in Scotland. There are three factors which lend significance to this case. First, it illuminates many of the problematic judicial issues which affected the prosecution of violence for gain across the 1660–1960 period and mentioned elsewhere in this chapter. Second, it offers a relatively early example of a well-planned, multifaceted and rather daring instance of violence for gain which involved numerous participants. Indeed, arguably, the case study occurs in a period of transition, where the crime of robbery effectively split into two types – (1) instances of impromptu interpersonal violent theft which were opportunistic and tended to occur between strangers and (2) instances of more elaborate, premeditated robbery involving a network of individuals with clearly identifiable roles where the spoils were great, but the need to evade justice was greater. The third interesting aspect to this case is the coverage it received and the opinion it fostered amongst popular audiences at the time. This can be considered alongside the attitudes of the authorities and the judicial response to the individuals involved. As we have already seen with the Gilder Roy case, robbers in Scotland were scorned rather than celebrated on the whole, but we should not assume from this that they were routinely ignored or considered to be dull or uninteresting...

Perhaps the first key thing to note about this case was that there was prolonged uncertainty amongst authority figures regarding the particular offence that the alleged defendants in the case ought to be charged with. On the 24th of March 1831, valuable property was stolen from a locked store inside the Prince Regent stagecoach whilst on its journey between Glasgow and Edinburgh. No interpersonal violence, abuse or threats were offered by the assailants involved, but the significant value of the amount stolen, £5,712 in banknotes and coin (equivalent to approximately £467,000 in today's money) meant that the authorities wanted this to be a prosecution where a capital sentence could result, rather than it be deemed a simple act of theft where the punishment would be relatively minor if conviction was achieved.[78]

Consequently, the prosecution went to some trouble in drafting and redrafting both the precognition and the subsequent indictment documentation, to charge the defendants, George Gilchrist, James Brown and William Gilchrist with '...a species of robbery' which they entitled 'theft by violent infraction'. Technically, there was no such offence on the statute books, nor it seems, had this specific category of stealing been deployed before, but, as the authorities pointed out in scribbled marginalia on the original court documents, in this instance, the offence perpetrated was deemed by them to be a species of robbery, because violence had been used to gain access to the locked store or 'boot' of the stagecoach.[79] However, other instances of shop-breaking or housebreaking which were brought before the Justiciary Court in the same year were not described in this way, nor placed in this category, even though they had also involved 'violent' lock breaking and 'aggressive' entry of premises. The approach adopted by the Scottish authorities in the case against George Gilchrist, James Brown and William Gilchrist was thus seemingly inconsistent, unwarranted and arguably reckless. Perhaps the judicial authorities were under pressure from the victims in this case, the Commercial Bank of Scotland, to make an example of those responsible for the theft that occurred. At any rate, the prosecution appeared to be attempting to set a legal precedent here which would broaden the definition of robbery to such an extent as to make it relatively meaningless and rather redundant as a categorisation of property crime.

Moreover, close reading of the trial material reveals that the prosecution would have been on safer ground in arguing that this episode was an instance of robbery, if they had paid attention to the statements and corroboratory evidence of their own witnesses, who clearly testified that one of the assailants in the case – George Gilchrist – was armed with a pair of pistols.[80] The carrying of a loaded weapon during the process of a theft, whether utilised or not, would have more easily led to this instance being defined as a capital crime, but the prosecution did not proceed on this basis which may seem rather curious to the independent observer. However, as the nature of the evidence which testified to this point was largely based on gossip and boastful hearsay, perhaps the authorities thought it not worth pursuing.

We have already seen elsewhere in this chapter that prosecuting episodes of violence for gain was something of a challenge for the Scottish authorities. Insurmountable evidence which directly and incontrovertibly linked a suspect to a robbery was often hard to come by and, as in the Hugh Bisland case study just examined, some victims were too afraid to testify in detail regarding what had transpired for fear of reprisal and further abuse. Threats which were made at the time of the robbery or subsequent to the offence were seemingly taken seriously and were evidently impactful in the courtroom, as the paltry conviction levels over time make clear. However, another factor which made the detection and prosecution of these types of offenders difficult was in relation to those episodes of robbery and violence for gain which were meticulously well planned, involved multiple assailants and their associated networks and were cleanly executed, with little or no incriminating evidence left behind by the protagonists. We see this kind of organised offending emerge much more in the modern era, and thus this current case study appears to be an early example or prototype of this variant of criminal enterprise. Indeed, the exploits of George Gilchrist and his comrades did attain a certain notoriety in this respect amongst contemporaries who were said to be both astonished and alarmed by their 'ingenuity', 'impudence', 'dexterity', 'determination' and 'daring effrontery.'[81]

The Glasgow branch of the Commercial Bank of Scotland sent a weekly parcel of money to the company head office in Edinburgh stagecoach. By way of preparation, the money was wrapped in paper, locked in an iron box which was effectively then pinioned with chains, and then the box was padlocked into the fore boot of the Prince Regent Coach which on this occasion left Glasgow at noon on the 24th of March 1831.[82] Initially on the journey east, there were no passengers on the inside of the coach, only the outside, which perhaps with hindsight, should have seemed a bit odd to the driver of the first leg of the route, John McDowall, as the six internal seats had all been bought and paid for. At any rate, two passengers did eventually join the stage about three miles into its journey: a man and a woman. They went inside and after about an hour and twenty minutes, when the coach was near the town of Airdrie, they disembarked. Although other passengers joined and departed the stage using the external seating provision, no further passengers took up the inside space for the rest of the journey.[83]

A new driver took over the stage at this point, John McMillan, but it wasn't until he got to Uphall in West Lothian that he realised something was amiss. When McMillan opened the door of the coach he found parcels scattered about inside. He quickly noticed that the lining of the inside of the coach was torn, the panel of the coach had been broken through and that there were pieces of wood lying about the floor. On further inspection, the driver and a local innkeeper who had come to his assistance (William Ross) discovered a large hole in the fore boot of the coach. Although the iron box was found to be still inside the boot space, the witnesses observed that '...it clearly had marks of violence upon it' and noted that its lock had been tampered with so that it was now difficult to open. When the box was finally accessed by the two men, it was found to be entirely empty. McMillan and Ross then raised the alarm with the authorities and an investigation began.[84]

So how did George Gilchrist and his accomplices manage to engineer this instance of 'theft by violent infraction'? Well, the court testimony reveals that they evidently went to elaborate lengths in the planning and execution of their crime, and their endeavours in this respect certainly testified to their tenacity and ingenuity, as the Scottish authorities were genuinely flummoxed when trying to figure out just how the 'robbery' had been perpetrated and by whom. Indeed, it was only after a tip-off and the subsequent arrest of two of the gang's members – James Morrison and Robert Simpson – that any meaningful details of this criminal enterprise came to light. These two individuals agreed, albeit reluctantly, to provide evidence for the prosecution and in return, the authorities vowed not to press any charges against them. According to the subsequent evidence they provided in court, George Gilchrist was the mastermind behind the crime and it was he who devised and organised the entire project. He enlisted the help of various individuals who he deemed to be essential in facilitating his grand criminal scheme, persuading them '...that the robbery could be easily done, and that there could be no risk.'[85]

George Gilchrist thought he had left nothing to chance and had planned for every eventuality. First, he became a partner in the coach company used by the Commercial Bank of Scotland and provided horses for the stage on the part of the route between Bathgate and Airdrie. Gilchrist used his position to find out the schedule of when the money was transferred, how this was done, and the details of the security provision related to its transfer.[86] Once he had this knowledge, Gilchrist then bought all of the tickets for the inside seats of the noon stagecoach from Glasgow to Edinburgh on the 24th of March under several false names to ensure no one could interfere with his plans en route. He also enlisted one James Brown (latterly his co-accused) to sit as a passenger on the outside of the coach to guarantee privacy. Accompanied by the aforementioned Robert Simpson, Gilchrist then disguised himself as a woman by donning an olive cloak on top of a black silk gown, a straw bonnet with a blue ribbon on top of a white muslin cap with a net frill, a pair of black gloves, a pair of snow boots, and even a black front piece of hair to complete the look, and they then joined the coach early into its journey.[87] Apparently, the reason for Gilchrist's adoption of the disguise was so that when the coach had to stop to pick him and Simpson up as impromptu passengers, suspicion of them would be minimised by posing as an innocent couple travelling together.

Once inside the coach and confident of being undisturbed, Robert Simpson opened the large bag he was carrying and laid out various tools (including a brace and bit, a chisel, a screw key, a saw, a screwdriver, some darning needles and a file) which he had brought along with him. Gilchrist, for his part, then brought out a box from the same bag, which contained two loaded pistols for security if they needed it.[88] The two men then set about getting at the fore boot of the stagecoach where the box containing the money was located. First, they ripped the fabric from the seats of the coach and then used the saw to cut away some of the wood panelling in order to gain access to the locked boot space. Once this had been achieved, they then bore five holes in the fore boot itself using the brace and bit, and then used the chisel to link the holes together to form a large opening which they could reach into. After having extracted the iron box from the boot, they then used the chisel to pry its lock open. They removed the paper money and coins and then left the stage at Airdrie where William Gilchrist, George's brother and his eventual co-defendant lay waiting for them with horses prepared for their getaway.[89] The loot was then passed in its entirety to James Morrison (aforementioned witness for the prosecution) who had passage for him organised by George Gilchrist on one boat down the Firth of Clyde and then another, with the switch of vessels another element in Gilchrist's elaborate attempts to maximise his chance of success and escape.[90]

Perhaps, however, George Gilchrist was a little too clever for his own good. His meticulous and carefully crafted plans necessitated the involvement of several individuals, not all of whom he knew well or trusted implicitly. Indeed, as he had to explain to them their separate and specific roles in the scheme, Gilchrist thus spread the knowledge of his illicit plans across a fairly wide radius of people and by doing so implicitly increased the risk of detection. Consequently, when Morrison and Simpson were heard boasting of their part in the robbery to members of the public at the same time that the Commercial Bank had offered a substantial reward to bring the culprits to justice, the inevitable happened and the two men were arrested and offered a deal by the prosecution team.[91]

On the basis of the testimony provided by Morrison and Simpson, the case against George Gilchrist was strong. He was clearly the ringleader of the gang and the central person involved in the robbery and so he became the focus of the prosecution's attention. It seems that the others indicted, James Brown and William Gilchrist, were considered to be ancillary participants in what had transpired, although it was evident that money from the robbery to the value of thirty sovereigns and five gold guineas had been found in James Brown's lodgings in Edinburgh.[92] Witness testimony in exculpation from three of George Gilchrist's servant maids, which attempted to provide an alibi for him regarding the day of the robbery, was largely ignored or undermined by the prosecution as unsubstantiated hearsay[93] and thus the verdict of assize against him was unanimous: guilty on all charges.

The cases against both William Gilchrist and James Brown on the other hand were both found not proven by a majority of the assize and in admonishing them, the Lord Justice Clerk advised the pair to '...strive by their future conduct to wipe off, if possible, the stain cast on their characters' by their involvement in this offence.[94]

After the verdicts had been read, two of the three judges involved in advising the Lord Justice Clerk in this case provided an interesting and detailed commentary on why they believed this crime merited the ultimate sanction of death, despite the fact that technically the offence did not meet the criteria required to be deemed a robbery in Scots law. Once again, in this case, there was an evident need to publicly justify the unusual approach taken. The vocal judges, Lord Mackenzie and Lord Moncrieff explained that in their view the crime was aggravated by various factors relating to both the planning and the perpetration of the offence. These factors included a complex conspiracy of many persons; the infraction of several lock-fast places using '...great violence'; the theft of a substantial sum of money; and in particular '...the exertion of wicked skill and boldness...[where]...there could be no doubt that this was as strong a species of theft as had ever come before this court.'[95] The Lord Justice Clerk heeded their advice saying:

> This crime was of such a daring nature, so destructive, and so utterly subversive of that security which the public are entitled to claim in conveyances of this nature, that I will only tell you that you have to prepare for eternity, and you ought to have the dispositions becoming a person standing in your situation. I advise you, in preparing for the fate that awaits you, to call to your assistance the ministers, and to take the instructions which they will afford you. And you ought to search the scriptures with an earnest scrutiny, and lose not a moment in the work of repentance and prayer, that God may extend to you, through the merits of your Redeemer, the pardon for this crime.[96]

George Gilchrist was then sentenced to death.

As was indicated in the introduction to this particular case study, the crime that the Gilchrist gang effected was one that evidently interested the Scottish populace in the first third of the nineteenth century. For instance, as well as a lengthy and detailed report of the trial and its proceedings which was published as a pamphlet in the immediate aftermath of the court case, there were also other shorter broadside publications produced at that time which offered the edited highlights of the sensational testimony provided.[97] Perhaps we should not be overly surprised by the attention afforded this case, given the evidence from elsewhere in this volume which suggests that the 1830s was a particular decade in Scottish history where social commentators and the Scottish press shone their spotlight upon crime and the individuals who perpetrated it. Indeed, and as with the trial at the Justiciary Court, it was very evidently George Gilchrist who became the particular focus for popular attention. Various broadsides recounted his conduct in prison, his behaviour towards his wife, family and friends in the wake of his fateful sentence and the preparations made for his execution. As was typical of these kind of contemporary works, they all offered religious and judicial justifications for the sentence meted out by the court.[98] Furthermore, somewhat unusually, three separate 'Lamentations' were published as broadsides in 1831 (purportedly authored by the convict from his gaol cell) and all constructed to emphasise that George Gilchrist himself applauded his own fate and went to his death a penitent man.[99]

Evidently, the interest generated by this case was not derived from any wish to idolise or romanticise the exploits of George Gilchrist and his accomplices, as might have happened south of the Tweed at this time, but rather, there were certain elements of the case that triggered and then kindled the curiosity of the populace and authorities across early nineteenth century Scotland. The first occurred in the immediate aftermath of the offence when George Gilchrist was arrested on suspicion of being involved in the robbery. Whilst being interrogated in the sheriff's chambers, Gilchrist made a dash for freedom and managed to lock his captors inside their own building before making his escape. He was recaptured not long after this episode, but his effrontery, coupled with the incompetence of the Scottish authorities, made headline news.[100] Then there was the undeniable and arguably idiosyncratic skill offered in the methodology of the robbery itself which was equally astonishing and intimidating to many and which raised various questions about the competence of security practices and the ways in which the wealthy were protected from the criminal elements of society.[101]

Finally, and arguably most importantly, there was the ongoing efforts made by the Commercial Bank of Scotland to recover the money stolen, which persisted for some time and which eventually came to be seen as desperate rather than appropriate. Commentators felt that the moneymen should be spending more time analysing what went wrong with their own security arrangements, rather than trying to recoup spoils long lost to them.[102] However, given the substantial sum involved and owing to significant pressure from their patrons, the bank remained determined and reports abounded in the aftermath of the trial which suggested that George Gilchrist had been offered a deal, where he would be able to avoid execution in return for revealing to the bank where he had hidden the stolen loot.[103] It is unclear whether such a deal was struck, and if it was, whether Gilchrist kept up his end of the bargain. At any rate, however, this aspect of the Gilchrist case perpetuated the story in the popular consciousness and led to some confusion over whether George Gilchrist was indeed executed, or whether, in the end, he was merely transported overseas.[104] All of this speculation resulted in well-publicised questions being asked of the omnipotence of judicial authority and whether the safety of the nation, or the wealth of a few select contemporaries, was paramount in the minds of the government of the day. Clearly, as this case study has shown, episodes of violence for gain could be fascinating in their own right due to the ingenuity and bravado involved, but they were also significant because of their ability to illuminate wider social and political agendas too.

(c) Anthony Miller and James Denovan (Twentieth Century)

The last case study in this chapter comes right at the end of our period of study in 1960, and is another which is notorious for highlighting broader social and political issues, albeit different ones from the George Gilchrist case analysed above. In this case, it was the capital sentence meted out to the convicted individual, more than the crime he had perpetrated, that roused particular interest in the case. In part, this was because the individual concerned was just eighteen years old at the time and in part, because the prevailing socio-political context was one when the campaign for the abolition of capital punishment was gathering momentum across Great Britain as a whole. In any event, what this case does illustrate, is that even in the modern era, robbery was deemed a very serious crime, especially when it resulted in loss of life (whether intentional or otherwise) during its commission.

On the 14th of November 1960, two teenagers were brought before the High Court in Glasgow: Anthony Joseph Miller aged eighteen and James Douglas Denovan aged sixteen.[105] Miller was charged with assault, robbery and capital murder and Denovan was similarly charged but had the offence of contravening the Criminal Law Amendment Act of 1885 (Section 11) added to his indictment.[106] It was clear from the evidence heard in court that Miller and Denovan had been working as part of a wider band of delinquents who attacked and robbed male victims looking for homosexual encounters in the toilets of Queen's Park Recreation Ground in Glasgow. Although in this case some details were bravely provided by erstwhile victims, the most damning evidence came from other members of the robber gang who agreed to testify for the prosecution in return for their own liberty. Once again then, just as in the Bisland and Gilchrist cases, the hidden nature of episodes of violence for gain, previously discussed in this chapter, could be overcome by the authorities' targeting specific gang members and persuading them to turn informer on their criminal comrades.

The court heard how on multiple occasions (five of which were referred to specifically in the indictment) Joseph Denovan set out to meet men looking for sex in the toilets at the park.[107] It would seem that Denovan did have some sort of reputation for offering casual homosexual encounters to strangers, because of the details relating to the extra charge on his part of the indictment, which pertained to an 'act of gross indecency' between himself and William Alexander Blue, where they were seen by a third party fondling each other's '…naked private member' in the same recreation ground. In any event, once a victim had agreed to go with Denovan, he was lured to an area where Tony Miller was waiting unseen, sometimes with accomplices and sometimes not. Miller would then attack his victims, usually by simply shoving them to the ground and then holding them there whilst he robbed them of their possessions before fleeing the scene, in a practice known as 'queer rolling'.[108] However, some victims testified to far rougher and more violent treatment at the hands of Miller. For instance, James Hugh McKay and Douglas Nicholl were both threatened with a knife when assaulted,[109] Matthew Keillar had a broken bottle pointed close to his face when robbed[110] and Robert Easdale was stabbed in the chest and hand after offering resistance to his attackers. He had to be hospitalised for some time and nearly died from his injuries.[111]

The rewards from this dangerous criminal activity were remarkably paltry, as typically, none of the victims carried valuables on their person. In the main the robbers' loot comprised watches, random keys and key rings, cigarette lighters, combs and some loose change.[112] It could be argued that these robbers repeatedly engaged in this species of criminal activity for the thrill it gave them in having power over other individuals, rather than for the prospect of substantial monetary gain. It is conceivable that James Denovan's motivations may have been more personal and nuanced than this, but this is impossible to tell from the evidence.

The attack that tipped the balance, made various former victims come forward and really focussed the minds of the authorities to put in the time and effort to investigate these attacks properly, occurred on the 6th April 1960. John Cremin met James Denovan at the side of the men's toilets in Queen's Park. Cremin was seemingly smelling of alcohol which Denovan welcomed as he knew this would make the robbery easier to facilitate. Cremin '...started touching' Denovan and suggested that they move to the air-raid shelters nearby for some privacy. Whilst they were moving in that direction, Anthony Miller appeared. According to testimony provided in court by various individuals, Miller then picked up a plank of wood that was about three and a half feet long as it was broad, stepped forward and hit Cremin over the back of the head with it. John Cremin, who had his hands in his pockets at the time, fell straight forward on to the ground. Denovan and Miller then rolled their victim on to his back and proceeded to rob him of a penknife, his wrist watch, a bundle of notes (to the value of £67) and a bank book. Noticing that a couple walking in the park had stopped to see what the commotion was about, Miller tried to lift Cremin off the ground whilst laughing, as if both he and Denovan were simply helping a drunk man who had stumbled. The couple seemed satisfied with this pretence and went on their way, and so Denovan and Miller dragged Cremin's body under some bushes and ran off.[113]

John Cremin was found dead at the scene a little later by a man out walking his dog. On initial inspection, the police assumed he had died of natural causes whilst out in the park. When they probed a bit further, however, it seemed that Cremin was something of a man of mystery. He had seemingly come to the area to watch an international match at the nearby Hampden Park football stadium and although he did have a criminal record for repeated acts of petty theft and homosexuality,[114] no one could fathom why he had signed into a nearby hotel under a false name.[115] With their curiosity piqued, the police ordered a postmortem to be carried out and it was quickly discovered that John Cremin had died from a subdural haemorrhage (bleeding on the brain) caused by a fractured skull. It was the view of the consultant pathologist for Renfrewshire, Mr Walter Pollock Weir, that John Cremin's fractured skull had been caused by '...a blow from a blunt weapon' but he did not speculate upon what kind of weapon that might have been.[116]

Although subsequent attacks were perpetrated by the robbers after the Cremin assault, the investigative net was closing in on their activities, with the police putting the park's public toilets under surveillance, and especially when James Denovan was picked up for the aforementioned 'gross indecency' offence and was found to have newspaper cuttings about the murder of John Cremin in his possession.[117] Although Denovan said nothing to the authorities about the robberies, he gave them enough information about the individuals he was associated with to enable them to make further arrests and this in turn allowed them to slowly begin to unravel the ties of the gang's membership. Indeed, three sixteen-year-old former members of the gang who had been involved in some of the robberies, either as look-outs or in helping fence the stolen goods after the fact, agreed to testify against Anthony Miller and James Denovan in court. The details Crawford McFarlean Mure, James Morrison Sinclair and George William Orr provided were crucial in establishing serial culpability and perhaps more importantly, in shaping and focussing the prosecution's case to be geared more towards the conviction of Miller rather than Denovan. In effect, they told the court that Miller had shown them his clothes from the night that Cremin was attacked and they were covered in blood. They explained how they watched Miller and Denovan burn the banknotes that they had stolen from Cremin to eradicate the main piece of incriminating evidence that could be laid against them. They also explained how Miller had boasted to them that it was he who had killed Cremin, not Denovan. Furthermore, they recounted how Denovan, for his part, had taken them to the spot in the park where the murder had happened saying 'This is where the man flaked...Let's have two minute's silence for the man who flaked.'[118]

The case against the two young men accused was very strong, but the evidence against Anthony Miller in particular, was pretty much overwhelming. This is probably why, on the penultimate day of the trial, both young men changed their pleas to guilty of all charges, save for the accusation of capital murder. In his eventual confession, Denovan admitted that he and Miller only ever preyed upon homosexuals. They did this, he explained, for two reasons. First, because these men were easy targets and rarely fought back and second, because the men would rarely, if ever, report what had happened to them given the oppressive context facing homosexuals at the time, so there was very little chance of the pair getting caught.[119] In summing up the case for Anthony Miller's defence, Mr Irvine Smith could offer little by way of rebuttal and indeed he described his own client as a 'thug' saying:

> Ladies and Gentlemen of the Jury, you cannot have heard the evidence of the past two days without a thrill of horror going over you; you cannot have heard these pleas that were tendered yesterday to those charges on that indictment without marvelling that these accused, not yet clean past their boyhood, should have been capable of descending to such utter villainy as those pleas testified they did descend to.[120]

Smith decided that the only way he could defend his client at this stage in the proceedings was to concentrate his arguments on the capital murder charge. By the Homicide Act of 1957, a murder committed in the further-ance of a theft was deemed a 'capital' murder if it could be proved that the actions of a specific individual caused the death of the victim concerned.[121] Thus Mr Smith tried to persuade the jury that James Denovan, not Anthony Miller, had killed John Cremin. His arguments held little weight, however, as they went against all the testimony that had already been heard. Unsur-prisingly, Anthony Joseph Miller was unanimously found guilty of *all* the charges against him, including capital murder. James Douglas Denovan, on the other hand, was also found guilty, but only as far as the plea he had en-tered. Consequently, although he was deemed to be guilty of murder, it was non-capital in nature. Due to his 'tender' age (only individuals over the age of eighteen could be sentenced to death under the Children and Young Persons Act of 1933[122]) Denovan was sentenced '...to be detained indefinitely at Her Majesty's Pleasure' and was in fact released just nine years later, on the 1st of May 1969.[123] Conversely, Miller (who had turned nineteen during the course of the trial proceedings) was sentenced to a short spell of imprisonment at Barlinnie Prison in Glasgow and was ordered thereafter '...to suffer death by hanging' in that same place.[124]

Although there was perhaps little surprise articulated by the verdict and sentence that Miller received, it was widely assumed that his capital sentence would be quashed to life imprisonment on appeal. After all, he was only a few years older than James Denovan, plus in recent years there had been an evident reluctance to hang convicts across Britain, and especially in Scotland it would seem, due to the burgeoning strength of the abolitionists' cam-paign. For instance, in 1960 itself, there were three capital murder trials in Scotland. One individual was acquitted on the grounds of insanity and the other two were convicted but latterly reprieved.[125] Indeed, since 1889, there had only been six capital cases in Scotland involving individuals under the age of twenty and all of these had resulted in acquittal or reprieve.[126] Con-sequently and perhaps with some optimism, Anthony Miller's mother and father went to visit the celebrated Glaswegian lawyer, Len Murray, to ask him to help with an appeal for their son.[127] When the Millers asked for Murray's assistance, they did not deny Tony's guilt as they considered it irrefutable, but rather they argued that the tender age of their son should surely afford him clemency from the Scottish authorities.

Murray shared their optimism and agreed to help. He and his legal team set out several grounds for appeal arguing (1) That the judge had misdirected the jury by not offering them the chance to consider a verdict of culpable homicide in the case; (2) That as the jury had convicted James Denovan, they deemed him criminal and culpable and his evidence against Miller ought to be called into question with regards to the charge of capital murder; and (3) That the verdict in the case was contrary to the evidence presented in court.[128] Like Miller's parents, however, Len Murray and his team knew that they did not have a strong legal challenge to the verdict and sentence of the High Court as the evidence against their client was so strong and because they had no new information to submit in defence.[129] So it was probably no great surprise when the appeal was rejected. However, according to Len Murray, what was galling and in his view '…thoroughly unwarranted' was that the trio of judges considering the appeal threw it out so quickly and arguably without due consideration saying that it was '…completely devoid of substance.'[130] So now, Anthony Miller's hope rested on a petition for reprieve to the Secretary of State for Scotland who at that time was John S. Maclay.

Miller's youth, his lack of previous convictions, the fact that the killing could be classified as an unpremeditated attack and the convict's evident remorse, made Len Murray very confident that this final chance for compassion would achieve the right result.[131] In addition, there was the case against Robert Dickson, brought to court at roughly the same time as Miller and Denovan who was convicted of shooting his fellow colleague and lighthouse keeper, Hugh Clark at close range with a .22 rifle. He had managed to earn a reprieve from the Secretary of State despite the explicitly violent nature of the crime perpetrated.[132] In addition, a public petition was initiated at the instigation of the Miller family and it had managed to garner thirty thousand signatures in a very short space of time, including those of fifty-nine MPs and three peers.[133] Moreover, in the context of abolitionism, where a recent amendment to the Criminal Justice Bill had been sought to raise the minimum age of hanging from eighteen to twenty-one years of age, things also looked positive, especially when a flurry of telegrams from various individuals were sent to prominent officials craving mercy for Anthony Miller.[134] However, Murray's confidence in success was misplaced and the public petitions for clemency fell on deaf ears.

After reviewing all of the evidence before him, including a damning submission by Lord Wheatley, the presiding judge at the trial who described the crime as '…vicious and sordid…with a depressing background of depravity, violence and callousness of a nature not normally found in or associated with people so young…',[135] the Secretary of State refused to grant Miller a reprieve. He said:

> …the completely sordid circumstances of the crime, the absence of any mitigating features in the story itself or in Miller's general character, the undoubted necessity of maintaining the deterrent effect of the sentence, and the considered advice which we have taken from the Home Office… make it very difficult to justify a recommendation to mercy. The law should be allowed to take its course.[136]

It was thought amongst the legal fraternity that Anthony Miller was incredibly unlucky. In effect, he had been chosen as the exception amongst a tide of convicted individuals who had attained reprieves, so that his punishment would act as a deterrent to other would-be violent delinquents. It is likely that the Miller case was treated differently from the other capital murder cases because it had been aggravated by robbery and because there had been proven multiple instances of violence for gain perpetrated in a context of what was considered at the time to be illicit sexual behaviour.[137] In addition, Miller's cause was probably not helped by persistent and detailed press reports of his long-standing obsession with fascism, his hero-worship of the Nazi leader Adolf Hitler, and accounts of him vandalising local properties with swastikas and fascist graffiti.[138]

Anthony Miller had initially struggled whilst in prison with the ongoing uncertainty of his fate. Once it was clear that no reprieve would be forthcoming, he became resigned to the inevitable and according to his lawyer, he '…acquired a maturity far beyond his years and far beyond anything he had shown so far.'[139] Miller wrote to each of his parents and to his brother Paul in the days that remained to him, despite the fact that his family visited him on a regular basis at this time. He simply wanted to make sure that they had something to remember him by after he was gone.[140]

On the 29th of December 1960, Anthony Miller was executed in the infamous hanging shed of Barlinnie Prison. He was the last teenager to be hanged in Britain.[141] As is clear from Len Murray's memoirs, the Tony Miller case had a significant impact upon the young lawyer at the time and his future opinions on judicial authority and capital punishment were shaped by his experience in this very case. As he recounted:

> The barbarity and futility of it all were inconsistent with our claims to be a civilised society. Not only were they going to destroy a life that did not belong to them, but, in addition, a punishment far greater than any other that man could possibly devise was being handed out to two totally innocent individuals – the parents of the condemned boy. What had they done to be so cruelly punished in this way by society? What was their crime?[142]

In a matter of days, Len Murray had changed his stance from being in favour of capital punishment to being '...a bitter abolitionist'[143] who by his own admission, would never fully recover from his involvement in the case against Anthony Joseph Miller.

Conclusion – The Violent North?

Throughout history, the nature and incidence of robbery has always been considered a useful gauge for broader trends of violence in specific localities and societies. Robbery offending rates equate to prevailing perceptions of safety and security, not only on a personal level, but also in a wider local regional and national sense too. Probably for this reason, and owing to the threat that robbery posed to both person *and* property, Scottish judicial attitudes to robbery have been persistently draconian in sentencing between 1660 and 1960, when sentences have been dispensed. To some extent this tough authoritative reaction seems to have been warranted, as data from the judicial statistics indicate that robbery was commonly indicted at the Scottish courts. Moreover, during the second half of the nineteenth and the twentieth centuries, rates of offending increased in contrast to all other forms of interpersonal violence. Given the significant influence robbery had on perceptions of violent behaviour more generally, these findings may well explain in part, the persistence of perceptions regarding Scotland's historic association with violence and violent behaviour.

Further fuel for such opinion may have been derived from the methodologies deployed in episodes of violence for gain in the Scottish context. Although techniques varied over time as the case studies in this chapter demonstrate, robbery and attempted robbery were often brutal, unpredictable instances of interpersonal violence perpetrated by individuals prepared to resort to whatever means was required to ensure the success of their criminal exploits. It was the blatant and indiscriminate nature of the threat offered by robbery which made it such a focus of concern in Scotland between 1660 and 1960. Moreover, it would seem from the evidence presented in this chapter at least, that the fears so routinely articulated by the authorities, social commentators and members of the general populace related to the nature and incidence of robbery in Scotland, were justified.

Notes

1 For further discussion of this observation throughout the history of robbery see T. Duke (2014) *Rogues of the Road: Highwaymen and Highway Robbery in Eighteenth Century England* (Union Bay: Duke Publications), p. 107; F. McDonald (2012) *Gentlemen Rogues and Wicked Ladies: A Guide to British Highwaymen and Highwaywomen* (Stroud: The History Press), p. 10; R. Sindall (1987) 'The London Garotting Panics of 1856 and 1862', *Social History*, 12, 3, pp. 351–359; A-M. Kilday (2013) 'Hell-Raising and Hair-Razing: Violent Robbery in

Nineteenth-Century Scotland', *The Scottish Historical Review*, XCII, 2, pp. 255–274 at p. 261 and C. Emsley (2011) *Crime and Society in Twentieth-Century England* (Harlow: Pearson Education Ltd), p. 31 and pp. 99–100. See also the evidence of change over time in the examples and commentary in M. Archibald (2012) *A Sink of Atrocity: Crime in Nineteenth-Century Dundee* (Edinburgh: Black and White Publishing), pp. 164–165; F. Linnane (2003) *London's Underworld: Three Centuries of Vice and Crime* (London: Robson Books), pp. 82–83 and pp. 131–159 as well as H. Croall (1998) *Crime and Society in Britain* (London and New York: Longman), p. 224.

2 For evidence of this throughout history see A-M. Kilday (2007) *Women and Violent Crime in Enlightenment Scotland* (Woodbridge: Boydell Press), p. 129; P. King (2003) 'Moral Panics and Violent Street Crime 1750–2000: A Comparative Perspective' in B.S. Godfrey, C. Emsley and G. Dunstall (eds) *Comparative Histories of Crime* (Cullompton: Willian), pp. 53–71 at p. 54 and F. McClintock and E. Gibson (1961) *Robbery in London: An Enquiry by the Cambridge Institute of Criminology* (London: MacMillan), p. vii.

3 For confirmation of this see J.M. Beattie (1986) *Crime and the Courts in England 1660–1800* (Oxford: Princeton University Press), p. 148 and B.J. Davey (1994) *Rural Crime in the Eighteenth Century: North Lincolnshire 1740–80* (Hull: University of Hull Press), p. 11.

4 Beattie (1986) *Crime*, p. 149; A. Macfarlane (1981) *The Justice and the Mare's Ale: Law and Disorder in Seventeenth-Century England* (Oxford: Basil Blackwell), p. 136 and Kilday (2007) *Women and Violent Crime*, p. 131.

5 For evidence of the fear associated with robbery which triggered or perpetuated moral panics across Britain between 1660 and 1960 see for instance H. Fielding (1751 edition) *An Enquiry into the Causes of the Late Increase in Robbers, With Some Proposals for Remedying this Growing Evil* (London: A. Miller) [Bodleian Reference: BOD 12 Theta 1972 (1)], pp. 2–3 and P. Colquhoun (1798 edition) *A Treatise on the Police of London Containing Detail of the Various Crimes and Misdemeanors by which Public and Private Property and Security Are, at Present, Injured and Endangered and Suggesting Remedies for their Prevention* (Philadelphia: Benjamin Davies), p. 2 from the Internet Archive at https://archive.org/details/atreatiseonpoli01colqgoog; R. Sindall (1990) *Street Violence in the Nineteenth Century* (Leicester: Leicester University Press), pp. 50–51; D. Philips (1977) *Crime and Authority in Victorian England: The Black Country 1835–1860* (London: Croom Helm), p. 250; Linnane (2003) *London's Underworld*, p. 81 and I. Donnachie (1995) '"The Darker Side": A Speculative Survey of Scottish Crime During the First Half of the Nineteenth Century', *Scottish Economic and Social History*, 15, 1, pp. 5–24 at p. 21. For further discussion of moral panics related to robbery in the eighteenth century see R.M. Ward (2014) *Print Culture, Crime and Justice in Eighteenth-Century London* (London: Bloomsbury), chapter three and R.B. Shoemaker (2006) 'The Street Robber and the Gentleman Highwayman: Changing Representations and Perceptions of Robbery in London, 1600–1800', *Cultural and Social History*, 3, 4, pp. 381–405 at p. 385. For the nineteenth century see J. Davis (1980) 'The London Garotting Panic of 1862: A Moral Panic and the Creation of a Criminal Class in Mid-Victorian England' in V.A.C. Gatrell, B. Lenman and G. Parker (eds) *Crime and the Law: The Social History of Crime in Western Europe Since 1500* (London: Europa Publications), pp. 190–213 and Sindall (1987) 'The London Garotting Panics', pp. 351–359. For the twentieth century see McClintock and Gibson (1961) *Robbery*, p. xv.

6 For evidence of these moral panics bearing little semblance to the reality of offending see Shoemaker (2006) 'The Street Robber', p. 383; Kilday (2013) 'Hell-Raising', p. 261; Sindall (1990) *Street Violence*, p. 5, p. 45 and p. 47;

H. Johnston (2015) *Crime in England 1815–1880* (London: Routledge), p. 32; Linnane (2003) *London's Underworld*, p. 98 and relating to the more modern era McClintock and Gibson (1961) *Robbery*, p. xv.

7 See for instance Sindall (1990) *Street Violence*, p. 100, pp. 146–147 and p. 159; Sindall (1987) 'The London Garotting Panics', pp. 351–359 and King (2003) 'Moral Panics', p. 70.

8 See for instance J.R. Ruff (2001) *Violence in Early Modern Europe* (Cambridge: Cambridge University Press), chapter seven and McClintock and Gibson (1961) *Robbery*, pp. 2–8.

9 For further discussion see A. Wright (2006) *Organised Crime* (Cullompton: Willan), p. 4, p. 9, p. 29 and p. 44; Linnane (2003) *London's Underworld*, pp. 105–106; B. McDonald (2010) *Gangs of London: 100 Years of Mob Warfare* (Wrea Green [Lancs]: Milo Books), p. 86, p. 97 and p. 233; R. Jeffrey (2002) *Gangland Glasgow: True Crime from the Streets* (Edinburgh: Black and White Publishing) but especially A. Davies (2013) *City of Gangs: Glasgow and the Rise of the British Gangster* (London: Hodder and Stoughton), *passim* but in particular, p. 21 and p. 204.

10 For further discussion see H. Shore (2010) 'Criminality, Deviance and the Underworld Since 1750' in A-M. Kilday and D.S. Nash (eds) *Histories of Crime: Britain 1600–2000* (Basingstoke: Palgrave Macmillan), pp. 120–140 at p. 125; Davies (2013) *City of Gangs*, *passim*; R. Jeffrey (2002) *Glasgow's Hard Men: True Crime from the Files of the Herald, Evening Times and Sunday Herald* (Edinburgh: Black and White Publishing), pp. 27–29; R. Matthews (2002) *Armed Robbery* (Cullompton: Willan); R. McKay (2016) *The Last Godfather: The Life and Crimes of Arthur Thompson* (Edinburgh: Black and White Publishing) and J. Crosbie (2007) *Armed and Dangerous: This is the True Story of How I Carried Out Scotland's Biggest Bank Robbery* (London: John Blake).

11 For further discussion of the entrepreneurial nature of criminal gangs see Linnane (2003) *London's Underworld*, pp. 116–125; Emsley (2011) *Crime*, p. 87; J. Morton (2003 edition) *Gangland – Volumes I and II* (London: Time Warner) and D. Thomas (2006 edition) *Villain's Paradise: Britain's Underworld from the Spivs to the Krays* (London: John Murray).

12 J.E. Conklin (1972) *Robbery and the Criminal Justice System* (Philadelphia: J.B. Lippincott Company), p. 4. My addition in parenthesis. For a similar definition see also Philips (1977) *Crime*, p. 246.

13 See for instance G. Walker (2003) *Crime, Gender and Social Order in Early Modern England* (Cambridge: Cambridge University Press), p. 190 and P. Linebaugh (1993) *The London Hanged: Crime and Civil Society in the Eighteenth Century* (London: Penguin), p. 54.

14 For further discussion see J. Ruff (1984) *Crime, Justice and Public Order in Old Regime France: The Sénéchausées of Libourne and Bazas, 1696–1789* (London: Croom Helm), p. 113.

15 Baron D. Hume (1797) *Commentaries on the Laws of Scotland Respecting the Description and Punishment of Crimes – Volume I* (Edinburgh: Bell and Bradfute), pp. 139–146. See also A.M. Anderson (1904 edition) *Criminal Law of Scotland* (Edinburgh: Bell and Bradfute), Part II, p. 183.

16 Baron Hume alludes to this point with respect to the early modern period at least see Hume (1797) *Commentaries – Volume I*, p. 146. For evidence, by contrast, of regular interference with legislation related to robbery in England see for instance Duke (2014) *Rogues*, pp. 27–29; C. Arnold (2012) *Underworld London: Crime and Punishment in the Capital City* (London: Simon & Schuster), p. 88; Ward (2014) *Print Culture*, pp. 109–110; F. McLynn (1991) *Crime and Punishment in Eighteenth-Century England* (Oxford: Oxford University Press), p. 58;

Philips (1977) *Crime*, p. 248; and Sindall (1990) *Street Violence*, pp. 9–10 and pp. 146–147.

17 *Ibid*, p. 139. For further discussion see Kilday (2007) *Women and Violent Crime*, p. 130.

18 The persistent nature of the serious regard for robbery amongst socio-political and judicial authorities in Britain over the 1660–1960 period is evidenced by Duke (2014) *Rogues*, p. 8; Beattie (1986) *Crime*, p. 148; McLynn (1991) *Crime*, p. 58 and pp. 25–27; Sindall (1990) *Street Violence*, pp. 146–147 and Croall (1998) *Crime*, p. 224.

19 For further discussion of the historically tough sanctions used against robbery convicts see Walker (2003) *Crime*, p. 194; P. Newark (1979) *The Crimson Book of* Highwaymen (London: Jupiter Books), p. 35 and p. 40; Kilday (2007) *Women and Violent Crime*, p. 133; Beattie (1986) *Crime*, p. 148; McLynn (1991) *Crime*, p. 75 and p. 77; G. Morgan and P. Rushton (1998) *Rogues, Thieves and the Rule of Law* (London: Routledge), pp. 149–150; Philips (1977) *Crime*, p. 248 and p. 252; C. Emsley (2005 edition) *Crime and Society in England, 1750–1900* (Harlow: Longman), p. 260 and Shore (2010) 'Criminality', p. 122.

20 It should be noted that the crime of arson would normally also fall under the category of crimes relating to violence for gain, but the number of indictments were so paltry in Scotland over the three centuries in question, that time-series trend analysis was pointless. It should further be noted that after 1882, the judicial statistics amalgamate the data for robbery and attempted robbery and the graphs here have been constructed to reflect that change.

21 See Kilday (2007) *Women and Violent Crime*, chapter seven.

22 For further discussion see Newark (1979) *The Crimson*, p. 30.

23 For further discussion of the reasons for the demise of highway robbery see G. Spraggs (2001) *Outlaws and Highwaymen: The Cult of the Robber in England from the Middle Ages to the Nineteenth Century* (London: Pimlico), p. 234; Duke (2014) *Rogues*, p. 112; McDonald (2012) *Gentlemen Rogues*, p. 10 and Beattie (1986) *Crime*, p. 155.

24 For further discussion see Beattie (1986) *Crime*, p. 152 and McLynn (1991) *Crime*, p. 60.

25 See for instance D. Brandon (2001) *Stand and Deliver: A History of Highway Robbery* (Chatham: Sutton Publishing), p. 163 and p. 165; Spraggs (2001) *Outlaws*, pp. 154–155; Sindall (1987) 'The London Garotting Panics', pp. 351–352 and Johnston (2015) *Crime*, p. 31.

26 See the examples in M. Archibald (2013) *Glasgow: The Real Mean City – True Crime and Punishment in the Second City of the Empire* (Edinburgh: Black and White Publishing), p. 234.

27 For further discussion see for instance Linnane (2003) *London's Underworld*, p. 83 and pp. 131–159; Conklin (1972) *Robbery*, p. 83; Emsley (2011) *Crime*, p. 31 and Croall (1998) *Crime*, p. 224.

28 See Emsley (2011) *Crime*, pp. 99–100 and Matthews (2002) *Armed Robbery*, *passim*.

29 For further discussion see McClintock and Gibson (1961) *Robbery*, p. ix.

30 See for instance Spraggs (2001) *Outlaws*, p. 6.

31 For evidence of this throughout history and Britain see B.A. Hanawalt (1979) *Crime and Conflict in English Communities 1300–1348* (Cambridge, MASS: Harvard University Press), p. 88; Brandon (2001) *Stand and Deliver*, p. 47; Spraggs (2001) *Outlaws*, p. 265; Walker (2003) *Crime*, p. 160 and p. 190; P. King (1999) 'Gender, Crime and Justice in Late Eighteenth- and Early Nineteenth-Century England' in M.L. Arno and C. Usborne (eds) *Gender and Crime in Modern Europe* (London: UCL Press), pp. 44–74 at p. 45 and p. 49; Philips (1977) *Crime*, p. 252;

Croall (1998) *Crime and Society*, p. 225; McClintock and Gibson (1961) *Robbery in London*, p. 21 and J. Katz (1991) 'The Motivation of the Persistent Robber' in M. Tonry (ed.) *Crime and Justice – A Review of Research: Volume 14* (Chicago: University of Chicago Press), pp. 277–306 at p. 281.

32 See for instance Kilday (2007) *Women and Violent Crime*, p. 129 and pp. 134–135 and Kilday (2013) 'Hell-Raising', p. 264.

33 For examples of this view see J.A. Sharpe (1999 edition) *Crime in Early Modern England 1550–1750* (Harlow: Longman), p. 109; E. Hobsbawm (2000) *Bandits* (London: Abacus), p. 147; Ruff (1984) *Crime*, p. 235; Philips (1977) *Crime*, p. 252 and Linnane (2003) *London's Underworld*, p. 81.

34 See for instance the examples in Kilday (2007) *Women and Violent Crime*, pp. 136–137; Kilday (2013) 'Hell-Raising', pp. 262–264 and M. Archibald (2014) *Bloody Scotland* (Edinburgh: Black and White Publishing), p. 110.

35 For further discussion of the broad victimology of robbery through history see Brandon (2001) *Stand and Deliver*, p. 24; McLynn (1991) *Crime*, p. 69; Archibald (2014) *Bloody Scotland*, p. 20; McClintock and Gibson (1961) *Robbery*, p. 16 and Emsley (2011) *Crime*, p. 101.

36 For more on the indiscriminate nature of robbery throughout history see Philips (1977) *Crime*, p. 126 and Croall (1998) *Crime*, pp. 224–225.

37 See Philips (1977) *Crime*, p. 249; Kilday (2007) *Women and Violent Crime*, p. 139; Conklin (1972) *Robbery*, p. 4 and McClintock and Gibson (1961) *Robbery*, p. 22.

38 For further discussion of the common deployment of violence in robbery offences across history see Brandon (2001) *Stand and Deliver*, pp. 23–24 and p. 162; Duke (2014) *Rogues*, p. 3 and pp. 9–10; Newark (1979) *The Crimson*, pp. 25–27; Shoemaker (2006) 'The Street Robber', p. 387; McLynn (1991) *Crime*, p. 71; Philips (1977) *Crime*, p. 248; Linnane (2003) *London's Underworld*, p. 81; McClintock and Gibson (1961) *Robbery*, p. ix, p. xiv and pp. 13–14; Croall (1998) *Crime*, pp. 224–225; Conklin (1972) *Robbery*, p. 121 and Katz (1991) 'The Motivation', p. 299.

39 See for instance Spraggs (2001) *Outlaws*, p. 89; McDonald (2012) *Gentleman Rogues*, pp. 43–49; McLynn (1991) *Crime*, p. 58; Kilday (2007) *Women and Violent Crime*, p. 138; Philips (1977) *Crime*, p. 250; Kilday (2013) 'Hell-Raising', p. 262 and p. 266; Archibald (2013) *Glasgow*, p. 234; McClintock and Gibson (1961) *Robbery* p. 25; Croall (1998) *Crime*, p. 227 and Conklin (1972) *Robbery*, pp. 110–111.

40 See the evidence in Kilday (2007) *Women and Violent Crime*, p. 129 and pp. 135–137; A. Adamson (2011) *Murder, Poaching and Lemonade: Crimes and Court Cases from Nineteenth Century West Lothian* (New York: Createspace), pp. 37–38 and pp. 45–46; Kilday (2013) 'Hell-Raising', pp. 262–265; Archibald (2013) *Glasgow*, pp. 49–52; Archibald (2014) *Bloody Scotland*, pp. 242–243 and p. 242 and R. McKay (2007) *Killers, Crooks and Cons: Scotland's Crimes of the* Century (Edinburgh: Black and White Publishing), pp. 71–75.

41 Sir John Fortescue (1885 edition) Charles Plummer (ed) *The Governance of England* (Oxford: Clarendon Press), pp. 141–142.

42 For further discussion of the robber as folk hero in the English context, see Spraggs (2001) *Outlaws, passim*; McDonald (2012) *Gentleman Rogues*, p. 9; Arnold (2012) *Underworld London*, pp. 80–81 and p. 90 as well as J.A. Sharpe (2005) *Dick Turpin: The Myth of the English Highwaymen* (London: Profile Books).

43 For evidence of robbers working together in teams throughout Britain and across history see Duke (2014) *Rogues*, p. 9; Spraggs (2001) *Outlaws*, p. 94; Brandon (2001) *Stand and Deliver*, p. 17 and p. 163; Newark (1979) *The Crimson* p. 20 and p. 31; Kilday (2007) *Women and Violent Crime*, pp. 139–140; Beattie (1986) *Crime* p. 149 and p. 159; Ward (2014) *Print Culture*, p. 99; Shore (2010)

'Criminality', pp. 122–123; Sindall (1990) *Street Violence*, p. 100, p. 61; Kilday (2013) 'Hell-Raising', p. 262; McClintock and Gibson (1961) *Robbery*, p. 24; Katz (1991) 'The Motivation, p. 278 and Conklin (1972) *Robbery*, pp. 64–65 and p. 107.

44 See for instance Croall (1998) *Crime*, pp. 225–226 and chapter thirteen as well as Conklin (1972) *Robbery*, p. 65.

45 For evidence of this across history see Colquhoun (1798 edition) *A Treatise*, pp. 73–74; McDonald (2012) *Gentlemen Rogues*, p. 20 and McClintock and Gibson (1961) *Robbery*, p. xiii.

46 For evidence of premeditation in the Scottish context of robbery see Kilday (2007) *Women and Violent Crime*, p. 131; Kilday (2013) 'Hell-Raising', p. 265; Archibald (2013) *Glasgow*, pp. 234–235; Archibald (2014) *Bloody Scotland*, pp. 21–27 and p. 47 and Archibald (2012) *A Sink*, p. 167.

47 For evidence of recidivism in robbery offending see Duke (2014) *Rogues*, p. 110; Archibald (2013) *Glasgow*, pp. 49–50 and Shore (2010) 'Criminality, p. 122.

48 For further discussion see Brandon (2001) *Stand and Deliver*, p. 209; Beattie (1986) *Crime*, p. 158; Kilday (2007) *Women and Violent Crime*, p. 144; Katz (1991) 'The Motivation', p. 280 and McClintock and Gibson (1961) *Robbery*, pp. 27–28.

49 For further discussion see Beattie (1986) *Crime*, p. 51; McLynn (1991) *Crime*, p. 10; Kilday (2007) *Women and Violent Crime*, p. 140 and Wright (2006) *Organised Crime*, p. 165.

50 Conklin (1972) *Robbery*, p. 87.

51 B. Henry (1994) *Dublin Hanged Crime, Law Enforcement and Punishment in Late Eighteenth-Century Dublin* (Dublin: Irish Academic Press), p. 108. For further detail on the types of goods stolen in robbery episodes throughout history see for instance G. Walker (1994) 'Women, Theft and the World of Stolen Goods' in J. Kermode and G. Walker (eds) *Women, Crime and the Courts in Early Modern England* (London: Routledge), pp. 81–105; Sindall (1990) *Street Violence*, p. 51; Croall (1998) *Crime*, pp. 225–226 and McClintock and Gibson (1961) *Robbery*, p. 27.

52 For further discussion of the relationship between robbery offending and economic conditions across history see Spraggs (2001) *Outlaws*, p. 4; Davey (1994) *Rural Crime*, p. 21; Ruff (1984) *Crime*, p. 120; Croall (1998) *Crime*, p. 226 and Conklin (1972) *Robbery*, p. 79.

53 Fielding (1751 edition) *An Enquiry, passim*. Similar sentiments were also voiced by Patrick Colquhoun, Daniel Defoe and Bernard Mandeville at this time see Colquhoun (1798 edition) *A Treatise*, pp. 69–70; D. Defoe (1728) *Augusta Triumphans: Or, the Way to Make London the most Flourishing City in the Universe* (London: J. Roberts) [Bodleian Reference: BOD Gough Lond.272 (8)]; D. Defoe (1728) *Street Robberies Consider'd: The Reason of their being so Frequent, with Probable Means to Prevent 'em* (London: J. Roberts) [Bodleian Reference: BOD Mar.849 (7)] and B. Mandeville (1725) *An Enquiry into the Causes of the Frequent Executions at Tyburn and Etc.* (London: J. Roberts) [Bodleian Reference: BOD Vet. A4 e.2124].

54 For further discussion see Fielding (1751 edition) *An Enquiry*, pp. 6–188.

55 For further discussion see Croall (1998) *Crime*, p. 226 and McClintock and Gibson (1961) *Robbery*, p. 105.

56 For further discussion see especially Spraggs (2001) *Outlaws, passim*.

57 There are numerous variants of this name in the primary source material consulted for this volume (including Gilderoy, Gilder-Roy) but I have employed the most common version Gilder Roy.

58 J. Cosgrave (1799) *A Genuine History of the Lives and Actions of the Most Notorious Irish Highwaymen, Tories and Rapparees, from Redmond O'Hanlon, the Famous Gentleman-Robber, to Cahier na Gappul, the Great Horse-catcher, Who Was Executed*

at Maryborough, in August 1735. To Which is Added, The Gold-finder, or, The History of Manus MacOneil, Who Under the Appearance of a Stupid, Ignorant Country Fellow (On the Bog of Allen, by the Help of His Man Andrew) Played the Most Notorious Cheats, And Remarkable Tricks on the People of Ireland, That Was Ever Known. Also, the Remarkable Life of Gilder Roy, a Murderer; Ravisher; Incendiary and Highwayman, With Several Others (Wilmington [DEL]: Bonal and Niles), p. 136.

59 *Ibid.*

60 *Jacobite Broadside – Colour Portrait of Gilder Roy in His Genuine Highland Garb*, reproduced with kind permission from The National Library of Scotland, Shelfmark: Blaikie.SNPG.9.9 found at http://digital.nls.uk/75240827.

61 G.H. Borrow (1825) *Celebrated Trials and Remarkable Cases of Criminal Jurisprudence from the Earliest Records to the Year 1825 – Volume II* (London: Knight and Lacey), p. 128.

62 *Ibid*, p. 129.

63 *Ibid.*

64 For details of the proclamation and reward see J. Spalding (1792) *The History of The Troubles and Memorable Transactions in Scotland: From the Year 1624 to 1645 – Volume I* (Aberdeen: Angus and Son), p. 71.

65 Cosgrave (1799) *A Genuine History*, p. 137.

66 Borrow (1825) *Celebrated Trials*, pp. 130–131.

67 National Records of Scotland (NRS), Justiciary Court, West Circuit Minute Books, JC13/14.

68 *Ibid.*

69 *Ibid.*

70 *Ibid.*

71 *Ibid.*

72 *Ibid.*

73 *Ibid.*

74 *Ibid.*

75 *Ibid.*

76 *Ibid.*

77 See National Library of Scotland (NLS), (1822) *Public Executions* (Edinburgh, n.p.), Special Collections (SpC), L.C. Fol. 73 (043) and (1868) *The Life of Calcraft: An Account of the Executions in Scotland for the Past 200 Years*, (Edinburgh, n.p.), SpC, L.C. Fol. 73 (132).

78 For a detailed breakdown of the amount stolen see the arrest warrant for George Gilchrist found at NRS, Justiciary Court Records, Precognition Papers, AD14/31/474/1/2.

79 See NRS, Justiciary Court, Precognition Papers, AD14/31/474/1/3 and Precognition Papers - Indictment, AD14/31/474/1/4.

80 See the testimony of James Morrison (deemed by the court to be a *socius criminis* or accomplice in crime) found in NLS (1831) *Trial of George Gilchrist, William Gilchrist and James Brown* (Edinburgh: n.p.), SpC, A.B. 8. 213.10, p. 8.

81 See contemporary reactions to the case found in *The Newgate Calendar* found at www.exclassics.com/newgate/ng860.htm.

82 See the testimonies of T.S. Lorrain and James Smith found in NLS (1831) *Trial of George Gilchrist*, pp. 2–3.

83 See NRS, Justiciary Court, Precognition Papers - Memorial, AD14/31/474/1/1.

84 See the testimonies of John McMillan and William Ross Smith found in NLS (1831) *Trial of George Gilchrist*, pp. 4–5.

85 The testimonies of James Morrison and Robert Simpson found in *ibid*, pp. 6–15 at p. 7 and pp. 15–18 respectively.

86 NRS, Justiciary Court, Precognition Papers – Memorial, AD14/31/474/1/1.

87 NRS, Justiciary Court, Precognition Papers, AD14/31/474/1/3.

88 See the testimony of James Morrison found in NLS (1831) *Trial of George Gilchrist*, pp. 6–15.

89 See the testimony of Robert Simpson found in *ibid*, pp. 15–18.

90 NRS, Justiciary Court, Memorial, AD14/31/474/1/1.

91 For the details of the reward offered see the eventual trial in the Court of Session brought against the Commercial Bank of Scotland for failing to pay the reward as promised which can be found in R. MacFarlane (1841) *Reports of the Jury Trials in the Court of Session* (Edinburgh: Thomas Clark), pp. 62–68.

92 See the testimony of Anthony Nish found in NLS (1831) *Trial of George Gilchrist*, p. 26.

93 See *ibid*, pp. 28–29.

94 *Ibid*, pp. 51–53.

95 *Ibid*, p. 52. My addition in parenthesis.

96 *Ibid*, p. 53.

97 *Ibid, passim*. See too for instance NLS (1831) *Trial and Sentence: A Full Account of the Trial and Sentence of William Gilchrist, George Gilchrist and Jame Brown, who were Tried on a Charge of Abstracting a Box from the Prince Regent Coach from Glasgow to Edinburgh, Etc.* (Edinburgh: n.p.), SpC, F.3.1.13 (51).

98 See for instance NLS (1831) *Execution* (Edinburgh: n.p.), SpC, Ry III A.2 (109) and NLS (1831) *Execution: Full, True and Particular Account of the Execution of George Gilchrist, at the Head of Libberton's Wynd on the Morning of the 3rd of August 1831 for the Robbery of the Prince Regent Coach* (Edinburgh, n.p.), SpC, Ry III A.2 (111).

99 See for instance NLS (1831) *Lamentation for George Gilchrist Under Sentence of Death in Edinburgh* (Edinburgh, n.p.), SpC, Ry III A.2 (109); NLS (1831) *Lamentation of George Gilchrist Now Under Sentence of Death in Edinburgh* (Edinburgh, n.p.), SpC, Ry III A.2 (110) and NLS (1831) *Lamentation of George Gilchrist who is to be Executed at Edinburgh on the 3rd of August Instant, Etc.*, (Edinburgh, n.p.), SpC, F.3.a.13 (52).

100 For further discussion of the escape made see Archibald (2013) *Glasgow*, p. 41.

101 See NLS (1831) *Execution*.

102 See NLS (1831) *Lamentations of George Gilchrist*, SpC, Ry III A.2 (110).

103 The most detailed piece of documentation indicating that a deal was brokered between the bank, the courts and Gilchrist is found in NLS, (1832) *Letter from Alexander Robertson Esq. W.S. to the Directors of the Commercial Bank of Scotland [In Connection with the Case of George Gilchrist Tried for the Theft of the Bank's Money]* (Edinburgh, n.p.), SpC, 1940.12(16), pp. 1–33.

104 The majority of contemporary broadsides report that George Gilchrist was executed, but some works do state that, after he provided information to the bank authorities, his sentence was commuted to transportation – see *The Newgate Calendar* found at www.exclassics.com/newgate/ng860.htm and a report written several years later in *The Pittsburgh Post-Gazette*, 17th March 1842, p. 23. Regardless of these publications, I believe the original sentence of the court was carried out.

105 *The Guardian*, 1st September 1960, p. 2.

106 NRS, Justiciary Court, Trial Transcripts and Proceedings, Indictment, JC36/266.

107 *Ibid*.

108 See J. Carron (2012) *Ghosts of Barlinnie: Ten Men, Ten Murder Trials, Ten Executions* (New York: Amenta Publishing), p. 104.

109 NRS, Justiciary Court, Trial Transcripts and Proceedings, Testimony of James Hugh McKay and Douglas Nicholl, JC36/266, especially pp. 20–26 and pp. 31–35 respectively.

110 *Ibid*, testimony of Matthew Keillar, especially pp. 118–119.

111 *Ibid,* testimony of Robert Easdale, especially pp. 59–70 and the testimony of Anne Margaret Stroyan Black, Senior House Officer at the Victoria Infirmary in Glasgow who looked after Easdale during his stay in the hospital, pp. 111–113.

112 For further details see NRS, Justiciary Court, Trial Transcripts and Proceedings, Indictment, JC36/266.

113 See for instance NRS, Justiciary Court, Trial Transcripts and Proceedings, Testimony of Detective Inspector John McLaren, JC36/266, especially pp. 219–221. See also *The Times*, 16th November 1960, Issue 54930, p. 7.

114 The fairly substantial list of John Cremin's previous convictions were shown in court, see NRS, Justiciary Court, Criminal Case File, HH16/426/1.

115 For further discussion see D.M. Fraser (2010) *The Book of Glasgow Murders* (Glasgow: Neil Wilson Publishing), p. 169.

116 NRS, Justiciary Court, Trial Transcripts and Proceedings, Testimony of Walter Pollock Weir, JC36/266, especially pp. 234–262.

117 NRS, Justiciary Court, Trial Transcripts and Proceedings, Testimony of Detective Inspector John McLaren, JC36/266, especially pp. 221–222. See also Fraser (2010) *The Book of Glasgow Murders*, p. 170.

118 NRS, Justiciary Court, Trial Transcripts and Proceedings, Testimonies of Crawfurd McFarlean Mure, James Morrison Sinclair and George William Orr, JC36/266, especially pp. 71–80, pp. 137–166 and pp. 206–207 respectively.

119 For further discussion of Denovan's confession see Fraser (2010) *The Book of Glasgow Murders*, p. 171.

120 NRS, Justiciary Court, Trial Transcripts and Proceedings, Summation in Defence of Anthony Joseph Miller by Mr Irvine Smith, JC36/266, p. 2. For more on Smith's personal opinion of the trial and the 'inevitability' of the verdict see I. Smith Q.C. (2012 edition) *Law, Life and Laughter: A Personal Verdict* (Edinburgh: Black and White Publishing), pp. 139–140.

121 See the explanation given at NRS, Justiciary Court, Trial Transcripts and Proceedings, Summation of Trial Proceedings by the Judge, JC36/266, pp. 10–11 and for the full details see also the Homicide Act, 1957 (5 and 6 Eliz. 2 c.11).

122 Children and Young Persons Act, 1933 (23 and 24 Geo. 5 c. 12).

123 For more on James Denovan's eventual release from prison see McKay (2007) *Killers*, p. 193.

124 NRS, Justiciary Court, Trial Transcript and Proceedings, Verdict and Sentence, JC36/266, pp. 54–56 and NRS, Justiciary Court, Death Warrant, HH/16/642/14. See also *The Guardian*, 17th November 1960, p. 2.

125 Smith Q.C. (2012 edition) *Law*, p. 145.

126 *Ibid*, p. 146.

127 For further discussion of this encounter see L. Murray (2002) *The Pleader: An Autobiography* (Edinburgh and London: Mainstream Publishing), pp. 13–14.

128 See NRS, Justiciary Court, Petition for Appeal, HH16/426/1. Anthony Miller declined to be present in court when the appeal was being heard. For further discussion on the deliberation over the grounds of appeal amongst Miller's legal team see Murray (2002) *The Pleader*, p. 22. See also *The Guardian*, 26th November 1960, p. 3.

129 See *ibid*, p. 23.

130 See *ibid*, p. 25; Fraser (2010) *The Book of Glasgow Murders*, p. 174 and also *The Guardian*, 8th December 1960, p. 3.

131 See Murray (2002) *The Pleader*, p. 23.

132 See Smith Q.C. (2012 edition) *Law*, p. 145 and especially a 2017 review of the Dickson case found at www.bbc.co.uk/news/uk-scotland-south-scotland-40875034.

133 For extracts from the petition itself and the accompanying signatories see NRS, Justiciary Court, Criminal Case File, HH16/426/2 and HH16/426/4.

134 For more on the utilisation of the Miller case by contemporaries campaigning to abolish or amend the legislation on capital punishment see *ibid*. For examples of the types of letters and telegrams sent to prominent individuals such as the Queen and the Secretary of State for Scotland (including some sent by Anthony Miller's parents) see NRS, Justiciary Court, Barlinnie Prison: Prisoners Records, HH16/642/1 and HH16/642/14 and NRS, Justiciary Court, Criminal Case Files, HH16/427.

135 NRS, Justiciary Court, Criminal Case File, HH16/426/1.

136 *Ibid*. See also *The Times*, 20th December 1960, Issue 54959, p. 7. The formal document dismissing the appeal and setting a new date for Miller's execution can be found at NRS, Justiciary Court, Barlinnie Prison: Prisoners Records, HH16/642/14.

137 For further discussion of this hypothesis see Smith Q.C. (2012 edition) *Law*, p. 146.

138 See various features in the *Daily Express*, 17th November 1960 cuttings from which are found at NRS, Barlinnie Prison: Prisoners Records, HH16/642/14. See also Carron (2012) *Ghosts*, p. 104.

139 Murray (2002) *The Pleader*, p. 28.

140 These intimate and at times humorous letters can be found at NRS, Justiciary Court, Barlinnie Prison: Prisoners Records, HH16/642/14. The reaction of Miller's parents to his impending execution can be found in several newspaper interviews with them published in the *Daily Express* on the 19th of December 1960 and the *Scottish Daily Mail* on the 20th December 1960. Cuttings relating to these publications are found at NRS, Barlinnie Prison: Prisoners Records, HH16/642/14.

141 For further details on the conduct of Anthony Miller immediately before and during his execution see NRS, Justiciary Court, Barlinnie Prison: Prisoners Records, HH16/642/1 and HH16/642/14. For confirmation of his death see the medical examiner's report in report in the same file and the *Edinburgh Evening Dispatch* on the 22nd of December 1960 a cutting of which is found in the same file and *The Times*, 23rd December 1960, Issue 54962, p. 4. For details of the burial of his remains at Barlinnie Prison see NRS, Barlinnie Prison: Prisoners Records, HH16/642/14.

142 Murray (2002) *The Pleader*, p. 29.

143 *Ibid*. See also *The Herald*, 6th June 1995; the *Daily Record*, 4th December 2010 and the *Scottish Daily Mail*, 22nd March 2014.

Chapter 6

The Violent North or The Enterprising Scot, 1660–1960?

Introduction

If Scotland was a violent nation and the Scots were truly a violent people, then we would expect this study to show a predominance of violent offences being brought before the judicial authorities throughout Scotland's recent history. Although the Scots could be fierce and aggressive when engaging in illegal exploits as we have already seen, it has also been made evident that the perpetration of extreme forms of violence was uncommon. Indeed, from 1660 to 1960, it was non-violent offences and property crimes in particular that overwhelmingly dominated court business. Thus, instead of thinking of the Scottish criminal as vicious and dangerous, should we not start to rethink this orthodoxy and consider the archetypal Scottish criminal as an individual who was more enterprising than enraged?

This notion of the enterprising Scottish criminal fits in well with the historic trope which made 'Scottishness' and 'enterprise' synonymous. It was the Victorians who first articulated the view that the Scots were '…the personification of progress' due to their inventiveness, their character and capabilities (which combined educational prowess and self-made expertise), and their perpetual commercial drive to invest and improve.[1] But were these qualities manifest in their illegal activities too? Were the Scots particularly entrepreneurial when it came to their participation in offences where money could be made and profit gleaned? Non-violent offences, and property crimes in particular, will be the focus of this chapter, so that we can better understand the endeavours of the more typical Scottish criminal.

Whether entrepreneurial or otherwise, the Scots should certainly be considered eclectic when it came to their involvement in non-violent criminality.[2] Their illegality was wide-ranging and extensive in terms of the types of offences perpetrated. However, due to the limits of space and the specific purview of the Scottish Justiciary Court, this chapter will not be able to explore *all* of the multifarious forms of non-violent criminal activity committed in Scotland between 1660 and 1960. Acts of petty theft, arson, vandalism, prostitution, extortion and blackmail for instance, will not be considered in this present analysis.[3] The other caveat about the specific focus and content of this chapter relates to changing official and societal preoccupations and how these have been reflected in the data relating to non-violent Scottish criminality across time.

Some offences, which were considered serious and regularly featured in the Scottish courtroom in the seventeenth, eighteenth and nineteenth centuries seemingly become ignored, forgotten or replaced in the obsessions of the Scottish judiciary by the more modern era. Conversely, other offences which were known to exist, but which were rarely considered by the Scottish authorities in the premodern period, began to grow in significance over the course of the twentieth century. These crimes became more frequently reported over time and as a result, they are eventually perceived as a menace or threat to the well-being and future preservation of the nation. The erratic nature of attitudes to certain types of non-violent offending causes problems for the historian of crime. As these offences were not indicted consistently over the entirety of the 1660–1960 period, they cannot be effectively analysed over a sustained chronology. Nor can they be accurately compared to crimes of violence which seem to have been more chronologically persistent in terms of committal rates and attitudinal gravitas.

To give an example, in premodern Scotland, and indeed elsewhere in Britain, forgery (and the uttering or passing of forged material) was considered an extremely serious offence akin to treason where capital punishment could result upon conviction.[4] Forgery was regarded as a threat to commercial sustainability in an era when the use of negotiable paper in the form of currency, credit, contracts and other documentation was at its height and open to exploitation in many ways.[5] Forgery trials were a relatively uncommon feature of Scottish judicial history from the seventeenth century until the late eighteenth century, when after that time, concerns over the offence seemed to wane and were replaced instead (but albeit not immediately or concurrently) by anxieties over the perceived threat from fraud.[6] This more recent disquiet intensified over the more modern era, especially with the advent of new technologies which have facilitated and extended the reach and significance of this type of criminal activity to an unprecedented degree.

Neither forgery nor fraud will be considered in this volume as both the qualitative and quantitative material relating to these crimes is insignificant, incomplete and unreliable for the three hundred years between 1660 and 1960.[7] Instead, this chapter will focus exclusively on the most persistent and most commonly reported type of non-violent property crime throughout Scottish history: theft and its allied offences.[8] Whilst it should be remembered that the primary utilisation of records from the Justiciary Court for this exploration limits the discussion of these crimes to the most serious larcenies and to the most infamous, recidivist offenders, we can, nonetheless, learn much about the entrepreneurial nature of Scottish criminality from this particular analysis.[9]

The Enterprising Scottish Criminal and the Law

Many variants of the non-violent illegal appropriation of goods have existed in history, but in Scotland at least, only a few offences have warranted separate legal categorisation from theft during the 1660 to 1960 period. In part, this is because, as historian Rab Houston explains, attitudes to land use and rights were very different north of the Tweed. Scottish statute law and Scottish common law had established what was legal and illegal from as early as the Middle Ages and this provided clarity for the populace. As a result, there was no need to codify or outlaw customary practices in the premodern period as was the case in England.[10] Whilst undoubtedly there was a clamour for better behaviour on the part of landowners and leaseholders at various points in the eighteenth, nineteenth and twentieth centuries in the Scottish context, this did not result in a flurry of legislative change.[11] So, for instance, there was no separate offence related to gleaning, poaching, or pilfering produce or fuel from the land in Scotland.[12] Although the theft of linen from a bleachfield and piracy were deemed separate capital crimes in the North, they were offences that were largely confined to the early modern period.[13] Neither wrecking nor smuggling appeared in the Scottish statute book in their own right either, but if the perpetration of these offences involved sustained or particularly aggressive violence towards authorities, as we saw in Chapter 3 of this volume, then the law could be flexed to render capital pains appropriate at the court's discretion.[14]

The simplicity of Scots Law extended to consideration of more obvious forms of the theft of goods from another person too. In England and elsewhere in Europe, especially during the premodern period, various elaborate distinctions were made in law, depending on the time, place, amount stolen, and degree of force used. As historian Alan Macfarlane describes:

> A theft occurring after the entry of another's premises, when the owner or his wife or his servants were present, was termed housebreaking (in the daytime) or burglary (at night). A theft from another's person was robbery, and if it took place in or near the king's highway it was highway robbery. Goods stolen from either houses or fields, in the absence of the owner, his family or servants, was termed larceny. Robbery of a person without his knowledge was pickpocketing. If the value of the object taken in larceny was one shilling or less, then it was petty larceny, if over that sum, grand larceny.[15]

Theft was considered a serious offence by the Scottish authorities as all three of the case studies in this chapter show. As Baron David Hume explains, the reason for the prevailing relatively staunch attitude was '...not so much the damage to the individual, as the violation of the order of civil society, by dishonesty prevailing over right, and the danger of seduction, by the spectacle of this as a practicable thing.'[16] Nevertheless, establishing an indictment for theft was relatively straightforward for the Scottish advocates of the 1660–1960 period in comparison with their counterparts elsewhere.

In Scots Law,

> Theft is committed when property is feloniously appropriated without the owner's or possessor's consent, and without the exercise of violence to the person, by one who has no special ownership in the property appropriated, and has not received it in trust under liability to account.[17]

There were only three necessary qualifications in Scots Law for a charge of theft to be regarded as viable. Firstly, there had to be not only a taking, but a carrying away of the item or items craved by the thief. Secondly, the taking and carrying away had to be committed with a felonious purpose, by an individual who knew that the item or items belonged to another person and who meant to deprive that person of their property. Finally, the taking and carrying away had to be for the sake of lucre or profit and not simply wilful destruction.[18]

It seems that the Scottish courts of the seventeenth, eighteenth and nineteenth centuries did not deal with a wide variety of different 'types' of indictments for theft. Having said this, however, there were several so-called 'aggravations' of a single act of theft which could result in a capital sentence being imposed on the accused. Two of these were related to the character of the thief and the other to the way in which the theft was carried out.[19] Of the former, the first kind of aggravation existed '…if it was the act of a common thief…one who is held and reckoned, or *habite and repute* (according to our phrase for it) to be one of that calling, and to make or help his livelihood by thieving.'[20] We can see reference to this aggravation in the 1822 case study below relating to Charles McLaren, Thomas Grierson and James McEwan. The second type of aggravation concerning the character of the accused, was applied to individuals who had previous convictions for repeated acts of theft.[21] Again, this is evident in the aforementioned case study from the nineteenth century as well as the more modern example featuring Johnny Ramensky. Both of these so-called aggravations were similar in that they were explicit attempts by the authorities to curtail the activities of 'professional' thieves, an issue which will be explored in due course.

The final type of aggravation applied to an act of theft related to the way in which the offence was carried out. '…theft which was accomplished by forcing or breaking any shut or fastened place of keeping…is held to be *furtum grave* [aggravated]; on account of the bold and deliberate character of the act.'[22] The only example of this kind of activity to receive a specific appellation in Scots Law was that of housebreaking. It was not possible for an individual to be indicted for a crime of housebreaking alone, as was the case in England, as Scots Law deemed the offence to be purely an aggravation of an act of theft. Nevertheless, the Justiciary Court considered this type of behaviour to be the most serious of the three aggravations and universally dealt with every such instance as a capital crime at common law until the middle of the nineteenth century, regardless of the existence of any extenuating circumstances. The reason for this severity of described by Baron Hume:

> Because the thing [act of housebreaking] is here done with that contrivance and deliberation, to which none but the practised thief is equal; and in thus venturing to take the property from the very sanctuary assigned for keeping it, and in contempt of all the obstacles contrived to deter him, he shows a resolute and daring spirit, such as threatens danger to the lives and persons of the inhabitants of the house, if they shall stay or oppose him in his purpose.[23]

Consequently, according to Hume, this aggravation of theft deserves '...the most particular attention...' of the law.[24] All three of the case studies below involve this type of aggravated theft, which in part explains why they were brought before the Justiciary Court.

According to Baron Hume, the study of resett (the receiving of stolen goods) is

> ...a proper sequel to that of theft and robbery, as being in some measure a continuation of them, and that by which its subserviency to the convenience of the thief, is one of the great means of attaching him to his unlawful course of life.[25]

We can see from this statement that not only was resett an offence that was wholly allied to theft, but that the discovery of stolen goods was often a key element in the detection and arrest of a given thief. This was evident in relation to the arrest of all five of the accused individuals in the case studies for this chapter. Eighteenth century commentators also voiced their concerns about the link between theft and resett. In the 1720s, Bernard De Mandeville commented that '...the mischief that one man can do as a thief, is a very trifle to what he may be the occasion of, as an agent...of felons.'[26] Then, in 1786, Henry Fielding argued that '...one of the great encouragements to theft of all kinds is the ease and safety with which stolen goods may be disposed of.'[27]

The Scottish word 'resett' literally meant to set goods before the public again and the crime of resett was defined in Scots Law as '...the receiving and keeping of stolen goods, knowing them to be such, and with an intention to conceal and withhold them from the owner.'[28] It should be noted that in the Scottish definition, there is no reference to the resale of the goods which was a prerequisite for a charge of resett in the English legal context. North of the Tweed, possession of stolen property sufficed for a charge to be warranted. The receiving of stolen goods was clearly regarded by both society in general, and the authorities in particular, as both a widespread and a serious offence. However, there appears to have been no capital statutory provision applied to the offence of resett in Scotland since a defunct act initiated by thirteenth century King Alexander II.[29] According to Baron Hume, the degree of punishment meted out upon an individual convicted of resett was completely left to the discretion of the judge in a given trial.[30] Having said this, however, he insists that in Scots Law at least, resett was considered to be a crime less serious than that of theft, and as a result, it was punished in a less severe manner.[31]

There were three simple qualifications which validated an indictment of resett. First of all, in Hume's description: 'It is the fundamental circumstance in the description of this crime that the stolen goods are to be received into the offender's possession.' Second, the resetter had to be in the knowledge that the goods received had been stolen. And finally, the act of resett had to be 'felonious'; that is, with the aim of detaining the property from its rightful owner.[32] It must often have been a difficult task for the authorities to fulfil these legal qualifications in order to substantiate a charge of resett. This suggests that this type of offence contributed significantly to the so-called 'dark figure' of unknown or unreported criminal statistics.

Trends in Criminal Enterprise and their Punishment

Figures 6.1 and 6.5 below show the relatively stable incidence of indictments for non-violent property crime in Scotland from 1836 to 1897, and the significant numerical surge after that date and into the twentieth century, as petty offences dealt with at the Burgh Courts were assimilated into the judicial statistics.[33] Figure 6.5 also illustrates that the trend in indictments over the modern era was generally upward. We can see from the high number of indictments that theft and its allied offences were commonly indicted at the Scottish courts and, in the nineteenth century at least, the indictment incidence was comparable with that of assault analysed in Chapter 3. What is also evident from Figures 6.2 and 6.6 is that it was instances of ordinary theft, rather than more serious larcenies that dominated court business. This was true, even after the jurisdictional data merge mentioned above. Figure 6.9 shows a relatively close correlation between indictments and convictions for non-violent property crime in Scotland between 1836 and 1899. This was probably due to juries being more willing to convict accused individuals when arbitrary punishments were the accepted sanction for proven acts of this kind of criminality. Conversely, Figure 6.11 shows that in the twentieth century, the gap between indictments and convictions grew quite substantially, despite supposedly improved detection methods. This pattern may have something to do with the sheer volume of non-violent property crime being processed by the Scottish authorities after 1900 and is perhaps indicative of a limited ability to manage the proliferation of criminal activity in a successful manner.

Interestingly, Figures 6.3, 6.4, 6.7 and 6.8 below show that the gap in offending between male and females increases over time in the Scottish context,

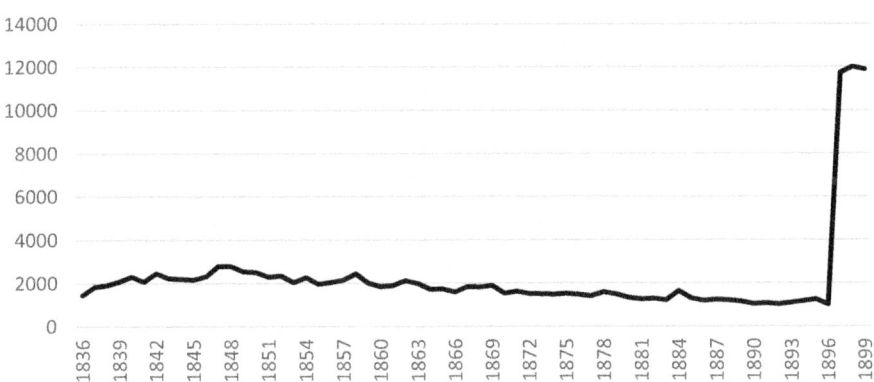

Figure 6.1 Indictments for Non-Violent Property Crime in Scotland, 1836–1899.

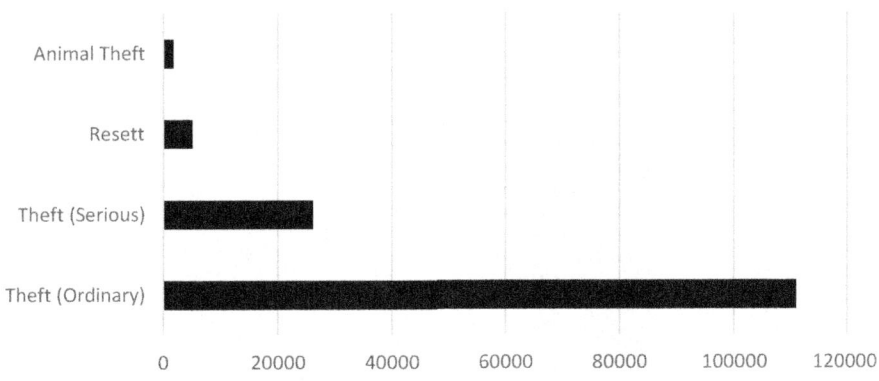

Figure 6.2 Types of Non-Violent Property Crime Indicted in Scotland, 1836–1899.

a pattern also mirrored in assault indictments. Although Scottish women were indicted for theft in large numbers over the twentieth century (especially when compared to the other offences we have looked at in this volume), men were far more likely to appear in court on a charge of this nature compared to their female counterparts. This gender disparity is especially acute if we consider women's involvement in the more serious forms of non-violent property crime. Scottish women were rarely prosecuted for breaking into property and stealing from therein. The data presented on convictions in Figures 6.10 and 6.12 reaffirms this incongruence but demonstrates that in the Scottish context, more women were convicted for non-violent property crimes than for any other offence.

Figures 6.13 and 6.16 below show indictment rates for resett as distinct from other forms of non-violent property crime in Scotland after 1836. As

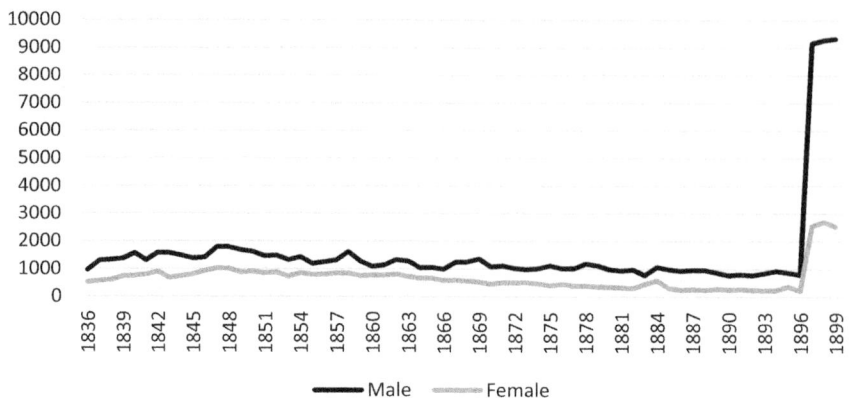

Figure 6.3 Indictments for Non-Violent Property Crime in Scotland by Gender, 1836–1899.

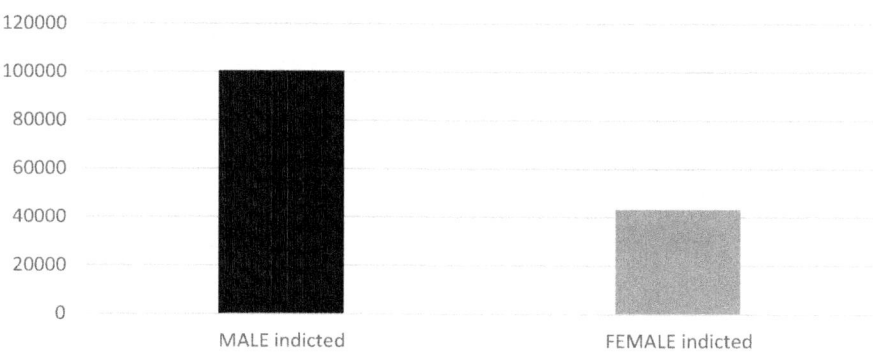

Figure 6.4 The Gendered Nature of Non-Violent Property Crime Indictments in Scotland, 1836–1899.

we can see, the indictment incidence for this offence was low until the jurisdictional data merge in 1897. Even then, the number of resett indictments was insignificant compared to those for non-violent property crime more generally, and for theft in particular. Interestingly, where the nineteenth century shows a slight but general downward trend in indictment incidence, a reversed trend is evident post-1900. The reason for specifically looking at resett is highlighted by Figures 6.14, 6.15, 6.17 and 6.18. As is evident, there was much less of a gender disparity in prosecutions for resett compared to the other offences examined in this work. This was particularly evident in the first half of the nineteenth century (see Figure 6.14) where at some junctures, the number of women indicted clearly outstripped the men and confirmed

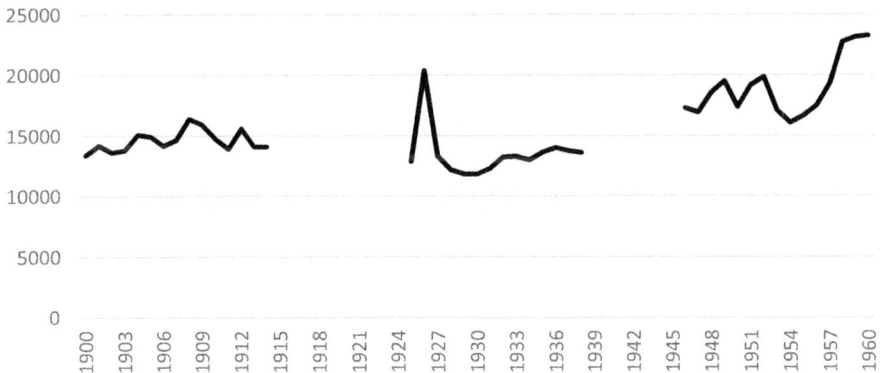

Figure 6.5 Indictments for Non-Violent Property Crime in Scotland, 1900–1960.

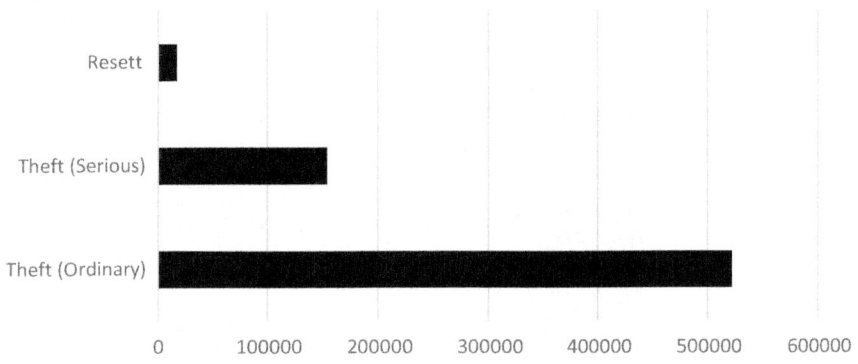

Figure 6.6 Types of Non-Violent Property Crime Indicted in Scotland, 1900–1960.

what we know about the earlier history of the offence in a Scottish context.[34] By the more modern era, however, the gender gap had widened to a degree more typical of the Scottish experience of recorded criminality, mirroring the trend seen in previous chapters where female felons largely disappeared from the modern Scottish courtroom. Disappointingly, conviction data for resett could not be disaggregated from the overall statistics.

There are two more significant issues to note regarding the available data on non-violent property crime. Firstly, juvenile delinquents did not make up a significant proportion of those indicted for non-violent property crime in Scotland between 1836 and 1960. This is likely due to them being dealt with by a separate judicial provision as has already been explained elsewhere in this volume. Secondly, both Figures 6.19 and 6.20 below show that recidivism did not have a significant part to play in indictments for non-violent property

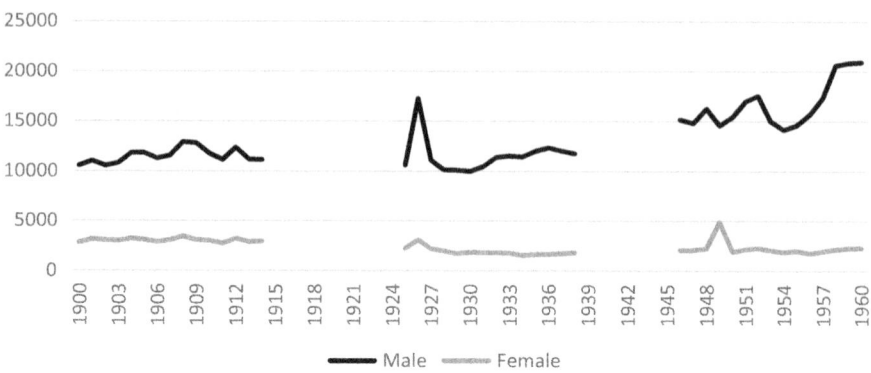

Figure 6.7 Indictments for Non-Violent Property Crime in Scotland by Gender, 1900–1960.

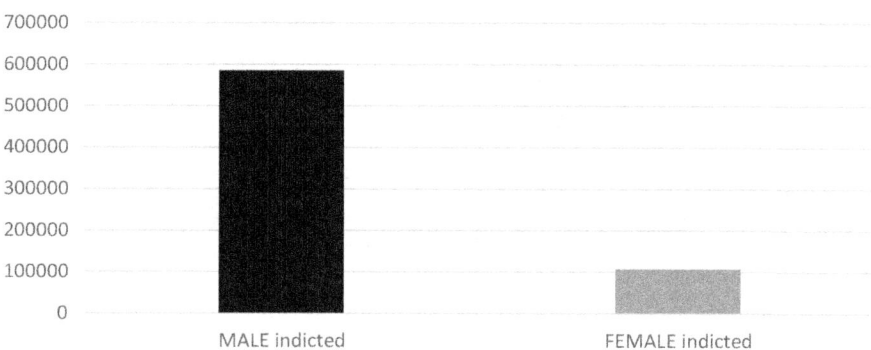

Figure 6.8 The Gendered Nature of Non-Violent Property Crime Indictments in Scotland, 1900–1960.

crimes in Scotland over the entirety of our period. This is perhaps surprising, as social observers regularly commented at different historical junctures about professional thieves and repeat offenders being a recurrent and intractable social problem, as is particularly exemplified in the second case study below. Yet, even in the more modern era, when we have a significant increase in indictment levels due to the jurisdictional data merge, we can clearly see that recidivism was not the acute problem commentators perceived it to be. When we compare this data, with the extent of recidivism in relation to interpersonal violence, seen in Chapter 3, it could be argued that the Scottish authorities were more intent on prosecuting individuals who were repeatedly violent, rather than those who were repeatedly acquisitive. This may, once again, have presented a false of impression of the nature of Scottish criminality over time.

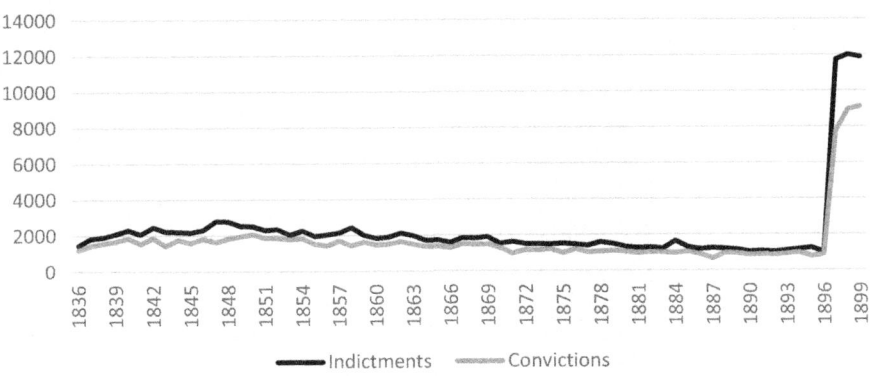

Figure 6.9 Indictments and Convictions for Non-Violent Property Crime in Scotland, 1836–1899.

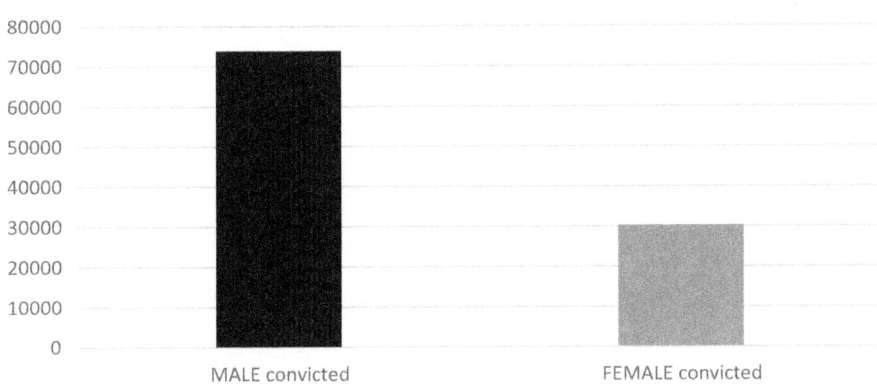

Figure 6.10 The Gendered Nature of Convictions for Non-Violent Property Crime in Scotland, 1836–1899.

Figure 6.11 Indictments and Convictions for Non-Violent Property Crime in Scotland, 1900–1960.

Figure 6.12 The Gendered Nature of Convictions for Non-Violent Property Crime in Scotland, 1900–1960.

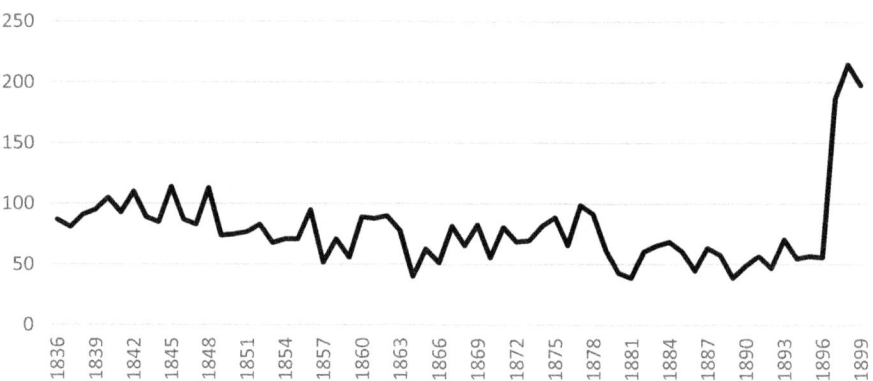

Figure 6.13 Indictments for Resett in Scotland, 1836–1899.

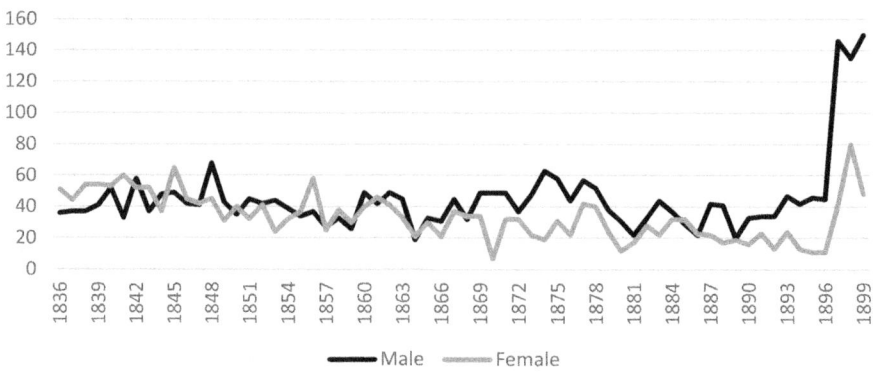

Figure 6.14 Indictments for Resett in Scotland by Gender, 1836–1899.

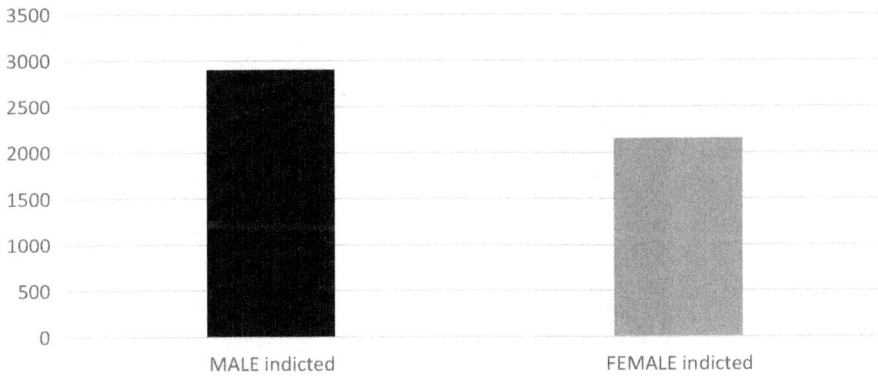

Figure 6.15 The Gendered Nature of Resett Indictments in Scotland, 1836–1899.

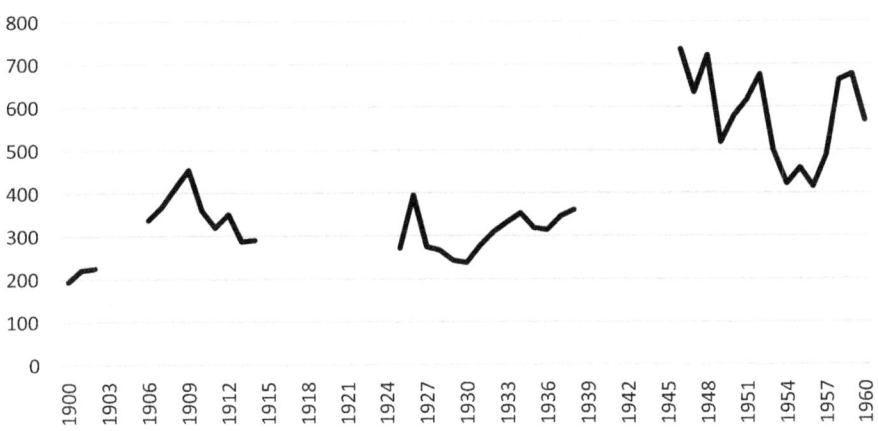

Figure 6.16 Indictments for Resett in Scotland, 1900–1960.

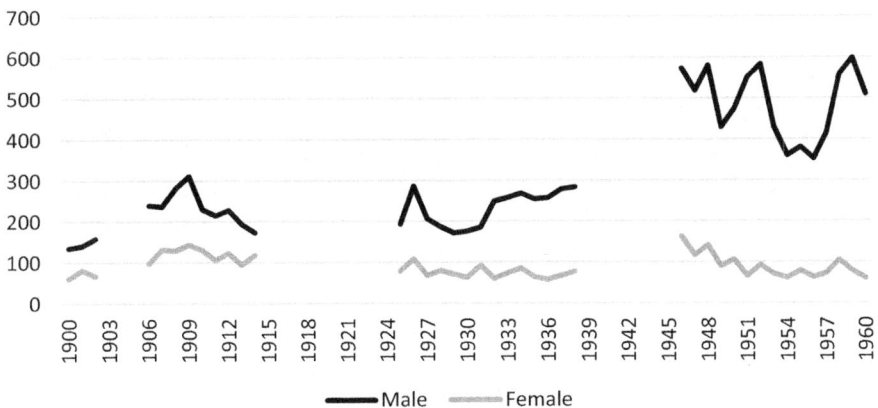

Figure 6.17 Indictments for Resett in Scotland by Gender, 1900–1960.

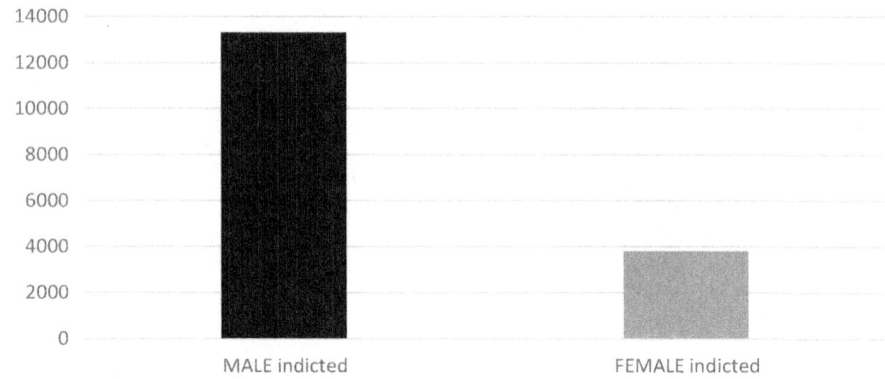

Figure 6.18 The Gendered Nature of Resett Indictments in Scotland, 1900–1960.

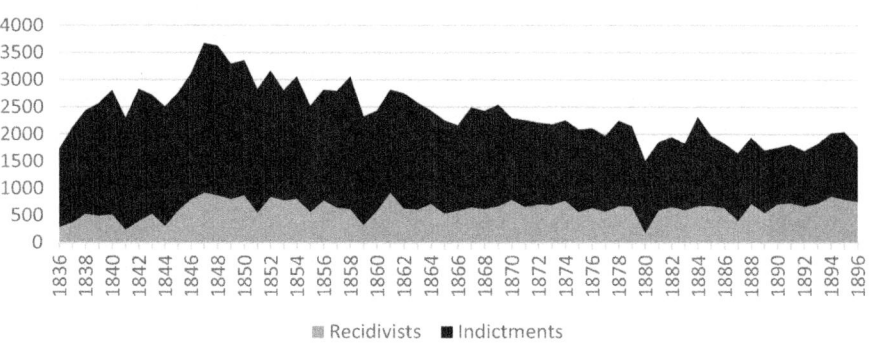

Figure 6.19 The Proportion of Recidivism amongst Indictments for Non-Violent Property Crime in Scotland, 1836–1896.

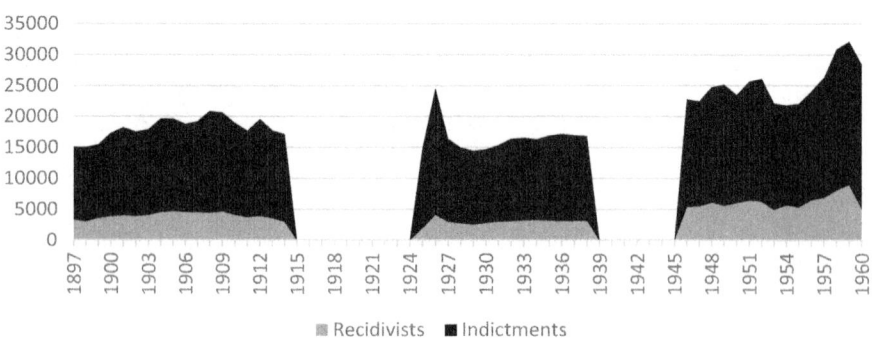

Figure 6.20 The Proportion of Recidivism amongst Indictments for Non-Violent Property Crime in Scotland, 1897–1960.

Offenders, Victims, Methods and Motive

It is evident from the masculine pronouns used in the legal definitions and descriptions of theft and reset provided earlier on in this chapter that both offences were considered gendered in that they were expected to be dominated by male offenders. Certainly, men did predominate in the number of individuals accused of stealing at the Scottish Justiciary Court between 1660 and 1960 as we have seen and as the three case studies in this chapter subsequently illustrate.[35] However, we ought to remember that more women were involved in non-violent theft than in any other type of crime in the three hundred years of our study.[36] In addition, closer analysis of the indictment evidence from the Justiciary Court reveals that male and female participation in this type of non-violent offending was more nuanced than we might have predicted.

For one thing, women were active, enterprising participants in *all* forms of theft from pickpocketing to housebreaking. Scottish women were autonomous criminal actors in this context and were not merely accomplices to male thieves.[37] In addition, and up until the twentieth century as we have seen, women tended to outnumber men when it came to the crime of reset. Yet, we should not surmise that they did this as an alternative to stealing or to avoid being directly or proactively involved in criminality. Rather, as women were more familiar with the value and price of goods and commodities in their role as keeper of the domestic purse, they were better placed to participate effectively in this particular offence compared to their male counterparts.[38] Lastly, when specific methodologies of theft are examined, it is evident that historically, women favoured some forms of property crime more than others. The same was also true for men. Women preferred pickpocketing, theft in the context of sexual encounters and shoplifting on the whole, whereas men were more inclined towards animal theft, smuggling ventures or thefts involving automobiles.[39]

The age range of the offenders accused of theft and reset in Scotland between 1660 and 1960 was also more diverse than we might have assumed given the recurring concerns over juvenile delinquency during our period of study and beyond in the English context at least, which are highlighted to some extent in the nineteenth century case study below.[40] Yet it seems that in Scotland, the age of the offender was less of a concern than was the case south of the Tweed, at least in terms of the cases brought before the Justiciary Court. There, youthfulness could function as a mitigation for the accused and as we have already noted, juvenile delinquents did not form a significant section of the Scottish criminal populace according to the judicial statistics.[41] Indeed, the Scots seemed to be more preoccupied with theft as a general and unpredictable threat to the property and status of the populace, rather than the involvement of the nation's youth in its perpetration.[42]

On the whole, theft tended to be a crime committed by strangers on strangers in an opportunistic fashion, unless it was carried out using inside knowledge of a location or workplace.[43] The threat posed by theft was unquestionably enhanced by the fact that it was a crime that was often associated with multiple assailants, either in relation to the act of stealing itself or in the disposal of stolen goods after the fact.[44] As is evident in the case study featuring Johnny Ramensky and the one involving the three youths, the more accomplices that were involved in a given theft, the richer the spoils tended to be; either because more elaborate crimes could be planned and perpetrated or because a greater quantity of loot could be carried off. Moreover, evidence from both theft and resett indictments between 1660 and 1960 highlight the existence of underground criminal networks across Scotland. These implied in turn, that this particular type of crime was potentially more hidden, extensive and 'professional' in nature when compared to many of the other types of offences considered by the Scottish judicial authorities over that period.[45]

In order to assess whether theft and its allied offences were carried out with enterprise and professionalism in the Scottish context, we need to examine the methodologies adopted by Scottish thieves. Were the Scots entrepreneurial in the *ways* in which they chose to steal and in the specific tactics deployed to facilitate this kind of criminality? Was any sort of professionalism reflected in their selection of targets and the items taken? To what extent was Scottish theft premeditated and planned? And, given that the incidence of recidivism was surprisingly low, can we learn more from the motives of Scottish thieves to indicate whether individuals participated in theft as a professional career or way of life or whether they did so owing to poverty-wrought desperation or sudden greed-based acquisitiveness?

Whilst not legally defined as separate entities in Scots Law, it is still possible to delineate distinct stealing methodologies from the indictment evidence brought before the Justiciary Court. As we might expect, numerous methodologies were deployed by Scottish thieves across the 1660–1960 period and these were mirrored in the exploits of thieves elsewhere during this period.[46] In the main, mechanisms for theft were determined by the immediate context in which a given thief was operating and these contexts became more varied and more complex over time. Methodologies were also influenced by commercial developments and technological advances and in response to contemporary official and societal reactions, such as the increased adoption of security measures and crime prevention strategies, especially in the more modern era.

Thus, from the seventeenth century, we find wreckers and smugglers stealing from ships, rustlers stealing animals from estates and opportunistic thieves helping themselves to items left unattended as well as the contents of other people's pockets.[47] In the eighteenth and nineteenth centuries we see pilfering poachers in the rural milieu and more of the tenacious pick-pocket skilfully operating in the busy crowds of urbanising areas. They stole along-side shoplifters who utilised their criminal dexterity in markets and fledgling commercial enterprises such as department stores.[48] We also see more work-place theft reported and embezzlement in particular, becoming a growing problem but one which was largely hidden from the gaze of the judiciary.[49] With wealthier households increasingly being filled with valuable commodi-ties, we also see housebreaking being committed with relative frequency and in more sophisticated ways during this period, with the use of false keys, prior planning and a degree of expertise.[50] In this sense, the Scottish thief could be considered entrepreneurial although perhaps not more so than his or her counterparts elsewhere. The spoils from breaking-and-entering were often substantial (as evidenced by two of the three case studies below), especially when multiple assailants were involved, and this was also true in the more modern era when businesses as well as personal residences became targeted.[51] In the twentieth century, and up until 1960 at least, non-violent theft typol-ogies had not changed significantly from the century before. However, the advent of the motor car offered greater mobility to thieves, it allowed escape to be better facilitated, and it could even be deployed as an expedient device in smash-and-grab raids.[52]

The types of goods stolen by Scottish thieves in the period 1660–1960 were also largely determined by *where* the theft was perpetrated. However, historians have argued that the gender of the offender also impacted upon loot selection, with thieves tending to steal items that they were familiar with or knew the value of.[53] In this respect, Scottish thieves could be con-sidered enterprising. As we can see in the case studies below, men were more likely to steal cash or to take items of potential value such as livestock, gold and silver plate, jewellery or vehicles.[54] Women, on the other hand, were often more inclined to steal items of clothing, fabric and a variety of accoutrements associated with fashionable attire.[55] Nevertheless, we should remember that both sexes also stole mundane items of low value which they knew could be readily got rid of either through consumption or through known networks of resetters. These types of offences had to be repeated on a regular basis if they were to aid in long-term subsistence or were to become profitable for the criminals concerned.[56] Consequently, some indi-viduals, like Johnny Ramensky whom we will encounter in the final case study of this volume, could become career thieves or professional pilferers, but this was typically because the paltry value of the treasures they stole necessitated recidivist behaviour, rather than because they were criminal entrepreneurs.[57]

As we saw in the previous chapter of this volume, and as the above analysis of the goods stolen by Scottish thieves demonstrates, the motives for the ille-gal appropriation of goods – whether violent or otherwise – tend to revolve around need rather than greed in the Scottish context and beyond between 1660 and 1960. As we have seen, many opportunist thieves grabbed items they could quickly utilise, but their actions tended to be borne of desperation rather than covetousness.[58] The exception to this may have been female shoplifters in the nineteenth and twentieth centuries who typically did not need the items they pilfered and indeed, could afford to pay for them if asked. These women, often more mature than the average thief, seemed to be suffering from some sort of mental malady, where the taking of items not their own was a compulsion that could not be controlled and is, as yet, not fully understood or satisfactorily explained.[59] Other individuals, such as Johnny Ramensky for instance, seem to have also been driven by an impulse to thieve, but this craving seems to have derived from the excitement generated by the perpetration of the offence and subsequent attempts to evade capture by the authorities.[60] Nevertheless, it could be argued, that the similarities between this kind of compulsion for excitement and the mental health problems associated with kleptomania referred to above, ought to be explored more thoroughly.

Whilst some Scottish thieves did steal items which might be considered luxurious or frivolous, as is evidenced in all three of the case studies to follow in this chapter, they rarely kept these goods for themselves. Rather, they selected items that they knew would bring the highest return from the network of resetters, pawnbrokers and members of the so-called 'hidden economy' that they were familiar with.[61] Thus, the majority of Scottish thieves could be considered entrepreneurial in terms of their motives for their offending and through the actions they perpetrated and the behaviour they displayed. Although the motives for participating in non-violent forms of property crime were undoubtedly diverse and dependent on the particular personal circumstances of the individual or individuals concerned[62], we can see, nonetheless, that theft was either something that was resorted to on occasion to supplement income or to help make ends meet, or it was a venture which could return a steady profit if engaged in regularly. Thus, it was evidently preservation and profit, rather than materialism and avidity, which lay at the heart of Scottish theft and its allied offences in the three centuries before 1960.

Case Studies and Attitudes to the Enterprising Scottish Thief

(a) Robert McLaymont (Eighteenth Century)

On the 3rd of September 1753, Robert McLaymont was brought before the South Circuit of the Justiciary Court held at Dumfries charged with theft, housebreaking, horse-stealing and using false keys.[63] The accused's defence team tried to argue that the supreme authoritative context of the Justiciary Court was no place for their client, as he was charged with minor transgressions and they tried to persuade the judge to restrict the potential scope of the trial to one where only an arbitrary punishment could occur. The judge rejected their plea, perhaps on the grounds that when Robert McLaymont was initially brought into court, it was explained that he also used the surname Galloway on occasion and it was well known to the authorities, that the use of aliases was a typical ploy exercised by established criminals (especially thieves or confidence tricksters) to avoid detection as they moved from one criminal context to another.[64]

The court went on to hear, through the testimony of Andrew Briggs, that in the middle of March 1753, a four-year-old gelding was stolen from his house in Burns, near Ferrytown of Cree in Kirkmabreck Parish, Kirkcudbright. The victim was able to give a pretty detailed description of his property, explaining that the horse was dark grey in colour with a whitish mane and a bell in his forehead. He also brought papers to court that clearly established him as the rightful owner of the horse and this was corroborated by two further witnesses. Briggs' neighbour, Michael McTaggart, then provided the court with some more detail regarding the methodology utilised during the horse-theft. He described coming to the stable and finding that a great deal of straw had been laid in the threshold of the stable and in the yard where the horse usually stood. McTaggart supposed that this had been done to prevent the horse's hooves making a noise upon the stones whilst being stolen.[65] From this evidence, it seems that the crime had been well thought through in advance of being perpetrated.

Eventually, the horse was found in a stable in Dumfries by some carriers (men employed to transport goods through the country by cart or carriage) who had recently visited Andrew Briggs and had been told of the theft. The owner of that stable, George Kerr, explained to the court that one morning the accused, Robert McLymont had come to his house, riding a grey gelding and asked Kerr to stable and feed the horse whilst he had some rest. Kerr agreed to do this, but a short time later, carriers delivering supplies to him suggested that the horse now technically in his possession was stolen property. Whilst McLymont was enjoying a nap, the authorities were called and quickly came to make an arrest, carrying their prisoner off to the house of the local Justice of the Peace for questioning. However, and as Kerr testified, the accused managed to make an escape through the window of the Justice of the Peace's house, but as he had done this without coat, vest or shoes, he did not get very far and was quickly recaptured. George Kerr and a further witness called Herbert Tweedie noted that when McLymont was arrested he left behind a saddle, a pocket book, three linen shirts and two coats – one big and brown in colour and one meet (fitted) and greyish blue in colour – all suspected to be stolen property, but only the saddle and the coats were later claimed to be so, as we will see in due course.[66] Two false keys were also found in the prisoner's possession which suggests an element of professionalism in his thieving exploits.[67]

George Kerr also testified to the court that he had encountered 'the rogue' Robert McLymont on a previous occasion. Earlier in 1753, at around Candlemas time, McLymont had come to Kerr's house and had sold him a tweed corn sack for two shillings. After Kerr had purchased the sack he fashioned some brown cloth into a letter 'K' and sewed it on the sack to mark it as his possession. Not long after this however, a neighbour of his, John Rule came to visit and upon seeing the sack, claimed that it had been recently stolen from his house. When this suggestion was authenticated by another neighbour, John Kennedy, Kerr returned the sack to its rightful owner and wrote off his financial loss.[68] Why George Kerr seemingly failed to learn any lessons from this episode when Robert McLymont came calling with a saddled horse and other fancy goods in his possession just one month later is difficult to discern, but perhaps Kerr's behaviour is indicative of his witting involvement in the possession and marketing of stolen goods.

The final testimony presented by the prosecution in this case was that of Alexander Houghan who was servant to a Mr John Welsh, Minister of Anwoth parish in Kirkcudbrightshire. In March of 1753, Mr Welsh died and Alexander Houghan was asked by Welsh's widow to move from the stable quarters into the kitchen of the house for her personal security and peace of mind. Houghan did so but left his belongings locked in the stable. These included a large chest which contained his Sunday-best clothes and two coats: one which was oversized and one which was fitted. On the morning of the eighth day of these living arrangements, Houghan awoke, went to the stable, unlocked the door and found the room in disarray. His master's saddle and bridle had been stolen along with his two coats. Houghan failed to provide any proof of ownership to reinforce his suggestion that he and his master were victims of housebreaking and theft. Nevertheless, it was implied by the court that this was the case and that the false keys found in Robert McLymont's possession had been utilised to affect this particular offence.[69]

The accused's blatant recidivist tendencies which commonly utilised cunning means and professional methodologies, his attempted flight from justice and the various stolen goods subsequently found in his possession, all meant that Robert McLymont had little to offer in mitigation of the multiple charges against him. The jury, for their part, did not need long to deliberate and they unanimously found McLymont guilty of all charges. The judge sentenced him to forty-seven days imprisonment in the Tolbooth of Dumfries and ordered that after this term, McLymont was to be hanged by the neck until dead at the hands of the common hangman.[70]

(b) Charles McLaren, Thomas Grierson and James McEwan (Nineteenth Century)

As with the McLymont case, recidivism was also the focal point for an indictment brought against three boys from Edinburgh in January 1823.[71] Charles McLaren (born in Paisley) who was fourteen-years-old, Thomas Grierson (born in London) who was thirteen and the youngest of the three, James McEwan (born in Crieff) who was just twelve-years-old upon his arrest, were indicted together at the High Court of Justiciary on charges of housebreaking, theft and being habite and repute thieves.[72] Despite their tender years, the boys had evidently been in a lot of trouble with the Scottish authorities. The Justiciary Court process papers detail numerous and previous complaints brought before the City of Edinburgh Police Court against the boys.[73] James McEwan alone, for instance, despite being the youngest of the three, had already been convicted twice for acts of petty theft from shops in the capital where, amongst other things, he had stolen twenty-three dram glasses, twenty-eight bottles of ale, ten horse-shoes, nine herrings and a large plum cake![74] Broadsides published during their trial reported that between them, the boys had more than sixteen convictions for previous offences and, as a result, all three had spent a considerable amount of time in the local bridewell at His Majesty's pleasure.[75] Indeed, it was whilst incarcerated in the Edinburgh gaol in the autumn of 1822, that the three individuals met one another and decided to collaborate in criminality.[76]

By January 1823, however, the boys had been brought to the Justiciary Court charged with two counts of housebreaking and theft. On the first charge, it was said that on the 9th of September 1822 the boys broke into the house of Thomas Riddel Esquire, a solicitor who resided in Newington, and proceeded to steal a variety of his possessions. The second charge related to an episode which occurred just three days after the first, when the boys were said to have broken into the house of a Colonel Munro who lived in the centre of Edinburgh. Munro worked for the Honourable East India Company and had several items of finery pilfered from his residence.[77]

More specifically in relation to the first charge, the court heard the testimony of Catherine Paton who was servant to the aforementioned Thomas Riddell. In July of 1822, Riddell had gone to the country for a time and with his permission, Catherine had gone to stay with a friend in his absence. She left the house in Newington on the 4th of September, ensuring that she took great care to secure the premises and even provided corroborating eye-witness testimony that she had done so.[78] Catherine returned to her place of work on the 10th of September 1822 and immediately noticed that something was amiss. From the outside of the property she could see that the window shutter of the servant's room was not shut as she had left it. Once she got inside the house, she could see that the said shutter was hanging by just one of its hinges, that its latch had been forced off and it was also evident that the central frame and pane of glass of the upper sash window had been taken out and latterly improperly replaced in its putty. She surmised from what she saw that one or more of the thieves had removed the frame and glass, undone the window latch, lifted the under sash, forced the shutter latch open and crawled through the space, thereby gaining entry to the premises. Once inside, the thief went to the front door, removed the chain and unlocked the door to let his accomplices inside.[79]

Catherine Paton then described how upon looking round the premises she noticed '...that things were very much disordered' and that various presses and trunks had been opened by force and their contents were either missing or had been strewn around the various rooms in the upstairs part of the house.[80] With time on their hands and with no one to stop them, the thieves had been relatively calculating and selective in deciding what loot to take. According to Thomas Riddle, eighteen silver forks, thirty-one silver table spoons, sixteen silver desert spoons, a soup ladle, eighteen tea spoons, a sugar basin, a number of plated candlesticks, a gold snuff box and, somewhat alarmingly, a brace of pistols were just some of the numerous items of value that had been stolen from his house and were yet to be accounted for.[81] The estimated value of the plunder from this crime alone was believed to be somewhere in the region of £150 in 1822, which equates to a relative value of some £12,540 in today's money.[82]

Much of the witness testimony in the precognition material relating to the Newington theft offers very little evidence which directly links any of the three suspects to the crime that occurred. However, fourteen-year-old Janet Allan (a neighbour of Thomas Riddle) resolved that prosecutorial problem. Indeed, her evidence almost negated the need for any further testimony to be heard about either this offence or the subsequent incident in the city centre. On the 9th of September 1822, Janet Allan saw a boy scale the wall of Thomas Riddle's house in an attempt to exit the grounds of the property. She challenged the lad as to what he was doing, and he told her that his friends had thrown his cap over the wall and he had gone to recover it, but he was unable to locate it. He then went back into Riddle's garden by the same method and eventually reappeared before Janet Allan after scaling the wall once again, but this time he had a cap on his head. Janet Allan also testified that she saw two other boys idly waiting for the agile boy in front of Thomas Riddle's property.[83] All of Janet Allan's testimony was corroborated by James Mackie, a local labourer, who saw what transpired as he was working on the roof of a neighbouring property. Initially, he had suspected that the boys were simply trying to steal fruit from Riddell's garden, but certainly he had surmised that they were up to no good.[84]

In any event, and crucially in relation to the prosecution case, Janet Allan was able to identify all three of the boys 'with certainty' when asked to do so at the police office a day or two after the Newington theft was discovered. She pointed out Thomas Grierson as the boy who scaled the wall and she recognised Charles McLaren and James McEwan as being the pair of miscreants who were hanging around outside her neighbour's property. Janet Allan was very confident in her identification of Grierson because she had talked to him in person during their minor altercation as described above. She was also unequivocal in her recognition of McLaren and McEwan as she explained that both of them had come to her father's house the weekend before this incident and had asked for a drink of water, which she duly provided for them.[85] We can of course only speculate whether this action on the part of the boys was part of a rouse to facilitate their recognisance of properties in the local area or whether they were genuinely thirsty.

The second charge in the indictment against the boys, related to a crime committed around the same time as the first offence, but this time in George Square, Edinburgh, at a house occupied by John Munro, Lieutenant Colonel in the Honourable East India Company. As was the case with the Newington crime, this property had also been left vacant at the time of the offence, as Munro and his family had gone on vacation.[86] Entry to the premises was quick and trouble-free it seems and was done by simply '...wrenching asunder' an iron stanchion from one of the windows using a hammer, propping up the window sash with the leg of an old chair, and slipping inside the building.[87] It was explained to the courtroom by John Munro's servant, Henrietta Taylor, that although the house had been locked and the shutters on the windows drawn, some of these had not been properly secured and this, alongside the fact that the under-sashes of the windows had '... no check or fastening to prevent their being put up', meant that the task of the thieves in this particular episode of housebreaking was ludicrously straightforward.[88]

Once inside, the thieves lit a lamp and some candles to illuminate their way around the house and proceeded to steal '...a tea-pot, a sugar bason [basin], sugar tongs, a cream ewer [large jug] and a waiter or salver [tray]', all of which were embossed with silver, as well as

> ...a silver tea scoop, a gold band for a child's hat, a white lace veil, several pieces of French lace, a lady's black satin dress, a black shawl, three silk gowns, and a fawn coloured silk or sarsanet [sarsenet] scarf.[89]

The maidservant, Henrietta Taylor, visited the property on the morning of the 11th of September 1822, and at first she considered everything to be normal as the house was locked up, just as she left it. However, upon entering the building, she discovered that several rooms were in disarray, with copious garments and items of wearing apparel littering the floor. Moreover, it soon became evident to her that various wardrobes, chests and closets had been broken into too and that certain items of her master's property were missing. Upon making this discovery, she alerted the authorities.

The court had heard evidence that two precocious acts of theft and housebreaking had occurred in Edinburgh and its environs in 1822. It had also heard that the three suspects before the bar had been positively identified by an independent witness as behaving suspiciously at the Newington break-in crime scene prior to its discovery. To make matters even worse for the accused, the prosecution also presented a declaration entered by Charles McLaren in which he confessed (in meticulous detail) to having planned and perpetrated all the offences libelled along with Grierson and McEwan. Moreover, McLaren admitted that the three had done so by themselves and for themselves, explaining that after selling on some of their loot, they had been able to afford food and lodgings for ten days, to buy themselves clothes and had enough left over to go '...and drink whiskey and strong ale in different publick [public] houses' across Edinburgh.'[90]

The boys' defence lawyers tried to claim that Charles McLaren was the victim of a false 'promise of safety' made to him by Captain Robertson, Superintendent of the Edinburgh Police. It was argued that Robertson had elicited a confession from the boy on the promise that all three would avoid punishment for the crimes for which they were charged, that they would be exonerated from all historic charges against them, that a suit of new clothes would be provided for Charles McLaren and that both he and Thomas Grierson would be found employment in the city. The defence also claimed that Captain Robertson had paid McLaren money to confess to the two sets of charges. None of these claims could be corroborated however, and as the credibility of the defence's claims effectively came down to choosing between the word of the Superintendent of the city's police force or the word of a convicted juvenile delinquent, the judge rejected or repelled the defence team's efforts and the assize was asked to deliberate on their verdict.[91]

It did not take long for a decision to be reached. However, the verdict was more nuanced that we might expect, given that some twenty-four witnesses had been heard for the prosecution and no witnesses were offered in defence. The assize found the pannels guilty of the first charge relating to the housebreaking and theft at Newington by a unanimous verdict. However, the second charge relating to the offences at the George Square property was deemed not proven. In addition, the assize recommended James McEwan to mercy on account of his tender years.[92] The judge in the case delivered a detailed speech to the courtroom in order to justify his chosen sentence. He explained:

> It is at all times to be deplored that persons of such tender years should become liable to such a punishment; but, though young in years, they

had been going on for a long period in a series of crimes. Much as crime had increased among society, it had increased in a ten-fold measure among youth, which would lead one to suppose that there were persons in this city, who made it a business to train up boys in the most easy and expeditious manner of committing crimes.

Not having profited by the wholesome discipline of Bridewell, the prisoners have persisted in a course of crimes which had brought them to this consummation. It remains only for the Court to deliver the dreadful sentence of the law, and it is most earnestly hoped that their awful situation will serve as an example to others. This would be the desired effect as it must never be again held that youth can be a protection to crime. It will convince your guilty associates of the hazard which they run, if they persist in the course in which you have been engaged; an occupation which sooner or latter must place them in a similar situation. I trust, however, that your example will have the desired effect upon those who were following such courses.

It is impossible to conceive that such young persons could have acted otherwise than as the instruments of their seniors; but I would advise all such to retrace their steps, and make a full disclosure of those sinks of infamy and vice, who prompted them on to their ruin, and to the certain forfeiture of their lives, to the offended laws of their country.[93]

The judge then proceeded to sentence all three boys to one month's imprisonment in the Tolbooth of Edinburgh and thereafter ordered that they be executed by hanging on a gibbet with all their moveable goods and property forfeited to the rights of the Crown.[94] In sentencing McLaren, Grierson and McEwan in this fashion, he had ignored the pleas of clemency from the assize and instead recommended that the three young pannels:

> ...prepare to appear before the judgement-seat of their Maker – to pray, and to read the scriptures; and if they could not reap themselves, they would get others that would do it for them; not to waste their time in idle expectations of mercy, for there was nothing in their case which could support such an idea: That they must entertain no other hopes of pardon but those which were to be derived through the salvation of Jesus Christ.[95]

Although the judge did suggest that McLaren, Grierson and McEwan may have been led astray and into a life of crime by adult offenders (a proposition which was not borne out by the evidence presented before the court), he nonetheless wanted to make examples of the three boys and use their convictions and sentence to deter other like-minded young criminals. It would seem that he did this in the context of one of the first moral panics about juvenile delinquency in the nineteenth century urban milieu. In any event, it was the boys' proven recidivism and their failure to learn any lessons from their previous encounters with judicial authority, more than any other element of their case, which marked them out for the ultimate exemplary punishment. Their execution date was then fixed for the 12th of February 1823.[96]

The public reaction to the sentence given was invariably mixed. Some contemporary commentators sided with the judge. In one publication for instance, it was argued that '...the crimes for which they were convicted has become of late so very prevalent in this place, and almost all, too perpetrated of youths of about their age that an example, perhaps, has become absolutely necessary.'[97] Others, conversely, were more sympathetic to the plight of the boys. One letter to the editor of the *Edinburgh Weekly Journal* dated 21st of January 1823 described the use of capital punishment for crimes short of murder as '...a feature of barbarity when enforced against persons of such tender years.'[98] As the author explained:

> I am far from being singular in viewing the probable execution of this sentence with feelings of deep regret and of considering the punishment of these unhappy boys as arising in great measure, if not wholly, from the untoward circumstances in which it has been their unhappy lot to be placed. Need I recapitulate the history of such beings? Born probably of vicious and depraved parents, neglected in their education, placed among the most worthless as companions, encouraged to pilfer by cunning and unprincipled resetters, and not arrived at the period of life, when the reasoning powers can enable them to counteract the errors of their education, they are brought to the gallows as mere victims of misfortune, whose fate can excite only pity and commiseration. Is it therefore, just, or consistent with the rules of enlightened jurisprudence, to inflict upon such young and misguided creatures, that punishment which is the doom of the murderer and assassin?[99]

Other individuals wrote to the journal to praise the 'sensible and considerate' content of the letter which did intimate that consideration should be given to the contextual factors or background details in the lives of the boys which may have contributed to their recurrent offending. Indeed, in the petitions for clemency submitted in the wake of their sentence, it was evident that the three boys had not enjoyed happy or privileged upbringings. McEwan lived with his father in abject poverty and stole food and provisions whenever he could just to keep himself and his infirm parent alive. McLaren's father died when he was young. His mother subsequently remarried, but his step-father threw both Charles and his younger sister out of the house and left them to fend for themselves. This rendered McLaren homeless and destitute at a very young age. Grierson had been orphaned when just a toddler, but he had managed to find work as a brass founder's apprentice. However, after being viciously abused and mistreated by his co-workers, he was forced to leave that employment and became homeless and penniless as a result.[100] Evidently all three boys were destitute and desperate, and we can assume that the opportunities open to them for earning a wage through legitimate means must have been limited.

Public discussion of these personal contextual details, along with letters like the one published in the *Edinburgh Weekly Journal* discussed above resulted in a popular outcry against the execution of McLaren, Grierson and McEwan. This popular discontent was accentuated by missives sent to Robert Peel (then Home Secretary) by Edinburgh's Lord Provost, a group of Magistrates from the city, the Duke of Montrose and several other important individuals of note. These communiqués argued that the hanging of such young boys would be repugnant to a civilised Scottish society. They suggested that the shame of the trial and the uncertainty of their fate was punishment enough and a sound deterrent to others. Indeed, they recommended that this uncertainty be prolonged to emphasise the seriousness of official attitudes towards this offending of this sort.[101]

This tide of opinion, which had rapidly intensified over just a short period of time, was effective. The Home Secretary took heed of the suggestions made and granted all three boys a month's respite from the hangman's noose and a new execution date was set.[102] Then, on the 13th of March 1823, after a further petition was submitted to the High Court of Justiciary, the three boys were granted a remission from their capital sentences. Instead, McLaren, Grierson and McEwan were ordered to be banished for life from Scotland and sent to the penal colony in New South Wales, Australia.[103] This sentence *was* effectively carried out against all three boys, although their fate once in the southern hemisphere is unknown.[104] Once again we see the Scots demonstrate their reluctance or uneasiness in dealing with certain types of offenders and it seems from the evidence relating to this particular case, that when it came to meting out the ultimate punishment at least, age could prove to be a mitigating factor in post-Enlightenment Scotland.

c) Johnny Ramensky (Twentieth Century)

Some individuals would argue that in many ways, Johnny Ramensky was one of the most enterprising Scottish criminals of the twentieth century era. He committed numerous instances of housebreaking and theft, and by using an innovative methodology which showcased his physical strength, flexibility and gallusness (bare-faced cheek), he stole a substantial array of reasonably valuable items. In the latter years of his prolonged life of crime, he regularly deployed explosives to blow 'lock-fast' places in an attempt to reap larger spoils from his theftuous activities and, infamously, he conducted several high-profile prison escapes. However, it could also be argued that Ramensky was a consummate failure as a criminal. For instance, we really only know about his enterprising illegal exploits because he was caught, tried and convicted so often. Ramensky spent much of his adult life incarcerated, and his prison breaks, whilst undoubtedly daring, were all short-lived and ultimately only served to lengthen his imprisonment and diminish any privileges afforded to him whilst behind bars. The life history of Johnny Ramensky has been mythologised and lionised by too many commentators for too long and now needs to be rewritten and reconsidered.

Johnny Ramensky was born in Glenboig, Lanarkshire in 1905 to Lithuanian parents. His father, a coalminer, died when Johnny was just a child, so he and his sisters moved with their mother to the Gorbals in Glasgow. There is little doubt that the Ramensky family endured a life of poverty, especially after Johnny's mother lost an arm in a factory accident, making it especially difficult for her to find work. It was likely for this reason that Johnny left school at fourteen and tried repeatedly, but unsuccessfully, to hold down a steady job.[105] Somewhat inevitably, it did not take long for Johnny Ramensky to drift into a life of crime and he had already been in trouble with the authorities on several occasions when, in 1921 at the age of sixteen, he was sent to the borstal at Polmont, near Falkirk. He was to get to know the facility and its regime well over the next few years, as he was intermittently sent there for acts of petty theft as a juvenile delinquent.[106]

With his extensive criminal record, there are numerous indictments involving Johnny Ramensky in the Scottish Justiciary Court Records which could have been selected for more detailed discussion in this chapter. However, in an attempt to challenge the folk-hero status of Ramensky and in particular, his sobriquet 'Gentleman Johnny' owing to his supposed abhorrence of violence, a case brought before the High Court in Glasgow in 1925 will be utilised.[107] On the 11th of November 1925, Johnny Ramensky was brought before the Justiciary Court charged with multiple counts of theft by housebreaking, housebreaking with intent to steal, attempted housebreaking and a single count of assault.[108] The court heard that between the 30th of September and the 24th of October 1925, Johnny Ramensky had broken into some seventeen different properties over an extensive *locus operandi* based in and around the city of Glasgow.[109]

It was explained before the assize that Ramensky (who was by then twenty years of age) spent his time wandering around residential areas trying to find unoccupied properties. Once he found a suitable target, he typically ascended a drain pipe at the back of that property, shimmied along the rhone pipe (or roof guttering), dropped down to his selected point of entry, raised an unlocked window sash or broke a pane of glass to enable him to put his arm inside in order to unfasten the snib which secured the remainder of the window and slid inside.[110] Evidently Ramensky was incredibly fit, dextrous and agile and was routinely able to scale buildings, hang on to ledges and squeeze into small spaces with commensurate ease. In terms of gaining entry to premises, he was, as one later commentator put it, '...the cat burglar extraordinaire.'[111]

In most of the thefts referred to in this particular indictment, Ramensky had stolen cash, jewellery or objects and personal effects that he knew could be readily sold on for a decent return. The non-monetary items he stole included pendants, earrings, brooches, watches, rings, bracelets, bangles, neck-chains, lockets, strings of beads and strings of pearls, sleeve links (or cufflinks), tie pins and scarf pins, an albert (watch chain), cigarette cases, spoons, cruets, knives, a pocket book, two pairs of spectacles and a pair of opera glasses, socks, scarves, a drinking cup, a poker, a clock and even a set of false teeth![112] Ramensky had clearly managed to accumulate a significant haul over his four week crime spree. He also stole war savings certificates (which he later returned to their rightful owner) and some interest warrants but it seems he was unsure about what he could do with either. In any event, the total value of the property stolen from the thefts libelled in 1925 was £1,431 which equates to approximately £74,900 in today's money.[113] Some of the stolen items were latterly recovered from Ramensky's mother's house upon his arrest, but a significant proportion remained unaccounted for.

On the 21st of October 1925, Ramensky broke into the house of Grace Scott at 270 Woodlands Road in Glasgow. Ramensky had entered the premises illegally using his standard method and in the knowledge that there was no one at home. However, Grace had forgotten something and returned to her house much earlier than Ramensky expected. Consequently, the court heard how Ramensky '...did seize her by the throat and compress the same, whereby she was put in a state of bodily fear and alarm.'[114] The prosecution admitted that the assault was a relatively minor one, but nonetheless, Ramensky's behaviour could hardly be described as 'gentlemanly' conduct. Initially, Ramensky denied this allegation of assault against him, but then as a letter to the Procurator Fiscal from an agent to the Crown on the 25th of November makes plain, Ramensky changed his mind and pled guilty to all charges.[115]

What is perhaps even more revealing in this particular indictment is that through a close reading of the precognition papers, a further, separate, and arguably more serious charge of assault was reported to the authorities as part of the spree of thefts that took place, but it was not levelled at Ramensky in the official list of charges and seems to have been forgotten or ignored by individuals who have written about Johnny Ramensky.[116] On the 24th of October 1925, Ramensky broke in to the house of Jane Stuart at 13 Clarence Drive in Hyndland in the west end of the City of Glasgow. Jane Stuart had returned from running an errand that day, to discover that a crowd of people had gathered outside her house. She learned from one of the individuals assembled '...that a burglar was supposed to be on the roof of the tenement.'[117] She pushed through the onlookers and went into her flat which was located on the third floor. She switched on the light in the drawing room and discovered the accused standing behind the door and he proceeded to '...rush past her knocking her to the floor.' Ramensky was then met in the hall by two men who had come to the victim's assistance. A lengthy struggle ensued and in trying to make his escape, Ramensky assaulted the men – on two separate occasions – with a poker he had stolen from the Stuart house.[118] We are not told why this particular charge was dropped by the prosecuting authorities, despite the unequivocal evidence of its occurrence and its distinctively serious nature. However, what the details of this account do suggest is that Johnny Ramensky did not solely exhibit non-violent tendencies in his perpetuation of offences, nor did he consistently go quietly into the hands of the authorities as has also been repeatedly stated.[119] Instead, it is evident that when threatened, desperate or frustrated, Ramensky seemingly only had self-preservation on his mind.

At the end of this lengthy indictment against Johnny Ramensky, the prosecution provided a detailed list of his previous arrests and convictions. These were all for theft or for housebreaking and theft, and it was made plain to all those present in the courtroom that a hardened recidivist stood before them.[120] His guilty plea and his established criminal history made the job of the court very straightforward. On the 25th of November 1925 the High Court sat in Glasgow. Johnny Ramensky was found guilty of all charges and was sentenced to eighteen months imprisonment in Saughton Jail, Edinburgh.[121]

The sentence given to Johnny Ramensky in 1925 did not deter him from his criminal exploits. Rather, court records document another two significant trials brought against him before his thirtieth birthday: one at the High Court in Glasgow in June 1927 and one at the Sheriff Court in Greenock in October 1932. On both occasions he was sentenced to further terms of imprisonment for housebreaking and theft.[122] Clearly, the reformative and deterrent theories of contemporary penal policy had little impact on Ramensky. Indeed, evidence held at the National Records of Scotland suggests that, if anything, Ramensky was becoming *more*, not less obstreperous towards authority as time went on. He continually petitioned the governor of whichever establishment he was in at the time to protest his innocence and the 'brutality' of the sentences he had received. He also regularly wrote to complain about his treatment by other prisoners (who he claimed racially abused him) and the conditions he had to endure whilst incarcerated (he contracted pneumonia whilst in prison in 1930).[123] He even climbed on to the roof of Barlinnie prison's 'E' Hall in July 1931, partly in protest and partly to flesh out a rather fanciful escape plan he had been working on. He proceeded to shower prison officials with slates from the roof and other missiles; arguably a further indication of his less than 'gentlemanly' demeanour.[124]

Things got serious for Johnny Ramensky in 1934. By this point he was married to a woman called Daisy (Margaret) McManus and they had a young child together. In April of 1934 Ramensky was indicted, along with his brother-in-law Marco Demarco, at the Sheriff Court in Aberdeen. The pair then had their case transferred to the High Court of Justiciary in Edinburgh, probably on account of the seriousness of the charge with the indictment papers recording a significant change in Ramensky's methodology. The charge noted that on the 24th or 25th of March 1934, Ramensky and Demarco broke into a bakery in Mount Street, Aberdeen. Whilst inside '…and by means of *explosives* [they] did force open a lock-fast safe and steal therefrom two hundred and forty-six pounds, fourteen shillings and ten pence of money.'[125] It was further brought to the court's attention that Johnny Ramensky had previous convictions for '…the dishonest appropriation of property.'[126]

This case marks a clear departure for Ramensky. He was now combining his cat-burglar capabilities with the use of explosives to maximise the returns gained from his criminal exploits.[127] Ramensky was arguably entrepreneurial and professional when contemplating his criminality, but he was evidently somewhat inept and amateur in terms of putting it into practice. He was quickly caught, arrested and latterly convicted and this time, in an escalation of sentencing that mirrored the escalation of his methodology, he was sentence to five years penal servitude at the notorious Peterhead prison in Aberdeen.[128] Undoubtedly, this harsher sentence was also a reflection of the burgeoning frustration amongst the Scottish judicial authorities who were likely fed up with having to deal with Johnny Ramensky and his tiresome, bungling criminal exploits on such a regular basis.

It was just six months into this particular sentence, that Ramensky made the first of five infamous escapes from the prison at Peterhead. Individuals intent on mythologising Johnny Ramensky's life story have argued that he did this in protest at not being allowed to go to his wife's funeral.[129] However, details from Ramensky's prison records state unequivocally that Daisy did not die until 1937.[130] Rather, Ramensky made his escape purely for sport and to impress his fellow inmates.[131] He was sent to the prison hospital suffering from depression and whilst there he picked a lock, cut across the prison yard unnoticed and climbed over the prison gate to freedom.[132] He was found by the authorities the next day just eight miles away wearing his 'prison garb' plus a brown jersey but only two pairs of socks. He had no shoes or boots on because he had been in the hospital ward. He was returned there for treatment on his 'broken feet' later that day.[133]

Ramensky's escape did not go unnoticed: he made national news headlines for two days straight.[134] Nor, however, did it go unpunished, and after his hospital treatment was concluded, Ramensky was ordered to be confined in leg irons in his cell for an indeterminate period of solitary confinement.[135] Owing to the publicity surrounding this incident, however, petitions and letters of concern started to flood government offices and press rooms, all complaining about the inhumane treatment that Ramensky was being subjected to in a modern, civilised society.[136] These pleas eventually reached the ears of Parliament in December of 1934, when the MP for Shettleston, John McGovern (1887–1968), asked a question of the Secretary of State for Scotland, then Sir Godfrey Collins (1875–1936), on whether he had heard about Ramensky's shackled treatment and whether he was '...prepared to put an end to this form of punishment?' The Secretary of State gave a short response which was very much to the point. He said '...orders had been given to discontinue the use of leg chains in Ramensky's case, and that this method of restraint is not to be employed in future.' He then added that 'the whole code of prison regulations' would be immediately reviewed and revamped as a consequence.[137]

Johnny Ramensky was now a household name. However, that scarcely indicated that he was a peaceable man. A further conviction for housebreaking and theft utilising explosives when placed alongside his prison files indicate that he was a perpetual troublemaker who would not defer to authority. He constantly petitioned against his poor treatment, regularly became involved in violent conflicts with his fellow inmates and perennially balked at the punishments he received as a result.[138] At the end of his sentence, Johnny Ramensky became part of the war effort, although the true extent of his contribution to the allies' cause is unclear.[139] Certainly we know that he trained as a commando and undoubtedly his knowledge of safe-blowing was put to good use in gathering intelligence information whilst he was in Italy and later in North Africa.[140] However, beyond this, the details are vague and unsubstantiated and it would seem that the description of him as a swashbuckling, medal-winning, war hero might have been somewhat overblown as part of the cult of Johnny Ramensky that was evidently created.

Once demobilised, Ramensky returned to what he knew best: criminality. Between 1947 and his death in 1972, Ramensky was brought before courts in York, Glasgow, Edinburgh, Aberdeen, Paisley, Stirling and Ayr charged with multiple counts of housebreaking and the opening of 'lock-fast' places.[141] Most of these instances did not involve interpersonal violence of any kind, although the deployment of explosive material was proving problematic as the force from the blasts often knocked passers-by off their feet, as happened to two policemen walking their beat in Rutherglen, near Glasgow in 1967 when Ramensky was attempting a bank raid close by and had misjudged the amount of gelignite required. This particular incident is also worthy of note as one of the aforementioned policeman also claimed that Ramensky assaulted him in the melee that ensued in their attempt to apprehend the culprit. Witnesses testified to seeing PC Neil Wilson 'bloodied and battered' as a result of his altercation with 'Gentleman Johnny'. Another conviction and a further four years imprisonment resulted from this particular incident.[142]

The determination of Ramensky to maintain his criminal career, even in his twilight years, was mirrored in his repeated refusal to bow to authority.

Earning the nickname, 'The Peterhead Papillion', Ramensky escaped from the northern prison a further four times.[143] His well-publicised efforts included one fairly comical incident in August 1952 where, after breaking from his cell and courageously climbing to the room of the institution, he bravely scaled the prison walls and thereafter heroically made his escape by 'furiously pedalling a girl's tiny pink bicycle'![144] Predictably, he did not get far, and was recaptured just thirty hours later. His defiance was celebrated by many who saw him as a champion of the people and his status as urban folk-hero became cemented in the popular consciousness.[145]

It is evident that after spending so much of his adult life in prison, Johnny Ramensky was wholly institutionalised. His post-war bride, Lily Mulholland, described prison as Ramensky's 'second home' which he thoroughly enjoyed going back to.[146] Clearly, Ramensky didn't really want to escape prison. He just wanted to see if he *could* escape and it was the excitement associated with making these attempts that motivated him. Similarly, the need to fuel his gambling habit and especially the challenge of trying to avoid capture by the authorities spurred Ramensky on to constantly reoffend.[147] As he said of himself in an interview with a journalist found in his archived prison files: 'I am a crook, always have been and there is no turning back. My heart is in the game and I would not have it otherwise…The game is what matters…'[148]

Ramensky's escapades resulted in hardship for him and some tough questions being levelled at the prison authorities.[149] On the 27th of January 1959 for instance, Johnny Ramensky was discussed in Parliament once again, but less sympathetically than on the previous occasion. Aberdeen North MP, Mr Hector Hughes (1887–1970) asked the Secretary of State for Scotland to make a statement in the House of Commons on Ramensky's repeated escape attempts and to outline what was being done to ensure that they ceased in order to avoid further embarrassment to the Scottish authorities. Mr Niall Macpherson (1908–1987), Joint Under-Secretary for Scotland replied by providing a summary of what had transpired and by noting that Ramensky had been '…punished by loss of remission and temporary deprivation of certain privileges' after each attempt. Unsatisfied with this response, Mr Arthur Woodburn (1890–1978), MP for Clackmannan and East Stirlingshire, suggested to his honourable friend that that Johnny Ramensky may as well be given a key to Peterhead prison![150] The upshot of this debate was that after his fifth and final escape, Ramensky had that particular prison sentence extended by a further eighteen months (reduced to twelve on appeal) to deter him from absconding in the future. This seems to have had the desired effect, albeit temporarily.[151]

Johnny Ramensky died at Perth prison from a brain haemorrhage on the 4th of November 1972. Three months earlier, at the age of sixty-seven, he had fallen from a roof in Stirling when attempting a break-in, probably due to his failing eye-sight. The fall was serious and Ramensky never fully recovered.[152] As his erstwhile QC, Sir Nicholas Fairbairn (1933–1995) commented on hearing of his client's demise: '...Ramensky was a compulsive criminal even until death – which is rare – breaking out of anything he was inside and into anything he was outside...He died where he had mainly lived – in prison.'[153] Johnny Ramensky was a compulsive criminal, a sensation seeker and to some extent, an enterprising Scot. He may well have been a 'likeable rogue'[154], however, he was no hero, no saint and no gentleman. By his own admission, he was just a thief. As he explained:

> Each man has an ambition and I have fulfilled mine years ago. I cherish my career as a safe blower. In childhood days my feet were planted on the crooked path and took firm root. To each one of us is allotted a niche and I have found mine. Strangely enough I am happy. The die is cast and for me there is no turning back.[155]

Conclusion – The Enterprising Scot?

This chapter has shown that it was non-violent offences, and particularly theft and its allied offences, which were most commonly brought before the Scottish courts over the 1660–1960 period. This conclusion immediately challenges the notion that the Scots were a predominantly and persistently violent people. The very nature and incidence of criminality north of the Tweed does not support that contention. Instead, this chapter has suggested that the activities of Scottish criminals may be more accurately depicted if we consider them to be more 'enterprising' than extreme in nature. Indeed, the data presented above has shown that theftuous activity in Scotland was relatively mundane in nature rather than serious. It was increasingly perpetrated by men (rather than by women or by juvenile delinquents) and it typically involved first-time offenders rather than recidivists. However, and as we have seen elsewhere in this volume, it is the more atypical thieves that have warranted the closest attention from the authorities and especially the press.

Whilst the methodologies for theft may have changed over time, due to technological advances and in response to commercial and personal security measures, the motives for this kind of criminality have remained relatively unaltered. We may consider Scottish criminals to have been 'enterprising' in the ways they stole from others, but they were not necessarily more creative in this respect than their counterparts elsewhere, given that the vast majority of offences were essentially opportunistic in nature, rather than pre-planned or premeditated. Moreover, thieves stole for largely the same reasons across time and across cultures: need, greed and sometimes just for the thrill of perpetrating the crime or trying to evade capture after the fact, as the case study of Johnny Ramensky so eloquently illustrates. In sum, there is no evident trend, trait or characteristic that sets the Scottish thief particularly apart from similar felons the world over. Crucially, this conclusion is mirrored in the evidence from the previous chapters of this volume too: Scottish criminals – violent or otherwise – were essentially unremarkable and thus undeserving of the historic characterisations associated with their illegality.

Notes

1 For further discussion see I. Donnachie (1992) 'The Enterprising Scot' in I. Donnachie and C. Whatley (eds) *The Manufacture of Scottish History* (Edinburgh: Polygon), pp. 90–105 at p. 90.

2 A point made about Scottish crime more generally but in relation to the twentieth century in A. Davies (1998) 'Street Gangs, Crime and Policing in Glasgow during the 1930s: The Case of the Beehive Boys', *Social History*, 23, 3, pp. 251–267 at p. 253.

3 Single acts of petty theft and offences associated with prostitution would not be heard by the Justiciary Court and would instead be dealt with in lesser courts. Although the data in this chapter will include all species of theft and reset recorded in the judicial statistics from multiple jurisdictions, the analysis will concentrate on the indictments of these offences at the higher courts. For historic scholarship on more minor non-violent offences in a Scottish context see for instance J.R.D. Falconer (2013) *Crime and Community in Reformation Scotland: Negotiating Power in a Burgh Society* (London: Pickering and Chatto), chapter three; L. Mahood (2013 edition) *The Magdalenes: Prostitution in the Nineteenth Century* (London and New York: Routledge); L. Settle (2016) *Sex for Sale in Scotland: Prostitution in Edinburgh and Glasgow 1900–1939* (Edinburgh: Edinburgh University Press) and R. Davidson and G. Davis (2012) *The Sexual State: Sexuality and Scottish Governance, 1950–80* (Edinburgh: Edinburgh University Press). Blackmail, racketeering and extortion have been written about for the inter-war and post-war periods but not in a Scottish context (see D. Thomas (2006 edition) *Villain's Paradise: Britain's Underworld from the Spivs to the Krays* (Edinburgh: John Murray), chapter four; P. Adey, D.J. Cox and B. Godfrey (2016) *Crime, Regulation and Control During the Blitz: Protecting the Population of Bombed Cities* (London: Bloomsbury) and M. Roodhouse (2013) *Black Market Britain: 1939–1955* (Oxford: Oxford University Press)). Most consideration of this type of offence in Scotland has been confined to the post-1960s period and has not been particularly academic in content (see for example R. McKay (2007) *The Last Godfather: The Life and Crimes of Arthur Thompson* (Edinburgh: Black and White Publishing) or R. Jeffrey (2008 edition) *Gangland Glasgow: True Crime from the Streets* (Edinburgh: Black and White Publishing)). Moreover, as there were only a few cases of this nature brought before the Justiciary Court between 1660 and 1960, this kind of criminality has not been considered in this present analysis.

4 See Baron D. Hume (1797) *Commentaries on the Laws of Scotland Respecting the Description and Punishment of Crimes – Volume I* (Edinburgh: Bell and Bradfute), pp. 200–201, pp. 501–502, p. 504 and p. 508. See also R. McGowen (1999) 'From Pillory to Gallows: The Punishment of Forgery in the Age of the Financial Revolution', *Past and Present*, 165, pp. 107–140; M. Gaskill (2000) *Crime and Mentalities in Early Modern England* (Cambridge: Cambridge University Press), chapter five; A. Macfarlane (1981) *The Justice and the Mare's Ale: Law and Disorder in Seventeenth-Century England* (Oxford: Basil Blackwell), pp. 61–62; D. Palk (2006) *Gender, Crime and Judicial Discretion 1780–1830* (Woodbridge: Boydell), p. 102; H. Shore (2015) *London's Criminal Underworlds, c. 1720–1930* (Basingstoke: Palgrave Macmillan, p. 120 and pp. 122–123; D. Philips (1977) *Crime and Authority in Victorian*

England: The Black Country 1835–1860 (London: Croom Helm), pp. 233–234; P. Handler (2005) 'Forgery and the End of the "Bloody Code" in Early Nineteenth-Century England', *The Historical Journal*, 48, 3, pp. 683–702; R. McGowen (2007) 'Managing the Gallows: The Bank of England and the Death Penalty, 1797–1821', *Law and History Review*, 25, 2, pp. 241–282 and S. Wilson (2016 edition) *The Origins of Modern Financial Crime: Historical Foundations and Current Problems in Britain* (Abingdon: Routledge), pp. 105–106.

5   A-M. Kilday (1998) 'Women and Crime in South-West Scotland: A Study of the Justiciary Records, 1750–1815' (Unpublished PhD Thesis, University of Strathclyde), pp. 236–239. For further discussion see J. Styles (1980) '"Our Traitorous Money Makers": The Yorkshire Coiners and the Law, 1760–83' in J. Brewer and J. Styles (eds) *An Ungovernable People: The English and Their Law in the Seventeenth and Eighteenth Centuries* (London: Hutchinson and Co.), pp. 172–249 and Gaskill (2000) *Crime and Mentalities*, chapter four.

6   For discussion of the regularity of forgery trials in the premodern period see the references at note five above. For discussion of the burgeoning moral panic over fraud see C. Emsley (1999 edition) *Crime and Society in England, 1750–1900* (London and New York: Longman), p. 141; Shore (2015) *London's Criminal Underworlds*, p. 118 and pp. 130–139; Philips (1977) *Crime and Authority*, p. 225 and pp. 227–228 and especially J. Taylor (2007) 'Company Fraud in Victorian Britain: The Royal British Bank Scandal of 1856', *The English Historical Review*, 122, 497, pp. 700–724; G. Robb (2002 edition) *White-Collar Crime in Modern England: Financial Fraud and Business Morality 1845–1929* (Cambridge: Cambridge University Press), *passim* and especially p. 1 and pp. 181–182; H. Croall (1992) *White Collar Crime: Criminal Justice and Criminology* (Buckingham: Open University Press); H. Croall (1998) *Crime and Society in Britain* (London and New York: Longman), Chapter fifteen; S. Wilson (2010) 'Fraud and White-Collar Crime: 1850 to the Present' in A-M. Kilday and D.S. Nash (eds) *Histories of Crime: Britain 1600–2000* (Basingstoke: Palgrave Macmillan), pp. 141–159 and Wilson (2016 edition) *The Origins of Modern Financial Crime*, p. 106. For the panic in a Scottish context see especially A. Adamson (2011) *Murder, Poaching and Lemonade: Crimes and Court Cases from Nineteenth Century West Lothian* (London: Createspace), p. 44; W.M. Meier (2011) *Property Crime in London, 1850 to the Present* (Basingstoke: Palgrave Macmillan), pp. 85–87; M. Archibald (2013) *Glasgow: The Real Mean City: True Crime and Punishment in the Second City of the Empire* (Edinburgh: Black and White Publishing), p. 170, p. 173 and for reference to the collapse of the Great City of Glasgow Bank in 1878 see pp. 175–179 as well as Robb (2002 edition) *White-Collar Crime in Modern England*, p. 56 and pp. 72–73.

7   Scholars interested in the data gathered on fraud and forgery in Scotland between 1836 and 1960 for this project should consult the database associated with this publication and made available via open access from the research data repository of Oxford Brookes University at https://radar.brookes.ac.uk/radar/home.do.

8   For evidence of the persistence and regularity of theft and its allied offences in a British context see for instance Baron D. Hume (1797) *Commentaries on the Laws of Scotland – Volume I*, p. 59; Kilday (1998) 'Women and Crime in South-West Scotland', pp. 207–208; A-M. Kilday (2014) '"Criminally Poor?" Investigating the Link between Crime and Poverty in Eighteenth Century England', *Cultural and Social History*, 11, 4, pp. 507–526 at p. 509; E. Moss (2011) 'Burglary Insurance and the Culture of Fear in Britain, c. 1889–1939', *The Historical Journal*, 54, 4, pp. 1039–1064; T. Morris (1989) *Crime and Criminal Justice Since 1945* (Oxford: Basil Blackwell), p. 35; C. Emsley (2011) *Crime and Society in Twentieth-Century England* (London and New York: Longman), p. 22 and p. 27; D.J.V. Jones (1996)

Crime and Policing in the Twentieth Century: The South Wales Experience (Cardiff: University of Wales Press), p. 69.

9 The potential link between theft and entrepreneurialism has been suggested for the Scottish context by D.A. Symonds, see (2006) *Notorious Murders, Black Lanterns and Moveable Goods: The Transformation of Edinburgh's Underworld in the Early Nineteenth Century* (Akron, OH: The University of Akron Press), p. 136.

10 See for instance Emsley (1999 edition) *Crime and Society in England*, chapter five; E.P. Thomson (1975) *Whigs and Hunters: The Origins of the Black Act* (London: Pantheon); E.P. Thompson (2009 edition) *Customs in Common* (London: Merlin Press); D. Hay, P. Linebaugh, J.G. Rule, E.P. Thompson and C. Winslow (2011 edition) *Albion's Fatal Tree: Crime and Society in Eighteenth-Century* England (London: Verso) and D. Jones (1982) *Crime, Protest, Community and Police in Nineteenth-Century Britain* (London: Routledge and Kegan Paul), chapters two and three.

11 For further discussion see R. Houston (2011) 'Custom in Context: Medieval and Early Modern Scotland and England', *Past and Present*, 211, pp. 35–76.

12 Baron D. Hume (1797) *Commentaries on the Laws of Scotland – Volume I*, pp. 98–99.

13 *Ibid*, p. 111 and p. 356–362.

14 *Ibid*, pp. 366–370 and pp. 371–381.

15 Macfarlane (1981) *The Justice and the Mare's Ale*, p. 120. For further discussion of the persistence of the complexities of English law with regard to non-violent property crime see G. Walker (2003) *Crime, Gender and Social Order in Early Modern England* (Cambridge: Cambridge University Press), p. 183; J.M. Beattie (2002 edition) *Crime and the Courts in England 1660–1800* (Oxford: Clarendon Press), pp. 182–183; D.D. Gray (2016) *Crime, Policing and Punishment in England, 1660–1914* (London: Bloomsbury), p. 111 and D. Taylor (1998) *Crime, Policing and Punishment in England, 1750–1914* (Basingstoke: Macmillan), pp. 39–40.

16 Baron D. Hume (1797) *Commentaries on the Laws of Scotland – Volume I*, p. 94.

17 A.M. Anderson (1904 edition) *The Criminal Law of Scotland – Part II* (Edinburgh: Bell and Bradfute), p. 174.

18 For further discussion see Baron D. Hume (1797) *Commentaries on the Laws of Scotland – Volume I*, pp. 70–76.

19 For further discussion see *ibid*, pp. 92–104.

20 *Ibid*, p. 92.

21 *Ibid*, p. 95.

22 *Ibid*, p. 98. [Author's note in parenthesis]

23 *Ibid.* [Author's note in parenthesis]

24 *Ibid.*

25 *Ibid*, p. 113.

26 B. de Mandeville (1725) *An Enquiry into the Causes of the Frequent Executions at Tyburn: And a Proposal for Some Regulations Concerning Felons in Prison, and the Good Effects to Be Expected from Them. To Which Is Added a Discourse on Transportation, and a Method to Render the Punishment More Effectual* (London: J. Roberts), p. 8. [Bodleian Library Ref. Vet. A4 e.2124].

27 H. Fielding (1751) *An Enquiry into the Causes of the Late Increase of Robbers, &c with some Proposals for Remedying This Growing Evil* (London: A. Miller), p. 105. [Bodleian Library Ref. G. Pamph. 885 (1)].

28 See Symonds (2006) *Notorious Murders*, p. 52 and also Baron D. Hume (1797) *Commentaries on the Laws of Scotland – Volume I*, p. 113.

29 *Ibid*, p. 117.

30 *Ibid*, p. 119.

31 *Ibid*, pp. 118–119.

32 *Ibid*, pp. 113–115.

33 The categories of non-violent property crime included in the judicial statistics for the nineteenth century are theft, animal theft, resett, housebreaking and entering into lock-fast places (without theft). It should be noted that as data was miscatalogued from 1805 to 1836 and no conviction data was available over that period either, it was decided to collate statistics from 1836 onwards. It should also be noted that the data for animal theft is merged with the data for general theft in 1914.

34 See Kilday (1998) 'Women and Crime in South-West Scotland', p. 229 and p. 231.

35 For further evidence of the dominance of men in indictments for theft throughout history see for instance D.W. Howell (2000) *The Rural Poor in Eighteenth-Century Wales* (Cardiff: University of Wales Press), p. 234; Gray (2016) *Crime, Policing and Punishment*, p. 68 and p. 89; Walker (2003) *Crime, Gender and Social Order*, p. 159; Beattie (2002 edition) *Crime and the Courts*, pp. 237–238; Kilday (2014) '"Criminally Poor?"', p. 512 and Croall (1998) *Crime and Society in Britain*, p. 215.

36 For further evidence of the dominance of theft in indictments for female criminals see J.M. Beattie (1975) 'The Criminality of Women in Eighteenth-Century England', *Journal of Social History*, 8, pp. 80–116 at p. 89; A-M. Kilday (2005) 'Women and Crime' in H. Barker and E. Chalus (eds) *Women's History: Britain, 1700–1850* (London: Routledge), pp. 174–193 at p. 178 and S. D'Cruze and L.A. Jackson (2009) *Women, Crime and Justice in England Since 1660* (Basingstoke: Palgrave Macmillan), p. 31.

37 For further discussion on the gendered assumptions relating to women's involvement in theft see G. Walker (1994) 'Women, Theft and the World of Stolen Goods' in J. Kermode and G. Walker (eds) *Women, Crime and the Courts in Early Modern England* (Chapel Hill, NC and London: University of North Carolina Press), pp. 81–105 at p. 82; Kilday (2005) 'Women and Crime', p. 178; W.M. Meier (2011) 'Going on the Hoist: Women, Work and Shoplifting in London, ca. 1890–1940', *Journal of British Studies*, 50, 2, pp. 410–433; Meier (2011) *Property Crime in London*, chapter three and Jones (1996) *Crime and Policing*, pp. 96–97.

38 For further discussion of Scottish women's involvement in resett see Kilday (1998) 'Women and Crime in South-West Scotland', p. 229 and p. 231; Kilday (2005) 'Women and Crime', pp. 178–179 and Symonds (2006) *Notorious Murders*, p. 52. For discussion of women involved in this offence elsewhere see Walker (2003) *Crime, Gender and Social Order*, p. 165; Gray (2016) *Crime, Policing and Punishment*, p. 158 and Meier (2011) *Property Crime in London*, p. 70.

39 For more on women's involvement in particular methodologies of theft see Palk (2006) *Gender, Crime and Judicial Discretion*, pp. 67–68; F. McLynn (1991) *Crime and Punishment in Eighteenth-Century England* (Oxford: Oxford University Press), pp. 92–93; D. Palk (2003) 'Private Crime in Public and Private Places: Pickpockets and Shoplifters in London, 1780–1823' in T. Hitchcock and H. Shore (eds) *The Streets of London: From the Great Fire to the Great Stink* (London: Rivers Oram Press), pp. 135–150 at pp. 137–139; Gray (2016) *Crime, Policing and Punishment*, pp. 159–160; Philips (1977) *Crime and Authority*, p. 208 and p. 210; T.C. Whitlock (2005) *Crime, Gender and Consumer Culture in Nineteenth Century England* (Aldershot: Ashgate), p. 6, p. 129 and p. 133; T. Whitlock (1999) 'Gender, Medicine, and Consumer Culture in Victorian England: Creating the Kleptomaniac', *Albion*, 31, 3, pp. 413–437; Meier (2011) 'Going on the Hoist', pp. 410–433 and D'Cruze and Jackson (2009) *Women, Crime and Justice*, pp. 36–41. For more on men's involvement in particular methodologies of theft see R. Platt (2011 edition) *Smuggling in the British Isles: A History* (Stroud: The

History Press), pp. 24–25 and Walker (1994) 'Women, Theft and the World of Stolen Goods', p. 82.

40   For more on the recurring moral panic about juvenile delinquency in the English context see for instance H. Shore (2002 edition) *Artful Dodgers: Youth and Crime in Early Nineteenth-Century London* (Woodbridge: Boydell); P. King (2006) *Crime and Law in England, 1750–1840* (Cambridge: Cambridge University Press), chapter two; J. Duckworth (2002) *Fagin's Children: Criminal Children in Victorian England* (London: Continuum); H. Johnston (2015) *Crime in England 1815–1880: Experiencing the Criminal Justice System* (London: Routledge), chapter nine; P. Cox (2013 edition) *Bad Girls in Britain: Gender, Justice and Welfare, 1900–1950* (Basingstoke: Palgrave Macmillan), pp. 26–33; P. Horn (1995) *Young Offenders: Juvenile Delinquency 1700–2000* (Stroud: Amberley); Jones (1996) *Crime and Policing*, p. 49; Emsley (2011) *Crime and Society in Twentieth-Century England*, p. 24 and J. Muncie (2009 edition) *Youth and Crime* (London: Sage).

41   For evidence of youth as an influential factor in judicial decisions elsewhere see Walker (2003) *Crime, Gender and Social Order*, pp. 184–185. For further discussion of the treatment of juvenile offenders in Scotland out with the Justiciary Court see L.A. Jackson and A. Bartie (2011) '"Children of the City": Juvenile Justice, Property, and Place in England and Scotland, 1945–60', *The Economic History Review*, 64, 1, pp. 88–113.

42   Anti-theft societies were established in various Scottish locations from the nineteenth century onwards, see Adamson (2011) *Murder, Poaching and Lemonade*, p. 35.

43   For further discussion see Kilday (2005) 'Women and Crime', p. 178; M. Archibald (2012) *A Sink of Atrocity: Crime in Nineteenth Century Dundee* (Edinburgh: Black and White Publishing), p. 145 and Cox (2013 edition) *Bad Girls in Britain*, p. 32.

44   For further discussion see Kilday (1998) 'Women and Crime in South-West Scotland', pp. 215–216 and pp. 232–233; Kilday (2014) 'Criminally Poor?', p. 512; Walker (2003) *Crime, Gender and Social Order*, pp. 170–171 and p. 175; Beattie (2002 edition) *Crime and the Courts*, chapter four and pp. 252–263; McLynn (1991) *Crime and Punishment*, p. 93; B. Henry (1994) *Dublin Hanged: Crime, Law Enforcement and Punishment in Late Eighteenth-Century Dublin* (Dublin: Irish Academic Press), p. 102 and p. 113; Palk (2006) *Gender, Crime and Judicial Discretion*, p. 64 and p. 83; A. Ager (2014) *Crime and Poverty in Nineteenth Century England: The Economy of Makeshifts* (London: Bloomsbury), p. 64; D. Brandon and A. Brooke (2010) *Edinburgh Murders and Misdemeanours* (Stroud: Amberley), p. 43; D.J.V. Jones (1992) *Crime in Nineteenth-Century Wales* (Cardiff: University of Wales Press), p. 125; Whitlock (2005) *Crime, Gender and Consumer Culture*, p. 131; Symonds (2006) *Notorious Murders*, p. 62 and Cox (2013 edition) *Bad Girls in Britain*, pp. 32–33.

45   For evidence of the relationship between theft, resett and wider criminal networks in Scotland and elsewhere over the 1660–1960 period see for instance H. Shore (2003) 'Crime, Criminal Networks and the Survival Strategies of the Poor in Early Eighteenth-Century London' in S. King and A. Tomkins (eds) *The Poor in England 1700–1850* (Manchester: Manchester University Press), pp. 137–165 at p. 154; Kilday (2005) 'Women and Crime', pp. 178–179; Walker (1994) 'Women, Theft and the World of Stolen Goods', pp. 91–92; Philips (1977) *Crime and Authority*, pp. 219–222; Symonds (2006) *Notorious Murders*, p. 55 and p. 72; Cox (2013 edition) *Bad Girls in Britain*, p. 32 and Croall (1998) *Crime and Society in Britain*, p. 217.

46   For further discussion of the diverse nature of theft across history see for instance S. Howard (2008) *Law and Disorder in Early Modern Wales: Crime and Authority in*

the Denbighshire Courts, c.1660–1730 (Cardiff: University of Wales Press), p. 100; Platt (2011 edition) *Smuggling*, p. 77; Taylor (1998) *Crime, Policing and Punishment*, pp. 40–43; Jones (1992) *Crime in Nineteenth-Century Wales*, chapter four; Gray (2016) *Crime, Policing and Punishment*, pp. 112–113, p. 130, p. 135 and p. 163; Cox (2013 edition) *Bad Girls in Britain*, p. 30; Davies (1998) 'Street Gangs', p. 260 and Croall (1998) *Crime and Society in Britain*, pp. 215–216.

47 For further discussion see variously C.B. Herrup (1985) 'Law and Morality in Seventeenth-Century England', *Past and Present*, 106, pp. 102–123 at pp. 114–116; Walker (2003) *Crime, Gender and Social Order*, pp. 185–186; Kilday (1998) 'Women and Crime in South-West Scotland', pp. 217–220; Walker (1994) 'Women, Theft and the World of Stolen Goods', p. 82; B. Lemire (1990) 'The Theft of Clothes and Popular Consumerism in Early Modern England', *Journal of Social History*, 24, 2, pp. 255–276 at p. 258 and p. 262; *Macfarlane* (1981) *The Justice and the Mare's Ale*, p. 148; Howell (2000) *The Rural Poor*, p. 227; Beattie (2002 edition) *Crime and the Courts*, p. 147, pp. 167–172, pp. 175–178 and p. 186; C. Winslow 'Sussex Smugglers', J.G. Rule 'Wrecking and Coastal Plunder' and D. Hay 'Poaching and the Game Laws on Cannock Chase' all in Hay, Linebaugh, Rule, Thompson and Winslow (2011 edition) *Albion's Fatal Tree*, pp. 119–166, pp. 167–188 and pp. 189–254 respectively; Philips (1977) *Crime and Authority*, p. 205 and p. 210; T.C. Barker (1954) 'Smuggling in the Eighteenth Century: The Evidence of the Scottish Tobacco Trade', *The Virginia Magazine of History and Biography*, 62, 4, pp. 387–399; R.C. Nash (1982) 'The English and Scottish Tobacco Trades in the Seventeenth and Eighteenth Centuries: Legal and Illegal Trade', *The Economic History Review (New Series)*, 35, 3, pp. 354–372; Platt (2011 edition) *Smuggling*, pp. 102–104 and *passim*; P. Monod (1991) 'Dangerous Merchandise: Smuggling, Jacobitism, and Commercial Culture in Southeast England, 1690–1760', *Journal of British Studies*, 30, 2, pp. 150–182; McLynn (1991) *Crime and Punishment*, p. 90 and chapter ten and D.D. Gray (2009) *Crime, Prosecution and Social Relations: The Summary Courts of the City of London in the Late Eighteenth Century* (Basingstoke: Palgrave Macmillan), p. 69.

48 For further discussion see Kilday (1998) 'Women and Crime in South-West Scotland', pp. 218–219; McLynn (1991) *Crime and Punishment*, pp. 92–93; Beattie (2002 edition) *Crime and the Courts*, p. 147 and pp. 178–181; Henry (1994) *Dublin Hanged*, pp. 115–116; Palk (2006) *Gender, Crime and Judicial Discretion*, p. 39; Palk (2003) 'Private Crime in Public and Private Places', pp. 135–150; M. Archibald (2014) *Bloody Scotland* (Edinburgh: Black and White Publishing), chapter seven; Adamson (2011) *Murder, Poaching and Lemonade*, pp. 42–43; D.J.V. Jones (1979) 'The Poacher: A Study in Victorian Crime and Protest', *The Historical Journal*, 22, 4, pp. 825–860; Whitlock (1999) 'Gender, Medicine, and Consumer Culture', pp. 413–437 and Meier (2011) 'Going on the Hoist', pp. 410–433.

49 See for instance Howell (2000) *The Rural Poor*, p. 229; Shore (2003) 'Crime, Criminal Networks and the Survival Strategies of the Poor', pp. 151–153; Emsley (1999 edition) *Crime and Society in England*, pp. 130–133; Jones (1992) *Crime in Nineteenth-Century Wales*, pp. 122–125; Taylor (1998) *Crime, Policing and Punishment*, pp. 41–42; Philips (1977) *Crime and Authority*, pp. 222–225 and B. Godfrey and D. Cox (2012) *Policing the Factory: Theft, Private Policing and the Law in Modern England* (London: Bloomsbury).

50 For further discussion and evidence see Walker (2003) *Crime, Gender and Social Order*, pp. 181–182; Gray (2016) *Crime, Policing and Punishment*, pp. 100–105; Adamson (2011) *Murder, Poaching and Lemonade*, p. 34 and Archibald (2014) *Bloody Scotland*, p. 211, pp. 219–220, pp. 223–229; Emsley (2011) *Crime and Society in Twentieth-Century England*, p. 22; Meier (2011) *Property Crime in London*, p. 37 and Croall (1998) *Crime and Society in Britain*, pp. 220–223.

51 For further discussion and evidence see McLynn (1991) *Crime and Punishment*, p. 88; Archibald (2014) *Bloody Scotland*, pp. 213–218 and pp. 226–227; Adamson (2011) *Murder, Poaching and Lemonade*, pp. 18–23 and pp. 32–33; Emsley (2011) *Crime and Society in Twentieth-Century England*, pp. 15–16; D'Cruze and Jackson (2009) *Women, Crime and Justice*, p. 32; Jones (1996) *Crime and Policing*, p. 145; Croall (1998) *Crime and Society in Britain*, pp. 218–220 and Meier (2011) *Property Crime in London*, chapters one, two and three.

52 The exception to this would arguably be the transformation seen in smuggling with the advent of the modern drug trade. For further discussion see Meier (2011) *Property Crime in London*, chapter six. In addition, the use of new information technologies has also significantly changed theft methodologies, but this development occurred after the 1960s era and is thus lies outside the scope of this present analysis.

53 For further discussion see Henry (1994) *Dublin Hanged*, pp. 109–113; Walker (2003) *Crime, Gender and Social Order*, p. 169; Walker (1994) 'Women, Theft and the World of Stolen Goods', p. 87; Kilday (1998) 'Women and Crime in South-West Scotland', p. 220; Kilday (2014) 'Criminally Poor?', pp. 514–516; Kilday (2005) 'Women and Crime', p. 179; Palk (2006) *Gender, Crime and Judicial Discretion*, p. 58; Gray (2016) *Crime, Policing and Punishment*, p. 164 and D'Cruze and Jackson (2009) *Women, Crime and Justice*, p. 34.

54 For further discussion and evidence of these conclusions in relation to Scotland and elsewhere across history see Walker (2003) *Crime, Gender and Social Order*, p. 162 and pp. 167–169; Walker (1994) 'Women, Theft and the World of Stolen Goods', p. 88; Kilday (2014) 'Criminally Poor?', pp. 514–516; Archibald (2014) *Bloody Scotland*, pp. 214–215 and p. 221; Symonds (2006) *Notorious Murders*, p. 140; Jones (1996) *Crime and Policing*, p. 149; Croall (1998) *Crime and Society in Britain*, pp. 218–219 and Jackson and Bartie (2011) 'Children of the City', p. 94 and p. 96.

55 For further discussion and evidence of these conclusions in relation to Scotland and elsewhere across history see Lemire (1990) 'The Theft of Clothes', p. 257; Walker (1994) 'Women, Theft and the World of Stolen Goods', pp. 88–91; Walker (2003) *Crime, Gender and Social Order*, pp. 162–164; Kilday (1998) 'Women and Crime in South-west Scotland', pp. 220–226; Kilday (2014) 'Criminally Poor?', pp. 514–516; Palk (2006) *Gender, Crime and Judicial Discretion*, p. 58; Adamson (2011) *Murder, Poaching and Lemonade*, p. 34; Symonds (2006) *Notorious Murders*, p. 140; Whitlock (1999) 'Gender, Medicine, and Consumer Culture', pp. 417–418; D'Cruze and Jackson (2009) *Women, Crime and Justice*, p. 34 and Jackson and Bartie (2011) 'Children of the City', p. 95.

56 For further discussion and evidence of this see Macfarlane (1981) *The Justice and the Mare's Ale*, p. 145; B.J. Davey (1994) *Rural Crime in the Eighteenth Century: North Lincolnshire 1740–80* (Hull: The University of Hull Press), p. 11 and pp. 22–24; Howard (2008) *Law and Disorder*, p. 116; Jones (1992) *Crime in Nineteenth-Century Wales*, p. 125; Ager (2014) *Crime and Poverty*, p. 65; Philips (1977) *Crime and Authority*, pp. 178–179, p. 196 and p. 199; Taylor (1998) *Crime, Policing and Punishment*, pp. 40–41; Davies (1998) 'Street Gangs', pp. 261–262 and Jones (1996) *Crime and Policing*, p. 106.

57 For further discussion on recidivism in the Scottish context and elsewhere see Kilday (1998) 'Women and Crime in South-West Scotland', pp. 217–218 and p. 232; Kilday (2014) 'Criminally Poor?', p. 512; Symonds (2006) *Notorious Murders*, p. 53; Gray (2016) *Crime, Policing and Punishment*, p. 100; Archibald (2012) *A Sink of Atrocity*, pp. 154–163; Meier (2011) *Property Crime in London*, p. 27 and Croall (1998) *Crime and Society in Britain*, p. 217.

58 For further discussion of economic desperation as a potential motive in epi-
    sodes of theft see Kilday (1998) 'Women and Crime in South-West Scotland',
    pp. 226–227; Kilday (2014) 'Criminally Poor?', pp. 516–522; Beattie (2002
    edition) *Crime and the Courts*, p. 188, p. 208; Howell (2000) *The Rural Poor*,
    pp. 231–232; McLynn (1991) *Crime and Punishment*, p. 89; Shore (2003) 'Crime,
    Criminal Networks and the Survival Strategies of the Poor', p. 140 and p. 150;
    Palk (2006) *Gender, Crime and Judicial Discretion*, p. 73; Henry (1994) *Dublin
    Hanged*, p. 113; Jones (1992) *Crime in Nineteenth-Century Wales*, p. 128; Ager
    (2014) *Crime and Poverty*, p. 62 and p. 64; Gray (2016) *Crime, Policing and Punish-
    ment*, pp. 121–122; Philips (1977) *Crime and Authority*, p. 198 and p. 204; D'Cruze
    and Jackson (2009) *Women, Crime and Justice*, p. 31; Jones (1996) *Crime and Po-
    licing*, p. 76; Jackson and Bartie (2011) 'Children of the City', p. 90 and Davies
    (1998) 'Street Gangs', p. 261.
59 See A-M. Kilday and D.S. Nash (2017) *Shame and Modernity in Britain: 1890 to the
    Present* (London: Palgrave Macmillan), chapter seven; Gray (2016) *Crime, Policing
    and Punishment*, pp. 162–163; Whitlock (2005) *Crime, Gender and Consumer Cul-
    ture*, pp. 185–189; Whitlock (1999) 'Gender, Medicine, and Consumer Culture',
    pp. 413–437; Meier (2011) 'Going on the Hoist', pp. 410–433 and D'Cruze and
    Jackson (2009) *Women, Crime and Justice*, pp. 38–41.
60 For further discussion of this see Gray (2016) *Crime, Policing and Punishment*,
    p. 122 and Croall (1998) *Crime and Society in Britain*, p. 213, p. 221 and p. 229.
61 For further discussion of the desire for profit as a motive in episodes of theft see
    Kilday (1998) 'Women and Crime in South-West Scotland', pp. 228–229 and
    pp. 235–236; Lemire (1990) 'The Theft of Clothes', p. 265 and p. 267; Morris
    (1989) *Crime and Criminal Justice*, p. 34 and Croall (1998) *Crime and Society in
    Britain*, p. 221 and pp. 228–229.
62 See Kilday (2014) 'Criminally Poor?', pp. 520–522; Beattie (2002 edition) *Crime
    and the Courts*, p. 252; Kilday (2005) 'Women and Crime', pp. 179–180; Gray
    (2016) *Crime, Policing and Punishment*, pp. 122–123; Archibald (2014) *Bloody
    Scotland*, p. 213; D'Cruze and Jackson (2009) *Women, Crime and Justice*, p. 41 and
    Croall (1998) *Crime and Society in Britain*, pp. 228–229.
63 The accused's surname is variously referred to as McLymont and McLaymont in
    the indictment papers of the Justiciary Court, but I have decided to utilise the
    name referred to at the point of sentencing: McLymont.
64 See National Records of Scotland (NRS), Justiciary Court Records (JC), South
    Circuit Minute Books, JC12/7.
65 See the testimony of Andrew Briggs, Michael McTaggart and Samuel McChesney
    in JC12/7.
66 For the identification of the greyish blue meet coat (or fitted coat) as being stolen
    property see the testimony of Alexander Houghan in JC12/7.
67 See the testimony of George Kerr, Herbert Tweedie and John Palmer in JC12/7.
68 See the testimony of George Kerr, John Rule and John Kennedy in JC12/7.
69 See the testimony of Alexander Houghan in JC12/7.
70 See the verdict and sentence against Robert McLymont in JC12/7.
71 The original precognition papers listed five adult individuals who charged
    alongside the three boys: William Humphrey, William Drummond, William
    Robertson, Elizabeth Lonie and Alexander Lonie. However, none of these in-
    dividuals were named in the eventual indictment. See NRS, Justiciary Court,
    Precognition Papers, AD14/22/21.
72 The ages of the accused were derived from the details evident in their dec-
    larations presented to the court. See NRS, Justiciary Court, Process Papers,

JC26/1823/217A/15 (James McEwan), JC26/1823/217A/16 (Charles McLaren) and JC26/1832/217A/17 (Thomas Grierson).

73 See NRS, Justiciary Court, Process Papers, JC26/1832/217A/13 noting hearings from the City of Edinburgh Police Court against Charles McLaren; JC26/1823/217A/14 noting hearings there against James McEwan; and, JC26/1823/217A/12 noting hearings there against Thomas Grierson.

74 NRS, Justiciary Court Process Papers, JC26/1832/217A/14.

75 See National Library of Scotland (NLS), (1823) *A Full and Particular Account of the Trial and Sentence of Charles MacLaren, Thomas Grierson and James McEwan, Accused of Housebreaking and Theft* (Edinburgh: n.p.), Special Collections (SpC), L.C. Fol. 74 (088) which notes that McLaren had eight prior convictions, Grierson had six and McEwan two.

76 See the declaration of Charles McLaren in NRS, Justiciary Court Process Papers, JC26/1832/217A/16.

77 See NRS, Justiciary Court Process Papers, JC26/1832/217A.

78 See NRS, High Court of Justiciary, Precognition Papers, AD14/22/221 – Testimony of Catherine Paton and Ann Fairbairn.

79 *Ibid* – see the testimony of Catherine Paton.

80 *Ibid.*

81 *Ibid* – see the testimony of Thomas Riddle. See also NLS, (1823) *A Full and Particular Account*, SpC, L.C. Fol. 74 (088) and (1823) *An Account of the Trial and Sentence of Charles MacLaren, Thomas Grierson and James McEwan* (Edinburgh: W. Glass), Spc, Ry III A. 2 (30).

82 Calculation made via www.measuringworth.com. I am grateful to Daniel Vicars for his help in generating this calculation.

83 See NRS, High Court of Justiciary, Precognition Papers, AD14/22/221 – Testimony of Janet Allan.

84 *Ibid* – see the testimony of James Mackie.

85 *Ibid* – see the testimony of Janet Allan.

86 See NRS, High Court of Justiciary, Precognition Papers, AD14/22/221 – Testimony of Henrietta Taylor. See also the testimony of fellow servant Margaret Milne.

87 NRS, Justiciary Court, Books of Adjournal, JC4/13.

88 NRS, High Court of Justiciary, Precognition Papers, AD14/22/221 – Testimony of Henrietta Taylor. This testimony was corroborated by that of the victim, Lieutenant Colonel John Munro.

89 NRS, Justiciary Court, Books of Adjournal, JC4/13.

90 See the declaration of Charles McLaren found at NRS, Justiciary Court Process Papers, JC26/1832/217A/16. [The author's addition in parenthesis.]

91 See NRS, Justiciary Court Minute Book, JC8/17.

92 *Ibid.*

93 See NLS, (1823) *A Full and Particular Account*, SpC, L.C. Fol. 74 (088).

94 See NRS, Justiciary Court Minute Book, JC8/17.

95 See NLS, (1823) *A Full and Particular Account*, SpC, L.C. Fol. 74 (088).

96 See NRS, Justiciary Court Minute Book, JC8/17.

97 See NLS, (1823) *Respite for a Month* (Edinburgh: J. MacLean), SpC, L.C. Fol. 74 (086).

98 See NLS, (1823) *Copy Letter, Relative to the Case of These Three Unfortunate Young Boys, Charles McLaren, Thomas Grierson and James McEwan Who Were Lately Sentenced to Be Executed* (Edinburgh: J. MacLean), SpC, Ry III A. 2 (31).

99 *Ibid.*

100 See the evidence provided in the petitions submitted by the three boys found in the National Archives (NA), Home Office, Criminal Petitions, Series I, HO 17/6/59.
101 See the various letters contained in the file found in *ibid.*
102 See NLS, (1823) *Respite for a Month*, SpC, L.C. Fol. 74 (086).
103 See NRS, Justiciary Court Books of Adjournal, JC4/14.
104 See the British convict transportation registers database (1787–1867) compiled by the State Library of Queensland from British Home Office Records: James McEwan (McEwen on register) was transported to New South Wales on the 16th of March 1824 on the *Countess of Harcourt* see Microfilm Roll 88, Class/Piece No. HO11/5, p. 122 found at https://convictrecords.com.au/convicts/mcewen/james/109650 [accessed 01/01/2018]; Charles McLaren was transported to New South Wales on the 8th of July 1824 on *Minerva;* see Microfilm Roll 88, Class/Piece No. HO11/5, p. 179 (91) found at https://convictrecords.com.au/convicts/mclaren/charles/77693; and lastly Thomas Grierson was transported to New South Wales but not until the 5th of August 1826 on the ship *Speke* see Microfilm Roll 88, Class/Piece No. HO11/6, p. 54 found at https://convictrecords.com.au/convicts/grierson/thomas/79608.
105 For further detail on the early life of Johnny Ramensky see his entry in the Dictionary of National Biography written by A.P. Baker at https://doi.org/10.1093/ref:odnb/58839 [accessed 15/12/2017].
106 For further discussion and detail of the very early criminal career of Johnny Ramensky see R. Jeffrey (2011 edition) *Gentle Johnny Ramensky: The Extraordinary True Story of the Safe Blower Who Became a War Hero* (Edinburgh: Black and White Publishing), chapters one and two.
107 For evidence of the entrenched view that Johnny Ramensky was a non-violent criminal throughout his career see *ibid, passim*; R. Jeffrey (2013) *Peterhead: The Inside Story of Scotland's Toughest Prison* (Edinburgh: Black and White Publishing), p. 68; G. Forbes (1996 edition) *Bible John and Such Bad Company – Crime Casebook* (Glasgow: Lang Syne Publishers), p. 48; N. Fairbairn (1987) *A Life Is Too Short – Autobiography: Volume One* (London: Quartet Books), p. 146; *Daily Record*, 13th November 2010, p. 9 and 16th February 2011, p. 11.
108 NRS, High Court of Justiciary, Precognition Papers, AD15/26/37/2 – Indictment.
109 *Ibid.*
110 NRS, High Court of Justiciary, Precognition Papers, AD15/26/37/3 – Statement of Facts against Johnny Ramensky.
111 *Daily Record*, 16th February 2011, p. 11.
112 NRS, High Court of Justiciary, Precognition Papers, AD15/26/37/2 – Indictment.
113 See note 16 above for detail on how this calculation was made.
114 NRS, High Court of Justiciary, Precognition Papers, AD15/26/37/2 – Indictment.
115 NRS, High Court of Justiciary, Precognition Papers, AD15/26/37/1 – Letter to Procurator Fiscal.
116 There is no mention of this incident in any published work on the life and crimes of Johnny Ramensky. See for instance Jeffrey (2011 edition) *Gentle Johnny Ramensky, passim.*
117 NRS, High Court of Justiciary, Precognition Papers, AD15/26/37/3 – Statement of Facts against Johnny Ramensky.
118 *Ibid.*
119 See the references at note 32 above as well as his entry in the Dictionary of National Biography written by A.P. Baker at https://doi.org/10.1093/

ref:odnb/58839 [accessed 15/12/2017] and the historical commentary on 'Johnny Ramensky' found at www.firstfoot.com [accessed 15/12/2017].

120 NRS, High Court of Justiciary, Precognition Papers, AD15/26/37/2 – Indictment.

121 NRS, Justiciary Court, Process Papers, JC26/1925/50 and High Court of Justiciary, Precognition Papers, AD15/26/37/1 – Indictment Notes.

122 See the details found in NRS, Justiciary Court, Process Papers, JC26/1927/80 and JC26/1934/82 which contains the extract conviction from the Sheriff Court.

123 NRS, Justiciary Court, Criminal Case File – John Ramensky (or Ramsay), HH16/297 and HH16/307. It should be noted that Ramensky repeatedly asked to change his name to Ramsay in order to curb the racist abuse he had suffered at the hands of fellow prisoners.

124 Sketched out plans of the prison yard and the prevailing security provision were found on his person when he was rescued off the roof – see NRS Justiciary Court, Process Papers, JC26/1927/80. See also Jeffrey (2011 edition) *Gentle Johnny Ramensky*, p. 31.

125 NRS, Justiciary Court, Process Papers, JC26/1934/82. [The author's addition in parenthesis and the author's italicisation for emphasis.]

126 *Ibid.*

127 It is suggested that Ramensky's knowledge of explosives may have come from his short-lived work experience as a miner or from listening to his father's descriptions of his work in that trade – see his Oxford Dictionary of National Biography entry written by A.P. Baker at https://doi.org/10.1093/ref:odnb/58339 [accessed 16/12/2017]. Alternatively, Ramensky may have learnt this methodology from a fellow prisoner during one of his spells of incarceration – see the detailed case histories of four infamous safe-blowers (known as Petermen) including Johnny Ramensky found at www.peterman. org [accessed 16/12/2017].

128 NRS, Justiciary Court, Criminal Case File – John Ramensky (or Ramsay), HH16/307.

129 See for instance his Oxford Dictionary of National Biography entry written by A.P. Baker at https://doi.org/10.1093/ref:odnb/58339 [accessed 16/12/2017] and Forbes (1992 edition) *Bible John and Such Bad Company*, p. 43.

130 NRS, Justiciary Court, Criminal Case File – John Ramensky (or Ramsay), HH16/304 and especially the letters between Ramensky and the prison governor which do state that he was not permitted to go to his wife's funeral, but which are clearly dated between August and November 1937.

131 For more on Ramensky's perpetual craving for excitement see Jeffrey (2011 edition) *Gentle Johnny Ramensky*, p. 20 and p. 146.

132 See NRS, Justiciary Court, Criminal Case File – John Ramensky (or Ramsay), HH16/297 and G. Kerr (2009) *Fugitives: Life on the Run* (London: Futura), pp. 49–50.

133 See Kerr (2009) *Fugitives*, p. 50.

134 See for instance *The Times*, 5th November 1934, Issue 46903, p. 14 and *The Manchester Guardian*, 6th November 1934, p. 11.

135 See NRS, Justiciary Court, Criminal Case File – John Ramensky (or Ramsay), HH16/297.

136 See for instance the examples in *ibid* and NRS, Justiciary Court, Criminal Case File – John Ramensky (or Ramsay), HH16/307.

137 *Hansard Parliamentary Debates (Fifth Series)*, 296, 21st December 1934: 1529–1538.

138 For numerous examples of Ramensky's bad behaviour see NRS, Justiciary Court, Criminal Case Files – John Ramensky (or Ramsay), HH16/304 and HH16/306 as well as Jeffrey (2011 edition) *Gentle Johnny Ramensky*, p. 47 and p. 182.

139 See his discharge papers from Peterhead prison in October 1942 and the particulars of his recommendation for licence along with the issue of a new identity card under the name John Ramsay found in NRS, Justiciary Court, Criminal Case File – John Ramensky (or Ramsay), HH16/299.

140 For some insight into Ramensky's military career see Jeffrey (2011 edition) *Gentle Johnny Ramensky*, chapter seven. Later in the same work, the author tentatively implies that Ramensky stole property, memorabilia and personal belongings from the Nazis during his war-time travels – see chapter fourteen. This inference was then picked up by the press when the book was published and was celebrated as a heroic achievement on Ramensky's part. See *Daily Record*, 13th November 2010, p. 9 and 16th February 2011, p. 11 and *The Scotsman*, 11th November 2010. However, the claims put forward by Robert Jeffrey were all based on hearsay and not on any substantiated facts or material evidence.

141 See the conviction record presented in Jeffrey (2011 edition) *Gentle Johnny Ramensky*, pp. 205–206; NRS, Justiciary Court, Criminal Case Files – John Ramensky (or Ramsay), HH16/300, HH16/301, HH16/303 and HH16/308; as well as various newspaper reports on his criminal exploits such as *The Manchester Guardian*, 23rd November 1955, p. 6; *The Guardian*, 20th September 1964, p. 7; *The Times*, 4th January 1967, Issue 56830, p. 3 and 22nd December 1971, Issue 58357, p. 2.

142 See NRS, Justiciary Court, Criminal Case File – John Ramensky (or Ramsay), HH16/308 and Jeffrey (2011 edition) *Gentle Johnny Ramensky*, pp. 138–143.

143 See Jeffrey (2011 edition) *Gentle Johnny Ramensky*, p. 3 and p. 207 and Jeffrey (2013) *Peterhead*, pp. 80–92. See also the following newspapers reports detailing these various escape attempts: *The Manchester Guardian*, 13th August 1952, p. 5, 18th October 1958, p. 1, 20th October 1958, p. 1, 18th December 1958, p. 1 and 27th December 1958, p. 10 as well as *The Times*, 18th October 1958, Issue 54285, p. 6, 20th October 1958, Issue 54286, p. 10, 18th December 1958, Issue 54337, p. 10, 27th December 1958, Issue 54343, p. 6 and 3rd February 1959, Issue 54065, p. 5.

144 *The Yorkshire Evening Post*, 11th August 1952, Issue 19265, p. 1.

145 Ballads, poems and songs were written about Johnny Ramensky – see *The Ballad of Johnny Ramensky* written by Norman Buchan found at www.firstfoot.com [accessed 16/12/2017] and *Let Ramensky Go!* Written by Roddy McMillan found at http://mysongbook.de/msb/songs/l/letramen.html [accessed 16/12/2017].

146 Jeffrey (2011 edition) *Gentle Johnny Ramensky*, p. 143.

147 *Ibid*, p. 35.

148 NRS, Justiciary Court, Criminal Case File – John Ramensky (or Ramsay), HH16/308 and Jeffrey (2011 edition) *Gentle Johnny Ramensky*, p. 38 and p. 178.

149 For evidence of action taken against prison officers at Peterhead prison in the wake of Ramensky's escape attempts see NRS, Justiciary Court, Criminal Case Files – John Ramensky (or Ramsay), HH16/302 and HH16/308 and *The Times*, 30th December 1958, Issue 54345, p. 2.

150 *Hansard Parliamentary Debates (Fifth Series)*, 598, 27th January 1959: 855–1036.

151 See NRS, Justiciary Court, Criminal Case File – John Ramensky (or Ramsay), HH16/302 and *The Times*, 27th May 1959, Issue 54471, p. 6.

152 For further details see NRS, Justiciary Court, Criminal Case Files – John Ramensky (or Ramsay), HH16/308 and HH16/309. See also Jeffrey (2011 edition) *Gentle Johnny Ramensky*, chapter 20.

153 Fairbairn (1987) *A Life is Too Short*, p. 146 and p. 210.

154 Jeffrey (2011 edition) *Gentle Johnny Ramensky*, p. 66.

155 NRS, Justiciary Court, Criminal Case File – John Ramensky (or Ramsay), HH16/308 and Jeffrey (2011 edition) *Gentle Johnny Ramensky*, p. 179.

Chapter 7

The Violent North – Fact or Fiction? Conclusion

This work is the first national history of crime in Scotland. Indeed, there are few, if any, truly national histories of crime for any other country in the West. Consequently, this volume makes a significant contribution to our understanding of crime, its perpetrators, its victims, and the official reactions to felonious behaviour in the past. Moreover, by producing a nationally extensive study over such a long chronology, this study is also unique, as to date, no other work has investigated the history of crime over the three centuries analysed here. For these reasons and owing to the depth of research conducted into a vast array of source material (both authoritative and popular in origin), this work makes a landmark contribution to scholarship on the history of crime.

The research and writing of such a history has been actively stimulated by the contention that Scotland has been persistently regarded as a violent nation. Of course, to some extent, it is fair to say that the legacy of this notion has been *advantageous* to some Scots in the more modern era, as it has facilitated the acceptance of the 'tartan noir' literary genre and has resulted in what has been deemed '…a golden age of crime fiction writing', where stories about gritty, brutal and violent criminality across Scotland's cities and countryside have taken centre stage.[1] The popularity of this dark writing shows no signs of abating, and it is likely that its success has contributed to the perpetuation of the belief that Scotland is a violent place, and the character of its people is hard, thrawn (stubborn) and aggressive. Yet, we must remember that this material is to be found in the *fiction* section of our bookstores and websites, not in the non-fiction or true-crime departments. Certainly, the volume and range of this kind of literature in existence is not indicative of the reality of Scottish crime, either now or in the past.

In a similar vein, this work has shown that the notion of Scotland as a violent nation has been founded on exaggeration and misinformation rather than on truth or fact. A further more modern example of this, and one which indicates the longevity of this fallacy, came in the autumn of 2005. A report was published by the United Nations in September of that year, which was based on data regarding instances of assault from twenty-one nations.

The report argued that according to its findings, Scotland was the most violent country in the developed world. However, senior Scottish police officers and politicians from all parties roundly criticised this conclusion. They said not only was the data erroneous (the report's figures for assault were more than ten times higher than the number of reported instances) but that the methodology of using telephone interviews alone to collect the data was wholly problematic, especially when cross-national comparisons were being drawn from the casual conversations that took place.[2] Despite this damning assessment, the media latched on to the report and its conclusions and sensationalised debates and discussions rapidly ensued in the press and on radio and television, all trying to determine the best means to curb the brutality and inhumanity still evidently besetting the Scottish context.

There was no let-up in interest on this topic and the following month, the press were roused by a further publication, this time produced by the University of California which had reportedly claimed that Scotland's murder rate now exceeded that of America. This report led to dramatic newspaper headlines such as 'SCOTLAND'S MURDEROUS HEART' and inspired the escalation of highly sensationalised popular and political soul-searching, all trying to find explanations for, and solutions to, the hideous moral decay that had once more been exposed.[3] Yet it soon became clear that the media had completely misread this report and had misquoted its findings to an outrageous degree. Consequently, retractions were quickly issued and corrections published in the British press. Meanwhile, just days later, the World Health Organisation produced a far more reliable and empirically sound study which noted that whilst Scotland's murder rate was 2.33 deaths per 100,000 people, that this was in fact far lower than the United States' rate which stood at 5.5 deaths per 100,000.[4] Once again sustained and credible evidence wholly undermines the enduring belief that Scottish identity is violent at heart.

As this volume has repeatedly and undeniably shown, the notion of Scotland as a violent nation is a piece of historic, and occasionally contemporary, hyperbole. Whilst acknowledging that recorded crime rates may not necessarily give a wholly accurate picture of the incidence of that type of activity, Figures 7.1 and 7.2 below show very clearly, that the Scottish experience of violence was never very great (at least in comparison with non-violent offences) and, that the rate of serious violent offending dissipated over time.[5] As we have seen in earlier chapters, episodes of serious and fatal interpersonal violence were relatively uncommon throughout the 1660–1960 period and forms of collective violence, which had once been almost ubiquitous in the Scottish context, were waning by the early Victorian era as popular protest evolved to become more peaceable and conventionally political.

As we have also seen, the involvement of women in instances of violent criminality similarly evaporated over time as they gained social independence and as their spheres of influence broadened to become more aligned to that of their male counterparts. Furthermore, even when we consider prosecutions

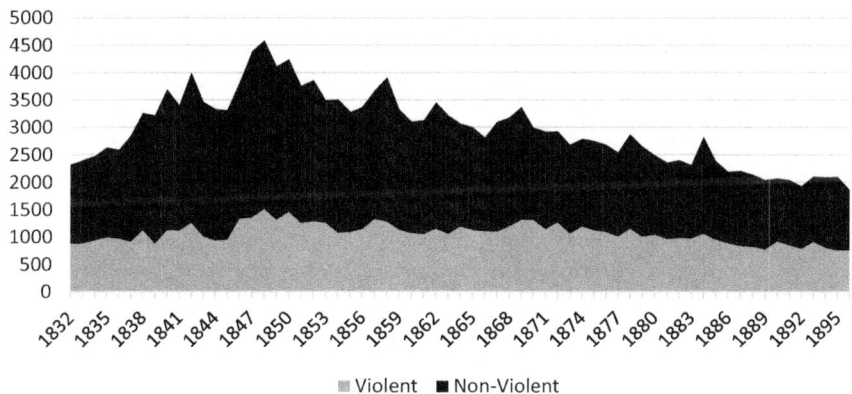

Figure 7.1 Criminal Indictments in Scotland 1832–1896.

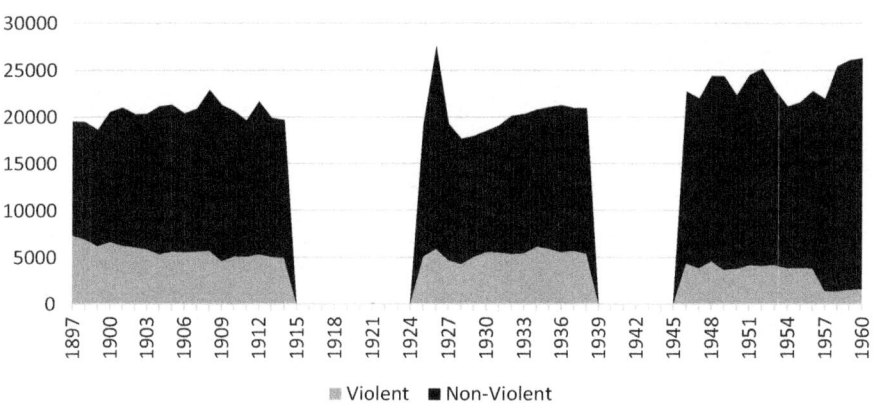

Figure 7.2 Criminal Indictments in Scotland 1897–1960.

for non-violent offences in Scotland since the early modern period, we can conclude that serious property crimes were rare and recidivism (which was such an importunate preoccupation amongst social commentators) was relatively unusual. The extent to which these trends in the Scottish history of crime are mirrored in the offending patterns of other countries over the 1660–1960 period cannot as yet be explored until other national comparative studies are conducted. Nevertheless, it is clear and irrefutable, that the notion of the Scots as a historically violent people is not really borne out by the judicial evidence.

Despite the persistence of the trope which associates Scotland with violence and extreme forms of bad behaviour, the true history of crime in Scotland between 1660 and 1960 was not particularly exceptional. From the evidence presented in this volume, it is unlikely that Scottish criminals were more common, more violent or more enterprising than their felonious counterparts elsewhere. Why would they be? Whilst we might expect it to be the case from the ingrained hyperbole perpetuated by others from without, the reality from within should not strike us as particularly surprising. From the methodologies deployed, to the characteristics of the accused and the motives for their actions, there was nothing particularly remarkable about the Scottish criminals uncovered in this study when compared with others we have encountered in research conducted elsewhere. There was also no evidence to suggest that the Highland region was more lawless than any other, as was apparently feared and articulated during the sixteenth and seventeenth centuries. Indeed, if anything, that part of the country was relatively peaceful in comparison to the more densely populated Lowland areas. Again, this should not come as a shock as crime typically occurs where people are to be found.

Of course, these conclusions should not imply that crime and violent offending were a rare occurrence in Scottish society between 1660 and 1960. As the data and case studies in this work have illustrated, Scottish history has had its fair share of serious crimes and violent offenders: male and female, young and old, individuals and groups. However, many of these particular and local episodes were sensationalised by the media and other interested parties and then extrapolated as if to be indicative of a broader national picture where violent criminality was endemic and aggression was an ingrained part of the Scottish psyche. This propaganda was not promulgated only externally, but internally too, as the Scottish authorities encouraged specific cases to be highlighted and certain criminals to be exposed to the public gaze in order to justify their approach to crime and the law over time. This was an especially shrewd idea, as it mirrored the penal policy north of the Tweed where punishment was used selectively to make examples of a few individuals in the hope that this would deter like-minded others. In the Scottish judicial system, the trial, and not its outcome, was regarded as the main mechanism for social control. The use of selected examples by the Scottish authorities also facilitated attempts to maintain the influence of religion in Scottish social life for as long as possible through the acknowledgement and articulation of the involvement of clerics at different junctures of the judicial process and crucially in encouraging the convict to exhibit remorse.

So examples of violent criminality and serious offences did exist in Scotland in the 1660–1960 period, but they were relatively isolated and infrequent events as Scottish commentators were regularly at pains to point out. Far more common were minor episodes of assault and trivial instances of theft. Thus the Scottish criminal could be described then as primarily ordinary and petty, than peculiar or petulant. Whilst Scotland may well have been more violent in earlier periods (especially with respect to the female involvement in aggressive criminality) this sort of behaviour was also evident in other locations in former times (albeit based on local or regional analyses rather than upon national perspectives). From 1660 to 1960, Scotland did *not* deserve its reputation as a violent nation. This book has challenged that long-held assumption, proven it to be an utter fallacy and laid it to rest once and for all.

Notes

1 *The Herald*, 13th September 2009 and *The Chicago Tribune*, 26th April 2013.
2 Reported on BBC News, 18th September 2005.
3 See for instance *The Guardian*, 20th October 2005.
4 *Ibid*. For further discussion see the blog post from 29th June 2017 by Professor Susan McVie (University of Edinburgh) entitled 'Can Scotland She Off its Violent Reputation' and found at www.research.aqmen.ac.uk/files/2017/06/Can-Scotland-shake-its-violent-reputation-FINAL.pdf [accessed 28/04/2018].
5 It should be noted that the content of these graphs consists of data from the judicial statistics relating to *all* offences prosecuted at the Scottish courts since 1832 and not just those crimes that were a focus for this particular study. It should also be noted, that, as with the stacked graphs elsewhere in this volume, the chronology was split at 1897 to reflect the jurisdictional data merge which results in a significant data inflation.

Bibliography

Primary Sources

Unpublished primary sources

National Archives (Kew, surrey)

Home Office Criminal Petitions (Scotland), HO 17/21/67.
Home Office Criminal Petitions, Series I, HO 17/6/59.

National Library of Scotland (Edinburgh)

(1711) *The Last Words and Declaration of Jannet Shank* (Edinburgh: John Reid), Special Collections, 6.314 (28) 104.

(1717) *A Declaration of Mr Robert Irving Who Murdered John and Alexander Gordon's* (Edinburgh: n.p.), Special Collections, Ry III c.36 (034f).

(1717) *The Last Confession of Mr Robert Irvine Who was Execute May 1st 1717 near Brughton between Leith and Edinburgh, for Murdering John and Alexander Gordons, Sons to James Gordon of Allan on Sunday the 28th of April 1717* (Edinburgh: n.p.), Special Collections, Ry III c.36 (034h).

(1717) *The Whole Trial, Confession and Sentence of Mr Robert Irving: Chaplain to Baillie Gordon, Who Was This Day Execute at the Green-Side Betwixt Leith and Edinburgh, for Murdering of John and Alexander Gordons* (Edinburgh: n.p.), Special Collections, Ry III C.36 (034g).

(1820) *A Full, True and Particular Account of the Execution of Andrew Hardie and John Baird* (Edinburgh: William Cameron), Special Collections, Ry III a. 2 (12).

(1820) *Execution: A Particular Account of the Execution of John Baird and Andrew Hardie Who Were Hanged and Beheaded at Stirling, on Friday the 8th day of September, 1820, Convicted of High Treason* (Glasgow: John Muir), Special Collections, L.C. Fol. 73 (014).

(1820) *The Following is a Particular Account of the Trial and Sentence: The Bonnymuir Prisoners for High Treason* (Edinburgh: W. Carse), Special Collections, L.C. Fol. 73 (009).

(1820) *Trials: A Particular Account of the Proceedings on the State Trials Which Commenced at Stirling on the 13th July, 1820* (Glasgow: John Muir), Special Collections, L.C. Fol. 73 (008).

(1822) *An Account of the Public Flogging of Edward Hand through the Streets of Glasgow, on Wednesday the 25th of September 1822, for Committing a Violent Assault on the Person of a Young Girl under 12 Years of Age at Greenock,* (Glasgow: John Muir), Special Collections, L.C. Fol. 73 (039).

(1822) *Public Executions,* Special Collections, L.C. Fol. 73 (043).

(1822) *Trials and Sentences of All the Different Prisoners Who Have Stood Their Trials at the Circuit Court of Justiciary, Which Opened at Glasgow on Monday the 16th of September 1822* (Glasgow: John Muir), Special Collections, L.C. Fol. 73 (038).

(1822) *Trial and Sentence of James Burtney before the High Court of Justiciary at Edinburgh, on Monday the 18th Nov. 1822 for Violating the Person of a Girl under Nine Years of Age at Prestwick, Near Ayr* (Glasgow: John Muir), Special Collections, L.C. Fol. 73 (041).

(1823) *An Account of the Trial and Sentence of Charles MacLaren, Thomas Grierson and James McEwan* (Edinburgh: W. Glass), Special Collections, Ry III A. 2 (30).

(1823) *A Full and Particular Account of the Trial and Sentence of Charles MacLaren, Thomas Grierson and James McEwan, Accused of Housebreaking and Theft* (Edinburgh: n.p.), Special Collections, L.C. Fol. 74 (088).

(1823) *Copy Letter, Relative to the Case of These Three Unfortunate Young Boys, Charles McLaren, Thomas Grierson and James McEwan Who Were Lately Sentenced to be Executed* (Edinburgh: J. MacLean), Special Collections, Ry III A. 2 (31).

(1823) *Respite for a Month* (Edinburgh: J. MacLean), Special Collections, L.C. Fol. 74 (086).

(1830) *An Account of the Execution of John Thomson and David Dobie for the Assault, Murder and Robbery of Margaret Paterson,* Special Collections, F.3.a.13(11).

(1830) *Execution and Confession: An Account of the Execution of David Dobie and John Thomson, at Edinburgh, on Wednesday the 18th August 1830, with an Account of Their Behaviour in Jail and on the Scaffold* (Edinburgh: n.p.), Special Collections, F.3.a.14(65).

(1830) *Execution of the Gilmerton Murderers, Dobie and Thomson* (Edinburgh: Forbes and Owen), Special Collections, F.3.a.14(66).

(1830) *Lamentations as of John Thomson and David Dobie* (Edinburgh: n.p.), Special Collections, F.3.a.14(63).

(1830) *Lines on the Gilmerton Murder* (Edinburgh: Robert Hodge), Special Collections, F.3.a.14(56).

(1830), *Lives and Transactions of the Gilmerton Murderers, Dobie and Thomson* (Edinburgh: n.p.), Special Collections, F.3.a.14(68).

(1830) *Melancholy Accident, with Further Particulars Relative to the Gilmerton Murder* (Edinburgh: F. O'Neill), Special Collections, F.3.a.13(7).

(1830) *Murder – Fourth Edition – Authentic Particulars* (Forbes and Owen: Edinburgh), Special Collections, F.3.a.14(53).

(1830) *Rioting!! A Full and Particular Account of the Great Riots and Mobs that took Place at Dundee, on Tuesday, Wednesday and Thursday last, the 6th, 7th and 8th July, 1830,* Special Collections, L.C. Fol. 74 (189).

(1830) *The Gilmerton Murderers, &c. A Sketch of the Conduct, Transactions and Behaviour of David Dobie and John Thomson Who Were Executed on Wednesday the 18th of August for Assault, Murder and Robbery, with Their Last Dying Confession and Behaviour on the Scaffold* (Edinburgh: R. Menzies), Special Collections, F.3.a.14(69).

(1830) *The Gilmerton Murders: Melancholy Address of Dobie and Thomson, with Dobie's Letter to His Wife* (Edinburgh: Forbes and Owen), Special Collections, RB1. 238 (62).

(1830) *The Recent Gilmerton Murder! The Latest Account of Interesting Particulars Relevant to these Most Iniquitous and Horrid Transactions, Which Lately Took Place Near Gilmerton, in the County of Edinburgh* (Edinburgh: John Craig), Special Collections, F.3.a.14(54).

(1830) *Third Edition of the Gilmerton Murders* (Edinburgh: n.p.), Special Collections, F.3.a.14(59).

(1830) *Thomson and Dobie's Lamentation* (Edinburgh: n.p.), Special Collections, F.3.a.14(62).

(1830) *The Trial, Sentence and Behaviour of John Thomson and David Dobie, Who are to be Executed at Edinburgh, on Wednesday the 18th of August Next, and Their Bodies Given for Dissection, for the Assault, Murder and Robbery of Margaret Paterson; Together with the Speeches of the Lords Justice Clerk, Meadowbank, and Moncrieff before Passing Sentence* (Edinburgh: R. Menzies), Special Collections, F3.a.14.f61.

(1830) *Trial and Sentence: A Full and Particular Account of the Trial and Sentence of John Thomson and David Dobie, Carters, Gilmerton, Who are to be Executed at Edinburgh, on Wednesday the 18th of August 1830, for the Assault, Rape, Murder and Robbery of Margaret Paterson, and Their Bodies to be Given for Dissection!* (Edinburgh: W. Robertson), Special Collections, F.3.a.14(57).

(1830) *Trial and Sentence of the Gilmerton Monsters* (Edinburgh: Forbes and Owen), Special Collections, F.3.a.14(58).

(1830) *Trials for Rape, &c. of D. Dobie, J. Thomson and D. Bertie before the High Court of Justiciary – July 12 and 14* (Edinburgh: n.p.), Special Collections, F.3.a.14(60).

(1831) *Execution* (Edinburgh: n.p.), Special Collections, Ry III A.2 (109).

(1831) *Execution: Full, True and Particular Account of the Execution of George Gilchrist, at the Head of Libberton's Wynd on the Morning of the 3rd of August 1831 for the Robbery of the Prince Regent Coach* (Edinburgh: n.p.), Special Collections, Ry III A.2 (111).

(1831) *Lamentation for George Gilchrist Now Under Sentence of Death in Edinburgh* (Edinburgh: n.p.), Special Collections, Ry III A.2 (110).

(1831) *Lamentation for George Gilchrist Under Sentence of Death in Edinburgh* (Edinburgh: n.p.), Special Collections, Ry III A.2 (109).

(1831) *Lamentation of George Gilchrist Who is to be Executed at Edinburgh on the 3rd of August Instant, Etc.,* (Edinburgh: n.p.), Special Collections, F.3.a.13 (52).

(1831) *Trial and Sentence: A Full Account of the Trial and Sentence of William Gilchrist, George Gilchrist and Jame Brown, Who Were Tried on a Charge of Abstracting a Box from the Prince Regent Coach from Glasgow to Edinburgh, Etc.* (Edinburgh: n.p.), Special Collections, F.3.1.13 (51).

(1831) *Trial of George Gilchrist, William Gilchrist and James Brown* (Edinburgh: n.p.), Special Collections, A.B. 8. 213.10.

(1832) *Letter from Alexander Robertson Esq. W.S. to the Directors of the Commercial Bank of Scotland [In Connection with the Case of George Gilchrist Tried for the Theft of the Bank's Money]* (Edinburgh: n.p.), Special Collections, 1940.12(16).

(1834) *Lamentation of Mary Braid, Who is to be Executed at Edinburgh on the 17th day of February for Incest with her Brother and the Murder of Her Own Child, Etc.* (Edinburgh: n.p.), Special Collections, F.3.a 13 (117).

(1834) *Trial and Sentence: A Full Account of the Trial and Sentence of Thomas and Mary Braid Who Were Tried for Incest and Murder* (Edinburgh: n.p.), Special Collections, F.3.a 13 (116).

(1868) *The Life of Calcraft: An Account of the Executions in Scotland for the Past 200 Years* (Edinburgh: n.p.), Special Collections, L.C. Fol. 73 (132).

Fraser, G. (1885) *The Story of the Wigtown Martyrs* (G. Ferguson: Wigtown) [NLS Ref. APS.1.78.188].

National Records of Scotland (Edinburgh)

Acts of the Parliaments of Scotland, PA2/13

Crown Office Criminal Appeals, AD24/62/7/1/11, AD24/62/7/1/21-44, AD24/62/7/1/76-85, AD24/62/7/1/91-92, AD24/62/7/1/103-106

High Court of Justiciary, Books of Adjournal, JC3/3, JC3/8, JC4/13, JC4/14, JC13/145, JC15/59

High Court of Justiciary, Minute Books, JC4/13, JC8/17

High Court of Justiciary, Process Papers, JC26/161, JC26/171, JC26/171/1/2, JC26/171/1/5, JC26/171/1/6, JC26/1834/354

Justiciary Court, Appeal Process Papers, JC34/2/240

Justiciary Court, Barlinnie Prison: Prisoners Records, HH16/642/1, HH16/642/14

Justiciary Court, Criminal Case Files, HH16/152-55, HH16/269/1-2, HH16/297, HH16/299-309, HH16/426/1-2, HH16/426/4, HH16/427

Justiciary Court, Death Warrant, HH/16/642/14

Justiciary Court, Murder Cases, HH60/703/1/108-117, HH60/703/1/184-195, HH60/703/1/217-220 and HH60/703/1/269-284

Justiciary Court, Precognition Papers, AD14/22/21, AD14/22/149, AD14/22/221, AD14/22/227, AD14/30/51, AD14/30/334/1-2, AD14/31/474/1/1-4, AD14/34/361/1-2, AD14/34/361/30, AD14/34/361/32, AD15/14/35, AD15/14/35/1, AD15/14/35/2, AD15/19/11, AD15/26/37/1-3

Justiciary Court, Process Papers, JC26/16/1, JC26/16/2/1, JC26/189, JC26/1822/180, JC26/1823/217A/12-17, JC26/1830/346/2-5, JC26/1914/105, JC26/1919/85, JC26/1919/85/40, JC26/1919/85/41, JC26/1925/50, JC26/1927/80, JC26/1934/82, JC26/1948/34

Justiciary Court, South Circuit Minute Books, JC12/1, JC12/2, JC12/7, JC12/11, JC12/17

Justiciary Court, Trial Reports, AD21/22/1, AD21/23/3, AD21/24/1,

Justiciary Court, Trial Transcripts and Proceedings, JC36/266, JC36/31/10

Justiciary Court, West Circuit Minute Books, JC13/14, JC13/16, JC13/53

Miscellaneous Small Collections of Family, Business and Other Papers, GD1/616/67

Plan of Crime Scene in the Case against Henry Watson by Neil Duff Architect, RHP 140365

Records of Church of Scotland Synods, Presbyteries and Kirk Sessions, Records of Penninghame Kirk Session, CH2/1387/1, Records of Kirkinner Kirk Session, CH2/228/1

Published Primary Sources

Official Documents and Publications (in chronological order)

Hansard Parliamentary Debates (Fifth Series), 296, 21st December 1934: 1529–1538

Hansard Parliamentary Debates (Fifth Series), 598, 27th January 1959: 855–1036

Parliamentary Papers, 21 Jac 1 c. 27 (1624)

Parliamentary Papers, 1. Geo. I. c. 5 (1715)

Parliamentary Papers, 4 Geo. I (1717)
Parliamentary Papers, 20 Geo II, c. 43 (1747)
Parliamentary Papers, 25 Geo 2 c. 37 (1751)
Parliamentary Papers, 39. Geo. III. c. 81 (1799)
Parliamentary Papers, 39 & 40 Geo III c. 106 (1800)
Parliamentary Papers, 43 Geo. 3 c. 58 (1803)
Parliamentary Papers, 49 Geo. 3 c. 14 (1809)
Parliamentary Papers, 5 Geo. 4 c. 95 (1824)
Parliamentary Papers, 3 & 4 Wm. IV, c. 46 (1833)
Parliamentary Papers, 4 and 5 Vict c. 56 (1841)
Parliamentary Papers, 20 & 21 Vict. c. 72 (1857)
Parliamentary Papers, 4 & 5 Geo. 5 c. 29 (1914)
Parliamentary Papers, 12 and 13 Geo. 5 c. 18 (1922)
Parliamentary Papers, 23 and 24 Geo. 5 c. 12 (1933)
Parliamentary Papers, 1 Edw. 8 and 1 Geo. 6 c 12 (1937)
Parliamentary Papers, 1 and 2 Geo. 6 (1938)
Parliamentary Papers, 5 & 6 Eliz 2 c. 11 (1957)
Parliamentary Papers, Judicial Statistics (Scotland), 1805–1960
Parliamentary Papers, The Murder (Abolition of Death Penalty) Act (1965)
Parliamentary Papers, The Criminal Justice [Scotland] Act (1980)
Parliamentary Papers, Children [Scotland] Act (1995)
Parliamentary Papers, Sexual Offences [Scotland] Act (2009)

Newspapers and Periodicals

Aberdeen Journal, 1st February 1919
Caledonian Mercury, 21st July 1764, 15th July 1830, 26th July 1830, 30th January 1834, 13th of February 1834
Daily Mail, 9th July 2015
Daily Record, 27th May 1958, 11th April 2009, 13th November 2010, 4th December 2010, 16th February 2011
Derby Daily Telegraph, 3rd February 1919
Dundee Courier, 1st February 1919
Edinburgh Evening Dispatch, 22nd of December 1960
Evening Times, 31st January 1919, 21st May 1958, 26th–27th May 1958, 29th May 1958, 6th June 1958, 21st June 1958, 24th–25th June 1958, 11th July 1958
Scottish Daily Express, 26th June 1958, 17th November 1960, 19th of December 1960
Scottish Daily Mail, 20th December 1960, 22nd March 2014
Socialist Worker, 8th May 2012
The Belfast News-Letter, 4th of February 1834
The Bury and Norwich Post, 9th June 1830, 12th February 1834
The Chicago Tribune, 26th April 2013
The Examiner, 6th June 1830
The Glasgow Herald, 31st January 1919, 27th February 1948, 27th May 1948, 28th May 1948, 12th May 1958, 14th–15th May 1958
The Guardian, 1st September 1960, 17th November 1960, 26th November 1960, 8th December 1960, 20th September 1964, 2nd April 1990, 18th May 2005, 19th September 2005, 20th October 2005
The Herald, 6th June 1995, 13th September 2009

The Hull Packet, 15th June 1830

The Lancaster Gazette and General Advertiser, 8th February 1834

The Leicester Chronicle, 12th June 1830

The Manchester Guardian, 6th November 1934, 13th August 1952, 23rd November 1955, 14th–24th May 1958, 21st June 1958, 29th June 1958, 6th July 1958, 29th July 1958, 18th October 1958, 20th October 1958, 18th December 1958, 27th December 1958

The Mirror (Perth, Western Australia), 13th March 1948

The Morning Chronicle, 3rd June 1830, 7th–8th June 1830, 16th June 1830, 31st January 1834

The Morning Post, 18th February 1834

The Pittsburgh Post-Gazette, 17th March 1842

The Scots Magazine, XI (June-December 1822), XXVI (May 1764)*The Scotsman*, 30th January 1919, 13th–15th May 1958, 19th September 2005, 11th November 2010

The Standard, 23rd July 1830

The Strike Bulletin, 1st–2nd February 1919

The Times, 5th June 1830, 5th November 1934, 27th February 1948, 14th–30th May 1958, 18th October 1958, 20th October 1958, 18th December 1958, 27th December 1958, 30th December 1958, 3rd February 1959, 27th May 1959, 16th November 1960, 20th December 1960, 23rd of December 1960, 4th January 1967, 22nd December 1971

The Yorkshire Evening Post, 11th August 1952

The York Herald, 12th June 1830

Western Daily Press, 1st February 1919

Western Times, 1st February 1919

Workers' Liberty, 9th April 2008

Yorkshire Evening Post, 31st January 1919, 1st February 1919

On-line Sources

Camden, W. (1722 edition) [Translated by Edmund Gibson] *Britannia: Or A Chorographical Description of Great Britain and Ireland, Together with the Adjacent Islands* (London: M. Matthew) available at https://archive.org/details.gri_331250111 16247.

Colquhoun, P. (1798 edition) *A Treatise on the Police of London Containing Detail of the Various Crimes and Misdemeanors by Which Public and Private Property and Security Are, At Present, Injured and Endangered and Suggesting Remedies for Their Prevention* (Philadelphia: Benjamin Davies) available at https://archive.org/details/atreatiseonpoli01colqgoog.

Jacobite Broadside – Colour Portrait of Gilder Roy in His Genuine Highland Garb, The National Library of Scotland, Shelfmark: Blaikie.SNPG.9.9. available at http://digital.nls.uk/75240827.

The Newgate Calendar available at www.exclassics.com/newgate/ng860.htm.

Other Works

(1822) The Acts of the Parliaments of Scotland – Volume IX: A.D. M.DC.LXXXIX – A.D. M.DC.XCV (London: HMSO).

(1840 edition) *Annals of the General Assembly of the Church of Scotland from the Origin of the Relief in 1752, to the Rejection of the Overture on Schism in 1766, Volume II* (Edinburgh: John Johnstone).

(1852) *The Kirk's Alarm: Or, A Present for the Priest Ridden* (Edinburgh: H. Robinson).

(1952) *The Holy Bible – The Old Testament: Revised Standard Version* (New York and Glasgow: Collins).

Alison, A. (1844) 'Causes of the Increase of Crime', *Blackwood's Edinburgh Magazine*, LVI, CCCXLV, pp. 1–14.

Alison, A. (1844) 'Imprisonment and Transportation – The Increase in Crime', *Blackwood's Edinburgh Magazine*, LV, CCCXLIII, pp. 533–545.

Anderson, A.M. (1904 edition) *Criminal Law of Scotland* (Edinburgh: Bell and Bradfute).

Borrow, G.H. (1825) *Celebrated Trials and Remarkable Cases of Criminal Jurisprudence from the Earliest Records to the Year 1825 – Volume II* (London: Knight and Lacey).

Boyer, A. (1717) *The Political State of Great Britain – Volume XIV* (London: T. Warner).

Boyle, E.V.G. (1900) *Seven Gardens and a Palace (with illustrations by F.L.B. Griggs and Arthur Gordon)* (London and New York: John Lane and The Bodley Head).

Chambers, R. (1858) *Domestic Annals of Scotland: From the Reformation to the Revolution – Volume I* (Edinburgh: Chambers).

Chambers, R. (1861 edition) *Domestic Annals of Scotland: From the Revolution to the Rebellion of 1745 – Volume III* (Edinburgh: Chambers).

Cosgrave, J. (1799) *A Genuine History of the Lives and Actions of the Most Notorious Irish Highwaymen, Tories and Rapparees, from Redmond O'Hanlon, the Famous Gentleman-Robber, to Cahier na Gappul, the Great Horse-catcher, Who Was Executed at Maryborough, in August 1735. To Which is Added, The Gold-finder, or, The History of Manus MacOneil, Who Under the Appearance of a Stupid, Ignorant Country Fellow (On the Bog of Allen, by the Help of His Man Andrew) Played the Most Notorious Cheats, And Remarkable Tricks on the People of Ireland, That Was Ever Known. Also, the Remarkable Life of Gilder Roy, a Murderer; Ravisher; Incendiary and Highwayman, With Several Others* (Wilmington [DEL]: Bonal and Niles).

Defoe, D (1728) *Augusta Triumphans: Or, the Way to Make London the Most Flourishing City in the Universe* (London: J. Roberts) [Bodleian Reference: BOD Gough Lond.272 (8)].

Defoe, D. (1728) *Street Robberies Consider'd: The Reason of Their Being So Frequent, with Probable Means to Prevent 'em* (London: J. Roberts) [Bodleian Reference: BOD Mar.849 (7)].

Fielding, H. (1751 edition) *An Enquiry into the Causes of the Late Increase in Robbers, with Some Proposals for Remedying this Growing Evil* (London: A. Miller) [Bodleian Reference: BOD 12 Theta 1972 (1)].

Flavel, J. (1840 edition) *A Blow at the Root of Antinomianism* (Philadelphia: Presbyterian Board of Publication).

Fortescue, Sir J. (1885 edition; edited by Charles Plummer) *The Governance of England* (Oxford: Clarendon Press).

Grant, J. (1880) *Old and New Edinburgh – Volume III* (London: Cassell, Petter, Galpin and Co.).

Harris Healey, G. (1955) (ed) *The Letters of Daniel Defoe* (Oxford: Clarendon Press).

Hume, Baron D. (1797) *Commentaries on the Laws of Scotland Respecting the Description and Punishment of Crimes – Volumes I and II* (Edinburgh: Bell and Bradfute).

Hume, Baron D. (1797) *Commentaries on the Laws of Scotland Respecting Trial for Crimes –
Volume I* (Edinburgh: Bell and Bradfute).

Jordan de Colombier, C. (1709 edition) *Historiques de Toutes Les Cours de L'Europe avec
L'Espion des Cours – Tome* IV (Brussels: Francois Foppens).

Kinsley, J. (1968) (ed) *The Poems and Songs of Robert Burns – Volume I Text* (Oxford:
Clarendon Press).

MacFarlane, R. (1841) *Reports of the Jury Trials in the Court of Session* (Edinburgh:
Thomas Clark).

Maclaurin, M. (1774) *Arguments and Decisions in Remarkable Cases, Before the High
Court of Justiciary, and Other Supreme Courts in Scotland* (Edinburgh and London:
Bell and Dilly).

Mandeville, B. (1725) *An Enquiry into the Causes of the Frequent Executions at Tyburn
and Etc.* (London: J. Roberts) [Bodleian Reference: BOD Vet. A4 e.2124].

McKay, A. (1858 edition) *The History of Kilmarnock* (Kilmarnock: Archibald McKay).

McShane, H. (1919) *Glasgow 1919: The Story of the 40 Hours Strike* (Glasgow: The
Molendinar Press).

Muncie, W. (1979) *The Crime Pond: Memoirs of William Muncie Formerly Assistant Chief
Constable, Strathclyde Police* (Edinburgh: Chambers).

Paterson, J. (1866) *History of the Counties of Ayr and Wigtown – Volume III: Cunninghame –
Part Two* (Edinburgh: James Stillie).

Spalding, J. (1792) *The History of The Troubles and Memorable Transactions in Scotland:
From the Year 1624 to 1645 – Volume I* (Aberdeen: Angus and Son).

Secondary Sources

Monographs and Key Edited Collections

Adamson, A. (2011) *Murder, Poaching and Lemonade: Crimes and Court Cases from
Nineteenth Century West Lothian* (London: CreateSpace).

Adams, S. and J. Goodare (2014) (eds) *Scotland in the Age of Two Revolutions*
(Woodbridge: Boydell Press).

Adey, P., D.J. Cox and B. Godfrey (2016) *Crime, Regulation and Control During the
Blitz: Protecting the Population of Bombed Cities* (London: Bloomsbury).

Ager, A. (2014) *Crime and Poverty in Nineteenth Century England: The Economy of
Makeshifts* (London: Bloomsbury).

Anderson, A.M. (1904 edition) *The Criminal Law of Scotland* (Edinburgh: Bell and
Bradfute).

Archer, J.E. (2000) *Social Unrest and Popular Protest in England 1780–1840* (Cambridge:
Cambridge University Press).

Archibald, M. (2012) *A Sink of Atrocity: Crime in Nineteenth Century Dundee*
(Edinburgh: Black and White Publishing).

Archibald, M. (2014) *Bloody Scotland: Crime in Nineteenth Century Scotland* (Edinburgh:
Black and White Publishing).

Archibald, M. (2014 edition) *Glasgow: The Real Mean City – True Crime and Punishment in the Second City of the Empire* (Edinburgh: Black and White Publishing).

Arnold, C. (2012) *Underworld London: Crime and Punishment in the Capital City*
(London: Simon & Schuster).

Bailey, J. (2003) *Unquiet Lives: Marriage and Marriage Breakdown in England, 1660–1800* (Cambridge: Cambridge University Press).

Barclay, K. (2011) *Love, Intimacy and Power: Marriage and Patriarchy in Scotland, 1650–1850* (Manchester: Manchester University Press).

Barrie, D.M. (2011 edition) *Police in the Age of Improvement: The Origins and Development of Policing in Scotland, 1775–1865* (Abingdon: Taylor and Francis).

Barrie, D.G. and S. Broomhall (2014) *Police Courts in Nineteenth-Century Scotland: Volume 2- Boundaries, Behaviours and Bodies* (Farnham: Ashgate).

Beattie, J.M. (1986) *Crime and the Courts in England 1660–1800* (Oxford: Oxford University Press).

Bennett, R.E. (2018) *Capital Punishment and the Criminal Corpse in Scotland, 1740–1834* (Basingstoke: Palgrave).

Bingham, J. (1973) *The Hunting Down of Peter Manuel: Glasgow Multiple Murderer (Written in Association with Detective Chief Superintendent William Muncie, Lanarkshire County Police)* (London: Macmillan).

Bloom, C. (2010 edition) *Violent London: 2000 Years of Riots, Rebels and Revolts* (Basingstoke: Palgrave Macmillan).

Bohun Lynch, J.G. (2008 edition) *Knuckles and Gloves* (London: Collins).

Bourke, J. (2013 edition) *Rape: A History from 1860 to the Present* (London: Virago Press).

Brailsford, D. (1988) *Bareknuckles: A Social History of Prizefighting* (Cambridge: Lutterworths Press).

Brandon, B. (2001) *Stand and Deliver: A History of Highway Robbery* (Chatham: Sutton Publishing).

Brandon, D. and A. Brooke (2010) *Edinburgh Murders and Misdemeanours* (Stroud: Amberley Publishing).

Brewer, J. and J. Styles (2007) (eds) *An Ungovernable People: The English and Their Law in the Seventeenth and Eighteenth Centuries* (London: Hutchison).

Brookman, F. (2005) *Understanding Homicide* (London: Sage).

Brown, K.M. (1986) *Bloodfeud in Scotland 1573–1625: Violence, Justice and Politics in an Early Modern Society* (Edinburgh: John Donald).

Bruce, S., T. Glendinning, I. Patterson and M. Rosie (2004) *Sectarianism in Scotland* (Edinburgh: Edinburgh University Press).

Cameron, J. (1983) *Prisons and Punishment in Scotland: From the Middle Ages to the Present* (Edinburgh: Canongate).

Carron, J. (2012) *Ghosts of Barlinnie: Ten Men, Ten Murder Trials, Ten Executions* (Edinburgh: Amenta Publishing).

Carter Wood, J. (2004) *Violence and Crime in Nineteenth-Century England: The Shadow of Our Refinement* (London: Routledge).

Charlesworth, A. (1983) (ed) *An Atlas of Rural Protest in Britain 1548–1900* (London: Croom Helm).

Charlesworth, A., D. Gilbert, A. Randall, H. Southall and C. Wrigley (1996) *An Atlas of Industrial Protest in Britain 1750–1900* (Basingstoke: McMillan).

Clark, A. (1987) *Women's Silence: Men's Violence – Sexual Assault in England 1770–1845* (London and New York: Pandora).

Cocks, H. (2003) *Nameless Offences: Homosexual Desire in the Nineteenth Century* (London: I.B. Taurus).

Conklin, J.E. (1972) *Robbery and the Criminal Justice System* (Philadelphia: J.B. Lippincott Company).

Conley, C.A. (2007) *Certain Other Countries: Homicide, Gender and National Identity in Late Nineteenth Century England, Ireland, Scotland and Wales* (Columbus: Ohio State University Press).

Conley, C.A. (1991) *The Unwritten Law: Criminal Justice in Victorian Kent* (New York and Oxford: Oxford University Press).

Cowan, E.J. (1980) (ed) *The People's Past* (Edinburgh: Polygon).

Cowan, E.J. and R. Finlay (2000) *Scotland since 1688: Struggle for a Nation* (London: Cima Books).

Cowan, E.J. and L. Henderson (eds) *A History of Everyday Life in Medieval Scotland, 1000 to 1600* (Edinburgh: Edinburgh University Press).

Cox, P. (2013 edition) *Bad Girls in Britain: Gender, Justice and Welfare, 1900–1950* (Basingstoke: Palgrave Macmillan).

Craig, M. (2011) *When the Clyde Ran Red* (Edinburgh and London: Mainstream Publishing).

Crawford, K. (2007) *European Sexualities, 1400–1800* (Cambridge: Cambridge University Press).

Croall, H. (1998) *Crime and Society in Britain* (London and New York: Longman).

Croall, H. (1992) *White Collar Crime: Criminal Justice and Criminology* (Buckingham: Open University Press).

Cronin, J. (1979) *Industrial Conflict in Modern Britain* (London: Croom Helm).

Crosbie, J. (2007) *Armed and Dangerous: This is the True Story of How I Carried Out Scotland's Biggest Bank Robbery* (London: John Blake).

Davey, B.J. (1994) *Rural Crime in the Eighteenth Century: North Lincolnshire 1740–80* (Hull: University of Hull Press).

Davidson, R. (2000) *Dangerous Liaisons: A Social History of Venereal Disease in Twentieth Century Scotland* (Amsterdam: Rodopi).

Davidson, R. and G. Davis (2014 edition) *The Sexual State: Sexuality and Scottish Governance, 1950–1980* (Edinburgh: Edinburgh University Press).

Davies, A. (2013) *City of Gangs: Glasgow and the Rise of the British Gangster* (London: Hodder and Stoughton).

D'Cruze, S. (1998) *Crimes of Outrage: Sex, Violence and Victorian Working Women* (London: Routledge).

D'Cruze, S. and L.A. Jackson (2009) *Women, Crime and Justice in England since 1660* (Basingstoke: Palgrave Macmillan).

Devine, T.M. (1990) (ed) *Conflict and Stability in Scottish Society 1700–1850* (Edinburgh: John Donald).

Devine, T.M. (1995) *Exploring the Scottish Past: Themes in the History of Scottish Society* (East Linton: Tuckwell Press).

Devine, T.M. (1991) (ed) *Irish Immigrants and Scottish Society in the Nineteenth and Twentieth Centuries* (Edinburgh: John Donald).

Devine, T.M. (2000 edition) *The Scottish Nation 1700–2000* (London: Penguin).

Devine, T.M. and D. Dickson (1983) (eds) *Ireland and Scotland 1600–1850: Parallels and Contrasts in Economic and Social Development* (Edinburgh: John Donald).

Devine, T.M. and P. Logue (2002) *Being Scottish: Personal Reflections on Scottish Identity Today* (Edinburgh: Polygon).

Devine, T.M. and R. Mitchison (1989) (eds) *People and Society in Scotland – Volume I 1760–1830* (Edinburgh: John Donald).

Devine, T.M. and J. Wormald (2012) (eds) *The Oxford Handbook of Modern Scottish History* (Oxford: Oxford University Press).

Dickinson, T. and J.H. Treble (1992) (eds) *People and Society in Scotland – Volume III: 1914–1990* (Edinburgh: John Donald).

Dickinson, W.C. and A.A.M. Duncan (1977 edition) *Scotland from the Earliest Times to 1603* (Oxford: Clarendon).

Doggett, M.E. (1993) *Marriage, Wife-Beating and the Law in Victorian England* (Columbia: University of South Carolina Press).

Donnachie, I. and C. Whatley (1992) (eds) *The Manufacture of Scottish History* (Edinburgh: Polygon).

Drummond, A.L. and J. Bulloch (1981) *The Scottish Church 1688–1843 – The Age of the Moderates* (Edinburgh: The Saint Andrew Press).

Duckworth, J. (2002) *Fagin's Children: Criminal Children in Victorian England* (London: Continuum).

Duke, T. (2014) *Rogues of the Road: Highwaymen and Highway Robbery in Eighteenth Century England* (Union Bay: Duke Publications).

Duncan, R. and A. McIvor (1992) (eds) *Militant Workers: Labour and Class Conflict on the Clyde 1900–1950 – Essays in Honour of Harry McShane 1891–1988* (Edinburgh: John Donald).

Durcan, J.W., W.E.J. McCarthy and G.P. Redman (1983) *Strikes in Post-War Britain: A Study of Stoppages of Work Due to Industrial Disputes, 1946–73* (London: George Allen and Unwin).

Elias, N. [translated by E. Jephcott] (1994) *The Civilising Process: The History of Manners and State Formation and Civilization* (Oxford: Wiley-Blackwell).

Emsley, C. (2005 edition) *Crime and Society in England, 1750–1900* (Harlow: Longman).

Emsley, C. (2011) *Crime and Society in Twentieth-Century England* (Harlow: Pearson Education Ltd).

Emsley, C. (2005) *Hard Men and Violence in England since 1750* (London: Hambledon and London).

Ewan, E. and M.M. Meikle (1999) (eds) *Women in Scotland, c. 1100–c. 1750* (East Linton: Tuckwell Press).

Fairbairn, N. (1987) *A Life is Too Short – Autobiography: Volume One* (London: Quartet Books).

Falconer, J.R.D. (2013) *Crime and Community in Reformation Scotland: Negotiating Power in a Burgh Society* (London: Pickering & Chatto).

Farmer, L. (1997) *Criminal Law, Tradition and Legal Order: Crime and the Genius of Scots Law, 1747 to the Present* (Cambridge: Cambridge University Press).

Ferguson, W. (1998) *The Identity of the Scottish Nation: A Historic Quest* (Edinburgh: Edinburgh University Press).

Findlay, J. (2000) *All Manner of People: The History of the Justices of the Peace in Scotland* (Edinburgh: Saltire Society).

Finlay, R.J. (2004) *Modern Scotland 1914–2000* (London: Profile Books).

Flegel, M. (2009) *Conceptualizing Cruelty to Children in Nineteenth-Century England: Literature, Representation, and the NSPCC* (Farnham: Ashgate).

Fletcher, R. (2004 edition) *Bloodfeud: Murder and Revenge in Anglo-Saxon England* (Oxford: Oxford University Press).

Forbes, G. (1996 edition) *Bible John and Such Bad Company – Crime Casebook* (Glasgow: Lang Syne Publishers).

Foyster, E. (2005) *Marital Violence: An English Family History, 1660–1857* (Cambridge: Cambridge University Press).

Foyster, E. and C.A. Whatley (2010) (eds) *A History of Everyday Life in Scotland, 1600 to 1800* (Edinburgh: Edinburgh University Press).

Fraser, D.M. (2010) *The Book of Glasgow Murders* (Glasgow: Neil Wilson).

Fraser, W.H. (2010) *Chartism in Scotland* (Pontypool: Merlin Press).

Fraser, W.H. (1988) *Conflict and Class: Scottish Workers 1700–1838* (Edinburgh: John Donald).

Fraser, W.H. and R.J. Morris (1990) (eds) *People and Society in Scotland – Volume II: 1830–1914* (Edinburgh: John Donald).

Freeman, M.D.A. (1979) *Violence in the Home: A Socio-Legal Study* (Farnborough: Gower).

Fry, M. (2005) *Wild Scots: Four Hundred Years of Highland History* (London: John Murray).

Furbank, P.N. and W.R. Owens (2016 edition) *A Political Biography of Daniel Defoe* (London: Routledge).

Gallagher, T. (1987) *Glasgow: The Uneasy Peace – Religious Tension in Modern Scotland* (Manchester: Manchester University Press).

Gane, C.H.W., C.N. Stoddart and J. Chalmers (2009 edition) *A Casebook on Scottish Criminal Law* (Edinburgh: W. Green).

Gaskill, M. (2000) *Crime and Mentalities in Early Modern England* (Cambridge: Cambridge University Press).

Gatrell, V.A.C. (1994) *The Hanging Tree: Execution and the English People 1770–1868* (Oxford: Oxford University Press).

Gilmour, I. (1992) *Riot, Risings and Revolution: Governance and Violence in Eighteenth-Century England* (London: Hutchinson).

Godfrey, B. and D. Cox (2012) *Policing the Factory: Theft, Private Policing and the Law in Modern England* (London: Bloomsbury).

Graham, M.F. (1996) *The Uses of Reform: 'Godly Discipline' and Popular Behaviour in Scotland and Beyond, 1560–1610* (Leiden: Brill).

Gray, A. (2006) *Crime and Criminals of Victorian London* (Chichester: Phillimore and Co).

Gray, D.D. (2016) *Crime, Policing and Punishment in England, 1660–1914* (London: Bloomsbury).

Gray, D.D. (2009) *Crime, Prosecution and Social Relations: The Summary Courts of the City of London in the Late Eighteenth Century* (Basingstoke: Palgrave).

Griffiths, T. and G. Morton (2010) (eds) *A History of Everyday Life in Scotland, 1800 to 1900* (Edinburgh: Edinburgh University Press).

Hain, P. (1986) *Political Strikes: The State and Trade Unionism in Britain* (London: Penguin).

Hammerton, A.J. (1992) *Cruelty and Companionship: Conflict in Nineteenth-Century Married Life* (London: Routledge).

Hanawalt, B.A. (1979) *Crime and Conflict in English Communities 1300–1348* (Cambridge: Harvard University Press).

Handley, J.E. (1945 edition) *The Irish in Scotland 1798–1845* (Cork: Cork University Press).

Hay, D., P. Linebaugh, J.G. Rule, E.P. Thompson and C. Winslow (2011 edition) *Albion's Fatal Tree: Crime and Society in Eighteenth-Century England* (London: Verso).

Henry, B. (1994) *Dublin Hanged Crime, Law Enforcement and Punishment in Late Eighteenth-Century Dublin* (Dublin: Irish Academic Press).

Hobsbawm, E. (2000) *Bandits* (London: Abacus).

Hobsbawm, E. and G. Rudé (2001 edition) *Captain Swing* (London: Phoenix Press).

Holmes, R.M. and S.T. Holmes (2010 edition) (eds) *Serial Murder* (Thousand Oaks: Sage).

Hook, A. and R.B. Sher (1995) (eds) *The Glasgow Enlightenment* (East Linton: Tuckwell Press).

Horn, P. (1995) *Young Offenders: Juvenile Delinquency 1700–2000* (Stroud: Amberley).

House, J. (2002 edition) *Square Mile of Murder: Horrific Glasgow Killings* (Edinburgh: Black and White Publishing).

Houston, R.A. and W.W.J. Knox (2001) (eds) *The New Penguin History of Scotland: From the Earliest Times to the Present Day* (London: Allen Lane).

Houston, R.A. and I.D. Whyte (1989) (eds) *Scottish Society 1500–1800* (Cambridge: Cambridge University Press).

Howard, S. (2008) *Law and Disorder in Early Modern Wales: Crime and Authority in the Denbighshire Courts, c.1660–1730* (Cardiff: University of Wales Press).

Howell, D.W. (2000) *The Rural Poor in Eighteenth-Century Wales* (Cardiff: University of Wales Press).

Hughes, A. (2010) *Gender and Political Identities in Scotland, 1919–1939* (Edinburgh: Edinburgh University Press).

Hurl-Eamon, J. (2005) *Gender and Petty Violence in London, 1680–1720* (Columbus: Ohio State University Press).

Jackson, L. (2000) *Child Abuse in Victorian England* (London: Routledge).

Jeffrey, R. (2002) *Gangland Glasgow: True Crime from the Streets* (Edinburgh: Black and White Publishing).

Jeffrey, R. (2011 edition) *Gentle Johnny Ramensky: The Extraordinary True Story of the Safe Blower Who Became a War Hero* (Edinburgh: Black and White Publishing).

Jeffrey, R. (2002) *Glasgow's Hard Men: True Crime from the Files of the Herald, Evening Times and Sunday Herald* (Edinburgh: Black and White Publishing).

Jeffrey, R. (2013) *Peterhead: The Inside Story of Scotland's Toughest Prison* (Edinburgh: Black and White Publishing).

Jeffrey, K. and P. Hennessy (1983) *States of Emergency: British Governments and Strike-breaking since 1919* (London: Routledge).

Johnston, H. (2015) *Crime in England 1815–1880: Experiencing the Criminal Justice System* (London: Routledge).

Jones, D. (1982) *Crime, Protest, Community and Police in Nineteenth-Century Britain* (London: Routledge and Kegan Paul).

Jones, D.J.V. (1973) *Before Rebecca: Popular Protest in Wales 1793–1835* (London: Allen Lane).

Jones, D.J.V. (1996) *Crime and Policing in the Twentieth Century: The South Wales Experience* (Cardiff: University of Wales Press).

Jones, D.J.V. (1992) *Crime in Nineteenth-Century Wales* (Cardiff: University of Wales Press).

Kehoe, S.K. (2010) *Creating a Scottish Church: Catholicism, Gender and Ethnicity in Nineteenth-Century Scotland* (Manchester: Manchester University Press).

Kenefick, W. (2007) *Red Scotland! The Rise and Fall of the Radical Left, c. 1872 to 1932* (Edinburgh: Edinburgh University Press).

Kennedy, A. (2014) *Governing Gaeldom: The Scottish Highlands and the Restoration State, 1660–1688* (Leiden: Brill).

Kermode, J. and G. Walker (eds) *Women, Crime and the Courts in Early Modern England* (London: Routledge).

Kerr, G. (2009) *Fugitives: Life on the Run* (London: Futura).

Kilday, A-M. (2013) *A History of Infanticide in Britain c. 1600 to the Present* (Basingstoke: Palgrave).

Kilday, A-M. (2007) *Women and Violent Crime in Enlightenment Scotland* (Woodbridge: Boydell Press).

Kilday, A-M. and D.S. Nash (eds) *Histories of Crime: Britain 1600–2000* (Basingstoke: Palgrave Macmillan).

King, B. (2011) *Undiscovered Dundee* (Edinburgh: Black and White Publishing).

King, P. (2006) *Crime and Law in England, 1750–1840* (Cambridge: Cambridge University Press).

Lees, S. (1997 edition) *Carnal Knowledge: Rape on Trial* (London: Penguin).

Lees, S. (1997) *Ruling Passions: Sexual Violence, Reputation and the Law* (Buckingham: Open University).

Lenman, B. (1981) *Integration, Enlightenment and Industrialisation: Scotland 1746–1832* (London: Edward Arnold).

Lenman, B.P. (1995) *The Jacobite Clans of the Great Glen 1650–1784* (Dalkeith: Scottish Cultural Press).

Leneman, L. (1998) *Alienated Affections: The Scottish Experience of Divorce and Separation, 1684–1830* (Edinburgh: Edinburgh University Press).

Linebaugh, P. (1993) *The London Hanged: Crime and Civil Society in the Eighteenth Century* (London: Penguin).

Linnane, F. (2003) *London's Underworld: Three Centuries of Vice and Crime* (London: Robson Books).

Logue, K.J. (1979) *Popular Disturbances in Scotland 1780–1815* (Edinburgh: John Donald).

Lynch, M. (2000) *Scotland: A New History* (London: Pimlico).

Macdonald, C.M.M. and E.W. McFarland (1999) (eds) *Scotland and the Great War* (East Linton: Tuckwell Press).

Macdonald, J.H.A. (1867) *A Practical Treatise on the Criminal Law of Scotland* (Edinburgh: W. Paterson).

Macdougall, N. (1983) (ed) *Church, Politics and Society: Scotland 1408–1929* (Edinburgh: John Donald).

Macfarlane, A. (1981) *The Justice and the Mare's Ale: Law and Disorder in Seventeenth-Century England* (Oxford: Basil Blackwell).

Macinnes, A. (1996) *Clanship, Commerce and the House of Stuart, 1603–1788* (East Linton: Tuckwell Press).

Mackie, J.D. (1991 edition) *A History of Scotland* (London: Penguin).

MacLean, M. and C. Carrell (1986) *As an Fhearann (From the Land): Clearance, Conflict and Crofting* (Edinburgh: Mainstream Publishing).

MacLeod, H. and M. McLeod (2010 edition) *Peter Manuel: Serial Killer* (Edinburgh: Mainstream Publishing).

Mahood, L. (2013 edition) *The Magdalenes: Prostitution in the Nineteenth Century* (London and New York: Routledge).

Mason, R. and N. Macdougall (1992) (eds) *People and Power in Scotland: Essays in Honour of T.C. Smout* (Edinburgh: John Donald).

Masson, D. (2004) (ed) *The Register of the Privy Council of Scotland. Volume III: 1578–1585* (Burlington: Tanner Ritchie Publishing).

Matthews, R. (2002) *Armed Robbery* (Cullompton: Willan).

McClintock, F. and E. Gibson (1961) *Robbery in London: An Enquiry by the Cambridge Institute of Criminology* (London: MacMillan).

McDonald, B. (2010) *Gangs of London: 100 Years of Mob Warfare* (Wrea Green [Lancs]: Milo Books).

McDonald, F. (2012) *Gentlemen Rogues and Wicked Ladies: A Guide to British Highwaymen and Highwaywomen* (Stroud: The History Press).

McDiarmid, C. (2010 edition) *Criminal Law Essentials (Scots Law Essentials)* (Edinburgh: Edinburgh University Press).

McFarland, E.W. (1990) *Protestants First: Orangeism in Nineteenth Century Scotland* (Edinburgh: Edinburgh University Press).

McGregor, A. (2005) *The Law Killers: True Crime from Dundee* (Edinburgh: Black and White Publishing).

McKay, R. (2007) *Killers, Crooks and Cons: Scotland's Crimes of the Century* (Edinburgh: Black and White Publishing).

McKay, R. (2016) *The Last Godfather: The Life and Crimes of Arthur Thompson* (Edinburgh: Black and White Publishing).

McLean, I. (1983) *The Legend of Red Clydeside* (Edinburgh: John Donald).

McLennan, J. (2009) *Blood in the Glens: True Crime from the Scottish Highlands* (Edinburgh: Black and White Publishing).

McLynn, F. (1991 edition) *Crime and Punishment in Eighteenth-century England* (Oxford: Oxford University Press).

McMullen, R.J. (1990) *Male Rape: Breaking the Silence on the Last Taboo* (London: GMP Publishers).

Meek, J. (2015) *Queer Voices in Post-War Scotland: Male Homosexuality, Religion and Society* (Basingstoke: Palgrave Macmillan).

Meier, W.M. (2011) *Property Crime in London, 1850 to the Present* (Basingstoke: Palgrave Macmillan).

Merely, G.C. and M.B. King (2000 edition) *Male Victims of Sexual Assault* (Oxford: Oxford University Press).

Mitchison, R. (2002 edition) *A History of Scotland* (London: Routledge).

Mitchison, R. and L. Leneman (1989) *Sexuality and Social Control: Scotland 1660–1780* (Oxford: Basil Blackwell).

Morgan, G. and P. Rushton (1998) *Rogues, Thieves and the Rule of Law: The Problem of Law Enforcement in North-east England, 1718–1800* (London: Routledge).

Morris, T. (1989) *Crime and Criminal Justice since 1945* (Oxford: Basil Blackwell).

Morton, J. (2003 edition) *Gangland – Volumes I and II* (London: Time Warner).

Muncie, J. (2009 edition) *Youth and Crime* (London: Sage).

Murray, B. (2000 edition) *The Old Firm: Sectarianism, Sport and Society in Scotland* (Edinburgh: John Donald).

Murray, L. (2002) *The Pleader: An Autobiography* (Edinburgh and London: Mainstream Publishing).

Newark, P. (1979) *The Crimson Book of Highwaymen* (London: Jupiter Books).

Nicol, A.M. (2008) *Manuel: Scotland's First Serial Killer* (Edinburgh: Black and White Publishing).

Palk, D. (2006) *Gender, Crime and Judicial Discretion 1780–1830* (Woodbridge: Boydell).

Peakman, J. (2004) *Lascivious Bodies: A Sexual History of the Eighteenth Century* (London: Atlantic Books).

Philips, D. (1977) *Crime and Authority in Victorian England: The Black Country 1835–1860* (London: Croom Helm).

Phillips, J. (2012) *Collieries, Communities and the Miners' Strike in Scotland, 1984–85* (Manchester: Manchester University Press).

Phillips, R. (1988) *Putting Asunder: A History of Divorce in Western Society* (Cambridge: Cambridge University Press).

Platt, R. (2011 edition) *Smuggling in the British Isles: A History* (Stroud: The History Press).

Quinault, R. and J. Stevenson (1974) (eds) *Popular Protest and Public Order: Six Studies in British History 1790–1920* (London: George Allen and Unwin).

Randall, A. (2006) *Riotous Assemblies: Popular Protest in Hanoverian England* (Oxford: Oxford University Press).

Randall, A. and A. Charlesworth (2000) (eds) *Moral Economy and Popular Protest: Crowds, Conflict and Authority* (Basingstoke: Macmillan Press).

Raynor, P., B. Lenman and G. Parker (1982) *Handlist of Records for the Study of Crime in Early Modern Scotland (to 1747)* (London: Swift).

Reed, M. and R. Wells (1990) (eds) *Class, Conflict and Protest in the English Countryside, 1700–1880* (London: Frank Cass).

Richards, E. (2008 edition) *The Highland Clearances: People, Landlords and Rural Turmoil* (Edinburgh: Birlinn).

Robb, G. (2002 edition) *White-Collar Crime in Modern England: Financial Fraud and Business Morality 1845–1929* (Cambridge: Cambridge University Press).

Robertson, I.J.M. (2013) *Landscapes of Protest in the Scottish Highlands After 1914: The Later Highland Land Wars* (Farnham: Ashgate).

Roodhouse, M. (2013) *Black Market Britain: 1939–1955* (Oxford: Oxford University Press).

Rosie, M. (2004) *The Sectarian Myth in Scotland: Of Bitter Memory and Bigotry* (Basingstoke: Palgrave Macmillan).

Rudé, G. (1964) *The Crowd in History: A Study of Popular Disturbance in France and England 1730–1848* (London and New York: John Wiley and Sons).

Ruff, J. (1984) *Crime, Justice and Public Order in Old Regime France: The Sénéchaussées of Libourne and Bazas, 1696–1789* (London: Croom Helm).

Ruff, J. (2001) *Violence in Early Modern Europe, 1500–1800* (Cambridge: Cambridge University Press).

Rule, J. and R. Wells (1997) *Crime, Protest and Popular Politics in Southern England 1740–1850* (London: Hambledon Press).

Sanderson, E.C. (1996) *Women and Work in Eighteenth-Century Edinburgh* (Basingstoke: Palgrave).

Settle, L. (2016) *Sex for Sale in Scotland: Prostitution in Edinburgh and Glasgow 1900–1939* (Edinburgh: Edinburgh University Press).

Sharpe, J.A. (1999 edition) *Crime in Early Modern England 1550–1750* (Harlow: Longman).

Sharpe, J.A. (2005) *Dick Turpin: The Myth of the English Highwaymen* (London: Profile Books).

Sheehan, W. and M. Cronin (2011) (eds) *Riotous Assemblies: Rebels, Riots and Revolts in Ireland* (Cork: Mercier Press).

Shepherd, I.A.G. (2006) *Aberdeenshire, Donside and Strathbogie: An Illustrated Architectural Guide* (Newcastle: Rutland Press).

Sher, R.B. (2015 edition) *Church and University in the Scottish Enlightenment* (Edinburgh: Edinburgh University Press).

Shoemaker, R.B. (1991 edition) *Prosecution and Punishment: Petty Crime and Law in London and Rural Middlesex, c. 1660–1725* (Cambridge: Cambridge University Press).

Shoemaker, R.B. (2004) *The London Mob: Violence and Disorder in Eighteenth-Century England* (London and New York: Hambledon and London).

Shore, H. (2002 edition) *Artful Dodgers: Youth and Crime in Early Nineteenth-Century London* (Woodbridge: Boydell).

Shore, H. (2015) *London's Criminal Underworlds, c. 1720–1930* (Basingstoke: Palgrave Macmillan).

Sindall, R. (1990) *Street Violence in the Nineteenth Century* (Leicester: Leicester University Press).

Slack, P. (1984 edition) (ed) *Rebellion, Popular Protest and the Social Order in Early Modern England* (Cambridge: Cambridge University Press).

Smith, I. (2012 edition) *Law, Life and Laughter: A Personal Verdict* (Edinburgh: Black and White Publishing).

Smout, T.C. (1997 edition) *A Century of the Scottish People 1830–1950* (London: Fontana Press).

Smout, T.C. (1998 edition) *A History of the Scottish People 1560–1830* (London: Fontana Press).

Smout, T.C. (2005) (ed) *Anglo-Scottish Relations from 1603 to 1900* (Oxford: Oxford University Press).

Spraggs, G. (2001) *Outlaws and Highwaymen: The Cult of the Robber in England from the Middle Ages to the Nineteenth Century* (London: Pimlico).

Stanko, E.A. (1985) *Intimate Intrusions: Women's Experience of Male Violence* (London: Routledge).

Stevenson, D. (1980) *Highland Warrior: Alisdair MacColla and the Civil Wars* (Edinburgh: Birlinn).

Stevenson, J. (1992 edition) *Popular Disturbances in England 1700–1832* (London and New York: Longman).

Stone, L. (1990) *Road to Divorce: England 1530–1987* (Oxford: Oxford University Press).

Symonds, D.A. (2006) *Notorious Murders, Black Lanterns and Moveable Goods: The Transformation of Edinburgh's Underworld in the Early Nineteenth Century* (Akron: University of Akron Press).

Symonds, D.A. (1997) *Weep Not for Me: Women, Ballads and Infanticide in Early Modern Scotland* (University Park: Pennsylvania State University Press).

Tarrow, S. (1998 edition) *Power in Movement: Social Movements and Contentious Politics* (Cambridge: Cambridge University Press).

Taylor, D. (1998) *Crime, Policing and Punishment in England, 1750–1914* (Basingstoke: Macmillan).

Thomas, D. (2006 edition) *Villain's Paradise: Britain's Underworld from the Spivs to the Krays* (London: John Murray).

Thompson, E.P. (2009 edition) *Customs in Common* (London: Merlin Press).

Thomson, E.P. (1975) *Whigs and Hunters: The Origins of the Black Act* (London: Pantheon).

Todd, M. (2002) *The Culture of Protestantism in Early Modern Scotland* (London: Yale University Press).

Todd, M.J. and G. Taylor (2004) *Democracy and Participation: Popular Protest and New Social Movements* (London: Merlin Press).

Underdown, D. (1987 edition) *Revel, Riot, and Rebellion: Popular Politics and Culture in England 1603–1660* (Oxofrd: Oxford University Press).

Vronsky, P. (2004) *Serial Killers: The Method and Madness of Monsters* (New York: Penguin).

Waddington, D. (1992) *Contemporary Issues in Public Disorder: A Comparative and Historical Approach* (London and New York: Routledge).

Walker, G. (2003) *Crime, Gender and Social Order in Early Modern England* (Cambridge: Cambridge University Press).

Walker, N. (1968) *Crime and Insanity in England – Volume One: The Historical Perspective* (Edinburgh: Edinburgh University Press).

Ward, R.M. (2014) *Print Culture, Crime and Justice in Eighteenth-Century London* (London: Bloomsbury).

Watson, F. (2002 edition) *Scotland: A History, 8000 B.C. – A.D. 2000* (Stroud: Tempus).

Watson, K.D. (2007 edition) *Poisoned Lives: English Poisoners and their Victims* (London and New York: Hambledon and London).

Whatley, C.A. (2000) *Scottish Society 1707–1830: Beyond Jacobitism, Towards Industrialisation* (Manchester: Manchester University Press).

Whetstone, A.E. (1981) *Scottish County Government in the Eighteenth and Nineteenth Centuries* (Edinburgh: John Donald).

Whitlock, T.C. (2005) *Crime, Gender and Consumer Culture in Nineteenth Century England* (Aldershot: Ashgate).

Whyte, I.D. (1995) *Scotland Before the Industrial Revolution: An Economic and Social History c1050–c1750* (London and New York: Longman).

Williams, D. (2011 edition) *The Rebecca Riots: A Study in Agrarian Discontent* (Cardiff: University of Wales Press).

Williams, G. (1994 edition) *A Dictionary of Sexual Language and Imagery in Shakespearean and Stuart Literature* (London: Athlone Press).

Wilson, D. (2009) *A History of British Serial Killing* (London: Sphere).

Wilson, J.G. (1959) *The Trial of Peter Manuel: The Man Who Talked Too Much* (London: Secker & Warburg).

Wilson, L. (2012) *Murder and Crime: Stirling* (Stroud: The History Press).

Wilson, S. (2016 edition) *The Origins of Modern Financial Crime: Historical Foundations and Current Problems in Britain* (Abingdon: Routledge).

Wood, A. (2002) *Riot, Rebellion and Popular Politics in Early Modern England* (Basingstoke: Palgrave).

Wormald, J. (1985) *Lords and Men in Scotland: Bonds of Manrent, 1442–1603* (Edinburgh: John Donald).

Wormald, J. (2005) (ed) *Scotland: A History* (Oxford: Oxford University Press).

Wright, A. (2006) *Organised Crime* (Cullompton: Willan).

Journal Articles

Abrams, L. (2013) 'The Taming of Highland Masculinity: Inter-Personal Violence and Shifting Codes of Manhood, c. 1760–1840', *Scottish Historical Review*, 92, 1, pp. 100–122.

Anderson, J. (2001) 'Pugilistic Prosecutions: Prize Fighting and the Courts in Nineteenth Century Britain', *The Sports Historian*, 21, 2, pp. 37–57.

Aspinwall, B. (1996) 'Scots and Irish Clergy Ministering to Immigrants, 1830–1878', *Innes Review*, 47, 1, pp. 45–68.

Barker, T.C. (1954) 'Smuggling in the Eighteenth Century: The Evidence of the Scottish Tobacco Trade', *The Virginia Magazine of History and Biography*, 62, 4, pp. 387–399.

Bartie, A. and L.A. Jackson (2011) 'Youth Crime and Preventive Policing in Post-War Scotland (c.1945–71)', *Twentieth Century British History*, 22, 1, pp. 79–102.

Bates, K. (2014) 'Empathy or Entertainment? The Form and Function of Violent Crime Narratives in Early-Nineteenth Century Broadsides', *Law, Crime and History*, 4, 2, pp. 1–27.

Beattie, J.M. (1975) 'The Criminality of Women in Eighteenth-Century England', *Journal of Social History*, 8, pp. 80–116.

Bingham, C. (1971) 'Seventeenth-Century Attitudes towards Deviant Sex', *The Journal of Interdisciplinary History*, 1, 3, pp. 447–468.

Chaytor, M. (1995) 'Husband(ry): Narratives of Rape in the Seventeenth Century', *Gender and History*, 7, 3, pp. 378–407.

Cockburn, J.S. (1991) 'Patterns of Violence in English Society: Homicide in Kent 1560–1985', *Past and Present*, 130, pp. 70–106.

Cole, W.A. (1958) 'Trends in Eighteenth-Century Smuggling', *The Economic History Review (New Series)*, 10, 3, pp. 395–410.

Conley, C.A. (2001) 'Homicide in Late-Victorian Ireland and Scotland', *New Hibernia Review*, 5, 3, pp. 66–86.

Conley, C.A. (1986) 'Rape and Justice in Victorian England', *Victorian Studies*, 29, 4, pp. 519–536.

Crowther, M.A. (1995) 'Criminal Precognitions and their Value for the Historian', *Scottish Archives: The Journal of the Scottish Records Association*, I, pp. 75–84.

Crowther, M.A. (1992) 'Scotland: A Country with No Criminal Record', *Scottish Economic and Social History*, 12, pp. 82–86.

Davidson, R. (2001) '"This Pernicious Delusion": Law, Medicine, and Child Sexual Abuse in Early-Twentieth-Century Scotland', *Journal of the History of Sexuality*, 10, 1, pp. 62–77.

Davies, A. (2006) 'Football and Sectarianism in Glasgow during the 1920s and 1930s', *Irish Historical Studies*, 35, 138, pp. 200–219.

Davies, A. (1998) 'Street Gangs, Crime and Policing in Glasgow during the 1930s: The Case of the Beehive Boys', *Social History*, 23, 3, pp. 251–267.

D'Cruze, S. (1993) 'Approaching the History of Rape and Sexual Violence: Notes towards Research', *Women's History Review*, 1, 3, pp. 377–397.

Devine, T.M. (1978) 'Social Stability and Agrarian Change in the Eastern Lowlands of Scotland, 1810–1840', *Social History*, 3, pp. 331–346.

Dickinson, H.T. and K. Logue (1976) 'The Porteous Riot: A Study of the Breakdown of Law and Order in Edinburgh, 1736–1737', *Journal of the Scottish Labour History Society*, 10, pp. 21–40.

Donnachie, I. (1995) '"The Darker Side": A Speculative Survey of Scottish Crime During the First Half of the Nineteenth Century', *Scottish Economic and Social History*, 15, pp. 5–24.

Donovan, R.K. (1979) 'Voices of Distrust: The Expression of Anti-Catholic Feeling in Scotland, 1778–1781', *Innes Review*, 30, 1, pp. 32–76.

Dunning, T. (2007) 'Narrow Nowhere Universes, Child Rape and Convict Transportation in Scotland and Van Diemen's Land, 1839–1853', *Scottish Historical Review*, 86, 1, pp. 113–125.

Edelstein, L. (1998) 'An Accusation Easily to be Made? Rape and Malicious Prosecution in Eighteenth-Century England', *The American Journal of Legal History*, 42, 4, pp. 351–390.

Eisner, M. (2003) 'Long-Term Historical Trends in Violent Crime', *Crime and Justice*, 30, pp. 83–142.

Ewan, E. (2010) 'Disorderly Damsels? Women and Interpersonal Violence in Pre-Reformation Scotland', *The Scottish Historical Review*, 84, 2, pp. 153–171.

Ewan, E. (2011) 'Impatient Griseldas: Women and the Perpetration of Violence in Sixteenth-Century Glasgow', *Florilegium*, 28, pp. 149–168.

Falconer, J.R.D. (2010) '"Mony Utheris Divars Odious Crymes": Women, Petty Crime and Power in Later Sixteenth Century Aberdeen', *Crimes and Misdemeanours*, 4, 1, pp. 7–36.

Fudge, E. (2000) 'Monstrous Acts: Bestiality in Early Modern England', *History Today*, 50, 8, pp. 20–25.

Gilbert, A.N. (1978) 'Sodomy and the Law in Eighteenth- and Early Nineteenth-Century Britain', *Societas – A Review of Social History*, VIII, 3, pp. 225–241.

Gray, D.D. (2007) 'The Regulation of Violence in the Metropolis: The Prosecution of Assault in the Summary Courts, c.1780–1820', *The London Journal*, 32, 1, pp. 75–87.

Grosclaude, J. (2014) 'From Bugger to Homosexual: The English Sodomite as Criminally Deviant', *Revue Française de Civilisation Britannique*, 19, 1, pp. 33–48.

Gurr, T.R. (1981) 'Historical Trends in Violent Crime: A Critical Review of the Evidence', *Crime and Justice*, 3, pp. 295–353.

Guthrie, C.J. (1910) 'The History of Divorce in Scotland', *Scottish Historical Review*, 8, 29, pp. 39–52.

Hair, P.E.H. (1971) 'Deaths from Violence in Britain: A Tentative Secular Survey', *Population Studies*, XXV, pp. 5–24.

Handler, P. (2005) 'Forgery and the End of the "Bloody Code" in Early Nineteenth-Century England', *The Historical Journal*, 48, 3, pp. 683–702.

Herrup, C.B. (1985) 'Law and Morality in Seventeenth-Century England', *Past and Present*, 106, pp. 102–123.

Honeyman, V. (2008) '"A Very Dangerous Place"?: Radicalism in Perth', *Scottish Historical Review*, 87, 224, pp. 278–305.

Houston, R. (2011) 'Custom in Context: Medieval and Early Modern Scotland and England', *Past and Present*, 211, pp. 35–76.

Houston, R.A. (2006) 'Poor Relief and the Dangerous and Criminal Insane in Scotland, c.1740–1840', *Journal of Social History*, 40, 2, pp. 453–476.

Hughes, A. (2004) 'Representations and Counter-Representations of Domestic Violence on Clydeside between the Two World Wars', *Labour History Review*, 69, 2, pp. 169–184.

Hughes, A. (2010) 'The "Non-Criminal" Class: Wife-Beating in Scotland (c. 1800–1949)', *Crime, History and Societies*, 14, 2, pp. 31–54.

Hughes, A. (2002) 'Working Class Culture, Family Life and Domestic Violence on Clydeside, c. 1918–1939 – A View from Below', *Scottish Tradition*, 27, pp. 60–94.

Hunt, M. (1992) 'Wife Beating, Domesticity and Women's Independence in Eighteenth-Century London', *Gender and History*, 4, 1, pp. 10–33.

Jackson, L.A. and A. Bartie (2011) '"Children of the City": Juvenile Justice, Property, and Place in England and Scotland, 1945–60', *The Economic History Review*, 64, 1, pp. 88–113.

Jenkinson, J. (2008) 'Black Sailors on Red Clydeside: Rioting, Reactionary Trade Unionism and Conflicting Notions of "Britishness" Following the First World War', *Twentieth Century British History*, 19, 1, pp. 29–60.

Johnston, C.N. (1907) 'The Punishment of Crime', *Juridical Review*, XX, pp. 316–340.

Jones, D.J.V. (1979) 'The Poacher: A Study in Victorian Crime and Protest', *The Historical Journal*, 22, 4, pp. 825–860.

Kelly, J. (1995) '"A Most inhuman and Barbarous Piece of Villainy": An Exploration of the Crime of Rape in Eighteenth-Century Ireland', *Eighteenth-Century Ireland*, 10, pp. 78–107.

Kennedy, A. (2016) 'Crime and Punishment in Early-Modern Scotland: The Secular Courts of Restoration Argyllshire, 1660–1688', *International Review of Scottish Studies*, 41, pp. 1–36.

Kilday, A-M. (2014) '"Criminally Poor?" Investigating the Link between Crime and Poverty in Eighteenth Century England', *Cultural and Social History*, 11, 4, pp. 507–526.

Kilday, A-M. (2013) 'Hell-Raising and Hair-Razing: Violent Robbery in Nineteenth-Century Scotland', *The Scottish Historical Review*, XCII, 2, pp. 255–274.

Kilday, A-M. (2016) '"Sugar and Spice and All Things Nice?" Violence against Parents in Scotland, 1700–1850', *Journal of Family History*, 41, 3, pp. 318–335.

King, P. (2011) 'Urbanization, Rising Homicide Rates and the Geography of Lethal Violence in Scotland, 1800–1860', *History*, 96, 3, pp. 231–259.

Knox, W.W. (2012) 'The Attack of the "Half-Formed Persons": The 1811–12 Tron Riot in Edinburgh Revisited', *Scottish Historical Review*, 91, 232, pp. 287–310.

Knox, W.W.J. (2015) 'Homicide in Eighteenth-Century Scotland: Numbers and Theories', *The Scottish Historical Review*, XCIV, 238, pp. 48–73.

Leeming, W. (1996) 'New Taboo? Some Observations on the Late Arrival of Changes to the Law of Incest in Scotland', *Journal of the Sociology of Law*, 24, pp. 313–336.

Lemire, B. (1990) 'The Theft of Clothes and Popular Consumerism in Early Modern England', *Journal of Social History*, 24, 2, pp. 255–276.

Leneman, L. (2000) '"A Natural Foundation in Equity": Marriage and Divorce in Eighteenth and Nineteenth-Century Scotland', *Scottish Economic and Social History*, 20, 2, pp. 199–215.

Leneman, L. (1997) '"A Tyrant and Tormentor": Violence against Wives in Eighteenth- and Early Nineteenth-Century Scotland', *Continuity and Change*, 12, 1, pp. 31–54.

Leneman, L. (1996) '"Disregarding the Matrimonial Vows": Divorce in Eighteenth and Early Nineteenth Century Scotland', *Journal of Social History*, 30, 2, pp. 465–482.

Lenman, B. and G. Parker (1980) 'Crime and Control in Scotland, 1500–1800', *History Today*, XXX, pp. 13–17.

Levack, B.P. (2010) 'The Prosecution of Sexual Crimes in Early Eighteenth-Century Scotland', *The Scottish Historical Review*, LXXXIX, 228, pp. 172–193.

Lythe, S.G.E. (1967) 'The Tayside Meal Mobs 1772–3', *Scottish Historical Review*, 46, 141, pp. 26–36.

Macpherson, H. (1947) 'The Wigtown Martyrs', *Records of the Scottish Church History Society*, IX, pp. 166–184.

MacWilliam, Rev. A.S. Canon (1967) 'Catholic Dundee: 1787 to 1836', *Innes Review*, 18, 2, pp. 75–87.

Marks, M.N. and R. Kumar (1996) 'Infanticide in Scotland', *Medicine, Science and the Law*, 36, pp. 299–305.

McGowen, R. (1999) 'From Pillory to Gallows: The Punishment of Forgery in the Age of the Financial Revolution', *Past and Present*, 165, pp. 107–140.

McGowen, R. (2007) 'Managing the Gallows: The Bank of England and the Death Penalty, 1797–1821', *Law and History Review*, 25, 2, pp. 241–282.

McLachlan, H.V. and J.K. Swales (1994) 'Sexual Bias and the Law: The Case of Pre-Industrial Scotland', *International Journal of Sociology and Social Policy*, 14, 9, pp. 20–43.

McReady, R.B. (1998) 'Irish Catholicism and Nationalism in Scotland: The Dundee Experience, 1850–1922', *Irish Studies Review*, 6, 3, pp. 245–252.

Meikle, H.W. (1909) 'The King's Birthday Riot in Edinburgh, June, 1792', *Scottish Historical Review*, 7, 25, pp. 21–28.

Meier, W.M. (2011) 'Going on the Hoist: Women, Work and Shoplifting in London, ca. 1890–1940', *Journal of British Studies*, 50, 2, pp. 410–433.

Monod, P. (1991) 'Dangerous Merchandise: Smuggling, Jacobitism, and Commercial Culture in Southeast England, 1690–1760', *Journal of British Studies*, 30, 2, pp. 150–182.

Moss, E. (2011) 'Burglary Insurance and the Culture of Fear in Britain, c. 1889–1939', *The Historical Journal*, 54, 4, pp. 1039–1064.

Mui, H–C. and L.H. Mui (1968) 'Smuggling and the British Tea Trade before 1784', *The American Historical Review*, 74, 1, pp. 44–73.

Muirhead, I.A. (1973) 'Catholic Emancipation: Scottish Reactions in 1829', *Innes Review*, 24, 1, pp. 26–42.

Nash, R.C. (1982) 'The English and Scottish Tobacco Trades in the Seventeenth and Eighteenth Centuries: Legal and Illegal Trade', *The Economic History Review (New Series)*, 35, 3, pp. 354–372.

Nugent, J. (2010) '"None Must Meddle Between Man and Wife": Assessing Family and the Fluidity of Public and Private in Early Modern Scotland', *Journal of Family History*, 35, 3, pp. 219–231.

Parker, G. (1986) 'Is a Duck an Animal? An Exploration of Bestiality as a Crime', *Criminal Justice History – An International Annual*, VII, pp. 95–109.

Phillipson, N.T. (1976) 'Lawyers, Landowners, and the Civic Leadership of Post-Union Scotland: An Essay on the Social Role of the Faculty of Advocates, 1661–1830, in Eighteenth-century Scottish Society', *Juridical Review* (New Series), XXI, pp. 97–120.

Richards, E. (1973) 'How Tame were the Highlanders during the Clearances?', *Scottish Studies*, 17, pp. 35–50.

Riggs, P.T. (2010) 'Prosecutors, Juries, Judges and Punishment in Early Nineteenth-Century Scotland', *Journal of Scottish Historical Studies*, 32, 2, pp. 166–189.

Ross, E. (1982) '"Fierce Questions and Taunts": Married Life in Working-Class London, 1870–1914', *Feminist Studies*, 8, 3, pp. 575–602.

Rushton, P. (1991) 'The Matter in Variance: Adolescents and Domestic Conflict in the Pre-Industrial Economy of Northeast England, 1600–1800', *Journal of Social History*, 25, 1, pp. 89–107.

Shoemaker, R.B. (1987) 'The London "Mob" in the Early Eighteenth Century', *Journal of British Studies*, 26, 3, pp. 273–304.

Shoemaker, R.B. (2006) 'The Street Robber and the Gentleman Highwayman: Changing Representations and Perceptions of Robbery in London, 1600–1800', *Cultural and Social History*, 3, 4, pp. 381–405.

Simpson, A.E. (1986) 'The "Blackmail Myth" and the Prosecution of Rape and Its Attempt in Eighteenth Century London: The Creation of a Legal Tradition', *The Journal of Criminal Law and Criminology*, 77, 1, pp. 101–150.

Sindall, R. (1987) 'The London Garotting Panics of 1856 and 1862', *Social History*, 12, 3, pp. 351–359.

Smart, C. (2000) 'Reconsidering the Recent History of Child Sexual Abuse, 1910–1960', *Journal of Social Politics*, 29, 1, pp. 55–71.

Sparks, R., L. Jackson, N. Davidson, L. Fleming and D. Smale (2017) 'Police and Community in Twentieth-Century Scotland: The Uses of Social History', *British Journal of Criminology*, 51, 1, pp. 18–30.

Stewart, M.M. (1995) 'In Durance Vile: Crime and Punishment in the Seventeenth and Eighteenth Century Records of Dumfries', *Scottish Archives: The Journal of the Scottish Records Association*, I, pp. 63–74.

Taylor, J. (2007) 'Company Fraud in Victorian Britain: The Royal British Bank Scandal of 1856', *The English Historical Review*, 122, 497, pp. 700–724.

Taylor, L. (1996) 'Food Riots Revisited', *Journal of Social History*, 30, 2, pp. 483–496.

Thompson, E.P. (1971) 'The Moral Economy of the English Crowd in the Eighteenth Century', *Past and Present*, 50, pp. 76–136.

Tomes, N. (1978) 'A "Torrent of Abuse": Crimes of Violence between Working-Class Men and Women in London 1840–1875', *Journal of Social History*, 11, 3, pp. 328–345.

Wallace, V. (2010) 'Presbyterian Moral Economy: The Covenanting Tradition and Popular Protest in Lowland Scotland, 1707–c.1746', *Scottish Historical Review*, 84, 227, pp. 54–72.

Walker, G. (2013) 'Everyman or Monster? The Rapist in Early Modern England, c.1600–1750', *History Workshop Journal*, 76, pp. 5–31.

Walker, G. (2013) 'Rape, Acquittal and Culpability in Popular Crime Reports in England, c. 1670–c.1750', *Past and Present*, 220, pp. 115–142.

Walker, G. (1998) 'Rereading Rape and Sexual Violence in Early Modern England', *Gender and History*, 10, 1, pp. 1–25.

Walker, W.M. (1972) 'Irish Immigrants in Scotland: Their Priests, Politics and Parochial Life', *The Historical Journal*, 15, 4, pp. 649–667.

Warner, J. and A. Lunny (2003) 'Marital Violence in a Martial Town: Husbands and Wives in Early Modern Portsmouth, 1653–1781', *Journal of Family History*, 28, 2, pp. 258–276.

Whatley, C.A. (2012) 'Custom, Commerce and Lord Meadowbank: The Management of the Meal Market in Urban Scotland, c.1740–c.1820', *Journal of Scottish Historical Studies*, 32, 1, pp. 1–27.

Whatley, C.A. (1994) 'Women and the Economic Transformation of Scotland' *Scotland Economic and Social History*, XIV, pp. 19–40.

Whitlock, T. (1999) 'Gender, Medicine, and Consumer Culture in Victorian England: Creating the Kleptomaniac', *Albion*, 31, 3, pp. 413–437.

Wiener, M.J. (2001) 'Alice Arden to Bill Sikes: Changing Nightmares of Intimate Violence in England, 1558–1869', *Journal of British Studies*, 40, 2, pp. 184–212.

Wood, I. (2006) '"The Bloodfeud of the Franks": A Historiographical Legend', *Early Medieval Europe*, 14, 4, pp. 489–504.

Wormald, J. (1980) 'Bloodfeud, Kindred and Government in Early Modern Scotland', *Past and Present*, 87, pp. 54–97.

Chapters from Edited Collections

Alison, A. (1850) 'Crime and Transportation', *Essays Political, Historical and Miscellaneous – Volume I* (Edinburgh: William Blackwood and Sons), pp. 543–617.

Anderson, M. and D.J. Morse (1990) 'The People' in W.H. Fraser and R.J. Morris (eds) *People and Society in Scotland – Volume II: 1830–1914* (Edinburgh: John Donald), pp. 8–45.

Archer, J. (2000) '"Men Behaving Badly"?; Masculinity and the Uses of Violence, 1850–1900' in S. D'Cruze (ed) *Everyday Violence in Britain, 1850–1950* (Harlow: Pearson), pp. 41–54.

Barclay, K. (2013) 'From Rape to Marriage: Questions of Consent in Eighteenth-Century Britain' in A. Greenfield (ed) *Interpreting Sexual Violence, 1660–1800* (London: Pickering and Chatto), pp. 35–44.

Block, M.R. (2013) '"For the Repressing of the Most Wicked and Felonious Rapes and Ravishments of Women": Rape Law in England, 1660–1800' in A. Greenfield (ed) *Interpreting Sexual Violence, 1660–1800* (London: Pickering and Chatto), pp. 23–33.

Broomhall, S. and D.G. Barrie (2012) 'Making Men: Media, Magistrates and the Representation of Masculinity in Scottish Police Courts, 1800–35' in D.G. Barrie and S. Broomhall (eds) *A History of Police and Masculinities, 1700–2010* (London: Routledge), pp. 72–101.

Brotherstone, T. (1992) 'Does Red Clydeside Really Matter Anymore?' in R. Duncan and A. McIvor (eds) *Militant Workers: Labour and Class Conflict on the Clyde 1900–1950 – Essays in Honour of Harry McShane 1891–1988* (Edinburgh: John Donald), pp. 52–80.

Broun, D. (2009) 'Attitudes of *Gall* to *Gaedhel* in Scotland before John of Fordun' in D. Broun and M. MacGregor (eds) *Mìorun Mòr Nan Gall, 'The Great Ill-will of* the Lowlander?' Lowland Perceptions of the Highlands, Medieval and Modern (Glasgow: University of Glasgow Press), pp. 49–82.

Brown, C.G. (1990) 'Protest in the Pews: Interpreting Presbyterianism and Society in Fracture during the Scottish Economic Revolution' in T.M. Devine (ed) Conflict and Stability in Scottish Society 1700–1850 (Edinburgh: John Donald), pp. 83–105.

Brown, K.M. (2001) 'Reformation to Union, 1560–1707' in R.A. Houston and W.W.J. Knox (eds) The New Penguin History of Scotland: From the Earliest Times to the Present Day (London: Allen Lane), pp. 182–275.

Brown, M. and S. Boardman (2005) 'Survival and Revival: Late Medieval Scotland' in J. Wormald (ed) Scotland: A History (Oxford: Oxford University Press), pp. 77–106.

Cairns, J.W. (2000) 'Historical Introduction' in K. Reid and R. Zimmermann (eds) A History of Private Law in Scotland, II: Obligations (Oxford: Oxford University Press), pp. 14–184.

Campbell, R.H. (1983) 'The Influence of Religion on Economic Growth in Scotland in the Eighteenth Century' in T.M. Devine and D. Dickson (eds) Ireland and Scotland 1600–1850: Parallels and Contrasts in Economic and Social Development (Edinburgh: John Donald), pp. 220–234.

Carson, K. and H. Idzikowska (1989) 'The Social Production of Scottish Policing 1795–1900' in D. Hay and F. Snyder (eds) Policing and Prosecution in Britain 1750–1850 (Oxford: Oxford University Press), pp. 266–297.

Clancy, T.O. and B.E. Crawford (2001) 'The Formation of the Scottish Kingdom' in R.A. Houston and W.W.J. Knox (eds) The New Penguin History of Scotland: From the Earliest Times to the Present Day (London: Allen Lane), pp. 28–95.

Clark, A. (2000) 'Domesticity and the Problem of Wifebeating in Nineteenth-Century Britain: Working-Class Culture, Law and Politics' in S. D'Cruze (ed) Everyday Violence in Britain, 1850–1950 (Harlow: Pearson), pp. 27–40.

Collins, B. (1991) 'The Origins of Irish Immigration to Scotland in the Nineteenth and Twentieth Centuries' in T.M. Devine (ed) Irish Immigrants and Scottish Society in the Nineteenth and Twentieth Centuries (Edinburgh: John Donald), pp. 1–18.

Conley, C.A. (2008) 'Atonement and Domestic Homicide in Late Victorian Scotland' in R. McMahon (ed) Crime, Law and Popular Culture in Europe, 1500–1900 (Cullompton: Willan Publishing), pp. 219–238.

Connolly, S.J. (1999) 'Unnatural Deaths in Four Nations: Contrasts and Comparisons' in S.J. Connolly (ed) Kingdoms United? Great Britain and Ireland since 1500 (Dublin: Four Courts Press), pp. 200–214.

Connolly, S.J. (1987) 'Violence and Order in the Eighteenth Century' in P. O'Flanagan, P. Ferguson and K. Whelan (eds) Rural Ireland, 1600–1900: Modernisation and Change (Cork: Cork University Press), pp. 42–61.

Croft Dickinson, W. (1958) 'The High Court of Justiciary' in Various Authors An Introduction to Scottish Legal History (Edinburgh: Stair Society, Series XX), pp. 408–412.

Cronin, J.E. (1989) 'Strikes and Power in Britain, 1870–1920' in L.H. Haimson and C. Tilly (eds) Strikes, Wars, and Revolutions in an International Perspective (Cambridge: Cambridge University Press), pp. 79–100.

Davies, S.J. (1980) 'The Courts and the Scottish Legal System, 1600–1747: The Case of Stirlingshire' in V.A.C. Gatrell, B. Lenman and G. Parker (eds) Crime and the Law: The Social History of Crime in Western Europe since 1500 (London: Europa), pp. 120–154.

Davis, J. (1980) 'The London Garotting Panic of 1862: A Moral Panic and the Creation of a Criminal Class in Mid-Victorian England' in V.A.C. Gatrell, B. Lenman and G. Parker (eds) *Crime and the Law: The Social History of Crime in Western Europe since 1500* (London: Europa Publications), pp. 190–213.

Devine, T.M. (1989) 'Social Responses to Agrarian "Improvement": The Highland and Lowland Clearances in Scotland' in R.A. Houston and I.D. Whyte (eds) *Scottish Society 1500–1800* (Cambridge: Cambridge University Press), pp. 148–168.

Devine, T.M. (1988) 'Unrest and Stability in Rural Ireland and Scotland, 1760–1840' in R. Mitchison and P. Roebuck (eds) *Economy and Society in Scotland and Ireland 1500–1939* (Edinburgh: John Donald), pp. 126–139.

Ditchburn, D. and A.J. MacDonald (2001) 'Medieval Scotland, 1100–1560' in R.A. Houston and W.W.J. Knox (eds) *The New Penguin History of Scotland: From the Earliest Times to the Present Day* (London: Allen Lane), pp. 96–181.

Donnachie, I. (1992) 'The Enterprising Scot' in I. Donnachie and C. Whatley (eds) *The Manufacture of Scottish History* (Edinburgh: Polygon), pp. 90–105.

Ewan, E. (2002) '"Many Injurious Words": Defamation and Gender in Late Medieval Scotland' in R.A. McDonald (ed) *History, Literature, and Music in Scotland, 700–1560* (London and Toronto: University of Toronto Press), pp. 162–186.

Falconer, J.R.D. (2008) 'A Family Affair: Households, Misbehaving and the Community in Sixteenth-Century Aberdeen' in E. Ewan and J. Nugent (eds) *Finding the Family in Medieval and Early Modern Scotland* (Farnham: Ashgate), pp. 139–150.

Forsyth, K. (2005) 'Origins: Scotland to 1100' in J. Wormald (ed) *Scotland: A History* (Oxford: Oxford University Press), pp. 1–38.

Foster, J. (1992) 'A Proletarian Nation? Occupation and Class since 1914' in T. Dickinson and J.H. Treble (eds) *People and Society in Scotland – Volume III: 1914–1990* (Edinburgh: John Donald), pp. 201–240.

Foster, J. (1992) 'Red Clyde, Red Scotland' in I. Donnachie and C. Whatley (eds) *The Manufacture of Scottish History* (Edinburgh: Polygon), pp. 106–124.

Foster, J. (2001) 'The Twentieth Century, 1914–1979' in R.A. Houston and W.W.J. Knox (eds) *The New Penguin History of Scotland: From the Earliest Times to the Present Day* (London: Allen Lane), pp. 417–493.

Foyster, E.A. (1999) 'Silent Witnesses? Children and the Breakdown of Domestic and Social Order in Early Modern England' in A. Fletcher and S. Hussey (eds) *Childhood in Question: Children, Parents and the State* (Manchester: Manchester University Press), pp. 57–73.

Fraser, W.H. (1988) 'Patterns of Protest' in T.M. Devine and R. Mitchison (eds) *People and Society in Scotland – Volume I: 1760–1830* (Edinburgh: John Donald), pp. 268–291.

Gallagher, T. (1991) 'The Catholic Irish in Scotland: In Search of Identity' in T.M. Devine (ed) *Irish Immigrants and Scottish Society in the Nineteenth and Twentieth Centuries* (Edinburgh: John Donald), pp. 19–43.

Gammon, J. (1995) '"A Denial of Innocence": Female Juvenile Victims of Rape and the English Legal System in the Eighteenth Century' in A. Fletcher and S. Hussey (eds) *Childhood in Question: Children, Parents and the State* (Manchester: Manchester University Press), pp. 74–95.

Gammon, J. (2013) 'Researching Sexual Violence, 1660–1800: A Critical Analysis' in A. Greenfield (ed) *Interpreting Sexual Violence, 1660–1800* (London: Pickering and Chatto), pp. 13–22.

Gollapudi, A. (2013) 'The Disordered Fundament: Sexual Violence on Boys and Sodomy Trial Narratives in the Old Bailey Proceedings' in A. Greenfield (ed) *Interpreting Sexual Violence, 1660*–1800 (London: Pickering and Chatto), pp. 45–56.

Hay, D. (2000) 'Master and Servant in England: Using the Law in the Eighteenth and Nineteenth Centuries' in W. Steinmetz (ed) *Private Law and Social Inequality in the Industrial Age: Comparing Legal Cultures in Britain, France, Germany and the United States* (Oxford: Oxford University Press), pp. 226–264.

Hay, D. (2011 edition) 'Poaching and the Game Laws on Cannock Chase' in D. Hay, P. Linebaugh, J.G. Rule, E.P. Thompson and C. Winslow *Albion's Fatal Tree: Crime and Society in Eighteenth-Century England* (London: Verso), pp. 189–254.

Houston, R.A. (1989) 'Women in the Economy and Society of Scotland, 1500–1800' in R.A. Houston and I.D. Whyte (eds) *Scottish Society, 1500–1800* (Cambridge: Cambridge University Press), pp. 118–147.

Houston, R.A. and W.W.J. Knox (2001) 'Introduction: Scots and their Histories' in R.A. Houston and W.W.J. Knox (eds) *The New Penguin History of Scotland: From the Earliest Times to the Present Day* (London: Allen Lane), pp. xiii–lviii.

Houston, R.A. and I.D. Whyte (1989) 'Introduction: Scottish Society in Perspective' in R.A. Houston and I.D. Whyte (eds) *Scottish Society 1500–1800* (Cambridge: Cambridge University Press), pp. 1–36.

Ingram, M. (2001) 'Child Sexual Abuse in Early Modern England' in M.J. Braddick and J. Walter (eds) *Negotiating Power in Early Modern Society* (Cambridge: Cambridge University Press), pp. 63–84.

Jackson, C. (2005) 'Judicial Torture, the Liberties of the Subject, and Anglo-Scottish Relations, 1660–1960' in T.C. Smout (ed) *Anglo-Scottish Relations from 1603 to 1900* (Oxford: Oxford University Press), pp. 75–101.

Jackson, L. (1999) 'Family, Community and the Regulation of Child Sexual Abuse: London, 1870–1914' in A. Fletcher and S. Hussey (eds) *Childhood in Question: Children, Parents and the State* (Manchester: Manchester University Press), pp. 133–151.

Jackson, L.A. (1999) 'The Child's Word in Court: Cases of Sexual Abuse in London 1870–1914' in M. Arnot and C. Usborne (eds) *Gender and Crime in Modern Europe* (London: UCL Press), pp. 222–237.

Jones, J. (2000) '"She Resisted With All Her Might": Sexual Violence against Women in Late Nineteenth Century Manchester and the Local Press' in S. D'Cruze (ed) *Everyday Violence in Britain, 1850–1950: Gender and Class* (London: Pearson), pp. 104–118.

Katz, J. (1991) 'The Motivation of the Persistent Robber' in M. Tonry (ed) *Crime and Justice – A Review of Research: Volume 14* (Chicago: University of Chicago Press), pp. 277–306.

Kilday, A-M. (2016) 'Britain's Most Wanted: Homicide and Serial Murder Since 1900' in D.S. Nash and A-M. Kilday (eds) *Murder and Mayhem: Crime in Twentieth Century Britain* (Basingstoke: Palgrave), pp. 31–61.

Kilday, A-M. (2014) 'The Barbarous North? Criminality in Early Modern Scotland' in T.M. Devine and J. Wormald (eds) *The Oxford Handbook of Modern Scottish History* (Oxford: Oxford University Press), pp. 386–404.

Kilday, A-M. (2016) 'Constructing the Cult of the Criminal: Kate Webster – Victorian Murderess and Media Sensation' in A-M. Kilday and D.S. Nash (eds) *True Crime Histories: Micro-Histories in Law, Crime and Deviance since 1700* (London: Bloomsbury), pp. 125–148.

Kilday, A-M. (2013) '"Outrageous Acts and Everyday Rebellions": Criminal Women in Eighteenth-Century Scotland' in K. Barclay and D. Simonton (eds) *Women in Eighteenth-Century Scotland: Intimate, Intellectual and Public Loves* (Farnham: Ashgate), pp. 253–270.

Kilday, A-M. (2005) 'Women and Crime' in H. Barker and E. Chalus (eds) *Women's History: Britain, 1700–1850* (London: Routledge), pp. 174–193.

King, P. (1999) 'Gender, Crime and Justice in Late Eighteenth- and Early Nineteenth-Century England' in M.L. Arnot and C. Usborne (eds) *Gender and Crime in Modern Europe* (London: UCL Press), pp. 44–74.

King, P. (2003) 'Moral Panics and Violent Street Crime 1750–2000: A Comparative Perspective' in B.S. Godfrey, C. Emsley and G. Dunstall (eds) *Comparative Histories of Crime* (Cullompton: Willian), pp. 53–71.

Knox, W.W. (1992) 'Whatever Happened to Radical Scotland? The Economic and Social Origins of the Mid-Victorian Political Consensus in Scotland' in R. Mason and N. Macdougall (eds) *People and Power in Scotland: Essays in Honour of T.C. Smout* (Edinburgh: John Donald), pp. 218–239.

Knox, W.W.J. and A. McKinlay (2010) 'Crime, Protest and Policing in Nineteenth-Century Scotland' in T. Griffiths and G. Morton (eds) *A History of Everyday Life in Scotland, 1800 to 1900* (Edinburgh: Edinburgh University Press), pp. 196–224.

Landsman, N.C. (1995) 'Liberty, Piety and Patronage: The Social Context of Contested Clerical Calls in Eighteenth-Century Glasgow' in A. Hook and R.B. Sher (eds) *The Glasgow Enlightenment* (East Linton: Tuckwell Press), pp. 214–226.

Lenman, B. (1984) 'The Limits of Godly Discipline in the Early Modern Period with Particular Reference to England and Scotland' in K. Von Greyerz (ed) *Religion and Society in Early Modern Europe 1500–1800* (London: George Allen and Unwin), pp. 124–145.

Liliequist, J. (1992 edition) 'Peasants against Nature: Crossing the Boundaries between Man and Animal in Seventeenth- and Eighteenth-Century Sweden' in J.C. Fout (ed) *Forbidden History: The States, Society and the Regulation of Sexuality in Modern Europe* (Chicago and London: University of Chicago Press), pp. 57–87.

Logue, K. (1980) 'Eighteenth-Century Popular Protest: Aspects of the People's Past' in E.J. Cowan (ed) *The People's Past* (Edinburgh: Polygon), pp. 102–123.

MacGregor, M. (2009) 'Gaelic Barbarity and Scottish Identity in the Later Middle Ages' in D. Broun and M. MacGregor (eds) *Mìorun Mòr Nan Gall, 'The Great Ill-will of the Lowlander?' Lowland Perceptions of the Highlands, Medieval and Modern* (Glasgow: University of Glasgow Press), pp. 7–48.

Maher, G. (2010) '"The Most Heinous of all Crimes": Reflections of the Structure of Homicide in Scots Law' in J. Chalmers and F. Leverick (eds) *Essays in Criminal Law in Honour of Sir Gerald Gordon* (Edinburgh: Edinburgh University Press), pp. 218–240.

Maxwell-Stuart, P.G. (2002) '"Wild, Filthie, Execrabill, Detestabill, and Unnatural Sin": Bestiality in Early Modern Scotland' in T. Betteridge (ed) *Sodomy in Early Modern Europe* (Manchester: Manchester University Press), pp. 82–93.

May, M. (1978) 'Violence in the Family: An Historical Perspective' in J.P. Martin (ed) *Violence and the Family* (Chichester: John Wiley and Sons), pp. 135–167.

McCormack, D. (2014) 'Highland Lawlessness and the Cromwellian Regime' in S. Adams and J. Goodare (eds) *Scotland in the Age of Two Revolutions* (Woodbridge: Boydell Press), pp. 115–133.

McLean, I. (1974) 'Popular Protest and Public Order: Red Clydeside, 1915–1919' in R. Quinault and J. Stevenson (1974) *Popular Protest and Public Order: Six Studies in British History 1790–1920* (London: George Allen and Unwin Ltd), pp. 215–242.

Mills, J. (2009) 'Rape in Early Eighteenth-Century London: A Perversion "So Very Perplex'd"' in J. Peakman (ed) *Sexual Perversions, 1670–1890* (Basingstoke: Palgrave Macmillan), pp. 140–166.

Nenadic, S. (1990) 'Political Reform and the "Ordering" of Middle-Class Protest' in T.M. Devine (ed) *Conflict and Stability in Scottish Society 1700–1850* (Edinburgh: John Donald), pp. 65–82.

Palk, D. (2003) 'Private Crime in Public and Private Places: Pickpockets and Shop-lifters in London, 1780–1823' in T. Hitchcock and H. Shore (eds) *The Streets of London: From the Great Fire to the Great Stink* (London: Rivers Oram Press), pp. 135–150.

Parker, G. (1988) 'The "Kirk By Law Established" and the Origins of "The Taming of Scotland": St Andrews 1559–1600' in L. Leneman (ed) *Perspectives in Scottish Social History – Essays in Honour of Rosalind Mitchison* (Aberdeen: Aberdeen University Press), pp. 1–32.

Richards, E. (1974) 'Patterns of Highland Discontent, 1790–1860' in R. Quinault and J. Stevenson (eds) *Popular Protest and Public Order: Six Studies in British History 1790–1920* (London: George Allen and Unwin Ltd), pp. 75–114.

Rowbotham, J. (2000) '"Only When Drunk": The Stereotyping of Violence in England, c. 1850–1900' in S. D'Cruze (ed) *Everyday Violence in Britain, 1850–1950* (Harlow: Pearson), pp. 155–169.

Rule, J.G. (2011 edition) 'Wrecking and Coastal Plunder' in D. Hay, P. Linebaugh, J.G. Rule, E.P. Thompson and C. Winslow (eds) *Albion's Fatal Tree: Crime and Society in Eighteenth-Century England* (London: Verso), pp. 167–188.

Sher, R. and A. Murdoch (1983) 'Patronage and Party in the Church of Scotland, 1750–1800' in N. Macdougall (ed) *Church, Politics and Society: Scotland 1408–1929* (Edinburgh: John Donald), pp. 197–220.

Shore, H. (2003) 'Crime, Criminal Networks and the Survival Strategies of the Poor in Early Eighteenth-Century London' in S. King and A. Tomkins (eds) *The Poor in England 1700–1850* (Manchester: Manchester University Press), pp. 137–165.

Shore, H. (2010) 'Criminality, Deviance and the Underworld since 1750' in A-M. Kilday and D.S. Nash (eds) *Histories of Crime: Britain 1600–2000* (Basingstoke: Palgrave Macmillan), pp. 120–140.

Snell, E. (2012) 'Trials in Print: Narratives of Rape Trials in the Proceedings of the Old Bailey' in D. Lemmings (ed) *Crime, Courtrooms and the Public Sphere in Britain, 1700–1850* (Farnham: Ashgate), pp. 23–41.

Stevenson, K. (2000) '"Ingenuities of the Female Mind": Legal and Public Perceptions of Sexual Violence in Victorian England, 1850–1890' in S. D'Cruze (ed) *Everyday Violence in Britain, 1850–1950: Gender and Class* (London: Pearson), pp. 89–103.

Stevenson, K. (2010) '"Most Intimate Violations": Contextualising the Crime of Rape' in A-M. Kilday and D.S. Nash (eds) *Histories of Crime: Britain 1600–2000* (Basingstoke: Palgrave Macmillan), pp. 80–99.

Stevenson, K. (2016) 'Offences against Children: Incest and Child Sexual Abuse' in D.S. Nash and A-M. Kilday (eds) *Murder and Mayhem: Crime in Twentieth Century Britain* (Basingstoke: Palgrave), pp. xx–xx at pp. 5–6 and p. 11 (on draft).

Styles, J. (1980) '"Our Traitorous Money Makers": The Yorkshire Coiners and the Law, 1760–83' in J. Brewer and J. Styles (eds) *An Ungovernable People: The English and their Law in the Seventeenth and Eighteenth Centuries* (London: Hutchinson and Co.), pp. 172–249.

Tilly, C. (1969) 'Collective Violence in European Perspective' in H.D. Graham and T.D. Gurr (eds) *Violence in America: Historical and Comparative Perspectives* (New York: Praeger), pp. 83–118.

Trumbach, R. (1989) 'Sodomitical Assaults, Gender Role, and Sexual Development in Eighteenth-Century London' in K. Gerard and G. Hekma (eds) *The Pursuit of Sodomy: Male Homosexuality in Renaissance and Enlightenment Europe* (New York and London: Harrington Park Press), pp. 407–429.

Walker, G. (1994) 'Women, Theft and the World of Stolen Goods' in J. Kermode and G. Walker (eds) *Women, Crime and the Courts in Early Modern England* (London: Routledge), pp. 81–105.

Walker, G. (1994) 'Women, Theft and the World of Stolen Goods' in J. Kermode and G. Walker (eds) *Women, Crime and the Courts in Early Modern England* (Chapel Hill and London: University of North Carolina Press), pp. 81–105.

Whatley, C.A. (1992) 'An Uninflammable People?' in I. Donnachie and C. Whatley (eds) *The Manufacture of Scottish History* (Edinburgh: Polygon), pp. 51–71.

Whatley, C.A. (1990) 'How Tame were the Scottish Lowlanders during the Eighteenth Century?' in T.M. Devine (ed) *Conflict and Stability in Scottish Society 1700–1850* (Edinburgh: John Donald), pp. 1–30.

Whatley, C.A. (2010) 'Order and Disorder' in E. Foyster and C.A. Whatley (eds) *A History of Everyday Life in Scotland, 1600 to 1800* (Edinburgh: Edinburgh University Press), pp. 191–216.

Whatley, C.A. (1992) 'Royal Day, People's Day: The Monarch's Birthday in Scotland, c. 1660–1860' in R. Mason and N. Macdougall (eds) *People and Power in Scotland: Essays in Honour of T.C. Smout* (Edinburgh: John Donald), pp. 170–188.

Wilson, S. (2010) 'Fraud and White-collar Crime: 1850 to the Present' in A-M. Kilday and D.S. Nash (eds) *Histories of Crime: Britain 1600–2000* (Basingstoke: Palgrave Macmillan), pp. 141–159.

Winslow, C. (2011 edition) 'Sussex Smugglers' in D. Hay, P. Linebaugh, J.G. Rule, E.P. Thompson and C. Winslow (eds) *Albion's Fatal Tree: Crime and Society in Eighteenth-Century England* (London: Verso), pp. 119–166.

Wohl, A.S. (1978) 'Sex and the Single Room: Incest among the Victorian Working Classes' in A.S. Wohl (ed) *The Victorian Family: Structure and Stresses* (London: Croom Helm), pp. 197–216.

Unpublished Theses and Dissertations

Brown, A. (2013) 'Social History of Scottish Homicide, 1836–1869' (Unpublished PhD Thesis, University of Leicester).

Honeyman, V. (2012) '"That Ye May Judge For Yourselves": The Contribution of Scottish Presbyterianism towards the Emergence of Political Awareness amongst Ordinary People in Scotland between 1746 and 1792' (Unpublished PhD Thesis, University of Stirling).

Kilday, A-M. (1998) 'Women and Crime in South-west Scotland: A Study of the Justiciary Records, 1750–1815' (Unpublished PhD Thesis, University of Strathclyde).

Merry, K.J. (2010) 'Murder by Poison in Scotland during the Nineteenth and Early Twentieth Centuries' (Unpublished PhD Thesis, University of Glasgow).

Vasser, M.B. (1995) 'Violence and the Central Criminal Courts in Scotland, 1603–1638' (Unpublished PhD thesis, Columbia University).

On-line Publications

Connelly, C. (2015) 'Effecting Change in the Legal Response to Domestic Abuse', *A History of Working-Class Marriage – Learning from the Past, Looking to the Future: Session 1 – Domestic Abuse and the Law* (University of Glasgow) available at http://workingclassmarriage.gla.ac.uk/wp-content/uploads/2013/11/clare_connelly.mp3, accessed 24th October 2016.

McVie, A. (2017) 'Can Scotland She Off its Violent Reputation' available at www.research.aqmen.ac.uk/files/2017/06/Can-Scotland-shake-its-violent-reputation-FINAL.pdf, accessed 28th April 2018.

Key Websites

https://convictrecords.com.au/convicts

http://mkheritage.co.uk/hdhs/fight.html

www.abusedmen inscotland.org/

www.founders-storylines.com/mugsheets/convicts/profile/6027/marybraid

www.founders-storylines.com/mugsheets/convicts/profile/6712/thomasbraid

www.gov.scot/Topics/People/Equality/violence-women/Key-Facts

www.measuringworth.com

www.oxforddnb.com/

www.peterman.org

www.scottishwomensaid.org.uk/

http://sites.scran.ac.uk/redclyde/redclyde/rc052.htm

www.stonewallscotland.org.uk

http://urbanglasgow.co.uk/archive-bloody-friday-glasgow-s-general-strike-of-1919._o_t_t_792.html

Index

Aberdeen 7, 57, 178, 273–5
'The Act Anent Murdering of
  Children' 31–2
Act of Indemnity 134
'An Act to Enable the Burghs in Scotland
  to Establish a General System of
  Police' 9
Adamson, John 176–7, 179
aggravated assault 116–18
aggravated murder 30
Agnew, Susan 137
Airdrie 222–4
Alexander, Helen 137–9
Alexander, Neil 180, 184, 185
Alexander II, King of Scots 248
Allan, Janet 264–5
Allied Trades Council 180
Anderson, Janet 96–8
Anderson, John 100–3
Anderson, Thomas 97
animal theft 249, 255, 280n33
anti-Irish riot 172–9, 175
Armour, Violet 11
assassination 30
assault: aggravated 116–18; common
  116–18; violent see violent assault
assault of authority 115–16; Alexander,
  Helen 137–9; convictions for 127–8;
  gendered nature of convictions for
  125, 128; and gendered nature of
  indictments 124, 126–7; indictments
  for 123, 125–6, 127–8; McGaa, Janet
  137–9; proportion of recidivism
  amongst indictments for 128–9
attempted murder: convictions for 121–2;
  gendered nature of convictions for
  121–2; gendered nature of indictments
  for 119–20; indictments for 118–19,
  121; see also murder

attempted rape: convictions for 87;
  indictments for 86–7; see also rape
attempted robbery 203; convictions
  for 204, 208; gendered nature of
  convictions for 205; gendered
  nature of indictments 204, 207, 208;
  indictments for 203, 204, 206, 207, 208
attitudes: to communal violence 167–86;
  enterprising Scottish thief 260–76; to
  fatal violence 50–66; to sexual violence
  90–105; to violence for gain 215–33
Auchincloss, Robert 92–3
Ayr 8, 98, 111n79, 132, 137, 138, 171, 274

Bannan, Alexander 100
Barrie, David 116
Bathgate 223
bestiality 78–9; as capital offence 78; as
  crime against God and nature 78
Bisland, Hugh 210, 217–20
Black, Margaret 220
blood feud, concept of 3–4
Bond, Edward 64
'bonds of manrent' 4
Boyd, James 90–3
Boyd, Margaret 132–4
Braid, Mary 52–6
Braid, Thomas 52–6
Brennan, Joseph 180, 185
Brookman, Fiona 28
Broomhall, Susan 116
Brown, Alexander 218
Brown, Callum 5, 167–8
Brown, James 220–7
Brown, Margaret 58–9
Bruce, William 115, 132–4
Burgh Police Courts 116
Burtney, James 94–100
Byrne, Simon 174–5, 178

Caledonian Mercury 170
Calikes, John Docherty 100–3
Camden, William 1
Cameron, Frederick 184
Campbell, Archibald 134–7
Campbell, Jeannie 142
Campbell, R. H. 167
capital murder 31, 60, 230
capital punishment: Manuel, Peter 60–1;
   in Scotland 8
Carlin, Helen 64
case studies: Alexander, Helen 137–9;
   Bisland, Hugh 217–20; Braid, Mary
   52–6; Brown, James 220–7; Bruce,
   William 132–4; Burtney, James 94–100;
   Campbell, Archibald 134–7; communal
   violence 167–86; Denovan, James
   227–33; enterprising Scottish thief
   260–76; fatal violence 50–66; Gilchrist,
   George 220–7; Gilchrist, William
   220–7; 'Glasgow Green Case' 100–5;
   Hand, Edward 94–100; Irving, Robert
   50–2; MacKinnon, Donald 134–7;
   Manuel, Peter 56–66; McGaa, Janet
   137–9; Miller, Anthony 227–33; sexual
   violence 90–105; Sword, James 90–4;
   Sword, John 90–4; violence for gain
   215–33; Watson, Henry 139–46
Catholic Emancipation Act 173
Chambers, Robert 1
Children and Young Persons Act of 1933
   117, 230
child sexual abuse 79–81
chronology, of Scottish communal
   violence 154–7
Church of Scotland 22n53, 167–9
Cochran, Charles 182
collective violence: modern 155;
   reactionary 155
Collins, Godfrey 274
Combination Act of 1800 159
Combination Act of 1799 159
*Commentaries on the Law of Scotland
   Respecting the Description and Punishment
   of Crimes* (Hume) 28
Commercial Bank of Scotland
   221–2, 226
common and/or aggravated assault 116–18
communal violence: anti-Irish riot
   172–9; attitudes to 167–86; case
   studies and 167–86; chronology of
   154–7; and the law 157–60; offenders,
   victims, methods and motive 164–7;
   overview 153; patronage riot 167–72;

punishment for 160–4; riot on Red
   Clydeside 179–86; trends in 160–4;
   violent North 186–7
Conklin, J. E. 213
Cooke, Isabelle 59
Coyle, William 177
Crawfurd, James 168, 171
Creelam, Robert 168
Cremin, John 228–9
criminal enterprise: and their punishment
   248–56; trends in 248–56
Criminal Law Amendment Act of
   1885 227
Croll, Nathan 176–7, 179
Cronin, James 156
culpable homicide 29; convictions for
   44, 45; gendered nature of 42, 43;
   gendered nature of convictions for 45;
   indictments for 41, 42, 44, 45; use as
   charge 30–1; and women indictments
   41–3; *see also* homicide
Cunningham, Elizabeth (Peg) 217
Cunningham, William 169

'dark figure' of unreported crime 16, 35,
   81, 94, 129, 248
Davies, Stephen 7
Davies, William 168
Dawson, Samuel R. 55
de Colombier, Claude Jordan 1
Defence of the Realm Act 182
Defoe, Daniel 1, 4
De Mandeville, Bernard 247
Demarco, Marco 273
Dempster, John 142
Denovan, James 210, 227–33, 228–9, 231
Devine, T. M. 4–5, 154
Dickson, Robert 231
'diminished responsibility' 31
Dingwall, Walter 13
Dobie, David 10–16
Docherty, Hugh Dearie 100–3
Domestic Abuse (Scotland) Act 118
Domestic Annals of Scotland (Chambers) 1
'domestic proximity,' and homicide 48
domestic violence 131; and England
   117–18; Watson, Henry 139–46
Dumfries 8, 19n24, 22n52, 261, 263
Dundee 173, 175–9
Dunlop, David 168
Dunn, Sydney 65

Easdale, Robert 228
East Kilbride 57

Eaton, William 99
Ebury, George 180, 185
Edinburgh 7, 10, 15, 50–3, 64, 69n58,
    71n78, 72n97, 96, 98, 111n79, 132,
    136, 144, 159, 179, 188n4, 191n43,
    216, 217, 220–4, 263–9, 272–4
Edinburgh Weekly Journal 268–9
England and Wales: child murder in 31,
    33; and domestic violence 117–18;
    and Scotland legislation on child
    murder 33
Enlightenment culture, of Scotland 7
enterprising Scot 276–7; case studies
    and attitudes to 260–76; enterprising
    Scottish criminal and the law 245–8;
    and the law 245–8; methods and
    motive 257–60; offenders 257–60;
    offenders, victims, methods and motive
    257–60; overview 243–4; trends in
    criminal enterprise and punishment
    248–56; victims 257–60
enterprising Scottish thief: attitudes to
    260–76; case studies 260–76
Esquire, Thomas Riddel 263

Fairbairn, Nicholas 275
Falkirk 270
Farmer, Lindsay 30
Farquharson, Alexander 177
fatal 'casual violence' 48
fatal violence: attitudes to 50–66; case
    studies 50–66; homicide 28–31;
    infanticide 31–5; methods 47–50;
    motive 47–50; offenders 47–50; and
    punishment 35–47; and Scotland
    28–35; trends in 35–47; victims 47–50;
    weapons used for 49; and women 47
Ferguson, William 184
Fielding, Henry 214, 247
Flavel, John 51
Forbes, Thomas 178
Fortescue, John 211
Forty Hours' Strike 159
Fraser, Alexander 134–5
Fraser, Hamish 4–5
Fry, Michael 6

Gallagher, Tom 172–3
Gallagher, William 180, 183–4, 185–6
gender disparity: and culpable homicide
    42, 43; and homicide 37–8, 40, 47–8
George, James 92–3
Gibson, Alexander 95
Gilchrist, George 220–7

Gilchrist, William 220–7
'The Gilmerton Monsters' *see* Dobie,
    David; Thomson, John
Glaister, John 101
Glasgow 8, 57, 61, 64, 65, 96, 139,
    142, 159, 179–84, 217–23, 227,
    230, 270–2
'Glasgow Green Case' 100–5
Gordon, Alexander 50–2
Gordon, James 50–2
Gordon, John 50–2
Greenock 272
Grierson, Thomas 246
The Guardian 187

Haldon, John 92
Haliburton, George 51
hamesucken 114–15; Bruce, William
    132–4; Campbell, Archibald 134–7;
    MacKinnon, Donald 134–7
Hand, Edward 81, 89, 94–100
Hart, James N. 143
Henry, Brian 213
Heritable Jurisdictions Act 7
High Court of Justiciary 7–8
Highland region (Scotland) 3–4, 6
highway robbery 209, 215
Hill, John 168
Hitler, Adolf 232
homicide 28–31; Brookman, Fiona
    on 28; and 'domestic proximity'
    48; and gender disparity 37–8, 40,
    47–8; gendered nature of 37–8,
    40; indictment pattern in Scotland
    between 1805 and 1960 36–7; judicial
    attitudes towards 28; low conviction
    rate for 38–40; types of 29–30
Homicide Act of 1957 31, 60, 230
Hope, Charles 51
Hopkins, Harry 180, 183, 185
Houston, Rab 245
Hughes, Hector 275
Hume, Baron David 28–31, 80–4,
    114–15, 157–8, 245, 247–8

Imrie, J. A. 101
incest 79–81
infanticide 31–5, 55; indictments and
    convictions for 46–7; reasons for
    50; and role of women 48; Scottish
    legislation on 33–5
Inverness 7, 134, 136
Irvine 168, 169
Irving, Robert 50–2

Jack, David 177
Jack, James 219–20
Jacobite Rebellions 4, 7, 10, 134
James VI, King of Scotland 168
John of Fordun 3
Justice of the Peace Court 7
Justices of the Peace 7

Keillar, Matthew 228
Kennedy, Allan 6
Kennedy, John 262
Kerr, George 261–2
Kettle, Martin 187
Kilmarnock 168, 169, 171
King, Thomas 91
King George I 134
King James VI 3, 27
Kirk 6, 9–10, 168
Kirkwood, David 180, 183–4, 185
Kneiland, Anne 57–8, 62
Knox, Bill 153
Knox, William 5

Lauder, Margaret 169
law: communal violence and 157–60;
    enterprising Scottish criminal and
    245–8; and sexual violence 78–84;
    violence for gain and 201–2; and
    violent assault 113–18
Lawson, Hellen 132
Lawson, Janet 178
Lee, Constantine 178
Lenman, Bruce 6
'lethal weapon' 29
Lindsay, Robert 137
Lobban, James 135
locus operandi 35
Lord Justice Clerk 7, 15, 154, 225
Lord Meadowbank 14, 53, 55
Lord Moncrieff 14, 225
Loudon, Robert 180, 185

McCartney, William 180, 184, 185–6
Macdonald, J. H. A. 30
McDowall, John 222
McEwan, James 246
Macfarlane, Alan 245
McGaa, Janet 137–9
McGovern, John 274
Macinnes, Allan 6
McKay, Alexander (Sandy) 174–5, 178–9
McKay, James Hugh 228
McKenzie, David 180, 185

Mackie, James 264
McKinlay, Alan 5
MacKinnon, Donald 134–7
McLaren, Charles 246
Maclay, John S. 231
McLymont, Robert 261–2
McManus, Daisy (Margaret) 273
McMillan, John 222–3
Maconochie, Alexander see Lord
    Meadowbank
Macpherson, Niall 275
McPike, John McKenzie 100–3
McTaggart, Michael 261
McWilliams, Martha 139–41
Manuel, Peter 31, 56–66; accusations
    against 57–60; criminal exploits 56–7;
    defenses against accusations 62
Manuel, Samuel 57
marital rape 83
Martin, James Bell 100
Maxwell, Thomas 137
Maxwell-Stuart, Peter 78
Mennie, Alexander Ferguson 182
Middle Ages 245
Miller, Anthony 210, 227–33, 229–31,
    231–2
Miller, Clerk Thomas 154
Miller, Tony 228, 232
'modern' collective violence 155
Moncrieff, James Wellwood see Lord
    Moncrieff
moral economy 166
moral panic, and rape 84
Morrison, James 223, 224
Motherwell 56
motive: of communal violence 164–7;
    enterprising Scot 257–60; fatal
    violence 47–50; sexual violence 87–9;
    for violence for gain 209–15; violent
    assault 129–32
Mulholland, Lily 275
Munro, Alexander 15
Munro, John 265
murder: capital 31; defined 30; see also
    attempted murder
Murder Act of 1751 29
murder 'free from all blame' 29
'murder under trust' 30
Murdoch, Alexander 167
Mure, Crawford McFarlean 229
Murray, Bill 173
Murray, James 180, 184, 185–6
Murray, Len 231, 233

Nenadic, Stana 155
Newington 263–6
Nicholl, Douglas 228
Nimmo, William 168

offenders: communal violence and 164–7;
    enterprising Scot 257–60; fatal violence
    47–50; sexual violence 87–9; violence
    for gain 209–15; violent assault 129–32
Oliver, Daniel Stewart 180, 185
Orr, George William 229
Orr, Janet 90–4
orthodoxy of passivity 4–5, 154

Paisley 90, 92, 181, 274
parricide 30
Paterson, Margaret 10–16
Paton, Catherine 263–4
patronage riots 167–72
Paul, George 141
Perth 7, 275
Peterhead 57, 273, 275, 288n139
Petrie, Ellen 64–5
petty theft 215, 229, 243, 263, 270, 277n3
poisonings 30
policing: 'An Act to Enable the Burghs in
    Scotland to Establish a General System
    of Police' 9; purpose of 9; as social
    control mechanisms 9
Porteous riots, Edinburgh 159
Practical Treatise on the Criminal Law of
    Scotland (Macdonald) 30
pre-Enlightenment Scotland 7
premeditated violence 49
Presbyterianism 167
Presbytery of Irvine 168–9
Privy Council 27
Protection from Abuse (Scotland) Act 118
punishment: communal violence and its
    160–4; criminal enterprise and their
    248–56; and fatal violence 35–47; for
    sexual violence 84–7; for violence for
    gain 203–8; for violent assault 118–29

Queen Anne 9

Ramensky, Johnny 258–60
Randall, Adrian 166
rape 81–4; attempted see attempted rape;
    convictions for 85; defined by Scots
    Law 81–2; indictments for 84–5; and
    'moral panic' 84; victims, treatment in
    court 83

'reactionary' collective violence 155
recidivism 123
Reid, Robert 219–20
religious protests 167
Renfrewshire 94, 229
Richardson, W. D. 101
Riddle, Thomas 264
Riot Act of 1715 158–9
riot on Red Clydeside 179–86
robbery: as capital crime 202;
    characteristic of 212; defined 201;
    highway 209, 215; indictments for
    203–8; nature and incidence of 233
Robbery Act 202
Robertson, William 176–7, 178
Rockhead, Margaret 132
Ross, William 223
Roy, Gilder 209, 215–17
Russell, Jannet 132
Rutherglen 142, 274

St Andrews 21n40, 147n2
Savage, Andrew 176–7
Savage, Elizabeth 95–6
Scotland: blood feud 3–4; Enlightenment
    culture 7; perception as violent nation
    1–10; see also specific terms
Scotophobia 2
Scots: perception, as violent people 1;
    persistence of violent 10–16; Whatley,
    Christopher on 4–5
Scots Law 245–8; bestiality and 78;
    mobbing and 157–8; rape and 81, 83;
    robbery and 202; sodomy and 78; types
    of homicide in 29–30
Scottish communal violence see
    communal violence
Scottish Justiciary Court 16–17,
    243, 257
Scottish policing see policing
Scottish Trades Union Council 180
Scottish violence 5–6, 16
Scottish women see women
'serial killer' 65
'sex crimes' 77
sexual violence: attitudes to 90–105;
    bestiality 78–9; case studies 90–105;
    child sexual abuse 79–81; incest
    79–81; and the law 78–84; methods
    87–9; motive 87–9; offenders 87–9;
    punishment for 84–7; rape 81–4;
    sodomy 78–9; trends in 84–7;
    victims 87–9

Shaw, John 218–19
Shearer, William 218
Sher, Richard 167
Sheriff Court 7
Shields, Agnes 98
Shinwell, Emmanuel 179, 183, 185–6
Shoemaker, Robert 166
Simpson, Robert 223
Sinclair, James Morrison 229
Smart, Campbell 182
Smart, Mary Ann 94
Smart, Michael 59–60
Smart, Peter 59–60
Smillie, James 184
Smith, Irvine 230
Smout, T. C. 4–5, 154
social control mechanisms: 'formal' 159; and penal sanctions 8; policing as 9; in Scotland 6, 9; trial as 292
sodomy 78–9; as capital offence 78; as crime against God and nature 78
Spence, Thomas 132–3
Steele, Anne 64
Steele, John 183–4
Stephenson, David 6
Stevenson, John 153, 166
Stirling 8, 22n54, 274, 275
street robbery (mugging) 210
Stuart, Jane 271–2
Substitution of Punishments of Death Act 83
Sunday Pictorial newspaper 64
Sword, James 90–4
Sword, John 90–4

Tannahill, Robert 91
Taylor, Henrietta 265
theft 8, 49, 56, 60, 177, 202, 213–15, 225, 230, 244–50, 253–9, 261–5, 270–2, 276, 280n33, 292
Thom, James Maxtone 142–3
Thompson, E. P. 166
Thomson, Alexander 168, 171
Thomson, Hugh 168
Thomson, John 10–16, 218
Tilly, Charles 155–6
Turner, Thomas 184
Tweedie, Herbert 261

United Nations 289
'unnatural offences' 84

victims: communal violence and 164–7; enterprising Scot 257–60; fatal violence 47–50; rape, treatment in court 83; sexual violence 87–9; of violence for gain 209–15; violent assault 129–32
violence see specific types
violence for gain: attitudes to 215–33; Bisland, Hugh 217–20; Brown, James 220–7; case studies and 215–33; Denovan, James 227–33; Gilchrist, George 220–7; Gilchrist, William 220–7; and the law 201–2; methods, offenders, victims and motive 209–15; Miller, Anthony 227–33; overview 200–1; punishment for 203–8; trends in 203–8
violent assault: introduction 113; and the law 113–18; methods 129–32; motive 129–32; offenders 129–32; punishment for 118–29; trends in 118–29; victims 129–32
'violent North': early perceptions and scholarship 2–10; thesis 1–2; see also Scotland

Wars of Independence 3
Watson, Agnes 139–46
Watson, Fiona 2
Watson, Henry 139–46
Watt, Vivienne 58–9
Watt, William 58–9
weaponry for fatal violence 49–50
Weir, Duncan 183
Weir, Walter Pollock 229
Welsh, John 262
Whatley, Christopher 4, 5
White, Adam 168
Whiteside, William 98
'wilful murder' 29
Wilson, Ann 178
Wilson, J. G. 61
Wilson, Neil 274
women: brutal assaults committed by 129; and fatal violence 47; indictments and culpable homicide 41–3; and infanticide 48; involvement in robbery 204–5; Scottish collective action and 161; theft and 249, 257
Woodburn, Arthur 275
World Health Organisation 290
Wormald, Jenny 8, 16
Wylie, William 168, 171

Printed in Great Britain
by Amazon

50777786R00196